Information Technology Encyclopedia and Acronyms

Springer-Verlag Berlin Heidelberg GmbH

Ejub Kajan

Information Technology Encyclopedia and Acronyms

With 244 Figures

Springer

Ejub Kajan
Softis
Bulevar Nemanjića 67a
18000 Niš
Yugoslavia
E-mail: eja@bankerinter.net

ISBN 978-3-642-62607-4 ISBN 978-3-642-56262-4 (eBook)
DOI 10.1007/978-3-642-56262-4

Library of Congress Cataloging-in-Publication Data

Kajan, Ejub, 1953-
Information technology encyclopedia and acronyms/Ejub Kajan.
p. cm.
Includes bibliographical references and index.
ISBN 978-3-540-41793-4 (alk. paper)
1. Information technology-Encyclopedias. 2. Information technology-Acronyms. I. Title.

T58.5.K33 2002
004'.03-dc21 2002020914

http://www.springer.de

Originally published by Springer-Verlag Berlin Heidelberg New York in 2002
Softcover reprint of the hardcover 1st edition 2002

Typesetting: Camera-ready by the author
Cover Design: KünkelLopka, Heidelberg
Printed on acid-free paper SPIN 10832831 - 06/3142SR - 5 4 3 2 1 0

Preface

Or I should say: "An Introduction to a Never Ending Story". This book contains over 4000 acronyms. By the time this book has reached the audience, there will be many new acronyms around. According to current estimates, as a rule of thumb, 100 acronyms appear every 3 months. From the early computing days, when the first computer was developed (ENIAC), up to today, computer jargon has always been full of acronyms. As a consequence of open systems, the appearance of the Internet and the Web, the increasingly rapid development of new technologies, and specifically the wide integration of computing and telecommunication technologies, the number of such acronyms, neologisms, etc. has risen to tens of thousands. One part of this jargon is still used by a relatively small group of professionals. Examples of such acronyms are pin assignments, names of registers, buffers and other functional units in computer architectures, commands in different operating systems, expressions used in a huge number of programming languages, etc. Thanks to the widespread use of computer and telecommunication technologies, and especially to the Internet and the Web, which have made computers a daily reality for millions of people, the rest of this jargon is of interest to an almost unlimited group of people. Managers, marketing people, salespersons, various IT professionals, end-users, and even scientists and researchers meet mysterious acronyms from time to time.

Sometimes this just awakens curiosity to find out more; at other times, however, this leads to the individual feeling frustrated due to his/her relative lack of knowledge. Often, the only way to satisfy this curiosity or to try to resolve the confusion is to consult the Web. Unfortunately, this takes time and may not produce an adequate answer. Let us suppose, for example, that the reader encounters the two acronyms CAVE and TWAIN, both well-known regular words in the English language. The usual fast Web searching will probably not reveal their IT meanings – TWAIN is "Technology Without An Interesting Name" and CAVE is "CAVE Automated Virtual Environment". This book explains these acronyms and over 4000 others.

In general, the chosen acronyms are classified into four groups. The most important group gives an up-to-date overview of modern architectures and technologies in use now or which are going to be in use very soon. Such acronyms require longer explanations than others, and very often they are supported with an appropriate illustration and many cross-references. Examples include AI, ATM, CAE, CAPI, CIM, COM, CORBA, C/S, DNS, DVB, DW, EC, EIS, EJB, FDDI, FTP, FTTC, GPS, GUI, HPCC, HTML, HTTP, I2-DSI, Internet, IP, ISDN, LAN, MIME, NGI, NII, ODBC, OO*, ORB, OSI, PGP, QoS, RAID, RDBMS, RISC, RP, RTS, SNA, SPI, TAPI, Tcl, TCP/IP, TCSEC, UAA, UIMS, UML, WAP, WWW, X.500 and XML. The second group covers major companies (e.g. AT&T, CDC, HP, IBM, NCR, SCO, SGI, etc.), research organizations (e.g. CERN, MIT, SRI, etc.), and organizations founded as standardization bodies or professional associations involved in specification and/or technology development (e.g. ACM, ANSI, DMTF, IEEE, IETF, ISO, OMG, OSF, W3C, etc.). Relevant journals, conferences and workshops are also covered in this group. In most cases, terms are supported by Web links to the relevant homepages, and many homepage screenshots are also included as figures to show their look and feel etc. Terms of common interest fall into the third group and include filenames, common electronics terms, chat terms, business terms, measurement units, miscellaneous terms, and also some terms which have been in use for a long period of time (e.g. COBOL, FORTRAN, RAM, ROM, OS, etc.). The fourth group covers some historical terms such as ARPANET, CP/M and ENIAC, and interesting acronyms such as S4L, WOMBAT and YANTSWIBTC, etc.

The main body of the book consists of 27 chapters that cover acronyms in alphabetical order from the numbers and symbols chapter ("#") to the letter "Z". For every acronym a clear explanation of its origin is given in red. In most cases where the acronym's pronunciation differs from the spelling, it's also given (e.g. GUI is pronounced "goo-ee"). The second part of the book has two chapters. The "Suggested Reading" chapter covers many reference books and/or important articles, websites, etc., where the reader may find deeper explanations. The last chapter is the "Subject Index" which covers all the terms explained in the main body of the book, categorizing them (e.g. "OSI Reference Model", "Conferences & Workshops", "Software Tools", "WWW", etc.) and listing the relevant main-body page numbers. Where an acronym can be classified in several categories, it's listed in its primary (wider) category.

While writing the book I referred to primary and definitive sources of information as far as possible – e.g. technical reference manuals, academic journal articles, established textbooks, international published standards, the websites of major corporations etc. However, the experienced reader will not be surprised to hear that this field is characterized by variations in definitions. By its nature the Web encourages the creation and proliferation of neologisms, but much information on the Web is inaccurate, and these errors replicate quickly. On the other hand, if even only a few people agree on and use a new term then it's not my role to tell them that they're "wrong". Thus, obviously, in this book I've tried to strike a balance on this issue, and to present here the terms and definitions that are most widely used, or that are of most benefit to the reader. Consistency in representation was another issue during the project, and while the websites of even major corporations show inconsistencies – one word vs. two, mixed capitalization and hyphenation etc. – I've tried here to accurately represent trademarks, product names and other "official" terms etc. and to consistently represent all others.

How to read the book

The following figure shows how this book can be read and used. The left branch of the diagram is for readers looking for a particular acronym (e.g. BIOS), while the right branch is useful for readers interested in a particular area (e.g. AI).

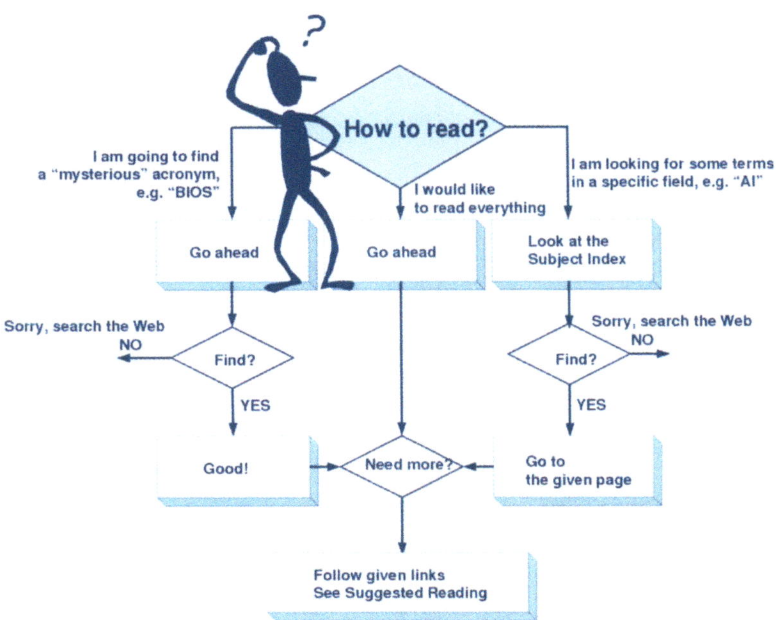

Acknowledgements

Many people helped me during the course of the project. I would like to thank first the people who have been involved in this since the early days. The idea was born seven years ago when my book about open systems appeared and I found that acronyms are very important in the understanding of the subject matter. The next trigger came from Prof. Dr. Živko Tošić who suggested that computer-related acronyms should be covered in a book. My wife, Prof. Dr. Slobodanka Djordjević-Kajan, immediately stood behind the idea, and I found myself deeply involved in the project before it had been formally recognized as a book proposal. So, the project had started.

Here I would like to put on record four names of people from whom I got significant support. First of all, Antonija and Dejan Mitrović gave me much useful advice during all stages of the project, and incredible support. They are definitely responsible for my final decision to make a book proposal. Dr. Antonija Mitrović also submitted several terms (e.g. CAPIT, KERMIT and ITS etc.). Then I met Alfred Hofmann, the Springer-Verlag editor, who immediately reserved the book for Springer-Verlag and put me into the checkmate position. That is not the end of the story, of course. During the summer of 2000 we had dozens of phone conversations and exchanged e-mails with useful advice about how to finish the project. And, thus, the whole summer holiday of 2000 disappeared. My relative, Alija Kajan, who works at CSIRO Australia, also had an important influence on turning the project into a book. Thus, the book grew from an idea, to a proposal, to a project, and finally to a book.

I asked a number of people to offer independent opinions on the book. Most reviewed a chapter or two, and they give their contributions in the section "First Impressions of Early Readers". These contributions by Phil Carroll, David Duce, Phil Ho, Bob Hopgood, Colin Jacka, Dejan Mitrović, J.J. O'Reilly, Rade Petrović, Vladimir Tošić, Živko Tošić, Ivan Veselinović and Aco Vidović were of specific and valuable importance – they gave me additional confidence in the project.

When I requested permission to use copyrighted materials in the book, such as screenshots of homepages etc., I was pleasantly surprised by the great efficiency and kindness shown. I'd like to thank, in alphabetical order of affiliation, Emilie David and Nan Broadbent (AAAS), Stacy Leistner (ANSI), Elizabeth Compton (AOL), Tina Geist (ASCILITE), Michael Clark (CDT), Renilde Vanden

Broeck (CERN), Julia O'Brien and Heather Harvey (DISA), Prof. Phil Willis (EG), Dr. Jason Leigh (EVL), Anke Varcin (ISO), Kara Herzog (MAPICS), Carol de Groot (TERENA), Dr. Hendrik Berndt (TINAC) and Jami Heldt (YAHOO! Inc.).

Finally, in the production stage, the Springer-Verlag professionals did their job just fine. From the technical point of view, the whole project was led by Ulrike Stricker, who is also responsible for the modern and nice layout of the book. She was working with me all the time, almost day by day, until the book was finished. Copyediting was done by Ronan Nugent, who did an excellent job, and he also contributed some terms and finetuned certain entries etc. I have to express especial thanks to Ulrike and Ronan as they gave me additional inspiration during the final stages of the project.

Trademarks

Many trademarks are mentioned in the book. Unfortunately, a full list of these would be unsuitable here – it would be too long, and there is the possibility that some would be unintentionally omitted. I believe that the book will be useful for readers who want to find out about products they require and vendors who can satisfy these requirements. Thus, I would like to list here just those trademarks closely related to the tools used in the manuscript preparation and/or which appear in certain figures (all material was prepared with the required permission from and/or courtesy of the respective owners, and taking EULAs into account etc.): AcuBench, ACUCOBOL and AcuODBC are trademarks of Acucorp; Adobe Acrobat Reader and Adobe Photoshop are trademarks of Adobe; Netscape 6 was used for screenshots of webpages and it's a trademark of Netscape Communications Corporation; the screenshot illustrations were made using HiJaak PRO, a trademark of Quarterdeck; CorelDRAW was used for drawings, and it's a trademark of Corel Corporation; finally, the book was written using Microsoft Word with Arial (a trademark of Agfa Monotype Corporation) font, and some 3-D drawings were prepared using either PowerPoint or Visio, and these are trademarks of Microsoft, as are Access, Excel and MSDN.

Niš, October 2001 Ejub Kajan

First Impressions of Early Readers

The aim of this chapter is to present some independent opinions on how the book may be used by readers. In order to provide such advice, the author asked various professionals – engineers, managers, programmers, researchers, academics, end-users etc. – to provide their opinions about the book, its content, and the approach it is based on. The author is extremely grateful for the contributions. The contributors and their impressions are given in alphabetical order.

I've noticed that in recent years IT has attracted specialists from outside the traditional computing and engineering disciplines, and this book will give them very useful knowledge about the technology underlying their work. In contrast, engineers now tend to move from working on technical projects to responsibility for their business applications, so I particularly like the fact that the book covers those terms you don't come across in your formal education, but are still somehow expected to know. The acronyms are explained as well as defined, so this book is much more informative than simple Web searching etc., and there are cross-references to related entries and original sources so that you get a good context for each term. The index classified by subject gives you a fast introduction to a whole field and not just a definition of a single term. This book will be very valuable for the modern engineer or IT practitioner. On a lighter note, I grew up watching "Road Runner" cartoons and I never knew what "ACME" stood for!

Phil Carroll
R&D Manager,
Europlex Technologies,
Dublin, Ireland

This book is a very valuable guide to the "acronym soup" that pervades our discipline. It will be of value to researchers, practitioners and students alike and should have a place in the reference section of every library. Readers are especially likely to appreciate the extensive diagrams which illustrate key concepts and terms.

Prof. David Duce
School of Computing
and Mathematical Sciences,
Oxford Brookes University, UK

I am impressed with this book for its comprehensive collection of technical acronyms that are everywhere in the Information Technology and Telecommunication industry. The author not only provides the origin of the abbreviation but also includes a brief technical explanation of the acronym itself. This will definitely be handy for a wide range of readers that are interested in the field. The overall information in the book is up to date and accurate. One thing I really enjoyed was "WOMBAT", I had never heard of it. Now I can arm myself with useful acronyms for some future project meetings.

Phil Ho
Research Engineer,
Telecommunications
and Industrial Physics (TIP),
CSIRO,
Marsfield, Australia

The idea that somebody would produce a book of this size completely devoted to describing acronyms in the IT industry took me by surprise. However, when I thought about it, the number of times per day that I come across an unknown acronym is quite high. So I tried to find a few of these in the dictionary and was pleasantly surprised. Not only did they appear, but there was sufficient information for me to understand the topic and where to look for more information. In places, there were URLs cited for the reader to find further information. The illustrations are very good and I was drawn into reading it; something that you do not normally do with a dictionary.

Prof. Bob Hopgood
W3C,
London, UK

The book covers a good selection of IT and telecommunications terms that are used by the professionals, and those that confront the layman as we begin the new millennium. Many people are turned away from being part of the new economy because of the language. This book could prevent that type of disillusionment. Both the computer and the telecommunication industries have for some time had their own bewildering vocabulary of acronyms. In today's convergent world the newcomer is confronted by the acronyms from both these industries, and in some cases they conflict or overlap. The inclusion of the three most commonly used definitions for ATM allows the layman to understand what is meant when he calls in to his bank, then proceeds to work where he prints out his PostScript documents, and then sends them down the broadband network. The book includes a good cross-section of IT terms that cover both the business/commercial sectors and the more technical environments of electronic engineering and computer science. The book would be an invaluable reference for the student of electronic engineering, telecommunications, or in fact any of today's university courses. Some of the definitions are extremely informative, e.g. C/S (Client/Server) has over one page devoted to it and provides an extremely good description. I would find it an invaluable book for my bookshelf, or close at hand at work or at home. It could well save some embarrassment when approached by "I believe you are an expert in the field of ..., so tell me what ... stands for".

Colin Jacka, Ph.D.
Discipline Leader,
Electronic Systems,
Telecommunications
and Industrial Physics (TIP),
CSIRO,
Marsfield, Australia

The computer industry and computer-related research cover a huge range of various technologies and products. For over half a century of computer history, many hundreds of thousands of people have worked in this area. In order to efficiently communicate, they have developed a separate computer jargon. Although this jargon has developed on top of the English language, it is often a mystery for non-specialists. Learning computer jargon is part of introductory computer courses, since it is not possible to develop a deeper understanding without knowing the jargon. Acronyms form a very important part of computer jargon. This book represents a unique attempt to help people to find their way through the ever-changing world of computer-related acronyms. It could be useful for both novices (to learn the basics of computer jargon) and experienced computer professionals. Due to extensive cross-references, this book could be used as a textbook for learning many computer topics, particularly new advances in computer networking. A large number of illustrations makes the reading and understanding of complex topics easy. Such a book should be part of the reference library of each computer professional.

Dejan Mitrović, M.Sc.
Solutions Development,
Trimble,
Christchurch, New Zealand

Modern telecommunications has changed rapidly from being a specialist's domain to one where decisions are made in meetings attended by engineers, application programmers, accountants, and sales and marketing managers etc., some of whom have only a sketchy understanding of the acronyms on the agenda. I'd recommend this book because it outlines the business environment as well as the literal meaning of telecommunications and IT acronyms. I'm often frustrated when reference material on the Internet is either inaccurate or too simplified, or when a search throws up too many "hits" etc. Using this book you can go directly to the acronym in question, or browse the subject index to skip to related topics and get a broader picture. Even people with expertise in the telecommunications and IT fields will discover new aspects in this book, while any reader's general knowledge can be improved by knowing the precise meaning of "ISO", the quirks of the main time zones, what "TÜV" stands for on a compliance sticker etc.

J.J. O'Reilly
Datacomms Manager,
Damovo
(Ericsson Business Communications),
Dublin, Ireland

Everybody can recall feeling helpless and frustrated by meaningless acronyms obstructing comprehension or constantly escaping one's short-term memory. A reference book like this could alleviate these feelings and aid the retention of information. It is particularly useful for professionals in other fields struggling through the ubiquitous acronyms in the area of computers and communications.

Rade Petrović, Ph.D.
Vice President of Technology,
Verance,
San Diego, CA, USA

I like that abbreviations of various research journals, magazines, and transactions are included and well explained. As space available for research papers is usually limited, one way to save it is to use abbreviations in references. Sometimes, this causes problems for the reader who has to "chase down" the references. Graduate students have to "chase" many research papers, and this is just one of many examples of how this valuable book can help them.

Vladimir Tošić
Ph.D. Student,
Carleton University,
Ottawa, Canada

Very often, people move towards rationalizing their activities as much as possible. As a consequence of such rationalization, there are many abbreviations in use, especially in computing and communications. Everyday, there are many times when people have unknown acronyms in front of them, while reading a journal, a book, a manual, or just searching the Web. Furthermore, the chances of coming across an unfamiliar computer acronym are sometimes independent of the current knowledge of the reader. This book represents a successful attempt to select the most important (and interesting) computer and communications acronyms and to explain them in an acceptable manner for most potential readers. In my opinion, this book could be valuable to a wide group of readers in their everyday work.

Prof. Dr. Živko Tošić
Dean of Faculty
of Electronic Engineering,
University of Niš,
Yugoslavia

Many years ago, in the early 1980s, I noted that reading some articles on IT achievements did not coincide with a complete understanding of the topics. *Additional "investigations" of the meaning of new acronyms occupied more and more of my time, and in the 1990s it became a real problem. Very often while* reading IT and communications articles I'm confronted with a lack of understanding of the substance. Discovering the meaning of a text swamped with acronyms becomes a real feat. The time needed for that discourages the thirst to be informed, but consolation that it happens to others, also to young engineers, is not an excuse. The appearance of this book was a pleasant surprise for me, particularly because it came from my friend and associate. During my first reading I discovered that I am not a lost cause any more. With this book close to hand I can come back and be "in" without any frustration. To be sincere, my incomparable surprise is that this dictionary can be read as a book, and not only used as a reference.

Ivan Veselinović, B.Sc.
General Manager,
Softis,
Niš, Yugoslavia

This is a comprehensive and sometimes fun book that covers the wide scope of IT terms, acronyms and definitions. It will be of great help for all those who need to stay in touch with the ever changing IT terminology. The website URLs and figures that accompany certain topics allow the readers to get more in-depth information on their areas of interest, which makes this book much more than another computer glossary, IYSWIM!

Aco Vidović
IBM International Technical
Support Organization,
Rochester, MN, USA

Content

# #

. – Star–dot–star. Any file, any filename extension. Used in some operating systems for the global copy, move or delete file operations under the specified directory. Also used in two other possible file combinations: any file with a particular file extension (for instance, *.doc), or a particular filename with any filename extension (dict.*).

1-2-3 – The name of the first publicly available spreadsheet program developed for personal computers by Lotus Corporation in 1982. The unusual name stands for the three basic functions of 1-2-3: graphics, spreadsheets and data management.

10-100 – Common name for a Ethernet/Fast Ethernet designation that has rates of both 10 and 100 Mbps, but not on the same port.

10Base2 – 10 Mbps Baseband 200 m. A kind of Ethernet LAN that uses 50-Ohm thin coaxial cable with a maximum length of 200 m per segment. See Fig. #-1.

10Base5 – 10 Mbps Baseband 500 m. A kind of Ethernet LAN that uses a thick coaxial cable (full specification) with up to 500-m-long segments. For longer-distance LANs, it is necessary to build in an appropriate number of repeaters.

10BaseF – 10 Mbps Baseband Fiber. An IEEE Ethernet specification for fiber-optic cabling. See also 10BaseFB, 10BaseFL and 10BaseFP.

10BaseFB – 10 Mbps Baseband Fiber Backbone. A part of the IEEE 10BaseF specification that provides a synchronous signaling backbone, a maximum of 2000 m long, that allows extra network segments and repeaters to be connected to the network.

10BaseFL – 10 Mbps Baseband Fiber Link. A part of the IEEE 10BaseF specification that provides an inter-repeater link, a maximum of 2000 m long.

10BaseFP – 10 Mbps Baseband Fiber Passive. A part of the IEEE 10BaseF specification that allows a number of computers to be organized in a star topology without repeaters. Segments can be up to 500 m long.

10BaseT – 10 Mbps Baseband Twisted Pair. An Ethernet that allows twisted pair cable as a backbone. The maximum speed of this kind of Ethernet is limited to 10 Mbps.

10BaseX – 10 Mbps Baseband any (X) Ethernet. A standard root for several baseband Ethernet specifications that operate at 10 Mbps or slower speeds. See 10Base2, 10Base5, 10BaseF and 10BaseT.

10Broad36 – 10 Mbps Broadband 36 MHz. An Ethernet network that uses a 75-Ohm coaxial cable based on the IEEE802.3 bus or a tree topology. It can operate at up to 10 Mbps. The distance supported is limited to 1800 m. Each of the two channels operates at 18 MHz, so the number 36 in the network name refers to twice 18 MHz.

Name	Cabling	Maximum segment distance
10Base2	thin coaxial	200 m
10Base5	thick coaxial	500 m
10BaseF	fiber cable	2000 m
10BaseFB	fiber cable	2000 m + extra segments
10BaseFL	fiber cable	2000 m + link
10BaseFP	fiber cable	500 m
10BaseT	twisted pair	100 m
100BaseFX	multimode fiber	400 m
100BaseT	unshielded twisted pair	100 m
100BaseT4	unshielded twisted pair 4	100 m
100BaseTX	twisted pair	100 m
100BaseVG	VG twisted pair	100–150 m
1000BaseCX	copper wire 150 □	25 m

Fig. #-1. Summary of baseband technologies

100BaseFX – 100 Mbps Baseband Fast Ethernet. The IEEE standard for Fast Ethernet (100 Mbps) over multimode fiber optic cabling. Segments can be up to 400 m long. See also 100BaseX.

100BaseT – 100 Mbps Baseband Twisted Pair. A series of IEEE802.3 standards for fast (100 Mbps) Ethernet using unshielded twisted pair cables.

100BaseT4 – 100 Mbps Baseband Twisted Pair (4). A series of IEEE802.3 standards for fast (100 Mbps) Ethernet using unshielded twisted pair cables with 4 wires.

100BaseTX – 100 Mbps Baseband Twisted Pair X. A Fast Ethernet specification based on twisted pair cables, either unshielded or shielded, with a segment length up to 100 m. The first pair of wires is used to receive data and the second pair is used to transmit data.

100BaseVG – 100 Mbps Baseband Voice Grade. An extension of 10BaseT Ethernet developed by HP and AT&T (IEEE802.12) based on voice grade (category 3) twisted pair cables (see UTP). Instead of CSMA/CD, used for ordinary Ethernet, 100BaseVG uses demand priority as the media access method. Furthermore, it requires 4-wire pairs and uses 5B/6B NRZ signal encoding. 100BaseVG/AnyLAN appears as an extension of 100BaseVG that can be used in either Ethernet or Token Ring in separated networks. It also supports isochronous data (e.g. voice or video). Compare with 10BaseT.

100BaseX – 100 Mbps Baseband any (X) Ethernet. The IEEE standard (IEEE-802.3u) for Fast Ethernet (100 Mbps based on Carrier Sense Multiple Access, see CSMA/CD). It appears in three variants (see 100BaseFX, 100BaseT4, and 100BaseTX).

1000BaseCX – 1000 Mbps Baseband Copper any (X) Ethernet. The IEEE standard (IEEE802.3z) for Fast Ethernet over copper cables.

1284 – The IEEE1284 parallel interface standard. See Enhanced Capability Port (ECP) and Enhanced Parallel Port (EPP).

1394 – A specification for a very fast external bus that supports data transfer rates of up to 400 Mbps. Also known as FireWire, which is a trademark of Apple for the original 1394 bus.

1G – First (1st)-Generation Wireless. A common name for an early wireless technology (from the late 1970s up to the late 1980s) based on radiotelephony and analog voice encoding. Compare with 2G and 3G.

1GL – First (1st)-Generation Language. A common name for a machine language that consists of a set of instructions and data in the form of a string of 0s and 1s. Before the second, third, etc. (see 2GL, 3GL, 4GL and 5GL) generations of languages appeared, 1GL was the only way to program computers.

1NF – First (1st) Normal Form. Normal forms commonly representing an approach to structuring information in a relational database (1NF, 2NF, 3NF, etc.) or metalanguages that allow the description of other languages (see BNF). 1NF represents groups of records organized as a table in which each column (information field) contains a unique indivisible piece of information. The other normal forms of relational databases extend 1NF by additional relationships between the information fields (see 2NF, 3NF, 4NF, 5NF, BCNF and DKNF).

1ST – 1st (First). Filename extension for Microsoft Windows Readme (first) files. Such files are used, for example, as installation guidelines, descriptions of system requirements, etc.

2B+D – Two (2) Base channels + D channel. A term associated with the Basic Rate Interface in ISDN communications. See BRI and ISDN. Compare with PRI.

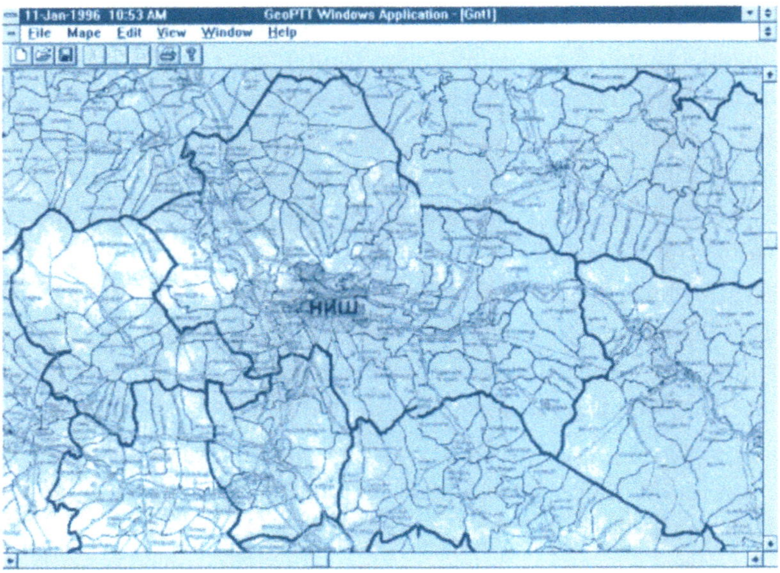

Fig. #-2. A map as an example of 2D graphics

2D – Two (2)-Dimensional. An umbrella term from the field of computer graphics that refers to a common attribute (two-dimensional, width and depth) of drawings, pictures, graphic systems, workstations, etc. 2D pictures can be native images (such as cartographic maps, as shown in Fig. #-2), schemes, or projections of 3D objects onto a particular plane.

2G – Second (2nd)-Generation Wireless. A common name for mobile wireless technology (first used in the 1990s) based on digital voice encoding. Examples are CDMA, TDMA and GSM. The technology is still under development in order to improve its bandwidth and routing, and include multimedia as well. With such capabilities the technology looks like something between 2G and 3G, so the term 2.5G is often used instead of 2G. Compare with 1G and 3G.

2GL – Second (2nd)-Generation Language. A common name for any assembly language (also known as an assembler) that uses particular processor-based commands and instructions at a higher level than that used by a 1GL. Such instructions are then translated into the machine-level code. For example, in GCOS6 (see GCOS) assembly language programming the instruction STORE $R1, LOC tells the computer to store the contents of register $R1 into a memory location with the symbolic name LOC. Compare with 1GL and 3GL.

2NF – Second (2nd) Normal Form. An approach to database design similar to 1NF but which introduces a primary key. More specifically, a relation R is in 2NF if it is in 1NF and also if every nonprime attribute is fully dependent on the primary key.

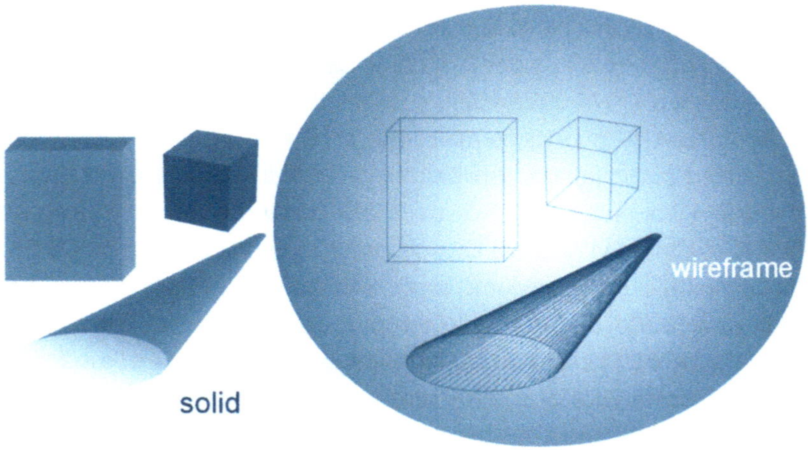

Fig. #-3. 3D graphics presentations

2PC – 2 (Two)-Phase Commit protocol. A protocol executed in distributed transactions to ensure atomicity (see ACID). It works as follows. When a transaction, initiated at a site, completes its execution, and all the sites at which the transaction has been executed inform the transaction coordinator that the transaction is completed, the transaction coordinator starts the 2PC protocol. During the first phase, 2PC asks transaction managers on sites where the transaction has been executed whether they are willing to commit their portion of the transaction. If the answer is "yes" from all the transaction managers called, 2PC commits the transaction in the second phase. If only one transaction manager answers "no", 2PC does not commit the transaction at all. See also TM (Transaction Manager). Compare with 3PC.

3Com – Computer, Communication and Compatibility. One of the world's leading manufacturers of internetworking equipment founded in 1979 by Robert Metcalfe (http://www.3com.com).

3D – 3 (Three)-Dimensional. A kind of computer graphics that allows object presentation in three dimensions, width, height and depth. Unlike 2D graphics, in addition to dimensions and colors, 3D graphics uses perspective, viewpoints, light sources etc. (see GKS-3D, VRC) to illustrate the real image of the object (scene). There are two techniques used, solid and wireframe, as shown in Fig. #-3.

3G – Third (3rd)-Generation Wireless. A common name for the next-generation wireless technology intended for fixed, mobile and portable communications. 3G systems should be able to operate from any location on Earth or over the Earth's surface, with rates greater than 2 Mbps and with routing using repeaters, satellites and LANs. All existing services are expected to be supported by 3G (paging, cellular phones, e-mail, web browsing, fax, videoconferencing, etc.). Enhanced multimedia capabilities are also required. It is expected that 3G will achieve full operability by the year 2005 in North America, Europe and Japan. The first attempt to offer 3G services happened on 1st October 2001, when NTT DoCoMo (http://www.docomo.com) launched its FOMA (Freedom of Mobile Multimedia Access), featuring plenty of bugs at that time. An article in "The Wall Street Journal" compared it with a powerful car which has bad styling, bad brakes, uses a lot of gas, etc. However, the technology pioneer didn't give up. "Mobile Media Japan" (http://mobilemediajapan.com) sent a message about DoCoMo. That part of NTT is expected to have 150,000 subscribers by the end of March 2002. Compare with 2G.

3GL – Third (3rd)-Generation Languages. A set of high-level language families that originated in the early 1960s. Typical examples are FORTRAN, COBOL and ALGOL. They introduced much improved programming possibilities compared to the low-level languages (assembly languages). They are more likely to be self-documented, they hide from programmers the low-level details of the target executing machine, the structure of the program follows the structure of the original problem under development rather than the structure of the processor design, architecture, etc. Due to their usefulness, legacy issues, and continuous standardization efforts, they have survived

#

down through the years. Figure #-4 illustrates the roots of famous 3GL families and their development tree from the 1960s up to today.

3NF – Third (3rd) Normal Form. In addition to 2NF features, 3NF requires that a relation has no transitive dependencies on nonprime key attributes.

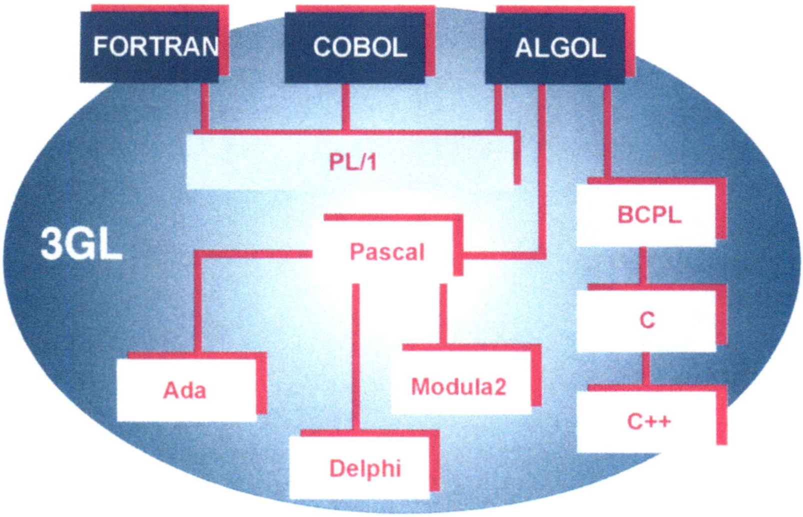

Fig. #-4. The 3GL family tree

3PC – 3 (Three)-Phase Commit protocol. A protocol executed in distributed transactions to ensure atomicity (see ACID). It is designed to avoid the possibility of blocking in a restricted case of possible failures. The first phase is identical to phase 1 of 2PC. In the second phase, in the case of a negative answer from any transaction manager, the transaction is aborted. If all transaction managers are ready to accept the committed transaction, 3PC precommits the phase, i.e. the transaction can still be aborted. Then, the transaction managers at the sites are informed that the transaction is in the precommit state. In the third phase, 3PC investigates whether a site has failed in the meantime and is waiting for an appropriate number of acknowledgments before making the final decision: commit transaction or abort transaction. See also 2PC.

3w – where, what and when. Term suggested (Djordjević-Kajan et al., 1997) for agent navigation in cyberspace when an agent requires some kind of interaction with other agents. Figure #-5 shows a typical example, where a mobile agent, in order to accomplish the delegated task, has to decide what to do, where to go, and when (3w space). To do that, communication with other agents on possibly different platforms may be required (see UAA). See also KIF and KQML.

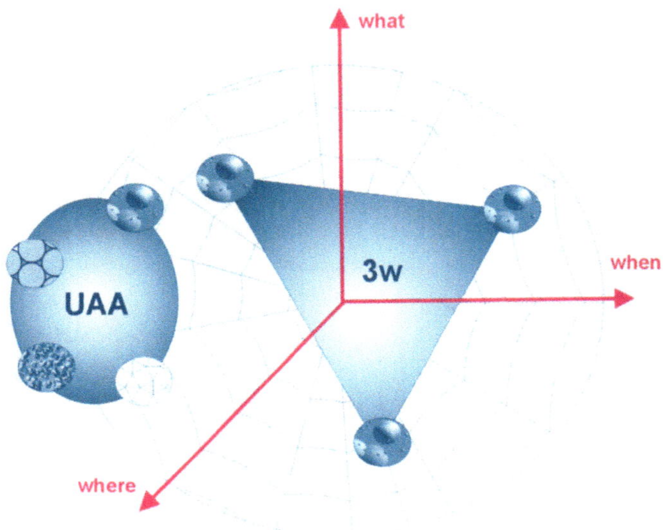

Fig. #-5. Mobile agent navigation in 3w space

404 – Not found. A status code returned by HTTP to a Web user when she/he tries to access a nonexistent site. Generally, there are two possible reasons for code 404, either the site no longer exists (also known as 404 limbo) or the wrong address was entered due to user typing errors. See also PURL.

4B/5B – 4-Bit/5-Bit local fiber. A fiber channel physical media and encoding scheme used for ATM and FDDI that allows speeds of up to 100 Mbps. In 4B/5B, every group of 4 bits is represented by a 5-bit symbol (explaining where the name comes from). This symbol is associated with a bit pattern that is then encoded using NRZI or another standard signal-encoding method. Sometimes abbreviated as TAXI (Transparent Asynchronous Transceiver/Receiver Interface). See also NRZI. Compare with 5B/6B and 8B/10B.

4GL – Fourth (4th)-Generation Languages. A common term related to programming languages that are oriented to end-users rather than to programming professionals. 4GLs speed up the application building process, minimize debugging problems, make user-friendly environments, reduce software maintenance costs, etc. They include application generators, report generators, query languages, etc. (see Fig. #-6). Some examples of such languages, also explained in this book, or in the references (e.g. Martin, 1986), are ADS, ADF, ADRSII, APL, AS, CSP, QBE, QMF, SQL, etc.

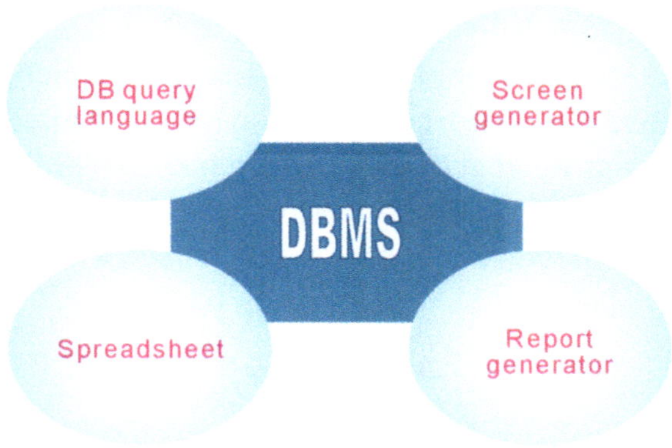

Fig. #-6. Some typical elements of a 4GL

4NF – Fourth (4th) Normal Form. A term from database design theory. A relation R is in 4NF if every nontrivial multivalued dependency is due to the keys. See 1NF, 2NF, 3NF and 5NF.

50X – 50 times X. The measurement term for the maximum data transfer rate in CD and DVD technologies. The term is expressed using a base of 150 KBps, which refers to the time required to read data from a compact disk in its original version (1X). Later improvements brought 2X, 4X, 8X, 12X, 24X, 32X, 40X and 50X.

5B/6B – 5-Bit/6-Bit encoding. An encoding scheme in 100BaseVG networks. In 5B/6B, every group of 5 bits is represented by a 6-bit symbol (explaining where the name comes from). This symbol is associated with a bit pattern that is then encoded using NRZI or another standard signal-encoding method. See also NRZI. Compare with 4B/5B and 8B/10B.

5GL – Fifth (5th)-Generation Languages. This term is used for programming languages having additional features compared with 4GLs. They originated in the field of artificial intelligence (see AI), especially in knowledge-based systems (see KBS), expert systems, speech recognition, decision support systems (see DSS), command, control, communication and intelligence systems (see C3I), active technologies such as mobile agents or active DBMS (see ADBMS), etc. The pioneering language in this field was PROLOG. The common underlying language is LISP and its variations.

5NF – Fifth (5th) Normal Form. An approach to database design that assumes that every join dependency in the relation is implied by the candidate keys of that relation. Compare with 1NF, 2NF, 3NF and 4NF.

6bone – IPv6 Internet Backbone. An international experimental network that serves as a testbed for the next-generation Internet Protocol (see IP, IPv6 and IPng). 6bone has been in operation since mid-1996. It involves around 200 organizations in 30 countries. Figure #-7 shows part of the 6bone network. Additional information can be found at http://www.6bone.net

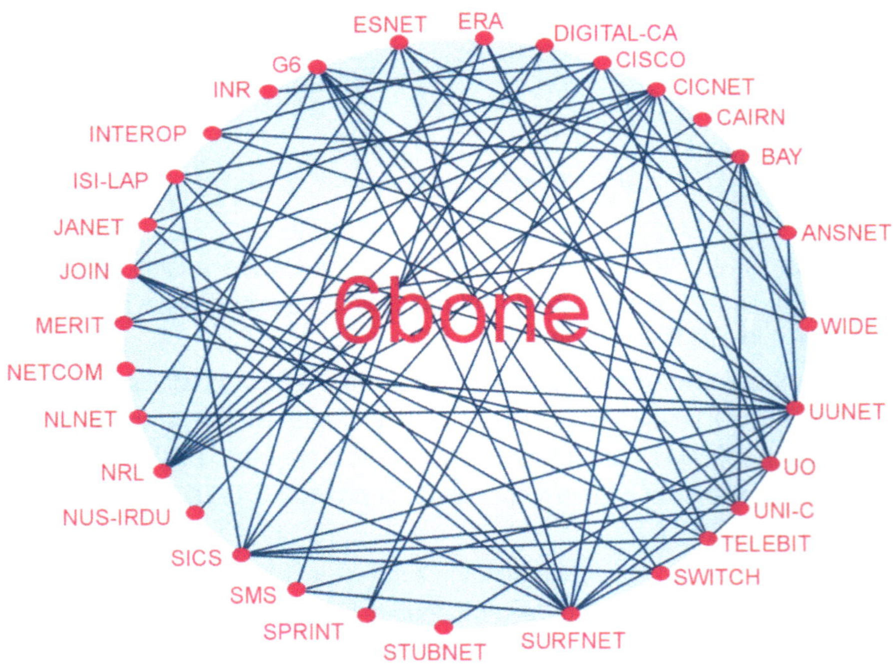

Fig. #-7. The 6bone backbone

6DOF – 6 Degrees Of Freedom. A term defining linear movement in either direction along each of three mutually perpendicular axes (i.e. x-, y- and z-axes), and rotation around each of the three axes in either direction. The term "Freedom" means that movement on any axis does not exclude any other simultaneous movement on any other axis; thus, a 6DOF device can interpret all possible motion within our 3-dimensional world.

6REN – IPv6 Research and Education Network. An initiative to promote IPv6 for high-quality high-performance operationally robust network services. See also IPv6 and 6bone.

802.x – A set of standards developed by IEEE to define methods of access and control of local area networks. They correspond to the ISO OSI Reference Model in the physical and data-link layers, but they also split the data-link layer into two sublayers (see LLC and MAC). The following are the IEEE 802.x standards:

- 802.1 specifies standards for network management at the hardware level. Adopted by ISO/IEC as the ISO/IEC8802-1 standard.
- 802.2 defines the operation of the LLC sublayer, making it transparent to upper layers. In particular, framing, addressing and error control are specified. Adopted by ISO/IEC as the ISO/IEC8802-2 standard.
- 802.3 describes the physical layer and the MAC sublayer for baseband networks that use a bus topology and the CSMA/CD accessing protocol (see CSMA/CD). Adopted by ISO/IEC as the ISO/IEC8802-3 standard.
- 802.3z describes the Ethernet at Gb speeds.
- 802.4 is similar to 802.3, but instead of CSMA/CD it uses token passing accessing, and either CATV or fiber-optic cable. Adopted by ISO/IEC as the ISO/IEC8802-4 standard. See also CATV.
- 802.5 describes the physical layer and the MAC sublayer for token ring networks (see TR) that use a ring topology and the token passing accessing protocol. Adopted by ISO/IEC as the ISO/IEC8802-5 standard.
- 802.6 describes standards for metropolitan area networks (see MAN). See also DQDB. Adopted by ISO/IEC as the ISO/IEC8802-6 standard.
- 802.7 describes the minimal physical, electrical and mechanical features of broadband cable, as well as the installation and maintenance of such cable. Adopted by ISO/IEC as the ISO/IEC8802-7 standard.
- 802.8 describes the use of optical fiber in networks defined in the standards 802.3–802.6. Adopted by ISO/IEC as the ISO/IEC8802-8 standard.
- 802.9 specifies the integration of voice and data over the same lines (see IVD). Adopted by ISO/IEC as the ISO/IEC8802-9 standard.

– 802.10 specifies the security issues in LANs, as well as in architectures that are compatible with the OSI Reference Model (see OSI). Adopted by ISO/IEC as the ISO/IEC8802-10 standard.
– 802.11 addresses wireless networking standards (see WLAN). Adopted by ISO/IEC as the ISO/IEC8802-11 standard.
– 802.12 addresses the issues relating to the 100BaseVG proposal.

80X86 – A microprocessor family originally developed by Intel, introduced in 1982 with the first microprocessor 286 (80286). Since then the Intel brand names (286, 386, 486, 586) have become de facto standards for PC microprocessor architecture.

8B/10B – 8-Bit/10-Bit local fiber. A fiber channel physical media and encoding scheme that allows up to 149.76 Mbps datarates over multimode fiber (see MMF). In 8B/10B, every group of 8 bits is represented by a 10-bit symbol (explaining where the name comes from). This symbol is associated with a bit pattern that is then encoded using NRZI or another standard signal-encoding method. See also NRZI. Compare with 4B/5B and 5B/6B.

8N1 – Eight (8) data bits, No parity, one (1) stop bit. In serial communications, the term used for the most common serial port setup. It means that every element consists of eight bits, with no parity. The stop bit is a return to the idle value of the signal and it is mainly used as a confirmation that the transmission of the previous element is finished.

@ – at sign. The delimiter which separates the username and the hostname in an e-mail address (for instance, user@hostname). The “at” sign can be found on any computer keyboard and it is coded as a special character with ASCII code 40 HEX. This simple, but brilliant, choice by Ray Tomlinson allows e-mail users to easily remember e-mail addresses. See e-mail.

A

A – Ampere. Measurement unit for the strength of electric current. The official definition is that 1 Ampere represents the constant current that, if maintained in two straight parallel conductors of infinite length, of negligible circular cross-section, and placed 1 meter apart in a vacuum, would produce a force between these conductors equal to 2×10^{-7} Newtons per meter of length.

AA – Auto Answer. A modem feature in which the modem is available to answer and establish a connection automatically.

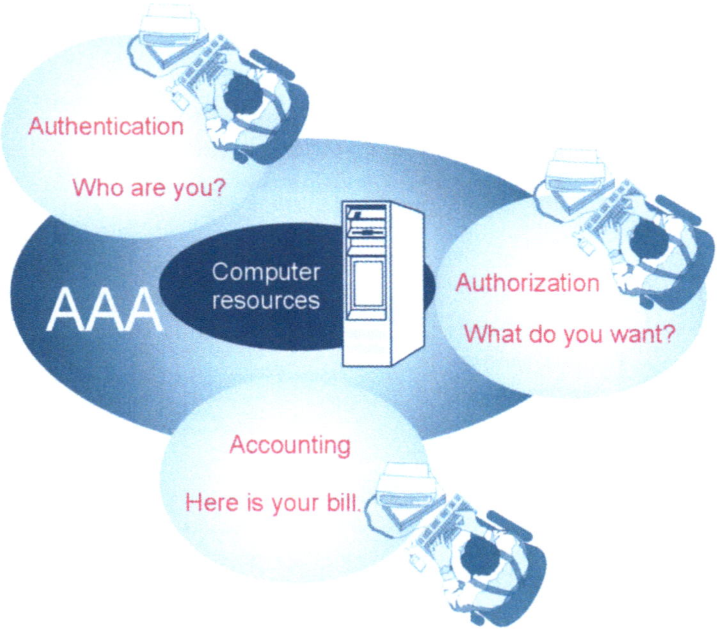

Fig. A-1. A simplified view of the AAA control mechanism

AAA – Authentication, Authorization, Accounting. A common term that describes three main access control mechanisms (see Fig. A-1). Authentication is the process used to identify the person who is trying to access some computer resources. Authentication is usually based on a user name and password. In more secure systems, in addition to authentication, an authorization process takes place, which gives access rights to the system based on the user identity. For example, the user is authorized to read files but has no rights to change anything. Finally, accounting measures the resources used during access, so that the measured data can be used either for billing the user or for resource planning. AAA services are often provided by a special-purpose AAA server such as the Remote Authentication Dial-In User Service (see RADIUS).

AAAI – American Association for Artificial Intelligence. A nonprofit scientific society founded in 1979 (http://www.aaai.org). AAAI is devoted to advancing the scientific understanding of artificial intelligence as well as to increasing public understanding of artificial intelligence, improving the teaching and training of AI practitioners, and providing guidance for research concerning the importance and potential of current AI developments and future directions.

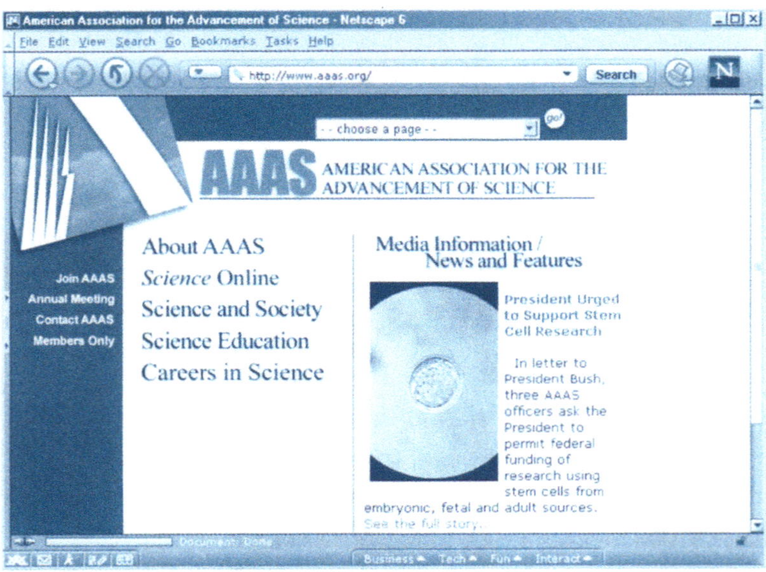

Fig. A-2. Homepage of AAAS (used with permission)

AAAS – American Association for the Advancement of Science. A nonprofit professional society (http://www.aaas.org) dedicated to the advancement of scientific and technological excellence across all disciplines, and to the public understanding of science and technology. It is one of the oldest societies in America, founded in Philadelphia in 1848. Pronounced “triple A-S”. See Fig. A-2.

AACE – Association for the Advancement of Computing in Education. An international, educational and professional organization founded in 1981 dedicated to the advancement of the knowledge, theory, and quality of learning and teaching at all levels using information technology.

AADN – American Association of Domain Names. The organization created by Chris Raines in May 1996. ADN offers to its members a comprehensive series of webpages to provide instruction and information to domain name owners, journalists, and even attorneys, etc. Also, there is a huge chronology of domain name disputes, including articles, policies, laws, legal documents etc.

AAF – Advanced Authoring Format. A multimedia file format introduced by Microsoft in 1998. It allows porting of multimedia presentations between different applications.

AAHE – American Association for Higher Education. The American national association of more than 8500 individuals (http://www.aahe.org) dedicated to improving the quality of American higher education. AAHE's members – faculty, administrators, and students from all sectors, as well as policymakers and leaders from foundations, government and business – believe that higher education should play a more central role in the national life and that their institutions can and must become more effective.

AAIM – Association for Applied Interactive Multimedia. An organization created to support professionals using and developing multimedia. AAIM conducts at least one major conference a year for the purpose of bringing together practicing multimedia professionals and those considering using multimedia and related activities (http://www.aaim.org).

AAL – ATM Adaptation Layer. An ATM layer (see ATM) used to transmit voice and video data, where fast delivery is more critical than accurate delivery. It is divided into two major parts: the upper layer is called the convergence sublayer dedicated to providing the interface to the application. The lower sublayer is called the Segmentation and Reassembly (SAR) layer and forms cell payloads by adding headers and trailers to the data units given to it by the convergence layer. These payloads are then passed to the ATM layer for transmission. The AAL supports four classes of services named A, B, C and D, also known as AAL1, AAL2, AAL3/4 and AAL5, respectively. Class A supports real-time connection-oriented communication with a constant bit rate for uncompressed video and other isochronous traffic. Class B has the same purpose, but with a variable bit rate. Class C is dedicated to connection-oriented communications with a variable bit rate but without real-time support. Finally, class D supports connectionless variable bit rate communications without real-time abilities. There is also an additional AAL called the Service-Specific Connection-Oriented Protocol (see SSCOP).

AAP – Association of American Publishers. An organization involved in the standardization of document preparation (http://www.publishers.org).

AAR – Automatic Alternate Routing. A network feature that allows automatic routing of network traffic in order to minimize distance, maximize throughput or balance channel usage.

AARP – AppleTalk Address Resolution Protocol. An implementation of the ARP protocol in the AppleTalk protocol suite. See also ARP.

AAS – Auto Area Segmentation. A technology used by Epson scanners, which detects and optimizes text and graphics on the same page.

AASERT – Augmentation Awards for Science and Engineering Research Training. A USDoD program that awards money to academic institutions to support graduate students training in science and engineering fields important to US national defense. The AASERT program is one element of the DoD's University Research Initiative (see URI).

ABBH – Average Bouncing Busy Hour. An approach for measuring traffic in various network trunks. It uses the peak hour of each day, over a certain period, and then the averaged traffic load for that period.

ABC – Atanasoff–Berry Computer. The first digital calculating machine that used vacuum tubes.

ABE – Agent Building Environment. An IBM toolkit intended for software developers that makes it easy to build an application based on agents or to add agents to an existing application. See also aglet, AWB and RP.

ABEL – Advanced Boolean Expression Language. A design language that allows complex logic designs to be entered, compiled, optimized, simulated and then implemented in the programmable logic. Although ABEL focuses on the programmable logic (see ASIC and FPGA), it can still be used to solve logic problems with discrete ICs. The power of ABEL is that it can produce an output with the simplicity needed for building with ICs, but gives the more advanced user the ability to design and build his/her own IC. The ABEL language uses minimization and optimization based on the Espresso optimization software from the University of California at Berkeley. The UNIX version of Espresso can be obtained via http://www-cad.eecs.berkeley.edu

ABEND – Abnormal End. A term used for abnormal termination of a task due to application errors.

ABF – Adobe Binary Font. Filename extension for files that contain Adobe Binary Screen Fonts.

ABI – Application Binary Interface. The interface by which an application program gains access to an operating system and other low-level services, designed to allow binary portability between machines with the same ABI. Also a part of the X/Open Common Application Environment (see CAE). Compare with API.

ABI+ – Application Binary Interface +. An Application Binary Interface (see ABI) specification dedicated to the Intel-based architectures intended for UNIX System V (see SVID). The specification addresses the ISO/ANCI C language, IEEE POSIX specification (see POSIX), SVID, UNIX System V ABI, and the Intel supplement for the System V ABI.

ABICC – Application Binary Interface C Compiler. C compiler available on SGI UNIX implementations (e.g. IRIX).

ABICC – Application Binary Interface Coordinating Committee. An industry group responsible for future editions of the System V Application Binary Interface (see ABI and ABI+).

ABIOS – Advanced Basic Input/Output System. A set of input/output routines inside IBM PS/2 microcomputers based on the Micro Channel Architecture (see MCA) which allows multitasking and the protected memory mode.

ABK – Auto Backup. A filename extension for a file that contains a CorelDraw automatic backup.

ABM – Asynchronous Balanced Mode. A High-Level Data-Link Control (see HDLC) communication mode supporting peer-oriented point-to-point communications between two stations in which both of them can initiate transmission.

ABR – Adobe Brush. A filename extension for a file that contains an Adobe PhotoShop brush (see Fig. A-3).

ABR – Available Bit Rate. ATM service that allows the transmission of huge amounts of data in burst traffic, the bandwidth range of which is roughly known. It is used for connections that do not require timing relationships between the source and destination. ABR is the only service with a rate feedback possibility, it allows for asking a sender to slow down when congestion occurs. A typical example is browsing the Web. This service does not control cell delay variation (see CDV), although admitted cells are not delayed unnecessarily.

ABR – Area Border Router. A common name for the router located on the border of one or more OSPF areas that connect those areas to the backbone network (see OSPF). ABRs are members of both the OSPF backbone and the attached areas.

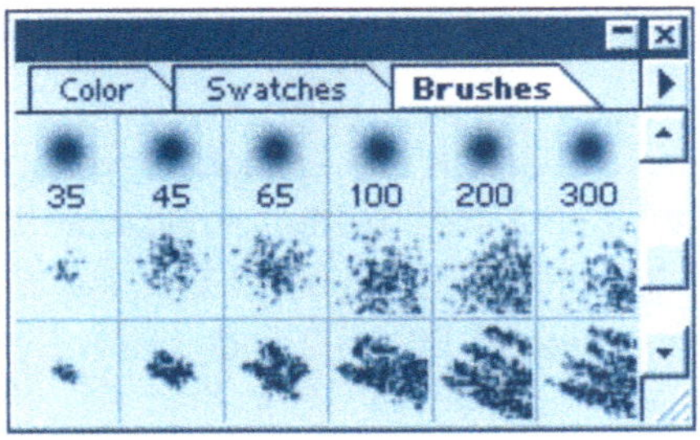

Fig. A-3. An example of an ABR file

ABX – Advanced Branch Exchange. A private branch exchange (see PBX) with advanced features, normally including the ability to handle both voice and data in an integrated manner.

AC – Access Control. A field in a token ring token or data frame.

AC – Accumulator. A register holding temporary results obtained using arithmetical or logical operations in microprocessors. Also abbreviated with ACC.

AC – Alternating Current. Electric current that periodically reverses its direction of polarity. In an average of time a “pure” AC power supply produces a sinewave. Its frequency is measured in cycles per second (Hertz, see Hz). This rate is not the same in all countries. For example, most European countries use AC at 50 Hz while North American countries use AC at 60 Hz. Consequently, some home electrical appliances or professional devices have either a 50/60-Hz switch or a power supply intended for a specific market area. Compare with Direct Current (DC).

AC – Application Context. A common term for all OSI application service elements (see ASE) required by an application in a particular context. In other words, in a peer-to-peer (see P2P) connection between two application layers AC provides the procedures for defining the particular relationship between them during the connection. Therefore, AC can determine the types of services that can be called during P2P connection and the manner in which information is to be exchanged. Therefore, such an application context is used as an input to another OSI element, called the common management information service (see CMISE), in order to provide the necessary system management.

ACAP – Application Configuration Access Protocol. An Internet protocol (RFC-2244) for accessing client program options, configurations, and preference information remotely, providing a solution for the problem of client mobility on the Internet. ACAP provides a protocol for arbitrary clients to store and retrieve client-specific configurations (address book, bookmarks, folders, etc.) from a server.

ACC – Accumulator. See AC (Accumulator).

ACC – Active Congestion Control. A technique under development that is intended for feedback congestion control across networks. ACC allows internal network nodes to act immediately when congestion occurs.

ACCU – Association of C and C++ Users. The society of C and C++ users all over the world (http://www.accu.org).

ACD – Automatic Call Distribution. A common name for a device or a service that automatically reroutes calls to a customer's geographically distributed locations served by the same central office (see CO). ACDs often provide some form of automatic caller identification such as Automatic Number Identification (see ANI) or Direct Inward Dialing (see DID), etc.

ACDC – Alternating Current–Direct Current. A common name for a device that transforms alternating current (see AC) into the required direct current (see DC).

ACDF – Access Control Decision Function. The term used in open systems (see PSI) to describe a function that uses access control information (see ACI) and other helpful data about how to access a particular resource in a given time and situation.

ACE – Access Control Entry. An entry in an Access Control List (see ACL). It contains a set of access rights and a security identifier (see SID).

ACE – Advanced Computing Environment. An industrial consortium founded to define an open architecture based on MIPS R4000.

ACE – Adverse Channel Enhancement. A modem feature that allows the modem to adjust itself for noisy lines.

ACE – Australasian Computing Education. An international conference focusing on the field of computing education.

ACEF – Access Control Enforcement Function. In open systems (see PSI and OSI), a function that implements the decision made by an Access Control Decision Function (see ACDF).

ACeS – Asia Cellular Satellite system. A digital communication service for mobile telephone and computer users in the Asia–Pacific region. It is the integrated GSM-based satellite system based on Ericsson technology. See also GSM.

ACF – Advanced Communications Functions. An IBM prefix attached to products that support SNA functions. For example, ACF/VTAM indicates that this version of VTAM supports SNA devices. See also SNA and VTAM.

ACF – Application Configuration File. In Microsoft Visual Studio, a filename extension for a file that contains configuration attributes for an application.

ACI – Access Control Information. Part of the X.500 Directory services used to control access to a file or directory.

ACI – Autonomous Citation Indexing. A citation indexing system that is capable of creating a citation index from literature in an electronic format.

ACIA – Asynchronous Communications Interface Adapter. An integrated circuit type that allows data access to RS-232 serial interfaces.

ACID – Atomicity, Consistency, Isolation, Durability. An acronym for desirable properties of transactions in a Database Management System (see DBMS). Atomicity refers to a transaction as an atomic processing unit either performed completely or not performed at all. Consistency assumes that correct execution of the transaction must hold the database in a consistent state. Isolation refers to the transaction update invisibility to other transactions until it is committed. Finally, durability does not allow changes that have occurred in the database to be lost due to subsequent failure.

ACISP – Australasian Conference on Information Security and Privacy. An international conference focusing on information security and privacy, including electronic commerce and network security.

ACK – Acknowledgment. A control code (ASCII character 6) sent to a sending computer by a receiving computer in order to acknowledge either its ready state to accept transmission or that error-free transmitted information has just arrived. Compare with NAK.

ACL – Accelerator file. A filename extension for a file that contains keyboard accelerator data, i.e. the most frequently used words.

ACL – Access Control List. One of the software security methods that asks a user about his/her rights to access a particular file. All ACL schemes associate with each file form a list of users who may access the file and how.

ACL – Agent Communication Language. A common term for a language used for agent-to-agent communication programming.

ACM – Address Complete Message. A call control message used in the B-ISDN User's Part (see BISUP) from the receiving exchange to the sending exchange indicating that the address information is complete.

ACM – Association for Computing Machinery. A well-known membership computer society established in 1947 (http://www.acm.org). The publisher of a number of highly rated scientific journals such as ACM Computing Surveys, Communications of the ACM (see CACM), Standard View, Multimedia Systems, Wireless Networks, Transactions on Database Systems, Transactions on Graphics (see TOG) etc. In addition, every year ACM organizes a large number of international conferences related to computers and communications. ACM has around 100,000 members who drive its publications, special interest groups (see SIG), conferences, awards etc.

ACM – Audio Compression Manager. A Microsoft utility that enables any Windows program to compress and decompress audio files in a variety of formats.

ACME – A Company that Makes Everything. A marketing term used to refer to a company that can make everything that the user needs to have. Sometimes ACME is just used as a phrase instead of referring to the real capability of a company, because the user's needs do not always match the capabilities of the vendor.

ACOSM – Australian Conference on Software Measurement. The Australian conference focusing on research in the field of software measurement.

ACPI – Advanced Configuration and Power management Interface. A specification from Intel, Microsoft and Toshiba that defines the interface between the operating system, the hardware and the BIOS software. Particular hardware platforms are described in ACPI tables. These descriptions allow the hardware to be built in flexible ways and can describe arbitrary operation sequences needed to make the hardware functions.

ACR – Actual Cell Rate. The current rate of a sender in ATM networks. The ACR lies between the minimum cell rate (see MCR) and the peak cell rate (see PCR).

ACR – Attenuation-to-Crosstalk Ratio. One of the factors that limits the distance a signal may be sent through a given media, usually expressed in decibels. It is the ratio of the power of the received signal, attenuated by the media, to the power of the NEXT crosstalk from the local transmitter (see NEXT).

ACS – Asynchronous Communications Server. A dedicated PC or expansion board used to provide network access to any of several serial ports.

ACS – ATM Circuit Steering. A method of routing ATM traffic to built-in test facilities in ATM equipment for monitoring and analysis.

ACSAC – Australasian Computer Systems Architecture Conference. An international conference focusing on all aspects of computer systems architecture. The proceedings are published by IEEE CS Press.

ACSC – Australasian Computer Science Conference. An annual conference focusing on research and novel applications in computer science.

ACSDE – American Center for the Study of Distance Education. The center established in 1988 (http://www.cdu.edu/ACSDE) seeks to promote distance education research, study, scholarship and teaching, and to serve as a clearinghouse for the dissemination of knowledge about distance education.

ACSE – Association Control Service Element. An application service element (see ASE) built into the seventh OSI layer (see OSI) in order to establish and clear a logical association (connection) between two application entities.

ACT – Actor. A filename extension for a file that contains a Microsoft Office Assistant Actor.

ACT – Australia Central (Darwin) Time. Time zone. UTC + 9.50 hours. No daylight saving applies in this zone.

ACTLU – Activate Logical Unit. In SNA communications, a command sent by a System Service Control Point (see SSCP) to a Logical Unit (see LU) to activate a session and establish session parameters. See also SNA.

ACTPU – Activate Physical Unit. In SNA communications, a command sent by a SSCP to a Physical Unit (see PU) to activate a session and establish session parameters. See also SNA.

ACTS – Advanced Communications Technologies and Services. The research and development program founded by the European Union in 1995. It has been devoted to projects for the European information highway.

ACTS – Application Conformance Test Suite. A test suite provided in a binary form used by application developers in order to test the conformance of their software to the ABI+ specification (see ABI and ABI+).

ACU – Automatic Calling Unit. A device that is capable of automatically initiating transmission calls.

AD – After Dark. A file that contains a screensaver program that can be set to randomly display a variety of screensaver patterns (see SCR) one after another.

A/D – Analog-to-Digital converter. A device that converts analog signals to appropriate digital signals. The A/D samples the input analog signal and converts each such measurement to the corresponding digital value. A reverse process is possible using digital-to-analog converters (see D/A or DAC).

AD – Administrative Domain. A set of hosts, bridges, routers, terminals, modems, etc., managed by a single administration authority.

Ad – Web Advertising. A large graphic image of a designated pixel size and byte size limit, usually animated, used to advertise something on the Web.

AD – Authorized Distributor. A marketing term used to designate a company that is authorized to distribute hardware or software having a brand name.

ADAM – Affordable Desktop Application Manager. The name of the CERN project trying to simplify user interactivity in the UNIX environment. ADAM is clearly inspired by the user interfaces offered by PC and Macintosh desktops in which applications and groups of applications are represented by icons and make use of the drag & drop paradigm. ADAM was developed in the object-oriented extension to Tcl/Tk (see Tcl/Tk). Documentation can be obtained via http://wwwinfo.cern.ch/umtf/adam

ADB – Active Database. The basic concept of an ADB is the ECA rule (see ECA) that defines the next state of a database. Once a set of rules has been defined, the ADBMS (see ADBMS) monitors the events, evaluates conditions associated with events, and triggers the relevant rules.

ADB – Ada Body. A filename extension for a file that contains the body part of an Ada program.

ADB – Apple Desktop Bus. A serial communications pathway built into some Apple computers (e.g. the Macintosh) that enables low-speed input devices, such as a keyboard or mouse, to communicate with the computer. The ADB can connect up to 16 devices, including graphics tablets, trackballs and light pens, to the computer. Although there are only two external ports, more than two devices can be linked in a series called a daisy chain.

ADBIS – Advances in Databases and Information Systems. An international conference which takes place in Eastern Europe, run by the ACM SIGMOD.

ADBMS – Active Database Management System. ADBMS provides mechanisms for ECA rule (see ECA) definition and execution. An ADBMS can support different event types, such as database events (update, deletion, querying, rule definition, transaction boundaries and other administrative operations), temporal events (periodic, at-a-particular-time, relative-timing, options) or general application signals. An event type may be primitive or composite. All ADBs have primitive event types, but some of them have combinations of primitive or composite events. The 10 mandatory features that are needed to qualify as an active database system, and the desired features which are nice to have, are given in Fig. A-4.

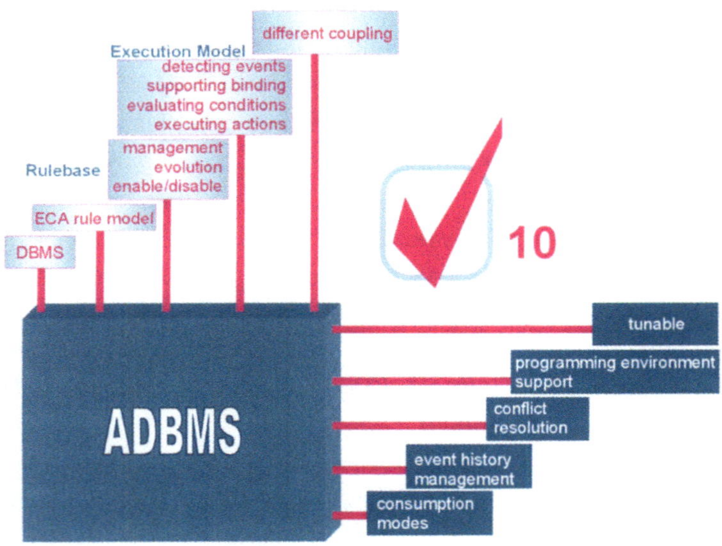

Fig. A-4. The mandatory features of ADBMS

ADC – Advanced Data Connector. The former name for Remote Data Services (see RDS).

ADC – Analog-to-Digital Converter. See A/D.

ADC – Australasian Database Conference. An annual conference focusing on research, development and novel applications of database systems. Topics include data mining, data warehousing, distributed and parallel databases, heterogeneity and interoperability, query processing and optimization, high-dimensional and temporal data, spatial data processing and management, web access to databases, etc.

ADCCP – Advanced Data Communications Control Procedure. An ANSI bit-oriented communication protocol (X3.66) based on the IBM SDLC protocol. All the bit-oriented protocols use the frame structure shown in Fig. A-5. The frame is recognized by flags (the 8-bit defined pattern) at the beginning and at the end of the frame. There are address, control, data and checksum fields between the flags. The data field has an unlimited bit length, the other fields inside the frame have limited lengths defined for particular bit-oriented protocols (e.g. see HDLC).

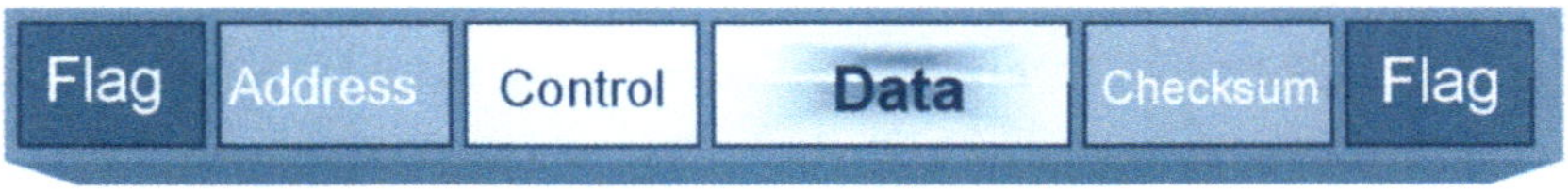

Fig. A-5. Frame format for bit-oriented protocols

ADCU – Association of Data Communications Users. A data communications users professional organization.

ADF – Application Development Facility. A very powerful application generator produced by IBM to reduce the design, coding, testing and documenting efforts.

ADI – AutoCAD Device-Independent file. A filename extension for a file that contains the device-independent binary plotter format generated by the AutoCAD drawing package.

ADL – Advances in Digital Libraries. The ACM/IEEE joint conference concerning digital libraries (see DL) research and technology. Among other things, the conference topics are agent technologies, data mining, collaborative research, testbed systems for DLs, document models, intellectual property, security and privacy, knowledge representation (see KR) and knowledge integration, resource discovery and management, multimedia libraries, standards and protocols, etc.

ADL – Architectural Description Language. A language used to describe system architecture.

ADM – Add-Drop Multiplexing. A way to demultiplex a high-speed traffic stream into its lower-speed components so that an additional low-speed channel can be added.

ADMD – Administration Management Domain. Based on RFC1208, this is a public service carrier for the X.400 Message Handling System (see MHS).

Some examples are MCI Mail and AT&T Mail in the US, British Telecom Gold-400mail, etc. Compare with Private Management Domain (PRMD).

ADN – Advanced Digital Network. Referring to a 56 Kbps leased line, this is a digital phone-line connection (leased line) capable of carrying 56,000 bps. At this speed, 10 Mb will take about 3 min to transfer. This is, for example, four times faster than a 14,400 bps modem.

ADN – Any day now. The chat term.

ADN – Automatic Digital Network. A digital network operated by the US Department of Defense (see DoD).

ADO – ActiveX Data Objects. A set of component interfaces developed by Microsoft that allows developers to build both desktop applications and Web applications. Essentially, ADO is the high-level interface for accessing OLE DB (see OLE). ADO can be used across all applications and tools already available, such as Visual Basic, C/C++, Java, IIS and Active Server Pages (see ASP), etc.

ADP – Automatic Data Processing. An early umbrella term related to some work performed by computers to achieve some specific goals. It usually refers to big computers (hosts)-oriented processing, and sometimes referred to company organization units in charge of company data processing. The term is also known as electronic data processing (EDP or just DP).

ADPCM – Adaptive Differential (or Delta) Pulse Code Modulation. A type of pulse code modulation technique (see PCM) used in data compression applications. Adaptive and differential attributes follow the method that uses the delta value between the current and the previous sample signal. ADPCM is useful in multimedia applications because it increases the effective bit resolution.

ADR – AfterDark Randomizer. A screensaver file that can be set to randomly display a variety of screensaver patterns one after another.

ADRS II – A Departmental Reporting System II. An IBM query/report language designed for end-users, such as accountants and executives, to allow them to produce some results without additional assistance from information technology professionals.

ADS – Ada Specification. A filename extension for a file that contains the specification of an Ada program.

ADSI – Active Directory Service Interface. A Microsoft programming interface based on COM objects used for accessing directory services.

ADSI – Analog Display Service Interface. An industrial standard protocol developed by Bellcore in 1993 that allows alternate voice and data services over the analog telephone network. It is possible to build ADSI into several communication devices such as pagers, personal digital assistants (see PDA), and personal computers with telephone applications, cable TV, etc.

ADSL – Asymmetric Digital Subscriber Line. A network service appropriate for applications such as video on demand (see VoD), designed to provide more bandwidth downstream from the central office (see CO) to the customer site. In addition, the abbreviation also applied to the ADSL Forum, the organization developing and defining xDSL standards (http://www.adsl.com).

ADSP – AppleTalk Data Stream Protocol. An AppleTalk protocol laid on a session layer that allows two nodes to establish a reliable connection.

ADT – Abstract Data Type. A term analogous to the system-defined data types characterized by their behavior. ADT differs from a conventional data type because its operations are user-defined and ADT encapsulates its definition. Generally, it is used to describe complex objects.

ADTF – ACR Decrease Time Factor. In ATM networks, the time permitted between sending Resource Management cells (see RM) before the rate is decreased to the initial cell rate (see ICR).

AE – Application Entity. An abstract term that represents an entity such as a computer, printer or software application. AEs exist in the seventh layer of the OSI Reference Model. For example, if a computer sends information to a printer, both the computer and the printer represent application entities.

AEDT – Australia Eastern Daylight Time. Time zone. UTC + 11.00 hours. It applies during the Australian summer, i.e. the calendar winter. The state of Queensland does not operate AEDT – it's on AEST all year round.

AENOR – Asociación Española de Normalización y Certificación. The Spanish national standards organization (http://www.aenor.es).

AEP – AppleTalk Echo Protocol. A transport-layer protocol used in AppleTalk network architectures.

AES – Application Environment Specification. A collection of Open Software Foundation (see OSF) specifications designed to provide a consistent application environment on different hardware platforms. It includes user commands and program interfaces for the operating system, user environment, and network services.

AEST – Australia Eastern Standard Time. Time zone. UTC + 10.00 hours.

AFAIK – As far as I know. The chat term.

AFC – Application Foundation Classes. Microsoft's version of the Java Foundation Classes (see JFC). AFC sits on top of the Java Development Kit (see JDK) and extends the Abstract Windows Toolkit (see AWT). Compare with Internet Foundation Classes (IFC).

AFDW – Active Framework for Data Warehousing. A data warehousing solution developed by Microsoft and Texas Instruments that represents Microsoft's standard for managing metadata. See also DW.

AFEB – African EDIFACT Board. The coordinating body for Electronic Data Interchange (see EDI) for the national standards organizations of Africa.

AFI – Authority and Format Identifier. A part of the address for the network service access point (see NSAP) in the OSI Reference Model (see OSI). The AFI is intended to specify the authority that allocates the values of the initial domain identifier (see IDI), as well as to specify the format of the IDI and the domain specific part (see DSP), both representing the other parts of the NSAP address.

AFIPS – American Federation of Information Processing Societies. The US association of computing and information-related organizations established in 1961. AFIPS is involved in education, research and standardization.

AFK – Away from keyboard. The chat term.

AFM – Adobe Font Metrics. A text file that defines a font metrics and pair kerning information used to change the spacing between letters for optical clarity and aesthetic reasons.

AFNOR – Association Française de Normalisation. The French national standards institute (http://www.afnor.fr), a member of ISO.

AFP – Advanced Function Printing. The ability to print text and images using all-points-addressable (see APA) printers. The term is connected with the IBM SAA (see SAA). Users are able to control formatting, the form of paper output, whether a document is to be printed or viewed online, and manage a document in a distributed network across different platforms (DOS, Windows, OS/2, OS/400, AIX, VMS, etc.).

AFP – AppleTalk File Protocol. An application/session-layer protocol used in the AppleTalk environment.

AFS – Andrew File System. A distributed file system developed at Carnegie Mellon University as part of the Andrew project. OSF adopts it as part of its Distributed Computing Environment (see DCE).

AFT – Application File Transfer. A prefix that identifies FTAM profiles in the International Standardized Profile grouping (see ISP). See also File Transfer Access and Management (FTAM).

AFTP – Anonymous File Transfer Protocol. A special kind of File Transfer Protocol (see FTP) that allows the user to retrieve documents, files, programs, and other data anywhere in the Internet without having to establish a "userid" and use a password. It is possible to use a special user identity ("anonymous") to bypass local security checks and get access to publicly accessible files on a remote system. Users have restricted access rights with anonymous FTP and usually can only copy files to or from a public directory, often named /pub, on the remote system. Many FTP sites do not permit anonymous FTP access in order to maintain security. Those that do permit anonymous FTP sometimes restrict users to only downloading files.

aglet – agile applet. A small application program (see applet) with the capability of serving as a mobile agent in a computer network (see RP). It is a class or template written in Java with object-passing capabilities, autonomy and the possibility of interacting with other program objects and/or of dispatching itself to run in parallel on different computers. The term originated from IBM (see AWB).

AGP – Accelerated Graphics Port. A bus specification made by Intel to allow high-quality low-cost graphics. It enables 3D graphics to be displayed quickly on ordinary PCs. AGP uses PC RAM for refreshing the monitor image.

AGRAS – Antiglare–Antireflective–Antistatic. An attribute combination usually used to refer to a monitor screen. Antiglare and antireflective refer to any measure taken to reduce reflections of external light on a monitor screen. The screen may be coated with a chemical (which may reduce its brightness), covered with a polarizing filter, or simply rotated so that external light is not reflected into the user's eye. Furthermore, antistatic refers to a device designed to minimize shocks caused by the buildup of static electricity, which can disrupt computer equipment or cause data loss. An antistatic device may take the form of a floor mat, a wristband with a wire attached to the workstation, a spray, a lotion, or other special-purpose device.

AGT – Argentina Time. Time zone. UTC – 3.00 hours. See TZ.

AH – Adaptive Hypermedia. An international conference focusing on the adaptive hypermedia and adaptive Web-based systems. Some of the major topics include information filtering in the Web context, intelligent tutoring systems (see ITS) on the Web, Web data mining, user modeling, etc.

AHA – Accelerated Hub Architecture. The microprocessor architecture developed by Intel that uses a dedicated bus for data exchange between processors. AHA replaces the PCI bus architecture. See also PCI.

AHFG – ATM-attached Host Functional Group. A group of functions performed by an ATM-attached host that is participating in a MPOA service.

AI – Adobe Illustrator. Filename extensions for files that contain drawings made by Adobe Illustrator.

AI – Applied Informatics. The IASTED international conference focusing on the latest research in the area of applied informatics.

AI – Artificial Intelligence. A common umbrella term for the computer science field which deals with a computer-supported human-brain emulation to solve a lot of problems. Such problems include speech recognition, natural language processing, intelligent retrieval from databases, expert consulting, creative response, theorem proving, learning from experience, automatic education and student modeling (see ITS), controlling the physical actions taken by robots, automatic programming, and so on. Thus, AI can be seen as an attempt to model aspects of human thought on computers. In order to achieve these goals, AI tries to understand how living things think and to find out how to implement that knowledge on computers. Some of the latest fields being focused on by AI researchers are network management by intelligent agents (see DAI), intelligent agents in electronic commerce (see EC), etc. See also RP (Remote Programming) and NCC.

AI – Authentication Information. A common term used in the network security area to determine whether a user is authorized to access the system.

AIEC – Artificial Intelligence and Electronic Commerce. The international workshop focusing on all areas related to the theoretical and practical aspects of AI technologies applied in electronic commerce.

AIF – Audio Interchange File. A filename extension for a file that contains a sound format used by Silicon Graphics and Macintosh applications.

AIFC – Audio Interchange File Compressed. The compressed version of an Audio Interchange File (see AIF and AIFF).

AIFF – Audio Interchange File Format. See AIF, an Audio Interchange File.

AIM – Advanced Informatics in Medicine. A 1988 research program on the development and application of information technology and telecommunications to medicine and healthcare for both medical practitioners and manufacturers of medical products and equipment.

AIM – Analog Intensity Modulation. A method of modulation that uses light signals (rather than electrical) where the intensity of the light source depends on the transmitted signal variations.

AIM – AOL Instant Messenger. A filename extension for AOL Instant Messenger launch files.

AIM – ATM Inverse Multiplexer. See AIMUX.

AIMSA – Artificial Intelligence: Methodology, Systems, Applications. The biennial international conference concerning the research and development of Artificial Intelligence (see AI) held in Bulgaria since 1984.

AIMUX – ATM Inverse Multiplexer. A device that allows multiple T1 or E1 communications facilities to be combined into a single broadband facility in order to transmit ATM cells. See E1 and T1. Also abbreviated as AIM.

AIN – Advanced Intelligent Network. The architectural concept for the creation of the next generation in telecommunications, which promises to bring advanced capabilities to residential, business, and mobile customers on the local network level. These capabilities have been previously available only in the long-haul networks.

AIOD – Automatic Identification of Outward Dialing. A PBX service that identifies the calling extension to provide cost accounting data. See also Private Branch Exchange (PBX).

AIP – Association of Internet Professionals. The organization founded to support, unify and represent the global community of Internet professionals.

AIS – Alarm Indication Signal. An all-ones signal used in the ISO/OSI network management (see OSI) as well as in broadband ISDN networks (see B-ISDN) to indicate that an error has occurred somewhere on the network.

AIT – Advanced Intelligent Tape. The proprietary 8-mm tape backup format.

AIX – Advanced Interactive eXecutive. The IBM proprietary name for its UNIX implementation for computers based on IBM RISC processors.

AKA – Also Known As. A common acronym used to note that some term is also known by another name. For example, CPI-C AKA XCPI-C.

AKDT – Alaska Standard Daylight Saving Time. Time zone. UTC – 8.00 hours. See TZ.

AKST – Alaska Standard Time. Time zone. UTC – 9.00 hours. See TZ.

AL – Application Layer. The topmost of the seven OSI layers (see OSI).

ALC – ACUCOBOL License. A filename extension for a file that contains ACUCOBOL license data (see COBOL), as shown in Fig. A-6.

ALENEX – Algorithm Engineering and Experiments. The annual international workshop focusing on original research in the implementation and experimental evaluation of algorithms and data structures.

ALGOL – Algorithmic Language. One of the root high-level programming languages (see 3GL) from the 1950s having its own programming language family, from the old grandpa ALGOL60 to its young grandchildren C and C++. Unlike FORTRAN which has been used widely throughout the years, ALGOL takes its place in programming language history thanks to its role in programming language development because many of the fundamental programming structures were first introduced in ALGOL.

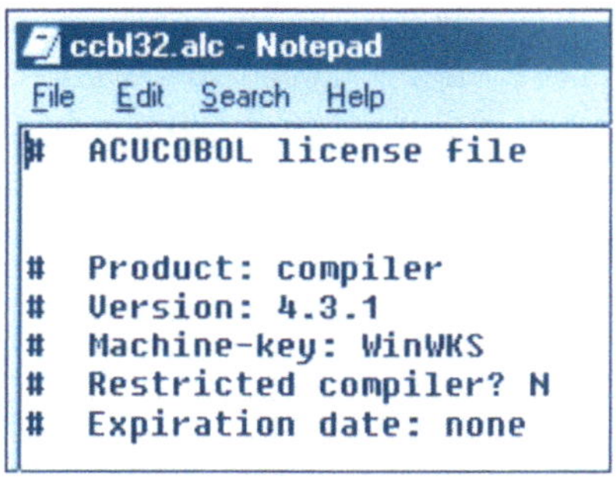

Fig. A-6. An example of an ALC file (part of it)

ALIBI – Adaptive Location of Internetworked Bases of Information. A resource discovery and information retrieval tool. ALIBI is neither a navigational system like the WWW nor a resource catalog like Archie. It is fully distributed and fully automatic, allowing users to quickly and easily retrieve data using a query-based interface.

ALIWEB – Archie-Like Indexing for the Web. A public service provided by NEXOR, UK (http://aliweb.emnet.co.uk). It proposes that people keep track of the services they provide in such a way that an automatic program can simply pick up their descriptions in a standard format, and combine them into a searchable database. Using ALIWEB, anybody can search this database.

ALM – Airline Miles. The method used to calculate distance (for rating purposes) of the point-to-point connections in the AT&T network.

ALT – Adult Literacy and Technology Network. A US national effort dedicated to finding solutions for using technology to enhance adult literacy. Additional information can be found at http://www.otan.dni.us/webfarm/alt

ALT – Algorithmic Learning Theory. An international conference concerning neural networks, learning dimensions, inductive inference, mathematical tools for learning, recursive functions learning, online learning, and the other aspects of algorithmic learning theory. The ALT proceedings are published by Springer-Verlag as part of the Lecture Notes in Computer Science (see LNCS).

ALU – Arithmetic Logic Unit. An integral part of the microprocessor chip dedicated to arithmetic, logical and comparative functions.

AM – Accounting Management. A function used in network management in order to obtain various data from a network, such as its performance, network usage, etc.

AM – Active Monitor. The node in a token ring network (see TR) that is responsible for creating, passing, and maintaining the token (see Fig. A-7). See also Standby Monitor (SM) and Active Monitor Present (AMP).

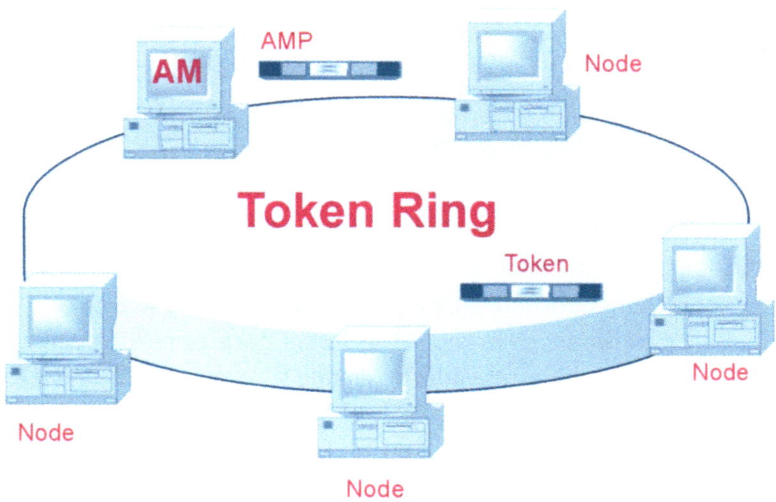

Fig. A-7. Active Monitor in a TR network

AM – Amplitude Modulation. A method used to perform information encoding by varying the amplitude of the electrical "carrier" which allows data to be transmitted across an analog network such as a switched telephone network.

AMAI – Annals of Mathematics and Artificial Intelligence. The scientific journal published by Baltzer that covers the influence of mathematical and computational techniques in the field of artificial intelligence.

AMAST – Algebraic Methodology and Software Technology. An international conference focusing on software technologies on a mathematical basis. In particular, the conference concerning the formal methods in software technology, concurrent and reactive systems, logic programming, object-oriented programming, functional programming, constraint programming, language and tools specification, theorem proving, relational and computational algebra, etc. The conference has been held every two years since 1989 in different countries and the proceedings are published by Springer-Verlag (see LNCS).

AMD – Advanced Micro Devices. An American company (http://www.amd.com) producing microprocessors, founded in 1969.

AME – Advanced Metal Evaporated. The Exatape data cartridge that allows up to 40 GB data storage.

AME – Asynchronous Modem Eliminator. A serial cable and connector that enable two computers to communicate directly. Also known as a null modem.

AMF – Account Metering Function. A function used in the OSI management model in order to hold records of every user's resource usage.

AMH – Application Message Handling. The prefix used in the International Standardized Profile model (see ISP) to identify the actions of the Message Handling System (see MHS).

AMI – Alternate Mark Inversion. The binary modulation code used by telephone companies for data and digital voice transmission. AMI uses RZ coding in an alternate bipolar scheme, with logical zeros corresponding to 0 V, and logical ones alternating between +3 V and –3 V. In the case of self-synchronization the number of continuous zeros must be limited. See also B8ZS and RZ.

AMI – American Megatrends Inc. An American company producing low-level system software for PC computers as well as RAID controllers. Additional information is available at http://www.megatrends.com

AMI BIOS – AMI Basic Input/Output System. The very popular BIOS, developed by AMI, stored in the ROM chip together with the configuration software. This allows modification of system settings without a separate configuration disk. See also BIOS.

AMP – Active Monitor Present. A packet issued (see Fig. A-7) every 3 s by an active monitor (see AM) used in token ring networks (see TR) in order to prove or disprove that the AM is still on duty and that a particular network can (or cannot) continue to operate properly.

A

AMPS – Advanced Mobile Phone System. An analog cellular communication technology that relies on frequency division multiplexing (see FDM). In AMPS, a particular geographic region is divided into relatively small cells, typically 10–20 km in diameter, each using some set of frequencies (825–890 MHz). AMPS was born in AT&T Bell Laboratories.

AMR – Audio/Modem Riser. The Intel specification for small modem boards equipped with a codec chip (see CODEC) that plugs directly into the motherboard of a computer. See also MDC.

AMS – Andrew Message System. A multimedia interface to electronic mail and bulletin boards developed as part of the Andrew project at Carnegie Mellon University. See also Andrew File System (AFS).

AMT – Address Mapping Table. A table used by routers or DNS servers to resolve IP addresses from a text entry such as a name. See also DNS and IP.

A/N – Alphanumeric. A common name for a string or data record consisting of letters, digits, control characters, space characters, etc., all of them belonging to ASCII, EBCDIC or some other character set.

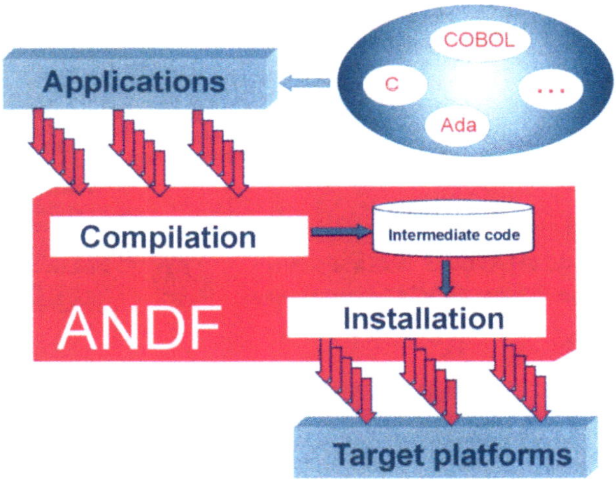

Fig. A-8. An overall view of the ANDF functionality

ANDF – Architecture-Neutral Distribution Format. This is a format proposed by the Open Software Foundation (see OSF), which allows software products to be distributed on a single magnetic tape format in an open way, independent of a target running machine (see Fig. A-8). The idea has been borrowed from the music industry where any distribution house can produce a compact disk or an audio tape and sell it without having to think of what kind of player will be used to deliver a beautiful sound to the customers. A full ANDF implementation can produce an amazing effect in software distribution and maintenance.

ANF – AppleTalk Networking Forum. An industrial consortium focused on the AppleTalk protocol encapsulation in other protocol suites.

ANI – Animated cursor. A Windows NT feature that allows a series of frames, one after another, to appear at the mouse pointer location instead of a single image, thus producing a short loop of animation. Also a filename extension.

Fig. A-9. ANSI Online home page (with permission of ANSI)

ANI – Automatic Number Identification. A service implemented by ISDN that enables the receiver of a phone call to see the phone number of the caller on a special display. Also known as caller ID (see CLID). See also ISDN.

ANM – Answer Message. A call control message used in B-ISDN BISUP from the receiving exchange to the sending exchange indicating an answer, and that a through connection should be completed in both directions.

ANN – Artificial Neural Networks. A family of massively parallel, nonlinear, distributed processing algorithms used to model a system from its past behavior. See also Artificial Intelligence (AI).

ANS – ANSI file. A filename extension for a file that contains ANSI text.

ANSI – American National Standards Institute. An acronym, pronounced "ann-see", for an organization of American industry, government, consumers and business groups dedicated to voluntary consensus standards and conformity assessment programs. ANSI works in numerous industry sectors and is the US representative in ISO. It is recognized all over the world for its work on computer and communication standards development, including programming languages (FORTAN, COBOL, C, etc.), and SCSI and SQL recommendations. Additional information is available at http://www.ansi.org. See Fig. A-9.

ANSI/SPARC – ANSI Standards Planning and Requirements Committee. See SPARC.

ANZEB – Australia/New Zealand EDIFACT Board. The coordinating body for Electronic Data Interchange (see EDI) for Australia and New Zealand.

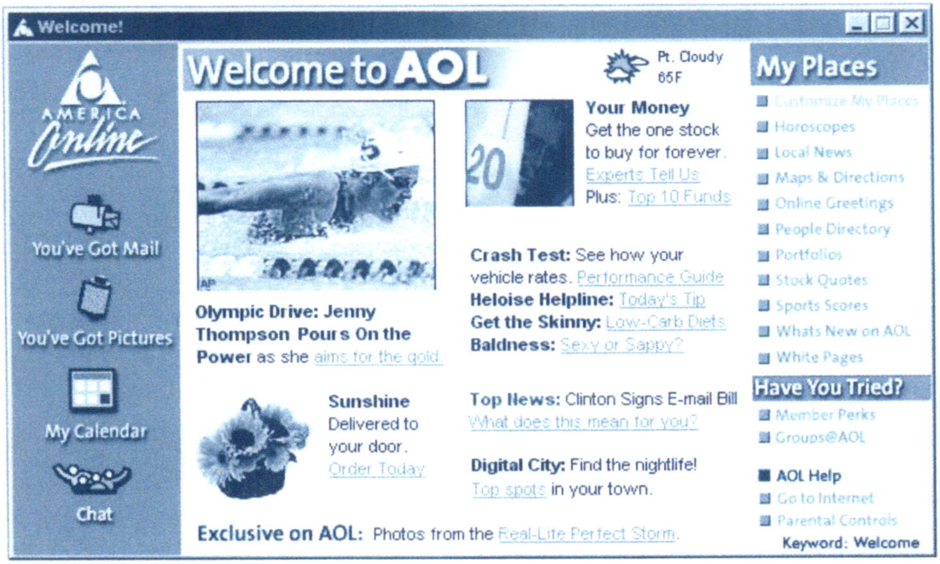

Fig. A-10. AOL welcome page.

AOL – America Online. One of the world's most popular Internet online services. It has over 28 million members worldwide (http://www.aol.com) and it is growing all the time. The service provides subscribers with a variety of interactive features: electronic mail, Internet access, news, sports, weather forecast, financial information and transactions, electronic shopping, and many more. See Fig. A-10.

AOM – Application OSI Management. The term related to the network management used in the International Standardized Profile model (see ISP).

AOP – Agent-Oriented Programming. A new approach to programming distributed systems, emphasizing explicit representation of time, beliefs, and commitments, including speech-act-like communicative commands.

AOP – Aspect-Oriented Programming. A new programming paradigm that tries to use the most appropriate paradigm to write the primary functionality of a system, and then the other aspects that do not fit into the chosen paradigm can be written in a more special-purpose language. Compilation of such different language-based programs requires a special kind of compiler called a weaver.

AOW – Asia–Oceanic Workshop. The regional organization in Pacific-Rim countries that performs the same functions as the European EWOS (see EWOS).

AP – Adaptive Programming. A programming paradigm, successor of the object-oriented paradigm (see OO).

AP – Application Process. An application that knocks at the door of the seventh OSI layer in order to ask for OSI services (see OSI).

APA – All Points Addressable. A computer graphics term related to the possibility of directly addressing any picture element on the graphics screen.

APAQS – Asia–Pacific on Quality Software. An international conference focusing on software quality. Some of the major topics include distributed, concurrent, real-time and Web-based systems testing, object-oriented models and design, metrics, software quality assurance, test case generation, etc. The proceedings are published by IEEE CS Press.

APAR – Authorized Program Analysis Report. An IBM term used for tracing bugs in programs that are discovered either by users or within IBM. A unique APAR for every program bug is used until it is fixed (see PTF).

APC – Asynchronous Procedure Call. In operating systems, a function call that executes separately from an executing program when a set of enabling conditions has occurred. A software interrupt is issued by the operating system's kernel to switch on the executing program to execute the call.

APDU – Application Protocol Data Unit. The highest-level view of the communication data exchanged between two applications over the ISO OSI-based communications (see OSI and PDU).

APE – Application Performance Explorer. A Microsoft tool that allows users to model their own application designs and test expected performances. A user's favorite design profiles can also be saved for later use, so the development of the next application should be faster and easier. According to the Microsoft Development Network (see MSDN), APE is a very suitable tool for the design of multitier (see EIS) client/server distributed applications. In addition, APE is able to simulate various deployment options and their implications on application functionality. Such options, for instance, could include the network bandwidth, machine boundaries, server capabilities, etc.

API – Application Programming Interface. A set of high-level routines used by an application program to call and take care of lower-level services offered by an operating system, database management system, graphics system, a network or the like. API is defined at the source code level. An API allows application programmers to stay out of the operating depth. It allows the programmer to fully concentrate on the application problem rather than to think about how to, for example, draw a line on a particular workstation under the UNIX environment and send it by TCP/IP to a workstation over FDDI. There are many APIs explained elsewhere in this book. To find them, just follow the arranged subject index at the end of the book. Compare with ABI.

APIA – Application Programming Interface Association. See XAPIA.

APL – A Programming Language. A very-high-level mathematics-oriented (especially for matrix and vector operations) interpreted programming language developed by Kenneth Iverson in the mid-1960s.

APL – Array Processing Languages. An international conference focusing on the array processing languages and their usefulness in rapid development, prototyping and toolbox creation.

APM – Advanced Power Management. An advanced display environmental feature that allows automatic power-off after a preset period of inactivity.

APN – Advances in Petri Nets. An international conference focusing on Petri nets. Topics include system design and verification using nets, structure, behavior, analysis and synthesis of nets, net models, timed and stochastic nets, symbolic net representation, case studies using nets, etc. The proceedings are published by Springer-Verlag (see LNCS).

APP – Application file. A filename extension for a file that contains a Visual FoxPro active document.

APP – Application Portability Profile. NIST standard SP500-187 intended to be used by computer professionals involved in system and application software development. It contains a lot of specifications required for application portability. See also PSI.

APPC – Advanced Peer-to-Peer Communication. See Advanced Program-to-Program Communication (APPC). See also P2P.

APPC – Advanced Program-to-Program Communication. An IBM protocol, part of the IBM SNA network analogous to the OSI session layer, designed to enable applications to be run on different computers and to exchange data directly.

APPEL – A P3P Preference Exchange Language. The specification that provides a syntax for policies and a mechanism for associating policies with Web resources (see P3P).

applet – mini application. A miniature program written in the Java language, dynamically loaded across the network, just like an image, sound file or video clip. Furthermore, an applet is an intelligent tiny program run inside the browser that can react to user inputs and dynamically change. It is based on agent technologies which are discussed here through a number of modern computer acronyms (see ACL, aglet, AWB, CS, DAI, JAT, MUA, MTA, RP, TACOMA, Tcl, UA, etc.).

APPN – Advanced Peer-to-Peer Networking. An IBM communication service that allows data routing among several APPC systems (see APPC). There is also an APPN+ that refers to the next generation of APPN, also called high-performance routing.

APSE – Ada Programming Support Environment. An integral part of the Ada processor for easy support of programming in Ada.

AR – Access Rate. The speed of the access channel of a frame relay network.

ARA – Attribute Registration Authority. A common term for an organization that allocates unique attribute values in the X.400 MHS.

ARAP – AppleTalk Remote Access Protocol. A data-link layer protocol sits on the AppleTalk protocol suite and allows a node to access a network from a remote location over a serial connection.

ARC – Advanced RISC Computing. A standard hardware architecture, that specifies the baseline hardware requirements for creating ACE-compatible systems (see ACE).

Archie – Archive. An Internet utility for finding files in public archives obtainable via anonymous FTP. See also AFTP. Compare with JUGHEAD and VERONICA. See also WWW.

ARCnet – Attached Resource Computer network. A network architecture originally developed as a proprietary network by Datapoint Corporation in the late 1970s. It operates at 2.5 Mbps, the newer version ARCnet Plus at 20 Mbps. It is a baseband token passing network. Any node requires an ARCnet network interface card. Associated cables can be coaxial, twisted-pair or fiber optic.

ARE – All Routes Explorer. In ATM networks, a specific frame initiated by a source that is sent on all possible routes in a Source Route bridging (see SR).

ARF – Alarm Reporting Function. A service provided by the OSI network management model that is capable of reporting failures, faults or problems that may cause faults. See also OSI.

ARIN – American Registry of Internet Numbers. The organization in the US that manages Internet address numbers in the US and assigned territories (http://www.arin.net). ARIN works closely with RIPE in Europe and APNIC in the Asia–Pacific region (see RIPE and APNIC).

ARJ – Archive Jung. A filename extension for a file compressed using the arj.exe program. The arj compression method was developed by Robert Jung.

ARLL – Advanced Run-Length Limited. A modified version of the Run-Length Limited (see RLL) method that allows denser storage of data on the disk as well as faster data rates.

ARM – Asynchronous Response Mode. A communication mode available in the HDLC protocol that allows a secondary node to establish communication with the primary node without being allowed to in advance. Compare with ABM and NRM.

ARP – Address Resolution Protocol. An Internet protocol defined by RFC826. It allows questions on how to find physical and IP addresses all over the Internet. ARP enables the Internet address independence of the Ethernet address. ARP is limited to physical network systems that support broadcasts that can be heard by all hosts on the network. Although ARP technically refers only to finding the hardware address, and RARP refers to the reverse procedure, ARP is commonly used for both. See also RARP.

ARPA – Advanced Research Projects Agency. A part of the US Department of Defense (see DoD). This is a research and development organization responsible for numerous technological improvements and advanced ideas in computers and communications (http://www.arpa.gov). See also DARPA.

ARPANET – ARPA Network. A packet-switching network established in 1969 by ARPA. According to many sources it was an initial embryo of the Internet. It served as the basis for early networking research as well as a central backbone during the development of the Internet. From 1990 ARPANET officially disappeared.

ARQ – Automatic Repeat request. A communication scenario in which the sender waits for a positive acknowledgment before advancing to the next data item. AKA PAR.

ARS – Automatic Route Selection. A PBX service that allows for automatic selection of the most efficient and cost-effective route. Also known as "least cost routing" or "alternate route selection".

ART – Arabic (Egypt) Standard Time. Time zone. UTC + 2.00 hours. See TZ.

ART – Asynchronous Remote Takeover. A kind of server that provides access to resources of the local machine or network to a remote caller. Also abbreviated as ARTS.

ARTDB – Active and Real-Time Database Systems. An international workshop focusing on advances in real-time software engineering, real-time system issues (see RTS), new directions in real-time database systems and active databases (see ADB).

artilect – artificial intellect. A very advanced term suggested by Dr. Hugo de Garis (the head of the Brain Builder Group at the Advanced Telecommunications Research Laboratory in Kyoto, Japan). According to him, an artilect is a computer intelligence superior to that of humans in one or more spheres of knowledge combined with an implicit will to use the intelligence. He assumes that artilects may appear within one or two generations.

ARTS – Asynchronous Remote Takeover Server. See ART (Asynchronous Remote Takeover).

AS – Application System. An IBM primary strategic product for end-user computing enabling a business professional to access data in a relational database as well as to manage that data using a variety of tools. A concept more than 10 years old in the IBM marketing strategy, it's still alive and focuses now on the new generation of AS/400e network-centric computing-oriented machines. See also NCC.

AS – Autonomous System. A common name (RFC1930) given to a collection of routers under a single administration authority as well as to an independent network. They use a common Interior Gateway Protocol (see IGP). An autonomous system must be assigned a unique 16-bit number by the Internet authority (see IANA). ASs communicate among each other using protocols such as BGP and EGP. The two most widely supported IGPs on the Internet are the OSPF and IS–IS protocols.

ASA – Active Server Application. A filename extension for a file that contains a Microsoft Visual Internet Development file.

ASAP – As Soon As Possible. A frequently used acronym in technical and business letters notifying the receiver that some priority action should take place.

ASC – Accredited Standards Committee. A body of ANSI involved with the development of information technology standards. See ASC X.3 and ASC X.12.

ASC – Artificial Intelligence and Soft Computing. The IASTED international conference focusing on the latest research in the field of artificial intelligence and soft computing. Some of the major topics include intelligent databases, fuzzy systems, neural networks, machine learning, knowledge acquisition and representation, computational linguistics, etc.

ASC – ASCII. A filename extension for a file that contains ASCII text only.

ASCII – American Standard Code for Information Interchange. A character set (pronounced "askee") that assigns some numeric values (decimal, hexadecimal or octal) to letters, numbers, punctuation marks, and certain other characters such as communication-oriented ACK, NAK and STX characters, and keyboard control codes such as backspace or carriage return. ASCII was developed in 1968 to standardize data transmission among disparate hardware and software systems and is built into most minicomputers and all personal computers. This scheme represents the total possible combinations of either 7 (originally) or 8 bits. The lower part of the ASCII table (hexadecimal 00–7F) is usually dedicated to English letters, numbers and special control and punctuation mark characters (see Fig. A-11), while the upper part (hexadecimal 80–FF) is often used to define a particular alphabet, either accent-oriented (such as French or German), non-Latin (such as Hebrew or Russian), or special graphical symbols for use in a nongraphic environment. All nonprinting characters are explained elsewhere in this book.

Bits b7–b5	000	001	010	011	100	101	110	111
Bits b4–b1								
0000	NUL	DLE	SP	0	@	P	`	p
0001	SOH	DC1	!	1	A	Q	a	q
0010	STX	DC2	"	2	B	R	b	r
0011	ETX	DC3	#	3	C	S	c	s
0100	EOT	DC4	$	4	D	T	d	t
0101	ENQ	NAK	%	5	E	U	e	u
0110	ACK	SYN	&	6	F	V	f	v
0111	BEL	ETB	'	7	G	W	g	w
1000	BS	CAN	(	8	H	X	h	x
1001	HT	EM	)	9	I	Y	i	y
1010	LF	SUB	*	:	J	Z	j	z
1011	VT	ESC	+	;	K	[	k	{
1100	FF	FS	,	<	L	\	l	|
1101	CR	GS	□	=	M	]	m	}
1110	SO	RS	.	>	N	^	n	~
1111	SI	US	/	?	O	_	o	DEL

Fig. A-11. ASCII character set in logical groupings (between 00 and 7F)

ASCILITE – Australian Society for Computers in Learning in Tertiary Education. An Australian society (http://www.ascilite.org.au) established to assist and advance educational uses of computers and allied technology in Australian universities, institutes of technical and further education, and postsecondary educational groups. It also provides a forum for those interested in the educational use of computer technology, and promotes and encourages research and evaluation related to the educational use of computer technology in tertiary education. And, last but not least, ASCILITE promotes cooperation and liaison with complementary organizations. See Fig. A-12.

ASC X.3 – Accredited Standards Committee X.3. An ANSI committee that creates standards for information processing systems.

ASC X.12 – Accredited Standards Committee X.12. An ANSI committee that creates electronic data interchange standards (see EDI).

ASE – Application Service Elements. A common acronym for the set of three application services built into the bottom of the seventh OSI layer (see ACSE, ROSE, RTSE), as shown in Fig. A-13. An application process (see

AP) or application entity (see AE) requests these services through predefined interfaces (e.g. appropriate API). Sets of ASEs are grouped into common application service elements (see CASE) and specific application service elements (see SASE). The entire set of ASEs required for a particular application is known as the application context (see AC) for that application.

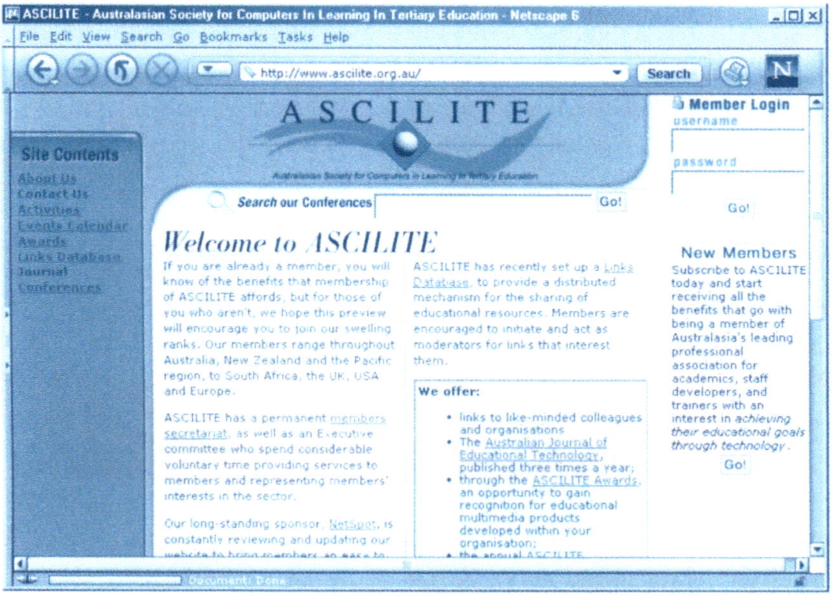

Fig. A-12. ASCILITE homepage (used with permission)

ASEB – Asia EDIFACT Board. The coordinating body for Electronic Data Interchange (see EDI) for the national standards organizations of Asia.

ASF – Automatic Sheet Feeder. A device attached to many dot-matrix printers that accepts a stack of paper and feeds it to the printer one page at a time, similar to laser printer paper trays.

ASI – Adapter Support Interface. An industrial standard developed by IBM that allows token ring (see TR) adapters to communicate with higher-level protocols. At least two components are included: Network Interface Card (see NIC) and a network-layer driver. Compare with NDIS and ODI.

ASIC – Application-Specific Integrated Circuit. A chip designed to perform a particular function. A special type of logic array at the start consists of a nonspecific collection of logic gates. Later, during a manufacturing process a layer is added to connect the basic circuit building blocks for a specific application. By changing the pattern of connection among gates, such a chip can be suitable for many application-specific requirements.

ASIO – Audio Stream Input/Output. A multichannel audio transfer protocol.

ASIS – Ada Semantic Interface Specification. A layered vendor-independent open architecture for interface between an Ada library and any tool requiring information in this library. ASIS has been designed to be independent of underlying compiler library implementations, thus supporting portability of CASE tools. Examples of tools from the ASIS interface include automated code monitors, browsers, compliance and metric tools, correctness verifiers, debuggers, analysis tools, design tools, etc.

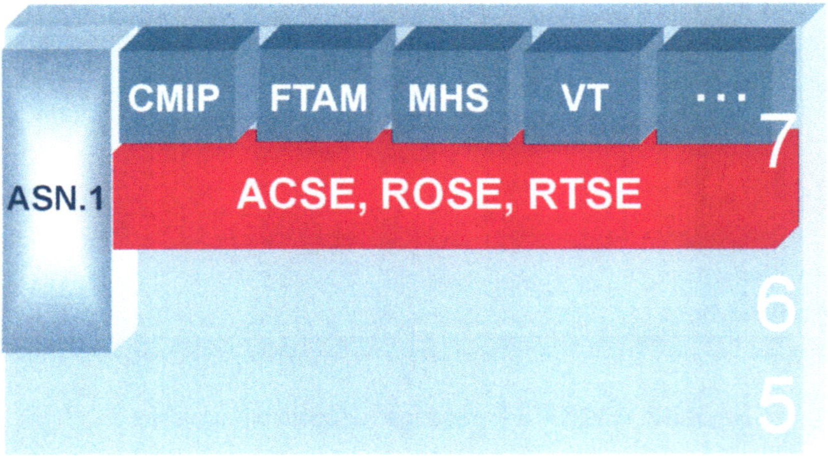

Fig. A-13. Application Service Elements in their environment

ASM – Applied Simulation and Modeling. The IASTED international conference focusing on the latest research in the field of applications of simulation and modeling.

ASN.1 – Abstract Syntax Notation 1. An abstract special-purpose language (ISO8824) used to describe OSI and other communication protocols. ASN.1 was developed by INRIA and then accepted by ISO. It is suitable for writing communication protocols because it describes data structures in a machine-independent way. OSI application-layer protocols such as electronic mail (see X.400), directory services (see X.500), etc. use ASN.1 to describe protocol data units they exchange (see PDU). In general, ASN.1 serves as a common syntax for transferring information between two end systems (see ES) that may use different encoding at each end. ASN.1 corresponds to CCITT X.208 on notation and X.209 on encoding rules.

ASP – Abstract Service Primitive. An implementation-independent description of an interaction between a service-user and a service-provider at a particular service boundary, as defined by OSI.

ASP – Active Server Pages. Webpages containing Java scripts or Visual Basic scripts (small embedded programs). On request, the scripts are executed by the Web server that sends a HTML document in return. Also, ASP is the file-name extension for these files. ASP has several built-in objects. The main five are listed below:

1. Application objects – for managing information for a web application created by ASP. Application objects are for the application as a whole and start when the web server starts.
2. Session objects – for managing information concerning the user's current Web session.
3. Response objects – for sending information to the client or user.
4. Request objects – for receiving information from the user.
5. Server objects – for providing information about the server.

In addition to these server-side objects, ASP has a number of server-side components. Components are objects that one must explicitly add to the ASP application, such as Database Access Objects (see DAO) and ActiveX Data Objects (see ADO). However, ASP is a feature of the Microsoft Internet Information Server (see IIS), but since the server is just building a regular HTML page it may be delivered to almost any browser.

ASP – Advanced Security Proxies. Project underway at NAI laboratories (see NAI) developing software architectures for the next generation of firewalls.

ASP – Application Service Provider. A type of Internet provider that allows a company to lease software on the ASP server and run the software without having to own it.

ASP – AppleTalk Session Protocol. A session-layer protocol used in the AppleTalk protocol suite.

ASPI – Advanced SCSI Programming Interface. A system software, consisting of a set of drivers, that allows easy configuration of the SCSI-based devices, such as hard disks, CD-ROMs, streamer tapes, etc.

ASPLOS – Architectural Support for Programming Languages and Operating Systems. The ACM SIGPLAN international conference focusing on the architectural support for programming languages and operating systems. The proceedings are published in the SIGARCH Computer Architecture News, SIGOPS Operating Systems Review and SIGPLAN Notices. See also SIGPLAN.

ASQ – Automated Software Quality. A common term for a set of procedures that use software tools as automated testing tools to improve the software quality.

ASR – Automatic Send/Receive. A teletypewriter that punches and reads paper tape offline and can transmit data from a paper tape or a keyboard.

ASSET – Application-Specific Systems and Software Engineering and Technology. The IEEE international symposium focusing on all aspects of software and system engineering as it applies to software development in specific application domains.

AST – Abstract Syntax Tree. A data structure used by compilers to perform code generation.

AST – Assistant. A filename extension for a file that consists of a guide which can be used by the user by asking a series of questions and then using the answers to perform a task.

AST – Aleutian Islands Standard Time. Time zone. UTC – 10.00 hours. See TZ.

AST – Atlantic (Canada) Standard Time. Time zone. UTC – 4.00 hours.

ASTA – Advanced Software Technology and Algorithms. Part of the High-Performance Computer and Communication program (see HPCC) for software and algorithms development for HPCC systems implementation.

ASTRAL – Alliance for Strategic Token Ring Advancement and Leadership. Part of the High-Performance Computer and Communication program (see HPCC) for software and algorithms development.

AT – Advanced Technology. The PC bus 16-bit technology on the motherboard. AT enables memory boards, video adapter boards and other peripheral device drivers to be connected to the motherboard.

ATA – Advanced Technology Attachment. ANSI name for a disk drive interface known as Integrated Drive Electronics (see IDE).

ATA – ARCnet Trade Association. An organization of vendors and others involved in ARCnet definition and standardization. See also ARCnet.

A

ATAL – Agent Theories Architecture and Languages. An international workshop focusing on the synergies between theories, infrastructures, architectures, formal methods and languages, all connected to intelligent agents. The proceedings are published by Springer-Verlag (see LNCS).

ATAPI – AT Attached Packet Interface. Part of the EIDE specification introduced by Western Digital in 1994 that allows CD-ROM drives to be connected to the same cable as the normal hard drive.

ATDP – Attention Dial Pulse. A command for pulse dialing in Hayes-compatible modems. Compare with ATDT.

ATDT – Attention Dial Tone. A command that initiates touch-tone dialing in Hayes and Hayes-compatible modems. Compare with ATDP.

ATE – Automatic Test Equipment. The combination of a hardware device used to perform test, diagnostics and measurement, and the appropriate software used to control such hardware.

ATK – Andrew Toolkit. A portable user-interface toolkit that provides a dynamically loadable, object-oriented environment wherein objects can be embedded in one another. Thus, one could edit a text that contains not only fonts and styles, but also embedded raster images, spreadsheets, drawing editors, equations, simple animations, etc. These embedded objects could themselves contain other objects. ATK is open, so programmers can create new objects that can be embedded as easily as those system-defined objects.

ATL – Active Template Library. A set of template-based C++ classes designed for COM objects implementation. ATL supports transaction server objects, active controls, etc. It is shipped with Microsoft Visual C++ 5.0. See also COM (Component Object Model).

ATM – Adobe Type Manager. A software tool that produces PostScript fonts output by rasterization of Type 1 fonts using their outline font files (see PS).

ATM – Asynchronous Transfer Mode. A standard which defines high-load high-speed (1.544 Mbps to 1.2 Gbps), fixed-size cell switching with dynamic bandwidth allocation. ATM is rapidly becoming a basic technology for the next generation of global communications, supporting diverse applications and a variety of interface speeds and distances. ATM uses very short fixed-size packets known as cells, each containing 53 bytes, five of which are for header information, and the other 48 are for data. The header carries Virtual Path/Virtual Channel Identifiers (see VPI/VCI) used for routing across an ATM network (see Fig. A-14). The HEC field is intended for error correction in the header, the GFC field for flow control, and the PT field for tariff. It is important to explain the key role of the virtual addressing mode and the short format of the ATM cell in efficiently supporting both data and voice and video transmission. Namely, it is well known that real-time voice and video transmission cannot wait for the communication channel to stay free. To solve this, ATM uses the CLC bit in the cell header to assign a priority to voice or video data. In that case, the maximum waiting time is the time required to transmit only one cell, usually several microseconds. Another essential attribute is virtual routing between ATM nodes. This feature means that any other ATM message and its cell can use the other free paths. The result is better efficiency for the global ATM network.

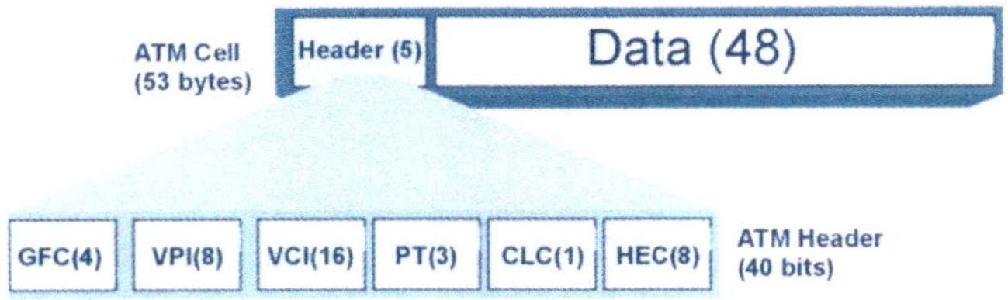

Fig. A-14. ATM cell

In the emerging field of high-speed virtual networking, ATM is a key component. In order to explain the ATM functionality, trends and importance, and due to the acronyms involved, this book addresses ATM in a huge number of terms explained (see AAL, B-ISDN, Convergence Sublayer (CS), FFOL, LAN, NNI, PM, QoS, SAR, SONET, SVC, TC, UNI, VPI, VCI, and many others). Most of these topics would justify a more comprehensive book than this one. Figure A-15 depicts how ATM uses two distinct address formats for SVC setups in public and private domains and between them. The ISO OSI Network Service Access Point format (see NSAP) has been used for private network addressing (see networks X, Y and Z) and the ITU-T E.164 format for public addressing. ATM Forum (http://www.atmforum.com) is the primary organization developing and defining ATM standards. It was founded in 1991 by Adaptive Corp., Cisco Systems Inc., Northern Telecom Ltd., and Sprint Corp. Currently, the forum consists of over 600 manufacturers, carriers, end-users, and other interested parties. ATM is defined in the broadband ISDN protocol at the levels corresponding to levels 1 and 2 of the ISO/OSI model (see B-ISDN). It is also known as the cell relay in order to distinguish it from the frame relay (see FR).

A

ATM – Automatic Teller Machine. A publicly available banking machine that allows a customer access to checking and savings accounts 24 h a day, for example to withdraw some cash. See also EFT.

AToM – ATM Management Objects. Specification RFC1695 that defines objects used for managing ATM devices, networks and services. ATM management objects allow network managers to consider groups of switches, virtual connections, interfaces and services as discrete entities. AToMs are used to manage ATM interfaces, ATM virtual links, ATM cross-connects, AAL-5 entities, and AAL-5 connections supported by ATM hosts, switches and networks. See also AAL-5, ATM and AToM MIB.

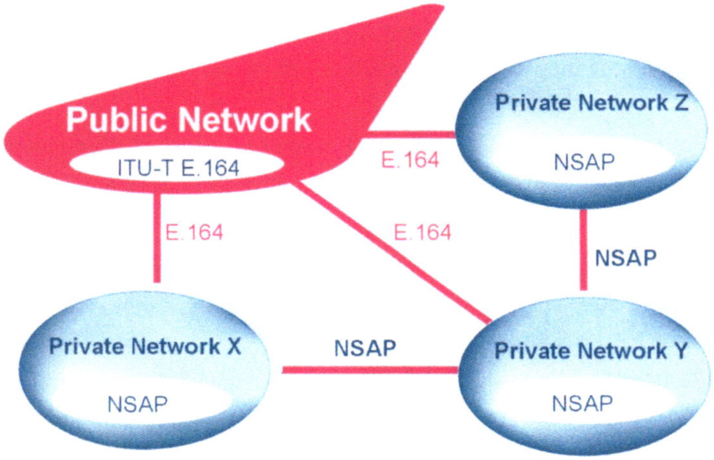

Fig. A-15. ATM addressing in public and private networks

AToM MIB – AToM Management Information Base. An agent defined in RFC-1695 that allows SNMP network management systems to monitor and configure ATM devices. Like other MIBs, AToM MIB reports on a device or traffic status and accepts configuration commands. See also AToM, MIB and SNMP.

ATP – Agent Transfer Protocol. An application programming interface (see API) developed by IBM for developing mobile agents (see RP). See also aglet and AWB.

ATS – Abstract Test Suite. Sets of abstract test cases for testing a particular protocol.

AT&T – American Telephone and Telegraph Company. The house where the UNIX operating system was born in 1969 and the C programming language as well. AT&T is a worldwide high-technology-oriented company. Additional information is available at http://www.att.com

AU – Access Unit. A device that provides ISDN access to Packet Switched Networks (see PSN). Also, a process inside the ITU-T Message Handling System (see MHS) that provides a gateway between the Message Transfer System (see MTS) and other ITU-T services.

AU – Audio. A common file format for sound files on UNIX.

Au – Authentication. See AAA.

AUE – Andrew User Environment. An integrated set of applications beginning with a generic object editor, a help system, a system monitoring tool, an editor-based shell interface, and support for printing multimedia documents. See AUIS.

AUI – Adaptable User Interface. A toolkit from Oracle that allows application portability between different graphical user interfaces (see GUI) and windowing systems.

AUI – Attachment Unit Interface. The IEEE802.3 interface between a Media Access Unit (see MAU) and a Network Interface Card (see NIC). For example, it connects the Ethernet module to an Ethernet hub. Also, the part of the ISO/OSI Reference Model at the physical layer (see OSI).

AUIC – Australasian User Interface Conference. An international conference focusing on techniques, tools and technology for user interface development in wide areas such as CSCW, virtual reality, multimedia and the Web.

AUIS – Andrew User Interface System. An integrated set of tools that allows the creation, use and mailing of documents and applications containing typographically formatted text and embedded objects. The Andrew archive is available via ftp://ftp.andrew.cmu.edu/pub/AUIS

AUP – Acceptable Use Policy. A set of guidelines describing a particular network usage, for instance, what kind of messages it accepts. These rules are different from network to network.

AURP – AppleTalk Update Routing Protocol. A routing protocol that exists in the AppleTalk protocol suite.

AUSTEL – Australia Telecommunications. The agency responsible for telecommunications regulation in Australia.

AUX – Auxiliary. A name reserved by the MS-DOS operating system for a standard auxiliary device (first serial port COM1).

A/UX – Apple UNIX. A version of the UNIX operating system made by Apple for various Macintosh computers and based on the AT&T System V, release 2.2 of UNIX with some enhancements. See also SVID.

AVAIL – Availability. The probability that the system is available for use at a given time. In other words, if, in every 1000 time units the system is probably available for 970 of these, its AVAIL is expressed as 0.970.

AVC – Average lines of Code. A measurement unit for complex software products, used in software cost estimation rather than in software metrics. See also LOC.

AVI – Advanced Visual Interfaces. An international conference that has taken place in Italy every two years since 1992. AVI is focused on the conception, design and implementation of visual interfaces. Topics include visual interface design, visual interaction, hypermedia and multimedia, adaptive and animated interfaces, computer-supported cooperative work (see CSCW), virtual reality (see VR), visual databases, WWW interfaces, etc.

AVI – Audio Video Interleaved. A Windows multimedia file format for sound and moving-pictures exchange. One of the hits on the Internet during the year 2000 was a baby playing many games, all available in the avi format. Look at http://members.aol.com/Cwong65803/Babypage, or just try to find any available page (among hundreds of thousands) using AltaVista or Yahoo!.

AVP – AntiViral Toolkit Pro. An antivirus utility from Kaspersky Labs Moscow (http://www.kasperskylab.ru) that runs under Windows 95/NT. It scans local disks, system memory, files or sectors of disks to eliminate computer viruses (detect, disinfect, clean, delete).

AVS – Adult Verification System. A service offered on the Internet used to restrict minors from entering adult-oriented sites. Many such sites are equipped with a security service (such as Adult Check) that checks the access rights of the visitor in terms of his/her age.

AW – Administrative Weight. The value set by the ATM network administrator to indicate the desirability of a network link.

AWB – Aglet Workbench. An IBM environment for building network-based applications that use mobile Java agents (see aglet) to search for, access, and manage data and other information on the Internet or on Intranets.

AWG – American Wire Gauge. A standardized method of specifying the size of copper wires. The system is based on the gauge, or diameter, of a conducting wire.

AWK – Aho, Weinberger and Kernighan. A pattern scanning and processing language named after the initials of its authors (Alfred Aho, Peter Weinberger and Brian Kernighan). There are also new versions of AWK, NAWK and GAWK. The Practical Extraction and Reporting Language (see PERL) was developed from AWK. AWK distributes with most UNIX and UNIX-like implementations as well as with some other operating systems.

AWT – Abstract Windows Toolkit. An abstraction, a part of the core Java class library, of a windowed operating system which describes the common functionalities and capabilities of all of them. AWT enables programmers to port Java applications from one window system to another. That means the AWT is able to provide access to the basic UI components such as colors, fonts, events, buttons, frames, panels, scroll bars, etc. See also UI and GUI.

AXX – ARJ xx. A filename extension for a file that contains a multivolume archive created by ARJ, where xx represents a number from 01 to 99. See also ARJ.

AZERTY. A keyboard in which the keys in the second-from-top row are labeled (from left to right): A, Z, E, R, T, Y, U, I, O and P. Compare with the QWERTY keyboard.

B

B – Bearer channel. The full duplex 64-Kbps channel used in Integrated Digital Service Networks (see ISDN). See also D channel.

b – bit (binary digit). The meanings of the terms bit and binary digit depend on the context; for example, (1010)b is a binary number, 100 bps is related to speed (see bps), etc. A bit is the smallest unit of storage that can take two possible values, 0 or 1.

B – Bridge. A networking device that allows linking of two networks together. Bridges are smart enough to know which computers are on which side of the bridge, so they allow only those messages that need to get to the other side to cross the bridge. This improves performance on both sides of the bridge. They are used to overcome incompatibilities between network layers of two different networks. That means that a bridge operates at the data-link layer. A bridge is independent of higher-level protocols so that different protocols can use the same bridge to send data to other networks. Two LANs connected by a bridge effectively become one LAN. Several different features, such as the bridged distance (local or remote), data-link level of operation (MAC or LLC), location (internal or external), type of routing (transparent or directed by source), etc., can categorize bridges. Compare with router (see R). See also brouter.

B – Byte. The basic computer data unit, the smallest memory capacity measurement unit, containing 8 bits. The bigger units are KB, MB, GB, TB, PB, etc.

B2B – Business-to (2)-Business. A common term applied to the exchange of information, products or services over the Internet between business partners. B2B Internet sites can be websites intended for some kind of web farming (see WF), brokering sites that act as intermediaries between people searching for products or services and potential providers, and information sites, which provide information about a particular industry. See also B2C, B2G, e-commerce (see EC) and e-tailing.

B2C – Business-to (2)-Consumers. A common term applied to the exchange of information, products or services over the Internet between companies and their customers. See also B2B, B2G, e-commerce (see EC) and e-tailing.

B2G – Business-to (2)-Government. A common term applied to the exchange of information, products or services over the Internet between companies and their government customers at any level.

B4N – Bye for (4) now. The chat term.

B8ZS – Binary 8-Zero Substitution. A type of line-code, used in T1 and E1 circuits, in which a special code is substituted whenever 8 consecutive zeros are sent over the link. This code is then interpreted at the end of the link.

b64 – base 64. A filename extension for a file that contains encoding data used by MIME.

BA – Broadcast Architecture. The Microsoft architecture that enables personal computers to serve as clients of broadband digital and/or analog broadcast networks. See also DVB.

BABEL – Broadcasting Across the Barriers of European Languages. A big effort to overcome barriers between European languages. Among thousands of available websites, the site http://www.geocities.com/ikind_babel/babel focuses on computer acronyms and is updated every 3 months by Irving and Richard Kind at Karlsruhe University in Germany.

BAC – Basic Access Control. The comprehensive set of access control guidelines in the X.500 standard. Compare with Simplified Access Control (SAC). See also X.500.

BACP – Bandwidth Allocation Control Protocol. A protocol used by ISDN, which allows a 2-channel ISDN circuit to use one channel to connect to the other host, and, as traffic increases, to activate the second channel as needed.

BACUG – Bay Area Cisco User Group. An organization of Cisco users in the local San Francisco area (http://www.bacug.com).

BAK – Backup file. A filename extension for a file that contains a backup version of the file. It is created by the system (such as system.bak) or by a Windows application, such as CorelDraw. Some applications have their own filename extensions for backup files (for instance, WinWord uses a WBK file).

BAK – Back at the keyboard. The chat term.

BARRNet – Bay Area Regional Research Network. The Northern California regional hub of NSFNET. The members are universities, government and private research laboratories, and corporate affiliates.

BARWAN – Bay Area Research Wireless Access Network. The project intended for the development of wireless overlay networks. The experimental testbed was created in the San Francisco Bay Area.

BAS – BASIC. A filename extension for code module files generated by Visual Basic (see VB). The .bus file contains procedures and variables used throughout the application.

BAS – Basic Activity Subset. One of the four subsets of the OSI session services.

BAS – Bit-rate Allocation Signal. A common name for signaling bits in a communication frame (ITU-T H.320) that enable transmission of code words. Such words are used to describe the capability of a terminal to structure the capacity of the channel or to synchronize multiple channels in various ways.

BASIC – Beginner's All-purpose Symbolic Instruction Code. A high-level programming language, very popular as a programming learning tool. It was developed in the mid-1960s at Dartmouth College by John Kemeny and Thomas Kurtz.

BAT – Batch. A filename extension for batch files (operating system commands in ASCII text). BAT files are either run automatically by the system (autoexec.bat in DOS, for instance) or run manually by typing a command at the command prompt line.

BBIAB – Be back in a bit. The chat term.

BBC – Broadband Bearer Capability. In ATM networks, a bearer class field that is a part of the initial address message.

BBL – Be back later. The chat term.

BBN – Bolt, Beranek and Newman Inc. A US company in Cambridge, Massachusetts, which has been involved in Internet development since 1968. The first network was made in 1969 with four nodes located at UCLA, SRI, University of California, Santa Barbara, and the University of Utah. This network, backbone, was able to operate at 50 Kbps. Since 1997, BBN has operated as BBNT (http://www.gte.com/AboutGTE/gte/bbnt).

BBS – Be back soon. A shorthand expression often seen in Internet discussion groups used by a participant leaving the group who wishes to be a temporary firewall to the rest of the group.

BBS – Bulletin Board System. A public computer system that serves as an information and message passing center for dial-up users. The requirements for a bulletin board are a computer, modem, and preferably some bulletin board software. A bulletin board can contain directories of files (for user downloading) and e-mail facilities (where users can exchange and/or post messages). Based on their access privileges, those using a bulletin board can read, download (copy from the bulletin board), upload (place on the bulletin board), and even modify stored files. Many software and hardware companies run proprietary BBSs for customers that include sales information, technical support, and software upgrades and patches.

Bcc – Blind Carbon Copy. An RFC822 recommendation for an electronic mail header that makes the addresses listed in Bcc invisible to the other mail recipients. Also known as "blind courtesy copy". Compare with carbon copy (cc).

BCC – Block Check Character. The result of a transmission verification algorithm normally calculated during transmission, appended to the end of a block, and then used for error detection by the receiver. Examples are Cyclic Redundancy Check (see CRC) and Longitudinal Redundancy Check (see LRC).

BCD – Binary Coded Decimal. A numbering system for encoding decimal numbers in a binary form. Each of the decimal digits 0 through 9 is coded using 4 bits and then separated by one space character (see Fig. B-1). This coding scheme is also known as 8-4-2-1 after the weight (powers of two) for each corresponding binary number. Thus, the decimal number 275 is 0010 0111 0101 in BCD notation, 409 is 0100 0000 1001, etc.

decimal	binary	decimal	binary
0	0000	5	0101
1	0001	6	0110
2	0010	7	0111
3	0011	8	1000
4	0100	9	1001

Fig. B-1. BCD coding scheme

BCN – Beacon. A frame used in token ring networks (see TR) to indicate that a hard error has occurred in the node sending the beacon frame or in this node's nearest addressable upstream neighbor (see NAUN).

BCNF – Boyce–Codd Normal Form. A special form of the Third Normal Form (see 3NF) in which every determinant, i.e. any attribute the value of which determines other values within a database row, is a candidate key.

BCOB – Broadband Connection-Oriented Barrier. In ATM networks, the message that indicates the type of service requested by the calling user. BCOBs can be class A for connection-oriented (see CO) constant-bit-rate service, class C for connection-oriented but variable-bit-rate service, or class X for transport service where the AAL, traffic type and timing requirements are transparent to the network. See also AAL and ATM.

BCP – Best Current Practices. The latest subseries of RFCs which are written to describe the best ways to use the Internet protocols and the best ways to configure options to ensure interoperability between various vendors' products (see RFC1818).

BCP – Bulk Copy Program. A command-line utility used for copying Microsoft SQL Server data to/from a file in a user-independent format.

BCP – Byte-Control Protocols. A common name for any protocol that is character-oriented rather than bit-oriented.

BCPL – Basic Combined Programming Language. A programming language from the ALGOL-like family developed in 1969 by Martin Richards. This is an imperative, block-structured, procedural programming language, originally intended to support the writing of compilers, but later it was used as a general system-programming tool. It is also a forerunner of the C language (see 3GL).

BCR – Bar Code Reader. A device capable of reading bar codes, the special identification codes printed as sets of vertical bars of different widths. The reader is used for rapid error-free input in libraries, grocery stores, production lines, warehouses, etc.

BCS – Basic Combined Subset. One of the four subsets of the OSI session services.

Bd – Baud. A unit of modulation rate. Named after the French engineer and telegrapher Jean Maurice Émile Baudot and originally used to measure the transmission speed of telegraph equipment. One baud corresponds to a rate of one unit interval per second, where the modulation rate is expressed as the reciprocal of the duration in seconds of the shortest unit interval. Also, a measure of signaling speed equal to the number of discrete signal conditions, variations or events per second, known as the baud rate (see BR).

BDT – Bulk Data Transfer. A protocol used in Xerox Courier for bulk data transfer between the client and server.

BEC – Backward Error Correction. The method of error correction when the receiving end detects an error and requests a retransmission from the sender. Compare with Forward Error Correction (see FEC).

BEDO – Burst EDO. A type of EDO DRAM (see EDO) that can process four memory addresses in one burst (transfer of data without a break). Introduced in 1995.

Bellcore – Bell Communications Research. One of the world's largest providers of networking software and professional services. According to information available on their site (http://www.bellcore.com), 80% of the US public telecommunication network depends on software invented, developed, implemented and/or maintained by Bellcore.

BER – Basic Encoding Rules. A set of standard rules for encoding data described by Abstract Syntax Notation 1 (see ASN.1). Using BER, it is possible to specify any ASN.1 element in the form of a byte string that includes three components (the type, the length and the value). The type (also known as identifier) indicates the class of an object and the form of a string (it may be BOOLEAN, INTEGER, OCTET, etc.). The length field is used to indicate the number of bytes used to encode the forthcoming value (also known as contents). The encoding itself may take one of the following forms: fixed length primitives, fixed length constructed or variable length constructed.

BER – Bit Error Rate. The probability that a single bit, when transmitted over a link, will be received in error. The BER depends on the type and length of the media involved in a transfer. Generally, BER is shown as a negative exponent (e.g. 10^{-8} means 1 out of 10^8 bits are in error). Compare with Block Error Rate (BLER).

BERT – Bit Error Rate Tester. A testing device that compares a received data pattern with a known transmitted pattern to determine the level of transmission quality. Compare with BLERT.

BEST – Best Education Sites Today. A search engine on the Internet dedicated to education (http://www.education-world.com). With over 10,000 URLs in its database, it is the most comprehensive source for education links on the Internet. It can be searched by a keyword, or by a topic list, or by browsing the awards for extensive reviews of the hottest education sites of the month.

BEST – BSDI Embedded System Technology. A set of BSDI activities intended to provide tools and services for Internet-based application development. Also known as e/BSD. More information is available at the BSDI site (http://www.bsdi.com). See also BSDI.

BFC – Briefcase. A system folder in Windows 95 used for synchronizing files between two computers, usually between desktop and laptop computers.

The Briefcase can be transferred to another computer via disk, cable or a network. When files are transferred back to the original computer, the BFC updates all files to the most recent version.

BFN – Bye for now. The chat term.

BFT – Binary File Transfer. Transfer of a file containing arbitrary bytes or words, as opposed to a text file containing only printable characters.

BG – Big grin. The chat term.

BGP – Border Gateway Protocol. An exterior gateway protocol (RFC1771) in the Internet Protocol Suite (see ISP). It is used for routing packets between networks that use different protocols (see EGP). Also, a kind of router (see R, Router).

BHLI – Broadband High-Layer Information. A Q.2931 information element that identifies an application-layer protocol used by the application. Compare with BLLI.

BHT – Branch History Table. A buffer used in RISC architectures to hold the history of previous branch paths taken during the execution of individual branch instructions.

BI – Business Intelligence. The essential attribute of the third-generation Business Information Systems (see BIS). Systems with business intelligence are focusing on prepackaged application solutions capable of accessing and delivering business data to both information providers and information users.

BIA – Burned-In Address. A unique address for a network interface card (see NIC) assigned by the manufacturer.

BIB – Bus Interface Board. A network interface card (see NIC) used for interfacing between the node and the network medium.

BICI – Broadband Inter-Carrier Interface. An ITU-T standard that defines the protocols and procedures for establishing, maintaining and terminating broadband switched virtual connections between public networks.

BIND – Berkeley Internet Name Domain. Implementation of a DNS server developed and distributed by the University of California at Berkeley. Many Internet hosts run BIND, and it is the predecessor of many commercial BIND implementations. A typical organization has one primary server, with one or more secondary servers that provide name serving on different LANs on the site. See also DNS.

BinHex – Binary to Hexadecimal. An encoding scheme that converts binary data into ASCII characters.

BIOS – Basic Input/Output System. A set of routines (pronounced "by-oss") built-in to the system ROM used to transfer information between system components.

BIP – Bit Interleaved Parity. A method used at the ATM PHY layer to monitor the error performance of the link. A check bit or word is sent to the link overhead covering the previous frame. Bit errors in the payload will be detected and may be reported as maintenance information. See also ATM and PHY.

BIS – Biologically Inspired Systems. An international symposium dedicated to discussion about artificial neural networks, sensors and sensory systems, computer vision, audition, high-level perception, smart human–machine interaction, autonomous robots, etc.

BIS – Business Information System. An information system that receives, processes, and stores business-oriented data (bills, payments, assets, sales, stocks inventory, giro account changes, salaries, etc.) and produces reports or printouts on demand. See also Enterprise Information System (EIS), Management Information System (MIS), Business Intelligence (BI) and Data Warehouse (DW).

B-ISDN – Broadband ISDN. The overall standard reference model for the exchange of different kinds of data, including synchronous, asynchronous and isochronous communications, defined by the CCITT Recommendation I.121. It represents a wide-area communication service offering live television, video on demand, full-motion multimedia electronic mail, LAN interconnection, high-speed data transport, and much more, all over the telephone line. The underlying technology for B-ISDN is ATM, as shown in the B-ISDN reference model in Fig. B-2. B-ISDN uses ATM technology over SONET-based circuits to provide data rates from 155 Mbps to 622 Mbps and beyond. B-ISDN is discussed in several ITU-T documents, such as I.113 which contains an ISDN vocabulary, I.121 which considers B-ISDN itself or B-ISDN and ATM together. Compare with Narrowband ISDN (see N-ISDN). See also ISDN. The reference model is divided into multiple planes as follows:

- User plane (U-plane) provides for transfer of user applications information. It contains the physical layer, ATM layer and multiple ATM AALs (see AAL and ATM) required for different service users.
- Control plane (C-plane) deals with call establishment and release and other connection control functions necessary for providing switched services.

- Layer management deals with the management between layers (inside the M-plane).
- Management plane (M-plane) provides management functions and the capability of exchanging information between the U-plane and the C-plane. Furthermore, the M-plane contains two sections: the layer management that performs layer-specific management functions, and the plane management that performs management and coordination functions related to the complete system.

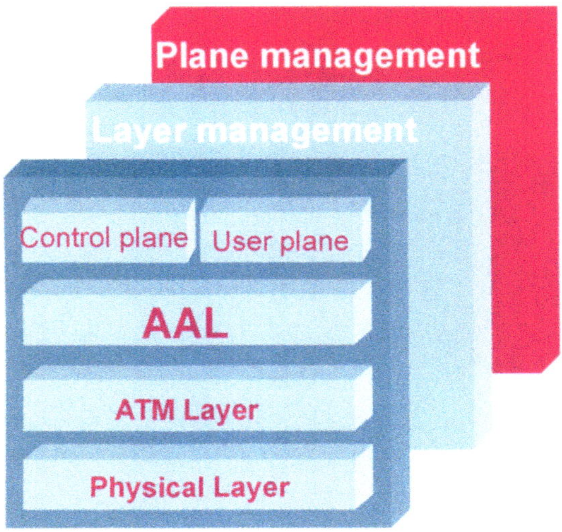

Fig. B-2. B-ISDN reference model

BIST – Built-In Self-Test. The capability of a circuit to test itself.

BISUP – B-ISDN User's Part. An SS7 protocol that defines signaling messages for controlling connections and services across ISDN networks. See also ISDN and SS7.

BISYNC – Binary Synchronous communications protocol. A communication synchronous standard protocol developed by IBM. Pronounced "by-sink". Messages are organized as variable-length frames, each frame is preceded and followed by special characters that enable the sender and receiver to synchronize their clocks.

BITBLT – Bit Block Transfer. A computer graphics programming technique (pronounced "bit-blit") that manipulates with bitmaps in memory, rectangular blocks of bits representing the attributes of the pixels forming an image. The key idea behind BITBLT is that one bit form is combined with another in such a way as to potentially alter the bitmap of the second form. It is based on 16 Boolean operations under the corresponding source (s) and destination (d) bits in bitmaps (see Fig. B-3). The Boolean operations represented by acronyms are explained elsewhere in this book via the appropriate truth tables (see NOR, NAND, XOR, etc.).

BITNET – Because It's Time Network. An academic computer network merged with the Computer+Science Network (see CSNET) to form the Corporation for Research and Educational Networking (see CREN). BITNET connects thousands of locations. Because in its early days BITNET used only IBM mainframes as network nodes, a gateway is required to connect it to the global Internet.

Bit pattern	Boolean operation	Bit pattern	Boolean operation
0000	d:= 0	1000	d:= NOT (s OR d)
0001	d:= s AND d	1001	d:= NOT (s XOR d)
0010	d:= s AND (NOT d)	1010	d:= NOT d
0011	d:= s	1011	d:= NOT ((NOT s) AND d)
0100	d:= (NOT s) AND d	1100	d:= NOT s
0101	d:= d	1101	d:= NOT (s AND (NOT d))
0110	d:= s XOR d	1110	d:= NOT (s AND d)
0111	d:= s OR d	1111	d:= 1

Fig. B-3. BITBLT combination rules

BIU – Basic Information Unit. The SNA data format that consists of the RH and RU information. See Request/Response Header and Unit (RH, RU).

BIU – Bus Interface Unit. A kind of Network Interface Card (see NIC) that serves as an interface between a node and the network. See also BIB.

BIX – BYTE Information Exchange. An online service (http://www.bix.com) originated by BYTE magazine, now owned and operated by Delphi Internet Services Corporation. BIX offers e-mail, software downloads, and conferences relating to hardware and software.

BL – Belly laughing. The chat term.

BLAST – Blocked Asynchronous/Synchronous Transmission. A popular communications method in which data is transmitted in blocks of a fixed number of bits. BLAST produces error-free transmission.

BLER – Block Error Rate. An error rate based on the proportion of blocks found in error during transmission. Compare with Bit Error Rate (BER).

BLERT – Block Error Rate Test(er). A control procedure (or device) designed to determine the number of erroneous blocks transmitted per unit time. Compare with BERT.

BLLI – Broadband Low-Layer Information. A Q.2931 information element that identifies a Layer-2 and a Layer-3 protocol used by the application. Compare with BHLI.

Fig. B-4. An example of a BMP picture (somewhere in Otago, New Zealand)

BLOB – Binary Large Object. A large block of bits (binary data) stored in a database, such as a picture or sound file. It is not interpreted by the database management system.

BLU – Basic Link Unit. The information contained in an SDLC frame. See also SDLC and SNA.

BMCV – Biologically Motivated Computer Vision. An international workshop focusing on the biologically based systems in the area of computer vision.

BMP – Bitmap Picture. A filename extension for files that contain bitmap pictures (see Fig. B-4).

BMS – Banyan Mail Service. A proprietary mail service used in the VINES environment. See also VINES.

BMTI – Block Mode Terminal Interface. A device which is used to create (and break down) packets to be transmitted through an X.25 network. This device is needed if block mode terminals are to be connected to the network without the use of an intermediate computer.

BN – Bridge Number. A locally administrated bridge identity used in Source Route Bridging (see SR) to uniquely identify a route between two ATM LANs.

BNC – Binary Network Connector. A connector type used to connect coaxial cable and appropriate devices. It locks when one connector is inserted into another and rotated through 90 degrees.

BNF – Backus–Naur Form. A metalanguage used for defining the syntax of formal languages. Named after John W. Backus and Peter Naur, who used BNF to define the ALGOL programming language.

BNU – Basic Networking Utilities. A version of UUCP distributed with UNIX System V release 3. Also known as Honey DanBer UUCP (after the login names of its inventors, Peter Honeyman, David Nowitz and Brian Redman). See also UUCP.

BOA – Binary-translation Optimized Architecture. An implementation of the IBM PowerPC family (see PPC) that combines binary translation with dynamic optimization.

BOC – Bell Operating Company. Any of the 22 operating companies that were stripped from the company AT&T by court order. See also RBOC.

BOF – Beginning-Of-File. A code placed before the first byte in a file used by the operating system to keep track of other records in a file relative to the first byte in it.

BOF – Business Object Facility. The infrastructure under Object Management Group consideration (see OMG) for supporting business objects operating as cooperative application components in a distributed environment.

BOM – Bill Of Material. An ordered list of parts, subassemblies and raw materials, that defines a product. It defines the type, number, quantity and relationships of parts and assemblies. It is used in Computer Integrated Manufacturing (see CIM), and also as a base document for purchasing.

BOND – Bandwidth On Demand. In ISDN, the ability to aggregate B channels (see B) as the data traffic increases.

BOOTP – Bootstrap Protocol. A protocol for booting diskless workstations (RFC951, RFC1084, RFC1542).

BOV – Business Operational View. The part of the Open-edi (see EDI) standard specification which defines the business aspects of the Open-edi scenario. Such aspects are, for example, the semantics of the business transactions, business rules, requirements, etc. Compare with FSV.

BPDU – Bridge Protocol Data Unit. A message type used by bridges to exchange management and control information.

bpi – bits per inch. A measurement unit for data storage density. It is the number of bits that fit into one inch of space on a magnetic data storage device (disk or tape). Actually, for disk storage it refers to bits per square inch.

BPI – Business Process Improvement. The improvement of an organization's business practices through the analysis of activities in order to reduce or eliminate non-value-added activities or costs, while at the same time maintaining or improving quality, productivity, timeliness, or other strategic or business purposes as evidenced by measures of performance. Also called functional process improvement (see FPI). Compare with BPR. See also BSM.

BPO – Business Process Objects. A part of the tiered architecture of the Lightweight Business Object Model (see LBOM). BPOs represent class modules that implement methods that perform business processes involving multiple business objects. See also DABO and UBO.

BPP – Bridge Port Pair. In ATM networks, the frame header information that identifies a bridge/LAN pair of a source route segment. Also known as the source routing descriptor.

BPR – Business Process Reengineering. A common term for careful investigation and redesign of a company business to achieve better productivity, better customer services, and so on. It requires a fundamental analysis and radical redesign of everything: business processes and management systems, job definitions, organizational structures and beliefs and behaviors to achieve dramatic performance improvements to meet contemporary requirements. Information technology (see IT) is an essential enabler in this process.

bps – bits per second. A basic measurement unit for communication speed. Higher rates are measured in Kbps, Mbps, Gbps, etc.

BPU – Bridge Processing Unit. The main board within a Multimedia Conference Server (see MCS) that processes the audio, video and data signals received from the conferencing systems. BPU appears as type I and type II. The BPU I is available in versions running at 33 MHz or 40 MHz. The 40-MHz version is required to support conferences that use a transfer rate of 768 Kbps or higher. The BPU II running at 40 MHz supports a 1920-Kbps conference with eight conferencing systems.

BR – Bit Rate. In a bitstream, the number of bits occurring per unit of time, usually expressed as bits per second (see bps).

BRA – Basic Rate Access. An interface that provides the access to the Basic Rate Interface of an ISDN (see BRI) either on B or D channels. Compare with Primary Rate Access (PRA).

BRB – Be right back. An expression used commonly in live chat services on the Internet and online information services by participants signaling their temporary departure.

BRI – Basic Rate Interface. An Integrated Services Digital Network (see ISDN) channel with a total data rate of 144 Kbps. It has two channels, B and D. Channel B is used for voice or data transfer while channel D is intended for control information. AKA 2B+D. Compare with PRI.

Brouter – Bridging router. A kind of router (see Router, R), also known as a routing bridge that represents a device that combines the features of a bridge and a router. It can operate in both the network layer or the data-link layer.

BRX – Browse Index. A filename extension for a file that contains a browse index on multimedia CDs.

BRZ – Bipolar Return to Zero. A bipolar signal in which each pulse returns to the zero amplitude before its period expires.

BS – Backspace. A control character (ASCII character 08).

BSA – Business Software Alliance. An association (http://www.bsa.org) established in 1988 by leading software developers all over the world (for example, Adobe, Autodesk, Corel, IBM, Lotus, Microsoft, Novell, Sybase, Symantec, etc.). BSA educates end-users on software copyrights, fights software piracy, and expands trade opportunities.

BSB – Backside Bus. Data bus between the processor and L1 and L2 cache memories inside Intel microprocessors that have a Dual Independent Bus (see DIB). See also L1 and L2.

BSC – Binary Synchronous Communication. See BISYNC.

BSC – Browser Content. A filename extension for a file that contains browser information.

BSD – Berkeley Software Distribution. A UNIX implementation developed at the University of California at Berkeley. It was based on the AT&T specification, but BSD innovations included paged virtual memory support, networking, interprocesses communication, enhancements of the file system, and some contribution to system security. "BSD" is usually preceded by the version number of the distribution, e.g. "4.3 BSD" is version 4.3 of the Berkeley UNIX.

BSDI – Berkeley Software Design Inc. The company (http://www.bsdi.com) that supplies the Berkeley Software Distribution operating system (see BSD) and networking product originally developed at the University of California, Berkeley. See also BSDI Embedded System Technology (BEST).

BSFT – Byte Stream File Transfer. The X/Open specification which defines a file transfer service between X/Open-compliant systems.

BSI – British Standards Institution. The British standardization body, a member of ISO (http://www.bsi.org.uk).

BSIA – Beijing Software Industry Association. The Chinese association established in 1986 by leading software developers in Beijing (http://www.bsia.org). It includes software companies, universities, research institutes, computer centers, etc.

BSM – Balanced Scorecard Methodology. An analysis methodology developed by Robert Kaplan and David Norton in 1992 used for business process improvement (see BPI). BSM maps the business strategy and mission statements of an organization into specific measurable goals, and the progress towards these goals is later checked.

BSR – Basic Semantic Repository. An Electronic Data Interchange (see EDI) term representing a technical infrastructure that provides storage, maintenance and distribution facilities for reference data about EDI semantic units.

BSS – Basic Synchronized Subset. One of the four subsets of the OSI session services.

BST – Bangladesh Standard Time. Time zone. UTC + 6.00 hours. See TZ.

BST – Brazil Standard Time. Time zone. UTC – 3.00 hours. See TZ.

BST – British Summer Time. Time zone. UTC + 1.00 hour. The correction also applies in Ireland (IST, Irish Summer Time) and in Portugal, but not in Iceland which uses GMT throughout the year.

BT – Baghdad Time. Time zone. UTC + 3.00 hours. See TZ.

BT – Burst Tolerance. A term applied to ATM connections supporting variable bit services (see VBR). It is also used as the limit parameter of the GCRA.

BTA – But then again. The chat term.

BTAC – Branch Target Address Cache. A small cache memory used in RISC architectures for branch prediction.

BTAM – Basic Telecommunications Access Method. An IBM mainframe subsystem that handles application access and routing within a network. BTAM is still used, but it is largely obsolete. Compare with TCAM and VTAM.

BTB – Branch Target Buffer. A buffer used in RISC architectures to hold the branch target addresses of previously executed branch instructions.

BTE – Broadband Terminal Equipment. An equipment category for B-ISDN that includes terminal adapters and terminals.

BTW – By the way. An expression often used to preface remarks in e-mail and Internet newsgroup articles. Also, the chat term.

BUS – Broadcast/Unknown Server. The kind of server in ATM LAN networks, which allows broadcasting. BUS also provides for delivery of a packet from some host in the network to an unknown host.

BUS – Bull Users Society. A users group interested in Bull computers. The members share common information about latest news from Bull, application development under Bull operating systems, available tools, interconnection methods, etc. Due to the BUS regional organization, it is better to use a higher-level site to find out something of interest. An example of such a site is http://www.enterprise.bull.com.

BW – Bandwidth. In communications, a numerical measurement of the throughput of a system or network. In general, the communication channel must have sufficient bandwidth to handle the amount of data that must be passed over it. Different measurement units are applied for different signals. Thus, digital signals are measured in bps, while analog signals are measured in Hz.

BWQ – Buzzword Quotient. An IBM term for the percentage of buzzwords in a speech or document.

C

C – C file. A filename extension for a file that contains C source code.

C1 – Certification level 1. A certification level for computer security (TCSEC).

C2 – Certification level 2. A higher certification level for computer security (see TCSEC).

C2 – Command and Control systems. A common term for systems that can react in their areas of responsibility. Sensors, the "eyes" and "ears", give real-time inputs, which then combine with the description of the system mission and its goals (see Fig. C-1). After several activities, such as estimation of the situation, options generation, choice of the best option, planning and instruction (orders) generation, the system is ready to act in the area of responsibility. Depending on the degree of artificial intelligence of such systems, the decision-making process can be more or less automatic, from simple support to offering a decision, and can be more or less distributed (see C3I).

C3 – Command, Control and Communication systems. C3 systems (see C3I).

Fig. C-1. Command and Control System

C3I – Command, Control, Communications and Intelligence. From the general point of view, C3I systems support prediction, prevention and intervention against any potentially dangerous situations caused by humans (aggression, terrorism, traffic accidents, etc.) or catastrophes (earthquakes, floods, fires, etc.). There are many examples of their usage, the typical ones are national defense, fireguard systems, hail suppression, air-traffic control, railroad control, anticriminal systems, etc. They are sometimes referred to as CCCI, C4I and C4I2 systems. Without artificial intelligence, such systems are known as C3 systems.

C4I – Command, Control, Communications, Computer and Intelligence. See C3I (Command, Control, Communications, and Intelligence).

C4I2 – Command, Control, Communications, Computer, Intelligence and Information. See C3I systems.

CA – Cellular Automata. A regular spatial lattice of "cells", each of which can have any one of a finite number of states. The state of each cell in the lattice is updated according to the local rule, which may depend on the state of the cell and its neighbors at the previous time step. The state of the entire lattice also advances in discrete time steps. Each cell in a cellular automata could be considered as a finite state machine which takes its neighbors' states as inputs and outputs its own state. See also FSA. (Source FOLDOC.)

CA – Certification Authority. A trusted organization or an entity that issues certificates for later use in some key-management techniques. For example, see PGP and PCA.

CA – Computer Associates International Inc. An independent software solution company (http://www.cai.com) founded in 1976 for multiplatform computing.

CA – Control and Applications. The IASTED international conference focusing on the most recent developments in the area of control and applications. Some major topics include control theory, linear and nonlinear control, optimization, modeling, simulation, intelligent and adaptive control, etc.

CAB – Cabinet file. A filename extension for a file that contains installation and setup data, all compressed into one file.

CAC – Connection Admission Control. A set of actions taken by each ATM switch during connection set-up in order to determine whether the requested Quality of Service (see QoS) would violate the QoS guarantees for the established connections. Two mechanisms (overbooking and full booking) are used to control the set-up of virtual circuits. Overbooking allows one connection to exceed permissible traffic limits, assuming that other active connections are not using the maximum available resources. Full booking limits network access once maximum resources are committed and only adds connections that specify acceptable traffic parameters.

CACM – Communications of the ACM. The journal issued by ACM every month. It covers all areas of computer science.

C

CACTUS – Carlos Addition for Clustered Terminal User Agents. An ESPRIT project from the late 1980s intended to provide the necessary components on personal computers for accessing X.400 using telephone lines. See also ESPRIT.

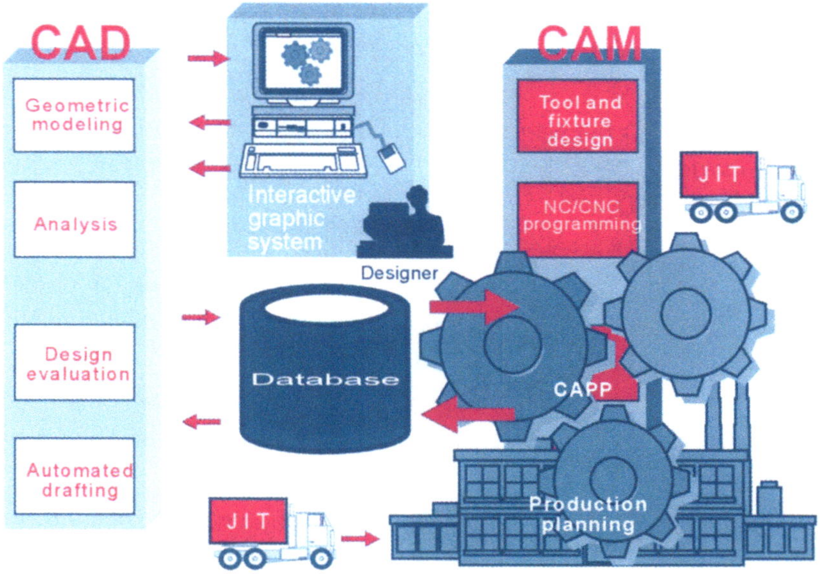

Fig. C-2. Components of CAD/CAM and their relationships

CAD – Computer-Aided Design. A common name for designing components and systems of mechanical, electrical, electromechanical, and electronic devices using interactive computer graphics. Various CAD applications create objects in two or three dimensions. Objects can be viewed as wireframe models, as models with shaded surfaces, or as solid objects. Often, such models are interpreted by a simulator that feeds back the behavior of the system under design for further interactive design and testing. Once objects have been designed, some CAD applications can produce parts lists, bills of materials (see BOM), or define numerical control tapes for use in manufacturing processes, and the like. Such applications rely on mathematics, allowing object resizing, rotation or other necessary geometrical transformations, so the hardware requirements for supporting a large number of vector and matrix operations are usually considerable. See also CADD.

CAD/CAM – Computer-Aided Design/Computer-Aided Manufacturing. A term describing both design and manufacturing supported by computers (see Fig. C-2). As noted above, CAD applications can output design data, which can be used later as inputs in manufacturing processes. For example, a bill of material (see BOM) can be used for purchasing the necessary components, parts lists for manufacturing line organization, control tapes for programming numerical machines on the line, etc. CAD/CAM-based production is crucial for any factory looking to achieve JIT (see JIT).

CADD – Computer-Aided Design and Drafting. A system of hardware and software similar to CAD but with additional features related to engineering conventions, including the ability to display dimension specifications and other notes. See also CAD.

CADDIA – Cooperation in Automation of Data and Documentation for Imports/Exports and Agriculture. An electronic information structure for collection, storage, transmission and exchange of information, using developments in information technology and telecommunications (http://www.caddia.org).

CADE – Conference on Automated Deduction. An international conference focusing on automated deduction. The proceedings are published by Springer-Verlag (see LNCS).

CAE – Common Application Environment. A set of standards, defined by the X/Open Company, for providing a complete support system for the development and running of application software in a full open environment, based on the portability, scalability and interoperability (see PSI) features of such applications. X/Open was founded in 1984 as an international nonprofit organization organized by a group of major computer manufactures to facilitate, guide and manage a transition process from closed to open systems. X/Open coordinates CAE development, and coordinates very closely with the Open Software Foundation (see OSF) via a common association named The Open Group (http://www.opengroup.org). X/Open adopted and adapted individual standards, both de jure (ISO, ANSI, IEEE, IEC, etc.) and de facto (well-known industrial standards approved because of their quality), and then put them into one cohesive and comprehensive superstandard known as the X/Open Portability Guide (see XPG).

Special attention from CAE is given to operating system services, programming languages, data management, networking, window management, and security. In 1988, X/Open introduced a brand to act as an easy identifier for products that conform to the specifications published in XPG2. In June 1990, X/Open launched the uniquely successful XPG3 branding program. This was followed by XPG4 in 1992. The X/Open CAE is a collection of both specifications developed by X/Open and its partners, and references to formal standards. Use of the X/Open brand is strictly controlled by a comprehensive licensing agreement, which clearly sets out the criteria for compliance for all types of X/Open-conformant products, and establishes stringent rules and obligations in the use of the trademark. See Fig. C-3.

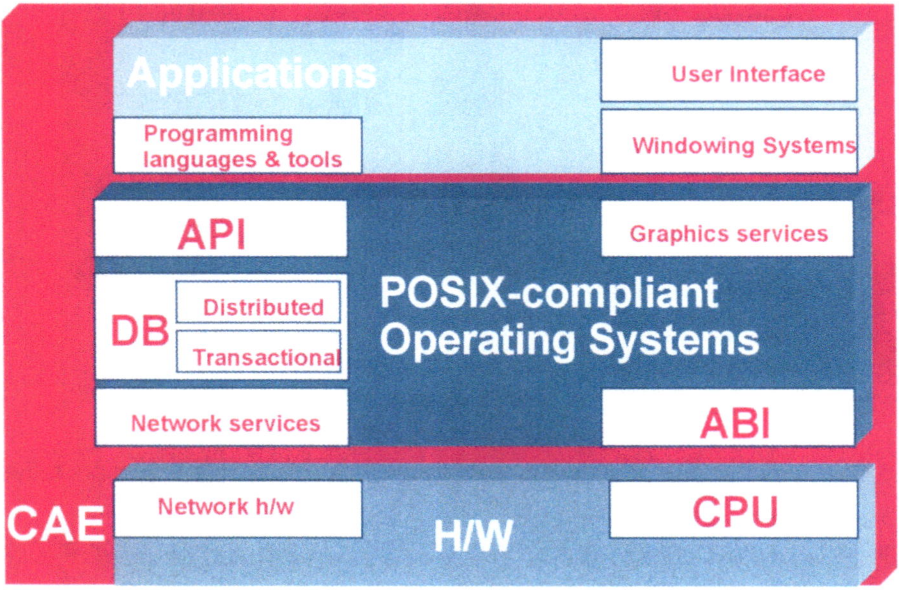

Fig. C-3. X/Open Common Application Environment

CAE – Computer-Aided Engineering. A common name for an application that enables users to perform some engineering tests and analyses.

CAG – Clip Art Gallery. The name of the folder in Microsoft Windows consisting of public-domain photographs, maps, videos, drawings and other such objects that can be "clipped" from the collection and incorporated into other documents. Figure C-4 depicts how it works, in the case where a user wants to include a cartoon from CAG into her/his own document.

CAI – Computer-Assisted Instruction. A learning technique where the cognitive processing is managed by a computer, but the learner (usually a university student) is a partner in the learning process. CAI improves critical thinking skills and encourages problem solving and decision making. See also Computer-Assisted Learning (CAL) and Intelligent Tutoring Systems (ITS).

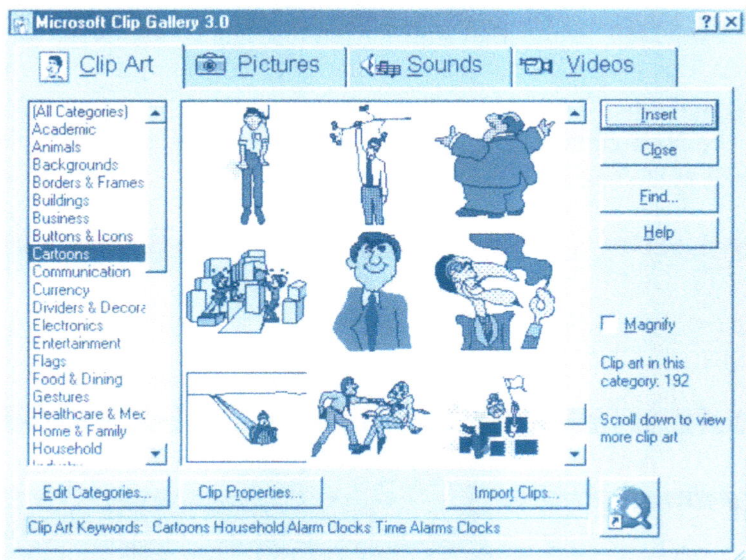

Fig. C-4. Some of the cartoons available in CAG

CAIDA – Cooperative Association for Internet Data Analysis. A collaborative organization (http://www.caida.org) promoting greater cooperation in the engineering and maintenance of a robust, scalable, global Internet infrastructure.

CAiSE – Conference on Advanced information System Engineering. An international conference focusing on advanced issues in information system engineering. The proceedings are published by Springer-Verlag (see LNCS).

cal – calendar. UNIX command used for the display calendar.

CAL – Computer-Assisted Learning. A type of educational program designed to serve as a teaching tool. See also CAI, CAT, CBL, CBT and ITS.

CALS – Continuous Acquisition Lifecycle Support. A DoD standard for electronic exchange of data with commercial suppliers. Formerly known as Computer-aided Acquisition and Logistic Support.

CAM – Computer-Aided Manufacturing. See CAD/CAM.

CAM – Content Addressable Memory. An associative memory often used in caches and memory management units. Write or read positions inside such memories are identified by memory contents rather than by addresses.

CAMP – Computer Architecture for Machine Perception. An international workshop focusing on architectures for machine perception. Some of the main topics are architectures for image understanding, sound recognition, smart sensors, rule-based systems, knowledge-based machines, distributed processing for machine perception, parallel video servers, languages, programming tools, neural networks, etc.

CAN – Campus Area Network. A network that connects nodes from multiple locations, which may be separated by a considerable distance. Due to limitations on the distances, CAN does not require modems and telephones between its nodes.

CAN – Cancel. A transmission control character used to indicate that the characters preceding it are in error and they should be canceled.

CANARIE – Canadian Network for the Advancement of Research, Industry and Education. A nonprofit Canadian organization (http://www.canarie.ca) established in 1993 dedicated to advanced Internet development in Canada.

CANPC – Communication Architecture and Applications for Network Parallel Computing. An international workshop sponsored by the IEEE Computer Society focusing on network-based parallel computing. The proceedings are published by Springer-Verlag (see LNCS).

CAP – Carrierless Amplitude/Phase modulation. The modulation technique based on QAM that stores segments of a modulated message in memory and reassembles it in the transmitted wave. See also QAM.

CAP – Complexity Adaptive Processors. An approach for reconfigurable microprocessor design.

CAPI – Common ISDN API. An API standard that allows access to both BRI and PRI ISDN equipment. It is designed to be the basis for a whole range of new protocol stacks for networking, telephony, file-transfer, application sharing, etc. It has been accepted by ETSI, as the ETS300 838 standard, as well as by ITU, as recommendation T200. CAPI can be used with MS-DOS, Microsoft Windows (95, 97, 98, NT), OS/2, Novell NetWare and UNIX. See also PRI (Primary Rate Interface) and BRI (Basic Rate Interface). Also, see ISDN (Integrated Service Digital Network).

CAPIT – Capitalization and Punctuation Intelligent Tutor. An Intelligent Tutoring System (see ITS) developed by the Intelligent Tutoring Group (headed by Dr. Antonija Mitrović) at the University of Canterbury, New Zealand. CAPIT teaches the mechanical rules of English capitalization and punctuation. Students must interactively capitalize and punctuate short pieces of unpunctuated lowercase text. CAPIT represents the domain as a set of constraints specifying the correct patterns of punctuation and capitalization, and feedback is given on violated constraints. The system was evaluated over several seasons in a classroom of 10–11-year-old school children with significant success.

CAPP – Computer-Aided Process Planning. An acronym for computer-supported process planning, the process that offers a number of potential advantages. These include process rationalization (more consistent, logical, and optimal), better productivity from process planners, improved legibility, and easier incorporation of other application programs.

CAQ – Computer-Aided Quality. Quality assurance in a manufacturing process supported by computers. See also Quality Assurance (QA).

CARL – Colorado Alliance of Research Libraries. An association that provides access to member and public library catalogs, current article indexes and document delivery, information databases, and library and system news (http://pac.carl.org). Some databases have restricted access to password holders, while the catalogs have free access.

CAS – Channel Associated Signaling. In telecommunications, a form of circuit state signaling in which one or more bits of signaling status are sent repetitively and are associated with that specific circuit.

CAS – Column Address Strobe. A signal sent to a DRAM memory in order to tell it that an associated address is a column address. A data bit is stored in a cell located using a column address and a row address. See DRAM. See also Row Address Strobe (RAS).

CASE – Common Application Service Element. A term used by ISO to describe certain application-layer services (see OSI and ASE). Examples include CCITT X.400, ISO FTAM, Association Control Service Elements (see ACSE), Remote Operation Service Element (see ROSE), Reliable Transfer Service Element (see RTSE), and Virtual Terminal (see VT).

CASE – Computer-Aided Software Engineering. A comprehensive term related to a working environment consisting of software tools that in all phases allow automatic software development. CASE tools are used for reengineering, debugging, program analysis, change management, documentation preparation, language processing, testing, editing, planning, etc. In general, CASE tools and workbenches are delivered as a single product that contains a useful subset of the above tool categories.

CAT – Catalog file. A filename extension for a file that contains a dBase catalog. See also dBase and D/D.

CAT – Common Authentication Technology. A specification for distributed authentication on the Internet. CAT supports both public and private key-encryption methods. Also, both client and server programs must use the services of a common interface connecting them to DASS or Kerberos security. See also Distributed Authentication Security Service (DASS).

CAT – Computer-Aided Teaching. See CAL.

CAT – Computer-Aided Testing. Procedures used by engineers to estimate the quality of some components or products, especially those created using CAD programs.

CAT – Computerized Axial Tomography. A medical procedure which makes a three-dimensional image of a body part. Inputs are made by a series of X-rays taken as cross-sections along the same axis.

CATE – Computers and Advanced Technology in Education. The IASTED international conference focusing on distance learning, advanced technology in education, and other topics related to computers in education.

CATS – Computing: The Australasian Theory Symposium. An international conference focusing on theoretical computer science. Some of the main topics include formal specification techniques, formal development methods, the theory of concurrent, parallel and distributed systems, algorithms and data structures, tools for automated reasoning, etc. The proceedings are published by Elsevier Science (see ENTCS).

CATV – Community Antenna Television. The local-area-network facility adapted using television techniques to produce flexible underlying data transmission over a LAN.

CAU – Controlled Access Unit. The term assigned to an intelligent hub in IBM token ring networks (see TR). Such hubs can connect and disconnect nodes, monitor nodes, and determine whether nodes are operating, etc.

CAUCE – Coalition Against Unsolicited Commercial Email. A voluntary organization (http://www.cauce.org) created by Netizens to advocate for a legislative solution to the problem of junk e-mails (also known as UCE). Such e-mails cost Netizens and Internet-based business millions of dollars every month. See also Netizen and S4L.

CAV – Computer-Aided Verification. An international conference focusing on computer-aided verification. The proceedings are published by Springer-Verlag (see LNCS).

CAV – Constant Angular Velocity. A feature of a CD-ROM drive that allows the drive to keep the rotation speed constant, but still enables it to read the data at different speeds. See also CLV.

Fig. C-5. I-wall as an example of a teleimmersive system
(courtesy of Dr. Jason Leigh, EVL, University of Illinois at Chicago)

CAVE – Cave Automated Virtual Environment. A projection-based virtual reality (see VR) system developed at the Electronic Visualization Laboratory (see EVL). CAVE creates for users, wearing special glasses, the illusion that objects surround them. This advanced virtual reality technology, integrated with audio and video conferencing, leads to so-called teleimmersive systems. When participants are teleimmersed they are not talking about a thing, they are standing inside it. See Fig. C-5. See also CAVERN and PARIS.

CAVERN – CAVE Research Network. An alliance of industrial and research institutions (http://www.evl.uic.edu/cavern) using CAVE and high-performance computing resources interconnected using high-speed networks to support collaboration in design, training, scientific visualization, and computational steering in virtual reality. See also CAVE.

CB – Clean Boot. A filename extension for a Microsoft clean boot file.

CBAIVL – Content-Based Access of Image and Video Libraries. An IEEE workshop working on algorithms and systems for content-based access of image and video libraries.

CBC – Cipher Block Chaining. An encryption technique where each encrypted block and previous block of ciphertext are additionally encrypted using Boolean XOR. The term ciphertext itself means encrypted data in contrast to plaintext which refers to nonencrypted data.

CBD – Component-Based Development. The building of software systems using prepackaged generic elements.

CBDS – Connectionless Broadband Data Service. A connectionless service similar to the Switched Multimegabit Data Service (see SMDS) defined by ETSI.

CBEMA – Computer and Business Equipment Manufacturers Association. An association of hardware vendors in the United States.

CBL – COBOL. A filename extension related to source files generated by ACU-COBOL or AcuBench IDE. See COBOL and IDE.

CBL – Computer-Based Learning. See Computer-Assisted Learning (CAL).

CBN – Call-By-Name. An argument passing mechanism where argument expressions are first passed and then evaluated. The contrasting strategy is call-by-value (see CBV).

CBQ – Class-Based Queuing. A bandwidth management technique based on multiqueue scheduling. In CBQ, bandwidth is assigned across a link to different traffic categories, according to a hierarchical structure.

CBR – Case-Based Reasoning. An AI technique for problem solving based on knowledge of similar cases from the past.

CBR – Constant Bit Rate. An ATM service category that provides constant-rate synchronous channels for real-time audio and video transmission.

CBT – Computer-Based Training. Job-oriented training using computers. CBT includes tutorials, drill and practice, simulations, testing, and may include embedded training.

CBV – Call-By-Value. An argument passing mechanism that evaluates arguments before the calling procedure is entered, and after that passes only the argument values. The contrasting passing strategy, described earlier, is call-by-name (see CBN).

CBX – Computerized Branch Exchange. A telephone routing exchange driven by a computer.

cc – C compiler. In UNIX, a command that invokes a C compiler.

cc – carbon copy. A directive used in e-mail to send a complete copy of a given piece of mail to another individual. The use of cc mail addressing, as opposed to directly addressing the mail to a person, generally implies that the recipient is not required to act; the message is for informational purposes only. In a cc directive, the fact that this recipient received the mail is printed in the mail header and is thus known to all other recipients. Also known as courtesy copy. Compare with Bcc.

CC – Clearing Center. A message-switching element in an Electronic Data Interchange (see EDI) environment used to pass EDI documents.

CC – Compiler Construction. An international conference focusing on the theory and practice of compiler construction. The proceedings are published by Springer-Verlag (see LNCS).

CC – Country Code. A set of digits within an address which signifies the country. This may be internationally agreed, as with the telephone country code, or the CCITT X.121 address may be used in X.25 networks, or the code may be vendor specific.

CC – Cyclomatic Complexity. In software engineering, the number of independent paths in a program.

CCB – Change Control Board. A supervisor team in a software organization responsible for the strategic and organizational impacts of requested changes (see CRF). The structure of such a team can vary from a single authority within an organization to a mixed board where people from both sides (client and developer) participate.

CCCI – Command, Control, Communications and Intelligence. See C3I.

CCD – Charge-Coupled Device. An electronic device in which semiconductor elements are connected and their combined charges can be measured using suitable applied control voltages. Arrays of photodiodes can be interrogated in this way, where the combined charges relate to the incident light intensities etc. An example is the light-detecting component in cameras and scanners.

CCH – Corel Chart. A filename extension for files that contain Corel Charts.

CCIDF – Common Citation Inverse Document Frequency. An algorithm used for scientific information dissemination, which works on the basis of similar citations in articles. Compare with TFIDF.

CCIR – Consultative Committee for International Radio. An international standards body that sets the rules and requirements for radio communications. CCIR is a committee within the ITU. See also ITU and CCITT.

CCITT – Comité Consultatif International Télégraphique et Téléphonique. The former name for ITU-T.

CCM – CORBA Component Model. The final part of OMG CORBA specification release 3.0 (see CORBA). CCM provides a framework for building, assembling and deploying plug-and-play CORBA objects in heterogeneous systems. The framework integrates components with applications written in Java, COBOL, COM/DCOM, C, C++, Ada, and Smalltalk. CCM also operates with other similar technologies, such as ActiveX, and Enterprise Java Beans (see EJB).

CCR – Commitment, Concurrency and Recovery. An OSI service element used to create atomic operations across distributed systems (see ACID). The component helps ensure that distributed data remains consistent by making sure that applications do not interfere with each other and that the actions involved are completed in full or not at all.

CCR – Current Cell Rate. In ATM networks, a field in the Resource Management cell (see RM) used to calculate the explicit rate (see ER) field in that RM cell.

CCRSE – Commitment, Concurrency and Recovery Service Element. See Commitment, Concurrency and Recovery (CCR).

Ccs – Hundred (C) call seconds. A method for measuring traffic in a telephone system. The first C is after the Roman “C” (hundred).

CCS – Common Channel Signaling. A signaling method used to send control signals across different channels instead of via voice and data channels.

CCS – Common Communication Support. One of the key parts of the IBM System Application Architecture (see SAA). This is one of the SAA stubs that supports data links, application services, session services, and datastreams.

CCS – Continuous Composite Servo. A compact disk (see CD) recording technique where the contents are stored on separate tracks laid out in concentric circles. Compare with Sampled Servo (SS).

CCS7 – Common Channel Signaling 7. A version of the CCITT Signaling System (see SS7) used in ISDN to provide some special services such as call forwarding and call waiting.

CCSDS – Consultative Committee for Space Data Systems. An international organization (http://www.ccsds.org) of space agencies and industries with mutual interests in space research.

CCT – China Coast Time. Time zone. UTC + 8.00 hours. See TZ.

CD – Carrier Detect. A communication signal sent from a modem to its computer to indicate that the modem is online.

cd – change directory. UNIX command that allows users to move to a new working directory.

CD – Compact Disk. A nonmagnetic audio and data storage medium in the form of a polished metal disk with a protective plastic coating that can be read by an optical scanning device. It is also called an optical disk. The disk is read by an optical scanning mechanism that uses a high-intensity light source, e.g. a laser, and mirrors. This technology forms the basis of media such as CD-DA, CD-ROM, CD-ROM/XA, CD-E, CD-I, CD-R and DVI etc. These media are all compact-disk-based, but store various types of digital information and have different read/write capabilities. The related standards are known as "Rainbow Books" after the colors of the lasers used in each particular technology. There are also several hybrid variants developed for special purposes, such as CD+G, CD-MIDI, CD-EB, CD-V, in order to allow recording of graphics, midi files, reference materials, and videos, respectively.

CDA – Communications Decency Act. An amendment to the US 1996 Telecommunications Act that went into effect on 8th February 1996, when thousands of Internet users turned their webpages black in protest. The main goal of the CDA was to prohibit telecommunication devices that make or make available any communications which are obscene, lascivious, or which harass other persons. At the same time no definitions were given as to what the terms obscene, lascivious, etc., exactly meant in the CDA. The protest by Internet users was supported by the Electronic Frontier Foundation (see EFF) to protect human rights, and the US 1st Amendment guaranteeing freedom of speech is so strong that on 12th June 1996, a three-judge panel in Philadelphia ruled that the CDA was unconstitutional.

CDB – Constraint Database. A type of database in which constraints are integrated as a basic data type. Constraints serve as a uniform data type for conceptual representations of different data with spatial and temporal behavior, for example. Such kinds of data behavior are very important in Geographic Information Systems (see GIS).

CDC – Control Data Corporation. An open system integrator founded in 1957 by William C. Norris to supply high-performance scientific and engineering systems (http://www.cdc.com). The company is now working on complex network reengineering. Control Data's credentials in network integration include implementing one of the first full-production frame-relay networks in the world, as well as designing and building the world's largest fully operational OSI network. Large organizations use its Rialto line of directory-enabled products and services to create client/server enterprise networks for a variety of digital commerce applications.

CDD – CERN Drawing Directory. A multiplatform utility at CERN that manages engineering drawings made in any part of CERN. See also CERN and CEDAR.

CD-DA – Compact Disk-Digital Audio. The first compact disk standard (see CD) developed for recording music. Since the appearance of the next-generation CD technologies, this kind of CD has become widely recognized by the term audio CD.

CDDI – Copper Distributed Data Interface. An FDDI implementation via copper wires. Such an implementation actually involves a misnomer because of FDDI's original fiber orientation. CDDI transmits over relatively short distances of about 100 m, providing data rates of 100 Mbps. Compare with FDDI. See also Shielded Distributed Data Interface (SDDI) and Twisted Pair DDI (TPDDI).

CD-E – Compact Disk-Erasable. A technological improvement in compact disks whereby information can be repeatedly changed on the CD. Older CDs are "write once, read many", i.e. the information originally written cannot be changed, but can only be added to.

CDE – Common Desktop Environment. Part of the COSE agreement among major UNIX vendors to present a common interface to all UNIX implementations. See COSE.

CDE – Cooperative Development Environment. An Oracle set of tools for client/server enterprise-wide application development.

CDF – Channel Definition Format. Provides a metadata vocabulary based on XML for describing inter-relationships between HTML pages and other Web resources. CDF clients may download Web content, and on the other hand CDF servers may distribute some content. See XML.

CDF – Comma-Delimited Format. A data file consisting of fields and records, stored as text, in which commas separate the fields from each other. Use of comma-delimited files allows communication between database systems that use different formats. If the data in a field contains a comma, the field can alternatively be enclosed within quotation marks.

CDF – Common Data Format. A library and toolkit for storing, manipulating and accessing multidimensional data sets. The basic component of CDF is a programming interface that gives a device-independent view of the CDF data model. All related information can be found at http://nssdc.gsfs.nas.gov/cdf

CDF – Cutoff Decrease Factor. In ATM networks, a parameter that controls the decrease in the Allowed Cell Rate (see ACR) associated with the Cell Rate Margin parameter (see CRM).

CDFS – CD-ROM File System. A 32-bit protected-mode file system that controls access to the contents of CD-ROM drives in Windows 95.

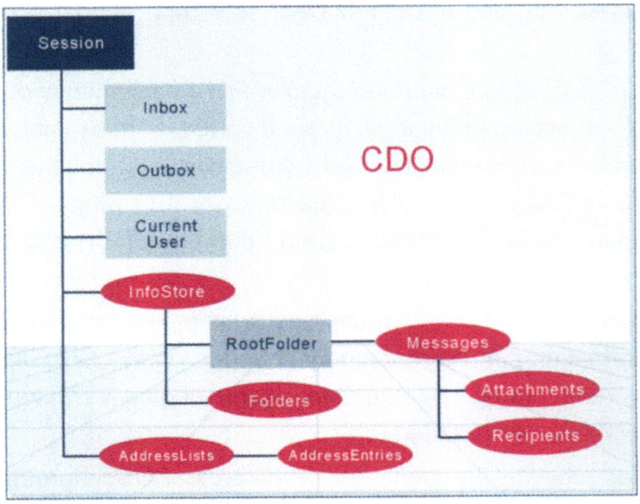

Fig. C-6. The CDO object model

CD-I – Compact Disk-Interactive. A standard for encoding, decompressing, compressing and displaying stored information on high-capacity optical disks, supporting audio, video and text data. CD-I is defined in the so-called "Green Book" (pronounced "see-dee-eye").

CDIF – CASE Data Interchange Format. An emerging family of standards for the interchange of data between CASE tools. CDIF was defined by the CDIF division of the EIA and is also being standardized via ISO/IEC JTC1/SC7/WG11. With the CDIF family of standards, each tool needs only one import and one export interface to be able to communicate with any other CDIF-compliant tool. Thus, CDIF improves the transfer of information among teams, projects, departments and whole organizations, and is one of the core enabling technologies for creating integrated systems and software engineering environments. Draft proposals can be obtained from http://www.cdif.org

CDMA – Code Division Multiple Access. A method for allocating a wireless channel which allows each station to transmit over the entire frequency spectrum all the time. Compare with TDMA.

CDO – Collaborative Data Objects. A Microsoft object model (see Fig. C-6) consisting of a refined set of COM objects that allows programmatic access to any MAPI provider (see MAPI). It is available by installing Microsoft Outlook 98. See also COM (Component Object Model).

CDPD – Cellular Digital Packet Data. A packet-switched digital connectionless datagram service for sending data over the existing cellular phones system. CDPD can be used, for example, to stay connected in a mobile computing environment. A CDPD modem and appropriate software are required. In order to protect users against unauthorized access to the data, CDPD uses encryption as well as data compression for cutting down transmission times and costs.

CDR – CorelDraw. A filename extension for files containing drawings made using the CorelDraw software package. All pictures in this book, except screenshots, were made using CorelDraw and then pasted into the appropriate pages using WMF files (see WMF) or TIFF files (see TIFF). Figure C-7 depicts such a scenario where the CorelDraw drawing named edbms1.cdr is exported to edbms1.wmf.

CD-R – Compact Disk-Recordable. An optical data storage medium (covered by the "Orange Book") characterized by its gold surface, intended for professional use. In fact, these are ordinary CD-ROM disks produced by special means. See also CD and CD-ROM.

CD-ROM – Compact Disk-Read-Only Memory. An optical data storage medium (covered by the "Yellow Book") characterized by high capacity (> 600 MB), which uses the same physical format as audio compact disks. It is very suitable for software, multimedia applications, or large database distribution. CD-ROMs are readable using CD-ROM drives that can be connected to a

SCSI, IDE or some kind of proprietary interface. Several features distinguish CD-ROM drives from each other, such as: the transfer rate, i.e. the amount of data that the drive can read from the disk in a second; the access time, which represents the average time needed to find a specified item on the disk; compatibility with various CD standards (see CD-ROM/XA, CD-I or any CD-*); the number of disks the drive can handle, etc.

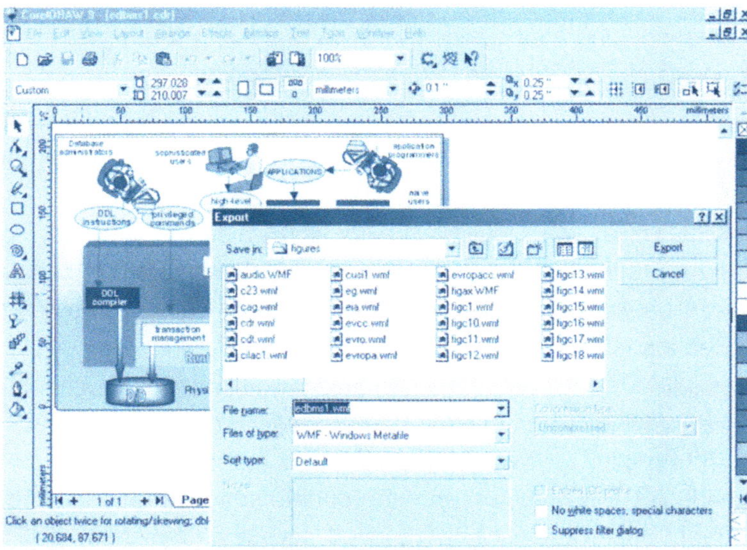

Fig. C-7. An example of a CDR file and WMF creation

CD-ROM/XA – Compact Disk-Read-Only Memory/Extended Architecture. An extended CD-ROM format developed by Microsoft, Philips and Sony which is compliant with the High Sierra ISO9660 standard, with the additional specification of adaptive differential pulse code modulation (see ADPCM) audio, images and interleaved data.

CDS – Cell Directory Service. Part of the OSF DCE (see DCE) that stores the names and properties of the resources inside a cell. In order to operate, every cell must have at least one running CDS server.

CDS – Cell Directory Server. A daemon process, the part of an OSF DCE Cell Directory Service that runs on a server machine in order to accept queries, look them up, and send back replies. The daemon process on the client side, the CDS clerk, has a different function, namely to do client caching.

C

CDS – Correlated Double Sampling. The technology that cleans an image signal and filters its noise during image scanning.

CDT – Central Daylight Time. Time zone. UTC – 5.00 hours. The Canadian province of Saskatchewan does not operate CDT – it's on CST all year round.

CDT – Center for Democracy and Technology. An organization concerned with free speech, data privacy, and other aspects of cyberspace usage. For more information visit http://www.cdt.org. See Fig. C-8.

Fig. C-8. CDT homepage (courtesy of CDT)

CDT – CorelDraw Template. A filename extension for files containing templates for drawing using the CorelDraw software package. See also CDR.

CDV – Cell Delay Variation. One of the ATM Quality of Service (see QoS) parameters that measures how uniformly the ATM cells are delivered. It is expressed in fractions of a second. When emulating a circuit, CDV measurements allow the network to determine whether cells are arriving too fast or too slow. See also CDVT.

CDVT – Cell Delay Variation Tolerance. The term applied to ATM layer functions (see AAL) when altering the traffic characteristics of an ATM connection (see CDV).

CD-WORM – Compact Disk-Write-Once Read-Many. One of the CD standards defined in the so-called "Orange Book". Also known as WORM.

CDX – Compound Index file. A filename extension for a file that contains multiple index entries.

CE – Concurrent Engineering. A systematic approach to software engineering where all aspects of a product's lifecycle are considered as early as possible during the design, manufacturing and maintenance processes.

CE – Connection Endpoint. In ATM terminology, a terminator at one end of a layer connection within a Service Access Point (see SAP).

Fig. C-9. The homepage for CERN (courtesy of CERN)

CEA – Cambridge Event Architecture. A project at Cambridge University focusing on middleware extensions development in order to provide a flexible, scalable approach to distributed application development (IEEE Computer, March 2000, pp. 68–76).

CEDAR – Center of Excellence for Document Analysis and Recognition. A research center (http://www.cedar.buffalo.edu) at which work is done on the science of recognition, analysis, and interpretation of digital documents.

CEDAR – CERN EDMS for Detectors and Accelerators. The Engineering Data Management System (see EDMS) used to manage the huge amounts of engineering and project data in CERN. See also CERN.

CEI – Connection Endpoint Identifier. The identifier of a Connection Endpoint (see CE) that can be used to identify the connection at a Service Access Point (see SAP).

CEN – Comité Européen de Normalisation. A body coordinating standardization activities in the EU and EFTA countries. By applying the CE marking a manufacturer declares compliance with CEN's relevant directives, e.g. the EMC directive. See http://www.cenorm.be

CENELEC – European Committee for Electrotechnical Standardization. See http://www.cenelec.org

CENIC – Corporation for Education Network Initiatives in California. A consortium (http://www.cenic.org) in California's higher-education community, established to coordinate the development, deployment, and operation of robust intercampus communications capable of supporting advanced research.

CER – Canonical Encoding Rules. A set of encoding rules used with Abstract Syntax Notation One (see ASN.1).

CER – Cell Error Rate (Ratio). The non-negotiable QoS parameter corresponding to the fraction of ATM cells delivered with errors (with at least one bit wrong). The measurement is taken over a time interval and should be measured on an in-service circuit.

CERN – Conseil Européen pour la Recherche Nucléaire. The European Laboratory for Particle Physics (http://www.cern.ch). The high-power research center in Europe, located in Geneva, Switzerland. The birthplace of the WWW. The above abbreviation is after the old French name. See Fig. C-9.

CERT – Computer Emergency Response Team. A Software Engineering Institute (see SEI) team at Carnegie Mellon University that provides round-the-clock international security services to the organizations on the Internet.

CES – Circuit Emulation Service. An ATM Forum specification for emulating time-division multiplexing (see TDM) circuits over ATM.

CET – Central European Time. Time zone. UTC + 1.00 hour. See TZ.

CETS – Compilation Environment Test Suite. The test suite used by compiler developers in order to test whether their software is capable of producing ABI+ compliant programs (see ABI and ABI+).

CFB – Cipher Feedback. An encryption technique where each byte of the following data is encrypted along with the previous seven bytes of ciphertext.

The result is that identical patterns in the plaintext appear as different patterns in the ciphertext. The term ciphertext itself means encrypted data, in contrast to plaintext which refers to nonencrypted data. Compare with CBC.

CFG – Configuration file. Filename extensions for files that contain configuration data in Microsoft Windows.

CFI – CAD Framework Initiative. A consortium working on interface standards for integrating CAD tools and data.

CFM – Cubic Feet per Minute. A measurement unit of the volume of air moved by a computer power-supply fan.

CFP – Call For Papers. An acronym often used by conference organizers in order to announce a conference, workshop, etc. (see Fig. C-10).

```
------------------------------------------------------------------------
ACISP'01      CALL FOR PAPERS
------------------------------------------------------------------------
                    The Sixth Australasian Conference
                   On Information Security and Privacy
                    2-4 July 2001, Sydney, Australia

General Information: Original papers pertaining to all aspects of computer
systems and information security are solicited for submission to the Sixth
Australasian Conference on Information Security and Privacy (ACISP 2001).
Papers may present theory, techniques, applications and practical
experiences on a variety of topics including:

    * Authentication and authority          * Cryptology
    * Database security                     * Access control
    * Mobile communications security        * Network security
    * Secure operating systems              * Smart cards
    * Security management                   * Risk assessment
    * Secure commercial applications        * Copyright protection
    * Key management and auditing           * Mobile agents security
    * Secure electronic commerce            * Software protection & viruses
```

Fig. C-10. An example of a CFP

CFP – Computers, Freedom and Privacy. The workshop focusing on legal remedies as essential instruments in the fight to ensure freedom and privacy.

CG – Computer Graphics. A common term for technologies that allow data manipulation and data presentation in some kind of graphic form. It covers graphical hardware (boards, I/O devices, workstations, displays, etc.), graphic systems such as GKS or PHIGS, GUIs, a numbers of graphical-based applications (CAD, GIS, etc.), as well as a number of appropriate algorithms.

CGA – Color Graphics Adapter. A video adapter board introduced by IBM in 1981. The adapter supports character modes of 40 or 80 columns by 25 vertical lines with 16 colors, and 640×200 or 320×200 graphic modes with two and four colors, respectively.

CG&A – Computer Graphics and Applications. The IEEE journal that covers the theory and practice of computer graphics (see CG). CG&A is published six times a year.

CGF – Computer Graphics Forum. The journal published by the Eurographics association (see EG) issued five times a year. The fifth issue is a special issue with EG conference proceedings.

CGI – Common Gateway Interface. A standard for handling "forms" data and for searching databases on the Web. It is an open platform-independent program resident on the Web server that can be activated by any client on the WWW via a simple CGI Uniform Resource Locator (see URL). When the program has completed its operation, it sends the results to the Web server as a document in a format the WWW browser can view, such as HTML, GIF, video clips, etc. Every form has both the HTML code, which controls its appearance, and the CGI script running on the server, which enables the form's content to be processed. Additional information can be obtained at http://hoohoo.ncsa.uiuc.edu/cgi

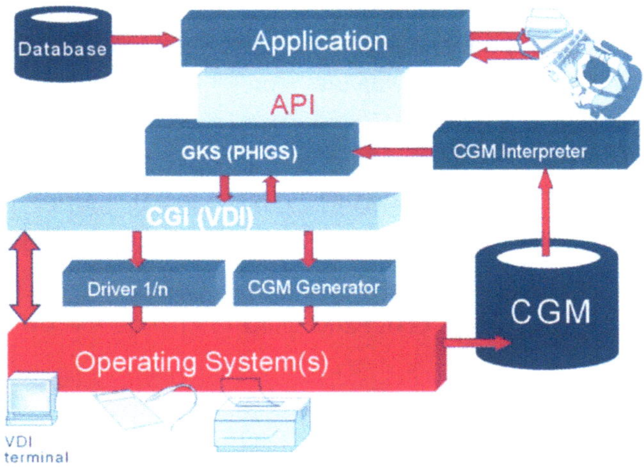

Fig. C-11. The role of a CGI and a CGM in a graphics system

CGI – Computer Graphics Interface. A standard (ISO9636) functional and syntactical specification of the control and data exchange between the device-independent graphics software and one or more device-dependent graphics drivers and appropriate input, output and input/output graphics devices (see Fig. C-11).

CGIM – Computer Graphics and Imaging. IASTED conference focusing on research and industrial practice in the field of computer graphics and imaging. Some of the main topics include rendering, modeling, animation, image processing, visualization, etc.

CGM – Computer Graphics Metafile. An ISO standard (ISO8632) that defines the way in which graphics images are stored for transfer to other systems and for later use. The role of the CGM in CG is shown in Fig. C-11.

CGMIF – Computer Graphics Metafile Interchange Format. An ISO standard that provides a vector-based representation for graphics files.

CGS – Centimeter–Gram–Second. An absolute system of metric units in which the centimeter, gram mass, and the second are the basic measurement units.

CHAP – Challenge–Handshake Authentication Protocol. A special kind of PPP authentication scheme specified in RFC1334 that allows validation of the originator's identity during connection, or later on.

chgrp – change group. UNIX command used to change the group affiliation of a file.

CHILL – CCITT High-Level Language. A problem-oriented real-time high-level language very similar to Ada. It was intended for telecommunication systems programming.

CHM – Compiled HTML. Filename extensions for compiled HTML files.

chmod – change mode. UNIX command used to change the access mode of files and directories. Changing the mode of a file is strictly allowed only for owners of a file or superusers.

chown – change owner. UNIX command used to change the ownership of a file.

CHP – Chapter file. A filename extension for a file that contains a chapter in Ventura Publisher.

CHRP – Common Hardware Reference Platform. A specification describing a family of machines, based on the PowerPC processor, that are capable of booting multiple operating systems, including Mac OS, Windows NT, AIX and Solaris. Apple, IBM and Motorola (also known as AIM) developed CHRP. See also the PowerPC platform (PPCO).

CHS – Cylinder/Head/Sector. A set of parameters applied to a hard drive (see HDD) that describes the technical specifications of the drive, determining the amount of data the drive can hold. Compare with LBA.

CI – Computational Intelligence. An international symposium focusing on computational intelligence. The main topics include adaptive and learning systems, artificial intelligence, cognitive and neural modeling, fuzzy systems, machine learning, image processing, multiagent systems, neural networks, pattern recognition, etc.

CI – Communications Interactive. The online version of the IEEE's Communications Magazine.

CI – Congestion Indicator. In an ATM environment, a field in an RM cell (see RM) used to cause the source node to decrease its Available Cell Rate (see ACR).

CIA – Cooperative Information Agents. An international workshop focusing on cooperative information agents. Some of the major topics include systems and applications of information agents, programming collaborative information agents, agent-based knowledge discovery and data mining, agents in open distributed and dynamically changing environments, mobile information agents, rational information agents and electronic commerce, human–agent interaction, security and privacy, etc. The proceedings are published by Springer-Verlag (see LNCS).

CIAC – Computer Incident Advisory Capability. A response team established in 1989 (http://www.ciac.org) to provide on-call technical assistance and information to US Department of Energy sites examining computer-security incidents. See also FIRST.

CICC – Center of International Cooperation for Computerization. An organization (http://www.cicc.org.sg) established in 1983 in order to cooperate with and assist developing countries in the introduction of computer and information technology, and to promote computerization as an important component of their economic and social development.

CICLing – Conference on Intelligent Text Processing and Computational Linguistics. An international conference focusing on the area of computational linguistics and intelligent text processing. The proceedings are published by Springer-Verlag (see LNAI).

CICS – Customer Information Control System. An IBM mainframe-based transaction-processing monitor that supports distributed transaction processing in SNA networks.

CIDR – Classless InterDomain Routing. The standard RFC1519 allows a more addressable space on the Internet. The key idea behind CIDR was to divide the Internet addresses all over the world into four zones (Europe; North

America; Central and South America; Asia and the Pacific), and give each about 32 million addresses to allocate, with another 320 million addresses reserved for the future. The main requirement for this addressing scheme is developing the routing protocols that support it, such as Border Gateway Protocol (see BGP) Version 4, Routing Information Protocol (see RIP) Version 2, Open Shortest Path First (see OSPF), IS–IS, etc.

CIE – Commission Internationale de l'Eclairage. A color model established by the international body mentioned in the acronym in 1931. This color model defined three standard primaries, X, Y and Z, as inputs to the color matching process.

CIEC – Citizens Internet Empowerment Coalition. An organization of Internet users, library groups, publishers, online service providers, and civil liberties groups fighting for the future of free speech on the Internet, and for the future of the US 1st Amendment (http://www.ciec.org). See also the Communications Decency Act (CDA).

CIF – Cells in Frames. A definition of how to encapsulate ATM cells in Ethernet and token ring frames, allowing ATM data to be sent to legacy desktops.

CIF – Common Intermediate Format. A video format specified by the International Telecommunications Union that governs the transmission of video signals over ISDN. The video format specifies 288 lines of 360 pixels.

CIFS – Common Internet File System. A protocol proposal intended to provide an open platform mechanism for client systems to request file services over a network. The protocol supports file access, file and record locking, read/write operations, file change notification, batch requests, unicode file names, distributed replicated virtual volumes, etc. It is intended to provide a more active Internet access than that usually provided by the classical FTP.

CIKM – Conference on Information and Knowledge Management. An international ACM conference focusing on improving information and knowledge management technologies. Topics include intelligent search, data mining, knowledge and resource discovery, cooperative and interoperable federated systems, view management, digital libraries, intelligent agents, data warehousing, mobile databases and wireless computing, advanced databases (active, temporal, spatial, object-oriented), etc.

CIL – Clip Gallery Installation Library. A filename extension for Microsoft Clip Gallery installation software.

CIM – Common Information Model. An approach to the management of systems and networks, under development by Desktop Management Task

Force Inc. (see DMTF), that applies the basic structuring and conceptualization techniques of the object-oriented paradigm, and allows the cooperative development of an object-oriented schema across multiple organizations to be supported.

CIM – Computer Input Microfilm. A technique that allows information stored on a microfilm to be converted into usable and manageable codes inside a computer.

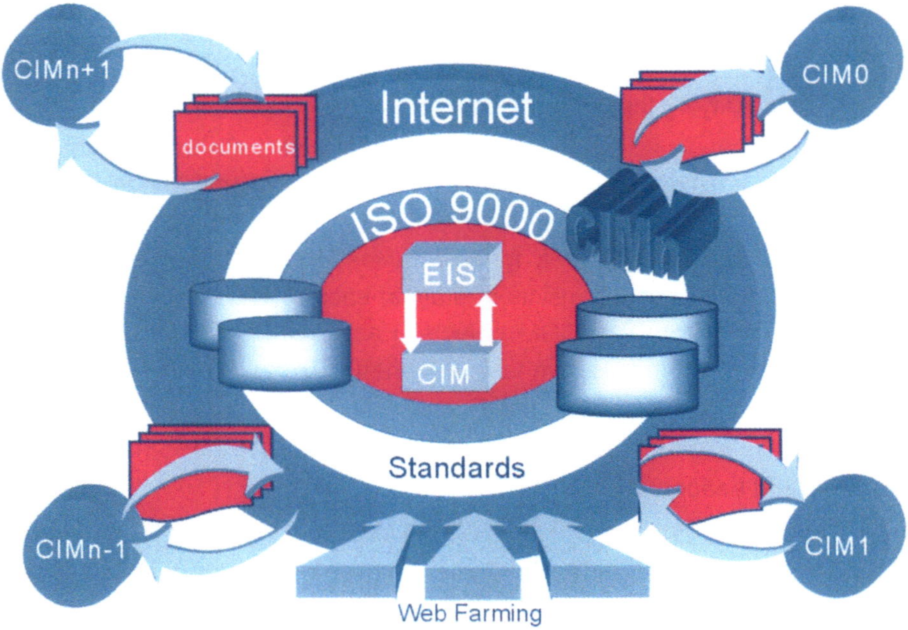

Fig. C-12. A strategic point of view of CIM development

CIM – Computer-Integrated Manufacturing. A common term addressing computer usage in a manufacturing process to automate both the management activities and the operational activities involved. It can be composed of some combination of several computer-aided activities, such as CAD, CAM, CAE, CAPP, CAQ, MIS, and related methods, strategies and standards, such as JIT, MRP or EDI. All of these acronyms are explained elsewhere in this book. Today, CIM systems are more and more communication-oriented via corporate Intranets and the Internet. The commercial, product, or any other relevant data are exchanged between business partners and their CIMs using standard data specifications and standard communication environments. In addition, all of that must conform to the ISO9000 series of standards. An open CIM development strategy is shown in Fig. C-12.

CIMOM – Common Information Model Object Manager. In the Common Information Model (see CIM), a program that manages the interactions between management applications and object providers.

CIO – Chief Information Officer. A job title given to a person responsible for the information technology and computer systems deployed in some kind of Enterprise Information System (see EIS, BIS, MIS) in an enterprise.

CIP – Carrier Identification Parameter. An identification code used in ATM networks for identifying the carrier to be used for the connection.

CIP – Common Interchange Pipeline. The Microsoft software for automatic business data exchange using standard Internet transport mechanisms such as e-mail or HTTP, or using Microsoft DCOM or MSMQ (Microsoft Message Queuing). Each pipeline is a framework that executes processes in sequence. The framework consists of stages, each of which has one or more pipeline components, i.e. COM objects. Each COM receives data from a previous one, performs its own task, and then makes the results available to the next COM. See also COM and DCOM.

CIPX – Compressed IPX. A variant of the IPX protocol (RFC1553) that uses a compressed header (and data).

CIR – Committed Information Rate. A bandwidth that represents the average level for a frame-relay network user. If the user's network activity exceeds this rate, the frame-relay controller will mark it in order to discard that user if necessary.

CIRCIT – Center for International Research on Communication and Information. The research center (http://www.circit.rmit.edu.au) established in 1989 in order to provide knowledge on communication and information technologies relevant to the Australian technology community, industry and the government.

CIS – CompuServe Information Service. A service provided by CompuServe (http://www.compuserve.com), which provides BBSs, online conferencing, financial transactions, weather forecasting, business news, travel, entertainment news, online editions, etc.

CIS – Contact Image Sensor. A scanner device sensor used on less expensive scanners instead of Charge-Coupled Devices (see CCD).

CIS – Cooperative Information System. A set of computers and associated applications connected using any kind of network (see LAN, MAN or WAN) that allows computer-supported cooperative work (see CSCW).

C-ISAM – C-written Index Sequential Access Method. An Index Sequential Access Method (see ISAM) written in the C language.

CISC – Complex-Instruction-Set Computer. A common term (pronounced “sisk”) related to processors that use complex instructions at the assembly-language level. Typical examples are Intel i86 processors. Compare with RISC.

CiSE – Computing in Science and Engineering. IEEE journal focusing on the large computational problems that appear in physics, medicine, astronomy, and the other hard sciences.

CIV – Cell Interarrival Variation. The measurement value in ATM networks that measures how consistently ATM cells arrive at the receiving end-station. The cell interarrival time is specified by the source application, and should vary as little as possible. For constant-bit-rate (see CBR) traffic, the interval between cells should be the same at the destination and at the source. If it remains constant, the latency of the ATM switch or the network itself (also known as the cell delay) will not affect the cell interarrival interval. Any variation in the latency could affect the quality of voice or video applications.

CIW – Certified Internet Webmaster. The title given to a person who has successfully finished a set of appropriate courses and exams supervised by some CIW certification organization. Such a person is capable of developing websites, administrating Web servers, etc.

CIX – Commercial Internet eXchange. A nonprofit trade association which coordinates Internet services (http://www.cix.org). Membership in CIX is open to organizations which offer TCP/IP or OSI services to the general public in one or more geographic regions.

CL – Compiler/Linker driver. A driver program (cl.exe) inside Microsoft Windows that controls C and C++ compilers and linkers.

CL – Connection-Less mode. Data transmission without prior establishment of a logical connection between the sending and receiving stations. It covers all the information required, such as the addressing, data transfer and error checking. Individual packets are directed from one intermediate node to the next until they reach their ultimate destination. Used by shared-media LANs like FDDI and token ring. CL is often termed “robust”. An example is the Connection-Less Network Protocol (see CLNP).

CLI – Call-Level Interface. A standardized programming interface for supporting SQL access to databases.

CLID – Calling Line Identification. A feature used in ISDN and some other telecommunications environments that includes the sender's identification number in the transmission so that the receiver knows who is calling. This feature is useful – for example, it can protect Internet users against theft of their paid time by various network intruders. It is also known as Automatic Number Identification (see ANI) and CallerID. See ISDN.

CLNP – Connection-Less Network Protocol. An OSI service (ISO8473) available on a network layer. It is a datagram protocol for the transmission of data and error indications. Also known as ISO IP.

CLP – Clipboard. A special memory resource maintained by windowing operating systems. The clipboard stores a copy of the last information that was "copied" or "cut". A "paste" operation passes data from the clipboard to the current program. A clipboard allows information to be transferred from one program to another, provided the second program can read the data generated by the first one. However, users should carefully use such a feature because some data attributes may be lost, such as text formatting attributes or image quality. Data copied using the clipboard is static and will not reflect later changes. See also DDE.

CLP – Cell Loss Priority. In an ATM network, a bit value used to specify whether a cell could be discarded.

CLR – Cell Loss Ratio. A negotiable ATM QoS parameter that measures the fraction of the transmitted cells that are not delivered at all, or are delivered too late and therefore lose their usefulness. Delay-sensitive voice and video require lower CLRs than data. The CLR is expressed as an order of magnitude, usually having a range of 10^{-1} to 10^{-15}.

CLS – Class. A filename extension for a file containing a so-called "Class Module", an object-oriented module used as the basis for COM components.

CLSID – Class Identifier. In Microsoft Windows, an identifier for a type of OLE object.

CLTP – Connection-Less Transport Protocol. An OSI service protocol that provides end-to-end transport data addressing via the transport layer, and error control via a checksum, but cannot guarantee delivery or provide flow control. It is the OSI equivalent of the User Datagram Protocol (see UDP).

CLTS – Connection-Less Transport Service. See Connection-Less Transport Protocol (CLTP).

CLU – Command-Line Utility. A program that can be executed at the appropriate command-line prompt. Used in some operating systems and some networking environments.

CLUT – Color Look-Up Table. See Look-Up Table (LUT).

CLV – Constant Linear Velocity. A feature of a CD-ROM drive that allows it to keep the data transfer rate fixed. See also CAV.

CLW – Class Wizard. A filename extension for a file that contains information about Visual Basic project classes.

CM – Configuration Management. The process of identifying, defining, recording and reporting the configuration items in a system and the changes requested.

CMA – Communications Managers Association. A US professional association (http://www.cma.org) servicing the needs of communications managers. CMA was established by Walter Young in 1948. CMA members include companies and their representatives (IT managers, usually).

CMC – Common Mail Calls. An API developed by the X.400 API association (see XAPIA) to enable programming of message handling agents to communicate with the message store components of a MHS. See also Message Handling System (MHS).

CMC – Computer-Mediated Communication. A common term for communication methods supported by computers, such as Usenet, e-mail, video conferencing, real-time chats, etc.

CMI – Computer-Managed Instruction. A common term related to any type of teaching that uses computers as educational tools (see CAI and CBT).

CMIP – Common Management Information Protocol. The ISO protocol (pronounced "see-mip") used in the OSI application layer to retrieve and send management-related information across an OSI network. Compare with SNMP. Also, a part of the Open Group TOGAF specification (see TOGAF).

CMIPDU – Common Management Information Protocol Data Unit. A packet existing in the OSI network management model that conforms to the CMIP. See also CMIP and CMISE.

CMIPM – Common Management Information Protocol Machine. The ISO protocol in the OSI application layer used to accept operations from a CMISE user and to initiate the actions needed to respond using valid CMIP packets to a CMISE user. See also CMIP and CMISE. Also, a part of the Open Group TOGAF specification (see TOGAF).

CMIS – Common Management Information Service. A part (pronounced "see-miss") of the Open Group TOGAF specification (see TOGAF). Basically, this is a set of management services (monitoring and control) provided in the ITU-T X.710 recommendation and ISO9595, used as the basis for ISO/OSI network management. See also CMISE.

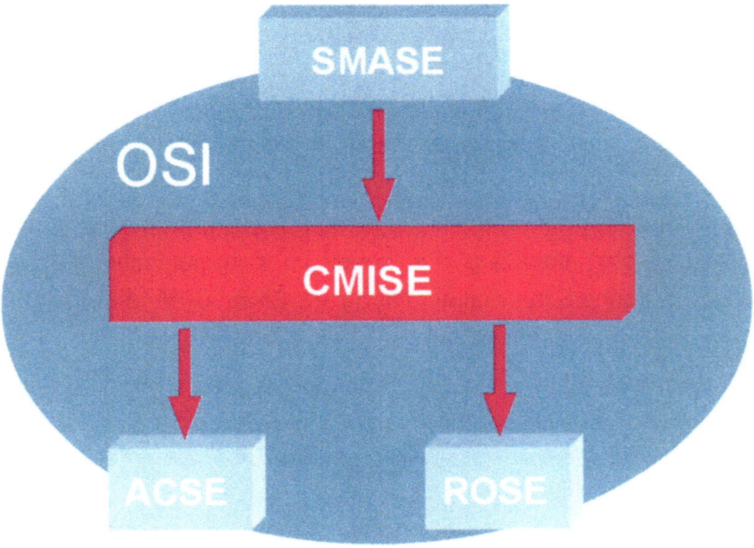

Fig. C-13. A CMISE in the OSI system management model

CMISE – Common Management Information Service Element. An entity (pronounced "see-mize") in the OSI network management model (as well as in TOGAF), that provides network management and control services (see Fig. C-13). The services provided by CMISEs are used by the system management functions (see SMF). A CMISE consists of two components, CMIS and CMIP. A CMISE provides three types of services. Management association services enable applications to establish connection with each other. In order to do that, CMISE uses an Application Control Service Element (see ACSE) that provides the ground rules for the connection. Management notification services report events and states about particular objects. Finally, management operation services manage the network. See also SMASE.

CML – Chemical Markup Language. A formal language derived from SGML for interchanging chemical information.

CMM – Capability Maturity Model. A software process capability model defined by the Software Engineering Institute (see SEI). The five levels of software process maturity are defined (see Fig. C-14). At the initial level there are no systematic organizational procedures defined, and therefore the software attributes are unpredictable. At the repeatable level of software maturity, it is possible to repeat software projects of the same type. The defined level represents the entry level for a software organization that has already defined its process and formal procedures. At the managed level software metrics are applied and used as feedback for software process improvement. Finally, the optimizing level allows continuous software process improvement with finetuning. See also Software Process Improvement (SPI).

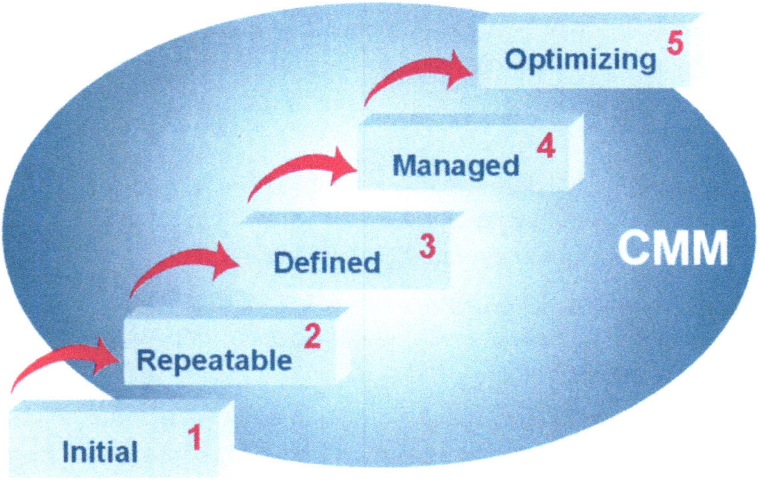

Fig. C-14. A Capability Maturity Model (CMM) from SEI

CMM – Color Management Module. A code used for color conversion and color mapping.

CMNP – Connection-Mode Network Protocol. An OSI service in the network layer.

CMNS – Connection-Mode Network Service. A specification extending local X.25 switching to a variety of media such as Ethernet, Token Ring or FDDI.

CMOS – Complementary Metal–Oxide–Semiconductor (Silicon). A semiconductor device (pronounced “see-moss”) that consists of two integrated N-type and P-type metal–oxide–silicon field-effect transistors. Such chips have very high speeds and low power consumption. CMOS technology is the dominant semiconductor technology for microprocessors, memories and ASICs. CMOS memory chips are used to hold the basic data about system hardware, etc.

CMOT – CMIP Over TCP. An effort to use the OSI CMIP to manage TCP/IP networks. CMOT was never finished, for various reasons such as the difficulties involved in porting the OSI model into the TCP/IP environment. See CMIP. See also CoMiX.

cmp – compare. UNIX command used to compare two files.

CMR – Cell Misinsertion Rate. One of the non-negotiable QoS parameters, representing the number of ATM cells that are delivered to the wrong destination due to an undetected error which occurred in the header.

CMS – Color Management System. A technology developed by Kodak and licensed to many other software vendors, used to calibrate and match colors that appear on video monitors and computer monitors and those that appear in any printed form.

CMS – Cryptography Message Syntax. An RFC recommendation (RFC2315) that describes a general syntax for data that may have cryptography applied to it, such as digital signatures and digital envelopes.

CMU – Carnegie Mellon University. A University in Pittsburgh, Pennsylvania, US, with a well-known School of Computer Science (http://www.cs.cmu.edu). See also CERT and SEI.

CMY – Cyan–Magenta–Yellow. A color model based on the three colors in the acronym. CMY starts with white and subtracts percentages of cyan, magenta and yellow to achieve the desired color. The black color is the result of a 100% subtraction of all three colors. CMY has a special usage when dealing with hardcopy devices that deposit colored pigments onto paper, such as inkjet printers.

CMYK – Cyan–Magenta–Yellow–Black. A color model very similar to CMY that uses black as the fourth color to ensure deeper blacks.

CNA – Certified NetWare Administrator. A title given to people who successfully complete Novell-authorized courses on administrating NetWare networks, ensuring their security, etc. See also CNE and CNI.

CNAME – Canonical Name. The official name for a host on the Internet. A host with multiple network interfaces may have a number of Internet addresses, each with its own canonical name (and possibly aliases).

CNC – Computer Numerical Control. A common term for systems that utilize a dedicated stored computer program to perform some or all of the jobs on particular production line, such as machine tool control, dynamic correction of the machine tool motions during processing, diagnostics, etc.

CNE – Certified NetWare Engineer. A title given to people who successfully complete Novell courses for NetWare networks on designing, installing and maintaining such networks. See also CNA and CNI.

CNET – Centre National d'Études des Télécommunications. The French national telecommunications research center at Lannion.

CNI – Certified NetWare Instructor. A title given to people who successfully complete training on teaching Novell courses. See also CNA and CNE.

CNI – Coalition for Networked Information. An organization (http://www.cni.org) founded in 1990 that promotes the creation of and access to information resources in networked environments in order to enrich scholarship and enhance intellectual productivity.

CNM – Customer Network Management. The ATM technique that allows users of ATM public networks to monitor and manage their portion of the carrier's circuits. Thus far, the ATM Forum has agreed that the CNM interface will give users the ability to monitor physical ports, virtual circuits, virtual paths, usage parameters and quality-of-service parameters. See also ATM, VC, VP and QoS.

CNMA – Communications Network for Manufacturing Applications. An ESPRIT project from the late 1980s. See also ESPRIT.

CNR – Complex Node Representation. A collection of nodal state parameters that provide detailed state information associated with a logical node.

CNRI – Corporation for National Research Initiatives. A nonprofit organization (http://www.cnri.reston.va.us) established in 1986 to speed up research and development for the National Information Infrastructure (see NII). Among other things, CNRI serves as the home of the IETF secretariat.

CNT – Canada Newfoundland Standard Time. Time zone. UTC – 3.50 hours.

CO – Central Office. A local telephone company office to which all local loops in a given area connect and in which circuit-switching of subscriber lines occurs.

CO – Connection-Oriented mode. A type of transport protocol with three distinct phases: session establishment, data transfer and session release. Once a connection has been established, information always traverses the same path between two nodes until the session is completed. For examples, see Internet TCP, OSI TP4, and CMNP. Other typical examples are ATM, ISDN and Frame Relay (see FR). Compare with Connection-Less mode (see CL).

COA – Certificate of Authenticity. The license on an original Microsoft product.

COB – COBOL file. A filename extension for a file that contains COBOL source code.

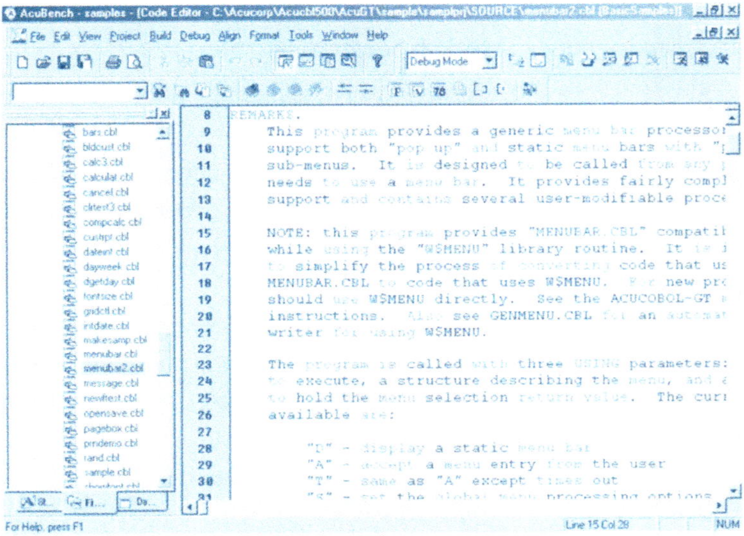

Fig. C-15. AcuBench in action creating a menu bar

COBOL – Common Business-Oriented Language. The most suitable third-generation programming language for business applications. One of the design aims of COBOL was that programs should be readable by non-computer specialists. After its initial issue in 1959 by a group coordinated by the US DoD, COBOL was standardized in 1968, 1974 and 1985. Because of its old-fashioned style, and character-based dialog at the user level (see CUI) etc., it was assumed that COBOL would disappear in the 21st century. However, due to protection investments in legacy applications, and the pioneering job done by the Acucorp (http://www.acucorp.com), COBOL today easily supports GUI applications (see Fig. C-15), ODBC, Java scripts, Intranet and Internet applications, and follows the OO paradigm and more modern application design techniques. For instance, AcuBench is an Integrated Development Environment (see IDE) that integrates the ACUCOBOL-GT compiler and runtime system with a central Project Manager, Code Editor, Screen Painter, and Screen Import Utility. AcuBench simplifies the development process and increases programming productivity. AcuBench uses common Windows GUI screen elements and layouts so that the interface screens are immediately familiar and easy to use. Development under AcuBench begins when the user creates a project and then populates the project with source files, copy files, and other files that are required by the application. Files can be added to or removed from the project at any time. As the project evolves, AcuBench keeps track of file dependencies and modification time stamps. When directed to by the user, AcuBench compiles only those files needed to bring the project up to date. Screens are saved as ".SMF" metafiles (see SMF), which can be edited with the Screen Painter and which are readily integrated into a project via the Project Manager. The Screen Painter is easy to operate and incorporates standard industry components, such as docking windows, a screened grid window, and a Property Sheet for detailing screen and graphical control behaviors. The controls and screen elements that can be created using AcuBench include labels, bars, entry fields, scroll bars, push buttons, bit-maps, check boxes, menus, radio buttons, toolbars, list boxes, tabs, combo boxes, grids and frames. All of these elements can have their own attributes. After the testing procedure, it is possible to generate the appropriate COBOL code (see CBL, MNU, PRD, SCR, SMF and WRK). The Code Editor automates many tasks, to accelerate the development process. It is possible to launch, compile, debug and execute program functions directly from the editor's environment. More than 50 easily customized hot keys are supplied with the Code Editor, enabling convenient macro recording for the most frequent editing operations.

COCF – Connection-Oriented Convergence Function. A function in the Distributed Queue Dual Bus architecture (see DQDB) that prepares data coming from or going to a connection-oriented service. The service first establishes a temporary connection, then transmits the data, and finally breaks the connection.

COCOMO – Constructive Cost Model. A well-documented empirical algorithmic cost-modeling method for evaluating the cost of a software package, proposed by Barry Boehm in 1981. The model exists in basic, intermediate and detailed forms. The COCOMO model follows the formula:

$$\text{Effort} = C \times PM^{s} \times M$$

where C is a complexity factor, PM is some product metric (program size or functionality), and M is a multiplier generated by combining different process, product and development attributes. The exponent s is usually close to 1. The original COCOMO model suggested four classes of attributes, as follows:

- Product attributes, such as reliability, database size and complexity.
- Attributes related to the hardware platform used (execution time, memory, etc.).
- Personnel attributes, taking into account the experience and skills of the people working on the project.
- Project attributes concerned with the use of software tools and the use of modern programming practice.

The COCOMO model is well documented, supported by commercial tools, and it is widely used. The most recent version was published in 1995.

COCOON – Computing and Combinatorics Conference. An annual international conference focusing on original research in the areas of algorithms, computational theory, computational complexity, and combinatorics related to computing. The proceedings are published by Springer-Verlag (see LNCS).

COD – Connection-Oriented Data. Data requiring sequential delivery of its component protocol data units (see PDU) to ensure the correct functioning of its supported applications.

CODASYL – Conference on Data Systems Languages. An organization (pronounced "code-a-sill") founded by the US DoD dedicated to the development of data management systems and languages, especially to COBOL (http://www.cbi.umn.edu/inv/codasyl.html).

CODEC – Coder–Decoder. A device that codes analog signals into digital signals for transmission and decodes digital signals into analog signals for receiving. For example, CODECs are used in ISDNs so that voice signals can be transmitted over digital lines and then converted to audio signals at the receiving end. The most common conversion method used is pulse amplitude modulation (see PAM).

COFF – Common Object File Format. A filename extension for a file that contains C or C++ compiled code. In Microsoft terminology it's also known as the Portable Executable (see PE) format.

COL – Commonwealth of Learning. An agency (http://www.col.org) founded with the purpose of improving the quality of education, utilizing distance education techniques and associated communications technologies to meet the particular requirements of member countries.

COLD – Computer Output to Laser Disk. The capture of large reports, generated by computers, on optical media.

COLT – Computational Learning Theory. An annual ACM international conference focusing on computational learning theory.

COM – Commercial. One of the top-level domains in the Internet Domain Name System (see DNS).

COM – Communication Port. A logical device name reserved by the MS-DOS operating system for up to four communications ports, COM1, COM2, COM3 and COM4.

COM – Compact executable file. A filename extension for a small (up to 64 KB) executable file.

COM – Component Object Model. The lowest-level element, the core of the Object Linking and Embedding Architecture (see OLE) that supports the creation and management of component software objects, and other low-level mechanisms such as dynamic loading of software components, shared memory management, etc. It is both an abstract model and a concrete implementation packed as a dynamically linked library (see DLL) or as executive files (see EXE). The COM model is a joint project of Microsoft and DEC. COM components can be written in a variety of languages, although most are written in C++, and they can be unplugged from a program at runtime without having to recompile the program. COM provides location transparency. Each COM object resides inside a server that can be either a DLL or an EXE file. These servers can be located on the same computer or on different computers on the network. In the case of a remote computer, DCOM is used for communications between remote COMs. See also DCOM and JOE.

COM – Computer Output to Microfilm. A term normally reserved for archival output to microfilm, when printed paper reports become too expensive and too bulky. The successor to COM is COLD (computer output to laser disk).

COM – Continuation of Message. An indicator used by the ATM Adaptation Layer (see AAL) in order to indicate that a particular ATM cell is a continuation of a higher-layer information frame which has been segmented.

COMA – Cache-Only Memory Architecture. Memory architecture used in scalable shared-memory multiprocessors. COMA uses large DRAM caches, called attraction memory. When a processor requests a block from a remote memory, the block is inserted in both the processor's cache and the node attraction memory.

COMAD – Conference on Management of Data. An international conference focusing on the management of data.

COMANDOS – Construction and Management of Distributed Office Systems. An ESPRIT project from the late 1980s. The overall goal of the project was to identify and develop an integrated application support environment for distributed applications.

CoMiX – Coexistence and Migration X. The X/Open guide to the coexistence of the Internet Protocol Suite (see IPS) and ISO Open System Interconnection (see OSI) protocol suite. CoMiX describes the key issues involved in the coexistence and migration between the IPS and OSI protocol suites, as an aid to planners and network designers in choosing the optimum strategy.

COMPSAC – Computer Software and Applications Conference. An annual IEEE international conference focusing on the recent research and development results in computer software and various applications.

COMSOC – Communications Society. IEEE society, a diverse group of professionals with a common interest in communications.

COMTI – COM Transaction Integrator. A Microsoft generic proxy that allows the combination of transaction programs from Microsoft Transaction Server (see MTS) and mainframes, for instance via the IBM SNA environment.

CON – Console. In minicomputers, a control unit, usually a terminal, through which a system administrator controls the system performance, boots the operating system, and makes other jobs available. Also, in the MS-DOS operating system, a logical device name for the console, the keyboard and the screen, as the primary input/output sources in DOS-based computer systems.

CONCISE – COSINE Networks' Central Information Service for Europe. Part of the COSINE project (see COSINE).

CONP – Connection-Oriented Network Protocol. An OSI protocol that provides connection-oriented operation for upper-layer protocols. See also CMNS.

CONS – Connection-mode Network Service. An OSI network-layer service that requires an established connection between the source and the destination before data transmission begins. CONS is common in wide area networks (see WAN). See also CO (connection-oriented) as a wider term. Compare with CLNS.

CoopIS – Cooperative Information Systems. An international conference focusing on cooperative information systems. The proceedings are published by IEEE Computer Society Press.

COP – Component-based OS Proxy. A joint project of Microsoft Research and Rochester University, a component-based API that acts like a traffic cop. COP directs operating system requests to the appropriate resource locations.

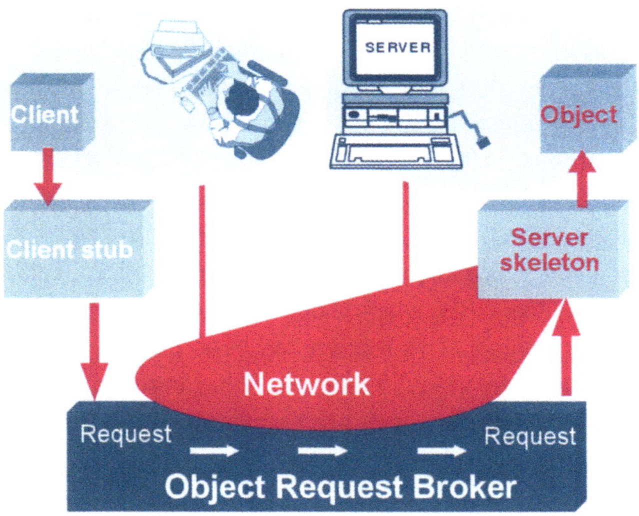

Fig. C-16. The simplified view of CORBA

CORBA – Common Object Request Broker Architecture. An architectural framework under Object Management Group (see OMG) development to allow integration of a variety of object systems. It is part of a wider OMG framework known as the Object Management Architecture (see OMA). The reference model has the following components:

- Object Request Broker – Enables objects to transparently make and receive requests and responses in a distributed environment. It is a basis for building applications from distributed objects and for interoperability between applications in heterogeneous and homogeneous environments.

- Object Services – Collection of services (interfaces and objects) that support basic functions for using and implementing objects. Services are necessary for constructing distributed applications, and are always independent of application domains.
- Common Facilities – Collection of services that many applications may share, but which are not as fundamental as the Object Services.
- Application Objects – Products of a single vendor in-house development group, which controls their interfaces. Application Objects correspond to the traditional notion of applications, so they are not standardized by the OMG. Instead, Application Objects constitute the uppermost layer of the Reference Model.

CORBA was the first component to be formally specified and is continuously being enhanced in order to support the technology emerging from the OMG and its affiliates. The first major specification, CORBA 1.1, was available as early as 1992. This specification was adopted based on a joint proposal by DEC, HP, Hyperdesk, NCR, ODI and SunSoft. CORBA was considered extremely simple (see Fig. C-16). Both client and object implementations are isolated form the Object Request Broker (see ORB) by their IDL interfaces, which are compiled into a client stub and server skeleton. Requests are always managed by the ORB, which hides the distribution details from application under development. This feature has been perfectly described by Jon Siegel in IEEE Computer (May, 1999). He noted that the distribution details reside only in the ORB, where they are handled by the software you bought, not by the software you built.

COS – Class Of Service. A way of describing a network connection or communications link in terms of one of its many variables. Variables include such aspects as security, priority, bandwidth, etc. Compare with QoS.

COS – Corporation for Open Systems. A membership-based non-profit research and development organization comprising computer and communications vendors and major users in the US. It is dedicated to developing OSI profiles and conformance testing.

COSE – Common Open Software Environment. An initiative by Hewlett-Packard, Sun, IBM, Novell and SCO to move towards consistency and interoperability among UNIX suppliers.

COSINE – Cooperation for OSI Networking in Europe. A European consortium with the same role in Europe as COS has in the US. Also, the name of an ESPRIT project from the late 1980s. See COS.

COSIT – Conference on Spatial Information Theory. An international conference focusing on spatial information theory. The proceedings are published by Springer-Verlag (see LNCS).

COSMOS – Cost Management with Metrics Of Specification. A European Strategic Programme for Research and Development in Information Technology (see ESPRIT) project.

COTS – Commercial Off-The-Shelf. A common term describing a software development method with reduced risk and cost and increased system functionality and capability. Building a system based on COTS components involves buying a set of pre-existing proven components, building extensions to satisfy local requirements, and integrating the components. COTS software components from different vendors are expected to integrate easily, work in a wide range of environments, and support extensions and local requirements. In practice, of course, there are several potential problems, which should be taken into account before COTS components are applied. For instance, components are often evaluated by vendors who don't check for full support of previous versions. Interoperability among COTS products from different vendors should be taken into careful consideration also, etc.

COW – Character-Oriented Windows interface. A System Application Architecture (see SAA)-compatible interface in OS/2.

CP – Constraint Programming. An international conference that deals with all aspects of computing with constraints. The proceedings are published by Springer-Verlag (see LNCS).

cp – copy. UNIX command used to make a copy of a file.

cpa – cost per action. One of the billing mechanisms used in Web advertising, that uses specifically defined actions taken by visitors to calculate how much an advertiser should pay, etc. Compare with cps and CPM.

CPAN – Comprehensive PERL Archive Network. A website that contains the collected wisdom of the entire PERL community (http://www.perl.com), hundreds of PERL utilities, several books, and the entire PERL distribution. See also PERL.

CPCS – Common Part Convergence Sublayer. The portion of the convergence sublayer (see CS) of an ATM Adaptation Layer (see AAL) that remains the same regardless of the traffic type.

CPE – Customer Premises Equipment. A common term for all telecommunications equipment located on the user side.

cpi – characters per inch. A measurement unit for the number of characters with particular sizes and fonts that can fit into a 1-inch line.

CPI – Common Programming Interface. Part of the IBM System Application Architecture (see SAA) that defines application programming interfaces (see API) that are consistent across all SAA-compliant systems.

CPI – Computer-to-PBX Interface. An interface used in digital telecommunications to provide communications between a computer and a PBX. See Private Branch Exchange (PBX).

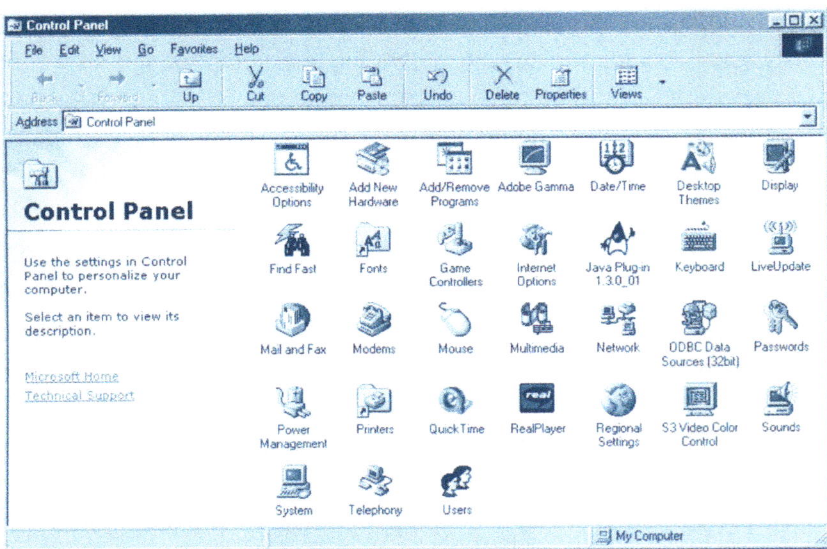

Fig. C-17. A set of CPL files

CPI-C – Common Programming Interface for Communications. The X/Open specification C210, published in 1992, for connection-oriented programming interfaces for applications that require program-to-program communications. Before data transfer can take place, a series of CPI-C function calls is needed to establish a connection between the two end-points. Program calls are used to establish the characteristics of the conversation and to exchange data and control information. CPI-C calls are designed to be the same across multiple languages, platforms and programming environments. They can be categorized as either starter-set calls or advanced function calls. The actual syntax used depends on the programming language used. Also known as XCPI-C.

CPL – Control Panel. A filename extension for files that contain control panel information in Microsoft Windows environments. Figure C-17 depicts an example of a Control Panel that has several CPL files, represented by their icons, e.g. Modems, Passwords, Network, etc.

CP/M – Control Program/Monitor. An operating system developed by Gary Kidall in 1975 for microcomputers based on Intel microprocessors.

CPM – Cost Per Thousand (M). An industry-standard measure for selling on the Web. The "M" is after the Roman numeral for a thousand.

CPM – Critical Path Method. A method of planning, terminating and managing large projects, by dividing such projects into smaller isolated tasks, with milestone events, etc. Inter-relationships are then shown using a graph that depicts the timetable between the events, defining the critical path which requires the longest time.

CPN – Calling Party Number. In ATM networks, a parameter of the initial address message that identifies the calling number and is sent to the destination carrier.

CPP – C++ (plus plus) file. A filename extension for C++ source code files.

cps – characters per second. A measurement unit for the speed of nonlaser printers, such as dot-matrix printers, as well as a measurement unit for communication speed.

cps – cost per sale. One of the billing mechanisms used in Web advertising, which uses sales resulting from Web advertising to calculate how much an advertiser should pay etc. Compare with cpa and CPM.

CPSR – Computer Professionals for Social Responsibility. An alliance of computer scientists and others concerned about the impact of computer technology on society (http://www.cpsr.org).

CPT – Corel Photo-Paint. A filename extension for Corel Photo-Paint images.

CPU – Central Processing Unit. The computer device that fetches, interprets and executes instructions. Mainframes and early minicomputers contained circuit boards full of integrated circuits that implemented the central processing unit functions. Single-chip central processing units are called microprocessors. Examples of such microprocessors are the Motorola 68000 family, the Intel x86 family, and the Intel Pentium.

CR – Carriage Return. A control character (ASCII decimal value 13) that advances the cursor or a printer to the next line.

CRA – Computing Research Association. An association (http://www.cra.org) comprising a huge number of North American academic computer science departments, laboratories, and industry and government research centers involved in basic computing research.

CRAYON – Create Your Own Newspaper. A website (http://www.crayon.net) that allows a user to create his/her own newspaper and publish it over the Internet.

CRC – Cyclic Redundancy Code (Check). A communication-error-detecting polynomial algorithm based upon treating bit strings as representations of polynomial coefficients of 0 and 1 only. After the polynomial code has been employed, both communication sides must agree in advance about the generator polynomial. The sender, before transmission, calculates the checksum based on a modulo 2 sum algebraic operation between the generator polynomial and the bit string 0 or 1 weight coefficients. The receiver, familiar with the generator polynomial involved, does the reverse algebraic calculation on the checksum field to determine whether there was an error-free message delivery. Three polynomials have become international standards (CRC-12 is used when the character length is 6 bits, the other two for 8-bit lengths):

CRC-12 $=x^{12} + x^{11} + x^3 + x^2 + x + 1$;

CRC-16 $=x^{16} + x^{15} + x^2 + 1$;

CRC-CCITT $=x^{16} + x^{12} + x^5 + 1$.

CRD – Cardfile. A filename extension for files that contain Cardfile information.

CREN – Corporation for Research and Educational Networking. The merger of CSNET and BITNET. It offers a wide variety of services, such as a store-and-forward electronic mail service using dial-up telephone lines, a full-service Internet using TCP/IP on top of X.25, a leased-line network that provides a low-cost protocol-independent packet-switching system, etc.

CRF – Cell Relay Function. The basic function that an ATM network performs in order to provide a cell relay service to an ATM end-station.

CRF – Change Request Form. The first phase in the software process change management where somebody makes a change request using an appropriate form. The complete CRF usually includes the recommendations for the change, and cost and time estimates, etc.

CRF – Connection-Related Function. A term used in ATM network traffic management to refer to a point in a network or a network element where peer connection functions are occurring.

CRI – Cray Research Inc. The company (http://www.cray.com) founded in 1972 by Seymour Cray to produce high-performance computing products. In 1996, the company merged with Silicon Graphics Inc. (see SGI).

CRLF – Carriage-Return Line-Feed. A carriage-return character (see CR) followed by a line-feed character (see LF), usually interpreted as a command to move the cursor or printer head to one line ahead on the leftmost position. Often abbreviated as NL (New Line).

CRM – Cell-Rate Margin. In ATM networks, a measure of the difference between the effective bandwidth allocation and that required for a sustainable rate measured in cells per second.

CRM – Communications Resource Manager. The X/Open specification that allows an instance of the model to access another instance, either inside or outside the current transaction manager (see TM) domain. For communication across multiple domains, CRMs use OSI TP services.

CRS – Cell Relay Service. A carrier service that supports the receipt and transmission of ATM cells between end-users in compliance with ATM standards.

CRSS – Composable Replaceable Security Services. A project at NAI Laboratories (see NAI) to develop security infrastructure that can support the next generation of survivable distributed systems.

CRT – Cathode-Ray Tube. The basic device for display screens and for television screens. It can be either monochromatic or color. A CRT display is built around a vacuum tube containing one or more electron guns. Electron guns emit streams of electrons that are accelerated using high voltages, typically between 15,000 and 20,000 V, applied near the face of the tube. Each electron beam moves from left to right, and from top to bottom, one horizontal scan line at a time. When the electrons hit the screen, the phosphor coated on the screen emits visible light. Due to the time dependence of the phosphor's emitted light, it is necessary to refresh the entire picture 30 times or more per second. The number of pixels on the screen determines the clarity of the image.

C/S – Client/Server. An architectural approach to either locally or wide area distributed networked environments. A client/server environment supports the division of complex applications into several tasks running on different hardware platforms, operating systems or even different networks. Furthermore, every task is developed and maintained separately, thus rapidly increasing the development and programming productivity.

Client/server applications consist of three basic components: client, server and network, as shown in Fig. C-18, having their own hardware and software, which can perform specific tasks. The client component is a complete, stand-alone personal computer, and it offers the user its full range of power and features for running applications. The server component can be a personal computer, a minicomputer, or a mainframe that offers the traditional strengths offered by minicomputers and mainframes in a time-sharing environment: data management, information sharing between clients, and sophisticated network administration and security features.

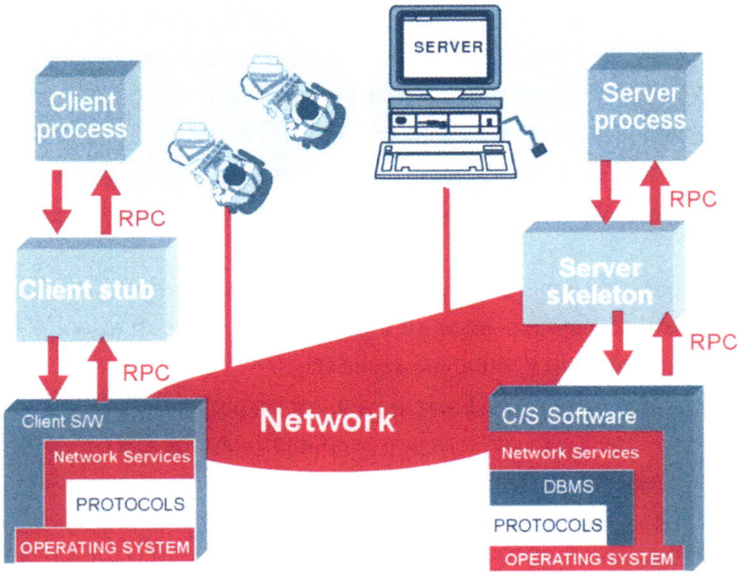

Fig. C-18. The components of a client/server environment

Nowadays, the components usually communicate using the Remote Procedure Call mechanism (see RPC). During a distributed application development, RPC hides a lot of the communication issues, such as data representation on different computers, knowing the remote server address, communication management, system errors, security, etc. The programming itself uses some kind of Interface Definition Language (see IDL) to meet the requirements of distributed applications. The communication scenario is very simple: the client calls a stub routine on its own machine that builds a message containing the name of the procedure and all associated parameters, then passes such a message to the communication driver for transmission. The server listens to the client requirements coming via RPCs, and when they arrive at the remote driver it gives them to its own stub, which unpacks them and makes ordinary procedure calls to the server (to its operating system). Having handled the request, the server returns the answers to the appropriate clients. Naive users can ignore the binding process, they need not even know the server location, and they can let the stubs take care of this and of establishing the binding process. Sophisticated users can control the binding process in detail.

CS – Client Server. See C/S.

CS – Computer Science. A common widely used term for many computer science-related fields. In addition, it is usually possible to use the term CS to find appropriate academic departments, research laboratories, shortcuts to research fields in, for example, university websites, etc.

CS – Convergence Sublayer. The part of the ATM adaptation layer (see AAL) used to convert non-ATM formats into ATM, and vice versa.

CSA – Canadian Standards Association. An independent nongovernment nonprofit association, the largest standards organization in Canada, established in 1919 (http://www.csa.ca). CSA standards are developed and written by volunteer committees representing a combination of government, industry, academia, special interest groups, consumer groups and the public.

CSC – Corel Script. A filename extension for a Corel script file.

CSCL – Computer-Supported Collaborative Learning. An international conference focusing on technology in collaborative forms for learning and teaching. The topics include tool designs and theoretical contributions.

CSCoRE – Computer Security in a Collaborative Research Environment. An international conference that explores the issues involved in providing a collaborative computational environment that is both open and secure.

CSCW – Computer-Supported Cooperative Work. A multidisciplinary research field focusing on how groups of people, located far from each other, can work together on the same data to accomplish a common task. Some representative CSCW applications are interactive education, C3I and C4I systems, multimedia teleconferencing, distributed enterprise systems, Open GIS, etc.

CSE – Computer Science and Engineering. An interdisciplinary field representing the intersection of applied mathematics, computer science, and engineering.

CSF – Common Software Foundation. A joint proposal by IBM, DEC, HP and other vendors to create a common system software interface for which applications can be developed. The result should be improved interoperability between multivendor systems.

CSFS – Cable-Signal-Fault Signature. A unique signal used to test the electrical activity on the line when using time-domain reflectometry (see TDR).

CSG – Constructive Solid Geometry. One of the most popular methods for 3D solid modeling using CAD systems. Simple primitives are combined by means of a regularized Boolean set of operators included directly in the representation. Furthermore, an object is stored as a tree with operators at the internal nodes and simple primitives at the leaves.

csh – C shell. A shell (interpretative language) distributed with BSD UNIX. See also BSD. See also ksh.

CSIRO – Commonwealth Scientific Industrial Research Organization. One of the biggest research organizations in the world, constituted in 1949 in Australia (http://www.csiro.au). According to the given site, on 30th June 1996, CSIRO had a total staff of 7497, including nearly 3000 scientists, working in laboratories and field stations all over Australia. Their work covers a broad range of areas of economic or social value to Australia, including agriculture, minerals and energy, manufacturing, IT standards, communications, construction, health and the environment.

CSL – Computer Science Logic. A European conference focusing on computer science logic. The proceedings are published by Springer-Verlag (see LNCS).

CSLIP – Compressed SLIP. An enhancement for the Serial Line Internet Protocol (see SLIP), where the 20-byte IP packet header can be compressed to, for example, 3 bytes. The compression strategy is known as Van Jacobson compression (RFC1141) after its inventor.

CSMA – Carrier-Sense Multiple-Access. A group of communication protocols which involve listening to the channel to see if it is busy. If it is, the station waits until it becomes idle and then transmits the appropriate frame according to the particular protocol. See CSMA/CA and CSMA/CD. See also LBT/LBW.

CSMA/CA – Carrier-Sense Multiple-Access/Collision Avoidance. One of the CSMA protocols with collision avoidance based on reducing the collision probability at the point where they are most likely to occur, i.e. directly after the channel has become free again.

CSMA/CD – Carrier-Sense Multiple-Access/Collision Detect. An Ethernet protocol (IEEE802.3, ISO8802-3), based on collision detection when the sender tries to send something and finds a busy communication line. In such circumstances the CSMA/CD protocol aborts the transmission and waits in a loop for a random time period before checking again (see Fig. C-19). See also LBT/LWT.

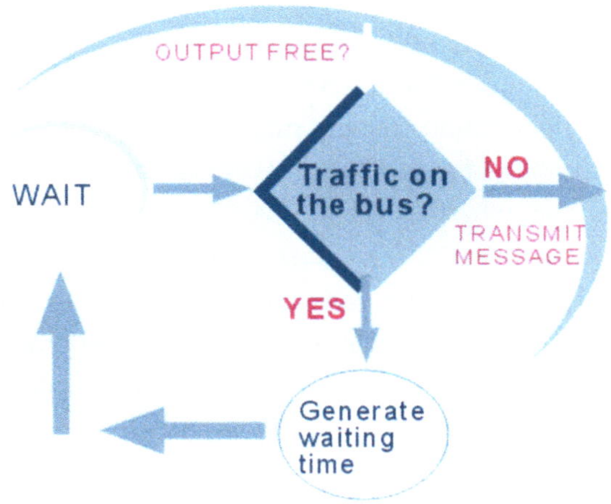

Fig. C-19. A simplified CSMA/CD protocol waiting loop

CS-MUX – Carrier-Switched Multiplexer. A component that belongs to the FDDI II architecture that passes time-dependent data (e.g. voice or video) to the MAC layer. See also FDDI, MAC and IMAC.

CSNET – Computer + Science Network. A large computer network, mostly in the US but with international connections. It merged with BITNET to form CREN. See also BITNET and CREN.

CSP – Cryptographic Service Provider. An independent software module that contains cryptographic algorithms or services that are integrated into the Microsoft Crypto API.

CSS – Cascading Style Sheets. An advanced tool for creating dynamic webpages. The new version, CSS2, includes audio style sheets as well as 3D preparation of webpages. CSSs allows authors of HTML documents and users to attach style sheets to HTML documents. The style sheets include information on how the page should appear. Also, a filename for a file that contains CSS. See also DHTML (Dynamic HTML), DOM (Document Object Model) and XML (Extensible Markup Language).

CSS – Centralized Structure Store. A data structure used in the Programmers Hierarchical Graphic System (see PHIGS). The fundamental entities of data are structure elements which are grouped together into units called structures, and which are organized as acyclic directed graphs (structure networks). A graphical output on a workstation is produced by traversing a structure and interpreting the structure elements.

CST – Central Standard Time. Time zone. UTC – 6.00 hours. See TZ.

CSTB – Computer Science and Telecommunications Board. The government body in the US that considers technical and policy issues pertaining to computer science, telecommunications and associated technologies. The CSTB monitors the health of these fields, paying attention, as appropriate, to human resources and infrastructure issues.

CSU – Channel Service Unit. An interface provided by a telecommunication carrier used for a terminal or computer connection to a digital medium so that customers can use their own equipment to regenerate incoming signals. In other words, a device replaces a modem on a digital line. Furthermore, the CSU is responsible for the appropriate timing and formation of all signals put on the line. See also DSU/CSU.

CSV – Comma-Separated Values. A file format in which a record and the fields in the record are separated by commas.

CSV – Common Service Verb. In SNA, an API that provides ways of translating characters, tracing, and sending network management data to a host.

CT – Conformance Testing. Testing of a candidate product for the characteristics required by a standard. Its primary goal is to ensure a specified implementation behavior. Additional benefits include: clarifying the standard, guiding future implementation; producing feedback for the standards authorities on improvements to the standard; encouraging commercial development by supporting a common baseline for all products; and providing greater confidence on the part of the potential enterprise user. Conformance-tested implementations increase the probability of successful operation and interoperation, but provide no guarantees.

CTC – Cornell Theory Center. The supercomputing center funded by the US National Science Foundation (see NSF), as well as by ARPA, the National Institutes of Health, IBM, etc. (http://www.tc.cornell.edu). They are involved in the high-performance computing and communication project (see HPCC), focusing on mass storage, I/O capability, networking, archival storage, data processing, and graphics power. The primary computing resources at CTC are a 512-processor IBM SP-2, a Silicon Graphics (see SGI) Power Onyx Array, consisting of two 8-processor Power Onyx Systems, and a 16-processor SGI Power Challenge.

CTD – Cell Transfer Delay. An acronym for the QoS parameter measuring the average transit time between the sender and the receiver. The CTD between two measurement points is the sum of the total inter-ATM node transmission delay and the total ATM node processing delay.

CTI – Computer–Telephone Integration. A technique that allows computers to integrate telephony functions, such as voice, fax receiving and sending, caller identification, etc. The full integration assumes message integration with databases, word processors, and a GUI environment, and integration with any other program used to generate or receive phone messages. Standards for CTI are defined at two levels: the physical, where connections between computers and appropriate switches are established; and the API level, where programmers provide CTI functions without accessing low-level protocols (see TAPI and TSAPI).

CTL – Certificate Trust List. A predefined list of items that have been signed by a trusted entity (see CA, Certification Authority).

CTL – Control key. A keyboard key used together with another key to produce a command for some special function. Abbreviated also as CTRL.

CTL – User Control. A filename extension for files produced by Visual Basic (see VB) that contain information about methods, properties, and the user interface required to create ActiveX control.

CTOS – Convergent Technology Operating System. An operating system produced by Convergent Technology (UNISYS) for its line of microcomputers. CTOS is a multitasking multiuser operating system that is similar in structure to UNIX.

CTRL – Control key. See CTL.

CTS – Clear-To-Send. A serial communications signal used to indicate that transmission can proceed, e.g. from a modem to its computer. Compare with RTS.

CTS – Conformance Testing Service. A series of guidelines and programs developed for testing whether or not a product conforms to a particular protocol correctly. CTS projects are defined for LAN and WAN protocols, as well as for ISO OSI seven-layer services (e.g. FTAM, X.400 and X.500).

CTT – China Taiwan Time. Time zone. UTC + 8.00 hours. See TZ.

CUA – Common User Access. A term used in the IBM System Application Architecture (see SAA) for user interfaces that should look consistent across applications and platforms.

CUE – Computer-Using Educators. The oldest and largest nonprofit organization in the US (http://www.cue.org) dedicated to learning, teaching and technology.

CUI – Character User Interface. An old-fashioned user-interface style based on characters. It was a pioneering technique in the batch-to-interactive processing transition. There are still many applications that use CUI. Compare with GUI.

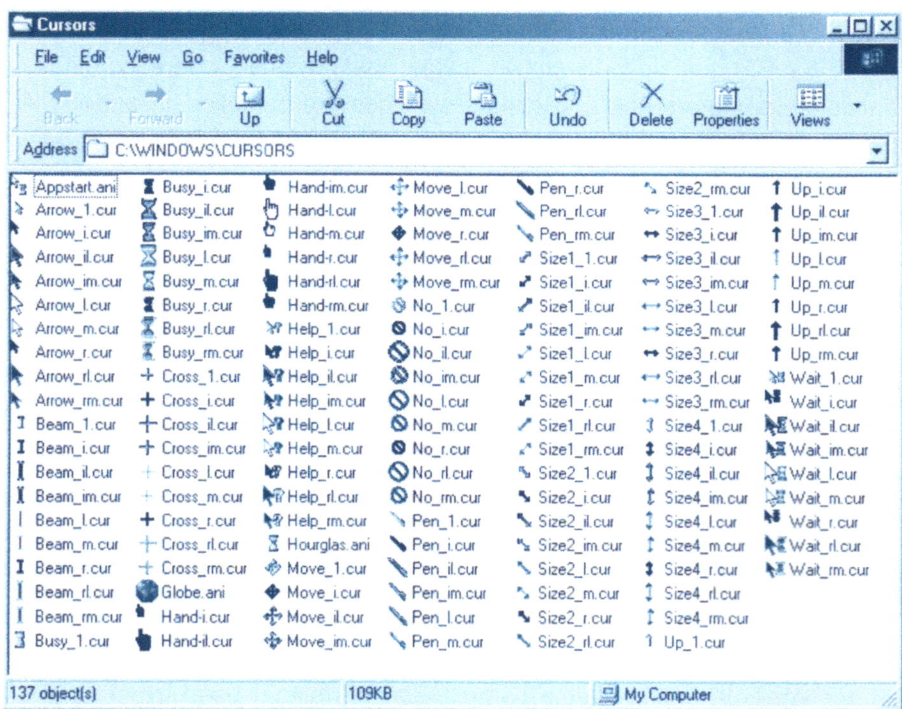

Fig. C-20. CUR folder contents

CUR – Cursors. The name of the folder in Microsoft Windows that contains the definitions of the available cursors (see Fig. C-20). An animated cursor (see ANI) is also shown (Globe.ani).

CUSI – Configurable Unified Search Index. An Internet search engine (http://cusi.emnet.co.uk) that allows, among other things, access to the other Web-searching services available (see Fig. C-21).

CUT – Control Unit Terminal. A term used by IBM for its general-purpose workstations with an operating mode that allows only one session. Compare with DFT.

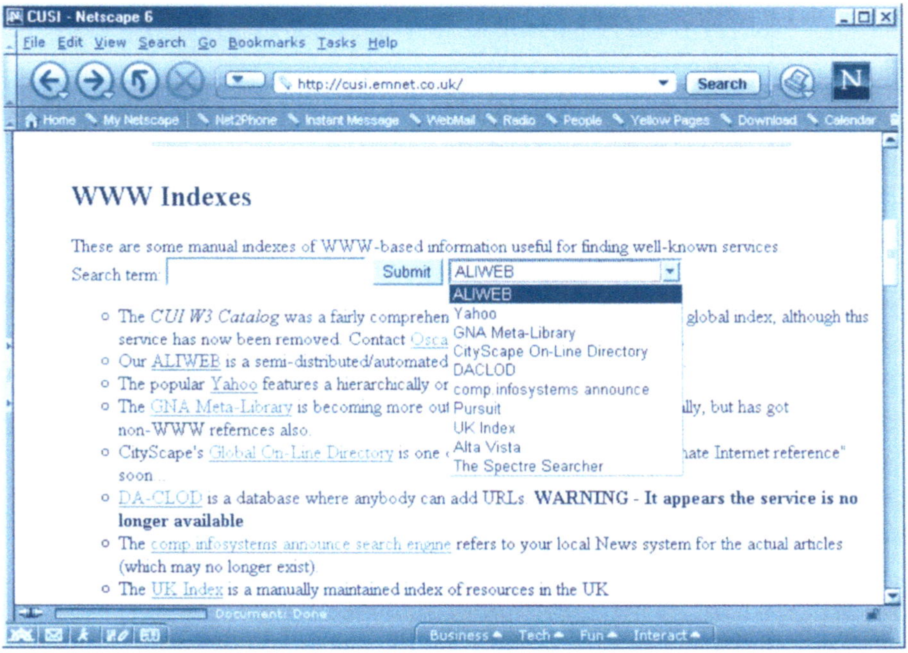

Fig. C-21. The CUSI engine in action

CUU – Conference on Universal Usability. An ACM international conference focusing on the universal usability of computers and computing. Topics include the policies, politics and economics of universal usability, evaluations and solutions that accommodate variations in hardware and software, and users with different skills, knowledge levels, ages, etc.

CVDT – Cell-Variation-Delay Tolerance. An ATM QoS parameter that governs how much variation is allowed in ATM cell transmission times.

CVE – Collaborative Virtual Environments. An ACM international biennial conference focusing on the design, development and use of collaborative virtual environments (computer-based, distributed virtual space). The main topics include CVE systems, architectures and applications, models and metaphors for collaboration, experiences, user–environment interactions, etc.

CVPR – Computer Vision and Pattern Recognition. IEEE international conference focusing on computer vision and pattern recognition. Some major topics include vision and learning, shape representation and recovery, color, texture, and physics-based vision, feature extraction, etc.

CVS – Concurrent Versions System. A source-code control system developed in April 1989 by Brian Berliner. CVS works by comparing new and old versions of files being checked and then creating patches for the changed code when a developer asks for an update. CVS is freely available on the Internet (http://www.cn.gnu.org, or http://www.cyclic.com).

CWI – Centrum voor Wiskunde en Informatica. An independent research institute for mathematics and computer science located in Amsterdam (http://www.cwi.nl).

CWIS – Campus-Wide Information System. A common name for a public online information service available in a university campus.

D

D – Data channel. An ISDN full duplex channel operating at 16 Kbps with a Basic Rate Interface (see BRI) or at 64 Kbps with a Primary Rate Interface (see PRI). See also ISDN. Compare with B channel (B) and H channel (H).

DA – Data Administrator. A person responsible for managing the entire data resources, either computerized or not.

DA – Desk Accessory. A common name for a small program in Microsoft Windows environments or on Macintosh computers that can be activated any time and then either closed or moved to a small part of the screen. Examples include a clock, calendar, phone dialer, and calculator, etc., as shown in Fig. D-1.

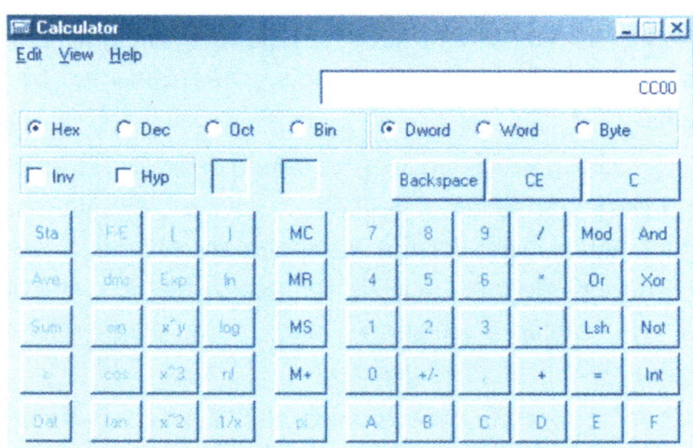

Fig. D-1. Calculator as a Desk Accessory in Microsoft Windows

DA – Destination Address. A header field very frequently used in many types of communication packets that specifies the node to which the packet is being sent. For example, see ADCCP and HDLC. See also Source Address (SA).

D/A – Digital/Analog converter. A device that translates digital input data to an analog signal at the output.

DAA – Data Access Arrangement. Interfacing equipment provided by a common carrier to allow privately owned communications equipment to be attached to that carrier's lines.

DAB – Digital Audio Broadcast. An ETSI standard that allows transmission of any combination of data, radio programs, and Web content with a 1.8-Mbps data rate. See also DVB.

DABO – Data Access Business Object. A tier in the Microsoft Lightweight Business Object Model (see LBOM) that represents the class modules that implement methods of performing all the data manipulation for the object. DABO can be installed on the client machine or in a distributed environment in Microsoft Transaction Server (see MTS). See BPO and UBO.

DAC – Digital/Analog Converter. See D/A.

DAC – Dual-Attachment Concentrator. An appliance used in FDDI to attach single-attachment stations or station clusters to both FDDI rings. See also Fiber Distributed Data Interface (FDDI).

DACL – Discretionary Access Control List. An Access Control List (see ACL) that is controlled by the owner of an object and that specifies particular rights given to a user or a group in that object access.

DAG – Data Acyclic Graph. An abstract data type often used to represent arbitrary relations between objects. Data objects are represented by nodes connected by paths.

DAI – Distributed Artificial Intelligence. A common term for an intelligence that is distributed across some kind of network. It covers distributed systems with knowledge, techniques used for the management of such systems, mobile agents, appropriate languages, active database systems, distributed network management by artificial intelligence, and many other related research fields. See also AI (Artificial Intelligence).

DAL – Data Access Language. An extension of SQL used in Macintosh-based client/server environments to provide a uniform access to any database that supports SQL. See also SQL.

DAM – Data Access Manager. A component inside MacOS System 7 used for accessing databases on a network.

DAM – Deferred Action Message. A message used to indicate that an action has been requested, but it cannot be performed due to the unavailability of the required resource.

DAMA – Demand-Assigned Multiple Access. A method for allocating access to communication channels. On request, one of the idle channels allocates the requested bandwidth, and is assigned to the party being asked for a channel.

Damovo – Data + Mobility + Voice. An independent company that evolved out of Ericsson Enterprise Solutions and offers integrated business telecommunications services (see http://www.damovo.com).

DAN – Departmental Area Network. A network that services a single government department.

DANTE – Delivery of Advanced Network Technology in Europe. A European network (http://www.dante.net) launched in July 1993 that provides advanced international computer network services for the European research community. Also, the name of the company responsible for DANTE development and maintenance.

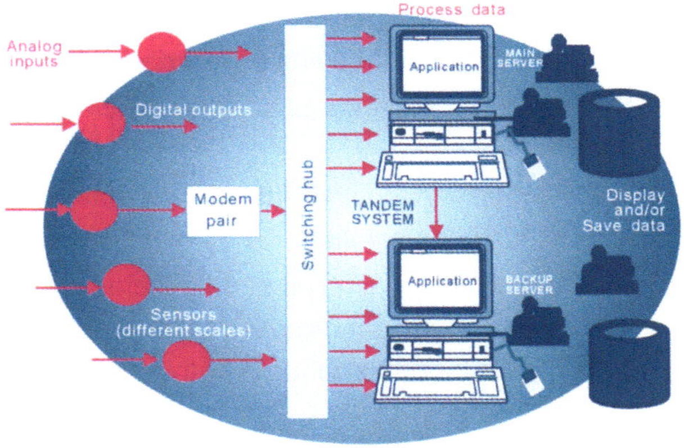

Fig. D-2. DAS architecture

DAO – Data Access Objects. A Microsoft collection of Component Object Model (see COM) objects organized in a single COM library that allows applications and applets to interact with the Microsoft Access database, as well as to access and manage ISAM files and ODBC databases.

DAO API – Data Access Objects Application Programming Interface. An API for Microsoft's Jet database engine that can query and edit Access databases, ISAM files and ODBC data. See also the Index Sequential Access Method (ISAM) and Open Database Connectivity (ODBC).

DAP – Data Access Protocol. A high-level software service in DEC implementation of the DNA architecture (see DECnet) which provides file transfer.

DAP – Directory Access Protocol. A protocol used in the X.500 Directory service for communications between a directory user agent (see DUA) and a directory system agent (see DSA). See also X.500.

DARPA – Defense Advanced Research Projects Agency. The US Defense Department Agency, well-known all over the computer world as a result of the ARPANET development. This network was a forerunner of the Internet.

DAS – Data Acquisition System. A class of real-time systems that collects data from sensors in order to process and analyze such data. Each sensor has an associated process that converts the analog input level into an appropriate digital signal. In real-time systems, which involve data acquisition and processing, as depicted in a given example (weight acquisition from different scales in a production line), the periods of the acquisition process and the processing process should be synchronized in such a way that no data must be lost. To solve this, most DASs buffer the input data and use tandem systems, as shown in Fig. D-2. Generally, DASs can use various kinds of data and different sensors at different stages of a processing unit.

DAS – Disk Array Subsystem. A whole set of carriage, cabling and electronics for multiple hard disks.

DAS – Dual Attachment Station. A device attached to both the primary and secondary FDDI rings that allows isolation of the ring failure. See also FDDI.

DASD – Direct Access Storage Device. A type of data storage device (pronounced "dazz-dee"). It supports direct data access regardless of the previously accessed data position or of the physical start of the storage area. A typical example is a disk unit.

DASS – Distributed Authentication Security Service. A type of security system intended for checking users logging into a network from untrusted or suspicious workstations.

DAT – Data file. A filename extension for a file that contains some data in Microsoft Windows.

DAT – Digital Audio Tape. A magnetic tape storage medium developed by Sony and HP designed to digitally record audio information. It uses a rotary head where the read/write head spins diagonally across the tape, like that of a video cassette recorder. The tape speed is much higher than a regular audio deck. DAT tapes are also very suitable for back-up data storage with high capacities (in GB).

DAT – Dynamic Address Translation. A mapping process used in operating systems that enables the virtual memory manager to map a virtual address into a physical address.

DATA – Decision Analysis by Tree Age. A modeling paradigm used in Decision Support Systems (see DSS) development, which deploys decision-making under the incertitude principle. DATA and other similar systems include methods for dealing with doubt about data values, user preferences, and other relevant aspects of decision problem solving. Also the name of the software offered by TreeAge Software Inc. (http://www.treeage.com).

DAVIC – Digital Audio-Visual Council. A nonprofit association registered in Geneva (http://www.davic.org). Its purpose is to advance the success of emerging digital audio-visual applications and services, by the timely availability of internationally agreed specifications of open interfaces and protocols that maximize interoperability across countries and applications or services (see MHEG). Membership in DAVIC is open to any corporation or individual firm, partnership, governmental body or international organization.

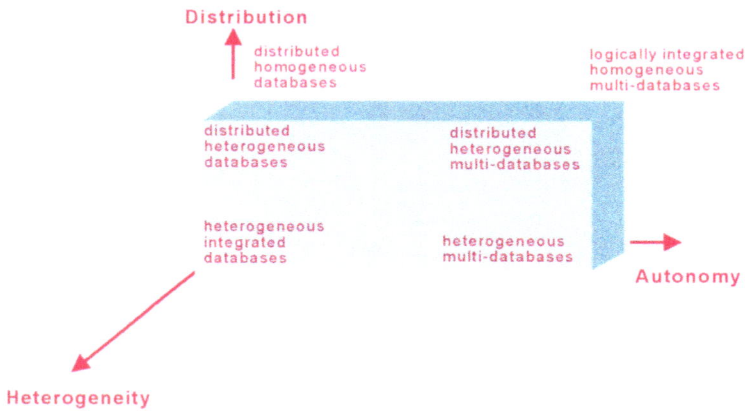

Fig. D-3. A categorization of databases

dB – decibel. A unit of relative measurement, based on a logarithmic scale between the measured quantity and a known reference. Named after Alexander Graham Bell. To find the number of decibels between two values the following formula is used:

$$dB = n \log (x/r)$$

where x is the measured quantity, r is the reference quantity, and n can take a value of 10 or 20 for voltage and current or power measurement, respectively.

DB – Database. A collection of data that is stored more or less permanently in a computer consisting of a number of records that can be searched, sorted, etc. The overall design of the database is called the database schema. Databases are loaded, updated, used and managed by database management systems (see DBMS). The collection of information stored in a database at a particular moment is called an instance of the database. Due to the degree of their heterogeneity, distribution and autonomy, databases can be categorized as shown in Fig. D-3.

DB-n – Data Bus connector number. A type of connector used to connect serial and parallel cables to a data bus. The number n represents the number of wires within the connector. DB connectors are defined by various EIA standards. See also EIA.

DB2 – Database 2. IBM's relational database management system (see DBMS) for mainframes running the MVS, VM or AS/400 operating systems.

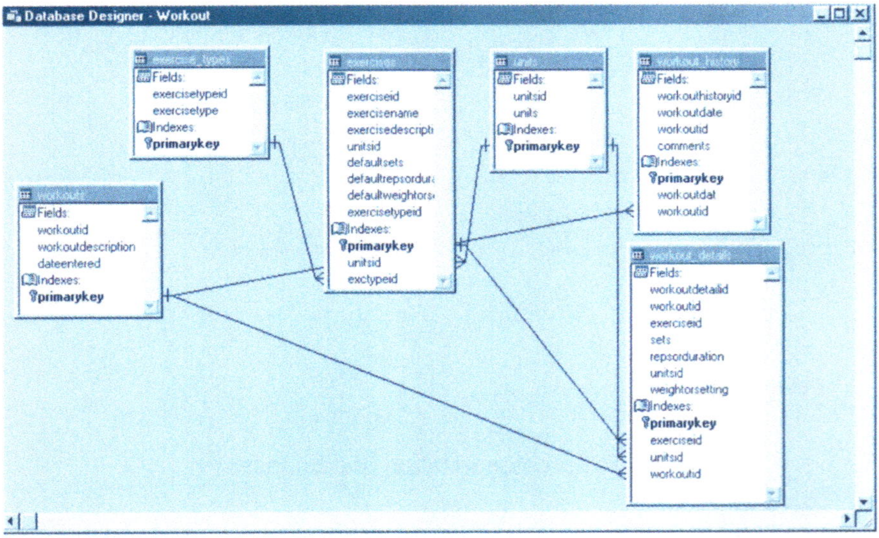

Fig. D-4. An example of a DBC file

DBA – Database Administrator. A person who has primary control of both the data in a database and the programs that access that data. He/she is responsible for arranging, organizing, controlling and monitoring of the centralized and shared database as well.

DBA – Doing business as. The chat term.

dBase – Database. A popular database management system (see DBMS) produced by Ashton Tate Corp., now owned by Borland Corp. The dBase format is supported by nearly all DBMSs.

DBC – Database Container. A filename extension for a file that contains Microsoft Visual FoxPro database container data (see Fig. D-4).

DBCS – Double-Byte Character Set. A character set used to represent ideographic characters (used in Far Eastern languages).

DBF – dBase file. A filename extension for a file that contains dBase data, the format originally developed by Ashton Tate, but understood by several other database programs.

DBF – Database File. A filename extension for several database formats.

DBG – Debugger file. A filename extension for a file that contains a Visual FoxPro debugger configuration.

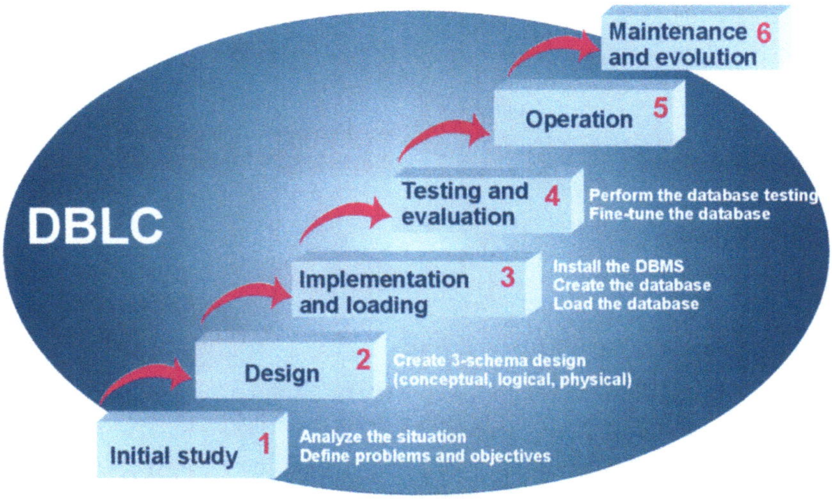

Fig. D-5. The overall view of a DBLC

DBLC – Database Life Cycle. The six-phase database history in an information system (see Fig. D-5). The phases are initial study, design, implementation and loading, testing and evaluation, operation, and maintenance and evolution.

DBMS – Database Management System. A collection of interrelated data and a collection of programs to access data. A DBMS manages all requests for database access, such as queries or updates. It provides users with an abstract view of data, hiding from them details of how data are stored and maintained. The structure of a DBMS is shown in Fig. D-6. Typical examples of commercial DBMSs are Oracle, Informix, Sybase, Ingress, Progress, Microsoft Access, DB2, etc. Every database and its DBMS is based on some kind of data model. Depending on the data model involved, the DBMSs can be categorized as relational (see RDBMS), object-oriented (see OODBMS), or network or hierarchical (see HDBMS). If a particular DBMS uses some set of rules (see ECA), we are talking about an active database management system (see ADBMS). In addition, databases in general can be categorized by the degree of their heterogeneity, distribution and autonomy (see Fig. D-3). Furthermore, they can be open or proprietary (closed). In order to understand the DBMS components given in Fig. D-6, see also Data Definition Language (DDL), Data Manipulation Language (DML) and Data Dictionary (D/D).

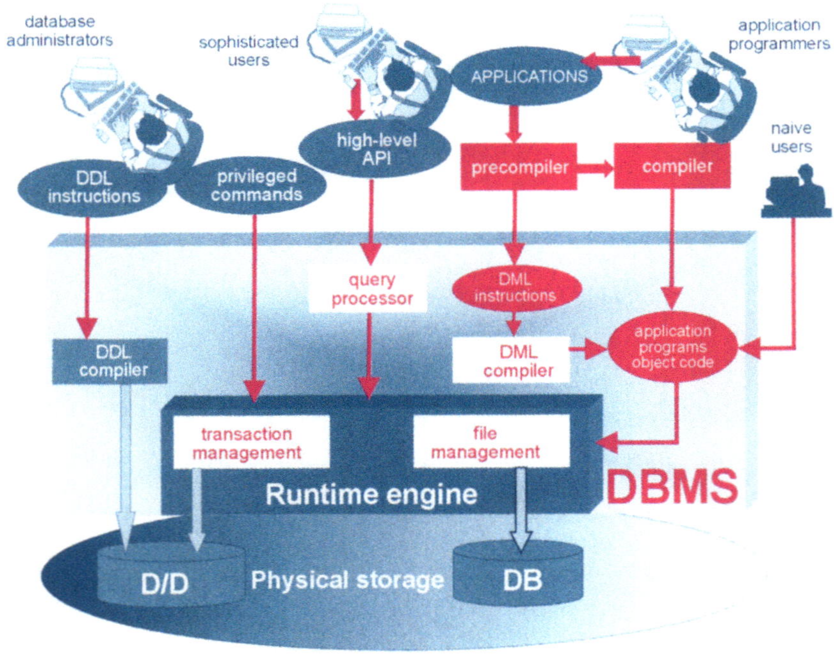

Fig. D-6. The structure of a DBMS

DBO – Design By Objectives. A method of software engineering for solving software development using techniques such as system function, system attribute, system solution specification, impact analyses tables, impact estimation tables, solution comparison methods, etc.

DBS – Direct Broadcast Satellite. A common name for a satellite that broadcasts signals directly to subscribers.

DC – Device Context. In Microsoft Windows, a structure used to define a set of graphic objects (such as a pen, a brush, a bitmap, etc.) and their associated attributes.

DC – Device Coordinate. The acronym used in computer graphics to describe a device-specific coordinate system and to represent absolute positions in the particular display space (see Fig. D-7).

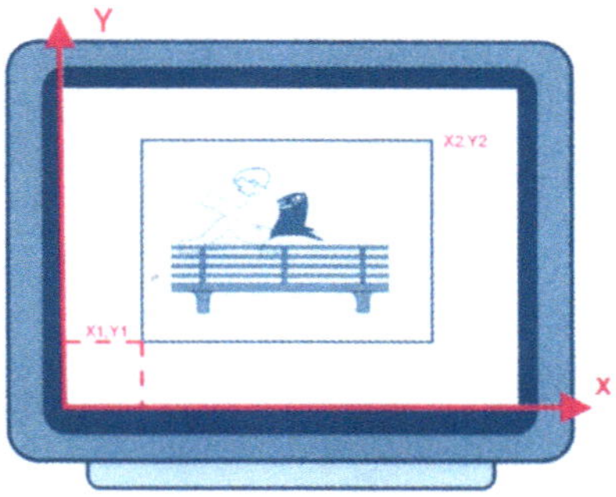

Fig. D-7. Device coordinate space

DC – Direct Current. A current provided from a battery. Its direction of flow is constant all the time. Compare with AC (Alternating Current).

DCn – Device Control n. One of the four control codes represented by ASCII characters DC1 (17), DC2 (18), DC3 (19) and DC4 (20).

DCA – Document Content Architecture. A formatting technique used in the IBM System Network Architecture (see SNA) that allows text-only documents to be exchanged between different computers. See also Revisable Form Text (RFT), Final Form Text (FFT), and Mixed Form Text (MFT). Compare with Document Interchange Architecture (DIA).

DCB – Disk Coprocessor Board. An expansion board used as an interface between the CPU and the hard disk controller. Also known as the Host Bus Adapter (HBA).

DCC – Data Country Code. One of the four addressing methods used by ATM devices. DCC, based on the NSAP format, identifies the location of ATM devices by country, using 2-byte ISO country codes.

DCC – Data Compression Conference. An international conference focusing on data compression and related areas. Topics of interest include compression algorithms, source coding, fractal-based methods, quantization theory, string searching, security, compression applications, etc.

DCC – Direct Cable Connection. A feature available in Windows 95 that allows two personal computers to be connected via a serial or parallel cable without a network interface card. A slower transfer rate than that with a true LAN is a disadvantage of DCC.

DCC – Direct Client-to-Client protocol. An Internet relay chat protocol (see IRC) enabling users to chat directly without IRC servers. Such a chat protocol does not need broadcasting, thus allowing more efficient use of the available bandwidth.

DCD – Data Carrier Detect. A serial communication signal used by a modem in order to tell an associated computer that it is online and therefore that it is ready to transmit. DCD is a hardware signal sent over line 8 in RS-232 connections.

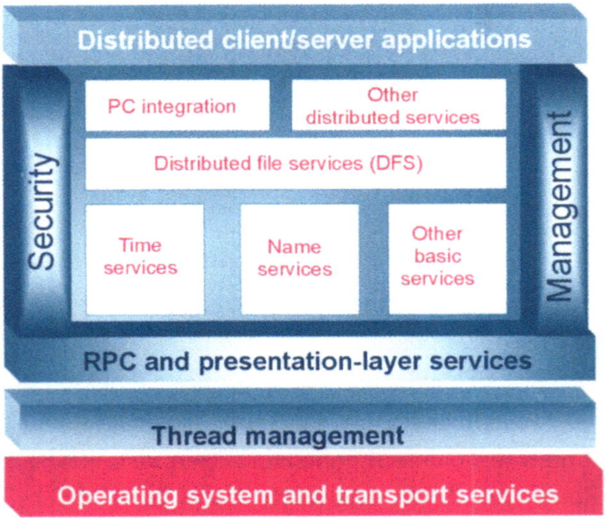

Fig. D-8. DCE tools and services

DCE – Data Communication Equipment. A common name for networking equipment such as analog and digital modems. In communications, an RS-232C DCE device receives data over line 2 and transmits over line 3. Compare with DTE (Data Terminating Equipment).

DCE – Distributed Computing Environment. This is the Open Software Foundation (see OSF) architecture consisting of a large number of tools and services that can be built on top of the existing operating system to allow distributed client/server applications development and a distributed heterogeneous run-time environment for their execution. DCE runs in an open environment consisting of computers from multiple vendors, different operating systems and networks. An application programmer need not worry about those differences because DCE hides them to allow easier application development as well as application portability. The DCE layered architecture (see Fig. D-8) offers a lot of tools and services. At the top of the operating system there is the DCE threads mechanism. If there is native thread support by the host operating system, the DCE thread library just enables conversion, otherwise DCE provides the full thread support. The next layer is the Remote Procedure Call layer (see RPC), the basic communication mechanism enhanced with some authentication services. See also CS (Client Server). Various DCE services, as shown in Fig. D-8, are at the top of the RPC layer. The supported services (time, directories and distributed files) are described elsewhere in this book (see CDS, DFS, DN, DNS, DTS, GDA, GDS and RDN). The security mechanism in DCE relies on authentication, authorization (see AAA), and Access Control Lists (see ACL) associated with each resource. The ACL decides which users may access a particular resource and what they may do with it. All of that is closely tied to the DCE cell structure, at least one computer or more having a common administration. The security of each cell is supported by one security service that the local principal has to believe.

DCG – Data Element Coordination Group. The part of the Technical Advisory Group 7 (see TAG) of the ISO that coordinates EDI data elements standardization (see DE and EDI).

DCM – Distributed Computing Model. The part of the open system strategy, introduced in the early 1990s by Bull, that allows customers to keep in touch with the emerging open systems and to protect their investments in Bull proprietary systems (see Fig. D-9). See GCOS. See also DCE, OCCA, PSI and TOGAF.

DCOM – Distributed Component Object Model. A binary standard that naturally extends the Component Object Model (see COM). Distributed COM extends the model for interaction between clients and component objects to the Internet. DCOM provides location independence, i.e. frees developers from restrictions about where components and their clients are physically located. It also abstracts the network so that the developers can build applications without worrying about network protocols. In other words, DCOM provides the infrastructure to catch calls to COM objects, route them to the appropriate server, and return the results to the client application. In addition, DCOM provides some kind of security. DCOM works with a wide variety of tools and languages, such as Java, Visual C++, Visual Basic, Delphi and Powerbuilder, without affecting component interaction. DCOM is available in Windows 95/98 and NT 4.0. Also called Distributed COM.

DCP – Definitional Constraint Programming. A declarative programming paradigm that integrates concurrent constraint programming, constraint logic programming and functional programming.

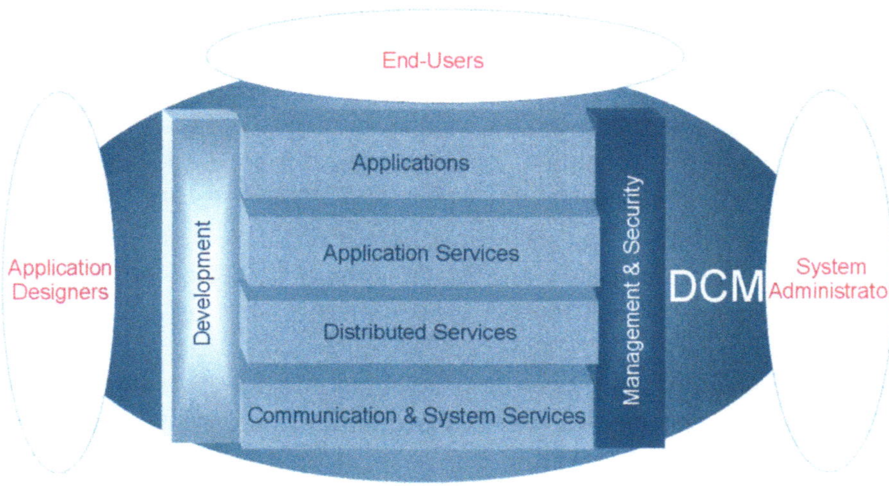

Fig. D-9. The overall view of the Bull DCM

DCS – Digital Cross-connect System. A network element that provides automatic cross-connection of a digital signal or its constituent parts.

DCT – Database Container. A filename extension for a file that contains a Microsoft Visual FoxPro database container (see Fig. D-4). Also used as a DBC file.

DCT – Dictionary file. A filename extension for a file that contains a database dictionary (see D/D).

D/D – Data Dictionary. In general, this is a special-purpose data structure to store data about the database itself. D/D is also called the system catalog (see Fig. D-6). A D/D may also include data that is external to the DBMS.

DDA – Digital Differential Analyzer. In computer graphics, an algorithm that determines whether a pixel is a part of a line or a curve or not.

DDB – Device-Dependent Bitmap. A bitmap format that contains bitmaps packed as required by a particular output device. Compare with DIB.

DDB – Distributed Database. A collection of several different data repositories that look like a single database to the user. A prime example is the Domain Name System (see DNS).

D

DDBMS – Distributed Database Management System. A database management system (see DBMS) capable of managing a distributed database, i.e. a database implemented on some kind of network in which both data and processing may be distributed among several sites. See also DDB.

DDC – Display Data Channel. A VESA standard specification for communication between a monitor and a video adapter. DDC is used by display monitors to facilitate personal computer Plug and Play (see P&P) settings.

DDC – Distributed Data Catalog. A data dictionary (see D/D) that contains the description of a distributed database such as fragment names, locations, etc.

DDCMP – Digital Data Communications Protocol. The data-link control protocol used by DEC for point-to-point transmission. May be used with asynchronous or synchronous transmission. It uses the byte count method for error detection. Also uses pipelining and piggybacking to improve efficiency.

DDD – Distributed Data Dictionary. See Distributed Data Catalog (DDC).

DDE – Dynamic Data Exchange. A form of interprocess communication mechanism implemented in Microsoft Windows and OS/2 for information and command exchange among simultaneously running applications. DDE has been superseded by a more efficient mechanism known as Object Linking and Embedding (see OLE).

DDEML – Dynamic Data Exchange Management Library. A Microsoft Dynamic-Link Library (see DLL) that provides a higher-level interface for dynamic data exchange than the traditional DDE specification.

DDF – Data Definition File. A filename extension for a file that contains Btrieve or Xtreive metadata.

DDI – Device Driver Interface. A common name for an interface between applications and device drivers.

DDI – Distributed Data Interface. The term used to represent all LAN types based on FDDI regardless of the media used in order to distinguish the fiber nature of the initial FDDI specification from its other implementations.

DDK – Device Driver Kit. A set of tools and libraries that allows programmers to write Windows-based software modules used to run hardware devices.

DDL – Data Definition (Description) Language. A language for database schema specification for things such as record layouts, key fields, properties, etc. DDL statements are compiled into a set of tables stored in a data dictionary (see D/D).

DDM – Distributed Data Management. An IBM defined set of rules that uses LU6.2 for the exchange of data between disparate systems implemented using APPC software. See APPC. See also DIA, LU6.2 and SNADS.

DDN – Defense Data Network. A global communications network serving the US DoD, composed of MILNET, other portions of the Internet, and classified networks, which are not parts of the Internet. The Defense Information Systems Agency (DISA) manages the DDN.

DDP – Datagram Delivery Protocol. A protocol in AppleTalk networks used for delivering packets between nodes on different subnetworks.

DDP – Distributed Data Processing. A type of data processing (see DP) that allows data to be located and processed on different places at different computers in a distributed environment.

DDR – Dial-on-Demand Routing. A routing technique used with ISDN that permits automatic initialization and closing of a circuit-switched session as the transmitting station demands.

DDR – Double Data Rate. A proposed standard for SDRAM memories in order to cover the requirements of high-speed workstations and servers. This new type of memory transfers data on both the rising edge and the falling edge of the input clock. Compare with Single Data Rate memory (SDR). See also SDRAM.

DDS – Digital Data Service. A leased line using digital transmission that can provide data communication rates of up to 56 Kbps. When DDS is employed, a Channel Service Unit (see CSU) and a Data Service Unit (see DSU) replace the modems used with analog lines.

DDS – Digital Data Storage. The industry standard for Digital Audio Tape (see DAT) formats.

DDV – Dialog Data Validation. In Microsoft Foundation Classes (see MFC), a method of data entry validation in a dialog box. See also DDX.

DDX – Dialog Data Exchange. In Microsoft Foundation Classes (see MFC), a method of data transfer between the controls of a dialog box and their associated variables. See also DDV.

DE – Data Element. In Electronic Data Interchange (see EDI), the term used for one or more data items, forming a unit or piece of information, as defined in the data dictionary of a system of EDI standards, and contained in an EDI message or transaction set. Data Elements are defined in an EDIFACT Data Elements Dictionary (see EDED).

DE – Discard Eligibility. A congestion control bit in a frame-relay (see FR) packet header that can be set if congestion on the network occurs, in order to discard such packets from the network traffic.

DEA – Data Encryption Algorithm. A common name for a rule, an algorithm, used for data encryption.

DEB – Debug Event Browser. In Microsoft Windows, a browser that is capable of displaying debug events, and their relevant properties and when they occurred.

DEC – Digital Equipment Corporation. The acronym for Digital, one of the biggest computer manufacturing companies in the world. To find out about DEC see http://www.dec.com

DECnet – Digital Equipment Corporation network. The combination of hardware and software services that is used to implement Digital Equipment Corporation's Digital Network Architecture (see DNA). In general, DECnet Phase V supports OSI-compliant protocols as well as its own protocols for backward compatibility with previous DECnet versions. There are also appropriate gateways for accessing IBM SNA networks.

DECT – Digital European Cordless Telecommunication. A standard for European digital mobile telephony. This system provides wireless PBX services (see PBX) with high speech quality and cordless data services for wireless LAN applications (see WLAN). DECT explicitly supports data applications by enabling the combination of up to twelve 32 Kbps time slots for one connection.

DECUS – Digital Equipment Computer Users Society. One of the largest and most respected user groups of its kind in the computer industry, established in 1961. More information can be obtained at http://www.decus.org

DEF – Definition file. A filename extension for a file that contains C++ definitions.

DEK – Data Encryption Key. A value used for the encryption of message text and for the computation of message integrity checks (signatures).

DEL – Delete key. An ASCII control key that deletes, somewhat depending on the application program used. It can be a character currently under the cursor, a selected part of a document, etc.

DELIVER – Desktop Link to Virtual Engineering Resources. A Web-based retrieval system developed at the University of Illinois at Urbana–Champaign, as one of the results of the DLI project. See also DL and DLI.

DELNI – Digital's Ethernet Local Network Interconnect. The product offered by DEC that allows up to eight active devices to be connected to a single Ethernet transceiver. The DELNI can be used as a stand-alone device to create a small DECnet network, or can be networked into a main LAN. Many other suppliers under various names manufacture similar devices. The functionality can be thought of as "Ethernet in a box".

DEMM – Database Schema Evolution and Meta-Modeling. An international workshop focusing on the foundation of models and languages for data and objects. The proceedings are published by Springer-Verlag (see LNCS).

DEP – Dependency file. A filename extension for a file that contains Visual FoxPro dependency data created by the setup wizard.

DER – Distinguished Encoding Rules. A set of encoding rules used with Abstract Syntax Notation 1 (see ASN.1). DER encodes data as a stream of bits for external storage or transmission.

DES – Data Encryption Standard. An IBM encryption standard adopted by the US government in 1977 for nonclassified documents. DES uses a single 64-bit value as a key and a private-key encryption strategy to convert ordinary text (known as plaintext) into encrypted text (known as ciphertext). A message is divided into 64-bit blocks and each of them is encrypted separately, one character at a time. During the encryption, the characters in the block are scrambled 16 times, and the encryption method changes after each scrambling. Four operating modes of DES are specified (see CBC, CFB, ECB and OFB). Compare with IDEA.

DES – Destination End-Station. In ATM, a termination point which is the destination for ATM messages and is used as a reference point for the ABR service (see ABR). Compare with SES.

DESPR – Digital Ethernet Single-Port Repeater. A device used to attach a ThinWire device to a standard Ethernet transceiver. Compare with Digital Ethernet Station Adapter (DESTA).

DESTA – Digital Ethernet Station Adapter. A device used to attach a standard Ethernet device to a ThinWire network. Compare with DESPR.

DFD – Data Flow Diagram. A graphical notation used to describe how data flows between processes in a system (see Fig. D-10). A tool of most structured system analysis techniques (see SSA).

DFS – Distributed File System. In general, a file system with files distributed on different machines, but accessible in the same way from the end-user point of view as if they are on a single computer. Also, a component of the Distributed Computing Environment (see DCE), a worldwide distributed file system that allows DCE distributed processes to access all files they are authorized to use. Intentionally, the basic interface to DFS is very similar to UNIX, but the security relies on the Access Control List protection method (see ACL) instead of the access bits (see RWX) used by UNIX. Each directory has three ACLs for giving access permission to the directory itself, the files in the directory, and the directories in the directory.

D

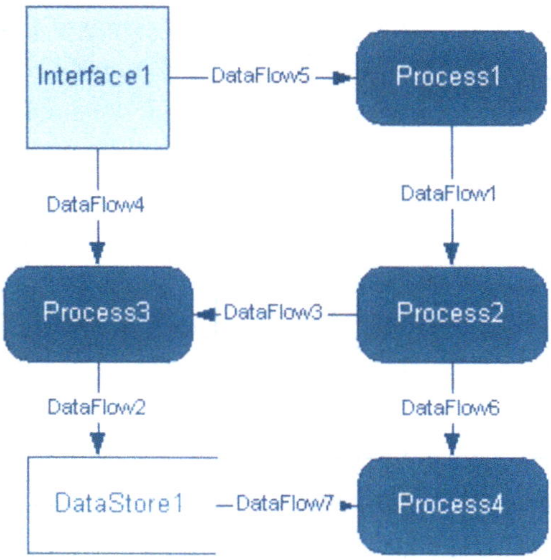

Fig. D-10. The DFD for an imaginary system

DFSK – Differential Frequency-Shift Keying. A modulation technique that uses changes in signal frequency to encode a signal. Compare with FSK.

DFT – Distributed Function Terminal. A terminal mode used in the IBM System Network Architecture (see SNA) in which a user may access up to five different applications. Compare with Control Unit Terminal (CUT).

DFWMAC – Distributed Foundation Wireless MAC. The IEEE802.11 specification of a medium-independent media access protocol (see MAC) for wireless communications. It is laid on top of the group of medium-dependent physical specifications. The lowest protocol level supports asynchronous communication between stations using the CSMA/CA protocol. The DFWMAC architecture accommodates both ad hoc and infrastructure WLANs, and guarantees interoperability for the rest of 802.x. See also 802.x.

DH – Diffie–Hellman algorithm. A public-key algorithm, invented by Whitfield Diffie and Martin Hellman, used for secure key exchange.

DHCF – Distributed Host Command Facility. An IBM product running as a remote processor. DHCF interfaces with the mainframe-resident HCF subsystem to provide distributed access. In a pure IBM environment, it is often used to achieve 3270 terminal access from a mainframe to a remote non-mainframe system. In the multivendor environment, DHCF is often emulated to allow 3270 terminals to access the non-IBM system via the HCF facility.

DHCP – Dynamic Host Configuration Protocol. A protocol (RFC1541) that allows dynamic allocation of IP addresses to IBM-compatible PCs running on a Microsoft Windows local area network. DHCP is similar to the BOOTP protocol. Actually, DHCP uses automatic allocation to assign a permanent IP address to the host, or dynamic allocation in which DHCP assigns a temporary IP address, or manual allocation where the network administrator assigns the address and DHCP just transfers it.

DHTML – Dynamic HTML. Object-oriented HyperText Markup Language (see HTML) developed by W3C. See also CSS and XML.

DIA – Document Interchange Architecture. A document-exchange specification used in IBM SNA, implemented on top of LU6.2, that defines methods of organizing and addressing documents for exchange between different computers and supported by IBM protocols (see APPC and LU6.2). The IBM implementation of DIA that runs under CICS is known as DISOSS.

DIAL-M – Discrete Algorithms and Methods for Mobility. An international ACM SIGMOBILE workshop focusing on discrete algorithms and methods for mobile and wireless computing and communications. Selected papers are published in a special issue of the Discrete Applied Mathematics journal.

DIB – Device-Independent Bitmap. A file format designed for bitmap graphics to guarantee the same bitmap appearance on different devices. DIB images are usually transferred in metafiles (see CGM, WMF), bitmap (see BMP) files, and via the clipboard.

DIB – Directory Information Base. The name of the entire directory structure inside the X.500 directory service. Each entry in the DIB consists of a name and a set of attributes. The full name of an entry corresponds to a path through the DIT from the root of the tree to the entry (similar to that applied in the UNIX file system). If the data required is not in the segment of the DIB held by the contacted server it will either invoke other servers to resolve the query or redirect the client to another server.

DIB – Dual Independent Bus. A bus architecture introduced in the Intel Pentium Pro and Pentium II. It uses two buses. One bus is used for processor-to-main-memory communication; the other one is used to pass data from the processor to the L2 cache. The processor can access both buses at the same time.

dibit – double information bit. A two-bit set representing one of the four possible bit combinations. It is used as a transmission unit in the modulation technique known as differential phase-shift keying (see DPSK).

DIC – Dictionary file. A filename extension for a file that contains a database dictionary.

DICOM – Digital Imaging and Communications. An industry standard for images transferred between medical imaging devices. It allows interoperability between diagnostic and therapeutic equipment from different vendors. Both the communication protocols and common data formats are defined.

DID – Direct Inward Dialing. A system that allows an outside caller to communicate with a number in a PBX directly, without going through the switchboard. Compare with DOD.

DIF – Data Interchange Format. A standard format for exchange of ASCII documents structured in a row-and-column order.

DII – Dynamic Invocation Interface. A part of the Common Object Request Broker Architecture (see CORBA) on the client side that allows a client direct access to objects without requiring IDL interface-specific stubs to be linked in the request. See also DSI (Dynamic Skeleton Interface).

DIKU – Do I know you? The chat term.

DIL – Dual In-Line package. See DIP.

DIME – Development of Integrated Monetary Electronics. An initiative in the European Union on the application of information technology to monetary electronics for both manufacturers and users.

DIMM – Dual In-line Memory Module. A memory module packed on a small circuit board with connections on both sides of the board.

DIN – Deutsches Institut fuer Normung. The German standardization body, a member of ISO (http://www.din.de).

DIP – Document Image Processing. A common term for storage, management and retrieval of images. Bitmapped images of paper documents are stored in a computer by scanning rather than in the form of text files. It takes more memory, of course, but it more readily incorporates drawings, photographs, signatures, etc. It is one of the key technologies required in order to achieve the paperless office.

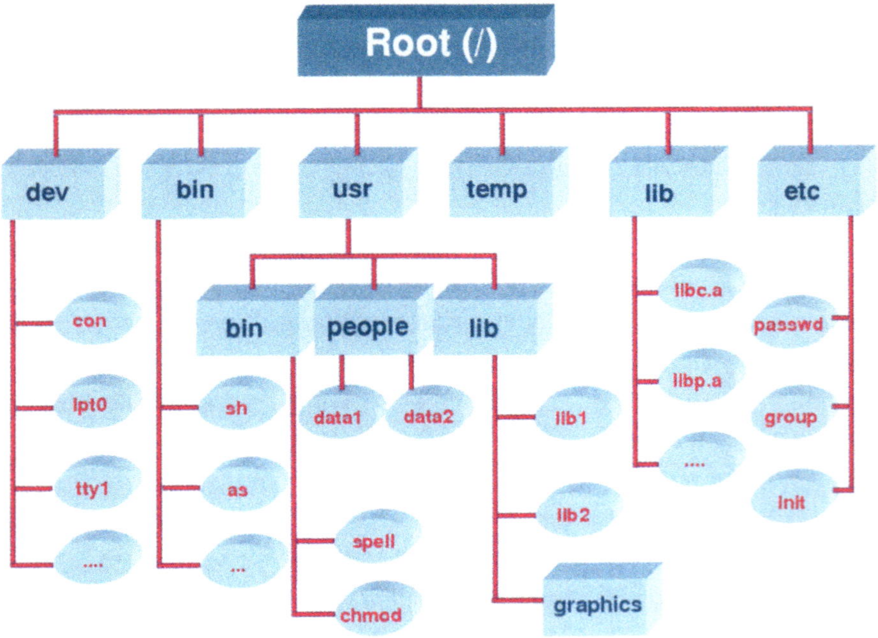

Fig. D-11. An example of a directory structure

DIP – Dual In-line Package. A standard for packing integrated circuits. Electronic circuits are enclosed in a rectangular plastic or ceramic housing and connected by downward-pointing pins that can be either soldered onto a printed circuit board or inserted into the appropriate socket. This technology is not suitable for modern chips that require very large numbers of connections. In that case it is better to use other packing technologies, such as a pin grid array (see PGA) or surface mounting (see SMD).

DIR – Direction. One-bit field in an ATM Resource Monitor (see RM) cell used to indicate the direction of the RM cell. If DIR consists of 0, then the RM cell is going from the source node, otherwise DIR is equal to 1 and the RM cell belongs to the destination node.

DIR – Directory file. A common name used by many operating systems to describe a root of a hierarchical file system. For instance, the DIR name is used by UNIX, DOS, GCOS, and other operating systems based on hierarchical file structures (see Fig. D-11). A directory is a way of organizing and grouping the files so that the user is not overwhelmed by a long list of them. The directories within a directory are called subdirectories. In order for a directory structure to be viewed by the user, different operating systems offer various ways. The directory structure can be an alphabetical list of names, sorted by date, by name, etc. In Microsoft terminology directories are known as folders.

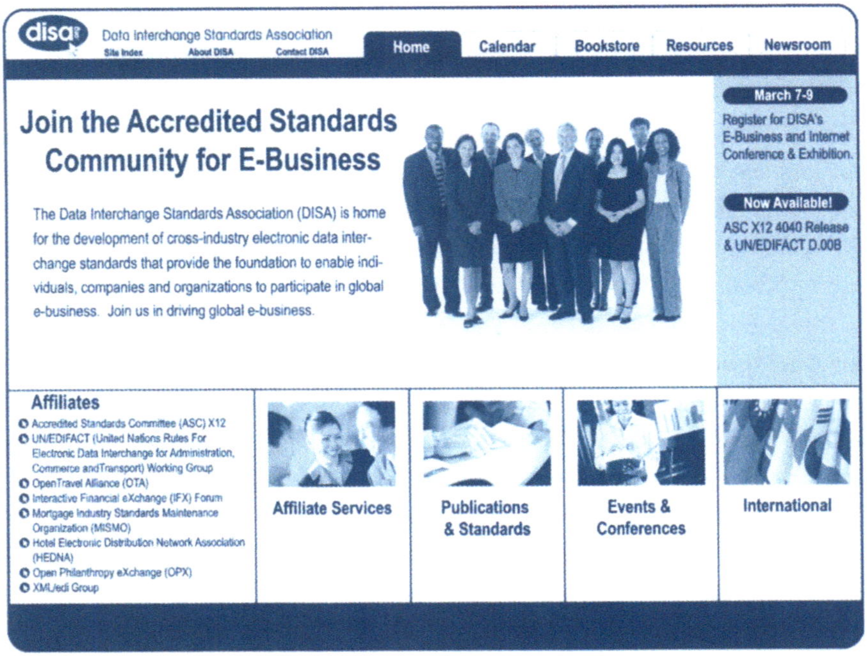

Fig. D-12. Homepage of the Data Interchange Standards Association (courtesy of DISA)

DIS – Draft International Standard. The second stage, after draft proposal, in adopting an ISO standard. The full process is described later (see ISO).

DISA – Data Interchange Standards Association. An organization created in 1987 by ANSI to take care of electronic data interchange standards (see EDI). Later, DISA extended its focus of interest to the electronic commerce area (see EC) too. Additional information is available at the DISA homepage (http://www.disa.org), see Fig. D-12.

DISA – Defense Information Systems Agency. The US government agency responsible for managing the DDN portion of the Internet, including the MILNET (http://www.disa.mil). Currently, DISA administers the DDN, and supports the user assistance services of the DDN NIC. See also Defense Data Network (DDN) and Network Information Center (NIC).

DiSC – Digital Symposium Collection. A yearly electronic journal issued by the ACM Special Interest Group on Management of Data (see SIGMOD). DiSC contains the most comprehensive source of information on database research. It includes the full contents of the previous year's SIGMOD Record and SIGMOD conference proceedings. The first issue of DiSC has 3700 HTML documents, over 400 PDF files, more than 2000 image files, and 11,000 links.

DISOSS – Distributed Office Support System. A collection of IBM software products for supporting office automation functions (see OA). It enables documents created by different products to be distributed and shared among IBM systems and it is commonly used as an interface point for transmitting documents to and from non-IBM computers.

DIT – Directory Information Tree. The name of the X.500 name tree that contains the information for a directory information base. The root of the DIT is an imaginary entry with a null name serving as a base for the naming elements in the tree. An object, which can be a country, an organization, a person, a device, etc., gets its name from the path between the root and the object itself. See X.500 and DIB.

DIVX – Digital Video Express. A type of CD drive similar to DVD CD technology. See also DVD.

DIX – Digital–Intel–Xerox. The common abbreviation for the three companies involved in the early days of Ethernet development.

DKE – Database and Knowledge Engineering. The scientific journal published by Elsevier Science concerning data engineering, knowledge engineering, and the interface of these two fields. Topics of interest include representation and manipulation of data and knowledge, appropriate architectures, construction of data/knowledge bases, applications, case studies, tools, etc.

DKNF – Domain-Key Normal Form. A normal form that takes into account all possible types of dependencies and constraints (functional, multivalued or join dependency).

DL – Digital Library. An umbrella term covering many modern techniques for making multimedia objects available to customers. Also, a wide-open research field in computer science. For instance, in May 1996, a special issue of IEEE Computer focused on a major US government initiative (see DLI). See also NZDL.

DL – Distribution List. A tool used in the CCITT X.400 Message Handling System (see MHS) for reaching multiple recipients with a single transmission.

DLC – Data-Link Control. A common name given to the functions provided in the data-link layer of the ISO/OSI Reference Model (see DLL and OSI). Also, an error-correction protocol used in the IBM SNA responsible for the transmission of data between two nodes over a physical link. See SNA (System Network Architecture).

DLCI – Data-Link Connection Identifier. A field in the frame-relay header (see FR) that represents the virtual circuit number associated with a particular destination.

DLE – Data-Link Escape. A transmission control character used in the Binary Synchronous Communications Protocol (see BISYNC). Used in conjunction with a second character that denotes a specific control function.

DLI – Digital Library Initiative. A project at the University of Illinois at Urbana–Champaign (see UIUC) sponsored by NSF, DARPA and NASA from 1994 to 1998. The aim of the project was to develop widely usable Web technology in order to effectively search technical documents on the Internet. See also DL (Digital Libraries).

DLL – Data-Link Layer. The second (from the bottom) layer of the OSI Reference Model. The DLL defines the protocols used to move data across the Physical Layer (for example, HDLC, LAP-B or IEEE802.2). The Data-Link Layer is sometimes also called the Logical Link Layer. See also OSI.

DLL – Dynamic-Link Library. A very useful feature of Microsoft Windows and OS/2 operating systems that allows executable code units to be stored as separate files (with .DLL, .DRV or .FON extensions) and to be loaded only when the calling program needs them. Also, DLLs are shared among different applications.

DLS – Data-Link Services. The services provided at the data-link layer (see DLL) in the ISO/OSI Reference Model (see OSI).

DLS – Distributed Link Services. A method used by IBM SNA Servers (see SNA) to connect to other SNA servers.

DLSw – Data-Link Switching. An interoperability standard (RFC1434) that provides a method for forwarding SNA and NetBIOS traffic over TCP/IP networks using the data-link layer.

DLT – Digital Linear Tape. A kind of magnetic tape drive that can transfer 5 MBps and can store 35 GB on a single cartridge. Data are usually compressed using the DLZ1 algorithm (see DLZ1).

DLU – Dependent Logical Unit. A type of Logical Unit (see LU) used in SNA communications that depends on the Signaling Connection and Control Part protocol (see SCCP) for establishing sessions with other Logical Units.

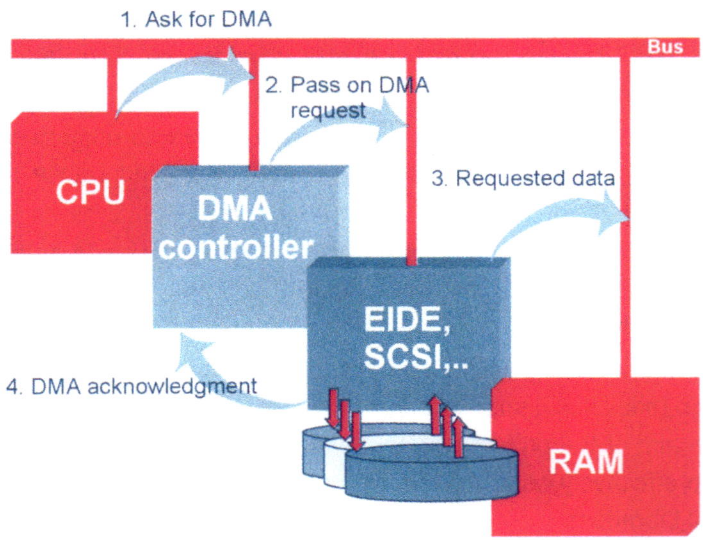

Fig. D-13. DMA transfer in brief

DLUR – Dependent Logical Unit Requester. The client part of the Dependent Logical Unit (see DLU) enhancement to APPN. See also APPN and DLUS.

DLUS – Dependent Logical Unit Server. The server part of the Dependent Logical Unit (see DLU) enhancement to APPN. The DLUS provides SSCP services to DLUR nodes over APPN. See also APPN.

DLZ1 – Digital Lempel–Ziv 1. An algorithm for data compression which maps variable-length input strings to variable-length output symbols. At the same time DLZ1 builds a dictionary of strings, which is accessed as a hash table.

Compression occurs when the input data matches a string in the table and is replaced by the output symbol.

DM – Digital (Delta) Modulation. A modulation method in which analog signals are encoded as a series of bits whose values depend on the level of the analog signal relative to the previous level. If the signal is increasing a logical 1 is set, otherwise a 0 code is set.

DMA – Direct Memory Access. The ability to transfer information directly between an input/output channel and memory rather than employing the microprocessor in that transfer (see Fig. D-13).

DMA – Document Management Alliance. An organization that creates the industry specification with the same name for enabling document management systems (see DMS) from different vendors to operate with each other (http://www.aiim.org/dma).

DMAC – Destination MAC. A MAC address specified in the destination address field of a packet. Compare with SMAC (Source MAC). See also MAC (Media Access Control).

DMD – Directory Management Domain. A collection of one or more directory system agents (see DSA) and directory user agents (see DUA), which are all managed by a single organization authority in the X.500 Directory Service.

DME – Distributed Management Environment. Sets of Open Software Foundation (see OSF) standards, which focus on tools that are necessary for managing heterogeneous environment.

DMI – Desktop Management Interface. An operating-system-independent and protocol-independent API for managing the personal computer defined by Desktop Management Task Force Inc. (see DMTF). The final specification was made available in April 1994. The DMI enables PC vendors to accentuate both standard and vendor-specific features in their products and supports existing standards, such as the SNMP and Plug and Play (see P&P). At a minimum, DMI identifies the vendor, the component name, the version, the serial number and the installation date and time for a particular component.

DMI – Digital Multiplexed Interface. A T1 interface between a private branch exchange (see PBX) and a computer. See also T1.

DML – Data Manipulation Language. A part of a database management system (see DBMS) that allows descriptions of how to search, move, update and delete database records. A DML can be either a high-level interactive query language or a procedural set of instructions embedded in a general-purpose language.

DML – Declarative Markup Language. A system of text-formatting codes used in text processing that indicates only that a unit of text is a certain part of a document. Document formatting is then done by another program, called a parser. SGML and HTML are examples of declarative markup languages. See also HTML and SGML.

DMM – Digital Multimeter. A test device, usually portable, used for the measurement of voltage, resistance, electric current or other electrical values.

DMS – Document Management System. A common name for software packages that are used to store, retrieve and manage unstructured data such as files, images, text, spreadsheets, sound clips, etc. Interoperability of such different-vendor systems is under consideration by the Document Management Alliance (see DMA).

DMSP – Distributed Mail System Protocol. The RFC1056 recommendation that allows users to download their e-mails to poorly connected workstations.

DMT – Discrete Multitone Modulation. An ADSL modulation technique that splits bandwidth usage into subchannels in order to obtain maximum data transfer. See also ADSL.

DMTF – Desktop Management Task Force. An industry-wide consortium committed to making PCs easier to use, understand, configure and manage. DMTF was founded in 1992 by Intel, Microsoft, Novell, SunSoft, SynOptics Communications Inc., HP, IBM and DEC (http://www.dmtf.org). Today, the DMTF's accomplishments represent the work of more than 350 hardware and software vendors, including leading companies in the PC industry. DMTF working committees define components, groups and attributes for PC systems, with the goal of making PCs selfconfiguring and identifiable to a wide range of management applications.

DN – Distinguished Name. An acronym for the full path name given by the X.500 directory service (see X.500).

DNA – Digital Network Architecture. The full layered network architecture developed by DEC. DNA is implemented with a combination of hardware and software products that are loosely referred to as DECnet (see DECnet). This is equivalent, for example, to IBM SNA or Sun ONC. See also SNA and ONC.

DNIC – Data Network Identification Code. Part of an X.121 address that consists of two addresses, the first specifying the country in which a particular Public Switched Network is located (see PSN), and the second specifying the PSN itself. See also X.121.

DNP – Distributed Network Protocol. The open (see PSI) and robust protocol developed for interoperability among systems deployed in the electric utility, oil and gas, water supply, and security industries.

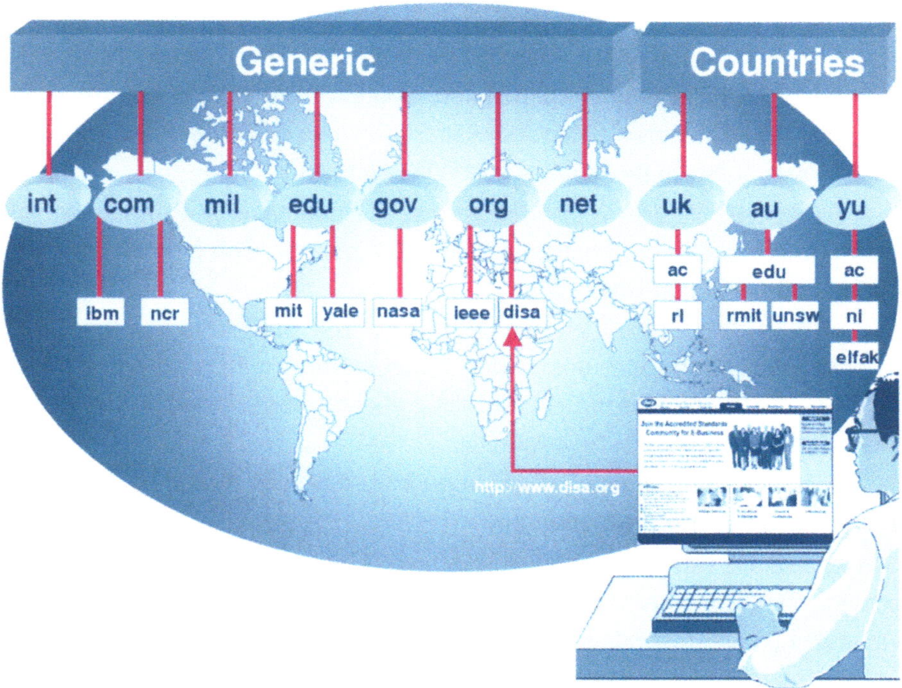

Fig. D-14. A portion of the Internet DNS

DNS – Domain Name System. The DNS (RFC1034, RFC1035) purpose is to provide a hierarchical domain-based naming scheme and a distributed database system capable of implementing that scheme. It is primarily used for mapping host names and e-mail addresses to IP addresses. The DNS is a tree-structured name space database with distribution both of information location and of administrative control. The database is spread over different name servers, each responsible for a portion of the name space tree. Each subtree in a DNS tree is known as a domain. Each domain is administrated by some organization that is responsible for ensuring that correct data is entered into that portion of the name space. DNS information is stored in each name server as a set of resource records (see RR) which contain data associated with one domain name. The style of host names now used in the

Internet is called "domain name", because this is the style of names used to look up anything in the DNS. Some important domains are .int (international), .com (commercial), .edu (educational), .net (network operations), .gov (US government) and .mil (US military), as shown in Fig. D-14. Most countries also have a domain. The country domain names are based on ISO3166. A full list is available at IANA (http://www.iana.org/cctld/cctld-whois.htm). For example, .us (United States), .uk (United Kingdom), .au (Australia), .nz (New Zealand), .yu (Yugoslavia), etc. See also FQDN and TLD. For a full picture of how it works, see also the Internet and WWW entries.

DOA – Distributed Objects and Applications. An international symposium focusing on research and practice in distributed objects. The proceedings are published by IEEE CS Press.

DOAM – Distributed Office Applications Model. The topmost sublayer of the OSI application layer that deals with document and data organization and transmission. It includes document filing and retrieval, document printing, data transfer, and MOTIS (see MOTIS).

DOC – Document. A filename extension dedicated to files made using the Microsoft WinWord text processor (see WinWord).

DOCSIS – Data Over Cable Service Interface Specification. A standard interface for cable modems that handle data between cable TV operators and personal computers or television sets. It specifies modulation techniques and the protocol for exchanging bidirectional signals over cable. It is now known as CableLabs Certified Cable Modem.

DoD – Department of Defense. The US government organization involved in the definition of many advanced computer and communication technologies. DoD also supports research and development work on such technologies. Additional information is available at http://www.defenselink.mil

DOD – Direct Outward Dialing. A service in a private branch exchange (see PBX) that allows a user to get an outside line directly, without going through the system's switchboard.

DOI – Digital Object Identifier. A permanent identifier given to a Web file or other Internet document that allows users to be redirected to a new address if the address of such a document has been changed.

DOM – Document Object Model. W3C specification intended for dynamic HTML (see DHTML). It will allow a platform-independent programming interface for HTML documents. It allows manipulation of the contents, structure and style of Web documents.

DOS – Disk Operating System. A common term related to any operating system that is loaded from disk devices while the system is starting or rebooting. Due to the popularity of Microsoft DOS, it is also used as a short term for that particular DOS (see MS-DOS).

DOV – Data Over Voice. A communication method which allows data and voice to be transmitted at the same time on the same conductor. The data is transmitted by modulating a carrier whose frequency is well above the audio range. Compare with Data Under Voice (DUV).

DP – Data Processing. An umbrella term for the work executed by computers to achieve specific goals, for example to calculate and display the total revenue of a particular company in a previous year. The term is also known as automatic data processing (ADP) and electronic data processing (EDP).

DP – Data Processor. In a distributed environment, a software component on each computer that stores data through a distributed database management system (see DDBMS and DBMS). It is also responsible for managing local data and coordinating access to such data.

DP – Draft Proposal. An older name for a preliminary version of an ISO standard intended for comments and critiques, before final voting to stand as an international standard (IS). Now the term Committee Draft (CD) is used.

DPA – Demand Protocol Architecture. A feature in Microsoft's LAN manager network architecture that allows protocol stacks to be loaded and unloaded dynamically. Using DPA, supporting other network environments on the same machine becomes possible.

DPC – Deferred Procedure Call. The name used in the Windows NT operating system for a called function, the task of which is less significant than the function under execution, so the DPC can wait until the higher-priority tasks are completed.

DPCM – Differential Pulse Code Modulation. A form of pulse code modulation where the efficiency is enhanced by only transmitting the difference between the current signal strength and the previous pulse signal strength, rather than the absolute values.

DPDU – Data-Link Protocol Data Unit. The form into which the data link control layer of the OSI network architecture formats data. See also PDU.

dpi – dots per inch. A measurement unit for the resolution of raster devices expressed as the number of discrete dots that a particular input device can transfer to a computer, or an output device can print or display per linear inch.

DPMI – DOS Protected Mode Interface. An older technique developed for Microsoft Windows 3.0 that enables MS-DOS-based applications to run in the protected mode. That allows them to overcome the native MS-DOS 640-KB memory restriction. The HIMEM.SYS driver provides this service.

DPS – Display PostScript. An extended form of PostScript that allows interactive use with bitmap displays in a multitasking environment.

DPSK – Differential Phase-Shift Keying. A communication method used by modems to encode data. In DPSK, there are four states available (see dibit) to describe the degree of phase shift (0, 90, 180, 270). For additional information about the phase-shift keying technique see PSK.

DQ – Distributed Queuing. A technique used in the Distributed Queue Dual Bus (see DQDB).

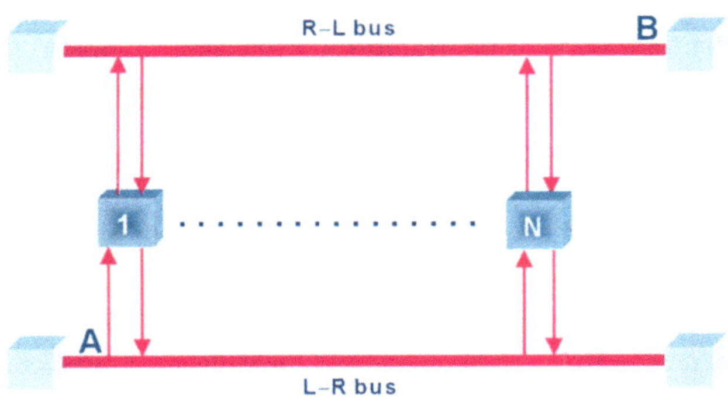

Fig. D-15. Architecture of DQDB

DQDB – Distributed Queue Dual Bus. The IEEE802.6 standard for metropolitan area networks (see MAN). DQDB consists of two unidirectional cables to which all the computers are connected, as depicted in Fig. D-15. Each cable (bus) has a device (head-end) that initiates transmission from the right to the left and vice versa. If the destination is to the right the sender uses bus A, otherwise bus B will be employed. The queuing is based on the FIFO order (see FIFO), each station sends up in a FIFO queue. In order to simulate a FIFO queue, each station maintains two counters. The request counter counts the number of downstream requests incremented until the station itself has a frame to send. The second one is the carrier counter, used to indicate the busy state of the A or B bus according to the FIFO rules. In order to support long distances, the cables mentioned above are based on fiber optics. DQDB operates in the bottom two layers of the OSI Reference Model (see OSI). In fact, in the data-link layer, DQDB operates in the media-access control (see MAC) sublayer. The number of nodes and the distance involved do not influence the performance of the DQDB configuration, so it is very suitable for high-speed communications.

DQMOT – Don't quote me on this. The chat term.

DQO – Data Quality Objectives. A process of planning tools for data collection activities. It provides a basis for balancing decision uncertainty with available resources.

DRAGOON – Distributed Reusable Ada Generated from an Object-Oriented Notation. A project from the late 1980s which was aimed at providing effective support for reuse in real-time distributed Ada applications. See also ESPRIT.

DRAM – Dynamic Random-Access Memory. A type of random-access memory (pronounced "dee-ram") in which the data is stored in capacitors. Since capacitors lose their charge over time, DRAMs have to be refreshed periodically. It is a very popular memory technology due to its high density and low price. There are many varieties of DRAM such as Pseudo-Static RAM (see PSRAM), page-mode DRAM, Extended Data Out DRAM (see EDO DRAM), Video RAM (see VRAM), Synchronous DRAM (see SDRAM), Rambus DRAM (see RDRAM), etc. Compare with Static RAM (SRAM).

DRAW – Direct Read After Write. A read/write technique used with optical recording that allows verification of a written record immediately after it has been recorded. If an error occurs the information is recorded once again in another location and the record table is updated with the address of the correct version. Another technique used to correct recording is DRDW.

DRDA – Distributed Relational Database Architecture. An IBM distributed architecture, which provides access to distributed relational data in IBM operating environments, for example in AIX, as well as in other non-IBM platforms that are compliant with the DRDA specification.

DRDW – Direct Read During Write. A recording technique used with optical disks that allows verification of the information accuracy during recording. If an error occurs the current recording is stopped at the faulty location and skips to a new section of the disk. Compare with DRAW.

DREN – Defense Research and Engineering Network. A sophisticated and robust DoD (see DoD) communications virtual private network on a commercial grid (http://www.dren.net). DREN is the long-haul communication service provider for the HPC community. See also HPC.

DRIVE – Dedicated Road Infrastructure for Vehicle Safety in Europe. A major initiative in the European Community, begun in 1988, to apply information technology to the improvement of road safety and the reduction of environmental pollution by road traffic.

DRO – Destructive Read Out. A reading technique used by some types of memory systems that destroys the memory contents that have just been read and passed on to the processor.

DRV – Driver file. A filename extension for a file that contains a device driver in Microsoft Windows.

DS – Dansk Standard. The Danish standards association (http://www.ds.dk).

DS – Directory Service. See X.500.

DS – Distributed Single-layer. An abstract test method for testing one protocol layer. The upper tester is located within the system under test and the PCO is located at the upper service boundary of the IUT. Test events are specified by abstract service primitives (see ASP) at the upper tester above the IUT and ASPs and/or protocol data units (see PDU) at the lower tester PCO. See also PCO (Point of Control and Observation) and IUT.

DSn – Digital Signal (Service) level n ($0 \leq n \leq 4$). A set of standard digital signals (channels). It uses pulse code modulation (see PCM) to encode an analog signal into digital form. The signal is sampled 8000 times per second, and each sample value is encoded in an 8-bit stream, which is transmitted using time division multiplexing (see TDM). DS0 allows transmission at a 64-Kbps rate. DS1 is a standard digital transmission format which allows a 24-voice channel to be demultiplexed to one simple digital channel, known as carrier T1 (1544 Mbps, US) or carrier E1 (2048 Mbps, Europe). DS2 allows transmission at the T2 rate (6312 Mbps). DS3 allows transmission at the T3 rate (44,736 Mbps). DS4 allows transmission at the T4 rate (273 Mbps).

DSA – Digital Signature Algorithm. A public-key algorithm used for digital signature generation. It is a part of the Digital Signature Standard (see DSS).

DSA – Directory Server Agent. Software with some kind of intelligence that provides the X.500 Directory Service (see X.500) for a portion of the directory information base. DSA handles incoming requests from Directory User Agents (see DUA), from both its own cell and from remote ones.

DSA – Distributed System Architecture. A well-known distributed system architecture implemented on Bull computers in the late 1980s.

DSAP – Destination Service Access Point. The service access point to be accessed at a destination. This information may be built into the data field of an IEEE802.3 transmission frame.

DS/DD – Double Sided/Double Density. A kind of floppy disk that allows both sides of a disk to be used for data storage with double density. For IBM-compatible PCs, there are 5.25" floppies with a capacity of 360 KB and 3.5" floppies with a capacity of 720 KB.

DSDM – Dynamic Systems Development Method. The consortium dedicated to defining, promoting and evolving standards for rapid application development (see RAD). See further information at http://www.dsdm.org

DSE – Data Switching Equipment. A common term used for equipment deployed in a switching network such as X.25.

DSE – Distributed Single-layer Embedded. A test method similar to Distributed Single-layer test (see DS) used for testing a protocol layer or sublayer.

DS/HD – Double Sided/High Density. A kind of floppy disk that allows both sides of a disk to be used for high-density data storage. For IBM-compatible PCs, there are 5.25" floppies with a capacity of 1.2 MB and 3.5" floppies with a capacity of 1.44 MB.

DSI – Distributed Storage Infrastructure. See I2-DSI (Internet2-Distributed Storage Infrastructure).

DSI – Dynamic Skeleton Interface. Part of the Common Object Request Broker Architecture (see CORBA) at the server side that allows an ORB to deliver a request. See also DII (Dynamic Invocation Interface).

DSL – Digital Subscriber Line. A remote transmission technology achieved using standard twisted-pair telephone cable. DSLs are established between the central post office and the user building, connected there to one or more phones, fax machines or modems. One special kind of DSL is the Asymmetric Digital Subscriber Line (see ADSL). There are also three other types of DSL: HDSL, SDSL and VDSL. Other solutions for the same purpose are FTTC and FTTH.

DSLAM – Digital Subscriber Line Access Multiplexer. An ADSL-based technology that provides high-speed Internet access over traditional twisted-pair (see TP) telephone wiring. See also ADSL.

DSM – Distributed Shared Memory. A memory system shared across a network (see Fig. D-16). More specifically, from the user point of view, memories associated with each distributed processor look like a memory organization in a local multiprocessor architecture. From the system design point of view the overall architecture is more complicated. For example, sharing the total address space can produce unpredictable and unnecessary network traffic, with significant congestion and application-processing overheads. To overcome these and other DSM architectural problems there are many approaches, such as Non-Uniform Memory Access (see NUMA), many consistency models, page-based DSMs, etc. See also SM (Shared Memory).

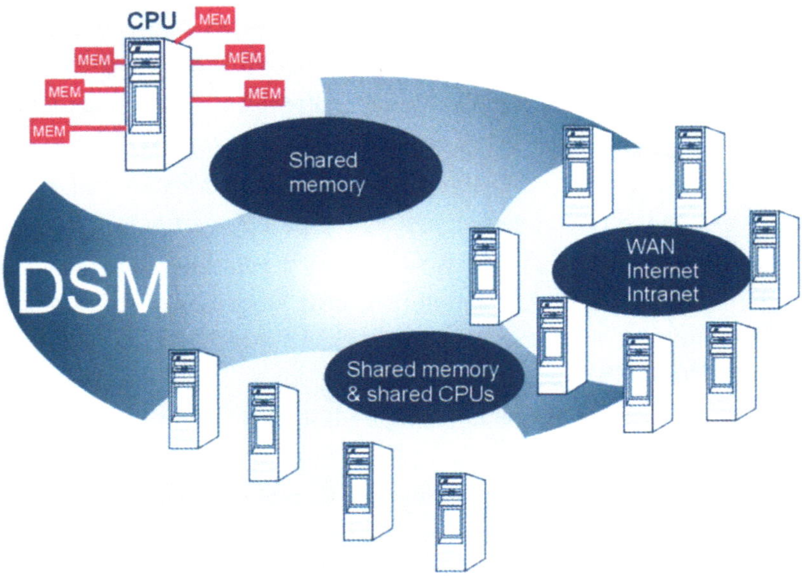

Fig. D-16. Several variations of DSM

DSML – Directory Service Markup Language. A markup language announced in 1999 that combines XML syntax and the Lightweight Directory Access Protocol (see LDAP).

DSMIT – Distributed System Management Interface Tool. An extension of the System Management Interface Tool (see SMIT) capable of working in a distributed environment. It is based on TCP/IP and the client/server model (see CS). DSMIT runs only in ASCII mode. It allows the SMIT interface to build system management commands and execute them over other clients on a network running on several UNIX implementations. Information is sent using TCP/IP sockets. The DSMIT program uses the same level of security as rsh does. See rsh (remote shell).

DSN – Data Source Name. The filename extension for the files containing the connection parameters from an application to a SQL Server database.

DSN – Dependable Systems and Networks. An international IEEE conference focusing on the field of dependable computing.

DSO – Database Security Officer. A person responsible for ensuring database security and integrity.

DSOM – Distributed System Object Model. The System Object Model (see SOM) developed by IBM as an implementation of CORBA's ORB. It allows binary class libraries to be shared between applications on distributed computers as well as on a given system (see CORBA and ORB).

DSP – Digital Signal Processor. An integrated circuit designed for high-speed data manipulations for audio and image management, as well as for data acquisition. In fact, the signals being processed were originally analog.

DSP – Domain-Specific Part. Part of the address for the network-layer service access point (see NSAP) used in the ISO/OSI Reference Model (see OSI). See also Service Access Point (SAP).

DSP – Developer Studio Project. A filename for a file that contains a Microsoft Developer Studio Project.

DSP – Directory System Protocol. A protocol used in the X.500 Directory Service for communications between Directory System Agents (see DSA).

DSPU – Downstream Physical Unit. A common name for a device that lies in the direction of packets traveling in a ring topology.

DSR – Data Set Ready. A serial communication signal employed by a modem to tell the connected computer that it is ready to operate. Compare with Data Terminal Ready (DTR). In most cases communication can take place only if both DTR and DSR are raised. In the full 25-pin RS-232C interface DSR is pin 6, in the 9-pin interface DSR is pin 4.

DSS – Decision Support System. A set of related programs and data required to help users analyze data, answer "what-if" questions, create financial or other models, and generally extract the truth from complex data. A DSS includes a database of information consisting of knowledge about a given area, a language for problem description and question formulation, and a modeling program for alternative testing. Other terms similarly used are Executive Information System and Management Information System (MIS).

DSS – Digital Signature Standard. A public-key cipher standard that specifies a digital signature algorithm (see DSA) and an appropriate message-hash algorithm. Such a signature is used to verify the identity of the sender as well as the origin of the message.

DSSSL – Document Style Semantics and Specification Language. An ISO standard addressing the semantics of high-quality composition in a way independent of the particular formatting systems or processes. DSSSL is intended to be a complementary standard to SGML.

DSU – Digital (Data) Service Unit. A device used to provide a standard interface to a user's terminal that is compatible with a modem. Often used together with Channel Service Unit (see CSU) as CSU/DSU.

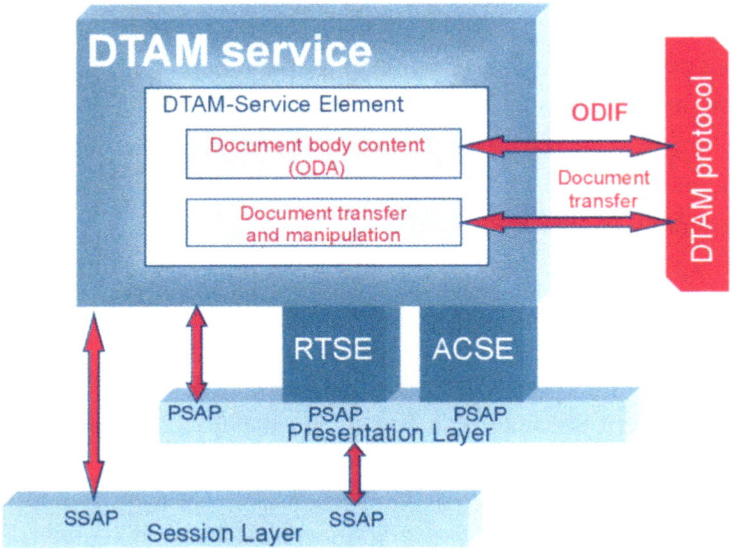

Fig. D-17. The architecture of the DTAM model

DSVD – Digital Simultaneous Voice and Data. A feature of some modems that allows voice and data to be transmitted simultaneously.

DSVIS – Design Specification and Verification of Interactive Systems. An international annual workshop focusing on formal representations in the design, specification, verification, validation and evaluation of interactive systems.

DSW – Developer Studio Workspace. Filename extensions for files that contain Microsoft Developer Studio workspaces.

D&T – Design & Test of Computers. The IEEE journal that covers the methods used to design and test electronic product hardware and supporting software.

DTAM – Document Transfer And Manipulation. The standard for telematics services (teletext, fax and handwritten material) in the upper part of the OSI application layer. In a general sense there are three classes of service: bulk transfer, document manipulation, and bulk transfer and manipulation. Documents that DTAM can handle must meet the Open Document Architecture (see ODA) requirements. The DTAM model is depicted in Fig. D-17. To transfer documents, DTAM uses either application-level support functions such as ACSE, ROSE or RTSE, or session-layer services. In some cases, when the recipient acts as an intermediary, DTAM sends the documents directly to the session layer. Finally, DTAM protocols provide communication between two applications using DTAM. See also ACSE, ROSE, RTSE, ODIF, PSAP and SSAP.

DTD – Document Type Definition. The definition of a document type in SGML, consisting of a set of markup tags and their interpretation. Also, a filename extension for such files.

DTE – Data Terminal Equipment. Equipment located at end-user stations, terminals, printers, etc. In communications, an RS-232C DTE device transmits data over line 2 and receives data over line 3. Compare with DCE (Data Circuit Equipment).

DTE – Domain and Type Enforcement. A project under development at the Network Associates International Laboratory (see NAI) concerning the access control mechanisms for UNIX kernels. DTE represents an enhanced form of table-oriented mandatory access control mechanism (known as type enforcement).

DTG – Digital Television Group. A consortium (http://www.dtg.org.uk) of manufacturers, networks operators and other interested parties, dedicated to the implementation of MHEG standards in digital TV. See also MHEG.

DTL – Designated Transit List. A list of nodes and optional link identifications in an ATM network that completely specifies a path across a single Private Network-to-Network Interface (see PNNI) group.

DTP – Desktop Publishing. A common term describing a computer application area used to layout text and graphics for printing. It allows text, graphics and images to be combined, font attributes (type, size, color, orientation, etc.) to be chosen, document organization in multiple columns, paragraph justification, and many other facilities for preparing a wide variety of documents. Well-known DTP applications are WinWord, Ventura Publisher, PageMaker, etc.

DTP – Distributed Transaction Processing. The X/Open standard that defines a distributed transaction processing architecture through which multiple application programs may share resources while coordinating their work in transactions that may be executed concurrently. The architecture defines application-programming interfaces and interactions among transactional applications, transaction managers (see TM) and resource managers (see RM), as shown in Fig. D-18. A minimal architecture definition consists of a set of component interfaces and a set of connections between those interfaces. Also, ISO standard 10026 defines the DTP in the upper application layer of the OSI protocol stack. See also OSI.

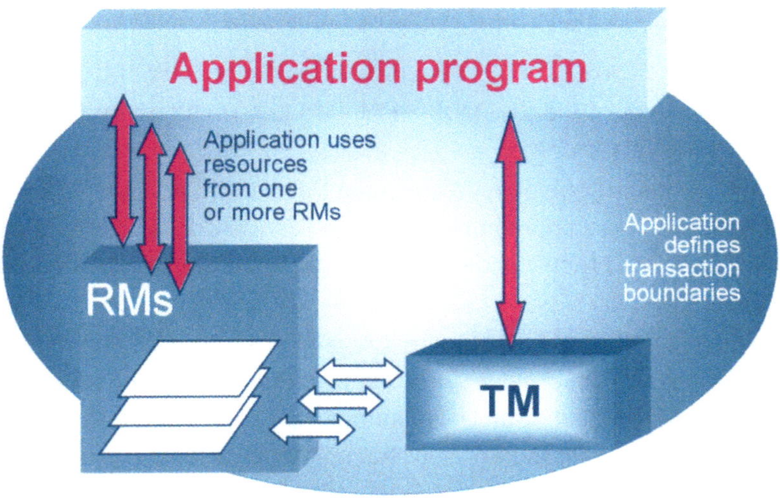

Fig. D-18. The X/Open DTP architecture

DTR – Data Terminal Ready. Serial communication signal initialized and sent by a computer to a modem on the line, in order to tell the modem that the computer is ready to accept incoming data. Also, the name of the pin (20) in an RS-232C interface connector or the pin on the chip dedicated to the same purpose. In the 9-pin interface specification, DTR is pin 4. Compare with Data Set Ready (DSR). In most cases communication can take place only if both DTR and DSR are raised.

DTR – Dedicated Token Ring. An advanced variant of the standard token ring topology (see TR). DTR allows a direct connection between a node and the token ring switch, so the node can deal with the entire network bandwidth while some other node is busy with its own communication needs.

DTS – Digital Termination Service. A service that allows private networks to get access to public networks.

DTS – Distributed Time Service. Part of the OSF Distributed Computing Environment (see DCE) addressing clock synchronization on separate distributed machines. It consists of timeservers asking each other "What time is it?" to achieve two important goals: keep the clocks mutually consistent, and keep them in touch with reality.

D

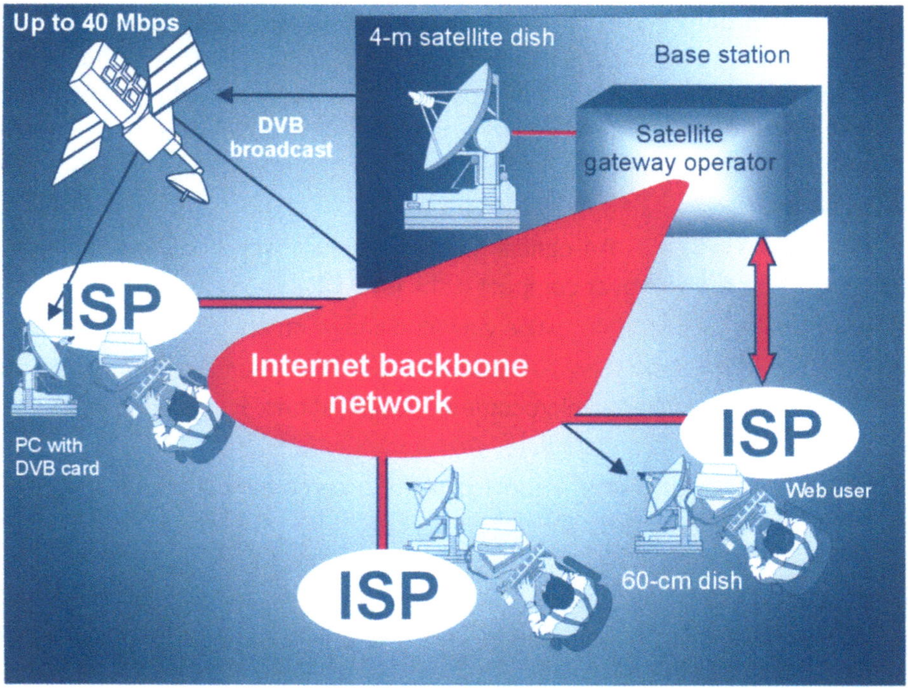

Fig. D-19. Web via DVB satellites

DUA – Directory User Agent. The software that accesses the X.500 Directory Service (see X.500) on behalf of the directory user. The directory user may be a person or another software agent.

DUNCE – Dial-Up Network Connection Enhancement. The software product (http://www.vecdev.com/dunce.htm) that automates dial-up Internet connections within Windows 95.

DUV – Data Under Voice. A strategy for transmitting voice and data over the same communication line. Compare with Data Over Voice (DOV).

DVB – Digital Video Broadcast. An advanced technique for providing Web services via satellites. The overall strategy is shown in Fig. D-19. Web users are connected to the Internet via regular Internet service providers (see ISP). Both the ISP and the Internet backbone network can be connected to a DVB base station equipped with a satellite gateway and a satellite dish (4-m radius). Instead of the required webpages returning via a standard phone line, ISP gives them to the DVB base station, which broadcasts them to its satellite. The user workplace is equipped with a small satellite dish (60-cm radius) and/or a DVB card inside its PC, and both are used to pick up requested pages from the satellite. DVB allows reception of a huge amount of multimedia data, such as MPEG-2 and webpages, as well as files with binary large objects (see BLOB). The DVB service is already available in France, Spain, Italy, Great Britain and Germany via Eutelsat, Astra, CanalPlus etc. See also DECT and GSM.

DVD – Digital Video Disk. An optical storage medium with improved capacity (in GB) and bandwidth over compact disks (see CD).

DVI – Diagonal Viewable Image. The viewable image on computer screens.

DV-I – Digital Video Interactive. A standard that implements compression of digital video and audio for microcomputer applications. It was developed by RCA, General Electric and Intel.

DVM – Data/Voice Multiplexer. A device used to combine voice and data signals on the same transmission line.

DVMRP – Distance Vector Multicast Routing Protocol. A routing protocol initially used by the Multicast Backbone (see MBone) making its choice based on the distance vector determining the best route between the source and destination nodes.

DVN – Digital Video Network. See I2-DVN (Internet2 Digital Video Network).

DVP – Distance Vector Protocol. A common name for routing protocols that use the distance-vector algorithm to determine the available connections. These connections are checked first based on the cost of reaching them via routers in neighbors in order to determine the best route between the source and destination. Examples include DVRMP, IDRP, RIP and RTMP.

DVST – Direct-View Storage Tube. A type of cathode-ray tube (see CRT) capable of displaying a detailed precise image on the screen without refreshment. That means a flicker-free display, supporting interactive graphics and the display of complex images without the high scan rate and bandwidth required by conventional CRTs.

DW – Data Warehouse. A modern approach to building a high-performance, often very large, information repository that serves as a strategic resource. A data warehouse is a repository (or archive) of information gathered from multiple sources, stored under a unified schema, at a single site (see Fig. D-20). A data warehouse is built on an active model of information and consists of key operational and historical data as well as relevant data from outside the organization. A DW can be distributed over several computers and may contain several databases and information from numerous sources in a variety of formats. Once gathered, the data are stored for a long time, permitting access to historical data. Thus, a DW provides the user with a single consolidated interface to data, making decision-support queries easier to issue. Data warehouses are going to be one of the key enabling technologies for building a new generation of decision-support systems, management information systems, and strategic CIM. Among others, some important issues in building a DW are: when and how to gather data, what schema to use, how to propagate updates, what data to summarize, etc.

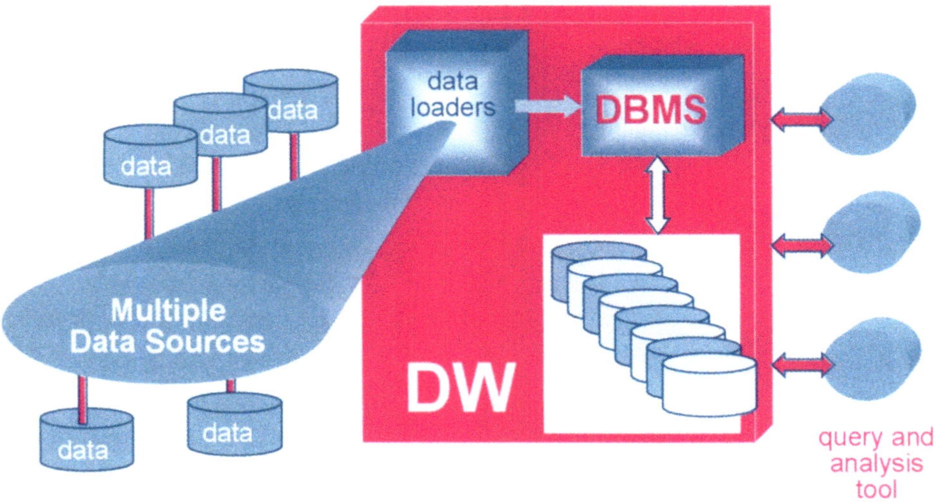

Fig. D-20. DW architecture

DWD – DiamondWare Digitized. An audio file format for high-quality interactive multimedia applications.

DWORD – Double Word. A unit of data consisting of four contiguous bytes treated as a single unit by microprocessors.

DX – Double Extension. A full 32-bit version of Intel 80386 or 80486 microprocessors. It means that the whole architecture supports 32-bit orientation (registers, data and address buses) in contrast to microprocessors designated with SX which are limited to a 16-bit data bus (compare with SX).

DXA – Directory Exchange Agent. In Microsoft Windows Exchange Server, a component that handles the transfer of directory information between the server directory and foreign mail systems.

DXF – Drawing Interexchange Format. A widely used computer-aided design (see CAD) file format for data transfer between CAD programs, such as AutoCAD etc.

DXI – Data Exchange Interface. A specification from the ATM Forum, described in RFC1483, that defines how network devices such as bridges, routers or hubs, can act as front-end processors (see FEP) in an ATM network.

E

E – Exa. A prefix meaning one quintillion (10^{18}). In computing, which is based on the binary numbering system, Exa has a value which is a power of 2 (2^{60}).

E – Exponent. An acronym often used in the case of large exponents such as 10^{24}, expressed as 10E+24.

E2PROM – E2 Programmable Read-Only Memory. See EEPROM.

E3 – Electromagnetic Environment Effects. A broad umbrella term used to cover electromagnetic compatibility, electromagnetic interference, radio-frequency interference, electromagnetic pulses, electrostatic discharges, radiation hazards, lightning, and the like.

EAB – Enterprise Access Builder. A feature of VisualAge for Java (see VA and VADD) that creates connections to enterprise server products such as CICS, Encina, IMS, TOC and the IBM MQ series.

EAI – Enterprise Application Integration. The common term for the set of processes together making one or more enterprise application (usually distributed) which acts as a single application. It requires the highest possible level of data integration and their distribution to the right application on time.

EAN – European Article Number. The European version of the article numbering and marking code. The main technology used is a bar code with two coding schemas EAN8 and EAN13.

EANCOM – EAN + Communications. A detailed implementation guideline of selected EDIFACT messages. As an integral part of total European Article Numbering (see EAN), EANCOM allows trading partners to exchange electronic documents for all normal commercial transactions in a simple, accurate and cost-effective manner. See also EDI and EDIFACT.

EARN – European Academic and Research Network. A European research community network originally sponsored by IBM, and connected to BITNET in the US.

EAROM – Electrically Alterable ROM. See EEPROM.

EAT – Eastern Africa Time. Time zone. UTC + 3.00 hours. See TZ.

EATCS – European Association for Theoretical Computer Science. An international organization founded in 1972 in order to facilitate the exchange of ideas between theoretical computer scientists.

EB – Encapsulation Boundary. The common name for two boundaries defined for delimiting encapsulated Privacy-Enhanced Mail (see PEM) messages. They are two strings: "BEGIN PRIVACY-ENHANCED MESSAGE" and "END PRIVACY-ENHANCED MESSAGE". The first boundary indicates that an encapsulated PEM message follows, the second boundary indicates that any text that follows is non-PEM text.

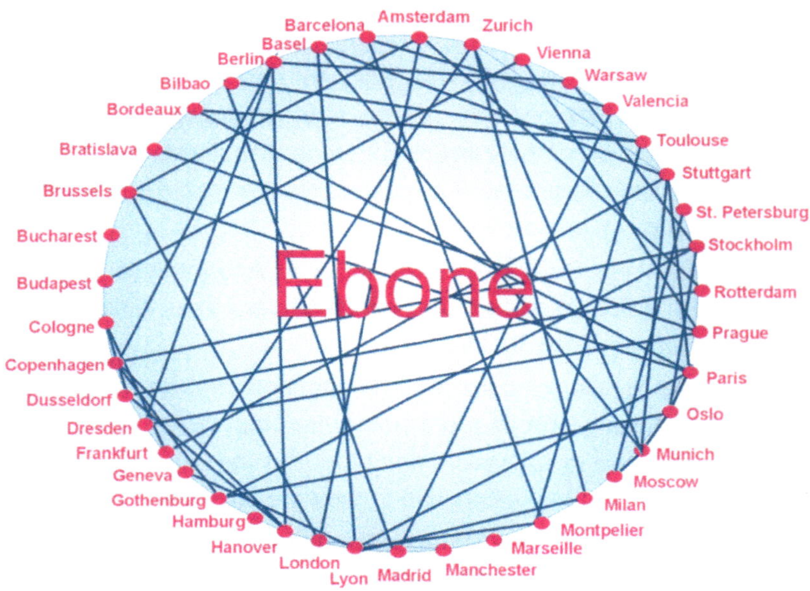

Fig. E-1. Part of the Ebone network (as of January 2001)

EB – Enterprise Bean. The part of the Sun Microsystems Enterprise Java Beans specification (see EJB), which describes a software component (non-visual) running on the server part of a distributed application based on EJB. Two kinds of EB are defined. The first involves objects associated with only one client and these are recognized as session beans. The second involves objects that represent data in a database and they are called entity beans. As opposed to session beans, an entity bean represents persistent data, i.e. it is an object view of an entity stored in a persistent database. An EB may be configured at deployment time by editing its properties. The EJB server is responsible for providing resources required by an EB, such as transactional services, storage services, security, naming, etc. An EB is composed of:

- a remote interface which represents the client view of the bean;

- a home interface holding the history of the bean lifecycle such as its creation, suppression or retrieval;
- the class of the bean that allows the particular bean to be managed in the EJB server; and
- the deployment descriptor containing the bean properties that may be edited at configuration time.

EB – Exabyte. Roughly 1 quintillion bytes, i.e. 2^{60} bytes.

EBCDIC – Extended Binary Coded Decimal Interchange Code. An acronym, pronounced "ebb-see-dick", that addresses an IBM coding scheme for assigning the binary-alphabetics, numerics, punctuation marks, and transmission control character mapping in a particular IBM way.

EBNF – Extended Backus–Naur Form. Extended BNF (see BNF). It uses additional constructs, such as square brackets, superscripts and subscripts, the suffixes + and *, and curly brackets.

Ebone – European Backbone. The European backbone network operated since 1991 that connects many networks all around Europe (see Fig. E-1). Descriptions of the most recent Ebone topology and future trends are available at http://www.ebone.com

E-broker – Electronic broker. A business model used in electronic commerce, in which an enterprise is essentially a middleman between a supplier and a buyer (for example, amazon.com).

EBU – European Broadcasting Union. Probably the largest professional association of national broadcasters in the world (http://www.ebu.ch).

EC – Electronic Commerce. A new computer and communication application field that supports efficient business on behalf of customers, sellers, manufacturers, and every possible intermediate actor (banks, national or regional chambers of commerce, etc.). The elements include EDI transactions, electronic mail, archives, audit trails, and all forms of records, including graphical images. See also EDI.

ECA – Event, Condition, Action. A rule that defines the next state of a database: when an event occurs, check the condition and if it holds, execute the action. There are many options for scheduling of events: immediate (executed directly after the event has been signaled), deferred (executed at the end of the triggering transaction), or decoupled (executed as a separate transaction or after a particular time interval). Scheduling algorithms define the coupling modes between triggering and the triggered transactions. An action formulates the reaction to an event and is executed after the rule has been triggered and its condition determined to hold. An action may refer to a transaction, or it may affect the database itself by performing some corrective or data retrieval operations or some arbitrary actions ranging from a complex application program to sending a series of signals. It is a key rule for active database implementation (see ADB and ADBMS).

e-cash – electronic cash. See e-money.

ECB – Electronic Codebook. An encryption strategy where every block of plaintext maps to exactly one block of ciphertext (see CBC). The disadvantage of this strategy is that the same source patterns always appear as the same encrypted patterns. Compare with CBC and CBT.

ECC – Elliptic Curve Cryptography. A security model based on an elliptical logarithm that gives higher level of security than the RSA algorithm.

ECC – Error Correction Code. A communication algorithm that allows recognition of an error that occurred during transmission. The receiving side can then request retransmission. Compare with Error Detection and Correction (EDAC).

ECCAI – European Coordinating Committee for Artificial Intelligence. The European organization (http://www.eccai.org) established in 1982 in order to promote the study, research and application of artificial intelligence (see AI) in Europe.

ECCV – European Conference on Computer Vision. An international conference focusing on computer vision. Topics include image features, texture, shading, color, visual motion, surface geometry, object recognition, active- and real-time vision, industrial applications, medical image understanding, etc. The proceedings are published by Springer-Verlag (see LNCS).

ECDL – European Conference on Digital Libraries. An international conference focusing on current research trends and perspectives in digital library systems. The proceedings are published by Springer-Verlag (see LNCS).

ECEG – European Conference on E-Government. An international conference focusing on the study, management, development, and implementation of Web-based technologies in the government sector. Some of the major topics include e-government portals and transaction sites, webocracy (Web democracy), security and confidentiality, integrated systems, citizen-centric information systems, web-enabled knowledge management, etc.

ECHO – European Commission Host Organization. A central repository and linkage network (http://www.echo.lu) providing access to several European Commission databases and information networks.

ECITE – European Conference on Information Technology Evaluation. An international conference that serves as a forum for academics and practitioners who have a special interest in how information systems may be evaluated.

ECKM – European Conference on Knowledge Management. An international conference focusing on the theory and practice of knowledge management. Topics include knowledge creation and sharing mechanisms, frameworks for conceptualizing knowledge management, knowledge assets valuation methods, impacts on organizational learning, impacts on business strategy, appropriate architectures, etc.

ECLiPSe – ECRC Constraint Logic Parallel System. A development environment for constraint programming developed by ECRC. For more information, visit the ECRC homepage (see ECRC).

ECMA – European Computer Manufacturers Association. A European association of computer manufacturers (http://www.ecma.ch).

ECML – European Conference on Machine Learning. An international conference focusing on current research trends in the area of machine learning. Topics of interest include artificial neural networks, case-based reasoning, cognitive modeling, genetic learning, inductive learning, information retrieval, knowledge acquisition, machine learning of natural languages, multiagent learning, robot learning, scientific discovery, Web navigation and mining, etc. The proceedings are published by Springer-Verlag (see LNCS).

ECN – Explicit Congestion Notification. A mechanism used in frame-relay networks (see FR) for indicating traffic congestion on the network. See also Backward and Forward Explicit Congestion Notification (BECN and FECN).

ECNE – Enterprise Certified NetWare Engineer. A title given to a person who already has a CNE title and who passes several additional courses in order to be qualified to maintain Enterprise NetWare-based networks. See also CNE.

ECOOP – European Conference on Object-Oriented Programming. A European conference dedicated to the latest research results and experience in the field of object-oriented programming (see OO and OOP). The proceedings are published by Springer-Verlag (see LNCS).

ECP – Extended Capabilities Port. A type of parallel printer port protocol proposed by HP and Microsoft that allows faster data transfer from computers to printers.

ECRC – European Computer-Industry Research Centre GmbH. A research organization (http://www.ecrc.de) founded in 1984 by Bull France, ICL UK and Siemens Germany, focusing on advanced information processing for the next generation of computers.

EC-Web – E-Commerce and Web. An international conference focusing on electronic commerce on the Web (see EC). The main topics include Web software development, XML, electronic payment, security aspects, electronic negotiations and trust, website engineering, user behavior, complex transactions, business models, etc. The proceedings are published by Springer-Verlag (see LNCS).

ED – End Delimiter. A field in a token ring (see TR) token that indicates the end of a token or data frame.

EDA – Electronic Design Automation. A collection of software tools for the development of integrated circuits and systems.

EDAC – Electronic Design Automation Consortium. An international association (http://www.edac.org) of companies involved in the development and manufacturing of the tools for electronic design automation (see EDA).

EDAC – Error Detection And Correction. A collection of methods used for error detection in transmitted or stored data and their correction. The simplest method is CRC (see CRC).

EDBT – European Database Technology. An international conference that serves as a forum for the exchange of the latest research results in data management. Topics include active databases, advanced query processing, authorization and security, constraint- and rule-management, data models, database design, data warehousing, OLAP, data mining, knowledge discovery, e-commerce, workflow, federated databases, GIS, legacy databases, OO and real-time databases, image and video databases, spatial and temporal databases, etc. The proceedings are published by Springer-Verlag (see LNCS).

EDCD – EDIFACT Composite Data Elements Directory. A subset of the UN Trade Data Elements Directory (see UNTDED).

EDED – EDIFACT Data Elements Directory. A subset of the UN Trade Data Elements Directory (see UNTDED).

EDEN – European Distance Education Network. EDEN was formally established in May 1991, following the first pan-European conference in Budapest in 1990. Its aim is to foster developments in distance education through the provision of a platform for cooperation and collaboration among a wide range of institutions, networks and individuals concerned with distance education in Europe.

EDGAR – Electronic Data Gathering, Analysis and Retrieval. A system deployed by the US Securities and Exchange Commission that performs automated data gathering, analysis and retrieval of time-sensitive corporate information (see http://www.sec.gov/eadux/wedgar.htm).

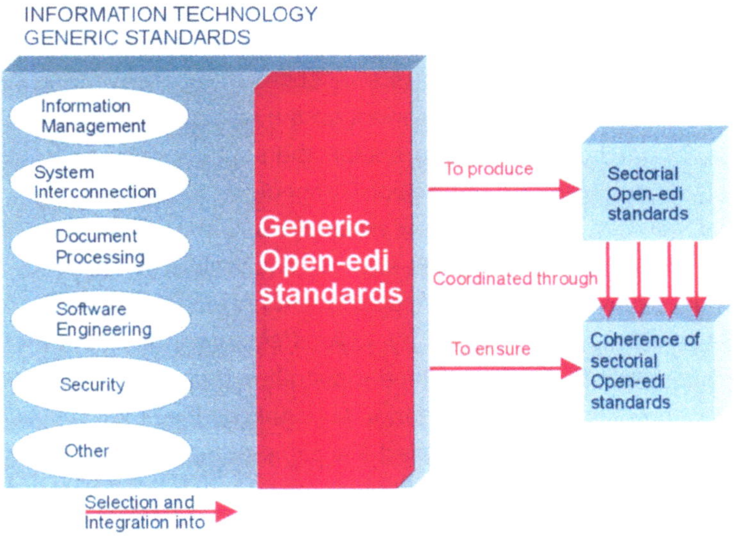

Fig. E-2. Relationships between Open-edi standardization and other standards

EDI – Electronic Data Interchange. The main aim of EDI is to eliminate redundant paperwork, delays and errors, replacing paper correspondence by electronic data interchange between business partners. EDI provides specifications for business transactions that are done electronically. EDI standards specify the type and the format of information that should be exchanged between business partners. The important move in the definition of electronic data interchange was the release of the Open-edi reference model, issued as the ISO/IEC CD 14662 document. Unlike classical EDI, in which most implementations have been successful only in long-term partnerships and among a limited number of partners, Open-edi introduced standard business scenarios and support services including business transactions that involve multiple types of data (text, images, voice and product description). The Open-edi reference model uses two views to describe the relevant aspects of business transactions, referred to as the Business Operational View (see BOV) and the Functional Service View (see FSV). The FSV focuses on the information technology aspects such as service capabilities, service interfaces and protocols including message handling, addressing, syntax, file transfer, network and data management, transaction processing, and so on. The Open-edi reference model provides the framework for coordination and integration of the existing and emerging standards and development of future standards for the interworking of organizations via Open-edi (see Fig. E-2). The sectorial Open-edi standards cover the contents and processes of the business transactions by defining Open-edi scenarios. This area is therefore dependent on the existence of the BOV-related standards. In addition, for a given sector, the sectorial Open-edi standards are closely related to other Information Technology Standards in this sector. Sectorial Open-edi standards may include existing EDI-related standards where these comply with the Open-edi reference model. Coherence of various sectorial Open-edi standards (see Fig. E-2) is ensured by harmonization of Open-edi scenarios developed by various sectors. It is done through the use of the common formalism and the registration procedures included in the generic Open-edi standards. In order to highlight the importance of EDI, many EDI promoters have often used the game of the letters in the acronym ("EDI or DIE" they say). The most active organizations in EDI standards development are the ISO (ISO9735) and ANSI X.12 committees.

EDIA – EDI Association. The oldest EDI association, founded in 1968 in the US.

EDID – Extended Display Identification Data. VESA standard data that describes basic information about a monitor and its capabilities. It includes vendor information, maximum image size, color characteristics, frequency ranges, etc. EDID information is used by the Display Data Channel (see DDC) for configuration purposes.

EDIF – Electronic Design Information Format. A framework for the definition and exchange of electronic design data, including masks, circuits and test data.

EDIFACT – EDI For Administration Commerce and Transport. A collection of internationally agreed standards, directories and guidelines for the electronic interchange of structured data, and in particular those that relate to trade in goods and services among independent computerized information systems. Recommended within the framework of the United Nations, the rules are approved and published by UN/ECE in the United Nations Trade Data Interchange Directory (see UNTDID) and are maintained under agreed procedures.

EDIN – Electronic Data Interchange Notifications. An additional mechanism used to provide message tracking in an Electronic Data Interchange connection (see EDI). EDIN is not supported by X.400, but it is supported by X.435 (see X.400 and X.435). In X.435 there are three possible EDINs. The positive EDIN is used to tell the sender that X.435 has examined the message and has determined that the receiving end should be able to process the EDI message. The negative EDIN is used to notify the sender that the EDI message couldn't be passed. The third EDIN is the forwarding EDIN that indicates that the message has been sent to another EDI user.

EDIWI – EDI World Institute. An international independent nonprofit organization created in April 1992 (http://www.ecworld.org), located in Montreal, Canada. The main goal of the institute is to address the strategic business issues in EDI implementation. The institute provides for national EDI associations an active forum for the exchange of ideas and information on such issues. The activities of the EDIWI are organized through research and implementation, information transfer, and education and training on an international basis.

EDMS – Engineering Data Management System. A crucial part of the CEDAR project at CERN (see CERN and CEDAR) that provides engineering data management for the people who need it, when they need it, regardless of the platform, vendor or distance involved (see PSI). However, an EDMS is much more than a simple data management system, it describes the equipment under development or production. That means that the EDMS is involved in the management of structures and associated engineering data in the product lifecycle, from design to implementation.

EDO – Extended Data Out. A type of dynamic RAM memory that allows faster data access than traditional DRAMs. See also DRAM.

EDOC – Enterprise Distributed Object Computing. An international IEEE conference in cooperation with ACM and OMG, focusing on distributed objects as core technologies in enterprise computing.

EDP – Electronic Data Processing. See ADP and DP.

EDSD – EDIFACT Segments Directory. A subset of the UN Trade Data Elements Directory (see UNTDED) that contains full descriptions of all the standard segments used in the United Nations Standard Message types (see UNSM).

EDT – Eastern Daylight Time. Time zone. UTC – 4.00 hours. Most of the US state of Indiana does not operate EDT – it's on EST all year round.

EDU – Education. The top-level Internet domain for educational organizations in the US and some other countries (cmu.edu, mit.edu, etc.). The equivalent domain in the UK, New Zealand, etc., is ".ac" (academic) followed by the country domain (ac.uk, ac.nz, etc.).

EDVAC – Electronic Discrete Variable Automatic Computer. The first stored-program digital computer.

EEI – External Environment Interface. The interface that supports information transfer between the application platform and the external environment. It's part of OSE and TOGAF.

EEMA – European Electronic Mail Association. A European association of developers and vendors of electronic mail products.

EEMS – Enhanced Expanded Memory Specification. A specification developed by AST, Quadram and Ashton Tate that allows a variable number of memory page frames (up to 64) as well as the storage of executable code in an expanded memory area. See also EMS.

EEPROM – Electrically Erasable Programmable ROM. Pronounced "ee-ee-prom". A nonvolatile storage device that can be erased by applying an electrical signal to one or more pins, after which it can be reprogrammed.

EER – Extended Entity-Relationship model. An extended version of the Entity-Relationship model (see ER) which includes specialization, generalization, higher-level and lower-level entity sets, attribute inheritance, and aggregation. Specialization enables an entity set to include subgroups of entities that are distinct in some way from other entities in the set. Generalization is a simple inversion of specialization that recognizes that a number of entity sets share some common features. Attribute inheritance is a crucial property of the higher-level and lower-level entities created by specialization and generalization depicting a hierarchy of entity sets. An aggregation is an abstraction through which relationships are treated as higher-level entities.

EET – Eastern European Time. Time zone. UTC + 2.00 hours. See TZ.

EEST – Eastern European Summer Time. Time zone. UTC + 3.00 hours.

EFCI – Explicit Forward Congestion Indicator. In ATM networks, an indication in an ATM cell header.

EFF – Electronic Frontier Foundation. A nonprofit advocacy organization of public interest (http://www.eff.org) established to address the social and legal aspects of computer communication issues. Mitchell Kapor and John Perry Barlow founded EFF in 1990. See also Communications Decency Act (CDA).

EFIS – Engineering Federated Information Systems. An international workshop focusing on the development of Federated Information Systems.

e-form – electronic form. An online document that contains blank spaces for a user to fill in with requested information and that can be submitted through a network to the organization or person requesting the information. Figure E-3 depicts an example of an e-form. An Internet user connected to an Internet service provider is required to fill out a given form if he/she wants to see, for example, the status of his/her account. On the Web, e-forms are often coded in CGI and secured via encryption. See also CGI (Common Gateway Interface).

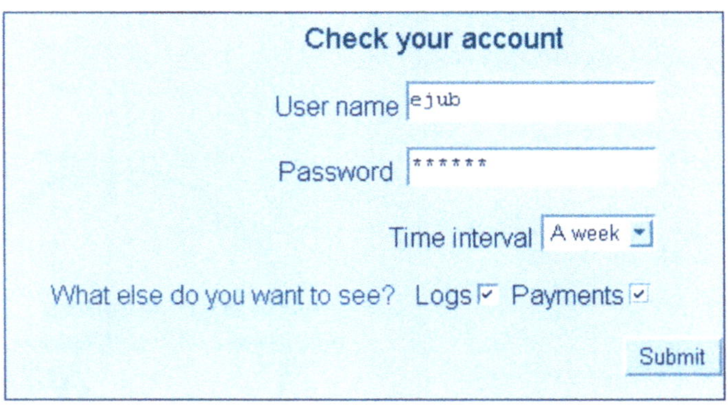

Fig. E-3. An e-form issued by an Internet service provider

EFS – Error-Free Seconds. A measurement unit used to specify the error performance of T carrier systems (see T), usually expressed as EFS per hour, day or week.

EFTPOS – Electronic Fund Transfer Point Of Sale. A well-known widely implemented electronic fund transfer system (see EFTS) based on point-of-sale terminals (see POS). Customers identify themselves and their accounts using personal identification numbers (see PIN), at the same time accepting the particular bill they have incurred, usually in a retail store. The bill amount is then electronically transferred from the customer's bank account to the account of the retail store.

EFTPS – Electronic Federal Tax Payment System. An electronic tax collection system developed and deployed in the US.

EFTS – Electronic Fund Transfer System. In general, a distributed system used to automatically transfer money between individuals or companies. It allows transfer of funds from the bank account of one person or organization to that of another. EFTS is also used to refer to the act of using this technology. It is an important addition to the organization that implements EDI. See also Electronic Data Interchange (EDI).

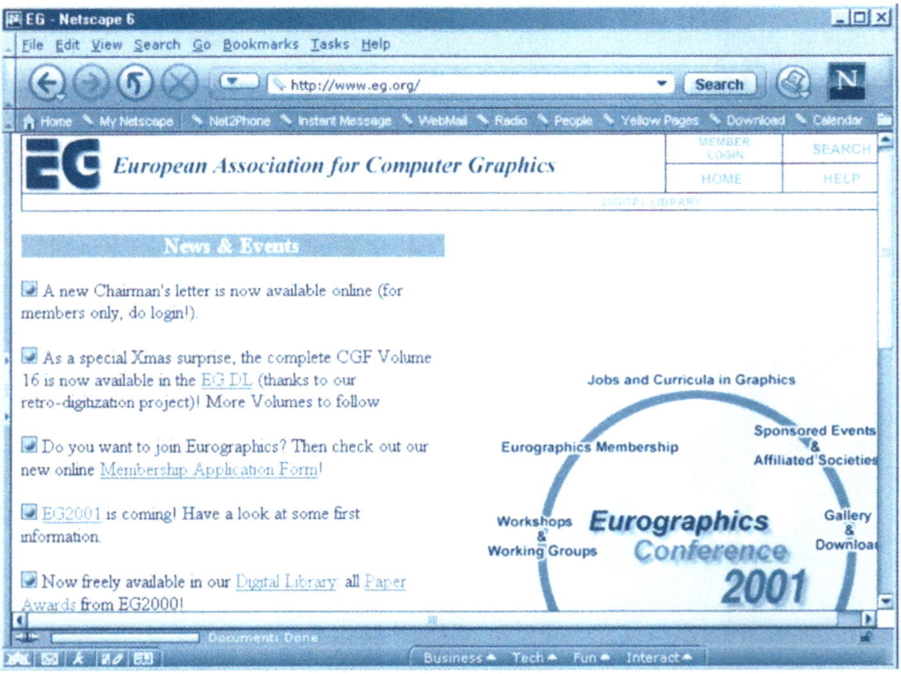

Fig. E-4. Eurographics homepage
(with the permission of Eurographics)

EG – Eurographics. A European association (http://www.eg.org) for computer graphics. Every year EG organizes an annual conference with the same name as well as several workshops. Also published by EG is the Computer Graphics Forum (see CGF). See Fig. E-4.

EGA – Enhanced Graphics Adapter. A video graphics adapter implemented by IBM in 1984 with a resolution of 640 horizontal pixels by 350 vertical pixels. It supports 16 colors chosen from a palette of 64 colors.

EGP – Exterior Gateway Protocol. A class of protocols used for communications between autonomous systems (see AS). Also, the specific Internet protocol (RFC904) used with a two-level routing algorithm to route an IP-based message between autonomous systems across the Internet. It has been replaced by the Border Gateway Protocol (see BGP).

EHF – Extremely High Frequency. Transmission frequencies between 30 GHz and 300 GHz.

EHLLAPI – Extended High-Level Language Application Programming Interface. An Application Programming Interface (see API) from IBM used to develop IBM 3270-based applications with the ability to integrate current applications development with earlier 3270 applications.

EIA – Electronic Industries Alliance. A Washington DC-based industrial organization (http://www.eia.org) notable for developing the group of RS standards including the well-known RS-232 and RS-422. There are also several joint standards which the EIA produced in close association with the Telecommunications Industry Association (see TIA), usually recognizable by the EIA/TIA prefix. An example is the standard for UTP cabling (EIA/TIA 568).

EIB – Enterprise Information Base. The information base containing management and performance information about the enterprise network. Such information is then used for network monitoring and management.

EICAR – European Institute for Computer Antivirus Research. A European organization (http://www.eicar.org) that works against the creation and delivery of malicious code, computer crime, misuse of computers and networks, malicious exploitation of personnel data, etc. EICAR organizes a conference of the same name.

EIDE – Extended Integrated Drive Electronics. An improved version of a disk controller with faster data rates, 32-bit transactions and, sometimes with DMA, EIDE accommodates drives as large as 8.4 GB. It is also referred to as Fast ATA-2. EIDE drives are cheaper than SCSI drives and provide much of the same functionality. See also IDE. Compare with SCSI.

EIS – Enterprise Information System. A common name for a modern business information system (see BIS) that is capable of delivering a wide variety of services to a broad range of users (customers, partners, employees, suppliers, etc.). Such services must be:

- Readily available, to meet the needs of today's global business environment; see Open-edi in the Electronic Data Interchange (EDI) definition.

- Secure, to protect the privacy of users and the integrity of enterprise data.
- Reliable and scalable, to ensure that business transactions are accurately and promptly processed.

In most cases, these services are developed as multitier applications (see Fig. E-5). The middle-tier of these applications is where the majority of the application development work is done. The middle-tier implements new services that integrate existing EISs with the business functions and data of the new service. The middle-tier shields first-tier clients from the complexity of the enterprise and takes advantage of rapidly maturing Internet technologies to minimize user administration and training. However, multitier applications are hard to design. They require bringing together a variety of skill-sets and resources, legacy data and legacy code.

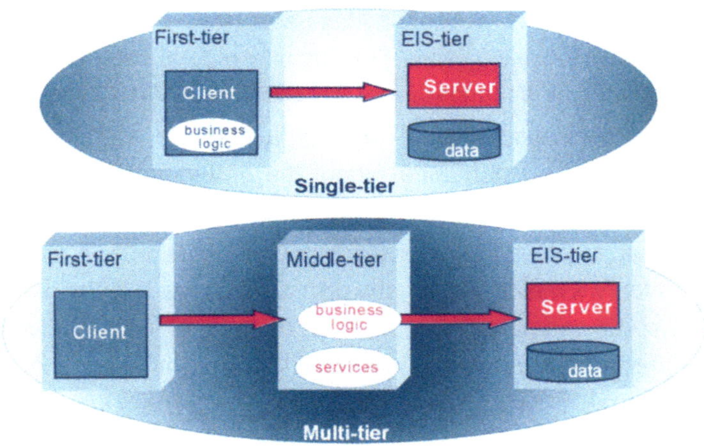

Fig. E-5. Single-tier versus multitier in EISs

In today's heterogeneous environment, enterprise applications have to integrate services from a variety of vendors with a diverse set of application models and other standards. Industry experience shows that integrating these resources can take up to 50% of the application development time. In the case of solving the Millennium Bug in legacy systems at the same time (see Y2K), the above percentage was significantly higher. In that case the better solution for designing new EISs was to proceed step-by-step. That meant the migration of legacy systems (programs and data) into an open environment, solving the Y2K problem, and then adjusting it for a new architecture. If legacy systems are based on old COBOL (which is usually the case) one of the best ways is to use ACUCOBOL or similar tools (see COBOL). See also Enterprise Java Beans (EJB) and Java 2 Enterprise Edition (J2EE).

EIS – Executive Information Systems. Another term used for Decision Support Systems (see DSS). Today executive information systems are usually integrated in an Enterprise Information System (see EIS, first definition).

EISA – Extended Industry Standard Architecture. A bus standard (pronounced "ee-sa") for IBM PC compatibles introduced in 1988 by "The Gang of Nine" consortium (AST Research, Compaq, Epson, HP, NEC, Olivetti, Tandy, Wyse and Zenith). It extends the Industry Standard Architecture (see ISA) bus to 32 bits and allows multiple CPU sharing as well as access to 4 GB of memory. Compare with ISA, MCA, PCI and VESA.

EJB – Enterprise JavaBeans. An architecture and set of interfaces specified by Sun Microsystems intended for developing and deploying distributed Java applications based on a multitier architecture. Such applications are typically open (see PSI), transactional, multiuser, database-oriented and secured. The EJB specification consists of two parts, describing the EJB server, in fact the necessary runtime environment, and some kind of programmer's guide explaining how an enterprise bean (see EB) should be developed, deployed and used. The interface between an EB and the EJB server is realized using an architectural component called a "container", generated using the tools associated with the EJB server. The role of such a "container" is to provide EB instances with lifecycles and persistence, and to interact with the transaction and security services. It is important to recognize the advantage of the EJB overall architecture where the client does not see any data access operation being used on the server side. This facility of EJB is enabled by the so-called persistence management. EJB components allow service developers to concentrate on the business logic and let the EJB server handle the complexities of delivering a reliable, scalable service.

EJNDP – Electronic Journal of Networks and Distributed Processing. An online journal that covers the broad range of topics related to computer networks and distributed processing.

EJO – Electronic Journals Online. A service offered by the Online Computer Library Center (see OCLC).

ELAN – Emulated LAN. An ATM network in which an Ethernet or Token Ring LAN is emulated using a client/server model. Multiple ELANs can exist simultaneously on a single ATM network. ELANs are defined by the LAN Emulation specification (see LANE).

ELAP – EtherTalk Link Access Protocol. The data-link layer protocol in the AppleTalk Ethernet networks.

ELF – Executable and Linking Format. An effort made by the Tool Interface Standards Committee (see TIS) to standardize the software interfaces (see ABI) visible to development tools for 32-bit Intel operating environments. ELF is a portable object file format that works in such environments for a variety of operating systems.

ELF – Extremely Low Frequency. Transmission frequencies between 0 kHz and 3 kHz.

Elisp – Emacs lisp. A language used to extend the Emacs editor (see Emacs).

EMA – Electronic Messaging Association. An association devoted to work on standardization of and education on electronic messaging systems such as e-mail, fax, voicemail, etc.

EMA – Enterprise Management Architecture. The network management architecture developed by DEC based on OSI network management (see CMIP).

Emacs – Editing Macros. An extensible and self-documented screen editor used with UNIX, VMS and other operating systems.

e-mail – electronic mail. A system for transmission of messages over a communication network. It is a computer-to-computer (or terminal-to-terminal) version of the postal service. Ray Tomlinson invented the system in 1972. Now, electronic mail is still the most used and beneficial feature of the Internet. Delivered messages are stored in electronic mailboxes assigned to users on the network (by a unique address username@destination-computer, e.g. eja@bankerinter.net, or by a company e-mail softis@bankerinter.net). They can be viewed, saved or deleted by the recipient. As a result of the widespread use of e-mail several standards for interoperability were developed, such as X.400 MHS, Simple Mail Transfer Protocol for IP (see SMTP), and Multipurpose Internet Mail Extensions (see MIME). As e-mail becomes increasingly popular in electronic commerce (see EC), and generally in EDI, the need to keep the content of e-mail messages hidden from unauthorized eyes also appears as an essential goal. Examples of such standards are Privacy-Enhanced Mail (see PEM) and Pretty Good Privacy (see PGP).

EMC – Electromagnetic Compatibility. CEN's EMC directive aims to reduce interference between electrical devices by reducing electromagnetic radiation and improving immunity. See CEN.

EMF – Enhanced Windows Metafile. A filename extension for a file that contains an enhanced Windows metafile.

EMF – Enterprise Modeling Framework. A research project for exploring enterprise integration technologies. The EMF consists of a methodology for modeling three major facets of an enterprise, function, information and dynamics, as well as the software tools for modeling the methodology.

EMI – Electromagnetic Interference. Unwanted electrical noise created by some kinds of electromagnetic sources, such as electric motors, fluorescent lights, production machines, etc. EMI affects the quality of the signal passing through a data transmission medium, reducing data integrity and increasing error rates.

EML – Element Management Layer. An abstraction of the functions provided by systems that manage each network element on an individual basis.

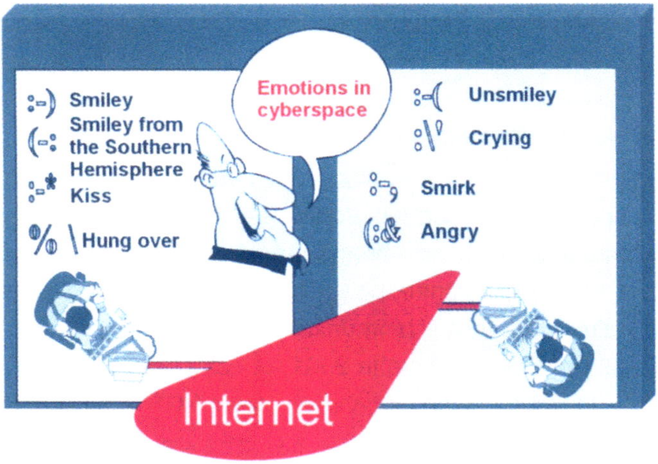

Fig. E-6. Examples of emoticons

EMM386 – Expanded Memory Manager 386. An expanded memory manager (see EMS) for IBM-compatible PCs with the Intel 80386 or higher processor. The EMM386 software is loaded into the CONFIG.SYS file by MS-DOS versions (release 5.00).

EMO – Evolutionary Multi-Criterion Optimization. An international conference that serves as a forum for the exchange of the latest research results in the field of evolutionary multicriterion optimization. The proceedings are published by Springer-Verlag (see LNCS).

e-money – electronic money. A generic name for the exchange of money through the Internet. Also called cybercash, digicash, digital cash or e-cash.

emoticons – emotional icons. A common name for a set of special icons either produced by a keyboard or imported from an image file used in e-mail messages or chat sessions in order to express the current emotion of the sender. Some emoticons are depicted in Fig. E-6. A good collection of emoticons is available at the website http://www.computeruser.com

EMS – Electronic Messaging System. An electronic mail system that incorporates an additional feature whereby the central facility assumes active responsibility for delivering the message to the intended address. It is quite different from the passive role of an electronic mail system, which merely delivers messages in response to a request by an addressee.

EMS – Element Management System. A management system that provides functions at the Element Management Layer (see EML).

EMS – Expanded Memory Specification. A specification for a memory paging scheme, also known as LIM EMS after the initials of the Lotus/Intel/Microsoft group which developed this technique. It enables access to memory beyond the conventional 640 KB memory in real mode.

EMSOFT – Embedded Software. A workshop that serves as a forum for discussing all aspects of embedded software. The topics include operating systems and middleware, programming languages and compilers, modeling and validation, software engineering, programming methodologies, scheduling, execution time analyses, communication protocols, and fault tolerance, etc. The first conference was held in 2001, at Lake Tahoe, CA, US. The proceedings are published by Springer-Verlag (see LNCS).

ENCINA – Enterprise Computing in a New Age. The software product line from Transarc Corporation, which provides an easy-to-use transaction processing environment for open systems, client/server systems, and a distributed computing environment.

ENIAC – Electronic Numerical Integrator And Calculator (Computer). The first digital computer based on 18,000 vacuum tubes and 6000 manual switches, developed in 1946 at the University of Pennsylvania by John Presper Eckert and John William Mauchly. It was in operation for almost 10 years. With a weight of 30 tons it was and is the mastodon of computing.

ENQ – Enquiry Character. A communication control code (05 HEX) used by a sender to assign a request, a response from the receiving device, or to ask for identification.

ENTCS – Electronic Notes in Theoretical Computer Science. An e-journal published by Elsevier Science (http://www.elsevier.nl/locate/entcs).

env – environment. UNIX command used to set up an environment for command execution.

EOF – End-Of-File. The mark code (1A HEX) residing at the end of a particular file telling the operating system that no additional data follows.

EOL – End-Of-Line. The traditional synonym for a new line, even though different systems use different characters, or combinations of them, to mark the end of a line.

EoN – Edge of Network. An initiative from IBM offering four new attributes for devices used in e-business and e-commerce (see EC). These attributes are end-use optimization, e-business readiness, e-lifestyle coordination, and effortless use.

EOR – End-Of-Record. A control character that marks the physical end of a record on a magnetic tape.

EOT – End-Of-Tape. A control character that marks the end of a tape or the end of a written tape.

EOT – End-Of-Transmission. The transmission control character (04 HEX) that marks the end of a communication session.

EPA – Environmental Protection Agency. The US agency (http://www.epa.gov) with the mission of protecting humans and the natural environment they live and work in.

EPC – Enterprise Process Continuum. The process model that includes a portfolio of processes, techniques and tools that support an enterprise's software delivery practice.

EPD – Early Packet Discard. A congestion control technique, proposed by S. Floyd and A. Romanow, for use in a classical IP over ATM (RFC1483 and 1577). When congestion occurs, EPD discards cells at the beginning of an IP packet, leaving the others intact. The last cell is preserved because it alerts the switch and the destination station to the beginning of a new packet. Since IP packets, from which cells have been discarded, receive no acknowledgment from the destination, they are automatically retransmitted. EPD is very useful when ATM networks carry data units that are many cells long, because a single lost cell could cause retransmission of the whole data frame, which would cause more and more congestion. Thus EPD prevents fragment of packets from consuming resources and contributing to further congestion.

EPHOS – European Procurement Handbook for Open Systems. The set of handbooks that serves as a procurement guide for the components of open systems. Each module has two parts. The first part contains only information considered of vital importance to the procurer and the basic information is easy to find and use. The second part contains more detailed relevant guidance, explanations, tutorials, etc.

EPIC – Electronic Privacy Information Center. A research center in Washington, DC, established in 1994 (http://www.epic.org) to focus public attention on emerging Netizens liberty issues, such as free speech, protection of the US 1st Amendment, etc. It is also a member of the Global Internet Liberty Campaign (see GILC). See also Communications Decency Act (CDA).

EPIC – Explicitly Parallel Instruction Computing. An architecture jointly developed by Intel and HP intended to be the foundation for the new 64-bit instruction set architecture.

EPOQUE – European Parliament Online Query System. A database of debates, reports and questions in the European Parliament.

EPP – Enhanced Parallel Port. A port dedicated to peripheral devices, commonly used for printers, external disk drives, or tape drives. Data and communications control lines are wired in parallel; each data line corresponds to 1 data bit. Data is transferred across all lines in a synchronous way. Initially developed by Intel, today EPP is one of the IEEE1284 standards. Compare with ESP.

EPROM – Erasable Programmable Read-Only Memory. A type of nonvolatile memory chip (pronounced “ee-prom”) that can be programmed several times after manufacture. Such chips can be erased by removing a protective cover from the top of the chip package and then applying ultraviolet light to the chip's surface through a quartz window. That allows the chip to be programmed once again. If many changes are expected to be required for a program stored in memory, for example, EPROMs can be more cost effective than PROMs even though they are more expensive. See also Programmable Read-Only Memory (PROM).

EPS – Encapsulated PostScript. An Adobe Systems extension of the PostScript file format that allows PostScript files to be included into other documents as independent entities. Many high-quality clip-art packages consist of such images. See also PS, PostScript.

EPSF – Encapsulated PostScript File. See Encapsulated PostScript (EPS).

EQ – Equal to. An acronym very often used in programming languages as a relational operator in logical expressions. For example:

```
if a EQ b then
    a=a+1
else
    b=b-1
endif
```

If the value of a is equal to that of b, the logical expression is true, therefore the "a=a+1" is executed, otherwise the statement "b=b-1" is executed. See also NE, LE, LT, GE and GT.

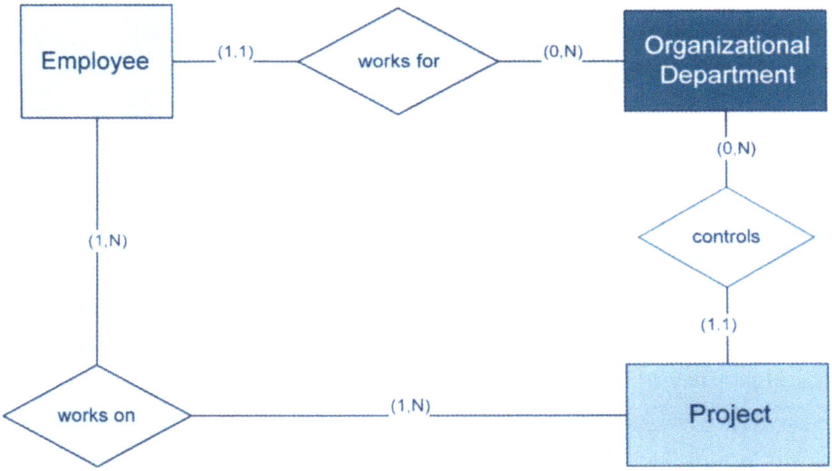

Fig. E-7. An example of an E-R diagram

E-R – Entity-Relationship model. A widely used data model developed by Peter Chen at MIT in 1975 and described in an ACM Transactions on Database Systems article entitled "The Entity-Relationship Model: Toward a Unified View of Data". It describes relationships (1:1, 1:M, M:N) among entities at the conceptual level using E-R diagrams which depict the three main components of the E-R model: entities, attributes and relationships. An entity is a "thing" or "object" in the real world that is distinguishable from other objects. They are described in a database by a set of attributes. E-R models also represent certain constraints to which the contents of databases must conform such as mapping cardinalities expressing the number of entities to which another entity can be associated via a relationship set. Also abbreviated as ER.

ER – Explicit Rate. An ATM RM cell field used to limit the source Actual Cell Rate (see ACR) to a specific value. See also ATM, RM and QoS.

ERA – Electronic Research Administration. A set of tools and systems that enables electronic reporting and submission of grant and contract information in research.

ERD – Entity-Relationship Diagram. A diagram that depicts E-R entities, attributes and relations. It also shows connectivities and cardinalities (Fig. E-7).

ERDM – Extended Relational Data Model. A data model based on the relational model with support for extensibility, complex objects, inheritance, procedure calls, and system-generated surrogates.

ERIC – Educational Resources Information Center. A common name for a number of websites that offer information relating to education. To be clear on what ERIC sites offer, three of them are listed below:

- http://www.indiana.edu/~eric_rec. Clearinghouse on reading, English, and communications. This site provides educational materials, services and coursework information to anyone interested in the language arts. Operated by the Smith Research Center at Indiana University in Bloomington, Indiana.
- http://gseis.ucla.edu/ERIC/eric.html. Provides free online searches of their database on community colleges and related topics. Maintained by the University of California, Los Angeles.
- http://www.ces.sped.org/ericec.htm. ERIC clearinghouse on counseling and student services. This site serves anyone with an interest in counseling and student services, including school social work, family counseling, career counseling, and student development.

ERLL – Enhanced Run-Length Limited. See ARLL and RLL.

ERP – Enterprise Resource Planning. The new generation of manufacturing resource planning (see MRPII) software. ERP's usefulness and power lie beyond the present function boundaries of MRPII. Beyond the standard functionality that is offered, other features are included, e.g. quality process operations management, and regulatory reporting. In addition, the base technology used in ERP will give users software and hardware independence as well as an easy upgrading path.

ERR – Error file. A filename extension for a file that contains Visual FoxPro compilation errors.

ES – End System. A common term for an end-user device on a network. In OSI terminology, this is a nonrouting host or node (see OSI).

ESA – European Symposium on Algorithms. An international symposium that focuses on all areas of algorithm research. Some of the main topics include approximation algorithms, combinational optimization, computational biology, databases and information retrieval, graph- and network algorithms, parallel and distributed computing, pattern matching, data compression, etc. The proceedings are published by Springer-Verlag (see LNCS).

ESC – Escape. A term used with different meanings: the character, the sequence, the code or the key. The ESC character represents one of the 32 ASCII control codes (1B HEX) used for event identification. It usually indicates the beginning of an ESC sequence, i.e. a string of characters that gives instructions to a device (such as a printer or a terminal). The ESC code represents a character or sequence of characters that indicates that the following character in a data stream is not to be processed in the ordinary way. Finally, the ESC key on the computer keyboard sends the ESC character to the computer.

ESCD – Extended System Configuration Data. A format for storing information about Plug-and-Play devices in the BIOS.

ESCON – Enterprise Systems Connectivity. An IBM optical fiber connection between a mainframe and its peripherals with a 200-Mbps data rate. ESCON uses a LED as the light source, sending signals at a wavelength of approximately 1325 nm with a 4B/8B encoding scheme.

ESD – Electronic Software Distribution. A means of directly distributing software to users online over the Internet or over leased lines. ESD systems provide secure communications that customers use to download and pay for software.

ESD – Electrostatic Discharge. The discharge of stored static electricity that can damage electronic equipment.

ESDI – Enhanced Small Device Interface. A standard that allows high-capacity hard disks, floppy disk drives and tape drives to communicate with processors at a high speed (10 Mbps). Due to its speed and density, ESDI is used in both personal computers and mid-range systems. Compare with IDE and SCSI.

ESI – End System Identifier. Usually an IEEE802 address.

ESIOP – Environment-Specific Inter-ORB Protocols. A part of the Common Object Request Broker (see CORBA) specification that defines an open-ended set of environment-specific protocols that would be used for interoperation among ORBs at user sites where a particular networking or distributed infrastructure is already in general use.

ES–IS – End System to Intermediate System. An Open Systems Interconnection (see OSI) protocol by which end systems (see ES) announce themselves to intermediate systems (see IS).

ESN – Electronic Switched Network. A telecommunication service that allows automatic switching between PBXs in a private network. See also PBX.

ESN – Equipment Serial Number. A number assigned by the manufacturer to equipment in order to keep track of equipment status at the customer site. The coding strategy is vendor-dependent, but is usually compliant with certain bar code specifications.

ESOP – European Symposium on Programming. An annual conference devoted to the design, specification and analysis of programming languages and programming systems. The topics include advanced-type systems, program analysis, program transformation and specialization, domain-specific languages, programming paradigms (OO, RP, AOP, logic, etc.), programming language solutions to practical issues in security, safety, real-time and embedded computing, etc. The proceedings are published by Springer-Verlag (see LNCS).

ESP – Enhanced Serial Port. A port dedicated to peripheral devices, commonly used for mice and external modems. Data transfer occurs as a sequence of bits and bytes on a pair of lines, either synchronously or asynchronously. See also UART. Compare with EPP.

ESPRIT – European Strategic Programme for Research and Development in Information Technology. A set of European projects funding information technology developments and their applications in the European Union.

EST – Eastern Standard Time. Time zone. UTC – 5.00 hours. See TZ.

e-tailing – electronic retailing. Yet another familiar old term (retailing) combined with the possibilities of cyberspace. In short, e-tailing is the selling of retail goods on the Internet. See also EC.

ETAPS – European Joint Conference on Theory and Practice of Software. An open confederation of conferences and other events in Europe that focus on software science. Some of the major ETAPS conference proceedings are published by Springer-Verlag (see LNCS).

ETEC – Emerging Trends in Electronic Commerce. An international conference focusing on the issues of Internet-based business.

e-text – electronic text. A book or other text-based work that is available online in an electronic format that can be read online or downloaded to a user's computer for offline reading.

ETR – Early Token Release. A frame used in 16-Mbps token ring networks (see TR) that allows multiple packets to be moving in the ring at any tome.

ETSI – European Telecommunication Standards Institute. The organization founded by the European PTTs and the European Union to propose telecommunication standards for Europe (http://www.ets.fr).

ETX – End-of-Text. A control character (03 HEX) used to indicate that there is nothing else to transmit in terms of a useful message. Also, a message followed by the EOT character indicates that the receiver has just received an error-free message.

EU – End-User. A term used very often but with several meanings. As a business term used by vendors, it usually refers to a company that uses some hardware and/or software products from that vendor. From the technical point of view the term end-user usually denotes a person who works with particular hardware or software.

EULA – End-User License Agreement. A document representing the legal contract between a software manufacturer and its customer in order to restrict software use, distribution or resale.

EUnet – European Internet. A European commercial Internet service provider. Regional EUnet providers are distinguished from each other by a country code (see DNS).

EUP – End-User Price. A business term used to denote the price of some equipment applicable to end-users (see EU). Compare with transfer price (see TP).

EURECA – European Research Coordination Agency. An agency within the European Union responsible for sponsoring projects within the European Program for High Technology Research and Development, which also incorporates other countries. Also known as EUREKA.

EUROCAST – European Conference on Computer-Aided System Theory. An international conference focusing on formal methods and tools for computer science. The proceedings are published by Springer-Verlag (see LNCS).

EUUG – European UNIX User Group. A European association interested in UNIX development.

EVL – Electronic Visualization Laboratory. The research laboratory at the University of Illinois at Chicago (http://www.evl.uic.edu) which focuses on visualization in teleimmersive environments (see CAVE).

EWAN – Emulator Without A good Name. A Telnet and terminal emulator for personal computers running with Microsoft Windows.

EWOS – European Workshop for Open Systems. An independent standardization body in Europe (http://www.ewos.be) that is principally concerned with functional profiles, i.e. with the development of subsets of open systems standards for particular functions. While profiles are fully international standards, the route to a standard is very much simpler than for other standards and is similar to the fast-track procedure in ISO, missing out the CD stage. It is also closely linked to other regional organizations with the same goals. Such organizations include AOW and OIW.

EWSPT – European Workshop on Software Process Technology. A European workshop that covers software process technology and the practical applications of this technology. The proceedings are published by Springer-Verlag (see LNCS).

EXE – Executable Program. An acronym, related to several operating systems methods, assigned to an executable code unit, sometimes used as a filename extension (.exe).

EXE2BIN – Executable to (2) Binary. A program used to convert an executable file (.EXE) to a binary format (.COM) file under the MS-DOS environment.

EXUG – European X User Group. A European user group interested in X Window System development and its implementation.

e-zine – electronic magazine. A regular publication distributed in digital form, usually via the World-Wide Web or on CDs. Examples include ACM SIGMOD DiSC and Elsevier Science ENTCS.

F

F – Farad. The measurement unit of electrical capacitance. A 1-Farad capacitor holds a charge of 1 Coulomb with a potential difference of 1 Volt between its plates. In practice, due to the huge charge represented by 1 farad, electrical capacitance is usually expressed in μF (10^{-6} F) and pF (10^{-12} F).

F – FORTRAN file. A filename for files that contain FORTRAN code.

F

F2F – Face-to (2)-face. The chat term.

F77 – FORTRAN 77 file. An extension for files that contain FORTRAN 77 code.

F90 – FORTRAN 90 file. An extension for files that contain FORTRAN 90 code.

FAC – Formal Aspects of Computing. The journal related to the formal aspects of computing, published by Springer-Verlag.

FADU – File Access Data Unit. A packet in OSI FTAM that contains information about accessing a directory tree in the file system. See also FTAM.

FAQ – Frequently Asked Questions. This is a common name for the documents that are maintained on the Web containing frequently asked questions and answers about selected topics. The main purpose of this service is to reduce traffic over the network due to the tendency of new users to ask the same questions repeatedly. Such FAQ pages are typically posted once or twice in a month.

FARNET – Federation of American Research Networks. An organization established in 1987 (http://www.farnet.org) acting as an executive forum for the exchange of information about the Internet and its applications and services.

FAT – File Allocation Table. A table (pronounced "fat") maintained by some operating systems to keep track of various segments of disk space used for file storage. It allows the operating system to know where available disk storage space is, as well as to connect scattered pieces of a particular file. A second copy of the FAT is also maintained in order to prevent a fatal crash of the file system. See also VFAT.

favicon – favorite icon. A customized image (pronounced "fav-eye-con") in Microsoft Internet Explorer (≥ 5.0) used as the navigation tool to go with a user-specified bookmark site. A free online favicon editor allows advanced webmasters to create their own favicons and use them during website development or maintenance (http://www.favicon.com).

FAX – Facsimile. The transmission of digitized text and/or graphics over telephone lines. Also, a filename extension of the file that contains a facsimile. The ITU-T has formulated a fax format and appropriate communications standards in the form of four groups as follows:

- Group 1, 100 dpi resolution, 6 min per page, FM;
- Group 2, 100 dpi resolution, 2–3 min per page, FM, AM;
- Group 3, 200 dpi resolution, QAM;
- Group 4, 200/400 dpi resolution.

FC – Feedback Control. A common name for the set of actions taken by the network and by the end-systems (see ES) to regulate the traffic on ATM networks.

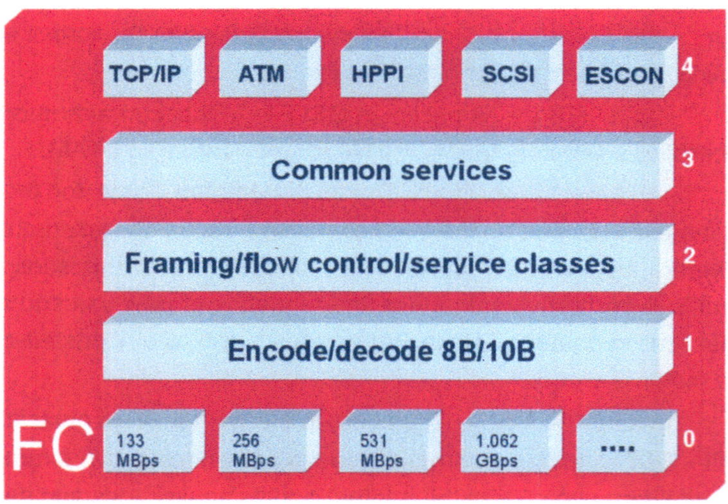

Fig. F-1. The five Fiber Channel layers

FC – Fiber Channel. Fiber Channel is an option for multivendor and multiprotocol-switched networks. Thanks to its five-layer OSI-like stack (see Fig. F-1), this technology runs on a wide range of data rates, from 100 MBps to 1000 MBps. It provides multiple classes of service to support different network applications and data types, including isochronous multimedia traffic. The five layers define physical media and transmission rates (FC-0), data encoding and decoding (FC-1), framing protocols and flow control (FC-2), common services (FC-3), and, finally, upper-layer protocols and application interfaces (FC-4). Frame sizes typically range from 36 bytes to 2 Kbytes. The FC frame is divided into five fields: Start-of-Frame (SOF), Frame Header, Data Field, CRC, and End-of-Frame (EOF). The amount of data volume for transmission is not dependent on the frame size. Thus, this makes the Fiber Channel very efficient for high-volume data transfers. A unique feature of the Fiber Channel is its four classes of FC-2 service. This allows it to satisfy a variety of communications needs, such as dedicated uninterruptible links, or guarantee delivery with receipt, and so on.

FC-AL – Fiber Channel-Arbitrated Loop. A SCSI-compatible fast serial bus interface offering a minimum base speed of 100 Mbps.

FCB – File Control Block. A memory block temporarily created by an operating system to hold information about a file that has been opened for use. An FCB typically contains some kind of file identification, its location on disk, last application position in a file, etc. After the file has been closed, the operating system releases the assigned memory block.

FCC – Federal Communications Commission. The US government organization (http://www.fcc.gov) which allocates the spectrum for AM and FM radio, television and cellular phones, as well as for special users.

FCIF – Full Common Intermediate Format. The video format (352×288) used in video teleconferencing.

FCS – Fiber-Channel Standard. A standard developed by ANSI X3T9.3 committees in order to specify Fiber-Channel architecture, physical media, packet encoding and framing, etc. See Fiber Channel (FC).

FCS – Frame Check Sequence. A common term given to the additional bits at the end of a transmitted message generated by the source and used as an error detection key at the destination side (for example, see FR and HDLC). See also EDAC.

FCS – First Customer Shipment. A business term used for the date when a new product is going to be delivered (or was delivered) to a customer for the first time.

FD – Floppy Disk. A data storage medium consisting of a round flat piece of Mylar coated with ferric oxide and protected by a plastic cover. Floppy disks (or just floppies) are usually made in sizes of 3.5" and 5.25", where the dimensions in inches represent their diameter lengths, and several capacities.

FDBMS – Federated Database Management System. Software that provides controlled and coordinated manipulation of component DBMSs in a Federated Database System (see FDBS). The key ideas of FDBMS and FDBS are shown in Fig. F-2.

FDBS – Federated Database System. A collection of cooperating, but autonomous database systems. An FDBS consists of a number of DB systems that are autonomous and yet participate in a federation allowing partial and controlled sharing of their data. FDBS represents a compromise between no integration (in which the users have to explicitly interface with multiple autonomous databases) and total integration (in which the autonomy of each component DB is sacrificed so that it can access data through a single global interface but cannot directly access a DBMS as a local user).

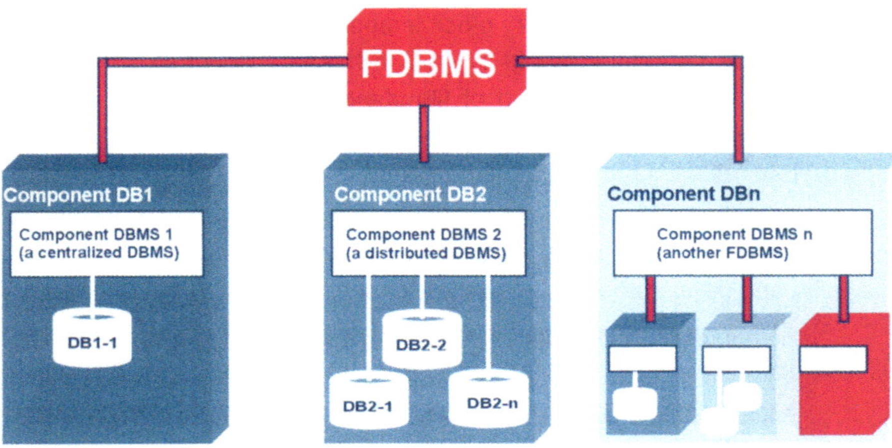

Fig. F-2. An FDBMS and its components

FDC – Floppy Disk Controller. A chip responsible for controlling a floppy disk drive (see FDD).

FDD – Floppy Disk Drive. An electromechanical device that writes data to or reads data from floppy disks.

FDDI – Fiber Distributed Data Interface. The standardized (ISO9314) high-performance fiber optic token ring LAN running at 100 Mbps over distances up to 200 km. The key idea of FDDI is based on dark fiber where the data carrier, instead of the current or voltage, is the binary amplitude-modulated light. The key feature of this approach is total internal reflection on the communication highway. The FDDI cabling consists of two fiber rings, one transmitting clockwise and the other transmitting counterclockwise. Should one of them break, the other can be used as a backup. The basic FDDI protocols are similar to the usual token ring protocols. A station first captures the token and then transmits a frame (see Fig. F-3 for the FDDI frame format) and removes it when it comes around again. The start delimiter (SD) and end delimiter (ED) mark the frame boundary fields. The frame control field (FC) tells us what kind of frame this is (data, control, etc.). The frame status field (FS) holds the acknowledgment data.

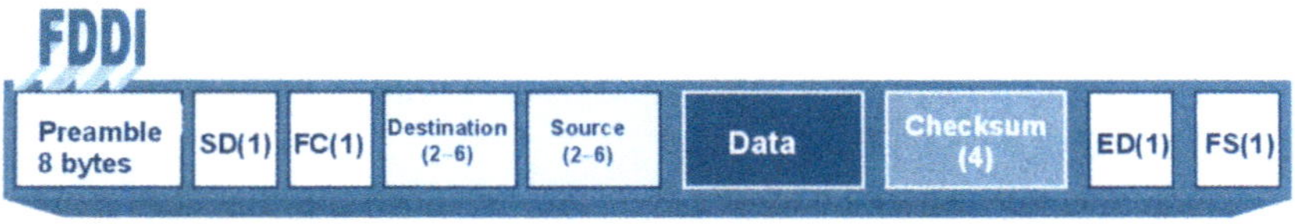

Fig. F-3. FDDI frame format

The FDDI standard has four layers: PMD, PHY, MAC and SMT, each of which describes a different facet of the FDDI architecture and each of which is explained elsewhere in the book (see PMD, PHY, MAC and SMT). FDDI is intended for a backbone of local metropolitan networks (see MAN) with a distance of over 100 km. FDDI overcomes two major LAN limitations, the speed and the distance. In addition to a regular asynchronous frame, FDDI also permits special synchronous frames for circuit-switched PCM or ISDN data. In summary, an FDDI network has the following characteristics:

- communications speeds up to 100 Mbps;
- singlemode or multimode fiber optic cabling is allowed;
- token-passing is the media access method;
- FDDI deploys a ring network topology;
- light, instead of electricity, is the only source of signaling;
- uses a 4B/5B encoding scheme;
- supports a 100-km-wide network area and nodes up to 2 km apart;
- supports hybrid networking, etc.

In addition to the original FDDI specification described above there are several variations, known as FDDI-II (real-time multimedia communications) and FFOL. See also CDDI, ESCON, FC, FCS, FO, SDH and SONET.

FDF – Forms Document File. A filename extension for files that contain Adobe Acrobat forms.

FDISK – Format Disk. A utility provided by MS-DOS and Microsoft Windows for preparing a hard disk drive to hold data and to logically partition the disk.

FDM – Frequency Division Multiplexing. A technique of loading multiple transmission signals onto distinct bands of a single bandwidth so that all signals can be carried simultaneously. Each user has exclusive possession of some frequency band.

FDMA – Frequency Division Multiple Access. A technique for assigning multiple channels within a large bandwidth. For example, FDMA is used by the existing cellular systems by dividing the total band allocated to a cellular operator (25 MHz) into discrete channels each of 30 kHz bandwidth. Compare with CDMA and TDMA.

FDSE – Full-Duplex Switched Ethernet. A kind of Ethernet link which allows data transmission in both directions simultaneously with double transmission capacity, i.e. changed from the usual 10 Mbps to 20 Mbps. See also FDX.

FDT – Formal Description Technique. A common name for formal methods of developing communication services and protocols. They can be either abstract- or implementation-oriented. Examples are Estelle, LOTOS and SDL.

FDX – Full Duplex. A kind of link or data communication in which data is transmitted in both directions at the same time. It consists of two channels, one for each transmission direction. Also, there exists a Full-Duplex Ethernet (both 10 Mbps and 100 Mbps), without collisions. See also FDSE. Compare with HDX.

FE – Form Effectors. A group of control characters intended for the control of the layout and format of data on an output device such as a printer or a terminal. Examples are carriage return (see CR), linefeed (see LF), etc.

FEA – Finite Element Analysis. The method used in computer-aided design (see CAD) to analyze the behavior of the object under design due to possible external influences such as stress, heat, etc. The object is divided into a large number of finite elements, usually rectangular or triangular shapes, which form an interconnecting network of concentrated nodes. After calculating the behavior of each node and determining the inter-relating behaviors of all the nodes in the system, the behavior of the entire object can be estimated.

FEAL – Fast Data Encipherment Algorithm. A family of algorithms used in developing various cryptoanalytic techniques. It uses byte-oriented operations based on 8-bit addition mod 256, two-bit left closed shifting, and XOR.

FEBE – Far-End Block Error. An error reported to the sender by the receiver in B-ISDN networks when the receiver-computed checksum differs from that of the sender. Compare with FERF.

FEC – Forward Error Correction. Used in AAL1 PDU to detect cell loss and prevent unnecessary transmission of cells belonging to faulty packets. It allows multiple ATM devices to share the same virtual circuit for real-time audio and video transmission with minimal added overhead and only slight performance degradation. See also AAL and PDU.

FED – Field Emission Display. A new type of flat-panel display in which electron emitters are arranged in a grid and individually controlled by "cold" cathodes. FED technology provides the high image quality of today's CRT displays (see CRT).

FED-STD – Federal Standard. The prefix used for standards issued by the US Federal Telecommunication Standards Committee (see FTSC).

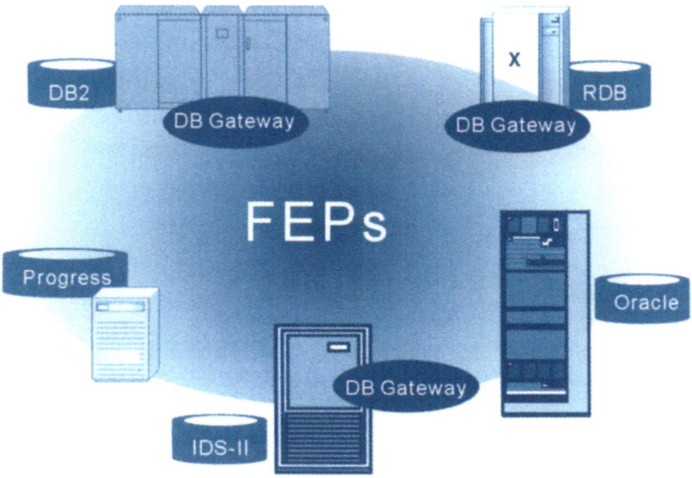

Fig. F-4. FEPs as DB gateways among different DBMSs

FEP – Front-End Processor. A common term for a processing unit that produces and manipulates data before another processing unit receives it. The common usage of FEPs is in data communications where they are used to relieve their hosts of necessary communications activities, such as error correction, encoding a message in the case of cryptography coding, communication management, and so on. In addition, they can be system-specific oriented, so they can serve as a connection element able to meet data from different database management systems, for example, making the data and their manipulation visible and understandable for both sides. Figure F-4 depicts the general situation.

FEPROM – Flash EPROM. A kind of nonvolatile memory similar to EEPROM, but where the erasing process is available only in blocks or for the entire chip.

FERF – Far-End Receive Failure. A signal sent upstream in B-ISDN networks in order to indicate that an error has occurred downstream. See also B-ISDN.

FEXT – Far-End Crosstalk. A leakage that occurs when a signal passes from a wire into another wire.

FF – Form Feed. A printer command (06 HEX) that tells a printer to move to the top of the next page. Also known as the page-eject character.

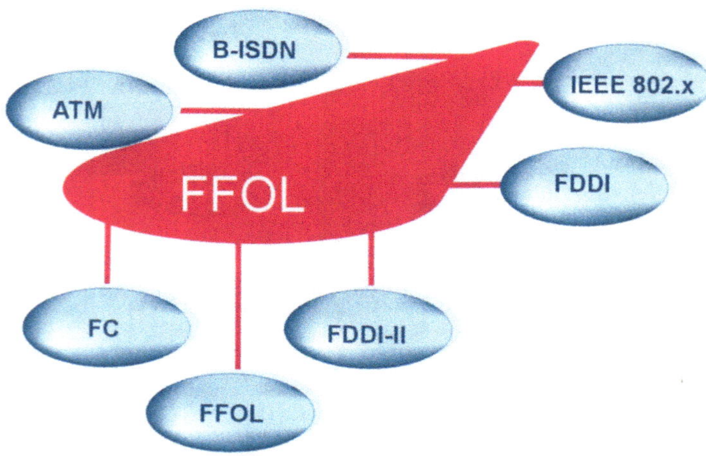

Fig. F-5. FFOL backbone

FFOL – FDDI Follow-On LAN. A standard proposal that defines higher rates of FDDI at 622 Mbps, 1240 Mbps and 2480 Mbps. One of the key features of FFOL is its easy connection to B-ISDN networks as well as ATM and IEEE 802.x (CSMA/CD, Token Ring, MAN etc.), as illustrated in Fig. F-5.

FFT – Fast Fourier Transform. An algorithm to compute the Fourier transform of a set of discrete data values. It is used in numerical analysis for different purposes. It can, for example, reconstruct a signal from the data frequency.

FFT – Final-Form Text. A filename extension for files that contain FFTDCA documents (see FFTDCA).

FFTDCA – Final-Form Text DCA. A standard in the Document Content Architecture (see DCA) for storing documents in a form ready to print. It allows different programs to exchange documents.

FG – Face and Gesture Recognition. IEEE International Conference on Automatic Face and Gesture Recognition.

FG – Functional Group. A set of ATM functions related in such a way that they will be provided by a single logical component. See AHFG, for example.

FGL – Fourth-Generation Language. See 4GL.

FHSS – Frequency-Hopping Spread Spectrum. A part of the IEEE802.11 standard that uses shifting frequencies for transmission header interception. See also DSSS and 802.x.

FIF – Fractal Image File. A filename extension for files that contain fractal images. Benoit Mandelbrot invented the term fractal in 1975. It comes from the Latin term “fractus”, meaning an irregular surface. Thus, fractals are non-regular geometric shapes that have some degree of nonregularity on all scales.

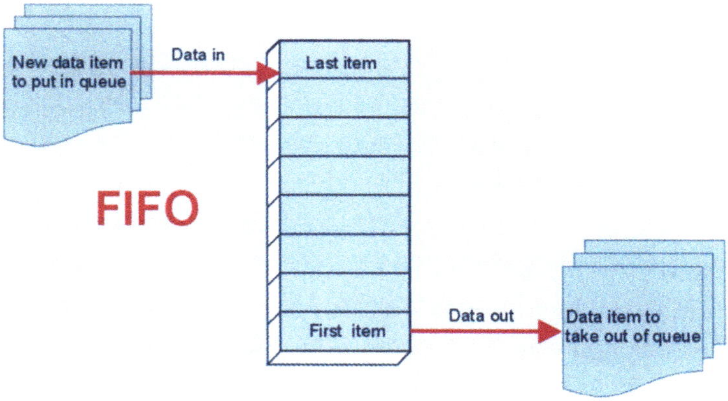

Fig. F-6. FIFO queue

FIFO – First-In, First-Out. A well-known linear data structure, a queue (pronounced “fie-foe”) in which items are taken out in the same order in which they were put in (see Fig. F-6). A common example of FIFO is the UNIX pipe mechanism. See LIFO, the opposite data structure.

FIP – Fair Information Practices. A general term for a set of standards dealing with the collection and use of personal data and addressing issues of privacy and accuracy.

FIPA – Foundation for Intelligent Physical Agents. An international organization (http://www.fipa.org) founded in 1996 to produce standards for heterogeneous agents and agent-based systems.

FIPS – Federal Information Processing Standard. Technical standards issued by the United States Government.

FIPS PUB – FIPS Publication. The prefix used to define documents that describe standards developed by the Federal Information Processing Standards group within the US Commerce Dept. See also FIPS. FIPS PUBs can be obtained at http://www.nist.gov.

FIRL – Fiber-optic Inter-Repeater Link. See FOIRL.

FIRST – Forum of Incident Response and Security Teams. FIRST is a coalition (http://www.first.org) that brings together a wide variety of computer security incident response teams.

FISH – First in, still here. The chat term.

FITCE – Federation of Telecommunications Engineers of the European Community. An organization founded in 1962 in Brussels, Belgium, focusing on telecommunication development in Europe and the rest of the world (http://www.fitce.org).

FITS – Flexible Image Transport System. The standard data interchange and archive format of the worldwide astronomy community. The complete standard and user's guide, some software, and test files are available from ftp://nsdc.gsfc.nasa.gov/pub/fits

FIX – Federal Information Exchange. One of the connection points between the American government Intranets and the Internet.

FIXML – Financial Information Exchange Markup Language. A messaging standard based on XML used in real-time electronic exchange of secure transactions. Find more information at http://www.fixprotocol.org

FLAP – FDDI TalkLink Access Protocol. The data-link layer protocol in the AppleTalk networking environment for FDDI support.

FLEA – Four-Letter Extended Acronym. A recognition of the fact that there are far too many TLAs. See also Three-Letter Acronym (TLA).

FLIH – First-Level Interrupt Handler. An interrupt handler used in a network environment to determine which device generated the interrupt and to invoke a second-level interrupt handler in turn to activate the required process.

FLIP – Fast Local Internet Protocol. An Internet protocol developed at the Vrije Universiteit in The Netherlands as an alternative to TCP/IP for internetworks made up of large-scale distributed systems.

FLL – FoxPro Link Library. A filename extension for files that contain a link library (see DLL) used by FoxPro.

FLOP – Floating-point Operation. An operation that performs arithmetic on data formatted as a normalized signed decimal number followed by a signed exponent.

FLOPS – Floating-point Operations per Second. A measure of the speed at which a computer can compute. It is usual to express this measure in larger, more suitable, units (see MFLOPS, GFLOPS).

FLP – Fast Link Pulse. In Fast Ethernet, a group of identical signals generated by the Ethernet adapter, bridge or switch at startup.

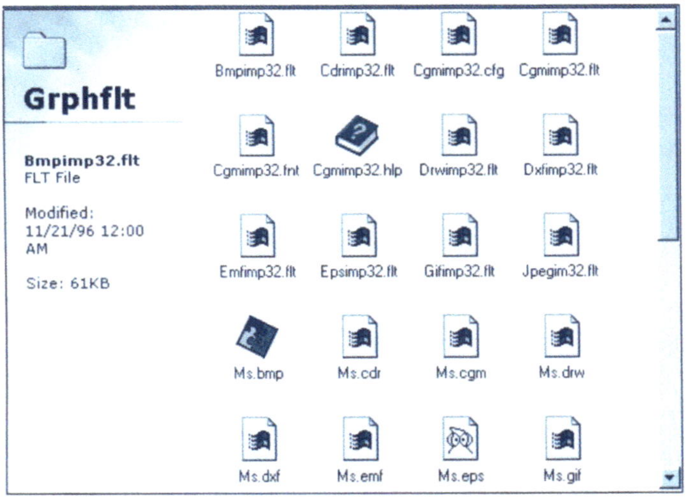

Fig. F-7. A list of several FLT files

FLT – Filter. A filename extension for files that contain graphics filters in Microsoft Windows environments (see Fig. F-7).

FM – Formal Methods. An international congress in the area of formal software and hardware development.

FM – Frequency Modulation. A way of encoding information in an electrical signal by varying its frequency.

FMB – Form Binary. A filename extension for files that contain Oracle binary source for forms.

FMH – Function Management Header. In SNA, an optional header sometimes used by Logical Units (see LU) that carries control information that is exchanged between LUs. FMH is placed between the request header (see RH) and the data. See also SNA.

FMI – Function Management Interface. In SNA, an interface that provides applications with direct access to SNA data flow and control by means of status messages.

FML – Forms Markup Language. A language proposed for enhancing the representation and handling of web application interfaces using dynamic forms, online wizards and multiple screen pages.

FMS – Flexible Manufacturing System. A kind of fully automated production system in which computer numerical control machines (see CNC) can work on a wider spectrum of similar parts, and sometimes even on different parts.

FMT – Form Text. A filename extension for files that contain Oracle text format for forms.

FMV – Full-Motion Video. A common term used for any system designed for delivering video images and sound on a computer, preferably on a compact disk.

FMX – Form Execute. A filename extension for files that contain Oracle executable forms.

FNC – Federal Networking Council. The coordinating group of federal agency representatives (http://www.fnc.gov) which are involved in the development and use of the US federal networks. Some of the members are representatives from DoD, DOE, ARPA, NSF, NASA, etc.

FNT – Font file. A filename extension for files that contain font information.

FO – Fiber Optics. The branch of optical technology concerned with the transmission of radiant power through fibers made of transparent materials such as glass including fused silica or plastic. Networks based on fiber optics offer a number of advantages over those based on copper wiring and electrical signals. See also FDDI and FC.

FOD – Fax On Demand. An automated system that makes information available on request by telephone. When a request is made, the system faxes the information to the telephone number given in the request.

FoIKS – Foundation of Information and Knowledge Systems. An international biennial symposium focusing on the theoretical foundations of information and knowledge systems.

FOIRL – Fiber-Optic Inter-Repeater Link. A fiber-optic signaling methodology based on the IEEE802.3 fiber-optic specification. It is a precursor of the 10BaseFL specification. AKA FIRL.

FOLDOC – Free On-Line Dictionary of Computing. A searchable dictionary of computer terms edited by Denis Howe. At the moment there are more than 10,000 terms described (http://wombat.doc.ic.ac.uk).

FOR – FORTRAN file. A filename extension for files that contain FORTRAN code.

FORTH – Fourth. A language from the late 1960s developed by Charles Moore, named as a shortened version of the word "fourth" because he believed that it was a 4GL.

F

FORTRAN – Formula Translation. An imperative and procedural programming language designed by John W. Backus and his team in the mid-1950s to solve problems involving numerical computations. It was one of the earliest high-level languages. FORTRAN includes a wide range of operators and predefined functions for the manipulation of numerical values. It has been standardized several times by ANSI and ISO (ISO1539) since 1966.

FOSDIC – Film Optical Scanning Device for Input to Computers. A device used to read documents on a microfilm and store them digitally on magnetic tape or a disk for further processing by a computer.

FOURCC – Four-Character Code. A code used to identify RIFF chunks. It is represented by 1–4 ASCII alphanumeric characters padded on the right using blank characters.

foxel – font (any, x) element. A data element that holds the average height and width of a character based on the current font in use.

FPA – Floating-Point Accelerator. A floating-point processor on a single integrated board, or in a single integrated circuit. This additional hardware allows different functions (multiplication, logarithms, exponentials, trigonometric etc.) to be performed on the floating-point numbers. Also called a numeric coprocessor or a math coprocessor. Examples include the 80x87 Intel family of chips.

FPA – Function Point Analysis. A metric for software complexity that can be used to estimate the relative size and complexity at an early stage of software development. It is useful as a relative measure of software team productivity and for estimating the development effort and time required for a project.

FPD – Full-Page Display. A video display with sufficient size and resolution to show at least one page in the letter format (8.5×11 inch) image.

FPGA – Field-Programmable Gate Array. See FPLA.

FPI – Functional Process Improvement. See Business Process Improvement (BPI) and Business Process Reengineering (BPR).

FPLA – Field-Programmable Logic Array. A gate array where the logic network can be programmed into a device after its manufacture. The programming can be performed only once.

FPM – Fast Packet Multiplexing. A form of time-division multiplexing which deals with packetized data from multiple channels and multiple source types. Unlike standard time-division multiplexing (see TDM), a fast packet device is capable of favoring channels (voice, for example), based on the source type and the interrupting channels (data, for example), to allow higher-priority signals (e.g. voice) to be transmitted first.

FPM – Fast Page Mode. A feature of DRAM memory that speeds up sequential access to data. Page-mode memory works by eliminating the need for a row address if the data is located in the row previously accessed. FPM is being replaced by new types of memory such as SDRAM. See also DRAM and SDRAM.

FPODA – Fixed Priority-Oriented Demand Assignment. An access protocol in which stations must reserve slots on the network. The allocation of slots depends on the station's priority levels.

FPS – Fast Packet Switching. A switching strategy that allows higher throughput by simplifying the switching process. Some of the methods used to achieve FPS are, for example, using fixed-size packets, leaving error checking to higher-level protocols, as applied in frame-relay networks (see FR), switching packets immediately upon arrival, etc.

FPT – FoxPro Table. A filename extension for a file that contains a FoxPro table memo.

FPU – Floating-Point Unit. See FPA (Floating-Point Accelerator).

FQDN – Fully Qualified Domain Name. The unique electronic address of every Internet host. It is the full name of a system rather then just its hostname. For example, "europa" is a host name and "europa.elfak.ni.ac.yu" is a FQDN. See also Domain Name System (DNS).

FR – Frame Relay. A connection-oriented packet-switched service used to transfer data from one location to another over WAN. It operates at the physical layer and the lower part of the data-link layer of the OSI Reference Model. FR packets are variable-length as shown in Fig. F-8. The FCS field in a frame has the usual purpose (see FCS) and there are also flag fields. The header for a FR packet consists of several fields, as depicted in Fig. F-8.

Header fields have the following purposes:

- DLCI (Data-Link Connection Identifier), represents the port to which the destination network is connected;
- CIR (Committed Information Rate), the estimated value of each node's average bandwidth requirements;
- EA (Extended Address), used in case the DLCI does not have sufficient space for the address;
- ECN (Explicit Congestion Notification), two bits used to inform either the destination node (FECN, F stands for forward) or the source node (BECN, B stands for backward) that congestion has occurred;
- DE (Discard Eligible) used in the case of a discard (see DE).

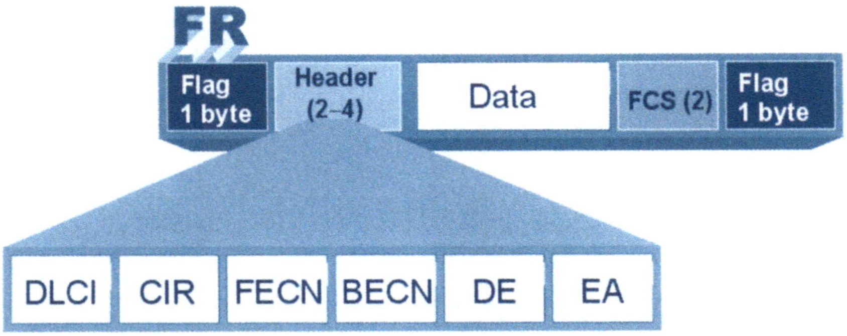

Fig. F-8. Frame Relay packet

Frame relay can have a bandwidth as high as 2 Mbps. FR discards any packets that cannot be delivered for some reason. Error correction and re-transmission requirements are left to higher-level protocols. It is being considered as a future replacement for X.25. Frame relay specifications can be found as ITU-T documents (I.233, I.370 and Q.922), and as ANSI documents (T1.606, T1.617 and T1.618). Additional information is also available at http://www.frforum.com

FRAD – Frame-Relay Access Device. A kind of computer that turns packets from TCP, SNA, IPX, and other protocols into frames that can be sent over a frame-relay-based (see FR) wide area network.

FRAM – Ferroelectric Random-Access Memory. A type of storage device (pronounced “eff-ram”) that permits data to be recorded on small cards or strips of material coated with ferric oxide magnetic film.

FRC – Functional Redundancy Check. A mode of Intel Pentium operation that allows us to run two chips side by side and compare their results.

FRM – Form. A filename extension for files generated by Visual Basic used to create the interface for an application .

FRMR – Frame Reject response. A signal used by the receiving end in an SDLC connection to indicate that an invalid frame or packet has arrived.

FRS – Frame-Relay Service. See Frame Relay (FR).

FRTT – Fixed Round-Trip Time. The sum of the fixed and propagation delays from the source to the furthest destination and back.

FRX – FoxPro Report. A filename extension for files that contain reports generated by FoxPro.

FS – File Separator. The identification character (ASCII decimal 28) that marks the end of a file.

FS – Frame Status. A field in a token ring (see TR) data packet.

FSA – Finite State Automata. An abstract machine consisting of a set of states, a set of input and output events and a state transition function.

FSB – Front-Side Bus. A type of bus used on some motherboards that connects the processor, chipset, DRAM and AGP socket. See also AGP and DRAM.

FSF – Free Software Foundation. An organization (http://www.fsf.org), based in Cambridge, Massachusetts, dedicated to promoting the development and use of free software. Richard Stallman heads the foundation. See also GNU.

FSK – Frequency-Shift Keying. A simple form of modulation in which the digital values 0 and 1 are represented by two different frequencies.

FSO – File System Object. An object-based tool that allows working with folders and files in Visual Basic.

FSP – File Service Process. A process that executes and responds to file handling requests on a file server.

FST – Flat Square Technology (Tube). A CRT monitor technology that reduces the picture tube curvature, yielding more accurate picture representations.

FSV – Functional Service View. The part of Open-edi (see EDI) that defines the information technologies for EDI (see IT) and the communications protocols.

FTAM – File Transfer Access and Management. An OSI application-layer protocol (ISO8571) which allows files, or their parts, to be transferred and accessed from remote systems, even if they have totally different file structures and data-handling methods.

FTN – Fido Technology Network. A system for exchanging e-mails and allowing discussion groups among the users of over 30,000 bulletin board services (see BBS). Also known as the FidoNet.

FTP – File Transfer Protocol. A well-known protocol (RFC959) that allows file transfer from a remote computer. A large number of FTP servers are available worldwide that allow people anywhere on the Internet to log in and download whatever files have been placed on them. See also AFTP.

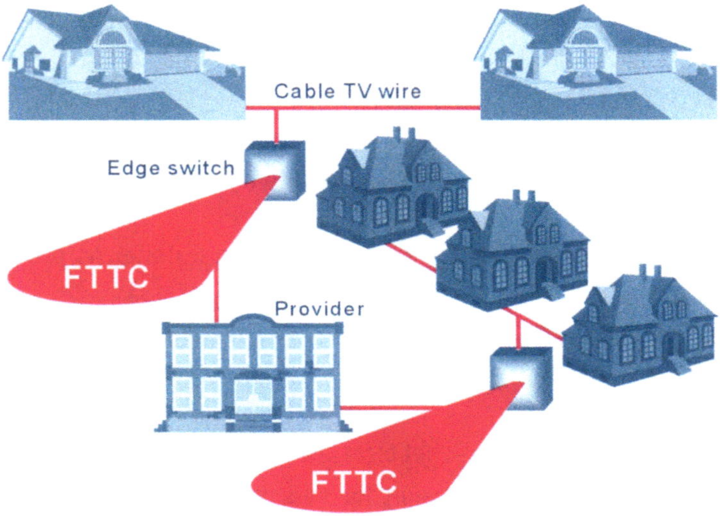

Fig. F-9. A possible FTTC solution

FTS – File Transfer Service. A common name for any one of a broad class of OSI application-layer services for handling files and moving them from one location to another. Some of them are explained elsewhere in this book. See CGM, EDI, FTAM, ILL, JTM, MHS, ODA, RDA, TP and VT.

FTS – Full-Text Search. A filename extension for the hidden files that contain an index, resulting from a full-text search of the Microsoft Windows help system files (see HLP).

FTSC – Federal Telecommunication Standards Committee. A US Government Agency established in 1973 to promote standardization of communications and network interfaces. FTSC standards are identified by the FED-STD prefix.

FTTC – Fiber To The Curb. A fiber implementation in the local loop that allows an optical fiber to be run from each end office into each neighborhood (the curb). The fiber is terminated in an edge switch that all local loops enter. A connection from the edge switch to the homes in the neighborhood can be implemented either via the telephone network or the cable TV network (see Fig. F-9). AKA FTTN. See also DAVIC.

FTTH – Fiber To The Home. An advanced future service running a fiber from the end office into every house. It is still too expensive for wider implementation. Compare with FTTC.

FTTN – Fiber To The Neighborhood. See FTTC.

FU – Functional Unit. The part of the Central Processing Unit (see CPU) where the actual instruction execution takes place. An example of an FU is Floating Point Unit (see FPA or FPU).

FUD – Fear, Uncertainty and Doubt. A general term for any strategy intended to discourage customers from adopting products from competitor companies.

FUNI – Frame User Network Interface. A service that performs protocol conversion between Frame Relay and ATM networks.

F/W – Firmware. The software stored in ROM or PROM memory during computer production, often responsible for system behavior when it is first switched on.

FWIW – For what it's worth. The chat term.

FXP – FoxPro. A filename extension for files that contain compiled FoxPro source code.

FYI – For Your Information. A subseries of RFCs that are not technical standards or descriptions of protocols. FYIs convey general information about topics related to TCP/IP or the Internet. FYI documents differ from most RFCs in that the FYIs are generally less technical. In order to see what FYIs look like, the following FYI can help: FYI18: "Internet Users Glossary", RFC1392, 1993. See also Request For Comments (RFC).

G

G – Giga. An order of magnitude meaning 1 billion, or 10^9. See GB, Gbps, GHz, GFLOPS and GIPS.

GA – Go ahead. The chat term.

GAL – Global Address List. In Microsoft MAPI, an address book container that holds recipient entries for an entire organization. See also MAPI.

GAM – Global Allocation Map. In Microsoft SQL Server, a disk space method used to record the allocation of extents. Each GAM covers 64,000 extents with nearly 4 GB of data. Compare with SGAM.

GB – Gigabyte. A measurement unit either for memory or disk storage capacity. It has 1024 megabytes or 10^9 bytes.

Gbps – Gigabits per second. A measurement unit for data rates.

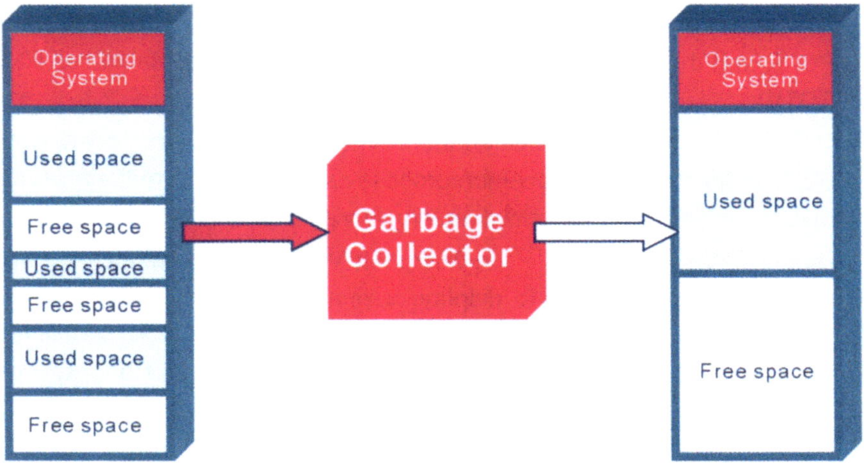

Fig. G-1. Garbage collection

GC – Garbage Collection. The technique of automatic storage compaction performed by an operating system in order to move all occupied areas of storage to one end or the other of the main storage area (see Fig. G-1). Automatic garbage collection is usually triggered during memory allocation for the next process when the amount of free memory falls below some threshold.

GCAC – Generic Connection Admission Control. In ATM networks, a process used to determine if a link has potentially enough resources to support a connection.

GCD – Greatest Common Divisor. The largest positive integer that divides both values of two given positive integers, without a remainder.

GCOS – General-purpose Comprehensive Operating System. The common name for several Honeywell (now Bull) proprietary operating systems. These include GCOS4, GCOS6, GCOS7, GCOS8 and GCOS9.

GCP – Ground Control Point file. A filename extension for the files that contain map projections.

GCR – Group Code Recording. A recording method used for some magnetic tapes. It uses a group of five bits to represent four bits of data.

GCRA – Generic Cell Rate Algorithm. An algorithm for using and enforcing the ATM quality of service parameters (see QoS). The algorithm, also called a virtual scheduling algorithm, works by checking every ATM cell to see if it conforms to the parameters for a particular virtual circuit. It uses two parameters, the first one specifies the maximum rate at which cells will be sent (see PCR), and the second one specifies the maximum acceptable cell jitter (see CDTV).

GDA – Global Directory Agent. A component of the OSF DCE directory service (see DCE) implemented as a daemon process used by a cell directory service (see CDS) to interact with a global directory service (see GDS) and DNS.

GDI – Graphical Device Interface. In Microsoft Windows, a graphics display system used by applications to display or print bitmapped text (TrueType fonts), images, and other graphical elements. The GDI is responsible for drawing dialog boxes, buttons, and other elements in a consistent style on the screen by calling the appropriate screen drivers and passing them the information on the item to be drawn. The GDI also works with GDI printers, which have limited ability to prepare pages for printing. Instead, the GDI handles that task by calling the appropriate printer drivers and moving the image or document directly to the printer, rather than reformatting the image or document in PostScript or another printer language.

GDMO – Guidelines for the Definition of Managed Objects. A standard (ISO/IEC10165-4) for defining data models using ASN.1 within the Telecommunication Management Network framework (see TMN). GDMO is a structured description language that provides a way of specifying the classes of objects, and their behaviors, attributes and class hierarchy.

GDS – Generalized Data Stream. The format for mapped data in APPC in IBM SNA networks. See APPC.

GDS – Global Directory Service. A part of the OSF DCE directory services (see DCE) used to locate remote cells. It is implemented as an X.500 (ISO9594) directory service and can work with other X.500 directory services. Every item in a global directory is stored as an object representing, for example, a country, a city, a company, a cell, etc.

GE – Greater than or Equal to. An acronym very often used in programming languages as a relational operator in logical expressions. See also EQ, NE, LT, LE and GT.

GED – Genealogical Data file. A filename extension for files that contain genealogical data.

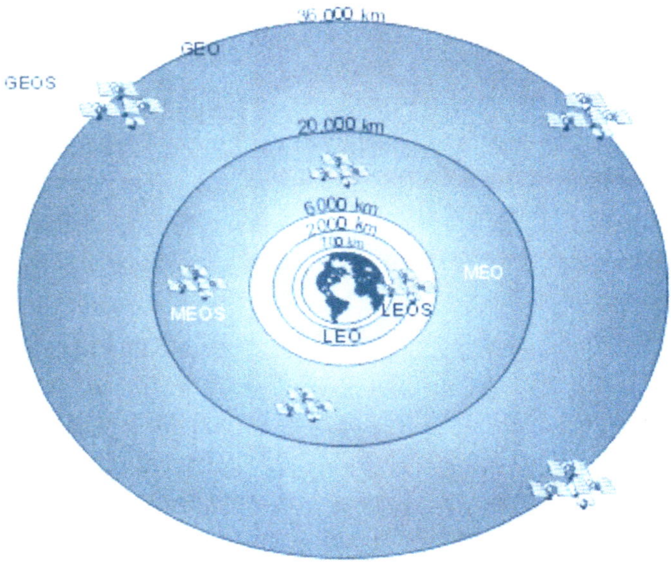

Fig. G-2. GEO, LEO and MEO positions above the Earth

GEO – Geostationary Earth Orbit. The traditional satellite orbit at 36,000 km above the Earth. Also, the common name for every satellite in that orbit. Compare with LEO and MEO. See Fig. G-2.

GEOS – Geostationary Earth Orbit Satellites. A common name for satellites that are in the GEO.

GETCO – Geometrical and Topological Methods in Concurrency. An international workshop focusing on geometrical and topological methods in concurrency. Some of the major topics include semantics, abstract interpretation, fault-tolerant protocols for distributed systems, geometrical/topological models, application of algebraic topology, etc.

GFC – Generic Flow Control. A protocol in ATM networks used to make sure that all nodes get access to the transmission medium.

GFI – General Format Identifier. A field in an X.25 packet that indicates the packet formats. See X.25.

GFLOPS – Giga Floating-point Operations per Second. A measure of computing speed, a billion floating-point operations per second.

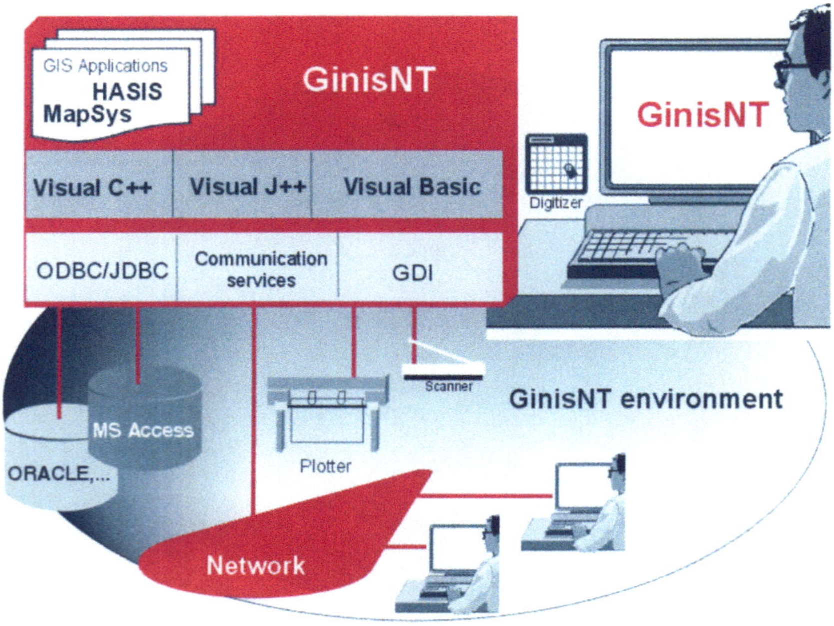

Fig. G-3. GinisNT architecture

GFR – Guaranteed Frame Rate. A standard from the ATM Forum. Sometimes called UBR+ (unspecified bit-rate plus). GFR lets users specify a connection-dependent minimum cell rate for transmissions. See also ATM and UBR.

GHz – Gigahertz. A measurement unit for a frequency equal to 1000 MHz.

GID – Global Index Directory. A filename extension for Windows 95 files that contain the help status.

GIF – Graphics Interchange Format. An industrial standard developed by CompuServe for digitized images compressed using the LZW algorithm. An image may contain up to 256 colors, including a transparent color. The size of the file depends on the number of colors actually used. See also LZW.

GIGO – Garbage In, Garbage Out. A computing axiom (pronounced "gi-goh") referring to the nonthinking nature of computers which will produce garbage data (incorrect or corrupted) every time when garbage data has been put into a process.

GII – Global Information Infrastructure. The name of the worldwide project with the same goals as those of the US National Information Infrastructure (see NII). Additional information can be obtained at http://www.giic.org

G

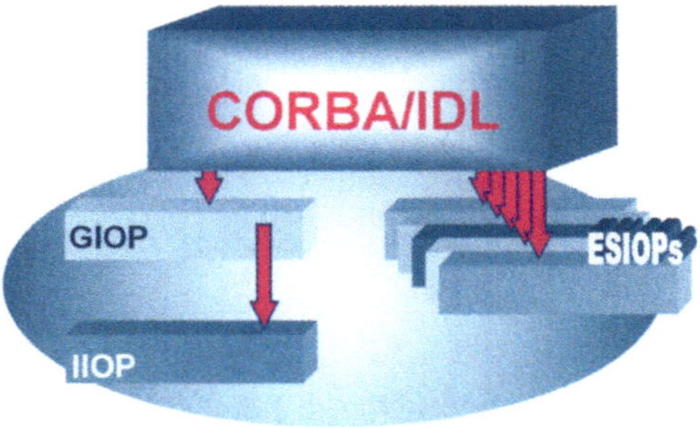

Fig. G-4. Inter-ORB protocol relationships

GILC – Global Internet Liberty Campaign. An organization (http://www.gilc.org) formed in 1996 to protect freedom of speech and the right to privacy in cyberspace. Some of the member organizations are: Internet Society (see ISOC), Amnesty International USA, Committee to Protect Journalists, Electronic Frontier Foundation (see EFF), Human Rights Watch, Privacy International, and many more. Unfortunately, it is clear that the main goals of this organization are not respected when government or security organizations think differently.

GinisNT – GIS Nis New Technology. An object-oriented scalable framework for GIS application development. The architecture and associated tools were developed at the Computer Graphics and GIS Laboratory in the Faculty of Electronic Engineering, University of Niš (which is where the middle part of the name comes from). The overall architecture of GinisNT is depicted in Fig. G-3. Figures #-1 and G-5 were produced using GinisNT tools. See also HASIS.

GIOP – General Inter-ORB Protocol. A part of the Common Object Request Broker (see CORBA) specification that defines a mandatory standard transfer syntax and a set of message formats for communications between Object Request Brokers (see ORB). The relationships between inter-ORB protocols, GIOP, the Internet Inter-ORB Protocol (see IIOP), and the Environment-Specific Inter-ORB Protocols (see ESIOP) are shown in Fig. G-4.

GIPR – Gigabit IP Router. An attempt to integrate IP routing and ATM switching technologies. Theoretically, a GIPR could deliver IP's interoperability benefits along with ATM's high speeds and quality of service support. The challenge for GIPR designers, however, is to construct an affordable device that delivers enough CPU and memory cycles to perform all IP packet processing at speeds that keep ATM circuits full.

GIPS – Giga Instructions Per Second. A measurement unit for the processing power equal to 1000 million instructions per second (see MIPS).

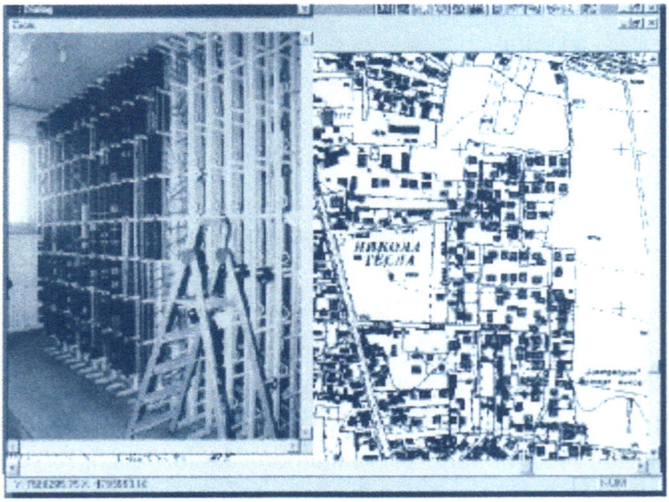

Fig. G-5. An example of a multimedia GIS
(courtesy of the CG & GIS Lab, University of Niš, Yugoslavia)

GIS – Geographic Information System. An information system used to capture, store, manipulate and display spatially referenced data for solving complex planning and management problems. Typically, a GIS is used for handling different kinds of maps (see Figures #-1, G-5 and G-6). These maps might be represented as several different layers, each holding data about a particular kind of feature, including the appropriate links for connecting to the next map layer or to a different presentation of an area, as shown in Fig. G-5. In general, GIS applications can be classified as cartographic, digital terrain modeling or geographic object applications. Examples include water resource management, landscape studies, and car navigation systems.

Fig. G-6. An example of a 3D map

GITM – Global Information Technology and Management. The annual international conference focusing on global IT management. Some of the topics include electronic commerce, IT in multinational companies, cross-cultural issues, frameworks for global information systems, the influence on economic development, EDI, distributed global databases and networks, etc. High-quality papers are published by the JGIM and JITCA journals.

GIWIST – Gee, I wish I said that. The chat term.

GKS – Graphical Kernel System. An ISO standard (ISO7492) that provides a language-independent nucleus of functions for computer graphics programming in two dimensions. GKS is a basic graphic system that can be used by the majority of applications that produce computer-generated pictures. It allows graphics applications to be easily portable between different platforms, and graphic methods to be easily understood and used by application programmers. GKS also helps manufacturers of graphic equipment as a guideline for providing useful combinations of graphic capabilities in a device. GKS provides a functional interface between an application program and a configuration of graphical input and output devices (see Fig. G-7). For integration into a programming language, GKS is embedded in a language-dependent layer containing particular language conventions. See also GKS-3D.

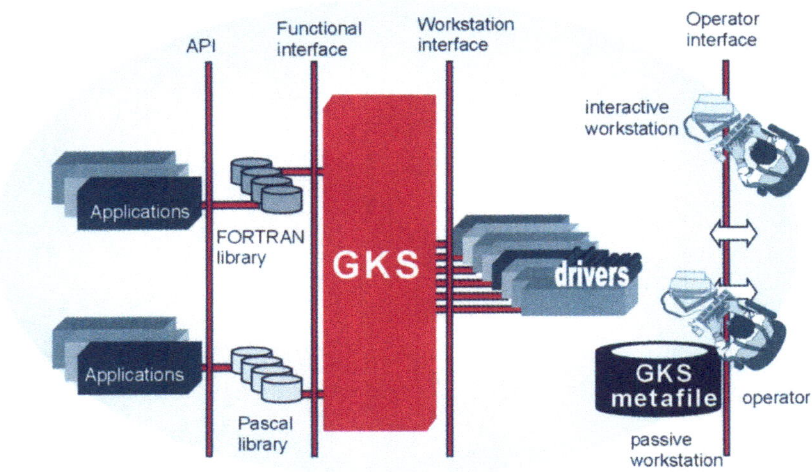

Fig. G-7. GKS functional overview

GKS-3D – Graphical Kernel System in 3D. An ISO standard (ISO8805) for the language-independent nucleus of functions for computer graphics programming based on the same principles as GKS with additional performance features for obtaining 3D graphics application programming.

GLONASS – Global Navigation Satellite System. The Russian satellite-based navigation system working on the same principles as the US Global Positioning System (see GPS), comprising three segments: space, control and user segment. GLONASS satellites are deployed in three orbital planes with 65° inclination at 19,100 km altitude, providing 24-h visibility for over 95% of the Earth's surface.

GML – Generalized Markup Language. An IBM document formatting language that describes documents in terms of their organization structures and contents parts and their relationships. GML was a precursor to the Standard Generalized Markup Language (see SGML).

GMT – Greenwich Mean Time. See Time Zone (TZ) and UTC.

GMTA – Great minds think alike. The chat term.

GND – Ground. A common term for a reference conductor at a 0-V potential, serving as the reference for other voltages in the circuit.

GNN – Global Network Navigator. A set of free-of-charge network services (http://www.gnn.com) representing something like a catalog of the whole Internet. The GNN catalog contains live links to the most useful network resources, such as business, news, sports, weather and travel information pages, etc.

GNOME – GNU Network Object Model Environment. A Windows-like desktop GUI that allows novices to use LINUX.

GNS – Global Name Service. A global naming technique designed by Butler W. Lampson et al. for providing facilities for resource location, mail addressing and authentication. GNS manages a naming database that is composed of a tree of directories holding names and values, something like that implemented in the UNIX file system. GNS is more adaptive to changes in the structure of the name space than DNS. See also DNS.

GNT – Generated code. A filename extension for files that contain MicroFocus executable code.

GNU – GNU's Not UNIX. A popular range of portable software from the Free Software Foundation (see FSF) based on the UNIX operating system. GNU is distributed under the GNU General Public License, which requires that anyone who distributes GNU or a program based on GNU may charge only for distribution and support and must allow the user to modify and redistribute the code on the same terms. See also LINUX, GNOME and GnuPG.

GnuPG – GNU Privacy Guard. A free-of-charge replacement for Pretty Good Privacy (see PGP).

GOL – Giggling out loud. The chat term.

GOSE – Geographic Open System Environment. The GIS standard reference model that defines the environment, applicable principles, and architectural framework for the field of geographic information, as shown in Fig. G-8. Structured within information technology standards, the reference model is independent of any application methodology and technology. This standardization effort has the following features:

- increases the understanding and usage of geographic information;

- increases the availability, access, integration and sharing of geographic information;
- promotes the efficient, effective and economic use of digital geographic information and associated hardware and software systems;
- contributes to a unified approach to addressing global ecological and humanitarian problems.

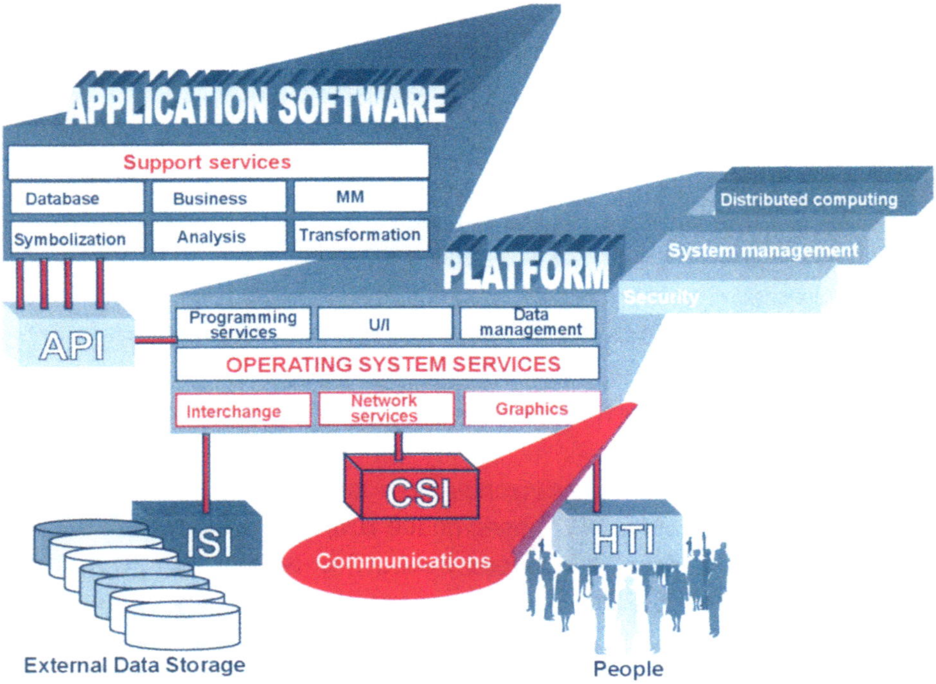

Fig. G-8. The GOSE reference model

GOSIP – Government OSI Profile. A common term for a standard defined by the US, the UK and some other countries for simplifying the purchase of computer equipment by government organizations.

GOV – Governmental. One of the top domain names on the Internet. See DNS (Domain Name System).

GP3 – Group 3 file. A filename extension for a file that contains a CCITT Group 3 compressed TIFF file. See also FAX and TIFF.

GP4 – Group 4 file. A filename extension for a file that contains a CCITT Group 4 compressed TIFF file. See also FAX and TIFF.

GPF – General Protection Failure (Fault). An error in addressing memory that cannot be attributed to any expected condition. This error condition occurs in an 80386 or in higher processors running in protected mode when an application attempts to access memory outside its given memory space or when an invalid instruction is issued.

GPIB – General-Purpose Interface Bus. The standard (IEEE488) for an industrial parallel bus, also known as HPIB after its development by Hewlett-Packard (see HPIB). It allows information exchange between computers and industrial automation equipment.

GPRS – General Packet Radio Services. A GSM extension that encapsulates data into short packets for transmission over the network at speeds of up to about 100 Kbps. See also GSM.

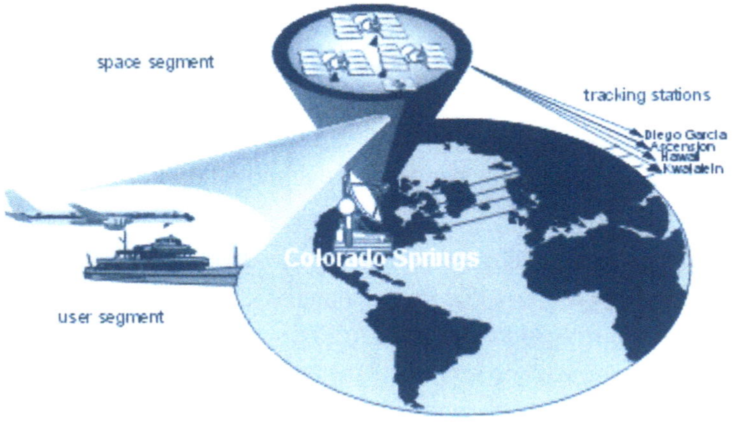

Fig. G-9. An overview of GPS

GPS – Global Positioning System. The US Navstar Global Positioning System based on 24 satellites in 6 orbital planes with 54° inclination at 20,100 km altitude providing a 24-h visibility over 95% of the Earth's surface (compare with GLONASS). GPS consists of three segments (see Fig. G-9): the space segment consisting of satellites which broadcast signals, the control segment steering the whole system, and the user segment including many types of receivers. The space segment provides global coverage with four to eight simultaneous observable satellites above 15° elevation. The control segment consists of the master control station located in Colorado Springs, Colorado, worldwide monitor stations, and ground control stations (see Fig. G-9). Using some kind of GPS receiver, any static or movable object in the user space can find out its position.

GQM – Goals, Questions, Metrics. A software engineering metrics paradigm proposed by Victor R. Basili and Dieter H. Rombach in 1988 to help decide what measurements should be taken and how they should be used to find out about the software process. As per the abbreviation given, GQM is based on the identification of organization goals, and questions for refining these goals, and appropriate metrics.

GRA – Graph. A filename extension for files that contain drawings made using Microsoft Graph.

GRD – Grid file. A filename extension for files that contain map projections.

GRIB – Grid In Binary. The World Meteorological Organization standard for gridded meteorological data. It may be downloaded using anonymous ftp from ftp://ncardata.ucar.edu/libraries/grib

GROW – GNU Remote Operations Web. Architecture for building networked applications and services using the Web.

GRP – Group. A filename extension for files that contain information about the program group in Microsoft Windows environments (e.g. Main, Desktop, WinWord, etc.).

GS – Geprüfte Sicherheit. German safety approval mark. See TÜV.

GSM – Global System for Mobile communications. European system for mobile communications currently in use in over 50 countries, some of them outside Europe. This is essentially a digital cellular radio of up to a maximum of 200 full-duplex channels per cell, each channel consisting of two frequencies. A downlink frequency is dedicated to communications from the base station to the mobile stations, an uplink frequency is used for the opposite direction.

GSS – Group-Sweeping Scheduling. A disk scheduling strategy based on the round-robin algorithm and intended to reduce disk arm movements.

GSS API – Generic Security Service API. An Internet standard proposed in RFC1508 and RFC1509 (made obsolete by RFC2743) defining an application-level interface to different system security services (RFC 2744 defines C API, RFC2853 defines Java API).

GST – Guam Standard Time. Time zone. UTC + 10.00 hours. See TZ.

GT – Greater Than. An acronym very often used in programming languages as a relational operator in logical expressions. See EQ, NE, LT, LE and GE.

GTRM – Going to read mail. The chat term.

GUI – Graphical User Interface. A type of user interface (pronounced "goo-ee") that uses pictures (icons) rather than just characters and words to describe the inputs and outputs of a program (see CUI). Figure G-10 gives a pictorial history of user interface development from the early 1980s. At the beginning, there were many human-related barriers. In the article "Etude and the Folklore of User Interface Design" published in the ACM SIGPLAN Notices in June 1981, Michael Good compared the status of user interface research at that time with weather. Everybody talks about it, but nobody does anything about it, he wrote. Today, user interfaces are typically GUIs based on windows, icons, menus and pointing devices (see WIMP) with graphical elements mixed with the text on the same display. GUIs are also characterized by undo possibilities for canceling previous operations, and sometimes by WYSIWYG attributes (as in document processing, see DP).

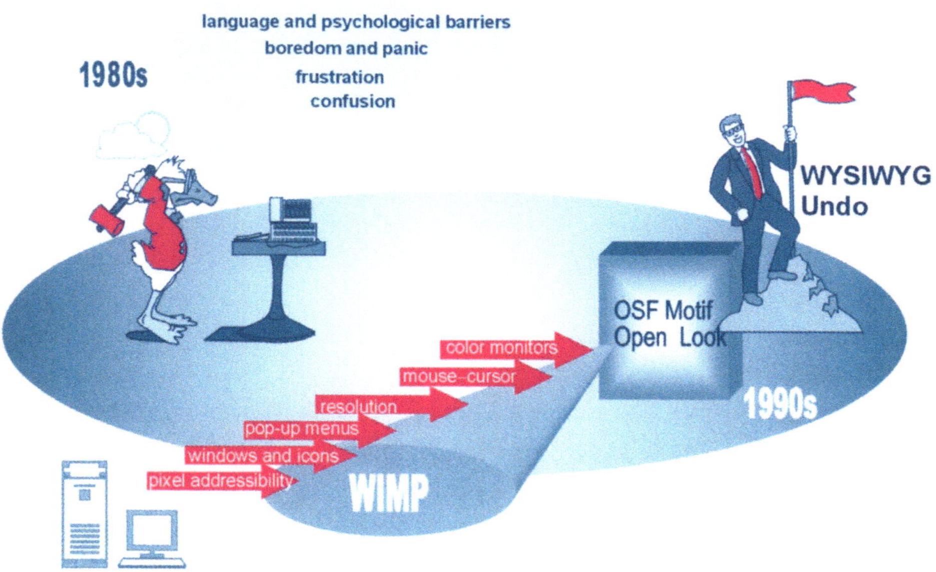

Fig. G-10. The evolution of the user interface

GUID – Globally Unique Identifier. The Microsoft implementation of the DCE Unique User Identifier (see UUID).

GVE – Graphics and Visualization Education. A joint Eurographics and ACM SIGGRAPH workshop considering the future of computer graphics education.

GWART – Gateway Address Routing Table. A table that holds information about the gateways, and their associated address types, which are available to the Microsoft Exchange Server.

GWES – Graphics, Windowing and Events Subsystem. In Microsoft Windows, a module that is responsible for the graphics and windowing functionality, as well as for processing user inputs and performing appropriate actions.

GZ – Gzip file. A filename extension for files that contain UNIX compressed files.

H

H – Header file. A filename extension for a file that contains header information. Used with C and C++ programs. For example, see STDIO.

H – High-speed channel. An ISDN bearer service that has a default speed, starting and stopping locations on a PRI and is contiguously transported from one PRI site to another. See also ISDN and PRI.

HAL – Hardware Abstraction Layer. In advanced operating systems, a layer in which assembly language code is isolated. A Hardware Abstraction Layer works similarly to an API and is used by programmers to write a device-independent code. An example is Windows NT.

HAND – Have a nice day. The chat term.

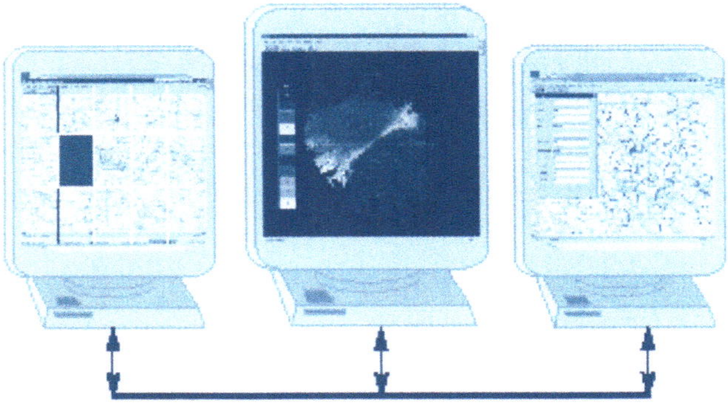

Fig. H-1. HASIS in action

HASIS – Hail Suppression and Information System. The C3I system developed at the Computer Graphics and GIS laboratory at the University of Niš, Yugoslavia (see Fig. H-1). HASIS hardware includes a main workstation for processing, displaying and analyzing radar signals, a workstation for coordination with the command center, a workstation for coordination between hail suppression stations, and an intelligent microwave link for communication between radar centers. Among other things, HASIS provides continuous observation of clouds, detection of clouds approaching storms, supports hail suppression commands and control processes, and recording and simulation, etc. See also C3I and GinisNT.

HAVi – Home Audio/Video interoperability. An industrial specification primarily intended for connecting digital home entertainment devices.

HBA – Host Bus Adapter. See Disk Coprocessor Board (DCB).

HBFG – Host Behavior Functional Group. A group of functions performed by an ATM-attached host that participates in an MPOA service. See also ATM and MPOA.

HCI – Human–Computer Interface. A general term for communication between people and machines. Other terms in use are Human–Technology Interface (see HTI) and User Interface (see UI).

HCSS – High-Capacity Storage System. A storage system used in a Novell NetWare environment (4.x) that includes optical disks as part of the file system.

HD – Hard Disk. A data storage device built from one or more inflexible platters coated with material that allows magnetic data recording. Every hard disk drive has its read/write heads, the head-positioning mechanism, and the spindle motor in a sealed case that protects it against outside contaminants. The protected environment allows the head to fly 10–25 millionths of an inch above the surface of a platter. Most hard disks contain from two to eight platters. HDs differ from each other in the interfaces and encoding techniques used (see ESDI, IDE, EIDE, SCSI and SMD). Compare with floppy disk (FD).

HDBMS – Hierarchical Database Management System. A database management system (see DBMS) that supports the hierarchical data model, in which records are organized as a collection of trees where all links point in the child to parent direction.

HDD – Hard Disk Drive. A disk drive used to read and write hard disks.

HDF – Hierarchical Data Format. A self-defining file format for transfer of various types of data between different operating platforms. Data can be either compressed or uncompressed raster images, or n-dimensional scientific data sets, together with information about the data such as labels, formats and scales for all dimensions. The source code and documentation are available from ftp://ftp.ncsa.uiuc.edu/HDF. A Web information server is available at http://hdf.ncsa.uiuc.edu:8001

HDL – Hardware Description Language. A kind of language used for conceptual integrated circuit design.

HDLC – High-level Data-Link Control. Part of the ITU-T X.25 recommendation. Also standardized by ISO as ISO7809 standard. HDLC defines a message format in packet public networks and transmission control. HDLC is a bit-oriented, synchronous protocol that applies to the data-link layer of the ISO Open System Interconnection (see OSI) architecture. A HDLC protocol frame is shown in Fig. H-2. The structure of the frame is the same as that described in ADCCP. The FCS fields are checksum fields using cyclic redundancy code and CRC-CCITT as the polynomial generator (see CRC). There are three kinds of HDLC frames: information, supervisory and unnumbered, and this is identifiable in the control field. The Information frame (I) contains data in the form of packets from higher-level protocols. The Supervisory frame (S) provides a separate way of controlling a session, while the Unnumbered frame (U) provides additional information for link control. HDLC can support half-duplex or full-duplex communications, circuit or packet-switched networks, point-to-point or multipoint network topologies, and transmission over cable or wireless media.

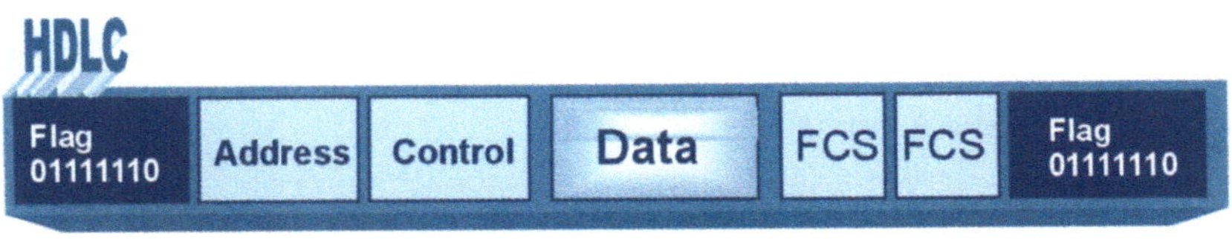

Fig. H-2. HDLC protocol frame

HDM – Hypermedia Design Method. The modeling method for DataWeb applications originating from the Entity-Relationship Model (see ER). In general, DataWeb applications are special kinds of information systems in which data can be navigated through, queried and updated by means of web browsers, regardless of the number and type of users. See also RMM and OOHDM.

HDML – Handheld Device Markup Language. A proposal for technology that will allow handheld devices, such as personal digital assistants (see PDA) and similar smaller devices, to provide Web services. These devices are characterized by small display sizes, limited input capabilities, limited resources, limited communication bandwidths, etc. HDML uses individual units of data called "cards" as the basic elements, with a "deck of cards" being required to make an application. The complete specification is available at http://w3.org/pub/WWW/TR/NOTE-Submission-HDML-spec.html

HDSL – High-bit-rate Digital Subscriber Line. A symmetric method for transmitting data at rates up to 1.5 Mbps in both directions. Compare with ADSL.

HDTV – High-Definition Television. A method for transmitting and receiving television signals that produces much better picture resolution and sharpness by roughly doubling the number of scan lines than applies for standard television technology. This emerging technology is not standardized yet. Actually, there are three HDTV systems under development, in Europe, Japan and the US, and all are different and mutually incompatible.

HDX – Half-Duplex. A communication setup whereby a device can receive or transmit but never do both at the same time. Compare with FDX.

HEC – Header Error Control. Part of the Asynchronous Transfer Mode (see ATM) header that covers the checksum of the header (without the payload field). The HEC CRC scheme uses a remainder after the 32 header bits have been divided by the polynomial generator (see CRC) $x^8 + x^2 + x + 1$ and then added to the number 01010101, which is sufficient to correct all single-bit errors and detect many multibit errors.

HENSA – Higher Education National Software Archive. An FTP archive dedicated to the UK academic community, located at the Universities of Kent and Lancaster (http://www.hensa.ac.uk).

HERP – Hazards of Electromagnetic Radiation to Personnel. The possibility that electromagnetic radiation can produce harmful biological effects in humans.

hex – hexadecimal. The base-16 number system that consists of digits 0 through 9, and letters A through F (equivalent to decimal numbers 10 through 15). Thus, the hexadecimal value C8 represents $12\times16+8$, i.e. 200. This system is very useful in programming because two hexadecimal digits (coded using 4 bits each) easily fit in one byte of memory (in the previous example C8 is stored in a byte of memory as 11001000). To avoid possible confusion with decimal numbers, hexadecimal numbers are usually followed by the letter H, or the abbreviation hex.

HF – High Frequency. Transmission frequencies in the range 3–30 MHz.

HFC – Hybrid Fiber Coax. A local distribution scheme for video on demand. Unlike Digital Subscriber Line (see ADSL, DSL), fiber to the curb, or fiber to the home (see FTTC, FTTH), which are all local distribution networks, the HFC solution is based on cable TV, with 750-MHz coax cables.

HGC – Hercules Graphics Card. An old video adapter card introduced in 1982 by Hercules Computer Technology. It was replaced with higher-resolution adapters (see VGA, SVGA).

HGL – HP Graphics Language. A filename extension for files that contain drawings made using HPGL. See also HPGL.

HICSS – Hawaii International Conference on System Sciences. An international conference focusing on computer system science. Topics are changed in accordance with the so-called minitrack for that year.

HiFD – High Floppy Disk. A type of high-density floppy disk developed by Sony that can hold 200 MB of data, with data transfer rates of up to 3.6 MBps.

HIPERLAN – High-Performance Radio LAN. A European wireless LAN that allows 20 Mbps data rates.

HIPPI – High-Performance Parallel Interface. A high-speed LAN for supercomputers, operating at 800 Mbps and 1.6 Gbps. The standard covers physical and data-link layers. For 800 Mbps rates HIPPI uses a cable containing 50 twisted pairs, while for 1600 Mbps two such cables (25-m long max.) are necessary. Messages are structured with a control word, a header of up to 1016 bytes, and a data part of up to 2^{32}–2 bytes broken up into frames of 256 words. Error control is based on a horizontal parity bit per word and a vertical parity word at the end of each frame.

hi-res – high-resolution. A common term applied to a high-quality screen or image with a good clarity of text or image detail. It depends on the number of pixels used. In raster printing, resolution is defined by the number of dots per inch (see dpi).

HITS – Hyperlink-Induced Topic Search. The searching algorithm for hyperlinked environments, such as the Web. The algorithm is based on the so-called authorities, i.e. webpages that provide the best sources of information on given topics, and the so-called hubs, i.e. webpages that provide collections of links to authorities. HITS works in two steps. The sampling step is used to find a set of webpages that look likely to be found in the relevant authorities. The second step is iterative numerical estimation of the largest weights of hubs and authorities.

HKUST – Hong Kong University of Science and Technology. One of the biggest world-class universities in Asia (http://www.ust.hk).

HLHSR – Hidden Line Hidden Surface Removal. A technique in computer graphics for determining visible lines and surfaces of 3D solid objects using the view point. See also 3D and VRC.

HLL – High-Level Language. A common term for any programming language that uses a higher level of abstraction than assembly languages. Statements in a high-level language generally use keywords similar to English words, which are then translated (during the compilation) into more than one machine-language instruction. In practice, every programming language above assembly languages is a high-level language. Also called high-order language. Examples include APL, FORTRAN, COBOL, Pascal, Ada, C, C++, Java and Visual Basic.

HLLAPI – High-Level Language API. An IBM API which allows communications between PC and mainframe applications. See also EHLLAPI.

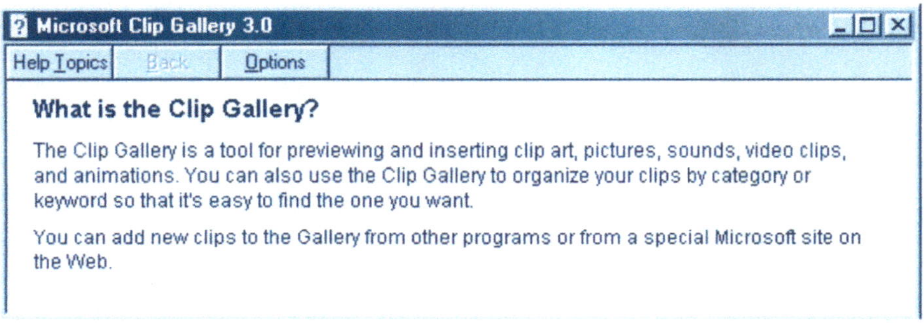

Fig. H-3. An example of a HLP file

HLP – Help file. A filename extension for a file containing help information for an application or utility in the Microsoft Windows environment. An example is shown in Fig. H-3.

HLS – Hue Lightness Saturation. A color model developed specifically for use with color displays introduced by Tektronix in the 1970s. The complete model can be represented by a double cone (see Fig. H-4). Using this model, any color can be specified in terms of an angle and two percentage values for hue, lightness and saturation, respectively. The model defines hue to lie on a circle centered on and at right-angles to 50% of the lightness scale, with blue at 0°, red at 120°, and green at 240°. Each hue is arranged so that it has its complementary color diametrically opposite on the circle. The black color is 0% lightness at the lower apex and white color is 100% lightness at the upper apex. Saturation increases from 0% to 100% on the circle itself. Another term for this is HSB (Hue Saturation Brightness).

HLT – Human Language Technologies. The common name for those technologies that are based on spoken or written languages used for communication between humans, or between human beings and machines or data sources. A typical example of such a technology would be a user interface based on the SILK metaphor (see SILK).

HMA – High Memory Area. The first 64 kilobytes of extended memory, which is memory beyond the 1 MB addressing space limit of MS-DOS. Version 5.0 of MS-DOS and later versions include the file HIMEM.SYS, which allows access to the high memory area.

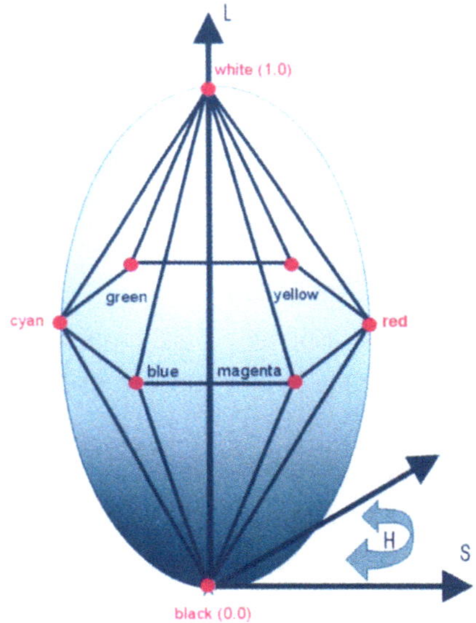

Fig. H-4. HLS color model

HMMA – HyperMedia Management Architecture. A new approach to network and system management proposed by the WBEM consortium (see WBEM), consisting of an object-oriented information model called the HyperMedia Management Schema (see HMMS) and a new management protocol called the HyperMedia Management Protocol (see HMMP).

HMMP – HyperMedia Management Protocol. A work in progress inside the Web-Based Enterprise Management (http://www.dmtf.org/wbem) initiative. HMMP is a protocol designed to help access to management information, allowing management solutions to be platform-independent and physically distributed across the enterprise. HMMP is based on modeling the managed environment as a collection of cooperating managed entities. Each entity can take one or more of four roles within the management environment: client, server, producer and consumer. The information content of the managed object is modeled using the schema defined by the Common Information Model (see CIM). It allows the HMMS to run over HTTP. See WBEM. See also HMMS and HMOM.

HMMS – HyperMedia Management Schema. An extendable data model representing the managed environment inside Web-Based Enterprise Management (see WBEM).

HMOM – HyperMedia Objects Manager. A kind of HMMP server which can switch server and client roles (see HMMP). It is a manager that analyzes the HTTP requests and translates them into native commands for the server. Typically, clients communicate with HMOMs, which are responsible for answering client requests by themselves or forwarding them to the appropriate HMMP server.

HMUX – Hybrid Multiplexer. A component that relies on the MAC layer in the FDDI-II network architecture. See FDDI.

HomePNA – Home Phoneline Networking Association. The industrial consortium (http://www.homepna.org) focusing on the compatibility standards between home-networking products.

HOOD – Hierarchical Object-Oriented Design. A method of hierarchical decomposition of the design into software units based on identification of objects, classes and operations reflecting problem domain entities or more abstract objects related to digital programming entities. It is intended for architectural and detailed design as well as for coding in programming languages such as Ada or C++. The HOOD method was originally developed to provide an object-oriented approach for large mission-critical real-time applications. It supports identification of the object architecture and leads naturally into detailed design where operations of objects are further refined for the target programming language. See also OOD (Object-Oriented Design).

HP – Hewlett-Packard. The worldwide computer manufacturing company represented in approximately 110 countries (http://www.hp.com) founded in 1939 by Dave Packard and Bill Hewlett. HP produces electronic instruments, calculators, a full range of computers, inkjet and laser printers, scanners, etc. The company developed the standard industry bus (see GPIB, HPIB) in 1975. The family of LaserJet printers is the company's most successful product ever.

HPA – High-Performance Addressing. A display technology used for portable computer screens.

HPC – Handheld Personal Computer. A computer that is small enough to fit in a jacket pocket. Compare with Personal Digital Assistant (PDA).

HPC – High-Performance Computing. See HPCC (High-Performance Computing and Communications).

HPCA – High-Performance Computer Architecture. The international symposium on high-performance computer architectures. Topics of interest include processor architectures, novel architectures for emerging applications, real-time and embedded architectures, simulation and performance evaluation, benchmarking and measurements, internetworking, etc.

HPCC – High-Performance Computing and Communications. An umbrella term from NASA, related to advanced high-power computer and communication technologies and architectures, such as supercomputer systems, large-scale parallel systems, high-speed networks, special-purpose systems (e.g. digital libraries, electronic commerce), software for high-performance computing, visualization and virtual reality, etc. There are several supercomputer science and technology testbed centers in the US. Some of them are:

- Cornell Theory Center (see CTC) in Ithaca, NY;
- National Center for Supercomputing Applications (see NCSA) in Urbana–Champaign, IL;
- Pittsburgh Supercomputer Center, Pittsburgh, PA;
- National Center for Atmospheric Research, Boulder, CO;
- The Center for Computer Graphics and Scientific Visualization at the University of Utah;
- The Center for Cognitive Science at the University of Pennsylvania.

More details can be found at http://www.hpcc.gov/blue97

HPCN – High-Performance Computing and Networking Europe. An international conference covering the field of high-performance computing and communications (see HPCC, for example).

HPF – High-Pass Filter. A signal-filter used in an ADSL modem at the customer's premises that allows only higher-frequency data to be delivered. Compare with LPF. See also ADSL.

HPF – High-Performance FORTRAN. A parallel language extension to FORTRAN90 that allows portable application development for a large number of target operating platforms.

HPFS – High-Performance File System. A file system available in OS/2 and Windows NT that supports long and mixed-case filenames, and uses sophisticated data structures and multilevel caching. In addition, it allows some extended free-form attributes to be associated with files and directories. For example, HPFS supports filenames of up to 255 characters, up to 64 KB of extended attributes for each file, and very-high-capacity hard disks (up to 64 GB).

HPGL – Hewlett-Packard Graphics Language. A graphic language designed by Hewlett-Packard for storing and interpreting vector graphical images. Originally it was intended for plotters. HPGL converts graphics into a metafile for later interpretation and original graphic restoration by the applications supporting HPGL.

HPIB – Hewlett-Packard Interface Bus. See GPIB.

HPJ – Help Project file. A filename extension for files that contain help information for Visual Basic (see VB) projects.

HPR – High-Performance Routing. A mechanism used in SNA networks to provide an SNA/APPN network with native access to a wide-area ATM network. See also ATM, APPN and SNA.

HP-UX – Hewlett-Packard UNIX. The Hewlett-Packard UNIX implementation compliant with X/Open Portability Guide Issue 4 (see XPG), FIPS 151.1, POSIX 1003.1, POSIX 1003.2 (see POSIX) and AT&T's SVID2 (see SVID2). This UNIX implementation has some of the features of 4.3 BSD (see BSD).

HQ – Headquarters. A business term used to assign a place where the general management of a company is located.

HR – Human Resources. A common term applied to the department of a company, university, etc. responsible for the legal aspects of employment.

HREF – Hypertext Reference. An attribute in a HTML document that defines a link to another document on the Web. See Fig. H-6. See also HTML.

HSB – Hue Saturation Brightness. A color model (see HLS).

HSLAN – High-Speed Local Area Network. A common term used to describe the generation of local area networks which are capable of running at 100 Mbps or at higher rates. Architectures that can meet the HSLAN requirements include 100BaseX, ATM and FDDI.

HSM – Hierarchical Storage Management. A data storage strategy in which data is distributed across three levels of storage media as follows:

- Primary storage, refers to disks that are immediately accessible;

- Secondary storage, refers to disks that are accessible without the operator's intervention, but their capacity is dormant for a while;
- Tertiary storage, refers to disks that must be requested and mounted or installed each time when extra data storage is required.

HSSI – High-Speed Serial Interface. A serial port that allows communication speeds of up to 52 Mbps.

HST – Hawaii Standard Time. Time zone. UTC – 10.00 hours. See TZ.

HSV – Hue Saturation Value. A color model (see HLS).

HT – Horizontal Tabulation. A control character (ASCII decimal 9) which causes the following character to be placed on the next "tab stop" position. Tab stops can be either at fixed equal distances (usually in text-based editors) or at changeable user-defined distances (usually in text processors).

HTH – Hope this helps. The chat term.

HTI – Human–Technology Interface. Another term for Human–Computer Interface (see HCI).

HTM – HyperText Markup. A filename extension for files that contain HTML documents.

HTML – HyperText Markup Language. A language for writing webpages where information (applications, videos) is stored in a network of nodes connected by hyperlinks (RFC2854). The nodes are meant to be viewed through an interactive browser, of which Mosaic, Netscape, Internet Explorer, Opera and Lotus Domino are the most popular. A hyperlink connects a piece of information on a webpage to another webpage. These links are implemented using Universal Resource Locators (see URL). Users can follow a link (usually underlined text marked by a special color, different to the rest of the information, or hidden behind an invisible object) by clicking on it. Pages that contain links to other pages are said to use hypertext. Markup (meaning that formatting commands, known as tags, are written directly into the source file) comes from actions taken by the page designer who tells the browser which font to use, what color to use, etc. Actually, HTML is an adaptation of ISO standard 8879 (see SGML), specialized for hypertext and the Web. A proper webpage consists of a head and a body enclosed by <HTML> formatting commands (tags) such as <HEAD> and <BODY>. The commands inside tags are called directives; examples include:

<TITLE>The title of the document</TITLE>; and

<FONT>Font name, size and color for document text</FONT>; etc.

Figure H-6 shows the HTML source file for the page shown in Fig. H-5. A program used to create and modify HTML documents (actually webpages) is called a HTML editor. In fact, instead of learning HTM commands, most HTML editors allow users to create webpages in a WYSIWYG manner (displaying the page being edited exactly as it will be shown on the Web). Of course, the additional attributes for modern webpage design, such as Java scripts, VBA scripts, cookies, ASPs, etc., are defined somewhere else and then referenced, as for any other external source (see the image reference in the given example). More information about HTML can be found at http://info.cern.ch/hypertext, and at a number of sites, as well as in written books and articles. HTML is also a filename extension for files that contain HTML documents. See also HTTP and WWW.

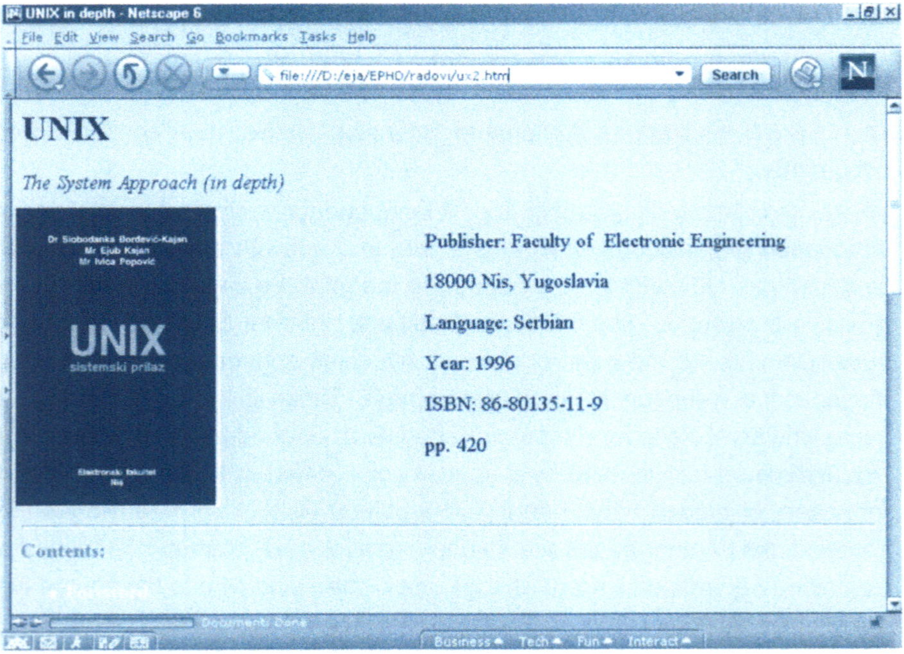

Fig. H-5. The formatted page of the HTML document in Fig. H-6

HTTP – HyperText Transfer Protocol. The standard Web transfer protocol consisting of two items: a set of requests from browsers to servers, and a set of responses. Two kinds of requests are supported: simple and full. A simple request is just a single command naming the page desired. The response is a raw page without headers, with no MIME, and no encoding. Full requests are recognized by the presence of the protocol version on the request line (GET, PUT, LINK, etc.). A full request can be issued as a set of multiple lines, first with the command line, and then a blank line for the end of the request indication, and then lines between, with RFC822 headers. HTTP specifications are available in RFC1945 and RFC2616.

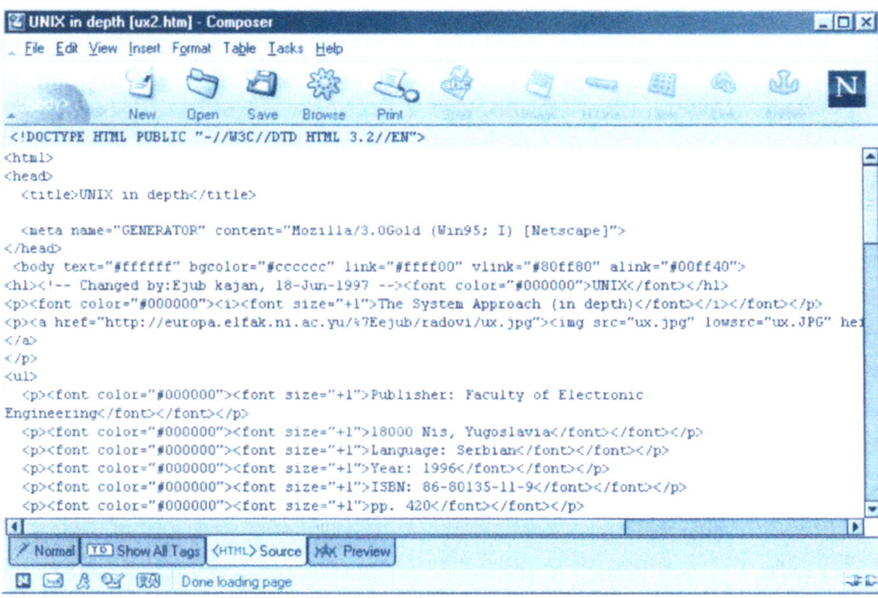

Fig. H-6. Part of the HTML for the page given in Fig. H-5

HTTPD – HyperText Transfer Protocol Daemon. The simplest form of Web server (see HTTPS), a program that can recognize and respond to requests using HTTP. The word “daemon” in the title follows earlier versions of HTTPDs dedicated to UNIX environments. See also HTTP.

HTTP-NG – HTTP Next Generation. A standard under development by the World-Wide Web Consortium (see W3C) for improving performance and enabling the addition of features such as security (see HTTPS).

HTTPS – HyperText Transfer Protocol, Secure. A Netscape variant of HTTP used for handling secure transactions. To specify an address on a HTTP server using the Secure Sockets Layer (see SSL) a user has to use https instead of http. The default port number of https is 443, as assigned by the Internet Assigned Numbers Authority (see IANA).

HTTPS – HTTP Server. Any machine (Web server) on which a HTTP server program can run. A HTTP server program is one that uses HTTP to serve up HTML documents and any associated files and scripts when requested by a client, such as a Web browser. The client/server connection is usually broken after the requested document or file has been served up. HTTP servers are used on Web and Intranet sites.

H/W – Hardware. The physical components of a computer system, including electronic boards, mechanical and plastic parts, cables, peripherals, etc. Computer manufacturers often use the abbreviation.

HWIH – Here's what I have. The chat term.

HyQ – HyTime Query. A language for use with HyTime defined in Annex A of the HyTime standard. It represents a sort of API by which computer systems can interact with HyTime systems using HyTime location. The HyQ language itself is a Lisp-like language where queries are specified by nesting HyQ functions within other functions. HyQ is not tied to any particular retrieval or search engine and therefore represents an interchange language for queries that would then be interpreted into concrete queries using proprietary query languages or mechanisms.

HYTELNET – Hypertext browser for Telnet. A menu-driven index of Internet resources that are accessible via Telnet, including library catalogs, databases and bibliographies, bulletin boards, and network information services. HYTELNET can operate through a client program on a computer connected to the Internet, or through the World-Wide Web. HYTELNET was written by Peter Scott at the University of Saskatchewan. See also Telnet.

HyTime – Hypermedia Time. An ISO standard (ISO/IEC10744) that defines an architecture for creating hypertext and hypermedia applications. HyTime primarily addresses the problem of hyperlinking as a problem of addressing, in other words, locating objects in space or time. A key aspect of addressing is the use of queries to find things based on their properties. It is designed using SGML as the notation language and defines a number of functions related directly to SGML constructs. See also SGML and HyQ.

Hz – Hertz. The unit for frequency measurement. 1 Hz equals one cycle per second. Bigger units (kHz = 1000 Hz, MHz = 1000 kHz, and GHz = 1000 MHz) are more often in practical use.

I

I2 – Internet 2. See NGI (Next Generation Internet).

I2C – Inter-IC. A type of bus used to connect integrated circuits (see IC). I2C was developed by Philips Semiconductors and is used in video devices (monitors, TV sets, etc.).

I2-DSI – Internet2 Distributed Storage Infrastructure. A project considering replicating hosting services for Internet content and applications. The result of I2-DSI should be keeping network traffic local and balancing it among the distributed servers. Such servers are operating at the moment in Indiana, North Carolina, South Dakota, Tennessee and Texas (US sites only). Several worldwide companies such as Cisco, IBM, and other companies support the project. Up-to-date information can be found at http://dsi.internet2.edu

I2-DVN – Internet2 Digital Video Network. An initiative in the US for a higher-education video network service capable of providing scalable and easy-to-use applications in order to deliver live or stored interactive high-quality digital video.

I2O – Intelligent Input/Output. An open standard (pronounced "eye-two-oh") that allows device drivers to operate across multiple operating environments. The architecture of I2O abstracts I/O operations (see I/O) into a set of messages, which allow the host and the I/O device to communicate.

I2OSIG – I2O Special Interest Group. An organization (http://www.i2osig.org) formed to define and promote a standard interface for high-performance I/O systems (see I2O). The organization was established at the beginning of 1996 by a group of leading enterprise-computing vendors.

I3E – IFIP Conference on E-Commerce, E-Business and E-Government. An IFIP conference that provides a forum for users, engineers and researchers in academia, industry and government, where they can present the latest results in e-commerce, e-business or e-government applications.

I18N – I-eighteen letters-N. The process of internationalization, i.e. planning and implementing products and services so that they can easily be adapted to particular languages (localization). Such processes, for example, support international character sets, allow translation of user interface dialog to a local language, etc.

IA5 – International Alphabet 5. A character set (ISO646) coded by seven bits used in ITU-T X.400 MHS for message transfer. IA5 is almost identical to the ASCII character set, but some character encoding can be changed (for example, ASCII # and ASCII $, and there is a redefinition of 10 characters for specific national purposes). In order to make a clear distinction between ASCII and IA5 there is a subset of IA5 (see IRV).

IAB – Internet Architecture Board. An Internet technical coordination body (http://www.iab.org) that has an influence on the quality of Internet-related standards. It has two task forces, IETF and IRTF.

IAC – In any case. The chat term.

IAC – Internet Access Coalition. An industrial organization involved in Internet access over telephone lines (see CTI, TAPI and TSAPI).

IAC – Inter-Application Communication. A process in MacOS System 7 used for communication between applications as well as for data exchange. Among others, IAC uses program-to-program communication, copy and paste by clipboard, events for program execution, etc.

IAIM – International Academy for Information Management. The annual conference organized by the association with the same name, dedicated to discussion about information-system instructional, pedagogical and curriculum-oriented topics.

IAL – International Algebraic Language. The first name of the ALGOL programming language (see ALGOL).

IANA – Internet Assigned Numbers Authority. The central Internet registry for various assigned numbers such as port, protocol, enterprise numbers, etc. For example, a TCP incoming port number for a HTTP server listening browser is port 80. It can be contacted at iana@isi.edu. See also ICANN.

IAP – Internet Access Provider. An organization which provides access to the Internet. It purchases an Internet link from another company that has a direct link to the Internet and resells portions of that bandwidth to the general audience (end-users).

IAPC – Instantly Available/OnNow Personal Computer. A technology for simplifying computers that allows personal computers to drop into a sleep state after a certain time of inactivity and at the same time to respond to an external stimulus (phone or fax calls, for example). The term is closely connected to the EasyPC initiative lead by Intel and Microsoft and supported by other PC manufacturers.

IAS – Information Access Service. Part of the IRDA protocol used so that the device can learn about the services offered by another device. See also IRDA.

IASG – Internetwork Address Subgroup. A range of internetwork-layer addresses summarized in an internetwork-layer routing protocol.

IASTED – International Association of Science and Technology for Development. An international organization (http://www.iasted.com) that provides a forum for scientists, researchers and industry members from all over the world to share their ideas and experience relating to the latest developments in the fields of science and engineering. In addition, IASTED has organized about 20 conferences each year since 1977.

IAT – Intelligent Agent Technology. The Asia–Pacific biennial international conference focusing on intelligent agent technologies. Its topics cover the future development of new models, new methodologies and new tools for building agent-based systems.

IAWTIC – Intelligent Agents, Web Technologies and Internet Commerce. An international conference for researchers and practitioners in the area of intelligent agents, Web technologies and e-commerce. The conference topics include agent architectures, intelligent business agents, mobile agents, virtual agent-based marketplaces, automated shopping and trading agents, virtual trading institutions, electronic payment systems, Internet marketing, etc.

IBD – Internet Business Directory. Internet search tool (http://www.ibdi.com) that allows users to find local, regional, national or international companies by name, city, state, zip, area code, or type of business. With over 20 million listings, this service provides free searches and listings for businesses.

IBG – Inter-Block Gap. An unused space between data blocks stored on a disk or tape that does not allow new data in a block to overwrite adjacent data in blocks.

IBM – International Business Machines. The biggest computer manufacturer in the world, known as "Big Blue" after its logo color. IBM produces and sells a wide variety of computer hardware, mainframes, servers, workstations, personal computers, printers, modems, etc., as well as system software and applications. In 2000 its total revenue was US$ 88.4 billion and the total number of employees was over 316,000. The IBM PC product line has been such a great success on the market that a lot of PC manufacturers have simply made IBM PC-compatible clones. In the spring of 1997 IBM definitively reserved a place in history, when its supercomputer named "Deep

Blue" won a chess match against the then world champion, Gary Kasparov. More information about IBM and its current product lines and development can be found at http://www.ibm.com

IBMNM – IBM Network Management. A protocol used for network management in an IBM Token Ring network.

IC – Integrated Circuit. An abbreviation used to refer to electronic components, such as transistors, resistors, diodes, etc., fabricated on a single chip of silicon crystal or other material. Jack Kilby (Texas Instruments) and Robert Noyce (Fairchild Semiconductor) developed the first ICs in the 1950s. Depending on the number of elements they incorporate, ICs are categorized by degree of integration, ranging from small-scale integration to ultra-large-scale integration (see SSI, MSI, LSI, VLSI, SLSI and ULSI).

IC – Internet Computing. IEEE journal that publishes the latest developments in Internet-based applications and supporting technologies (online version, http://www.computer.org/internet).

IC3N – International Conference on Computer Communications and Networks. IEEE international conference focusing on the design, implementation and applications of computer communications and networks. The topics include optical communications, ATM networking, QoS issues, network interoperability, intelligent networks, network management and security, video on demand, communication software, real-time communications, wireless, mobile and satellite networks, protocol design and testing, etc.

ICA – Intelligent Communication Adapter. Part of the VINES networking environment that provides serial connections from a VINES server to other environments. See also VINES.

ICA – International Communication Association. An international membership organization (http://www.ica.org) composed of academic institutes concerned with the promotion and use of international communication facilities.

ICA3PP – International Conference on Algorithms and Architectures for Parallel Processing. An international conference focusing on theory and technologies in parallel and distributed computing. The topics concentrate on architectures, algorithms, networks, systems and applications of such computing. See Fig. I-1 and visit the given address.

ICAI – Intelligent Computer-Assisted Instruction. A common term for computer programs that help people to learn by using artificial intelligence techniques. They adapt instructional sessions to the needs, knowledge and learning capabilities of their users. Such programs, or systems, are also known as intelligent tutoring systems (see ITS).

ICANN – Internet Corporation for Assigned Names and Numbers. An agency (http://www.icann.org) formed to manage a newly privatized and competitive system for registering, coordinating and maintaining Internet domain names. ICANN is usually pronounced "eye-can". This service was previously performed by the Internet Assigned Number Authority (see IANA).

Fig. I-1. Homepage of ICA3PP 2000

I-CASE – Integrated Computer-Aided Software Engineering. A collection of software tools that perform software engineering functions such as fully automated program design, coding and debugging.

ICC – Iterative and Collaborative Computing. An international conference focusing on agent-based systems, adaptive and adaptable systems, computer-mediated communications, CSCW, computer-supported cooperative learning, digital libraries, ergonomics, interface and cognitive issues, HCI, multimedia and hypermedia, wearable computing, etc.

ICCAD – International Conference on Computer-Aided Design. An international conference focusing on physical design and test, synthesis and system design, and verification, modeling and simulation.

ICCCM – Interclient Communications Conventions Manual. A data communication format in the X Window System environment.

ICCCN – International Conference on Computer Communications and Networks. See IC3N.

ICCV – International Conference on Computer Vision. IEEE international conference focusing on computer vision. The topics include real-time vision, visually guided robotics, image segmentation, integrating speech and image understanding, tracking of gestures, etc. More information is available at the address given in Fig. I-2.

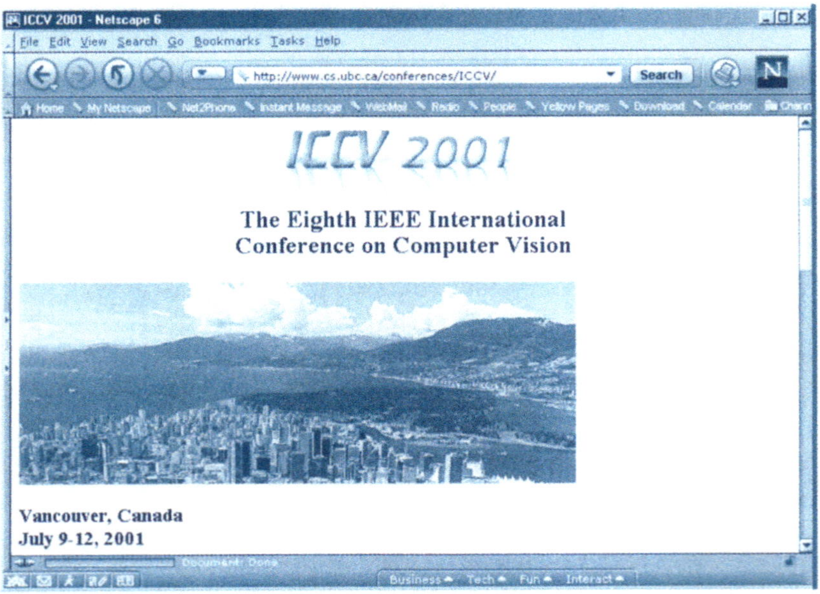

Fig. I-2. Homepage of ICCV 2001

ICD – International Code Designator. A code used to identify an international organization. The British Standards Institution (see BSI) handles ICD registration.

ICDCS – International Conference on Distributed Computing Systems. An international conference sponsored by IEEE that focuses on aspects of distributed and parallel computing. Some of the major topics include clustered architectures, distributed systems, fault-tolerant systems, protocols, mobile computing and the Internet, multimedia, digital libraries, multiagent systems, etc. The proceedings are published by IEEE Computer Society Press.

ICDL – International Centre for Distance Learning. A documentation center that specializes in collecting and disseminating information on distance education worldwide (http://www.icdl.open.ac.uk).

ICE – Information and Content Exchange. A protocol that allows one provider to pass information to another provider by using a HTML page.

ICECCS – International Conference on the Engineering of Complex Computer Systems. IEEE international conference focusing on all aspects of complex computer systems. Some of the major topics are tools, environments and languages for complex systems, complex data management including distributed, real-time and mobile databases, formal methods for achieving dependability in complex systems, human factors, interoperability, standardization, security, etc.

ICEIS – International Conference on Enterprise Information Systems. An international forum for researchers and practitioners interested in enterprise information systems (see EIS). The conference covers different aspects of enterprise computing such as enterprise database applications, AI, DSS, system analysis and specification, and Internet and electronic commerce (see EC).

ICF – International Cryptography Framework. A new security solution for the Internet and electronic commerce (see EC). It has a four-part architecture consisting of a host system which delivers secure applications to the end-user, a hardware-based encryption engine (cryptographic unit), a policy token (software that tells the cryptographic unit what level of encryption is desired), and a network security server run by a certified organization.

ICL – International Computers Limited. A UK hardware and software vendor (http://www.icl.co.uk) that specializes in system integration in selected areas. It operates in over 80 countries worldwide. Now a part of Fujitsu.

ICMIT – International Conference on Management of Innovation and Technology. The new IEEE international conference focusing on product and process innovation, technology and R&D management, supply-chain management, TQM, management of intellectual properties, management of information technology, software engineering management, economics and the legal impact of the Internet, financial engineering, etc.

ICMP – Internet Control Message Protocol. An extension to the Internet protocol (IP) defined by RFC792 that allows error events on the Internet to be reported. A wide variety of messages can be generated by ICMP, classified according to unreachable destination, expired time, invalid header field, necessary redirection, echoes, etc. There are also four message types dealing with Internet addressing to allow hosts to discover their network numbers and solve some other possible addressing problems.

ICN – Implicit Congestion Notification. A way to determine if there is congestion on a network. In the case of congestion, some transport protocols can produce implicit inferences. Compare with explicit congestion notification (ECN).

ICN – International Conference on Networking. An IEEE conference focusing on network technologies. Topics of interest include communications modeling, security, switching and routing, ATM, VoIP, MPLS, QoS, wireless networks, active networks, Java, TINA, CORBA, traffic engineering, multimedia and multicast communications, etc.

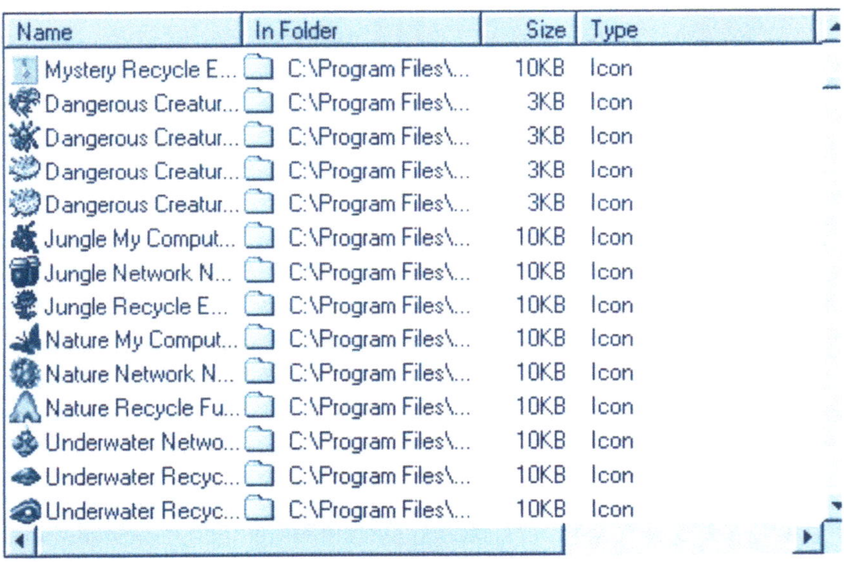

Fig. I-3. Examples of ICO files

ICO – Icon. A filename extension for a Microsoft Windows file that contains an icon (see Fig. I-3).

ICOIN – International Conference on Information Networking. An international conference focusing on all aspects of communication networks and distributed computing systems. Some of the major topics include communication protocols and architectures, security and privacy, distributed database systems, mobile and nomadic computing, internetworking and the World-Wide Web, high-speed communications, multimedia communications, groupware, personal communication systems, distance learning, QoS, etc. The proceedings are published by IEEE CS Press.

I-Commerce – Internet Commerce. See e-commerce (EC).

ICP – IMA Control Protocol. A mechanism that enables IMA (inverse multiplexing over ATM) cell streams to be reassembled at the receiving end. Control cells inserted into each link enable endpoints to continually negotiate and configure connections. Data fields within the control cells transmit information about the state of the link. See also IMA.

ICP – Independent Content Provider. A person or a company that delivers broadcast content. Such content can be television programs, websites, software, etc.

ICP – Internet Cache Protocol. A protocol used by one proxy server to query another for a cached webpage instead of trying to retrieve it from the original location.

ICP – Internet Content Provider. An organization that provides news, reference material, audio or video content for websites.

ICPADS – International Conference on Parallel and Distributed Systems. An international conference for discussing and sharing experiences and new ideas on all aspects of parallel and distributed systems. Topics include parallel/distributed architectures, algorithms, applications, databases, compilers and languages, distributed operating systems, programming environments, distributed object systems, high-speed networking and protocols, interoperable autonomous systems, fault-tolerant systems, multimedia systems and communications, mobile and real-time computation and communication, CSCW, security and privacy, distributed agent systems, etc.

ICPP – International Conference on Parallel Processing. An international conference that focuses on the latest research in the field of parallel and distributed computing. Major topics include network embedding, parallel and distributed algorithms, resource management, distributed shared memory, network monitoring, adaptive communications, groupware, compiler optimization, parallel applications, job scheduling, mobile computing, etc.

ICR – Intelligent Character Recognition. A technology that employs either software only or software and hardware techniques to recognize and translate raster images into a structured text.

ICR – Initial Cell Rate. An ATM Available Bit Rate (see ABR) service parameter that represents the rate at which a source should send initially and after an idle period. ICR is expressed in cells/s. See also ATM and QoS.

ICSE – International Conference on Software Engineering. An international conference focusing on the software engineering field, especially on program comprehension.

ICSM – International Conference on Software Maintenance. An international conference in the field of software and systems evolution, maintenance and management.

ICSR – International Conference on Software Reuse. An international conference that focuses on the latest research in the field of software reuse. Some of the major topics include object-oriented methods, product-line architectures, formal domain languages, generative reuse, design patterns, etc.

ICSTM – International Conference on Systems Theory and Management. An international conference intended for research and industrial people interested in the contemporary developments in systems theory and contemporary experiences in the practice of systems management. Some major topics include action learning and research, adaptive and strategic planning, chaos and complexity, cognitive processes in systems thinking and learning, community and soft operational research, cybernetics, information systems implementation and management, management strategy for information technology, quality management systems, philosophy of systems thinking, etc.

ICTEC – International Conference on Telecommunications and Electronic Commerce. An international annual conference dedicated to emerging electronic commerce research (see EC) and telecommunications aspects of it.

ICTS – Implementation Conformance Test Suite. The test suite used by system vendors in order to compare the run-time behavior of their system to the appropriate Application Binary Interface specification (see ABI and ABI+).

I-D – Internet Draft. A working draft document of the IETF and its Working Groups, valid for a maximum of six months; it may be updated, replaced or made obsolete by other documents at any time. Very often, I-Ds are precursors of RFCs. See also Internet Engineering Task Force (IETF) and Request For Comments (RFC).

ID – Interrupt Identifier. A unique value used by an operating system kernel (see OS) in order to identify the device that raised the interrupt and that requires more processing. Also used to check whether the interrupt handling is complete or whether to invoke an interrupt service thread (see IST).

IDA – Intelligent Data Analysis. A paper- and Web-based refereed journal published by Elsevier Science. It covers the research and applications of AI techniques in data analysis across a variety of disciplines. Techniques such as data visualization, database mining, data fusion, editing, transformation, filtering, sampling, machine learning, fuzzy logic, statistical pattern recognition, etc. are discussed. Also, IDA is the name of the international symposium with similar topics, the proceedings are published by Springer-Verlag (see LNCS).

IDAPI – Integrated Database Application Programming Interface. An API set that puts emphasis on the navigational access to data. IDAPIs are rich enough to support basically any ISAM type of data source and yet efficient enough so that they do not add unnecessary overheads while doing basic data access. They also incorporate the query concept, either SQL or QBE, into the same unified framework. IDAPI was developed by Borland, IBM and Novell as an alternative to ODBC (see ODBC). See also ISAM, SQL and QBE.

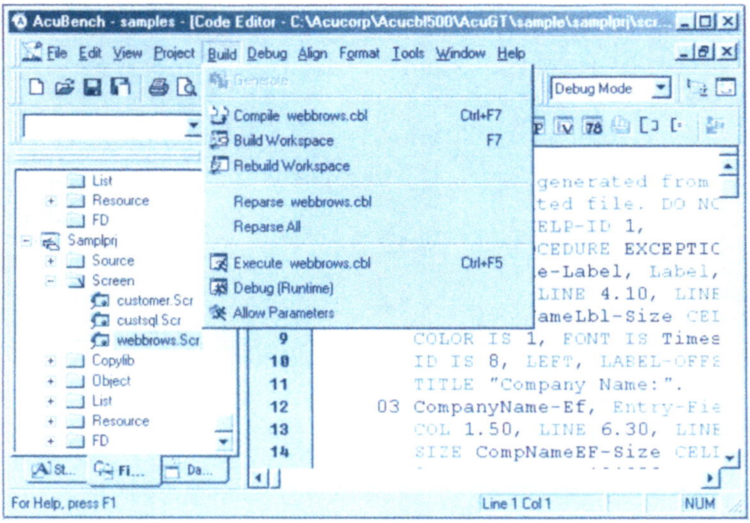

Fig. I-4. AcuBench as an example of an IDE

IDC – Internet Database Connector. A method for accessing database files indirectly over some type of network.

IDD – Internet Data Distribution. Software developed by Unidata for distributing real-time data over the Internet.

IDD – Installable Device Driver. A user-level dynamic-link library (see DLL) that drives devices connected to a Windows CE-based platform by means of standard input/output.

IDE – Integrated Device Electronics. A type of disk drive interface in which the controller resides in the drive itself.

IDE – Interactive Development Environment. A collection of interactive software tools for supporting software development processes. Such systems may include appropriate graphical tools, syntax-directed editors, integrated compilers, appropriate run-time environments, and so on. Well-known examples are Visual C++ and Visual Basic (see VB). Another example is AcuBench, the tool developed by Acucorp, intended for fast COBOL application development (http://www.acucorp.com), with a look and feel as depicted in Fig. I-4. AcuBench is described elsewhere (see COBOL).

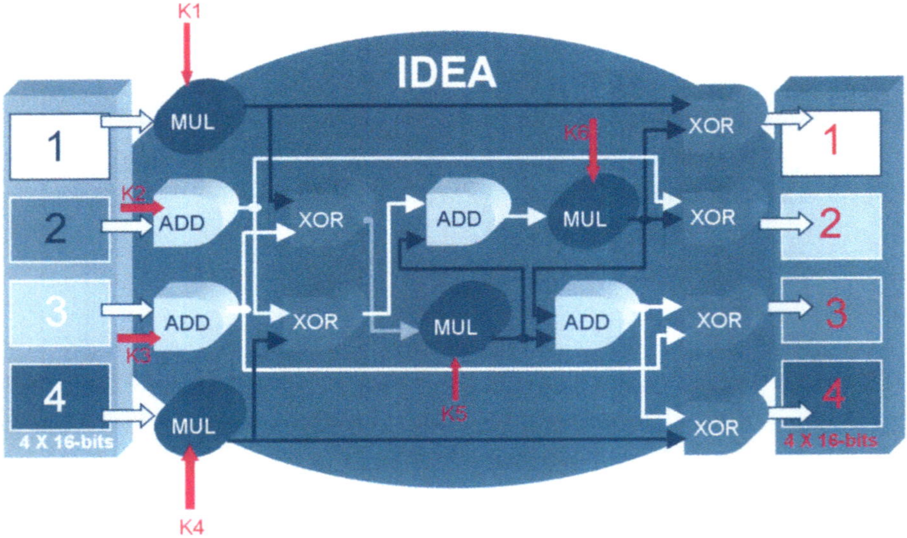

Fig. I-5. The “top secret” details of one IDEA iteration

IDEA – International Data Encryption Algorithm. An encryption algorithm written in Switzerland by Xuejia Lai and James Massey in 1992 that uses a 128-bit key. The basic structure of IDEA uses 64-bit blocks that are managed in a sequence of eight parameterized iterations (see Fig. I-5) to produce 64-bit output ciphers. For iteration, every output bit depends on every input bit. The whole algorithm uses only three operations: 16-bit addition modulo 2^{16}, 16-bit multiplication modulo $2^{16}+1$, and XOR implemented on four 16-bit input blocks and on every intermediate result after iteration. The 128-bit key mechanism is used to generate six keys (K1, K2, ...and K6) for each of eight iterations and four for the final transformation. There is no currently known technique capable of breaking a message encrypted using IDEA. For instance, it is used in the Pretty Good Privacy (see PGP) package.

IDEAL – Intelligent Data Engineering and Automated Learning. An international biennial conference focusing on the latest developments in data engineering and learning. The proceedings are published by Springer-Verlag (see LNAI).

IDI – Initial Domain Identifier. The part of a network address in the OSI Reference Model (see OSI) that represents an administrative unit (i.e. a domain).

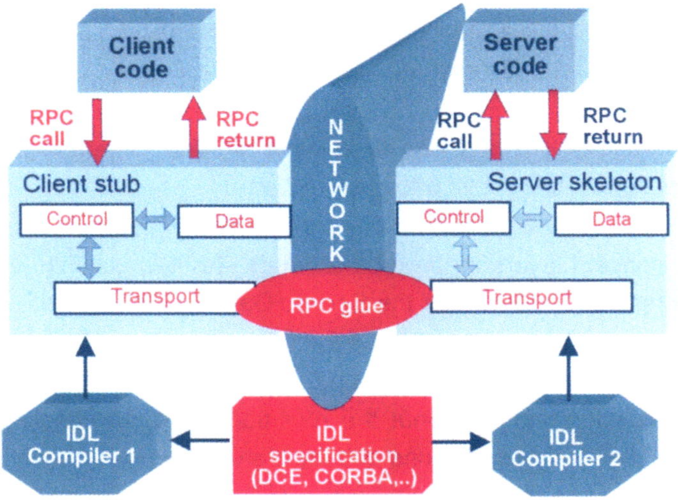

Fig. I-6. Generation of a client stub and server skeleton using IDL

IDL – Interface Description (Definition) Language. A common term for a platform-independent description language used in distributed computing frameworks. There are several standardized IDLs. In the OSF Distributed Computing Environment (see DCE), IDL is used as a tool for defining RPC stubs (see RPC). In the Common Object Request Broker Architecture (see CORBA), IDL is the base mechanism for object interaction with mapping specifications to C++, Ada, Smalltalk, COBOL, etc. For a given IDL, compilers translate interface definitions into client stub and server skeleton code in a target programming language (see Fig. I-6). Thus, this code provides the marshaling and unmarshaling glue (see DCE) between the infrastructure (network environment) and the client and server application code.

IDLE – International Data Line East. An imaginary line that represents UTC + 12.00 hours to the east of UTC. See TZ (Time Zone) and UTC.

IDLW – International Data Line West. An imaginary line that represents UTC – 12.00 hours to the west of UTC. See TZ (Time Zone) and UTC.

IDP – Internet Datagram Packet. A network-level routing protocol in the XNS protocol suite. It can be used to route packets from any of several transport-layer protocols such as the Routing Information Protocol (see RIP), Packet Exchange Protocol (see PEP), or Sequenced Packet Exchange (see SPP). It was the basis for the NetWare IPX protocol. See also XNS.

IDRP – Interdomain Routing Protocol. An ISO protocol for routing transmission between different administrative domains. It is based on the Border Gateway Protocol (see BGP).

IDSS – Intelligent Decision Support System. A decision support system (see DSS) that uses artificial intelligence techniques.

IDU – Interface Data Unit. A term related to the communication scenario between two adjacent layers of the protocol stack. An IDU consists of both the interface control information and the Service Data Unit (see SDU).

IDX – Index file. A filename extension for a file, generated by Visual FoxPro, that contains one header record and one or more node records. The header record contains information about the root node, the current file size, the length of the key, the index options and the signatures.

IE – Information Engineering. A methodology that translates a company's strategic goals into data and applications that will help to achieve specific company goals.

IE – Internet Explorer. The popular Web browser developed by Microsoft (see MSIE).

IEC – International Electrotechnical Commission. An international standards organization founded in 1906, which, together with ISO, defines a lot of international standards related to information technologies (http://www.iec.ch).

IEEE – Institute of Electrical and Electronics Engineers. Probably the largest professional organization in the world (http://www.ieee.org) relating to computer and communications technologies. In addition to its publishing activities (famous journals such as IEEE Computer, IEEE Communications Magazine, IEEE Expert, IEEE Journal on Selected Areas in Communications, and many more), it runs a large number of international conferences. IEEE has a standardization group as respected as either ANSI or ISO.

IEEE CS – IEEE Computer Society. The world's largest association of computing professionals (http://computer.org). The society publishes IEEE Computer, a monthly magazine containing tutorials and in-depth articles of relevance across the computer field, news, conference announcements and calls for papers, information on industry trends, etc. In addition, the society publishes 11 magazines and 9 research-oriented transactions (see TOPAMI, TPDS, TSE, TKDE, TC, TVCG, TMM, TON and TVLSI). Over 150 titles (books and conference and workshop proceedings) are also published by the society every year.

IEF – Information Engineering Facility. A fully integrated set of CASE tools (see CASE) that generates COBOL code for a wide variety of platforms (PC, MVS, VMS, AIX, HP-UX, etc.).

IEPG – Internet Engineering Planning Group. A group (http://www.isc.org/iepg) primarily composed of Internet service operators, the goal of which is to promote a globally coordinated Internet operating environment.

IESG – Internet Engineering Steering Group. The executive committee of IETF (http://www.ietf.org/iesg.html). It provides the first technical review of Internet standards and is responsible for the day-to-day management of IETF.

IETF – Internet Engineering Task Force. An Internet group that makes technical and other contributions to the development of the Internet and its technologies. It is a wide-open international community (http://www.ietf.org) for all organizations or individuals interested in Internet development.

IETM – Interactive Electronic Technical Manual. A computer-based collection of the technical information needed for the diagnosis and maintenance of a defense system, visually arranged and formatted for interactive presentation to the end-user on an electronic display system.

I/F – Interface. A common term for the point at which a connection is made between two elements so that they can work with one another. In hardware, interfaces are usually physical connectors with specified electrical characteristics (PCI, SCSI, etc.). Typical examples in software are user interfaces (see UI), APIs, etc.

IFC – Internet Foundation Classes. A set of Java objects, classes and frameworks written by Netscape that helps speed up the development of network-based complex and robust applications. It is possible to access these classes via Java, JavaScript, C and C++. IFC is freely available both in object code and in source code. The five basic frameworks provided by IFC are animation, concurrency, drag and drop, event and localization. Furthermore,

IFC contains support for multifont text, persistence, UI widgets and windowing systems.

IFD – Interface Device. A hardware device that allows humans to interact with computers or other electronic systems. See also HCI. In general, an IFD must have an input interface (a mouse, a keyboard, a tablet, etc.) and an output interface (display screen, audio output, etc.).

IFIP – International Federation for Information Processing. A multinational organization (pronounced "eye-fip") founded in 1960 representing over 60 member nations concerned with information processing. The IFIP secretariat is located in Laxenburg, Austria (http://www.ifip.or.at). The US counterpart of IFIP is AFIPS.

IFS – Installable File System. A file system that can be loaded dynamically into an operating system. Windows NT has an IFS that can read directories using FAT, CDFS or HPFS, and read and write files using the formats appropriate for the file system.

IGC – Institute for Global Communications. An organization (http://www.igc.org) dedicated to the use of computer networks in areas such as human rights, peace and environmental protection.

IGES – Initial Graphics Exchange Specification. A standard file format for computer graphics data storage supported by ANSI, especially intended for describing models created with CAD programs. It includes a wide variety of basic primitives that enable a standard way of describing drawings and engineering diagrams.

IGMP – Internet Group Management Protocol. The Internet multicasting protocol (RFC1112) having only two kinds of packets: query and response. It uses class D addresses (see IP). Special multicast routers implement multicasts, each of them sending hardware multicasts to the hosts on its LAN every minute (approximately), asking them to report back on the groups their processes currently belong to. Each host sends back responses for all the class D addresses of interest.

IGP – Interior Gateway Protocol. An Internet protocol distributing routing information within an autonomous system (see AS), i.e. within each network. To expand these capabilities between networks an exterior gateway protocol is used (see EGP). The term gateway in the abbreviation follows an old convention. The preferred modern concept that represents the same function is the router. The most widely supported IGPs are the Routing Information Protocol (see RIP) and Open Shortest-Path First (see OSPF).

IHA – I hate acronyms. The chat term.

IHL – Internet Header Length. A field in an Internet Protocol (see IP) datagram or packet (see Fig. I-10).

IHW – Information Hiding Workshop. An international workshop focusing on the protection of digital intellectual property. The proceedings are published by Springer-Verlag (see LNCS).

IIA – Information Interchange Architecture. An IBM standard for exchanging documents between different systems.

IICS – International Interactive Communications Society. The worldwide non-profit organization (http://www.iics.bc.ca) for interactive media professionals. Dedicated to the advancement of interactive arts and technologies since 1983, members of the IICS include professionals involved in the rapidly integrating digital "convergence" industries: multimedia, computing, telecommunications, education, mass media, consumer electronics, publishing and entertainment, among others.

IINREN – Interagency Interim National Research and Education Network. An evolving network system under development since 1992. A smooth evolution of this networking infrastructure into the future gigabit network is expected (see NREN).

IIOP – Internet Inter-ORB Protocol. Part of the CORBA document that specifies how General Inter-ORB Protocol (see GIOP) messages are exchanged using TCP/IP. The protocol is suitable for use by any ORB to interoperate in an IP domain.

IIS – Internet Information Server. Microsoft's Web-based Windows NT server that allows web browsers to access applications and information on Windows NT servers. IIS 3.0 adds Active Server Pages (see ASP), allowing business information to be embedded into HTML pages. The latest information about IIS can be found at http://www.microsoft.com/products/prodref/81ov.htm

IIXNET – Internet–Intranet–Extranet. The common term related to all networks that use the TCP/IP protocol and Web-based technologies. The term "Internet", as a global network, is explained later in this chapter. The term "Intranet" refers to a network that may also be distributed to some extent, and may be owned by a corporation and accessible only by authorized people. An Intranet is protected against unauthorized access using so-called firewalls. The term "Extranet" refers to an Intranet with a door provided for external viewers (usually business partners) that have some kind of limited access rights with appropriate authorization.

IJAIS – International Journal of Accounting Information Systems. An academic and professional international journal that publishes articles related to relationships between accounting and information systems.

IJCIO – International Journal of Computational Intelligence and Organization. A quarterly international journal (http://www.ecst.csuchico.edu/~ijcio) focusing on the theories, methods and applications of computational intelligence in organizations.

IJCIS – International Journal of Cooperative Information Systems. The journal published by World Scientific addressing all aspects of cooperative information systems, such as requirements, functionality, implementation, deployment and evolution.

IJHCS – International Journal of Human–Computer Studies/Knowledge Acquisition. A journal published monthly by Academic Press. Some of the major topics of the journal are intelligent user interfaces, natural language interaction, human factors, computer-supported cooperative work, speech and graphical interaction, knowledge acquisition, knowledge-based systems, user modeling, user interface management systems, requirements engineering, etc.

IJIM – International Journal of Information Management. The journal focusing on the responsibility for designing and managing complex information systems.

ILK – Incremental Link. A filename extension for a file that contains status information for later incremental linking to the program.

ILL – Interlibrary Loan. A standard (ISO10160, ISO10161) that defines how to share books and other documents among libraries all over the world.

ILP – Instruction-Level Parallelism. In microprocessor design, the concept of executing two or more instructions in parallel.

ILY – I love you. The chat term. In cyberspace, the term has a wider meaning than that used in real life. Also, the name of the very dangerous virus that appeared at the beginning of May 2000.

IM – Intelligent Messaging. Part of the VINES network operating system that provides for generalized information transfer. IM refers to e-mails and message handling (see BMS), BBSs, calendars, workflow automation, reporting and scheduling, faxes, etc.

IM – Input Method. A mechanism that allows a user to input text by means of a touch-sensitive screen.

IMA – Interactive Multimedia Association. A trade organization founded in 1988 involved in areas of networked services, scripting languages, data formats and intellectual property rights.

IMA – International MIDI Association. A nonprofit international industrial organization that promotes the Musical Instrument Digital Interface (see MIDI) specification.

IMA – Inverse Multiplexing over ATM. An ATM Forum specification that defines how a stream of ATM cells can be distributed in a round-robin fashion over several links and then reassembled into the original order at the receiving end.

IMAC – Isochronous Media Access Control. An element used in the FDDI-II MAC layer that handles isochronous (time-dependent) data such as voice, video, etc. See also FDDI and FDDI-II.

IMAP – Internet Mail Access Protocol. The RFC recommendations (RFC1064, RFC1730, RFC1731, RFC1732 and RFC1733) that allow a client to access and manipulate electronic mail on the server side in the same way that local mailboxes can. Unlike POP3, IMAP allows a user to retrieve messages from more than one computer. IMAP4 was introduced in December 1994. It runs on top of TCP/IP. Compare with POP3.

IMHO – In my humble opinion. A shorthand used in e-mail and in online forums that flags a statement that the writer wants to present as a personal opinion rather than as a statement of fact. See also IMO.

IMINT – Imagery Intelligence. A technique that involves gathering information from the study of images in various forms, i.e. visible, infrared, radar, etc. This type of intelligence can be used to reveal new systems, estimated capabilities, developmental stages, and patterns of movement and activity.

IMO – In my opinion. A shorthand phrase used often in e-mail and Internet news and discussion groups to indicate an author's admission that a statement he or she has just made is not strictly a fact. Compare with IMHO.

IMQ – Istituto Italiano del Marchio di Qualità. Italian quality and safety association (http://www.imq.it).

IMR – Internet Monthly Report. Published monthly. The purpose of the IMRs is to communicate the Internet Research Group's accomplishments, or milestones reached, or problems discovered by the participating organizations.

IMS – Information Management System. A hierarchical database management system (see HDBMS) used in IBM SNA communications. See also SNA.

IMS – Instructional Management System. The common term for any network-based instructional process. An IMS is typically able to establish learning objectives, create learning materials, determine student skill or knowledge levels, assign appropriate materials to students, track progress of a student's work and knowledge, provide and manage student-to-tutor and student-to-student communications, evaluate student learning, and report learning outcomes.

IMSA – Internet and Multimedia Systems and Applications. The IASTED international conference focusing on the subject given in its title. Topics include Internet and Web tools and applications, Internet architectures, Internet and multimedia search technologies, software engineering over the Internet, multimedia database systems, multimedia networking and communications, operating systems for multimedia, video on demand, distance learning, and collaborative systems.

IMTC – International Multimedia Teleconferencing Consortium. The mission of the IMTC is to bring together all organizations involved in the development of interactive multimedia teleconferencing products and services to help create and promote the adoption of industry-wide interoperability standards.

IN – Intelligent Network. Network architecture originated by Bellcore that served as the backbone for a number of advanced telecommunication services. The features of IN are its service-independent architecture, flexible distribution of code to process the services, user-friendly and flexible service-creating functions, open architecture with a set of standard interfaces, compatibility with existing networks, and self-awareness, self-adaptability and self-provisioning capabilities. See also AIN (Advanced Intelligent Network).

INCOSE – International Council on System Engineering. An international organization formed to develop and enhance the system engineering approach to multidisciplinary system development. Its goals are to provide a focal point for systems engineering knowledge, provide collaboration in systems engineering education and research, improve the professional status of all persons engaged, encourage governmental and industrial support for activities in this field, etc.

inetd – Internet daemon. A UNIX command that manages many common TCP/IP services (see FTP etc.).

INF – Information file. A filename extension for Microsoft Windows files that contain setup installation information, either for hardware or software installation. An example of such a file is shown in Fig. I-7.

INFOSEC – Information Security. A common name for the protection of information against unauthorized disclosure, transfer, modification or destruction, whether accidental or intentional.

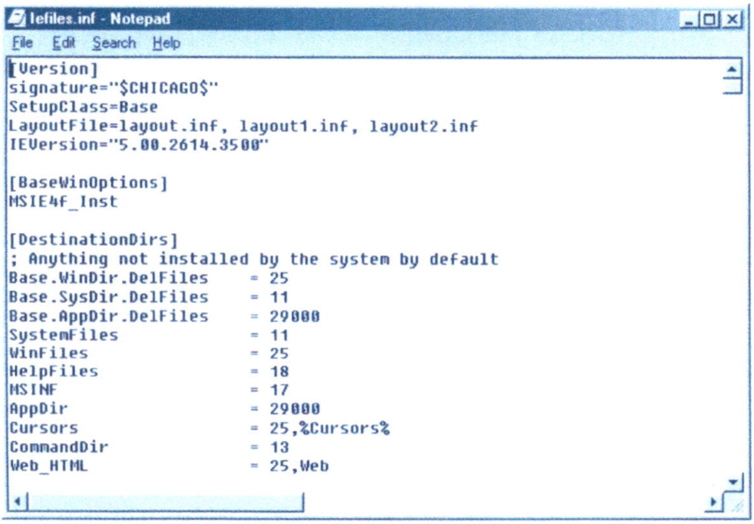

Fig. I-7. An INF for Internet Explorer

INGRES – Interactive Graphic Retrieval System. A set of software tools developed by Computer Associates International (see CA). The current version, Ingres II, includes Ingres RDBMS that offers a new approach to n-tiered relational database application management, OpenROAD, Ingres-/OpenAPI, and embedded SQL precompilers. Furthermore, Ingres/ICE (Internet Commerce Enabled) is a unique database solution that supports Internet and corporate Intranets. Also includes connectivity options (CA ODBC driver and Ingres/Net). Ingres/Visual DBA, Ingres/Replicator and Ingres/Star support distributed databases. Ingres runs on a wide range of platforms, including Windows desktops, Windows NT and UNIX, with connectivity to legacy data.

INI – Initialize. A filename extension for files that contain initialization information about a system and/or its components (such as sys.ini and win.ini). Figure I-8 shows an example of such a file.

INRIA – Institut National de Recherche en Informatique et en Automatique. French computer science research institute (http://www.inria.fr). Among other things it developed Abstract Syntax Notation One (see ASN.1).

INS – Insert key. A key on the keyboard, labeled "Insert" or "Ins", the usual function of which is to toggle a program's editing setting between an insert mode and an overwrite mode, although it may perform different functions in different applications.

INT – International. One of the top-level domains (see TLD) on the Internet. See also DNS (Domain Name System). The INT domain belongs to international organizations such as the International Telecommunication Union (see ITU).

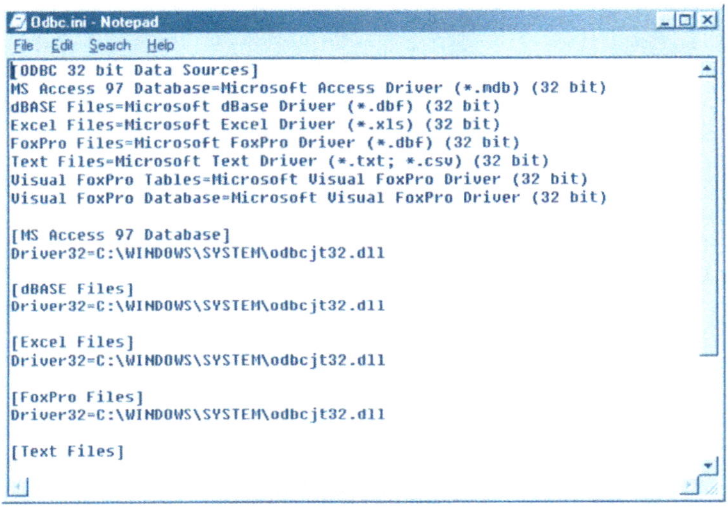

Odbc.ini - Notepad

File Edit Search Help

```
[ODBC 32 bit Data Sources]
MS Access 97 Database=Microsoft Access Driver (*.mdb) (32 bit)
dBASE Files=Microsoft dBase Driver (*.dbf) (32 bit)
Excel Files=Microsoft Excel Driver (*.xls) (32 bit)
FoxPro Files=Microsoft FoxPro Driver (*.dbf) (32 bit)
Text Files=Microsoft Text Driver (*.txt; *.csv) (32 bit)
Visual FoxPro Tables=Microsoft Visual FoxPro Driver (32 bit)
Visual FoxPro Database=Microsoft Visual FoxPro Driver (32 bit)

[MS Access 97 Database]
Driver32=C:\WINDOWS\SYSTEM\odbcjt32.dll

[dBASE Files]
Driver32=C:\WINDOWS\SYSTEM\odbcjt32.dll

[Excel Files]
Driver32=C:\WINDOWS\SYSTEM\odbcjt32.dll

[FoxPro Files]
Driver32=C:\WINDOWS\SYSTEM\odbcjt32.dll

[Text Files]
```

Fig. I-8. An INI file for Microsoft ODBC

Intel – Integrated Electronics. A well-known company, probably the most famous microprocessor chip manufacturer in the world. From the first 4-bit Intel 4004 chip to today's Pentium, the brand name Intel is associated with high-quality microprocessor technologies. See the history of microprocessors at the Intel museum http://www.intel.com/intelis/museum

internet – internetwork. A collection of networks interconnected using routers and other devices that work in general as a single network. Not to be confused with the Internet.

Internet – Interconnected networks. The largest network in the world, "the network of all networks". Developed from a classified proposition to the US Department of Defense made by The RAND Corporation in 1964 for a communication network without a central authority, that would survive a nuclear holocaust, the Internet has grown and gained popularity even among people who do not use computers. In 1969, the first node was installed on a computer at UCLA. It was quickly joined by three others: at the Stanford Research Institute, the University of California at Santa Barbara, and the University of Utah. In 1971, ARPANET, as the network was named, was expanded to 15 nodes (23 hosts), and in 1972 it grew to 37 nodes. In 1974, this network began to use TCP. In the 1980s, different groups linked their computers to the "network of networks", which was by then no longer primarily a military tool. Connecting was easy, and was financed by each connecting entity. Commercial computers and an increasing number of foreign computers were linked to the Internet. Prof. Leonard Kleinrock is often referred to as the father of the Internet. ARPANET formally expired in 1989, a victim of its own success. In addition to maybe hundreds of books written about the Internet, here are some online sources of Internet history:

http://altavista.software.digital.com/inethistory/nfintro.htm;

http://www.totally.com/live/gc/hist.html; http://info.isoc.org

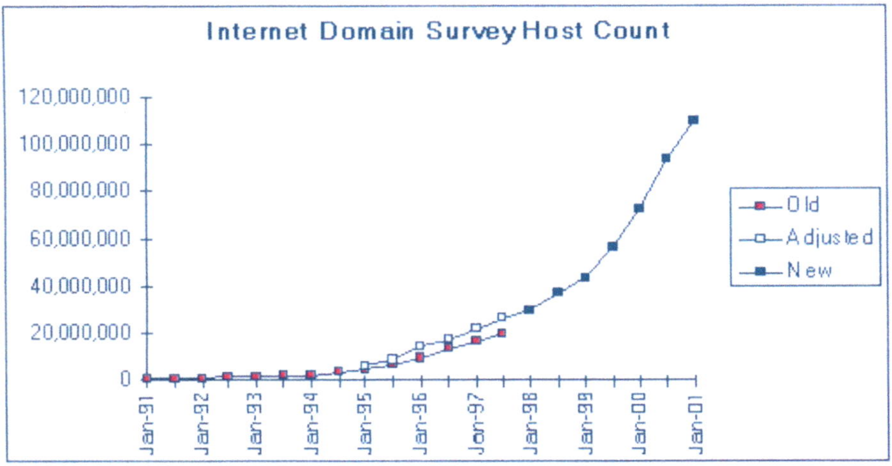

Fig. I-9. The growth of the Internet up to January 2001
(source: Internet Software Consortium, http://www.isc.org)

The Internet continues to grow exponentially. By 1990, it had grown to 3000 networks and 200,000 computers. By 1995, there were multiple backbones, hundreds of regional networks, tens of thousands of LANs, millions of hosts, and tens of millions of users. In addition to the traditional services such as e-mail, news, remote login and file transfer, in 1992 WWW services became available on the Internet. Statistics about the Internet can be found at http://www.openmarket.com/intindex, or at http://www.isc.org, or at http://www.nw.com. According to the Network Wizard Internet Domain Survey, by July 1997 there were 19,540,000 hosts connected to the Internet with more than 1,300,000 domains. The rapid Internet growth trends are shown in Fig. I-9. The figure speaks for itself (more than 109,500,000 hosts connected up to January 2001). During a period of 3.5 years the number of Internet hosts increased more than five-fold. And it is continuing to grow. In order to have a clear picture about why the Internet is so popular, we can take a look at the available services. These include Archie a service for gathering, indexing, and displaying information, WWW and WWWW, a number of browsers (see MSIE, for example), ftp as a basic service, Gopher and Veronica as advanced services, IRC, e-mail, etc. In order to see who is who in the Internet world, look at several bodies associated with running the Internet, such as the IAB, IANA, IETF, W3C, etc., each of which is explained elsewhere in the book.

InterNIC – Internet Network Information Center. The organization that is charged with registering domain names and IP addresses as well as distributing information about the Internet (http://www.internic.net). InterNIC was formed in 1993 as a consortium involving the US National Science Foundation, AT&T, General Atomics, and Network Solutions Inc.

Interpedia – Internet Encyclopedia. A proposed public-domain encyclopedia to be created for and maintained on the Internet.

INTUG – International Telecommunications Users Group. An international users group dedicated to the promotion and use of telecommunications and the satisfaction of users' needs.

I/O – Input/Output. A common term for computer activities and associated hardware and software connected with the "outside world". It refers to the tasks of gathering data for processing and making the results available to users or machines. There are many terms used together with I/O, some of them are:

- I/O buffer: a part of memory dedicated to temporary storage of incoming and outgoing information;
- I/O bus: a part of the computer architecture used for transferring information to and from the CPU and various I/O devices;
- I/O channel: a hardware path from the CPU to the I/O bus;

- I/O controller: a chip or a board associated with an input or output device, interfacing between the device and the microprocessor, also called a device controller;
- I/O device: a hardware component used to provide information to the computer and to receive information from it; for instance, a terminal, modem, etc.;
- I/O processor: a device for handling I/O without disturbing the CPU;
- I2O: a new approach for future input/output (see I2O).

IOC – Interoffice Channel. In digital telecommunications, a communication link between two carrier offices or between points-of-presence (see POP) for two interexchange carriers (see IXC).

IONL – Internal Organization of the Network Layer. The Open System Interconnection (see OSI) standard (ISO8648) for the detailed architecture of the OSI network layer, partitioning the network layer into subnetworks interconnected by convergence protocols. IONL recognizes three sublayers of the network layer. The bottom sublayer, called subnetwork access, provides an interface over which to send data across a network. The middle sublayer, called subnetwork-dependent (or SNDCP), assumes a particular type of subnetwork, i.e. an Ethernet LAN. Finally, at the top of this mininetwork protocol stack is a subnetwork-independent sublayer (see SNICP) that provides internetworking capabilities for the layers above it.

IOP – Interoperability. One of the main attributes related to open systems. IOP is the ability of equipment from different vendors to work together and exchange data, programs, etc., without any limitation. See also PSI (Portability, Scalability and Interoperability).

IOTP – Internet Open Trading Protocol. A set of standards (RFC2801) designed to handle a variety of business transactions between different parties, such as merchant, bank, credit checker, customer, etc., regardless of the payment system. IOTP supports Secure Electronic Transaction (see SET), e-checks and other payment systems.

IOW – In other words. The chat term.

IP – Internet Protocol. The network layer for the TCP/IP protocol suite (see IPS). An IP datagram consists of a header part and a text part. The IP header (see Fig. I-10) has a 20-byte fixed part and a variable-length optional part, together making up a 60-byte maximum length. The version field keeps track of which version of the IP protocol the datagram belongs to. The header length (IHL) field provides information on how long the header is, in

32-bit words. A default value of 5 indicates a header without options. The type of service field tells the subnet what kind of service is required, according to speed and reliability. The total length field covers both the header and data, with a maximum possible length of 65,533 bytes. The identification field allows the destination host to recognize which datagram a newly arrived fragment belongs to. The next bit is unused (U), and the following two indicate whether there is any fragment yet to arrive. The fragment offset has information on where in the current datagram this fragment belongs. The time to live (see TTL) field is a counter used to limit packet lifetimes. The protocol field indicates what kind of transport service is required, TCP, UDP or something else defined in RFC1700 (see TCP/IP). The header checksum verifies the header only. The options field may include some information about security, the exact path from the source to the destination, timestamps and route records.

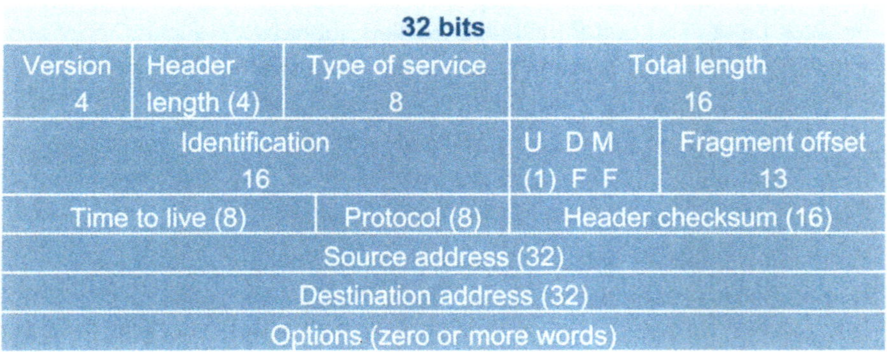

Fig. I-10. IP header (field lengths in bits)

The source address and destination address indicate the network number and host number, as per the addressing schema given in Fig. I-11. The addressing combination is unique and it is assigned by the Internet Assigned Number Authority (see IANA). No two machines have the same IP address. Also, due to the network field in the IP address, the same hosts connected to multiple networks have different IP addresses on each network. The IP addressing schema within classes A, B, C and D allow, for example, 2 million networks with up to 254 hosts each, and multicasting. The values 0 and –1 have special meanings: this network, and all hosts on the indicated network, respectively. In IP addressing, schema class A is used for very large networks (128 class A networks are possible). Class B is used for medium-size networks. Class C is used for small networks with no more than 255 nodes. Class D is used for multicast addressing, while Class E is reserved for experimental purposes. The fast Internet growth, as per Fig. I-9, and the more services already available mean the existing addressing schema are not going to be enough. The IP protocol shown here is also going to be inappropriate, so the Internet community is looking for a new addressing schema (see CIDR) and for new IPs as well (see IPv6).

Class		
A 0	Network	Host 1.0.0.0 to 127.255.255.255
B 10	Network	128.0.0.0 to 191.255.255.255
C 110	Network	192.0.0.0 to 223.255.255.255
D 1110	Multicast address 224.0.0.0 to 239.255.255.255	
E 11110	Reserved for future use 240.0.0.0 to 247.255.255.255	

Fig. I-11. IP addressing schema (32-bit fields)

IPC – Inter-Process Communication. A common term for an operating system service for data exchange between two processes, either within the same computer or across a network. Some well-known examples are shared memory, UNIX sockets and semaphores, OS/2 named pipes, Microsoft Windows DDE, etc.

IPCCC – International Performance Computing and Communications Conference. An EEE international conference serving as a forum for the exchange of current research work in computers, communications, their synergism, and their applications.

IPCP – IP Control Protocol. The protocol that establishes and configures IP over the Point-to-Point Protocol (see PPP).

IPDC – Internet Protocol Device Control. An effort from 1998 to define an improved standard for voice over IP (see VoIP) communications. See also SGCP.

IPDPS – International Parallel and Distributed Processing Systems. An international conference focusing on all aspects of parallel computation. Some of the major topics include scientific computing, special-purpose processors, parallel and distributed architectures, parallel programming languages, programming tools and environments, operating system support for parallel and distributed computing, etc.

IPDS – Intelligent Printer Data Stream. A printing mode used in the SNA environment that allows access to advanced printer capabilities.

IPDS – International Performance and Dependability Symposium. An IEEE international symposium focusing on the performance and dependability of computer systems and networks. Major topics include analytical, simulation and measurement techniques, and fault injection for performance and dependability applied to hardware/software, real-time systems, communication systems, distributed systems, parallel and clustered systems, multiprocessing systems, etc.

IPI – Intelligent Peripheral Interface. A hard disk drive that supports transfer rates of up to 25 Mbps and storage capacities of several GBs. IPI has been defined by two standards, ANSI/ISO9318-3 for magnetic and optical drives, and ANSI/ISO9318-4 for magnetic tape drives.

IPL – Information Processing Letters. An international journal published by Elsevier Science. Some of the main topics of the journal are algorithms, computational geometry, distributed computing, computational complexity, computer architectures, data structures, functional programming, fault tolerance, formal languages, cryptography, information retrieval, software design and implementation, program correctness, theory of computation, etc.

IPL – Initial Program Load. The part of a booting procedure used to start or restart a computer system by copying the kernel into the main memory and running it.

IPL – Initial Program Loader. A bootstrap loader which performs the booting procedure. See IPL above.

IPL – Internet Public Library. The first public library on the Internet that provides free library services to the Internet community (http://www.ipl.org).

IPM – Interpersonal Messaging. In general, a process of exchange messages by humans rather than applications or processes. Part of the X.400 Message Handling System (see MHS and X.400). IPM represents a type of message handling for use in business or private correspondence. The IPM takes place under the control of the Interpersonal Messaging System (see IPMS).

IPMS – Interpersonal Messaging System. A user-to-user service in the 1984 version of the X.400 Message Handling System (see MHS and X.400) that provides e-mail capabilities. See also IPM.

IPng – Internet Protocol next generation. See IPv6.

I-PNNI – Integrated Private Network-to-Network Interface. An extension to the Private Network-to-Network Interface (see PNNI) protocol used by ATM switches.

IPOM – IP-oriented Operations and Management. IEEE workshop focusing on SNMP, Web-based network management, operations of IP networks, SNMP versus TMN, IP over SONET/SDH, management of QoS, IP security, management of VoIP, debugging routing problems, integrated management of multilayer networks, new IP-level services, IP over ATM, IP traffic modeling and management, etc.

I-POP – I-WAY Point of Presence. In the Information Wide Area Year (see I-WAY) infrastructure, dedicated hardware at each site that provides a trusted locale for management, scheduling and other functions. See also POP.

IPP – Internet Presence Provider. A company that offers the disk space, high-speed Internet Access, and optionally the design of websites for companies, organizations or individuals who wish to have a visible presence on the Internet. Many Internet Service Providers (see ISP) are also IPPs.

IPP – Internet Printing Protocol. An application-level protocol (RFC2910) that can be used for distributed printing on the Internet. It describes what the end-user, operator and administrator need in the context of printing documents from a variety of sources, such as desktop applications, documents selected by reference, and documents created by batch or background applications.

IPPP – Internet Presence Provider and Promoter. A company that offers to create a website, maintain it, provide Internet access for that website and promote an audience for it. Many Internet Service Providers (see ISP) are also IPPPs. See also IPP (Internet Presence Provider).

IPRA – Internet Policy Registration Authority. The ultimate arbiter for certification of authority policies (see PCA) for the Privacy-Enhanced Mail service (see PEM) on the Internet.

IPS – Internet Protocol Suite. See TCP/IP.

IPSE – Integrated Project Support Environment. See SEE.

IPsec – Internet Protocol security. The IETF security protocol of the network layer that provides authentication and encryption over the Internet.

IPv4 – Internet Protocol version 4. The classic IP version (see IP).

IPv5 – Internet Protocol version 5. An advanced experimental IP for real-time streams (see RTS).

IPv6 – Internet Protocol version 6. A proposal for a future IP that has to meet the requirements issued by the IETF in RFC1550. The next generation of IP has to support a billion hosts, reduce the size of routing tables, simplify the protocol itself, provide better security, pay more attention to the type of service, permit old and new protocols to work together for a few years, allow the protocol to evolve in the future, etc. The following features have been proposed: 16-byte addresses instead of the current four bytes, embedded encryption, simplification of the header so that it contains only 7 fields, better support for options, and more attention to the type of service. More information about IPv6 can be found at http://www.ietf.cnri.reston.va.us

IPX – Internet Packet Exchange. The connectionless internetwork datagram protocol running on Novell NetWare networks. It is based on the old Xerox protocol (see IDP) but with various modifications. It passes packets transparently from source to destination, even if the source and destination are on different networks. IPX packets can be encapsulated in Ethernet packets or Token Ring frames. IPX operates at ISO/OSI levels 3 and 4 but does not perform all the functions of those levels. In particular, IPX does not guarantee that a message will be complete (no lost packets). It is similar to IP and XNS. See IP and XNS. See also ISO/OSI.

IPXODI – Internet Packet Exchange Open Data-link Interface. A protocol driver in the NetWare environment that can prepare workstation requests intended for the network. Such preparation may be in the form of attaching a header to the packet, packaging it in an appropriate way, etc. Data are packed as datagrams.

IQ – Information Quality. An international conference dedicated to the exchange of knowledge about the research into and practice of information quality. Topics include information quality in the context of the Internet and the Web, e-commerce, data mining and data warehousing, I/O tools, metrics, measures and technologies, standards, cost/benefits analyses, etc.

IR – Information Retrieval. The process of finding, organizing and displaying information, particularly using computers.

IR – Infrared. Electromagnetic radiation at frequencies just below that of visible red light. Infrared radiation is directly proportional to the temperature of the object generating it.

IR – Internet Registry. A central repository that contains the network addresses of machines and ID numbers of domains on the Internet. IR maintenance is delegated by IANA and is currently carried out by DDN NIC.

IRAM – Intelligent RAM. A project under the supervision of David Patterson at the University of California at Berkeley. IRAM combines a processor and memory in a single chip to reduce the memory delay.

IRC – Internet Relay Chat. A public service on the Internet that allows interactive talk among huge numbers of Internet users. It was invented by Jarrko Oikarinen of Finland in 1988. There is no restriction on the number of people who can participate in a given discussion, or the number of channels that can be formed. An IRC channel, maintained by an IRC server, transmits the text typed by each user who has joined the channel to all other users who have joined the channel. Generally, a channel is dedicated to a particular topic, which may be reflected in its name.

IRD – Integrated Receiver/Decoder. A subscriber terminal used for satellite television systems.

IRDA – Infrared Data Association. The industry organization (also known as IrDA) of computer, component, and telecommunications vendors who established the standards for infrared communication between computers and peripheral devices such as printers.

IRDP – ICMP Router Discovery Protocol. A protocol similar to ES–IS, but used with IP allowing the determination of the address of a router that it can use as a default gateway. See ES–IS.

IRDS – Information Resource Dictionary System. A set of ISO standards that defines data dictionaries (see D/D) to be implemented on top of relational databases.

IRG – Inter-Record Gap. See IBG (Inter-Block Gap).

IRG – Internet Resource Guide. An online book that describes many services available on the Internet. The NSF Network Service Center also distributes the IRG electronically on demand. The IRG is available via ftp://nnsc.nsf.net, followed by the command cd resource-guide.

IRGB – Intensity Red Green Blue. A supplement to the standard RGB color model (see RGB) generated by adding four bits that increase the intensity of the red, green and blue signals, resulting in a total of 16 colors.

IR-L – Information Retrieval Letter. A journal issued by the ACM Special Interest Group on Information Retrieval (see SIGIR).

IRL – Inter-Repeater Link. A cable segment between two repeaters in an Ethernet network. If optical cable is used, the IRL is known as a Fiber-Optic Inter-Repeater Link (see FOIRL).

IrLAP – Infrared Link Access Protocol. A data-link layer reliable point-to-point protocol.

IrLMP – Infrared Line Management Protocol. A multiplexing protocol that allows multiple sessions over a single point-to-point link.

IrLPT – Infrared Line Printer. A protocol used to print via a serial infrared connection. See also IRDA.

IRM – Information Resource Manager. See Data Administrator (DA).

IRMJ – Information Resources Management Journal. An applied research international journal focusing on the managerial and organizational facets of information technology resource management.

IRP – Interdomain Routing Protocol. The ISO equivalent (see IDRP) of the Internet Exterior Gateway Protocol (see EGP).

IRQ – Interrupt Request. A common name for a hardware signal or software event found on many processors seeking processor attention for some task. When accepted, the IRQ causes the processor to temporarily suspend the execution of normal instructions, to save the status of its work, and to transfer control to an interrupt handler routine. Interrupts can occur for many reasons, ranging from normal to highly abnormal. The number of the IRQ determines which interrupt handler will be used. In the AT bus, ISA and EISA, 15 IRQs are available; in MCA, 255 IRQs are available; each device's IRQ is hard-wired or set by a jumper or DIP switch. The VL bus and the PCI local bus have their own interrupt systems, which they translate into IRQ numbers. See also AT, ISA, EISA, MCA, PCI and VL bus.

IRQL – Interrupt Request Level. In Windows NT, a measure of relative priority for IRQs. A processor uses a cutoff IRQ level in order to mask all IRQs below and to handle all IRQs above that level.

IRSAIS – International Research Symposium on Accounting Information Systems. An international symposium on interdisciplinary research that draws from accountancy, behavioral and cognitive sciences, computer science, economics and information technology. The proceedings are published in the journal IJAIS.

IrSOCK – Infrared Sockets. An implementation of Windows sockets (see WINSOCK). See also IRDA.

IRTF – Internet Research Task Force. The Internet group (http://www.irtf.org) responsible for long-term Internet-related research projects from the theoretical point of view.

IRU – Indefeasible Right of Use. The term refers to the long-term leasing of a portion of the capacity (a certain number of channels of a given bandwidth) of an international cable.

IRV – International Reference Version. A particular variant of IA5 that is identical to ASCII encoding. See IA5.

IS – Information System. A general term used to denote a collection of people, procedures and equipment designed, built, operated and maintained to collect, record, process, store, retrieve and display information.

IS – Intermediate System. An Open Systems Interconnection (see OSI) system, which performs the same job as an IP router, i.e. forwarding messages at the network layer. Also, bridges, repeaters and X.25 circuits are all ISs at the appropriate lower levels (physical, data-link and network). Also known as Internetworking Unit (see IWU). Compare with End System (ES).

IS – International Standard. In general, any de jure standard, which passed the whole standardization process and was approved by the International Organization for Standardization (see ISO).

IS – Internet Standard. A specification related to an Internet technology that has proven stability and has been widely implemented.

ISA – Industry Standard Architecture. A bus design (pronounced "eye-sa") for the IBM PC/XT, AT and models based on the 386, 486 and higher chips, which allows various adapters to be added by inserting plug-in cards into expansion slots. This architecture provides for 8-bit and 16-bit access to the bus. Compare with EISA, MCA, PCI and VESA.

ISA – Information Systems Architecture. The output of Information Engineering (see IE), which serves as the basis for planning, development and control of future information systems.

ISA – Intelligent Systems and Applications. An international congress dedicated to the latest developments in intelligent systems, such as computational intelligence, interactive and collaborative computing, and biologically inspired systems.

ISADS – International Symposium on Autonomous Decentralized Systems. An international symposium focusing on the latest research in the field of autonomous decentralized systems. Some of the major topics include heterogeneous distributed systems, control systems, mobile agents, CSCW, distributed software development and maintenance, object management architectures and frameworks, novel applications, intelligent networks, etc.

ISAKMP – Internet Security Association and Key Management Protocol. A protocol (RFC2408) that defines authentication of communication between two peers.

ISAM – Index Sequential Access Method. A scheme (pronounced "eye-sam") to locate a data record in a large database using the unique key for that record. The record can then be searched sequentially for the desired data.

ISAPI – Internet Server Application Programming Interface. A Microsoft API between applications and their Internet Information Servers (see IIS). ISAPI uses its own Windows dynamic-link libraries (see DLL) to perform the same set of functions as a common gateway interface (see CGI). Using DLLs ISAPI has an important advantage over CGI, because multiple ISAPI application DLLs can reside in the same process as the HTTP server, while conventional CGI applications run in different processes.

ISBN – International Standard Book Number. A unique number assigned to a book title by its publisher for tracking and ordering purposes. Very often, it is marked with an EAN code on the cover. Compare with ISSN.

ISC – Intelligent Systems and Control. The IASTED international conference focusing on expert systems, fuzzy systems, adaptive and robust control, nonlinear systems, optimum control and other aspects of intelligent systems and control.

ISC – Internet Software Consortium. An organization (http://www.isc.org) that produces high-quality reference implementations of Internet standards. In addition, every six months ISC publishes the Internet Domain Name Survey (see Fig. I-9).

ISCA – International Symposium on Computer Architecture. The joint ACM and IEEE symposium dedicated to all aspects of computer architecture. Some of the major topics are multiprocessors, multicomputers and distributed architectures, novel computing techniques and architectures, application-specific, embedded or special-purpose architectures, performance evaluation and measurement of real systems, memory hierarchies, I/O, etc.

ISCC – IEEE Symposium on Computers and Communications. An international forum to exchange ideas in the areas which connect computers and communications. Some of the major topics are Internet services and applications, electronic commerce, digital libraries and content hosting, multimedia information management and exchange, nomadic computing, data mining and knowledge discovery, active networks, wireless, cellular and mobile computing, network design, operation and management, etc.

ISD – Information Systems Development. An international conference for information systems researchers and practitioners.

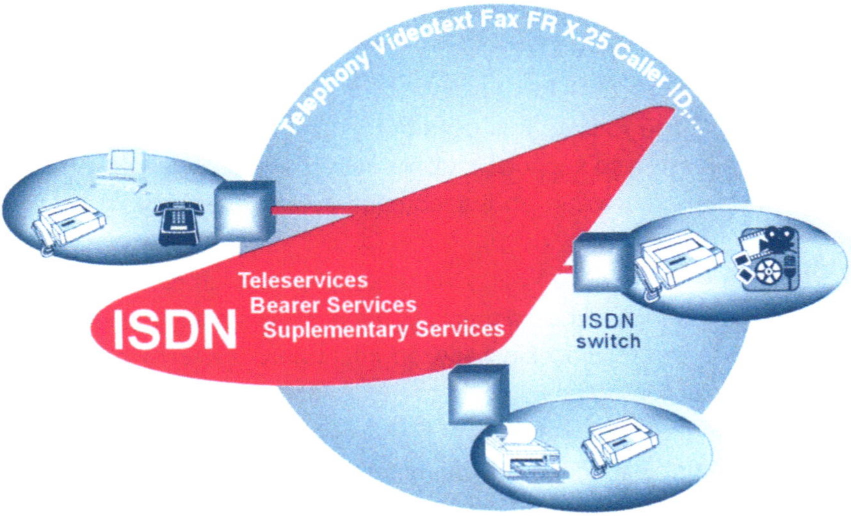

Fig. I-12. ISDN services

ISDN – Integrated Services Digital Network. A worldwide emerging telecommunications network technology that supports voice, video and data communications using digital techniques (see Fig. I-12). ISDN provides teleservices for information processing, such as fax, teletext, videotext, telephony, etc., bearer services for communications handling (e.g. Frame Relay, X.25, etc.), and some supplementary services such as CID, call forwarding, call waiting, line hunting, conference dialing, etc. It is intended to eventually replace the plain old telephone system (see POTS) with it. ISDN supports bandwidths of about 2 Mbps. The ISDN general definitions are described by ITU-T recommendations I.112, I.120 and I.200. See also B-ISDN, BRI and PRI.

ISECON – Information Systems Education Conference. An international conference focusing on information systems education. Topics include leading edge and emerging technologies, Internet course and curriculum delivery, best practices in IT education, human factors in IT, women and minorities in computing, etc.

ISESS – International Software Engineering Standards Symposium. An international IEEE symposium focusing on the latest directions in software engineering standards.

ISH – Information Superhighway. A term introduced by the US Clinton/Gore administration for a proposed high-speed communication system to enhance education in the US in the 21st century. With the growth in the Internet and Web (see Fig. I-9), many people have viewed the Internet as an information superhighway.

IS–IS – Intermediate System–Intermediate System. The OSI interior gateway protocol for message routing. It is used in numerous Internet backbones. At the same time IS–IS also supports multiple network-layer protocols. An IS–IS protocol may be used within an autonomous system (see AS) or between them.

ISJ – Information Systems Journal. An international journal published by Blackwell Science focusing on aspects of information systems, with particular emphasis on the relationship between information systems and people, businesses and organizations.

ISN – Information Systems Network. A high-speed switching network developed by AT&T that can connect to many known network architectures such as SNA or Ethernet.

ISN – Internet Society News. The official newsletter of the Internet Society (see ISOC).

ISO – International Organization for Standardization. See Fig. I-13. The members of many national standards organizations from a number of countries founded this international organization (http://www.iso.ch) in 1946. These members include ANSI from the United States, DIN from Germany, BSI from the United Kingdom, JSA from Japan and many more (as per January 2001, 138 national standards bodies). ISO has almost 200 Technical Committees, each dealing with a specific subject divided into particular working groups. The ISO membership is based on the above-mentioned national organizations, but the real work is done by thousands of volunteers worldwide. These "volunteers" are often sponsored by their employers who want to make sure that their new products will meet international standards. Other volunteers are academics trying to help define useful, scientifically supported ways of finding new and realizable technologies. A standard usually starts with a proposal for a New Work Item (NWI). If this is approved (by a vote of the participating members), it is assigned to an appropriate Subcommittee which then produces the first Working Draft (WD). Once the draft has reached a reasonable degree of maturity, it is registered as a Committee Draft (CD, previously known as a Draft Proposal (DP)). After a six-month ballot, the standard can be registered as a Draft International Standard (DIS) provided that two-thirds of the P-members (Participating members, i.e. those who have registered their desire to participate in that particular standardization work) vote in favor of progression and less than one quarter of all the member bodies vote against. It may then be registered as a full International Standard (IS) following a similar procedure but requiring a 75% majority.

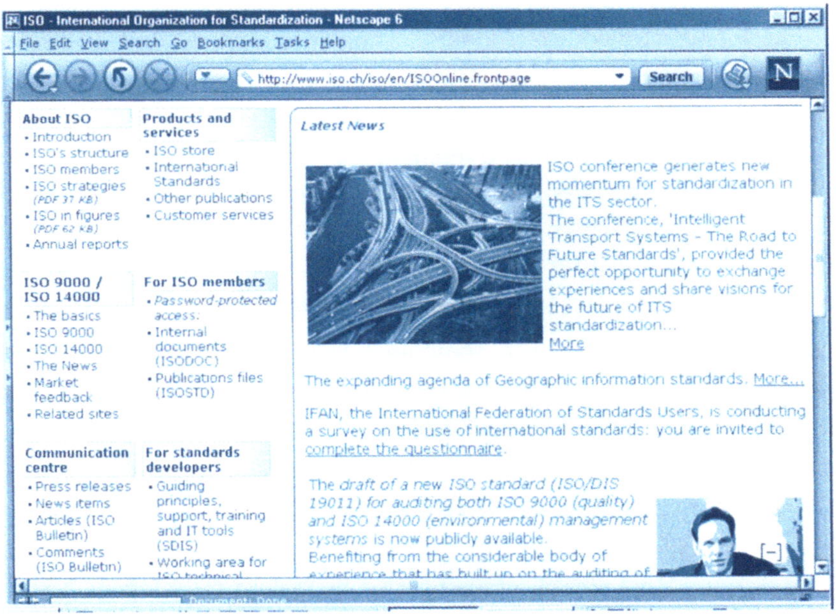

Fig. I-13. ISO homepage
(printed with the permission of ISO)

The ISO decision-making process is based on voting, by consensus, by the official national members, and therefore it is sometimes inefficient for the current market requirements. However, the results are still impressive. By the end of 2000, ISO had developed 13,025 international standards totaling 391,582 pages in English. An international standard is known as ISOxxxx-n:dddd, where xxxx is the number of the standard, n is the part number (which may be omitted in the case of single-part standards) and dddd is the date of its issue (e.g. ISO8571-1:1988, a general introduction to FTAM).

Standards developed under JTC1 (see JTC1) have ISO replaced by ISO/IEC. One or more letters in parentheses following the standard denotes the language(s) in which it is printed. The official languages of ISO are English, French and Russian. The term "ISO" is not an acronym, it comes from the Greek word "isos" meaning "equal".

ISOC – Internet Society. The professional membership nonprofit organization (http://info.isoc.org) which promotes wider Internet usage and its growth. Among other things, the ISOC provides a forum for discussion and collaboration in the operation and use of the global Internet infrastructure, publishes a quarterly newsletter, the Internet Society News, and holds a conference.

ISODE – ISO Development Environment. Tools (pronounced "eye-so-dee-ee") that implement OSI upper-layer services.

Isoenet – Isochronous Ethernet. An Ethernet enhancement developed by National Semiconductor for handling real-time voice and video over the Ethernet category 3 UTP cable (see UTP). Isoenet can be integrated into an existing network by adding an appropriate hub in the wiring closet and replacing standard Ethernet adapters with Isoenet adapters.

ISO/OSI – ISO Open Systems Interconnection. See OSI.

ISP – Internet Service Provider. A company which provides Internet access to other companies or individuals. Such companies include America Online (see AOL), CompuServe, Microsoft Network, EUnet, etc.

ISP – International Standardized Profile. A clearly defined subset of an emerging ISO standard that allows early valid implementations.

ISPASS – International Symposium on Performance Analysis of Systems and Software. The IEEE annual international symposium focusing on performance analysis in the design of systems and software.

ISQED – International Symposium on Quality Electronic Design. An international IEEE symposium focusing on the latest research in the field of quality integrated circuit design.

ISR – Information Systems Research. A journal dedicated to the productive application of information technology in order to improve economic and social welfare.

ISR – Interrupt Service Routine. A small routine that resides in the OEM adaptation layer (see OAL) which is executed in the kernel mode (see OS) and has direct access to the hardware registers. ISR is used to map physical interrupts to logical interrupts.

ISSN – International Standard Serial Number. A unique number assigned to a series (journals, magazines, etc.) by its publisher for tracking and ordering purposes. Compare with ISBN.

ISSRE – International Symposium on Software Reliability Engineering. An international symposium focusing on software reliability engineering for a broad range of applications. Some of the major topics are measurement for software reliability assessment, software reliability models, software testing and verification, reliability tools, education, technology transfer, appropriate standards, etc. More information is available at the homepage of ISSRE 2001 (see Fig. I-14).

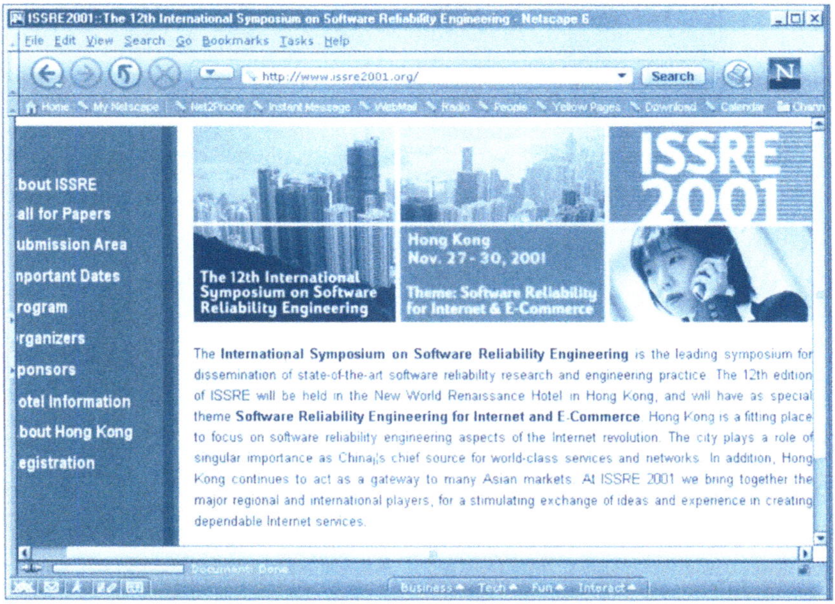

Fig. I-14. Homepage of ISSRE 2001

IST – India Standard Time. Time zone. UTC + 5.50 hours. See TZ.

IST – Irish Summer Time. Time zone. UTC + 1.00 hour. See TZ.

IST – Interrupt Service Thread. A thread created by a device driver to wait on an event.

ISTE – International Society for Technology in Education. A nonprofit professional organization dedicated to the improvement of education through computer-based technology.

ISU – Install Shield Uninstall. Filename extensions for files in Microsoft Windows environments used for installing or removing Microsoft applications. It is strongly recommended to use isu files (via the appropriate wizard, see Fig. I-15) for removing applications, rather than the delete command. Simple deleting usually leads to an unstable Windows environment, and probably something will not work at all.

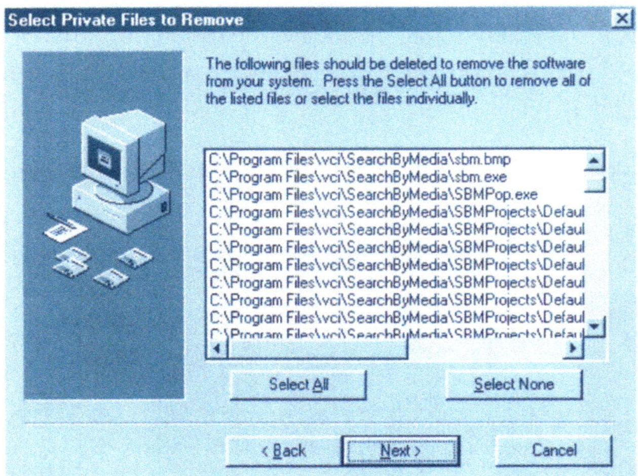

Fig. I-15. An example of an ISU wizard

ISU – Integrated Service Unit. The combination of a channel service unit (see CSU) and data service unit (see DSU) in one device. The ISU is used to interface computers and terminals to a digital data service (see DDS) line.

ISV – Independent Software Vendor. A company, sometimes an individual, that independently develops software products. Such products then appear on the market as third-party software, usually offered by big hardware and software manufacturers, or directly by the ISV.

ISWC – International Symposium on Wearable Computers. IEEE international conference focusing on advances in wearable computing. Some of the main topics include ubiquitous computing, CSCW, personal imaging, consumer, industrial and medical applications, software agents, special-purpose hardware, the ergonomics of wearable hardware, networking, etc.

IT – Information Technology. A common name for any kind of technology, hardware and/or software used to get, process and give information. It covers the whole area of computer and telecommunication technologies.

IT – Iran Time. Time zone. UTC + 3.50 hours. See TZ.

ITAA – Information Technology Association of America. An organization (http://www.itaa.org) that defines performance standards, improves management methods, and monitors the adherence to the US government regulations in the computer services field.

ITCA – International Teleconferencing Association. A professional association linking users, providers, strategists, educators, learners, managers and employees that use teleconferencing, telecollaborative and distance-education technologies.

ITCC – Information Technology: Coding and Computing. An international conference intended to serve as a forum bringing together researchers and practitioners to exchange ideas and experience from different areas of specialization in information technology. Topics include digital image processing, document image analysis, data compression, multimedia computing, information databases, error control codes, enterprise architectures and enterprise-wide information management, etc. The proceedings are published by IEEE CS.

ITE – Information Technology Equipment. The equipment used in Information Technologies (see IT) for receiving data from external sources, processing and then providing appropriate outputs.

ITI – Information Technology Industry Council. The new name for the Computer and Business Equipment Manufacturers Association (see CBEMA). The latest news can be found at http://www.itic.org

ITiCSE – Innovation and Technology in Computer Science Education. The ACM conference sponsored by the SIGCSE and SIGCUE ACM groups. Some of the main topics include intelligent tutoring systems (see ITS), teaching material and aids, graphics/visualization, teaching methods, distance learning, evaluating learning and teaching, closed laboratories, computer-supported collaborative learning, mobile computing in computer science, cultural impacts, information technology and ethics, etc. See also SIGCSE and SIGCUE.

ITR – Internet Talk Radio. A common name for the audio programs distributed over the multicast backbone (see MBONE).

ITS – Intelligent Tutoring System. A knowledge-based system (see KBS) for intelligent education, focusing on knowledge communication rather than on the transfer of knowledge. ITS allows the student to actively participate in the instruction process, which is individualized according to the student's knowledge, learning capabilities and preferences. The area of intelligent education is a complex one, incorporating topics from artificial intelligence (see AI), psychology, cognitive science, human–computer interaction, anthropology, linguistics and computer science. An example, a screenshot from SQL Tutor, an ITS for SQL programming, is given in Fig. I-16. SQL Tutor was developed by Dr. Antonija Mitrović and is intended for student education on SQL. The illustration in Fig. I-16 shows how SQL Tutor helps the students to learn SQL statements by searching a database containing data about famous movies, actors and directors. More information about SQL Tutor is available at http://www.cosc.canterbury.ac.nz/~tanja/sql-tut.htm

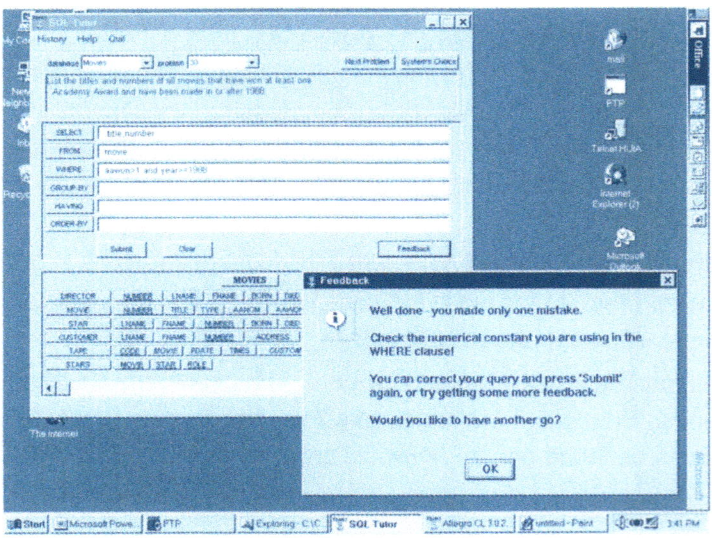

Fig. I-16. SQL Tutor in action, an example of an ITS
(courtesy of Dr. Antonija Mitrović, University of Canterbury, New Zealand)

ITT – Invitation To Transmit. The token frame in an ARCnet network architecture. See ARCnet.

ITU – International Telecommunication Union. An international organization (http://www.itu.int) founded in 1865 having its head office in Geneva, Switzerland. ITU works closely with all standardization organizations as well as with governmental organizations. ITU coordinates the development of telecommunications technologies and their use at international and national level. ITU has three main sectors: radio communications (see ITU-R), telecommunications (see ITU-T), and development.

ITU-R – ITU-Radio Communications Sector. Part of ITU concerned with allocating radio frequencies worldwide.

ITU-T – ITU-Telecommunication Sector. Formed as CCITT in 1956, it changed its name in 1992. ITU-T is concerned with telephone and data communication systems, and makes technical recommendations for them. These recommendations often become internationally accepted standards, such as the well-known V.24 (EIA RS-232), X.400 or X.25. ITU-T produces more than 5000 pages of recommendations per year. They can be found at many sites, e.g. ftp://src.doc.ic.ac.uk/pub/computing/ccitt and ftp://croton.inria.fr/ITU/ccitt. ITU-T has the following study groups: service definition, network operation, tariff and accounting principles, network maintenance, protection against electromagnetic environment effects, outside plants, data networks and open systems communication, terminals for telematic services, television and sound transmission, languages for telecommunication applications, switching and signaling, end-to-end transmission, modems and transmission techniques, and transmission systems and equipment.

ITXC – Internet Telephony Exchange Carrier Corporation. A company (http://www.itxc.net) that provides routing, authorization and billing services to Internet telephony service providers throughout the world.

IUI – Intelligent User Interfaces. The annual conference focusing on research and development into intelligent user interfaces. Some of the main topics are knowledge-based tools for IUI, intelligent agents and agent-based interaction, automated presentation of information, integration of multimedia/multimodal inputs, adaptive user interfaces, appropriate architectures and environments, application-specific intelligent interfaces, etc.

IV – Initialization Vector. In cryptography, a sequence of random bytes appended to the front of the plaintext before encryption by a block cipher (see CBC) used to ensure that two identical initial ciphertext blocks do not occur.

IVD – Integrated Voice and Data. The physical integration of voice and data in a single network as specified by the IEEE802.9 working group. It specifies the interface between equipment that produces packetized or time-sensitive (known as isochronous) data and an access unit, which uses TDM to combine the data for further transmission. See IVDT, an example of IVD implementation.

IVDS – Interactive Video and Data Services. The wireless implementation of interactive TV.

IVDT – Integrated Voice Data Terminal. A terminal device in which a telephone and one or more other devices, such as a video display unit, keyboard or printer, are integrated into one unit and used over a single circuit.

IVR – Interactive Voice Response. A software application that accepts a combination of voice telephone inputs and touch-tone keypad selections and provides appropriate answers in the form of faxes, e-mails, voice, etc. See also Computer Telephony Integration (CTI).

IV&V – Independent Verification and (&) Validation. The process of software verification and validation (see V&V) by an independent group, unlike V&V where the V&V team and the development team work closely together.

I-WAY – Information Wide Area Year. A project started in the US in 1995. It was an experimental high-performance network based on ATM technology that linked over a dozen of the fastest high-performance computers and advanced visualization machines across the US. Among other things, I-WAY was used as a testbed for a teraflop wide area computing system and for identifying future network research areas. Today, it is a large international network that offers many network services.

IWSSD – International Workshop on Software Specification and Design. An international forum for research on requirements specification and design methods, software architecture, concurrent, distributed and real-time systems, and formal models.

IWU – Internetworking Unit. A common name for a device used for interconnecting LANs, such as a bridge or router. See also Intermediate System (IS).

IXC – Inter-Exchange Carrier. A common carrier providing long-distance connectivity between Local Access and Transport Areas (see LATA).

IY2KCC – International Y2K Cooperation Center. A temporary organization created in February 1999 under the auspices of the United Nations, with funding from the World Bank. IY2KCC promoted strategic cooperation and action among governments, people and the private sector to minimize the adverse effects of the so-called Millennium Bug (see Y2K) on the global community and economy. Just after the critical date, and after a positive acknowledgment that the Y2K problem had been solved, IY2KCC closed its physical offices.

IYSWIM – If you see what I mean. The chat term.

J

J++ – Java++. The Visual Java from Microsoft, a fully integrated development environment (see IDE) for Java that runs on Windows 95 and Windows NT. J++ has several great tools (Applet Wizard) that make developing applications in Java extremely easy and fast.

J2EE – Java 2 Enterprise Edition. The Java platform that defines the standard for developing multitier enterprise applications (see EIS). J2EE simplifies enterprise applications by basing them on standardized, modular components, by providing a complete set of services to those components and by handling many details of application behavior automatically, without complex programming. It consists of the following elements:

- J2EE Application Programming Model: A standard programming model for developing multitier thin-client applications.
- J2EE Platform: A standard platform for hosting J2EE applications as a set of required APIs and policies. The primary element is the list of Java technology standards that all J2EE products are required to support.
- J2EE Compatibility Test Suite: A suite of compatibility tests for verifying that a J2EE product is compatible with the J2EE platform standard.
- J2EE Reference Implementation: A reference platform for demonstrating the capabilities of J2EE and for providing an operational definition of the J2EE platform.

J2EE takes advantage of many features of the Java 2 Standard Edition, such as portability, JDBC API for database access, CORBA technology for interaction with the existing enterprise resources, and a security model that protects data even in Internet applications. Building on this base, J2EE adds full support for Enterprise JavaBeans (see EJB) components, Java Servlets API, and JavaServer Pages technology (see JSP).

JACL – Java Command Language. A Tcl interpreter written in Java that enables Tcl to be used in "100% pure Java" environments for such applications as web browsers for use on network computers. See also Tcl.

JACM – Journal of the ACM. An ACM journal published bimonthly. JACM covers the most significant work from a wide group of interests in computer science. Topics include artificial intelligence, complexity of algorithms, computational geometry, computer architecture, cryptology, database systems, networks and theory, digital libraries, data structures, distributed computing, formal languages, graph theory, logic in computer science, machine learning, operational research, parallel algorithms, programming languages, scientific computing, etc.

JAE – Java Application Environment. The source code release of the Java Development Kit.

JAIR – Journal of Artificial Intelligence Research. A scientific journal appearing in both electronic form and in paper form published by Morgan Kaufmann (http://www.cs.washington.edu/research/jair). JAIR focuses on all aspects of artificial intelligence (see AI).

JAM – Just Another Metafile. A document markup scheme for producing LaTeX, HTML or RTF outputs.

JANET – Joint Academic Network. The UK academic and research network (http://www.ja.net) that connects several hundred institutions, including all universities, most colleges of higher education, and most research and other organizations that work in collaboration with the academic community. It is fully connected to other Internet service providers in the UK as well as to the National Research Networks in Europe. The high-speed part of JANET (SuperJANET) provides an advanced fiber broadband network.

JAR – Java Archive. A compressed collection of platform-independent files stored in a way that makes it possible to associate each file with digital signature information stored separately in the same archive.

JAR – Journal of Automated Reasoning. An interdisciplinary journal published by Kluwer (http://www.wkap.nl/journalhome.htm). JAR covers automated theorem proving, logic programming, expert systems, artificial intelligence, robotics, computational logic, program synthesis, program validation, and other aspects of automated reasoning.

JASIS – Journal of the American Society for Information Science. A journal published by Wiley, focusing on the generation, recording, distribution, storage, representation, retrieval and dissemination of information.

JAT – Java Agent Template. An approach under research for Web-based agents that will allow us to write Java agents capable of sending KQML messages (see KQML).

JavaOS – Java Operating System. A Java-based operating system optimized to run applications written in the Java programming language directly on different hardware platforms without requiring a host operating system.

JBIG – Joint Bilevel Image Experts Group. A joint experts group of ISO, IEC and ITU-T (JTC1/SC2/WG9) which defines a compression standard for lossless image coding (the result after compression and decompression is the same as the original). Also, a filename extension for such a format.

JCDL – Joint Conference on Digital Libraries. The ACM/IEEE joint conference focusing on research and development in digital libraries (see DL).

JCE – Java Cryptography Extensions. An extension of the Java Development Kit (see JDK) that allows developers using Java and JDK to work with a number of standard encryption technologies and build encryption wrappers around Java applets that create virtual private tunnels. The security enhancements include new cryptographic extensions and a new permissions-based access model in JDK that gives users control and access via Java applets over specified local computer resources and directories. JCE will open the door to building heavyweight Internet-based enterprise applications. JCE supports the Digital Encryption Standard (see DES) and X.509 for digital certifications.

J

JCK – Java Compatibility Kit. A set of tools used to certify an implementation conformance with a Java platform.

JCKBSE – Joint Conference on Knowledge-Based Software Engineering. An international conference focusing on knowledge and software engineering.

JCL – Job Control Language. An old term from the batch-processing era related to a script language used to control the execution of IBM batch programs on OS/360 machines.

JCN – Journal of Communications and Networks. A quarterly published journal (http://jcn.or.kr) that covers all topics in communication theory and techniques, communication systems, and networks.

JCSS – Journal of Computer and System Sciences. An international journal published bimonthly by Academic Press. JCSS presents original research papers in computer science and related subjects in system science, paying attention to the relevant mathematical theory. Some of the major topics are theories of algorithms and computability, formal languages, automata theory, parallel and distributed computing, computer networks, complexity theory, neural networks, computer modeling of complex systems, etc.

JDA – Joint Development Agreement. A relatively old agreement between IBM and Microsoft to develop a joint operating system environment for personal computers. Later, each partner chose its own direction: OS/2 for IBM, Windows NT for Microsoft.

JDA – Journal of Discrete Algorithms. An international journal published quarterly by Hermes Science Publishing, UK. JDA topics include all areas of finite and discrete design and analysis. JDA appears in both electronic and paper forms.

JDBC – Java Database Connectivity. A collection of open database drivers written in Java which allows programs to query and edit databases on any platform with a Java Virtual Machine implementation (see JVM). In order to free developers from thinking about specific drivers, JDBC has its own API (see JDBCAPI). JDBC drivers can either be entirely written in Java, so that they can be downloaded as part of an applet, or they can be implemented using native methods to bridge the gap to existing database access libraries. The most important interfaces which are used to build the JDBC framework are java.sql.Connection, java.sql.DriverManager, java.sql.Statement and java.sql.ResultSet.

JDBCAPI – Java Database Connectivity API. An open standard Java API, very similar to ODBC, which allows Java applications to work with any RDBMS via the same API regardless of the target database engine. JDBCAPI is implemented via a driver manager that can support multiple drivers connected to different databases. The JDBCAPI work is based on the X/Open SQL Call-Level Interface (see CLI) and on Microsoft's ODBC specification.

JDK – Java Development Kit. The JavaSoft development tool that allows users to develop applets that run in browsers supporting Java 1.1 and to develop Java applications as well. It supports several advanced features (in version 1.1) such as signed applets, the JAR file format, an application window toolkit (see AWT), the JavaBeans component model (see EJB), database connectivity, remote method invocation (see RMI), etc.

JDM – Journal of Database Management. An international journal with major articles on a variety of database issues.

JEA – Journal of Experimental Algorithms. An electronic journal published by the ACM. JEA is devoted to experimental work on the design and analysis of algorithms and data structures. The following areas are covered: combinatorial optimization, computational biology and geometry, graph manipulation, graphics, heuristics, network design, routing and scheduling, searching and sorting, parallel processing, and VLSI design.

JEDI – Joint Electronic Document Interchange. A project studying the popular formats for word processing (see WP) that exist in both academic and commercial environments. The project aims to identify format conversion methods for popular de facto standards and their relationships with internationally recognized standards such as SGML and ODA. Some of the general aims of the project are the design and implementation of multimode converters capable of converting documents into formats recognized by SGML, the investigation of the transfer of such documents using the MIME e-mail technique, the investigation of the searchable forms of such documents using WAIS, etc. See also Multipurpose Internet Mail Exchange (MIME) and Wide Area Information Service (WAIS).

JEDMICS – Joint Engineering Data Management Information and Control System. The system designed to provide a modern means of storing and retrieving engineering drawings and data in electronic repositories.

JEPI – Joint Electronic Payment Initiative. A joint project of the World-Wide Web Consortium (see W3C) and CommerceNet in the field of electronic payment via the WWW.

JEUC – Journal of End-User Computing. A journal focusing on research and development in end-user computing in organizations. In addition to scientific research papers, JEUC offers readers a special section with practical advice.

JFC – Java Foundation Classes. An extension of the Abstract Windows Toolkit (see AWT) that adds graphical user interface class libraries to the AWT.

JFIF – JPEG File Interchange Format. A portable file format for exchanging JPEG files between different software packages, created by Eric Hamilton in 1992.

JFLP – Journal of Functional and Logic Programming. An electronic journal published by MIT Press. Integration of the functional programming and logic paradigms and their common foundations are covered by the journal articles.

JFP – Journal of Functional Programming. An international journal published by Cambridge University Press. The journal provides scientific information about anything related to functional programming. In particular, four basic categories are recognizable: the foundation of functional programming, the implementation of functional languages, linguistics, and applications.

JGIM – Journal of Global Information Management. An international multidisciplinary journal focusing on the applications and environments of global information technology. Some of the major topics of JGIM are frameworks and models for global information management, electronic commerce, the social impacts of IT in developing countries, human resources, the influence on economic development, EDI, distributed databases, networks, etc.

JIBC – Journal of Internet Banking and Commerce. An electronic journal focusing on electronic commerce and banking over the Internet.

JIC – Just in case. The chat term.

JIIS – Journal of Intelligent Information Systems. An international journal published by Kluwer. The mission of the journal is to present research and development results focused on the integration of artificial intelligence and database technologies in the creation of intelligent information systems. JIIS includes research papers, survey papers, meetings, workshops and conference announcements and reports, tutorial articles, and book reviews.

JIP – Journal of Internet Purchasing. An electronic free-of-charge journal issued bimonthly that informs professionals and executives on the principal developments, benchmark practices, and future trends in Internet-based purchasing.

JIT – Just-In-Time. A method used, especially in mass production, to provide the best ratio between the stocks of production material and final products, practically trying to keep stocks of both empty in any moment, a so-called zero inventory.

JIT – Just-In-Time Compiler. A platform-specific compiler often contained within JVMs (see JVM).

JIT – Journal of Information Technology. An international journal published by Taylor & Francis, focusing on advanced information and communication technologies.

JITCA – Journal of Information Technology Cases and Applications. An international quarterly journal focusing on IT cases and applications in organizations of varying sizes all over the world. JITCA is published by Ivy League Publishing in the US.

JITI – Journal of Information Technology Impact. An international journal focusing on the social impacts of information technologies (http://www.jiti.com).

JITM – Journal of Information Technology Management. An international journal (http://www.baltzer.nl/jitm/itm.asp) focusing on corporate information and technology management.

JITTA – Journal of Information Technology Theory and Application. An electronic journal (http://www.rutgers.edu/~ejournal) focusing on the IT theories used to solve business problems.

JK – Just kidding. The chat term.

JLP – Journal of Logic Programming. An international journal published by Elsevier Science. All aspects of logic programming are covered, including theory and foundations, implementation issues, applications involving novel ideas, and relationships to other programming methodologies.

JMAPI – Java Management API. The Java user interface interaction model that addresses the configuration and troubleshooting tasks of system administrators in small-to-large networking environments. This model is an extension of the page metaphor that is common on the Web. Objects and object information are presented via pages and dialogs. Navigation among object information and services is primarily via page-to-page. A JMAPI page provides a number of mechanisms to support the navigation among pages, such as menus, link tables, default mouse double-click actions, etc. Every page is constructed from a standard JMAPI page template. Standard pages provide fixed collection methods and display styles for managed objects and services. Objects are typically displayed using one of the UI elements, such as lists, icons or hierarchies.

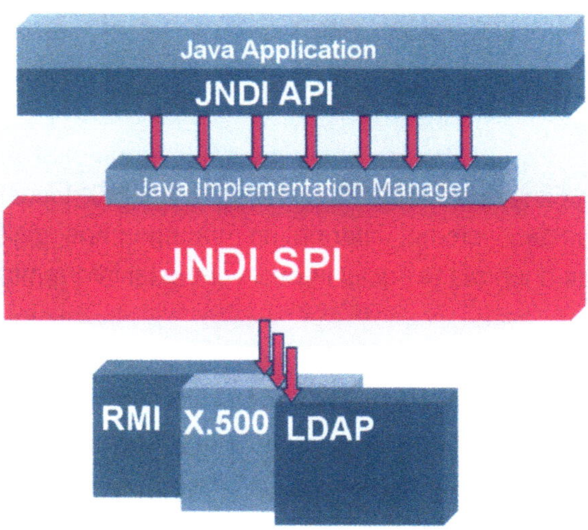

Fig. J-1. JNDI architecture

JMF – Java Media Framework. The Java API that specifies a unified architecture, messaging protocol and API for media players, video capture and conferencing.

JMS – Java Message Service. An API for using several enterprise messaging systems.

JNDI – Java Naming and Directory Interface. An API specified in the Java programming language that provides directory and naming functionality for Java applications. It is defined so as to be independent of any specific directory service implementation, such as the Domain Name System (see DNS), X.500, Lightweight Directory Access Protocol (see LDAP), etc. The JNDI architecture (see Fig. J-1) consists of the JNDI API and the JNDI SPI. The JNDI API allows Java applications to access a variety of directories in a common way. See also JNDI SPI.

JNDI SPI – JNDI Service Provider Interface. This interface provides the means by which different naming and directory service providers can develop and hook up their implementations so that the corresponding services are accessible from applications that use the Java Naming and Directory Interface (see JNDI). In addition, because JNDI allows the use of names that span multiple namespaces, one service provider implementation may need to interact with another in order to complete an operation. The SPI provides methods that allow different provider implementations to cooperate to complete client JNDI operations. See also X.500.

JNI – Java Native Interface. An application programming interface supported in Java that allows Java code to call and be called by routines in other languages.

JoDI – Journal of Digital Information. An electronic journal published by the British Computer Society and Oxford University Press. JoDI focuses on digital libraries, hypermedia systems, information management, digital information design, intelligent agents, the social impacts of digital information, etc.

JODL – International Journal on Digital Libraries. An international journal published quarterly by Springer-Verlag. Topics of interest include the theory and practice of the acquisition, definition, organization, management and dissemination of digital information via global networks.

JOE – Java Objects Everywhere. A product offered by Sun, allowing applications to be built as Java front-ends connected to back-end servers using NEO. The NEO (it's not an acronym, thankfully) core is a complete suite of environments: an operating environment, a development environment, and a set of system administration tools based on a CORBA-compliant ORB, making it a standards-based product. JOE is the interfacing technology between Java/Web front-ends and NEO/CORBA application services. Together, they attempt to solve the problems encountered by developers when trying to offer large and complex Web-based applications, which use data and services already available. JOE includes an internal ORB that connects Java applets on Web browsers to NEO objects running on corporate networks and providing the functional engines for application services. Messages are automatically routed from Java applets to CORBA objects and back. Using JOE and NEO, existing applications can be deployed on the Web without rewriting entire systems. This backward compatibility allows corporations to capitalize on their existing systems. In addition, JOE provides some advanced features such as asynchronous event notification support for Java applets, developer productivity tools, administration tools, and firewall support.

JOL – Journal of Online Law. An electronic publication about law and online communications over wide networks (http://www.wm.edu/law/publication/jol).

JPE – JPEG file. A filename extension for files that contain JPEG images. See also JPEG.

Fig. J-2. An example of a JPG file (Sydney Harbour)

JPEG – Joint Photographic Experts Group. The name for the joint ITU-T and ISO group and the standard (pronounced "jay-peg") designed by the group for compressing either full-color or grayscale digital images. There are four modes of operation: sequential, progressive, lossless and hierarchical. In sequential encoding, a picture is encoded from top to bottom, and in the progressive method the picture builds up in multiple scans, each time getting a better sharpness. In lossless encoding, there are no data lost after decompression. In hierarchical encoding, the image is encoded with different resolutions. The JPG encoder works on one color component at a time; for grayscale pictures the encoding is straightforward. Originally implemented only in hardware, JPEG compression schemes are now available in many image viewing or handling packages. For nonrealistic images (cartoons) there is another standard (see JBIG); for moving pictures there is a group of standards (see MPEG).

JPG – Joint Photographic Experts Group. A filename extension for JPEG images. Figure J-2 shows a pictorial representation of Sydney Harbour taken from a ferry using a standard camera and later converted into a JPEG image using a scanner. Beautiful, isn't it?

JRE – Java Runtime Environment. A subset of the JDK dedicated for end-users and developers who then redistribute the runtime alone. See also JDK and JVM.

JRI – Java Runtime Interface. A standard C/C++ interface in the Java environment. It defines a standard interface to the JVM and to Java services, allowing decoupling between applications and the JVM internals. This in turn allows native methods to be independent of the Java runtime system, allows Java class upgrades without affecting native methods, and allows runtime upgrades without affecting Java classes. See JVM (Java Virtual Machine).

JRTS – Java Runtime System. An implementation of a Java Virtual Machine (see JVM) for a specific hardware platform.

JS – JavaScripts. A filename extension for files that contain JavaScript source code.

JSA – Japanese Standards Association. The Japanese standardization body (http://www.jsa.or.jp), a member of ISO.

JSAC – Journal on Selected Areas of Communications. Journal published by the IEEE Communication Society (see COMSOC). Each issue is dedicated to a certain subject area according to a call for papers (see CFP).

JSC – Journal of Symbolic Computation. An international journal published by Academic Press for mathematicians and computer scientists who have particular interests in symbolic computation. Topics include computational algebra, computational geometry, automated theorem proving, automatic programming, design and implementation of symbolic computation languages and systems, and applications.

JSP – Java Server Pages. An extensible Web technology that uses template data (HTML or XML), custom elements, scripting languages, and server-side Java objects to return dynamic content to a client. Also, the filename extension for files that contain HTML pages that refer to Java servlets.

JSSS – JavaScript Style Sheets. The Java-language-based style sheets developed by Netscape (Netscape Communicator 4.01 and up) to support style sheets on the Web (see CSS and DSS).

JST – Japan Standard Time. Time zone. UTC + 9.00 hours. See TZ.

JT – Java Time. Time zone. UTC + 7.00 hours. See TZ.

JTA – Java Transaction API. An API that allows J2EE servers and applications to access transactions.

JTC1 – Joint Technical Committee # 1. A Joint Technical Committee established by ISO and IEC to cover information technology standardization, especially for OSI.

JTM – Job Transfer and Manipulation. An ISO standard (ISO8831, ISO8832), part of the OSI application level, which specifies how to transfer a job defined in one system to another system somewhere on the network. See also TOP.

JTS – Java Transaction Service. A specification that defines the implementation of a transaction manager which supports a Java transaction API (see JTA) and implements the Java mapping of the OMG Transaction Service (see OTS) at the level below the API.

JUGHEAD – Jonzy's Universal Gopher Hierarchy Excavation And Display. A Gopher-oriented search that supports keyword searches and the use of logical operators (AND, OR and NOT). The result of a JUGHEAD search is a display of all menu items matching the search string at some location. Compare with VERONICA and WAIS.

JUNET – Japanese UNIX Network. A research network in Japan dedicated to noncommercial institutions and organizations.

JUS – Jugoslovenski Standard. The Yugoslavian standards written by the Yugoslavian Federal Standards Association. In practice, they are usually adopted from ISO standards and translated into the local language.

JVM – Java Virtual Machine. An operating environment that allows interpretation of Java compiled programs in a virtually platform-independent way. JVM defines an abstract rather than a real operating environment and specifies an instruction set, a set of registers, a stack, a garbage-collected heap, and a method area. The output of compiled Java source code is called bytecode and can be interpreted by a JVM one instruction at a time or can be compiled later for the real microprocessor. See also VM (Virtual Machine).

JvNCnet – John von Neumann Computer Network. The Northeast Research Regional Network which connects research organizations concentrated in the Northeastern United States, with access to the NSFNET backbone, and international connections to the several Scandinavian countries (Norway, Finland, Iceland, Sweden and Denmark) and the United Kingdom.

K

K – Kilo. An order of magnitude meaning 10^3 in the metric system. In computing, based on powers of 2, kilo is most often used to mean 2^{10}. To clearly distinguish between the metric and binary contexts, the lowercase letter k is often used to indicate 1000, while uppercase K is used for 1024.

KAD – Knowledge-Aided Design. A knowledge-based design system that represents, stores, integrates and manages various types of design knowledge. The representation should be able to model and express information such as requirements, versions, design rationale, etc., and have the ability to reason about them.

KAIS – Knowledge and Information Systems. A quarterly journal published by Springer-Verlag (in electronic and paper form) that serves as an international forum for researchers and professionals interested in knowledge systems and advanced information systems. The topics focus on the theoretical foundations, infrastructure and enabling technologies.

KAoS – Knowledgeable Agent-oriented System. An open distributed architecture for software agents, supporting reuse, interoperability and extensibility, developed by Dr. Jeffrey Bradshaw. The KAoS architecture describes agent implementations and interactive agent-to-agent messaging communications. KAoS is optimized to work with component integration architectures such as OLE and Java and with distributed objects such as those provided by CORBA and COM. See RP (Remote Programming).

Kb – Kilobit. The measurement unit for 1024 bits.

KB – Kilobyte. The measurement unit for 1024 bytes.

KB – Knowledge Base. A component of an expert system that contains knowledge about a specific domain. Knowledge can consist of facts, complex objects and their attributes, relationships between objects, and rules for processing knowledge and for deriving new knowledge.

KBD – Keyboard. An input-only device that usually includes keys for a standard set of printable characters (letters, numbers, punctuation marks) usually laid out in the QWERTY pattern, a calculator-like numeric keypad at one side, and optionally a set of function keys (F1, F2, ..., F10, Delete, Insert, Alt, Home, Print Screen, etc.).

Kbps – Kilobits per second. A measurement unit for data-transfer speed, measured as the number of Kb transferred per second.

KBS – Knowledge-Based System. A common term for computer systems that contain explicitly represented domain knowledge.

KDC – Key Distribution Center. An authentication method that uses a trusted center that shares user keys with each of its users in privacy. Authentication and session key management always goes through the KDC. The idea behind it is simple. The message passing from the sender Sx to the receiver Ry is passed through the KDC. From the Sx to the KDC a message is encrypted with the key shared between the Sx and the KDC. In the KDC, the incoming message is decrypted and formed again, this time with the key shared between the KDC and the Ry. After the message's arrival, the Ry knows that the sender Sx wants to talk with him, and also which key the Sx wants to use.

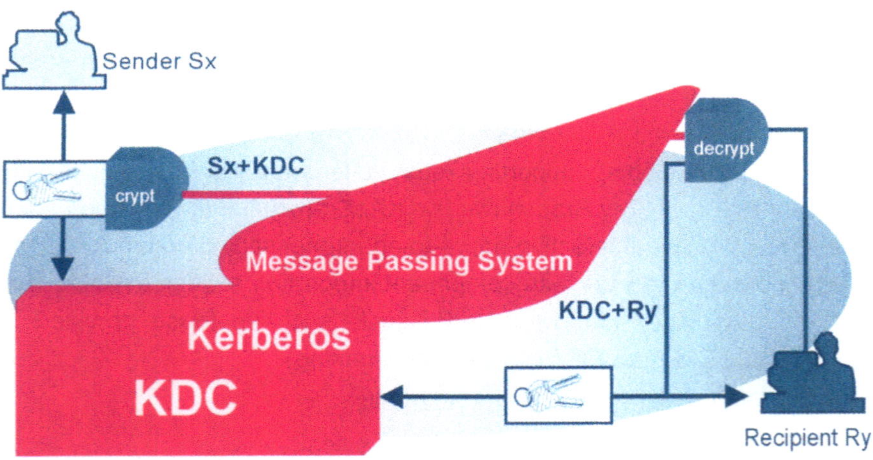

Fig. K-1. Kerberos KDC in action

This scenario is depicted in Fig. K-1, where the KDC is based on the Kerberos authentication system. Kerberos (in Greek mythology, the name of a three-headed watchdog that guards the entrance to Hades) is an authentication service developed as part of the well-known MIT Athena project. Kerberos assumes in advance that there are no trusted parties, and requires identification every time a service is requested. Identifications (such as passwords) are never sent across the network in cleartext (see Fig. K-1), and the only entity that knows all the passwords is the authentication server.

KDD – Knowledge Discovery and Data Mining. An ACM international conference sponsored by ACM SIGKDD focusing on knowledge discovery and data mining. See also SIGKDD.

KE – Knowledge Engineering. A technique that allows acquisition of knowledge from a human expert or a similar source and its representation in an expert system.

KEE – Knowledge Engineering Environment. A knowledge-system development product that provides software developers with a set of programming tools and techniques for building applications to represent and analyze knowledge.

KERMIT – K1-10 Error-free Reciprocal Micro Interconnect over TTY. A popular file-transfer protocol developed by Columbia University. Kermit runs in most operating environments, it provides an easy method of file transfer with variable-length units which are normally up to 96 bytes long. Control characters are converted into standard visible ASCII characters, which both communication sides can understand.

KERMIT – Knowledge-based Entity-Relationship Modeler for Intelligent Tutoring. A problem-solving environment for ER modeling (see ER) developed by the Intelligent Computer Tutoring Group at Canterbury University in New Zealand. The main aim of the system is to individualize pedagogical instructions for each student. Three separate windows are built into the KERMIT user interface (see Fig. K-2). The top window displays the given problem that should be solved by the student, the middle window is the Microsoft Visio ER stencil embedded into KERMIT as the workspace for problem solving, and the bottom window is the KERMIT feedback.

kHz – kilohertz. A measurement unit for a frequency equal to 1000 Hz (see Hz).

KIF – Knowledge Interchange Format. A standard language for interchange between various knowledge representation (see KR) languages. It can express beliefs, rules, facts, partial descriptions of procedures, etc. KIF reduces the number of translators needed for KR language communication.

KIS – Knowbot Information Service. A "white pages" service that allows a query for a service and then a search of several other address databases of various sorts for addresses matching the given query. KIS uses Knowbot programs to search the directories (see Knowbot).

KLOC – Kilolines Of Code. In software metrics, a measurement unit for the size of a source code.

KMAC – Knowledge Management Conference. An international conference focusing on theory, practice and support for knowledge-management soft-

K

ware. Some of the main topics include case studies about knowledge management, cross-cultural issues, knowledge creation, transfer, sharing, storage and use, data mining, intranets, workflow, etc.

KMP – Key Management Protocol. A protocol used for checking security keys in a secure network.

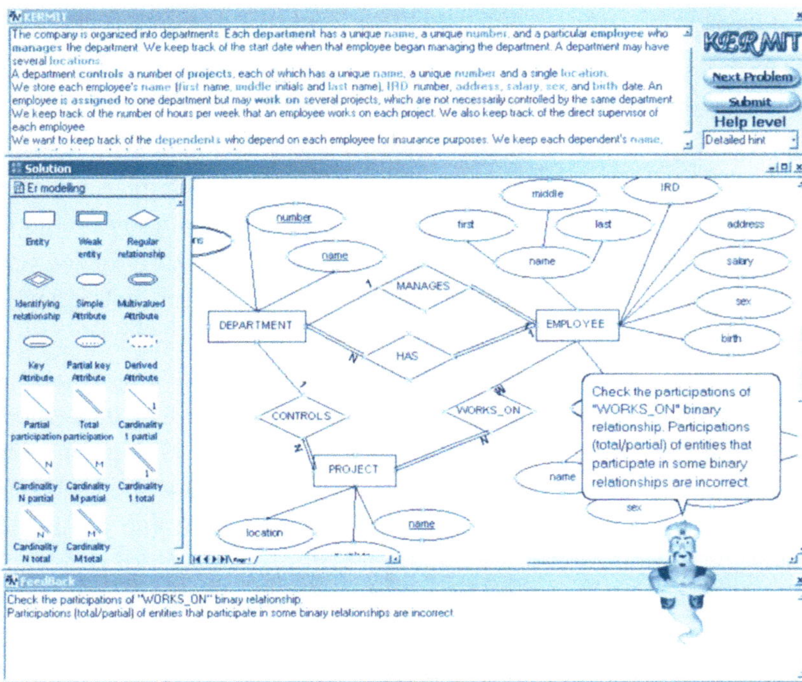

Fig. K-2. The KERMIT user interface
(courtesy of Dr. Antonija Mitrović)

KMT – Key Management and Distribution Toolkit. A toolkit used for Internet key management and distribution that consists of two primary components. A source code library has a set of comprehensive functions to create, maintain, retrieve and use cryptographic keys. The second component is the user tools, designed so that users can maintain their own database of keys.

Knowbot – Knowledge Robot. An agent-based program that seeks out information based on specified criteria. "Knowbot", as trademarked by CNRI, refers specifically to the search engine for Knowbot Information Services (see KIS). See also CNRI.

KQML – Knowledge Query and Manipulation Language. A high-level protocol and language for agent service and for agent-to-agent interaction. It is part of a larger effort, the ARPA Knowledge Sharing Effort, which aims to build large-scale reusable and sharable knowledge bases. KQML consists of three layers: a communication layer describing low-level communication parameters such as sender, recipient and communication identifiers; a message layer which indicates the interpretation protocol and contains an action; and a content layer which has information pertaining to the action submitted. KQML can be used as a language for an application program to interact with an intelligent system, or for two or more intelligent systems to share knowledge in support of cooperative problem solving.

KR – Knowledge Representation. Methods for representing formalized and structured knowledge in expert systems and other AI systems, such as semantic networks, production rules, etc. See also KRL.

K&R – Kernighan and (&) Ritchie. An abbreviation referring to the original version of the C programming language described in the book written by Brian W. Kernighan and Dennis M. Ritchie. It has been closely associated with the UNIX operating system, since it was developed on that system, and since UNIX and related software are written in C. The language, however, is not tied to any operating system or machine. Although it has been called a "system programming language", because it is convenient for writing operating systems, it has been used equally effectively to write other programs.

KRL – Knowledge Representation Language. The term used to refer to the language used by a particular system to encode knowledge. See also Knowledge Representation (KR), KQML and KIF.

KSE – Knowledge Sharing Effort. A distributed research program which is developing a methodology and the software tools for coordination and knowledge sharing in intelligent information systems. Specific components include the Knowledge Interchange Format (see KIF), the Knowledge Query and Manipulation Language (see KQML), and Ontolingua.

ksh – Korn shell. In the UNIX operating system, a program that resides between an interactive user and the kernel (see OS). "Korn" refers to its developer David Korn. See also csh.

KSR – Keyboard Send/Receive. A communication device that is limited to using a printer to receive and a keyboard to transmit. Because some such devices have no storage, the messages are printed as they are received and transmitted as they are typed at the keyboard.

KVM – Keyboard, Video, Mouse. A type of switch that allows multiple KVM devices to be connected, and allows switching between them.

KWIC – Keyword-In-Context. An automatic search methodology used to create indexes of text or titles, in which the keyword is stored along with some surrounding text.

KWIM? – Know what I mean? The chat term.

L

L1 – Level 1 cache. A term used for the cache memory that is nearest to the CPU, when there is more than one cache in the processor architecture. Also known as the primary cache. See also L2 and L3.

L2 – Level 2 cache. A term used for the cache memory that resides between the L1 cache and the main memory. Also known as the secondary cache. See also L1 and L3.

L2F – Layer 2 Forwarding. A protocol that supports the creation of secure virtual private dial-up networks over the Internet.

L2TP – Layer 2 Tunneling Protocol. An extension of the Point-to-Point Protocol (see PPP) that makes a virtual PPP connection at the second layer of the OSI protocol stack (RFC2661). See also OSI.

L3 – Level 3 cache. A term used for the cache memory that resides between the L3 cache and the main memory. See also L1 and L2.

LAA – Locally Administered Address. A parameter used by a controller in order to determine whether the node of a Token Ring network can access the mainframe connected to a Token Ring.

LADS – Local Area Data Set. A name sometimes used for a short-haul modem. A device that is used to accomplish data transmission on a privately owned "wire" where the distance exceeds the communication interface driver specifications.

LAM – Lobe Attachment Module. A box in a Token Ring network used as a multiple interface to which new nodes (known as lobes) can be connected.

LAN – Local Area Network. A group of computers and other devices (terminals, printers, modems, routers, bridges, etc.) connected together in a network over a relatively limited area (office, building, group of closed buildings, etc.). LANs are distinguished from each other by their topology, their transmission technology, and their speed. Topology refers to the way the interconnection paths between nodes (a place where a computer or device is connected to the network) are arranged. Various LAN topologies can be applied; two of the most common are the bus and ring topologies (see Fig. L-1). In the bus topology, a common pathway called a bus is shared by many computers (users) which can be connected to the bus at any point at any time. Because all the computers use the same path, an arbitrary mechanism is required, such as that implemented in the Ethernet (see CSMA/CD). In the ring topology, all the computers are connected in a large ring. Data from any computer must pass through the other computers along the way until it reaches the intended receiver. It is a very useful topology, with a simpler protocol than that for bus protocols. The main drawback is that any failure at any computer may cause the entire network to fail. Today, it is often preferable to use two rings. It is also possible to use a mixed LAN topology, as depicted in Fig. L-2, where a star topology has been applied to connect VT100-compatible terminals, while PC workstations are running on the bus topology. In addition to the logical topologies described above, topologies can also be distinguished by their physical characteristics, i.e. the electrical characteristics of the connections.

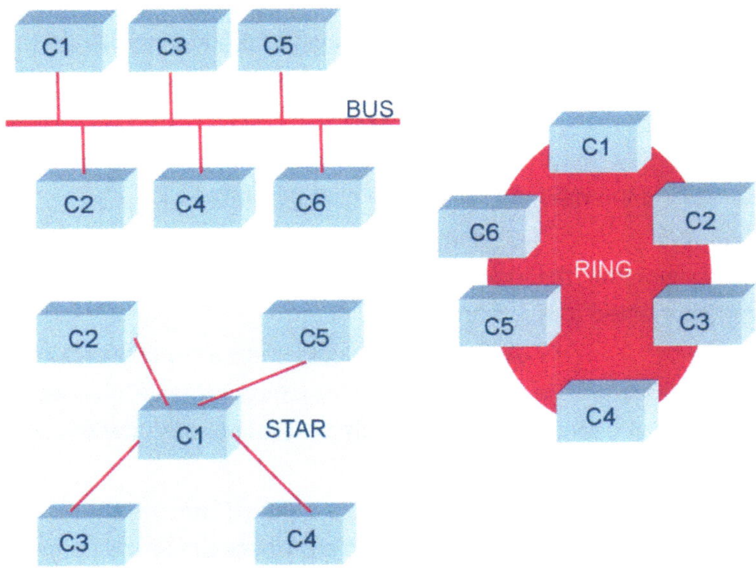

Fig. L-1. Three LAN topologies, a bus, a ring and a star

According to the administrative relationship between the nodes, LANs can be server-based or peer-to-peer-based. In a server-based LAN, a server controls access to some resources (such as a database or a printer) and serves as a host for the workstations connected to the server, as shown in Fig. L-2. Such a configuration is typical for client/server computing (see C/S). Unlike server-based LANs, each node in a peer-to-peer LAN can initiate some actions and provide services for other nodes without requiring a server's permission. In - order to manage a network, a server uses an installed network operating system (see NOS), which may replace the native operating system or run as a program on top of it. Workstation software, usually known as client software, works using workstation native operating systems. However, there are network configurations in which workstations do not have disks (known as diskless workstations). In such cases, the network software is booted from the server to each node and all processing is handled by the server. According to the technology applied, LANs can be based on Ethernet (IEEE802.3, ISO8802-3), Token bus (IEEE802.4, ISO8802-4), Token ring (IEEE802.5, ISO8802-5), Fast Ethernet (IEEE802.3u), or ATM. In the case of FDDI, it is normal to refer to call such large fast networks as Metropolitan Area Networks (see MAN). Also, the emerging wireless communications have introduced a new kind of LAN (see WLAN). The speeds vary according to the applied technology. They range from 10 Mbps typically on Ethernet, to 100 Mbps over Fast Ethernet or FDDI, to Gbps rates available on FFOL and HIPPI.

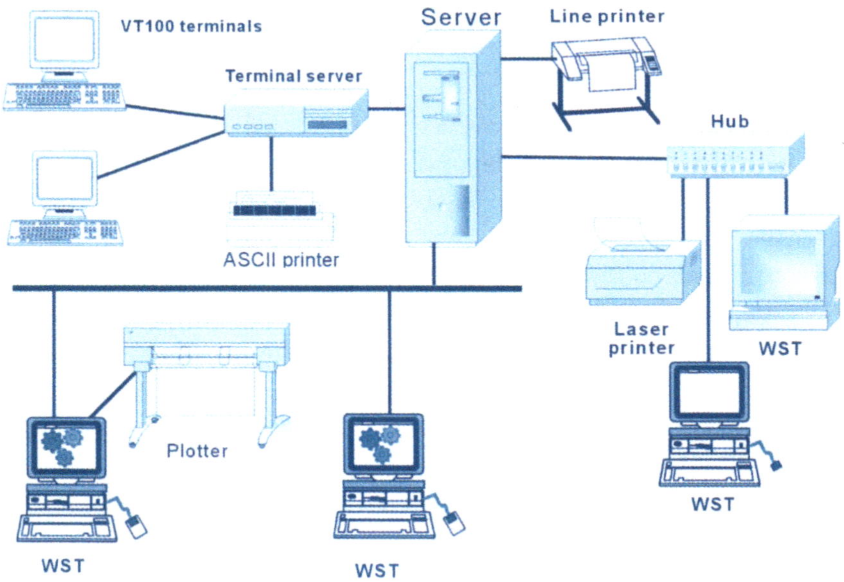

Fig. L-2. An example of a mixed LAN topology

LANE – LAN Emulation. A technology that allows an ATM network to work as a LAN backbone. Also, it defines Ethernet and Token Ring ELANs. See ELAN.

LAN/RM – LAN Reference Model. A term used for the IEEE802.x series of specifications dedicated to LANs (see 802.x).

LAP – Language Action Perspective. An international workshop focusing on the theory and practice of the so-called language action perspective. The term was introduced by Terry Winograd, Fernando Flores and Juan J. Ludlow who stated that human beings are fundamentally linguistic beings who act through language.

LAP – Link Access Procedure. The CCITT recommendation for a bit-oriented data-link layer protocol modified from the ISO HDLC protocol. Later on, LAP was modified again into LAPB and LAPD (see LAPB and LAPD).

LAPB – Link Access Procedure Balanced. A modified version of the initial LAP specification. LAP-B is most widely known as the protocol of choice for connecting a computer to a packet-switching X.25 network. See also Link Access Procedure (LAP).

LAPD – Link Access Procedure on the D channel. A modified version of the initial LAPB specification defined by the ITU-T recommendations Q.920 and Q.921. It is an ISDN data-link layer protocol for the D channel. See also Link Access Procedure (LAP).

LASER – Light Amplification by Stimulated Emission of Radiation. A device that produces coherent light in the visible, infrared or ultraviolet spectrum by certain quantum effects. Such effects can be obtained in many different kinds of materials: gases, liquids and solids. Lasers are widely used in high-quality page printers, fiber-optic cables, to read and write data on CD-ROMs, etc.

LAT – Local Area Transport. A set of de facto industry protocols developed by DEC to control the transfer of data between a terminal server and its "target" host utilizing a LAN.

LATA – Local Access and Transport Area. A geographic telephone dialing area serviced by a single local telephone company. Calls appearing within LATAs are called "local calls".

LaTeX – Lamport TeX. A well-known document preparation system based on TeX, developed by Leslie Lamport at the SRI AI Laboratory.

LATIN – Latin American Theoretical Informatics. An international Latin American symposium on theoretical computer science. The main topics include algorithms, automata theory, coding theory, computational biology, combinatorics, computational geometry, symbolic computation, data compression, cryptography, discrete mathematics, formal languages, graph theory, pattern matching, etc. The proceedings are published by Springer-Verlag.

LawTech – Law and Technology. The IASTED international conference focusing on the most current technology-related developments relevant to legal practice and scholarship.

LB – Leaky Bucket. A term associated with ATM networks used to describe the algorithm used for conformance checking of cell flows from a user or network. See also GCRA, UPC and NPC.

LBA – Logical Block Addressing. A set of parameters stored in BIOS/CMOS used to describe the configuration of the hard disk drive (see HDD). It is used by hard drives that are larger than 540 MB. See also BIOS. Compare with CHS.

LBE – Language-Based Editor. An editor that is aware of the syntactic, semantic and in some cases the structural rules of a specific programming language and which provides a framework for the user to enter source code. Programs or changes to the previously stored programs are incrementally parsed into an abstract syntax tree and automatically checked for correctness.

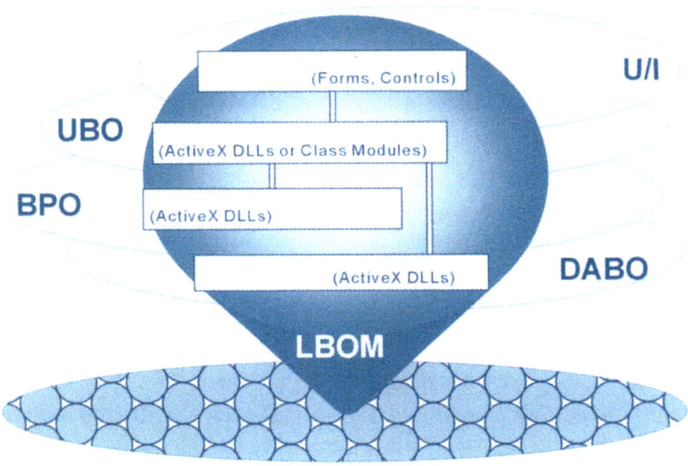

Fig. L-3. The LBOM architecture

LBOM – Lightweight Business Object Model. A three-tier model (see EIS) that separates: the business logic required for the user interface; the data access code required to insert, update and delete the data; and the business logic that implements more sophisticated business processes (UBO, BPO and DABO, respectively); see Fig. L-3. See also BPO, DABO and UBO.

LBS – LAN Bridge Server. In an IBM Token Ring network, a server used to keep track of and provide access to any bridges connected to the network.

LBT/LWT – Listen Before Talk/Listen While Talk. A fundamental rule used in the CSMA/CD media-access method. In order to send a packet onto the network, a node must first listen (LBT) to sense a free network pathway and keep listening (LWT) even while transmitting. See also CSMA/CD.

LCD – Liquid-Crystal Display. A type of display that consists of a very thin layer of liquid-crystal compound sandwiched between two transparent insulating layers. When an electric field is applied, light leaving the crystal is then aligned to pass through the upper polarizing layer. A grid of electrodes can selectively turn on a cell, or pixel, containing the liquid crystal material, turning it dark.

LCI – Logical Channel Identifier. See Virtual Channel Identifier (VCI).

LCID – Locale Identifier. A 32-bit standardized numerical value used to identify a locale for an environment in which a computer system and programs are deployed (or are going to be deployed). The locale determines the language used for menus and messages, the keyboard layout, the sorting order of strings, and date/time conventions.

LCN – Local Computer Networks. An IEEE conference focusing on practical solutions to important problems in computer networking. Some of the topics are internetworking, anything over IP, wireless networks, high-speed networks, performance analysis, real-time networks, active networks, ATM/Gb Ethernet, virtual private networks, multicast algorithms, QoS, congestion control, etc.

LCN – Logical Channel Number. See Virtual Channel Number (VCN).

LCP – Link Control Protocol. Part of the Point-to-Point Protocol (see PPP) dedicated to bringing lines up and down, testing them, and negotiating options. It is activated after the physical connection between the calling modem (usually at or inside a PC) and the called provider's router has been established. The PC sends the router a series of LCP packets to select PPP parameters to be used. LCP is described in RFC1548 and RFC1570. There are 11 types of LCP packets defined by RFC1661. In addition to TCP/IP settings, if the user wants to connect he/she has to apply for connection using a user name and password.

LCR – Languages, Compilers and Run-time Systems. An international biennial workshop focusing on languages, compilers and run-time systems for scalable computers. The proceedings are published by Springer-Verlag.

LCR – Least Cost Routing. In a PBX telephone system, a feature that allows selection of the cheapest path to a destination. See also PBX.

LCTES – Languages, Compilers and Tools for Embedded Systems. The ACM workshop focusing on recent embedded system development and future trends. The proceedings are published by Springer-Verlag (see LNCS).

LDAP – Lightweight Directory Access Protocol. The Internet standard (RFC1777, RFC1778) defined by IETF that allows directory lookups on the Internet. LDAP directory entries are arranged in a hierarchical structure that represents political, geographic and organizational boundaries. At the top of the tree appears a country; the lowest entries can represent people, organizational units, documents, etc. LDAP Version 3 is defined in RFC2830.

LDB – Lock Database. Filename extensions for Microsoft Access lock files.

LDCM – LANDesk Client Manager. Software developed by Intel as an implementation of the Desktop Management Interface standard (see DMI). LDCM allows LAN administrators to see configurations and monitor the status of personal computers on the LAN.

LDL – Logic Data Language. A project at MCC started in 1984. LDL is a deductive DBMS that combines the expressive capabilities of PROLOG with the functionality of a general-purpose DBMS. See also PROLOG and MCC.

L

LDM – Legacy Data Management. The process of identifying and evaluating historical information and defining potential solutions and requirements for long-term usage of that data in a cost-effective manner.

LDM – Limited-Distance Modem. A short-haul modem normally used on a privately owned circuit that conditions and strengthens a digital signal for higher baud rates (greater than 1 Mbps) over short distances.

LDM – Local Data Manager. The software that allows Unidata sites to select, capture, process and distribute real-time data. A modified version for the Internet is known as the Internet Data Manager or Internet Data Distribution (see IDD).

LDR – Long-distance relationship. The chat term.

LE – LAN Emulation. See LANE.

LE – Less than or Equal to. An acronym very often used in programming languages as a relational operator in logical expressions. See also EQ, NE, LT, GE and GT.

LEC – LAN Emulation Client. An entity in an end system (see ES) that performs data forwarding, address resolution, and other control functions for a single end system within a single ELAN. Each LEC is identified by a unique ATM, and is associated with one or more MAC addresses reachable through that ATM address. See also ELAN and MAC.

LEC – Local Exchange Carrier. Local or regional telephone company that operates a telephone network and the customer lines. Also known as Local Carrier.

LECID – LAN Emulation Client Identifier. An identifier contained in the LANE header that indicates the identity of the ATM host or ATM LAN bridge.

LECS – LAN Emulation Configuration Server. In an ATM LAN, an entity that assigns individual LANE clients to particular ELANs.

LED – Light-Emitting Diode. A semiconductor device that converts electrical energy into light. LEDs are usually used as indicators if something is on or off, to read an output for control purposes, etc. They are available in green, yellow, red and blue colors, among others.

LEN – Low-Entry Networking. An SNA standard that enables adjacent nodes to initiate and terminate communications with one another using LU 6.2 APPC.

LEOS – Low Earth Orbit Satellites. A common name for the communication satellites which use low orbit (in general 700–2000 km above ground) to provide high bandwidth for video on demand, television, or some Internet services. Examples of such satellites are Iridium, TELEDisc and GLOBALSTAR. See also GEOS.

LES – LAN Emulation Server. In an ATM LAN, an entity that implements the control function for a particular ELAN.

lex – lexical analyzer. A compiler generator under the UNIX operating system. It is a lexical analyzer generator based on regular expressions. It accepts a table of patterns and produces a table-driven C program capable of recognizing an input string that satisfies the patterns. Input to lex consists of one file with three parts separated by lines beginning with %%. While the first and the third parts are optional, the second part consists of a table of patterns and C statements dealing with appropriate actions.

LF – Linefeed. A control character (ASCII character, decimal 10) that commands a computer or printer to advance one line below the current line, without moving the cursor or printer head position.

LF – Low Frequency. Transmission frequencies between 30 kHz and 300 kHz.

LFN – Long File Names. A feature of Microsoft Windows that allows filenames to be up to 255 characters.

LFN – Long Fat Network. A very-high-bandwidth (several hundred Mbps) long-haul network.

LGN – Logical Group Node. In ATM networks, a single node that represents the lowest-level peer groups in the respective higher-level peer group.

LGO – Logo file. Filename extension for a logo file.

LIAC – Limited Inquiry Access Code. A code used by a device that responds to an inquiry for limited purposes. An inquiry may be a specific event, limited period of time, etc.

LIDOS – Literature Information and Documentation System. The information system that provides access to bibliographic data and associated online information in the area of artificial intelligence research.

LIFO – Last-In, First-Out. A protocol for a data structure called the stack in which elements can be added and removed only from the front (top) of the stack (see Fig. L-4). Thus, the element removed from the stack is the element that has been held for the least amount of time. Compare with FIFO.

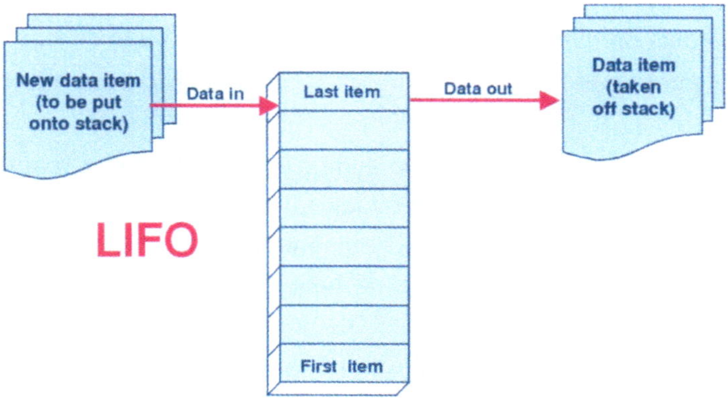

Fig. L-4. LIFO queue

LILO – LINUX Loader. The booting program which resides in the boot sector of a hard disk which is executed when the system is booted from the hard disk. LILO can also be used as a first stage boot loader for several operating systems.

LIMDOW – Light-Intensity Modulation/Direct Overwrite. A technology for magneto-optical (see MO) drives developed by Nikon.

LIM EMS – Lotus/Intel/Microsoft Expanded Memory Specification. See EMS.

LINUX – Linus Torvalds' UNIX. A freely available, very popular 32-bit operating system for personal computers that is compatible with the POSIX 1003.1 standard and which includes many UNIX system V and BSD4.3 functions. The name LINUX (pronounced "linnucks") is named after Linus Torvalds, a Finnish student of computer science who developed the operating system and placed the program source code on the Internet in November 1991. LINUX supports almost all of the requirements demanded by modern UNIX-type operating systems, such as multitasking, multiuser, paging and dynamic cashing, shared libraries, various formats for executable files, national keyboards and fonts, BSD sockets, System V IPC, TCP/IP, SLIP and PPP protocols, etc.

LIP – Large Internet Packet. A packet format used in NetWare that allows packets larger than the regular 576-bytes size of NetWare packets.

LIS – Land Information System. A subset of Geographic Information Systems (see GIS).

LIS – Logical IP Subnet. A group of IP nodes, such as a host and routers, that acts like a virtual LAN. Hosts on the same LIS may exchange IP packets directly, but hosts on different ones are required to go through a router.

LISA – Local Integrated Software Architecture. A personal computer made by Apple.

LISP – List Processing. An applicative, symbolic, functional and recursive language developed in 1959 by the MIT Artificial Intelligence Group led by John McCarthy and Marvin Minsky. The fundamental data structure handled by LISP is a list. LISP uses the same representation for programs and data, and that provides very powerful facilities for symbol manipulation and list processing. LISP is widely used in the field of artificial intelligence (see AI). The ideas of LISP have also had great influence in the study of the theoretical aspects of computer science.

LL – Logical Length. In SNA, a part of a logical record that holds 2-byte-long information of its length.

LL – Left-to-right-scan, Leftmost derivation. A class of language grammars, which can be parsed without backtracking. A grammar is said to be LL (k) if a top-down parser can be written for that grammar which can make a decision as to which process to apply at any stage by simply examining the next k symbols of the input. The term LL is derived from the fact that the input is read from left to right and the parser constructs the leftmost derivation of the sentence in reverse. Compare with LR.

LLA – Logical Layered Architecture. A development concept based upon hierarchical principles in which the architecture can be thought of as being based on a series of layers, and the scope of each layer is broader than the layer below it. An example of LLA is the ISO/OSI layered architecture of network communications (see OSI).

LLAP – LocalTalk Link Access Protocol. A data-link layer protocol implemented in the AppleTalk protocol suite.

LLC – Logical Link Control. The upper portion of the data-link layer, as defined in IEEE802.2. The LLC sublayer presents a uniform interface to the user of the data-link service, usually the network layer (see Fig. L-5). The LLC handles error control, flow control, framing and MAC addressing. Below the LLC sublayer is the MAC sublayer.

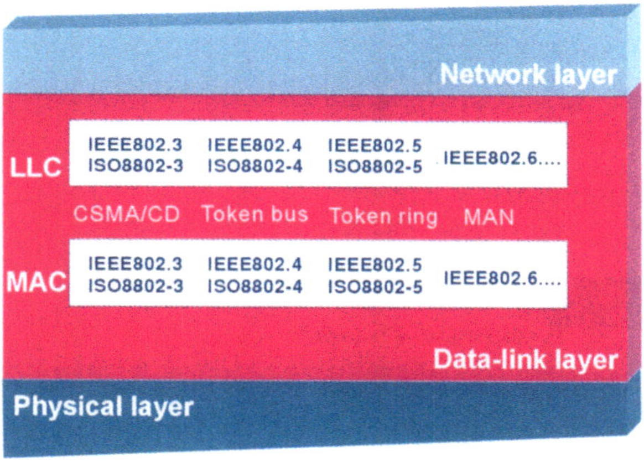

Fig. L-5. LLC in brief

LLTA – Lots and lots of thunderous applause. The chat term.

LME – Layer Management Entity. A mechanism used in the OSI network management in order to provide communication between OSI layers and to access management elements at different layers. Each layer has its own LME. See also OSI, SMAE and SMAP.

LMI – Local Management Interface. A specification for use by frame-relay (see FR) products that defines a method of exchanging status information between devices, such as routers sending or receiving data in the networks.

LMID – Logical Media Identifier. In Microsoft Windows NT, a logical representation of a physical storage location.

LMMP – LAN/MAN Management Protocol. A protocol for network management that provides the OSI CMIS/CMIP network management services to be implemented directly on the logical-link control sublayer (see LLC). The initial name of LMMP was CMIS/CMIP over LLC, also known as CMOL. See also CMIP and CMIS.

LMU – LAN Manager for UNIX. An implementation of the Microsoft product LAN Manager dedicated to UNIX servers.

LM/X – LAN Manager for UNIX. A common term for LAN monitor devices in the UNIX environment.

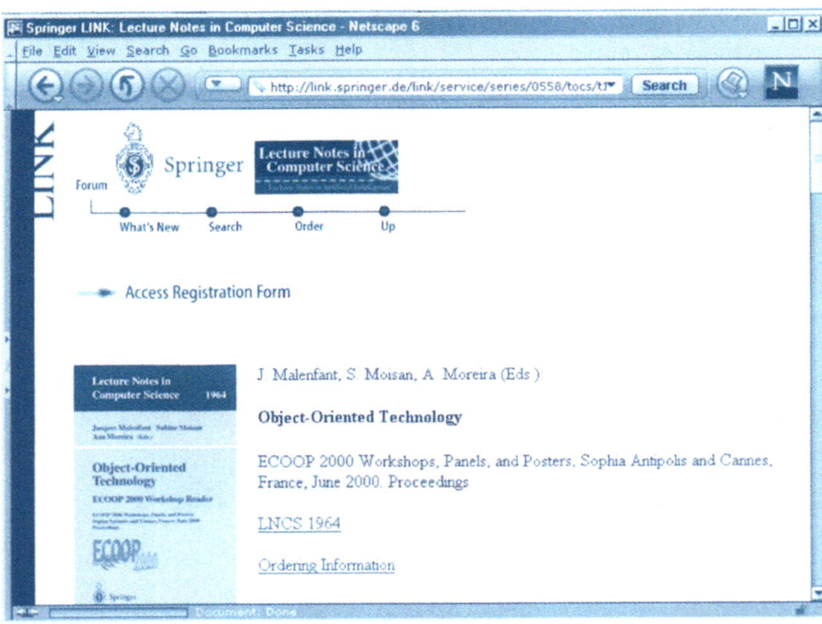

Fig. L-6. Part of the LNCS online digital library

LNAI – Lecture Notes in Artificial Intelligence. The subseries of the Springer-Verlag Lecture Notes in Computer Science (see LNCS) covering research (conference and workshop proceedings) and tutorials and textbooks in the area of AI (http://www.springer.de/comp/lncs/index.html).

LNCS – Lecture Notes in Computer Science. The series of books published by Springer-Verlag covering developments in computer science research. A number of international conference and workshop proceedings are published in the LNCS, as well as surveys, tutorials and textbooks. Depicted in Fig. L-6 is an example of an LNCS offering. Online information about new volumes of LNCS can be found at http://link.springer.de/series/lncs. See also LNAI.

LNK – Link file. A filename extension for Windows shortcut files. LNK files contain links to executable files of Windows applications.

LNNI – LAN emulation Network-to-Network Interface. Enables one vendor's implementation of LAN emulation (see LANE) to work with another's. This specification is essential for building multivendor ATM networks and is currently under development at the ATM Forum. LNNI can be established as BUS–BUS, LES–LES, LECS–LECS and LECS–LES interfaces. See also BUS, LES and LECS.

LOC – Lines Of Code. In software metrics, a measurement unit for the size of source code. Usually expressed in 1000 LOCs (see KLOC).

LOC – Loss Of Cell delineation. A signal used in ATM networks for monitoring the performance of the PHY layer (see PHY).

LOF – Loss Of Frame delineation. A signal used in ATM networks for monitoring the performance of the PHY layer (see PHY).

L

LOG – Logarithm. A common acronym for a logarithm based on 10; i.e. $\log_{10}(x) = y$, thus $x = 10^y$ (e.g. log 1 = 0, log 10 = 1, log 100 = 2, etc.).

LOL – Laughing out loud. The chat term.

LOOPS – LISP Object-Oriented Programming System. An object-oriented LISP extension, developed by the Intelligent Systems Laboratory at Xerox PARC, used in knowledge-based systems development.

LOP – Loss Of Pointer. A signal used in ATM networks for monitoring the performance of the PHY.

LOPSTR – Logic-based Program Synthesis and Transformation. An annual international workshop for presenting recent research and discussing future trends in the synthesis and transformation of programs. The best papers are published by Springer-Verlag (see LNCS).

LOS – Loss Of Signal. A physical-layer alarm sent by the receiver to indicate a cessation in signal transmission. For example, LOS is declared if a fiber-optic cable is cut and the receiving end no longer detects any signal transmissions. The LOS alarm continues until it is manually suppressed or the problem is fixed.

LOTOS – Language Of Temporal Ordering Specification. An ISO standard (ISO8807) related to the OSI communications model that defines a formal specification language based on temporal ordering used for protocol specification.

LP – Line Printer. A common name for any printer that prints one line at a time. They are high-speed devices and are often used with mainframes, minicomputers or networked machines. Compare with LPT.

LP – Linear Programming. The process of program development that allows us to find optimal solutions for systems of equations composed of linear functions, in which there are insufficient terms for a straightforward solution.

LPC – Local Procedure Call. A common term for a mechanism that allows us to call some procedure in a local environment. Compare with Remote Procedure Call (RPC).

LPD – Line Printer Daemon. A protocol used to send print jobs between UNIX systems.

LPF – Low-Pass Filter. A signal filter that can be installed in a customer premises ADSL modem in order to prevent delivery of high-frequency data. Compare with HPF.

lpm – lines per minute. A measurement of printer speed, the number of lines of characters printed in 1 min.

LPP – Lightweight Presentation Protocol. A presentation-layer protocol, dedicated to use in CMIP over TCP (see CMOT); it was never completed.

lpstat – line printer status. UNIX command used to obtain information about the print requirements of a printer, i.e. the number of tasks that are waiting for a printer and the origins of the requested tasks.

LPT – Line Printer. A logical device name for line printers. Also, a name reserved by the MS-DOS operating system for up to three parallel printer ports.

LQ – Letter Quality. A level of print quality for dot-matrix printers which is supposed to result in crisp and dark characters for use in business letters. Also, a common attribute name for dot-matrix printers which allow LQ printing. Most of them can achieve only near-letter-quality printing (see NLQ).

LR – Left-to-right-scan, Rightmost derivation. A grammar is said to be LR (k) if a bottom-up parser can be written for that grammar which makes a single left-to-right pass over the input while examining at most the next k symbols of the input. The term LR is derived from the fact that the input is read from the left to the right and the parser constructs the rightmost derivation of the sentence in reverse. Compare with LL.

L&R – Later. The chat term.

LRC – Longitudinal Redundancy Check. A system of error control based on the formation of a block check following preset rules. In communications, the LRC procedure adds a calculated value to a block of data representing a transmitted message. The value is based on the data in the message and is calculated both before and after the transmission. If discrepancies are not found, the transmission is assumed to be accurate, otherwise a retransmission is required.

LRU – Last Recently Used. An algorithm used in a memory management system, taking into account the patterns of program behavior by assuming that the page used in the most distant past is least likely to be referenced in the near future.

ls – list. UNIX command used to list the files in directories (see DIR) and to list information about files.

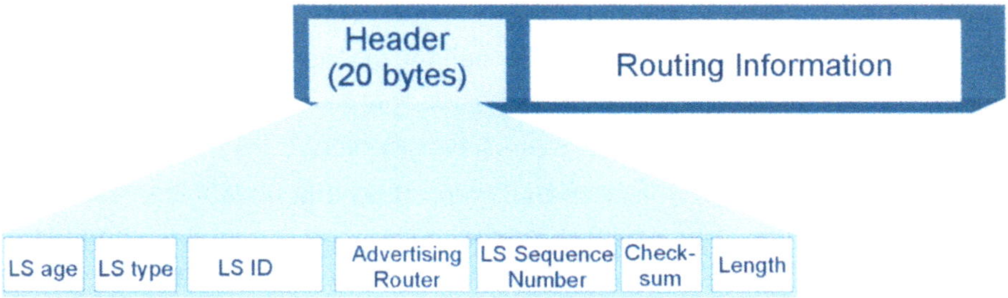

Fig. L-7. LSA frame format

LSA – Link-State Advertisement. A kind of broadcast packet used by link-state protocols that contains information about neighbors and path costs, used by the receiving routers to maintain their routing tables. Sometimes called a link-state packet (LSP). For instance, in RFC2740 (OSPF for IPv6) there are seven distinct types of LSAs defined, each describing a piece of the OSPF routing domain. All LSAs begin with a common 20-byte header (see Fig. L-7). This header contains enough information to uniquely identify the LSA (LS type, LS ID, and Advertising Router). Multiple instances of the LSA may exist, and thus the LS age, LS sequence number and LS checksum fields are used to determine which instance is recent. The LS age represents the time (in seconds) since the LSA was originated. The LS type is used to indicate the function performed by the LSA. The routing information fields that follow the LSA header may have different data depending on the LS type. Such information may include the IDs of the neighborhood interfaces or routers, the cost of those paths, further data about the router (boundary, area border, or multicast), etc.

LSAP – Link Service Access Point. Any of several Service Access Points (see SAP) in the logical-link control sublayer (see LLC) of the OSI data-link layer.

LSAPI – License Service Application Programming Interface. A standard set of functions that provides license-tracing services within an application.

LSB – Least Significant Bit. The lowest-order bit (rightmost) in a normal representation of a binary number.

LSC – Least Significant Character. The lowest-order (rightmost) character in a string.

LSD – Least Significant Digit. The lowest-order (or rightmost) digit in a normal representation of a number.

LSI – Large-Scale Integration. A term describing a concentration of between 100 and 5000 circuit elements on a single chip. Compare with MSI and VLSI.

LSL – Link Support Layer. Part of ODI serving as an intermediate layer between the NIC and the higher-level services. See also NIC and ODI.

LSP – Link-State Packet. See Link-State Advertisement (LSA).

LSP – Link-State Protocol. A kind of routing protocol that uses a link-state algorithm to determine the available connections. The link-state algorithm is based on the distances from a router to all its immediate neighboring routers. Examples include the NetWare Link Service Protocol (see NLSP), Open Shortest Path First (see OSPF), and Intermediate System–Intermediate System (see IS–IS). See also Link-State Advertisement (LSA). Compare with Distance Vector Protocol (DVP).

LSP – LISP file. Filename extensions for files that contain LISP code.

LSR – Leaf Setup Request. A type of setup message used in communications when a leaf node requests a connection to an existing point-to-multipoint connection or requests the creation of a new multipoint connection.

LSRR – Loose Source and Record Route. An IP option that enables the source for a datagram to specify the routing information and to record the actually used route.

LT – Less Than. An acronym very often used in programming languages as a relational operator in logical expressions. For example:

```
if a LT b then
   a=a+1
```

```
else
   b=b–1
endif
```

If the value a is less than that of b, the logical expression is true, therefore the "a=a+1" is executed, otherwise the statement "b=b–1" is executed. See also EQ, NE, LE, GE and GT.

LTA – Line Turnaround. The amount of time required to set-up the line in the reverse direction in half-duplex communications (see HDX).

LTE – Lite Terminating Equipment. ATM equipment that terminates a communication facility using a SONET Lite Transmission Convergence layer (see TC).

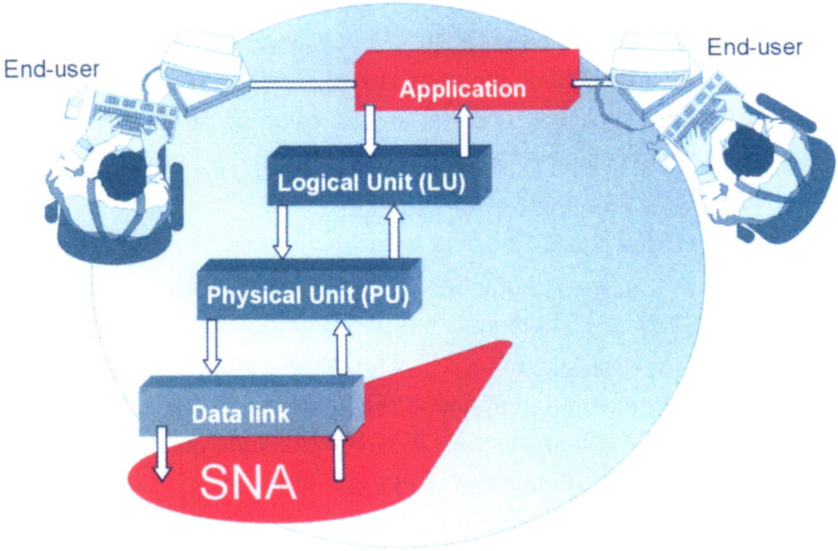

Fig. L-8. The role of LUs and PUs in SNA communications

LTM – Laugh to myself. The chat term.

LTM – Line Traffic Monitor. A device for monitoring LAN traffic.

LTNS – Long time no see. The chat term.

LTO – Liner Tape Open. A scalable tape architecture technology with two available formats. Ultrium is used for high capacity and performance, whilst Accelis is optimized for fast access.

LTR – Long-term relationship. The chat term.

LU – Logical Unit. A primary component of the IBM SNA that enables end-users to communicate with each other and gain access to SNA network resources (see Fig. L-8). In fact, an LU is a connection and the software controlling the connection. There are several LU types distinguished from each other by their associated numbers. The first four (LU0–LU3) involve master–slave relationships between the program and the device under control. LU4 may be used either for the master–slave or for the P2P relationship. LU6 is intended for P2P communications. See System Network Architecture (SNA). The other two units types are known as PU and SSCP.

LU6.2 – Logical Unit 6.2. A type of logical unit (see LU) that governs peer-to-peer SNA communications between programs in a distributed processing environment. See also APPC.

LUA – Logical Unit Application. In SNA, both the name for a conventional Logical Unit application (see LU) and for an API that allows LU applications to be written which are capable of communicating with host applications.

LUID – Locally Unique Identifier. A 64-bit unique value generated by the operating system every time it's restarted.

LULAB – Love you like a brother. The chat term.

LULAS – Love you like a sister. The chat term.

LUN – Logical Unit Number. A number between 1 and 7 used on each device connected to a SCSI chain to identify the particular device. See also SCSI.

LUNI – LANE User-to-Network Interface. The ATM Forum standard for LAN emulation on ATM networks. It defines the interface between the LAN Emulation Client (see LEC) and the LAN Emulation Server (see LES) components. See also ATM (Asynchronous Transfer Mode).

LUT – Look-up Table. A table used by color-generation systems that in each position contains three values, each related to one of the primary colors (see RGB). The value of each primary color usually ranges from 0 to 255 (2^8–1) or from 0 to 4095 (2^{12}–1). According to that value and the frame buffer pointer to the LUT (see Fig. L-9) a video processor can extract the three required color values, one for each of the electron guns in the CRT.

LVD – Low Voltage Differential. A type of SCSI disk-drive interface that operates at 80 MBps in 16-bit SCSI mode for cable lengths of up to 12 m. Also known as Ultra2 SCSI. See also SCSI.

LWP – Lotus WordPro. A filename extension for a file that contains a document made using Lotus WordPro.

Lynx – Less Insecure (any) UNIX. A character-based browser developed at the University of Kansas for students who use UNIX workstations.

LZ – Lempel–Ziv compression. An entropy compression algorithm developed by Abraham Lempel and Jacob Ziv. Actually, there are two of them, LZ77 and LZ78, and both are dictionary-based algorithms: they build up a dictionary of previously used strings of characters. The output streams of such encoders consist of characters or references to the dictionary. A combination of a reference with a character generates a new reference in the dictionary. For example, a reference to "Hi" in the dictionary followed by the character "s" results in a new reference "His". ARJ and ZIP files are derived from LZ77.

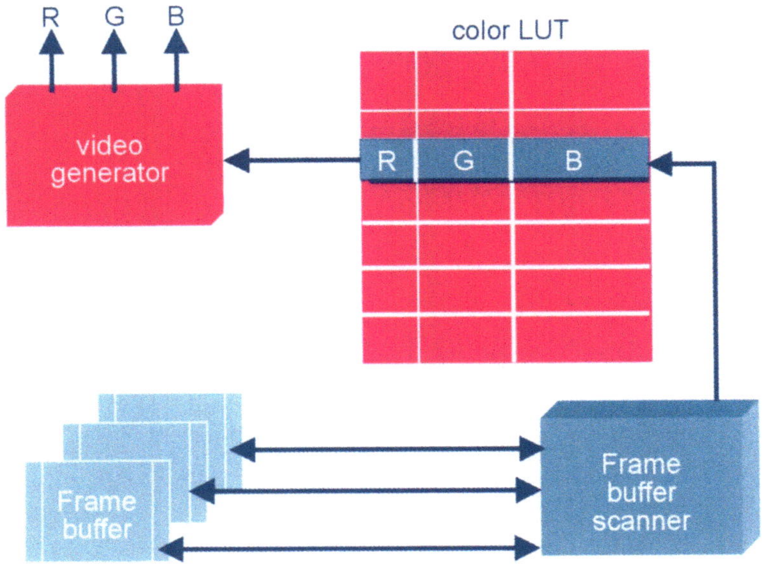

Fig. L-9. The color look-up table

LZH – Lempel–Ziv–Huffman. A compression algorithm derived from the LZ algorithm (see LZ entry) with additional compression applied to the output of the LZ compressor using dynamic Huffman coding (developed in the 1950s by D.A. Huffman).

LZW – Lempel–Ziv–Welch. An improvement of LZ78 made by Terry Welch in 1984 for implementation in hardware for high-performance disk controllers. LZW uses a table of entries with an index field and a substitution-string field. This dictionary is preloaded with every possible symbol in the alphabet.

Thus, every symbol can be found in the dictionary by using a reference. The encoder searches in the dictionary for the largest possible reference to the string at the input. This reference plus the first symbol of the input stream after the reference are stored in the output stream. The decoder reads the encoded stream and replaces the reference with the substitution string that is stored in the associated entry of the dictionary. The symbol that follows the reference is stored directly in the decoded stream. The best-known LZW implementations are the UNIX "compress" utility and GIF.

M

μ – micro. This symbol, the Greek letter "mu", is used to indicate micro (from the Greek word "mikros" or "small"), and as a prefix it represents 10^{-6}, for example 1 μA is 10^{-6} A etc.

M – Mega. An order of magnitude (10^6). In computing, that really means 1,048,576 which is the power of two (2^{20}) closest to 1 million in decimal. See MB and Mb.

m – milli. An order of magnitude representing one-thousandth (for example 1 mV is equal to 0.001 V, 1 ms is equal to 0.001 s, etc.).

M3D – Motion 3D. A filename extension for a file that contains Corel Motion 3D animation.

MAC – Media Access Control. ISO OSI and IEEE sublayer in the data link layer which controls access to the physical medium of a network. The MAC sublayer is especially important in LANs, where communications are based on multi-access channels. There are two main classes of access methods, probabilistic and deterministic. In the probabilistic method the line is checked to see when the node wants to transmit (see CSMA/CD). In the deterministic method, nodes get access to the network in a predetermined sequence (polling, for example). Typical examples of MAC protocols are IEEE802.3 for CSMA/CD, IEEE802.4 for Token Bus, IEEE802.5 for Token Ring, and IEEE 802.6 for DQDB.

MAC – Message Authentication Code. A keyed hashing algorithm that uses a symmetric session key.

MACA – Multiple Access with Collision Avoidance. An early protocol for wireless LANs used as the basis for the IEEE802.11 standard. The basic idea is receiver stimulation by a short frame sent from the sender, so that the receiving station can detect this and avoid transmitting itself until the incoming large frame has arrived. See also MACAW.

MACAW – Multiple Access with Collision Avoidance Wireless. A finetuned MACA in existence since 1994. See MACA.

MacOS – Macintosh Operating System. The proprietary operating system from Apple for its Macintosh family of personal computers.

MAE – Macintosh Application Environment. A system shell for open RISC-based systems that provides a Macintosh interface within an X Window

System window. The Macintosh Application Environment is both Mac- and UNIX-compatible and will support all off-the-shelf products for the Macintosh. See also RISC and X.

MAE – Metropolitan Area Ethernet. A Network Access Point (see NAP) where Internet Service Providers (see ISP) can connect with each other.

MAM – Microsoft Access Macro. A filename extension for a file that contains macros in a Microsoft Access database. Access to those files as well as to the others (see MAQ, MAR and MAT) relevant for seeing the database content is available via a very simple user interface, as depicted in Fig. M-1.

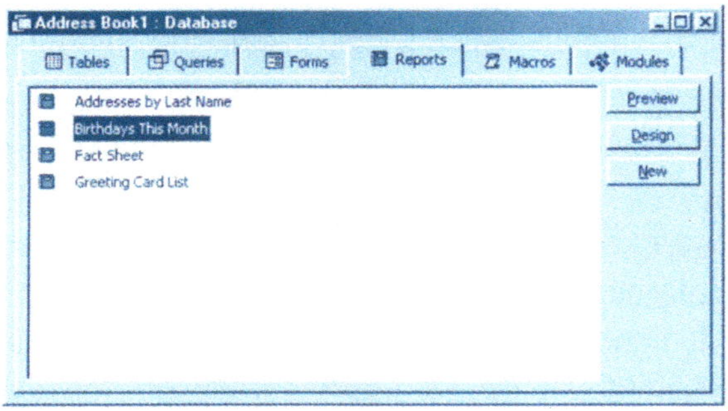

Fig. M-1. Microsoft Access user interface for a database review

MAMA – Multi-Agents and Mobile Agents. An international symposium focusing on agent technologies and electronic commerce. Major topics include agents (architectures, information agents, mobile agents, network agents, behavior modeling, user modeling, standards), multiagents (agent platform, agent-based software engineering, agent communications and languages, coordination, collaboration, simulation, verification, organization, scalability), CSCW and agent technologies, virtual organizations, and electronic commerce. The proceedings are published by Academic Press.

MAN – Metropolitan Area Network. A type of local area network, actually a set of LANs that can be spread over several hundred kilometers (for example, all over a town or metropolitan area) based on the DQDB standard (see DQDB).

man – manual. The UNIX command used to locate and print citations from the UNIX system manual, where the printed manual is unavailable.

MANTLE – Mid-Atlantic Network for Teaching Learning Enterprises. The MANTLE organization was created to build a forum for sharing and disseminating knowledge about distance education. A particular focus of the organization is promoting the professional development of educators engaged in this type of instruction in the mid-Atlantic region of the US.

MAP – Manufacturing Automation Protocol. A set of protocols developed by General Motors based on the IEEE802.4 Token Bus specification intended for its factory automation program. The MAP protocol stack follows the OSI model and guarantees access to each host within a certain maximum time. The MAP model recognizes three types of networks depending on the manufacturing hierarchy level at which the network is defined, as follows:

- Type 1: Networks that operate at the highest level in the automation hierarchy. They support information management, task scheduling, and resource allocation.
- Type 2: Networks that connect work cells and workstations serving as process or machine controllers.
- Type 3: Networks that connect machines and their components that operate in real-time.

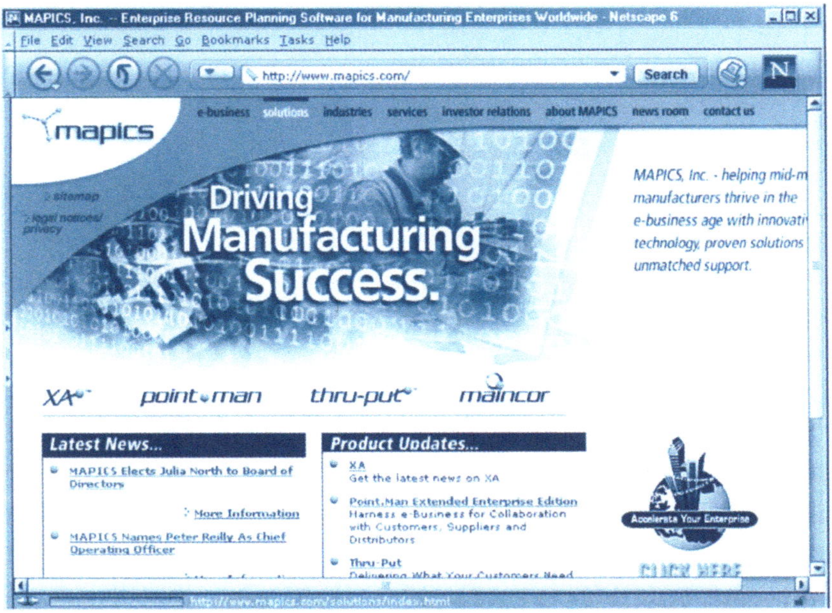

Fig. M-2. MAPICS homepage (with permission of MAPICS Inc.; Copyright 2000 MAPICS Inc., All Rights Reserved)

MAPI – Messaging Application Programming Interface. Microsoft system designed to send electronic mail across a local area network. MAPI solves a critical problem for developers by separating the messaging requirements of applications from messaging services with an intermediary layer called the MAPI subsystem. Windows applications can use MAPI calls through the subsystem to interact with any MAPI-compliant messaging system. MAPI eliminates the need for the client application to know how a particular messaging system provides services. Microsoft chooses a client/server approach for MAPI to help reduce bottlenecks that increased messaging generates on a LAN. The client/server architecture distributes tasks between the client side and the server side. Servers store the procedures and executable modules most commonly used by clients. MAPI is an architectural approach, not just a set of APIs. It exists as a subsystem of the entire operating system.

MAPICS – Manufacturing, Accounting and Production Information Control System. One of the most widely used manufacturing software packages worldwide. As an IBM official business partner, the MAPICS company (http://www.mapics.com) is responsible for the development and implementation of the MAPICS package worldwide. See Fig. M-2. See also Enterprise Resource Planning (ERP), Executive Information Systems (EIS), and Enterprise Product Data Management (EPDM).

MAQ – Microsoft Access Query. A filename extension for a file that contains Microsoft Access queries.

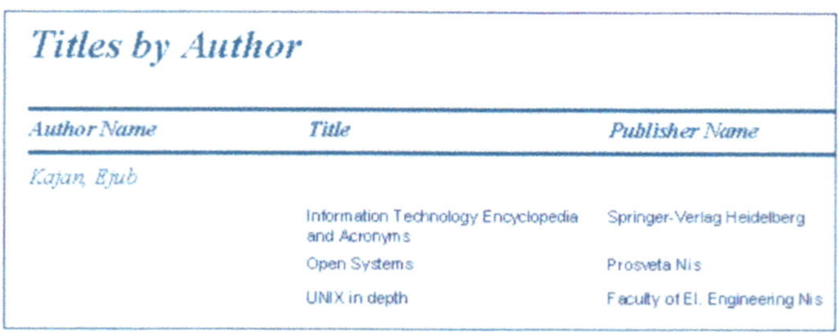

Fig. M-3. The contents of the MAR file for a simple database

MAR – Microsoft Access Report. A filename extension for a file that contains a Microsoft Access report (Fig. M-3).

MARS – Multicast Address Resolution Server. A mechanism for supporting IP multicast. A MARS serves a group of nodes (known as a cluster); each node in the cluster is configured with the ATM address of the MARS. The MARS supports multicast through multicast messages of overlaid point-to-multipoint connections or through multicast servers. Compare with ARP.

MARVEL – Machine-Assisted Realization of the Virtual Electronic Library. A global information system (http://marvel.loc.gov) that combines the vast collection of information available at and about the US Library of Congress with many electronic resources accessible through the Internet. Specific menu items included in MARVEL are research and reference, the US Congress, US federal government information, and copyright.

MAS – Multi-Agent System. The term from the Distributed Artificial Intelligence (see DAI) research field. Agents and agent technologies are described elsewhere in the book (see RP, Remote Programming). As for the agent definition, various definitions have also been proposed for the term MAS. The following one appeared in the IEEE Knowledge and Data Engineering journal (KDE-1(1), 1989, pp. 63–83: "A MAS is a loosely coupled network of problem-solver entities that work together to find answers to problems that are beyond the individual knowledge of each entity". In order to provide communications between different agents in a multiagent system, it is necessary to provide an appropriate communication mechanism. A common agent communication may be achieved by open scripting languages such as Java or Tcl (see AWB, RP and Tcl), by declarative languages such as KQML, or by shared ontologies such as Ontolingua or Knowledge Interchange Format (see KIF). In order to achieve a real MAS, i.e. a MAS where agents may communicate without any restrictions, several standardization efforts have taken place (for example, see FIPA, KAoS and UAA).

MAT – MATLAB. A filename extension for a file that contains MATLAB (an interactive program for high-performance numeric computation and visualization, see http://www.mathworks.com) binary variables.

MAT – Microsoft Access Table. A filename extension for a file that contains a Microsoft Access table.

MAU – Media Access (Attachment) Unit. A device used in Ethernet and IEEE 802.3 networks that provides the interface between the Attachment Unit Interface (see AUI) port of a station and the common medium of the Ethernet. It can be built into a station or can be a separate device such as a network interface card, repeater, hub, etc. It performs physical-layer functions, including conversion of digital data from the Ethernet interface, collision detection, and injection of bits onto the network. Internal MAUs are built into the network device; external MAUs usually plug directly onto the AUI port of the device. A multiport MAU, or transceiver, allows a number of workstations to be attached to a single connection on the Ethernet bus.

MAU – Multistation Access Unit. In the IBM Token Ring architecture, a term used for a wiring hub. MAU serves as the termination point for multiple nodes (lobes in IBM terminology) and can be connected to the network or to another hub.

Mb – Megabit. A measurement unit for 1,048,576 bits.

MB – Megabyte. A measurement unit for 1,048,576 bytes.

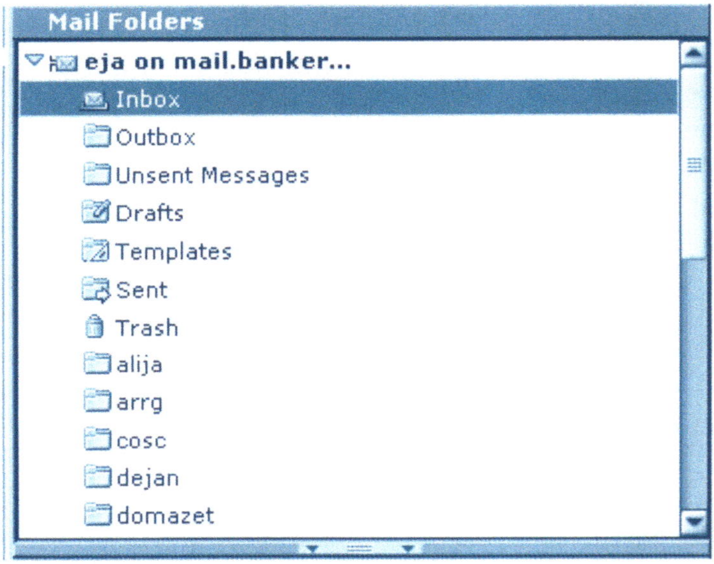

Fig. M-4. Typical structure of a MBX

MBCS – Multiple-Byte Character Set. A character set in which characters are represented as either 1-byte or 2-byte values. See also DBCS.

MBONE – Multicast Backbone. A virtual network on top of the Internet to support routing of IP multicast packets intended for multimedia transmission, implemented by Steve Deering at Xerox PARC. MBONE is organized as clusters of networks that operate on IP multicasting using class-D addresses. The concept was adopted at the March 1992 IETF in San Diego, during which it was used to audiocast to 40 people throughout the world. At the following meeting in July 1992, in Cambridge, the name MBONE was adopted. See RFC1112 and RFC1122 for the details. See also 6bone.

MBOX – Mailbox. A filename extension for a file that contains a mailbox created by Berkeley UNIX.

MBR – Master Boot Record. A small program that resides on the first sector of the hard disk. MBR is executed during the booting process.

MBS – Maximum Burst Size. An ATM traffic parameter that specifies the maximum number of cells that can be transmitted at the ATM's peak cell rate (see PCR). MBS plays a key role in measurement, in capacity planning and network management.

MBX – Mailbox. An e-mail term related to electronic mailboxes that have the same purpose as regular post mailboxes (see Fig. M-4). In other words, somebody can leave the letter in your mailbox, or you can leave your letter in the mailbox waiting for the postman to pick it up and deliver it. Also, a file-name extension for a file that contains a mailbox created by Microsoft Outlook. Figure M-4 shows the typical structure of a Netscape mailbox (see SNM) consisting of default folders (Inbox, where incoming messages are stored; Unsent Messages, for messages being prepared for sending later; Sent, for messages already sent; Outbox, for messages being sent; Trash, for deleted messages) and several user-defined folders.

MCA – Micro Channel Architecture. IBM's proprietary 32-bit bus used in their PS/2 personal computers as well as in their servers and mainframes, based on RISC technology. Now, IBM does not officially use MCA as an acronym after the lawsuit by the Music Corporation of America.

M

MCC – Microelectronics and Computer Technology Corporation. One of the first and one of the largest computer industry research and development consortiums in the US (http://www.mcc.com), founded in late 1982 by major computer and semiconductor manufacturers. MCC works on system architectures, advanced microelectronics design, process control, intelligent systems, distributed technologies, etc.

MCF – MAC Convergence Function. A function used in the DQDB network in order to prepare data for a connectionless service (see CL). See also DQDB.

MCI – Media Control Interface. A device-independent interface for multimedia devices and media files. Conceptually, this control is a set of pushbuttons that provides users with access to devices such as audio boards, CD-ROM devices, etc. (see Fig. M-5).

MCIF – Miniature Card Implementers Forum. An industrial consortium working on specifications for new cards which are about a quarter of the size of current PC cards. It was founded by Compaq, Fujitsu, HP, Intel, Microsoft, Nokia, Philips and Sharp.

MCLR – Maximum Cell Loss Ratio. An ATM QoS parameter that indicates the highest acceptable number of dropped cells compared with the total number of cells received for a given transmission. See also ATM (Asynchronous Transfer Mode) and QoS.

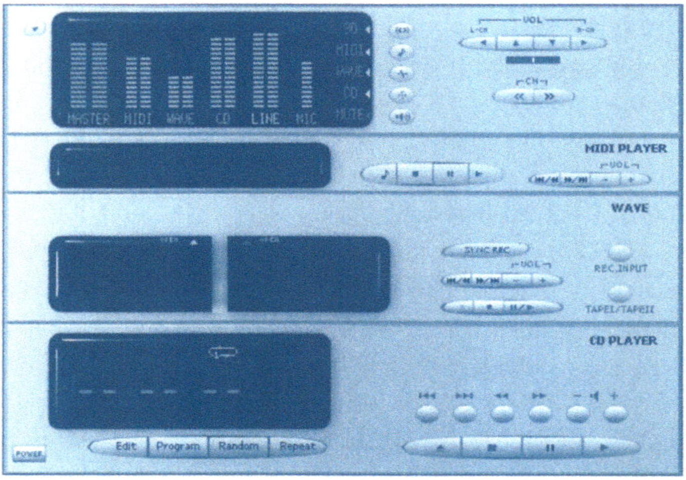

Fig. M-5. An example of an MCI application

MCR – Minimum Cell Rate. An ATM QoS parameter, representing the minimum number of cells per second that is considered acceptable by the customer. If the carrier is unable to provide this required rate, it must reject the connection. See Quality of Service (QoS). Compare with Available Bit Rate (ABR).

MCS – Multiple Classifier Systems. An international workshop focusing on the state of the art of the theory and applications of multiple classifier systems. Some of the major topics include theoretical foundations, neural networks, mixture models, hybrid systems, appropriate data mining, intelligent agents, and a number of application areas. The proceedings are published by Springer-Verlag (see LNCS).

MCS – Multimedia Conference Server. Server that makes it possible for several sites (conference endpoints) to participate in a real-time conference with audio, full motion video, and document sharing.

MD – Management Domain. In the ITU-T X.400 MHS, a limited area for message handling that operates under the control of a single management authority. See also ADMD and PRMD.

MD – Message Digest. A message digest (MD-2 described in RFC1319, MD-4 in RFC1320, and MD-5 in RFC1321) is an algorithmic operation, generally performed on text, which produces a unique 128-bit signature for that text. Message digests differ in their operating speeds and resistance to crypto-analytic attack. The word digest is a checksum value calculated by an algorithm using a message, an authentication key, and time information.

MDA – Mobile Data Access. An international conference dealing with the important aspects of supporting data over hybrid wireless and wired networks. The proceedings are published by Springer-Verlag (see LNCS).

PubID	Name	Address	City	State
1	ACM	11 W. 42nd St., 3rd flr.	New York	NY
2	Addison-Wesley	Rte 128	Reading	MA
3	Bantam Books	666 Fifth Ave	New York	NY
4	Benjamin/Cummings	390 Bridge Pkwy.	Redwood City	CA
5	Brady Pub.	15 Columbus Cir.	New York	NY
6	Computer Science Press	41 Madison Ave	New York	NY
7	ETN Corporation	RD 4, Box 659	Montoursville	PA
8	Gale	835 Penobscot Bldg	Detroit	MI
9	IEEE	10662 Los Vaqueros Circle	Los Alamitos	CA
10	Intertext	2633 E. 17th Ave.	Anchorage	AK
11	M&T Books	501 Galveston Dr.	Redwood City	CA
12	Macmillan Education	175 Fifth Ave.	New York	NY
13	McGraw-Hill	1221 Ave of the Americas	New York	NY
14	Microsoft Press	One Microsoft Way	Redmond	WA
15	Morgan Kaufmann	2929 Campus Dr., Suite 260	San Mateo	CA
16	Osborne	2600 Tenth St	Berkeley	CA
17	Prentice-Hall	15 Columbus Cir.	New York	NY
18	Prentice-Hall International	Rte. 9W	Englewood Cliffs	NJ
19	Q E D Information Sciences	P.O. Box 82-181	Wellesley	MA
21	SRA	155 N. Wacker Dr.	Chicago	IL
22	Slawson	165 Vallecitos de Oro	San Marcos	CA
24	TAB	P.O. Box 40	Blue Ridge Summit	PA
25	Waite Group Press	100 Shoreline Hwy., Suite A285	Mill Valley	CA

Fig. M-6. An example of an MDB file (only part of it is visible)

MDB – Microsoft Access Database. A filename extension for a file that contains a database created by Microsoft Access. An example of such a file (a database of publishers) is given in Fig. M-6.

MDBS – Multidatabase System. A database system that drives other database systems and allows the users to simultaneously access independent databases using a single data definition and manipulation language. An MDBS provides a single global schema that represents an integration of the relevant positions of the underlying local databases. Users may formulate queries and updates according to the global schema.

MDC – Metadata Coalition. A standards group (http://www.mdc.com) dealing with the metadata interchange format standard.

MDC – Mobile Daughter Card. An audio/modem riser (see AMR) equivalent board used in mobile computers.

MDD – Model Device Driver. The platform-independent layer of a built-in device driver supplied by Microsoft.

MDDS – Mobility in Databases and Distributed Systems. The IEEE international workshop focusing on the mobility of users, hardware, software and data. Some of the major topics cover the impact of mobility in distributed applications, appropriate data models, theoretical frameworks for mobility, wireless communications, appropriate object-oriented technologies, operating systems support, mobile agents, distributed mobile objects, resource allocation and management in mobile environments, etc. The proceedings are published by IEEE CS Press.

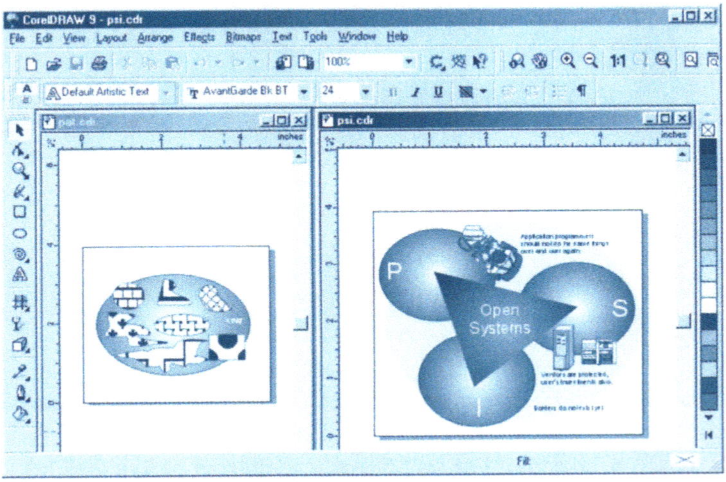

Fig. M-7. An example of an MDI

MDI – Multiple-Document Interface. A Windows API that enables development of an application that allows the user to have more than one document open at the same time. Figure M-7 depicts such an application (CorelDraw) with two CDR files open at once. Compare with SDI (Single Document Interface).

MDT – Mountain Daylight Time. Time zone. UTC – 6.00 hours. Most of the US state of Arizona does not operate MDT – it's on MST all year round.

MDZ – Microsoft Access Database Wizard. A filename extension for a file that contains a wizard template used by Microsoft Access to create a new database (see Fig. M-8).

MEMS – Microelectromechanical System. A technology that combines computers with tiny mechanical devices such as sensors, valves, mirrors and actuators embedded in semiconductor chips.

MEN – Management Event Notification protocol. An application-level protocol proposed by DEC for use in its Digital Network Architecture (see DNA). Used for communication between an event (happening) source and an event sink. A part of the protocol suite used for overall network management.

MEO – Medium Earth Orbit. A common name for satellites which reside between 6000 km and 20,000 km above the ground. Compare with GEO and LEO.

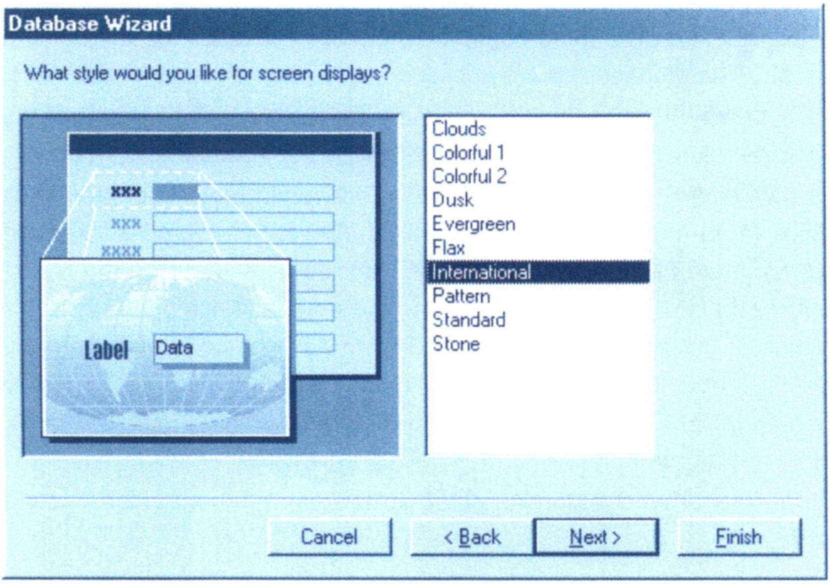

Fig. M-8. One of the MDZ files available in Microsoft Access

MESCH – Multi-WAIS Engine Search for Commercial Hosts. A CGI program written to query multiple remote sites running freeWAIS. MESCH runs on a server site (http://www.ip.net, for example) and participating client sites run freeWAIS and make their indices available for searches. It currently allows searches through commercial shops on the web. See also WAIS.

MESI – Modified, Exclusive, Shared or Invalid. A cache coherence protocol for a single-bus multiprocessor where each cache line exists in one of four stages, M, E, S or I, as mentioned in the given acronym.

MET – Metafile. A filename extension for a file that contains a metafile created by Presentation Manager.

MET – Middle European Time. Time zone. UTC + 1.00 hour. See TZ.

METDST – Middle European Time Daylight Saving Time. Time zone. UTC + 2.00 hours. See TZ.

MF – Medium Frequency. Frequencies in the range 300–3000 kHz.

MFCS – Mathematical Foundations of Computer Science. An international symposium focusing on research on all aspects of theoretical computer science. MFCS has a long history, in fact MFCS2000 was the 25th symposium. The main topics include algorithms, computational geometry, learning theory, automata, formal languages, cryptography, security, knowledge-based systems, parallel and distributed computing, quantum computing, artificial intelligence, etc. The proceedings are published by Springer-Verlag (see LNCS).

MFLOPS – Million Floating-point Operations per Second. A measure of computing speed, a million floating-point operations per second.

MFM – Modified Frequency Modulation. A widely used method of storing data on disks. MFM encoding is based on an earlier technique called frequency modulation (see FM) but improves on its efficiency by reducing the need for synchronizing information and by basing the magnetic coding of each bit on the status of the previously recorded bit. MFM encoding stores more information on a disk than does frequency modulation encoding and is used on many hard disks. It is not, however, as efficient a space saver as the technique known as run-length limited encoding (see RLL).

MFS – Macintosh File System. An older file system used in earlier Macintosh systems.

MFT – Multiprogramming with a Fixed number of Tasks. An operating system for the family of IBM System/360 computers.

MGCP – Media Gateway Control Protocol. An effort to make a protocol for gateways allowing voice, video and data traffic over IP networks (RFC2805).

MH – Mobile Host. A common term for portable computers which allow access to e-mail and normal file systems from anywhere in the world.

MHEG – Multimedia/Hypermedia Expert Group. An ISO/IEC standard (ISO/IEC 13522) that specifies a coded representation of final-form multimedia and hypermedia information objects (pronounced “M-heg”). These objects define the structure of multimedia/hypermedia presentation in a system-independent way. The MHEG standard has several parts, as follows:

- MHEG-1 defines the multimedia objects, their behavior, the actions that can be applied to them, and their interchange representation in ASN.1, which allows MHEG interpreters to share MHEG objects.
- MHEG-2 was intended to define SGML-based encoding for the framework defined by MHEG-1. However, due to a lack of resources it was cancelled before finalization.
- MHEG-3 defines executable code dedicated to a virtual machine.
- MHEG-4 is a "supporting" standard, which defines the ISO official procedure for assigning identifiers for content formats used by other MHEG parts. MHEG-4 reached International Standard status in 1995.
- MHEG-5 is intended to support the distribution of interactive multimedia/hypermedia applications in client/server architectures across different platforms. The applications reside on the server, and as parts of the application are needed they are downloaded to the client. The MHEG-5 interpreter resides on the client, and it is its responsibility to interpret the application parts, to present them to the user, and to handle local user interactions.
- MHEG-6 is an extension of MHEG-5 that allows data processing and communication with the external environment, such as servers, local device drivers, etc. It uses Java as an interchange format and the Java Virtual Machine (see JVM) to interpret this format.
- MHEG-7 is intended to specify interoperability and conformance testing of MHEG-5 interpreters.

MHS – Message Handling System. The standard defined by ITU-T as X.400 and by ISO (ISO10021) as the Message-Oriented Text Interchange Standard (MOTIS) in the OSI application layer. It provides the functions for global electronic mail transfer among local mail systems and Message Transfer Agents (see MTA), as shown in Fig. M-9. The whole scenario is similar to work done by the post office and postal workers. It also provides temporary storage for messages before they are forwarded to their destination (see MS). See also e-mail, MTS and User Agent (UA).

MHz – Megahertz. The frequency measurement unit for millions of cycles per second, used to measure the clock rates of modern digital logic.

MI – Marketing Identifier. A business term used by a vendor to refer to its product on the market. Usually, MIs appear in pricing lists, offers, sales contracts, etc.

MIA – Multivendor Integration Architecture. A proposal for a standardized architecture for the interconnection of multivendor systems issued by NTT.

MIB – Management Information Base. A database used to hold the management information related to a network or internetwork. MIB can be accessed via network management protocols such as SNMP or CMIP. The details on the MIB format depend on the network and network management model being used. Standard minimal MIBs have been defined.

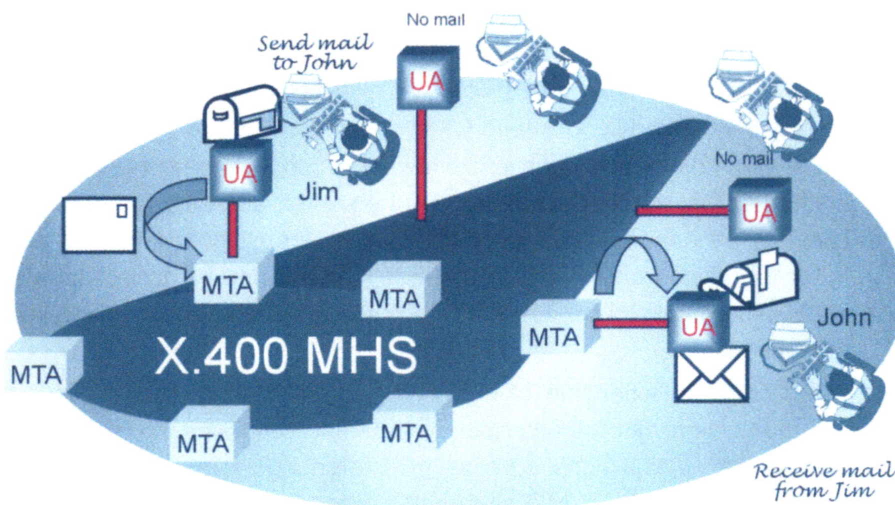

Fig. M-9. An overview of a MHS

MIC – Modeling Identification and Control. The IASTED international conference dedicated to presenting and discussing the recent developments in the area of modeling, identification and control.

MICAI – Medical Image Computing and Computer-Assisted Intervention. An international annual conference focusing on computer-assisted interventions, medical robotics, image computing, and surgical navigation.

MICE – Management Information Control and Exchange protocol. An application-layer protocol used in DEC's Digital Network Architecture (see DNA) to implement various network management functions.

MicroVAX – Micro Virtual Address Extended. The low end of DEC's VAX line. The MicroVAX line includes the MicroVAX 2000, MicroVAX II, and MicroVAX 3000 series. See also VAX.

MicroVMS – Micro Virtual Machine System. DEC's implementation of the VMS operating system for the MicroVAX computers. See also MicroVAX, VAX and VMS.

MID – Message Identifier. A field in an ATM cell used to associate cells that carry segments from the same higher-layer packet.

MIDAS – Multitier Distributed Applications Services. A Borland product intended for multitier distributed application development. The essential component of MIDAS is the Remote Data Broker, which can be divided into three distinct sections, the client, the data transfer protocol, and the server. The client portion consists of Delphi components and a single tiny DLL providing connectivity to the middle-tier application servers, which in turn provide connectivity to a variety of databases (Access, DB2, dBase, FoxPro, Informix, Oracle, Sybase, and any ODBC). The basic scenario looks like this:

1. The client makes a DCOM request to the server.
2. The server creates a special protocol called a DataPacket used to transfer the data from the server to the client.
3. The result is returned to the client.

The other components of MIDAS are intended for middle-tier business object building, maintenance of data integrity, reducing network traffic, etc. The multitier architecture is described in the entry for EIS. Further information about MIDAS is available from the Borland website (http://www.borland.com).

M

MIDI – Musical Instrument Digital Interface. A high-speed serial interface standard (pronounced "middy") that allows connection of musical synthesizers, instruments, and computers. In addition to the hardware specification (the connector and the cable), it is also the software specification describing the way in which music and sound are encoded and communicated between MIDI devices. MIDI devices exchange information in a form called a MIDI message that allows various aspects of sounds (e.g. volume) to be encoded in a digital way. There are 127 "instruments" specified by MIDI with unique codes assigned. In addition to classic musical instruments such as the violin or piano, some codes are reserved for common special effects. Therefore, MIDI devices can be used for creating, recording and playing back music. Separate connections are defined for input, output and for passing through.

MIDL – Microsoft Interface Definition Language. The Microsoft implementation of the OSF DCE Interface Definition Language (see IDL). See also DCE (Distributed Computing Environment).

MIF – Minimum Internetworking Functionality. An ISO definition of the minimum functionality required by a local area network node which also has the capability of interconnecting to a wide area network.

MII – Media-Independent Interface. A standard specification for the interface between network controller chips and their associated media interface chip(s). The MII automatically senses 10- and 100-MHz Ethernet speeds.

MIIS – Microsoft Internet Information Server. See IIS (Internet Information Server).

MIL – Military. One of the top-level domains on the Internet. See MILNET. See also DNS and TLD.

MILNET – Military Network. This network was created in 1984 from parts of the original ARPANET. Military users wanted to have an operational production network, while the research community wanted to have a network on which to continue experimenting in networking. Therefore, the military users were placed on MILNET, the research users were placed on ARPANET, and the two networks were connected using mail bridges and gateways. Today, MILNET is one of the class-A networks on the Internet (see MIL).

MIM – Multipart Internet Mail. Filename extensions for files that contain multipart messages in the MIME format. See also MIME.

MIMD – Multiple Instruction Multiple Data. A type of parallel computer architecture, or processor, that uses multiple processing elements which operate independently of each other with a separate code. Processing elements very often execute the same program. They can achieve a high efficiency for general types of computations. However, since processors may even start at different times and may process data at different rates, synchronization and load balancing are very important and difficult goals. Compare with SIMD.

MIME – Multipurpose Internet Mail Extensions. This IETF standard (RFC1521, RFC2231, RFC2646) defines a mail message format which can support messages in different languages (with accents, in non-Latin alphabets, etc.) as well as messages not containing text at all (e.g. audio and/or video). MIME is independent of specific platforms and operating environments. The standard mail format defined in RFC822 (To:, Cc:, Bcc:, From:, Sender:, Received:, Return-Path:) is extended by MIME to add structure to the message body and define encoding rules for non-ASCII messages. Figure M-10 explains text, image, audio and video MIME types. The MIME application type allows users to attach any file, which can then be interpreted at the destination. Actually, two subtypes are defined: an octet-stream as an uninterpreted byte sequence, and printable documents. Multipart MIME allows mixed, alternative, parallel and digest subtypes which provide independent parts of messages in the specified order, the same messages in different formats, a simultaneous view of the message parts, and every part of the message to be viewed as a complete message, respectively. The MIME message type allows RFC822-compliant messaging, partial message transmission, and fetching the message itself as an external body.

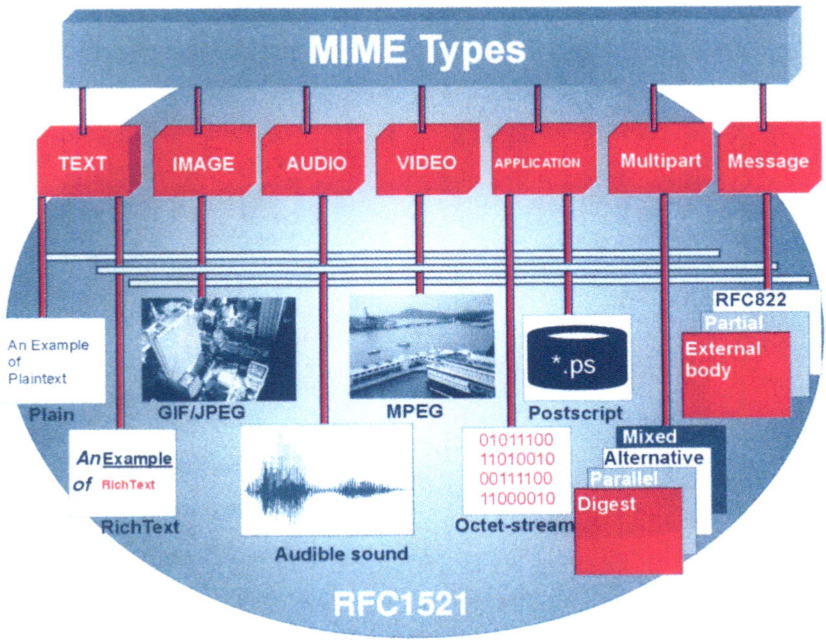

Fig. M-10. The MIME types and subtypes defined in RFC1521

MIME defines five new message headers as follows: (1) an identification of the MIME version, (2) a description of the contents, (3) a unique identifier of the contents, (4) the way the message body is wrapped for transmission, and (5) the nature of the message. MIME user agents (see Fig. M-11) are responsible for creating, transmitting, receiving and parsing multimedia or multipart messages. To create a multimedia message, a MIME user agent uses separate composition agents for each message type supported, as shown in Fig. M-11 for three different input data types (RichText, audio and video). Composition agents can handle such data either as a file (as an MPEG input in Fig. M-11) or as a signal (as an audio signal in Fig. M-11), where the particular composition agent has an appropriate driver for it. The Message Designer calls the appropriate composition agents to create the desired message and the Message Builder converts the composed message into the format required for sending, providing an interface between the MIME user agent and the mail service. At the receiving end, things are done in the reverse order. The Parser identifies the different parts in a message and passes them to the Dispatcher. The Dispatcher calls appropriate viewers, which are capable of showing the message to an end-user.

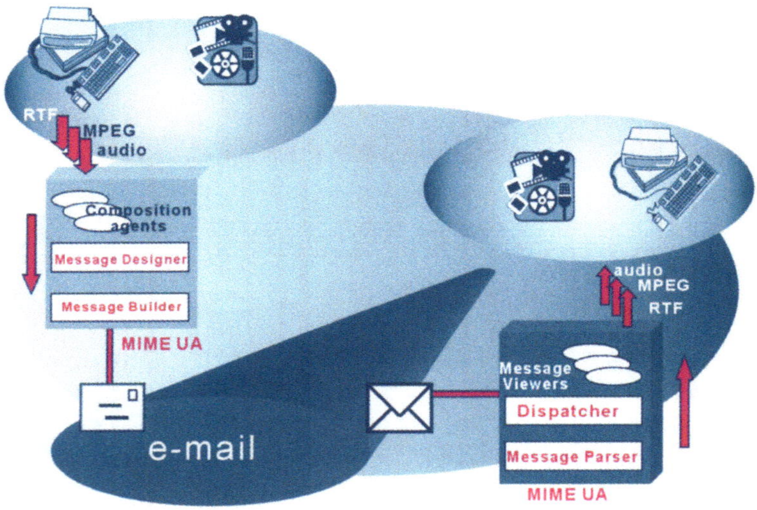

Fig. M-11. MIME agents in action

MIPS – Microprocessor without Interlocking Pipeline Stages. A family of RISC processors, the architecture of which was developed at Stanford University. MIPS uses the pipeline approach to enable a number of instructions to be active at once. See also RISC.

MIPS – Million Instructions Per Second. A common measure for processor speed.

MIS – Management Information System. An information system capable of providing various levels of management within an organization, with the accurate information required for supervising, decision making, problem solving, etc. It is very often directly connected with a Business Information System (see BIS). See also Decision Support System (DSS), Data Warehouse (DW), Enterprise Information System (EIS) and Web Farming (WF).

MIT – Massachusetts Institute of Technology. An independent coeducational university (http://web.mit.edu) located in Cambridge, MA, US. MIT admitted its first students in 1865. Today MIT is one of the world's outstanding universities. Education and research, with relevance to the practical world as a guiding principle, continue to be its primary purpose. It is organized into five schools that contain 21 academic departments, as well as many interdepartmental programs, laboratories and centers, the work of which extends beyond traditional departmental boundaries. According to "MIT Facts 2000" over 2500 researchers were working with MIT in 1998–1999. Forty-six present and former members of the MIT community have won the Nobel Prize. MIT's computing environment gives access to a rich array of technologies and information resources. Those services and facilities include the campus network MITnet, the Athena Computing Environment, hardware and software sales, and a variety of support activities (helplines, consulting, training, publications) to help members of the MIT community make effective use of information technology.

MIT – Midway Islands Standard Time. Time zone. UTC – 11.00 hours. See TZ.

MITM – Man In The Middle. A type of hacker attack, where a user expects to communicate with a second user, and receives an encryption key from a third party. The user trusts that encryption message and therefore he/she establishes the communication with the third party time believing that the conversation is taking place with the second user.

mkdir – make directory. The UNIX command used to create directories.

MLI – Multiple-Link Interface. Part of the ODI generic network driver interface. See also Open Data-link Interface (ODI).

MLP – Multilink Procedures. A protocol used with multiple network connections running in parallel.

MLT – Multiple Logical Terminals. A feature of an IBM 3174 establishment controller, in an SNA environment, that allows support of multiple sessions simultaneously. See also SNA.

MM – Multimedia. An advanced computer term that refers to the integration of text, images, audio and video in a variety of application environments.

MMA – Marketing Monitoring and Analysis. The part of the Manufacturing, Accounting and Production Information Control System (see MAPICS) that provides high accessibility to current and historical sales information. MMA applications are intended for sales managers, representatives, financial planners, and others who need marketing data on time.

MMA – MIDI Manufacturers Association. An industrial group composed of MIDI instrument manufacturers and MIDI software companies. See also MIDI.

MMC – Microsoft Management Console. A common Microsoft console framework for management applications. MMC will run on both the Windows NT Workstation and Server (4.0 and later versions) and Windows 95 operating systems. The goal of MMC is to support simplified administration through integration, delegation, task orientation, and overall interface simplification. The site http://msdn.microsoft.com/library provides additional information.

MMCD – Multimedia Compact Disc. A standard for storing 4.7 GB of data, including video.

MMCN – Multimedia Computing and Networking. An international conference focusing on recent developments in multimedia computing and high-speed networking. Some of the major topics include multimedia computing systems, multimedia networking, multimedia and the Internet, measurement, modeling and appropriate application areas.

MMDS – Multichannel Multipoint Distributed System. A system invented in the 1980s by the Federal Communications Commission (see FCC) which broadcasts terrestrial or satellite microwave transmissions directly to consumers' homes.

MME – Multipart MIME. Filename extension for files that contain multipart messages in MIME format. See also MIME.

MMF – Microsoft Mail File. A filename extension for a file that contains Microsoft Mail.

MMF – Multimode Fiber. A fiber-optic transmission element which is designed to carry more than one frequency at the same time.

MMIS – Multimedia Information System. A kind of information system that allows creation, processing, storage, management, retrieval, transfer and presentation of multimedia information.

MMM – Microsoft Multimedia Movie. Filename extensions for files that contain multimedia movies.

MMR – Microsoft Multicast Router. A computer that enables a content server to send a datastream to any broadcast output device.

MMS – Manufacturing Message Service. In the OSI Reference Model, a part of the Manufacturing Automation Protocol that enables an application on a control computer to communicate with an application on the production line.

MMU – Memory Management Unit. A hardware device used to support mapping of virtual memory addresses to physical memory addresses. In most modern microcomputers the MMU is built into the CPU chip. The MMU maintains a page table in which each entry gives the physical page number corresponding to the virtual one. This is combined with the page offset to give the complete physical address. Page table entries may also contain information such as whether the page has been written to, when it was last used, what kind of access permission is given for a particular process, etc. The MMU also takes care of the memory fragmentation.

MMX – Matrix Math Extensions. A set of 57 extra instructions built into some versions of Intel Pentium processors to allow SIMD operations on multimedia and communication data types. See also Single Instruction Multiple Data (SIMD).

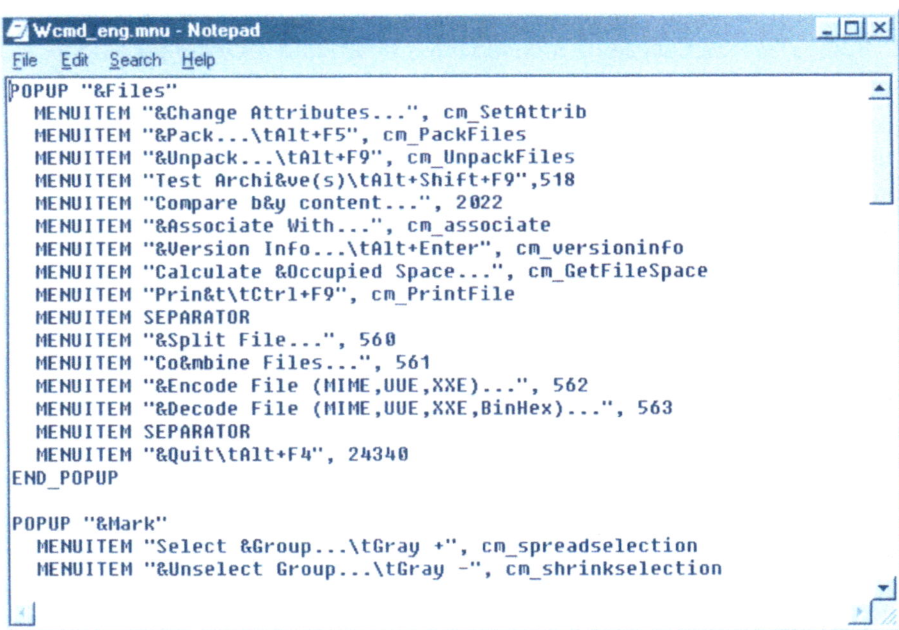

Fig. M-12. Part of a MNU file for Windows Commander (see Wincmd)

Mn – Management interface n. A common term for a series of management interfaces of ATM networks. The number n relates to different management capabilities of ATM networks, as follows:

- M1: The management of ATM end devices.

- M2: The management of private ATM networks or switches.
- M3: The management of links between public and private networks.
- M4: The management of public ATM networks.
- M5: The management of links between two public networks.

MNP – Microcom Networking Protocol. A family of protocols used by high-speed modems, developed by Microcom, intended for error correction and data compression.

MNU – Menu file. A filename extension generated by an Interactive Development Environment (see IDE) under Microsoft Windows. One example is AcuBench (see COBOL) where a developer creates a menu. The code inside a .mnu file is intended to be in the program at compile time and this is achieved using the COPY statement. Another example is shown in Fig. M-12, where the .mnu file is read by Notepad.

MO – Magneto-Optical. In rewritable optical technology, a technique for recording data. MO utilizes a focused laser beam and an external magnet that can reverse polarity. The recording film on the media is made of metal alloys that, on a formatted blank disk, have the polarities aligned in a single direction.

MOBICOM – Mobile Communications. An international conference focusing on mobile communications. Some of the major topics include applications, architectures, protocols, data management, performance, security, integration, operating systems, mobile agents, and other aspects of mobile computing and communications. Selections of the best articles are published by ACM/Baltzer journals (see MONET and WINET).

MOD – Module file. A filename extension for a file that contains digitized sound samples.

MODEM – Modulator/Demodulator. A device that converts digital signals to analog signals and vice versa. At the source, a modem converts digital signals to a form suitable for transmission over analog communication facilities. At the destination, the analog signals are returned to their digital form. Modems are distinguished from each other by their speed, the distance supported, the modulation method used (see ADM, ADPCM, AM, ASK, DASK, DFSK, DM, DPSK, FM, QAM, QPSK, PCM, PDM, PPM, TCM and TQM), the kind of available connection (see SDX, HDX and FDX), the error correction and detection supported, whether they are in-built or external, etc.

MOEMS – Micro-Optical Electromechanical System. A flat panel monitor.

MOF – Meta-Object Facility. The facility under Object Management Group consideration (see OMG) for defining the services for metamodel creation and management.

MOM – Message-Oriented Middleware. A distributed event-driven asynchronous computing model consisting of messages that are brokered by one or more "post offices" which then forward these messages to the interested parties with guaranteed delivery (see Fig. M-13). MOM software makes the transport of the messages simpler to code and support than the more 'raw' technologies, such as operating system services or network-level programming interfaces. Message shipping and receiving are network-transparent. MOM tools also do not require the two sides to be in direct communication to exchange messages. The MOM architecture, approach and leading MOM products (with relevant web links) can be found in an overview online article by Markku Korhonen from the Helsinki University of Technology (go to the http://www.tml.hut.fi/Opinnot and search for "mom").

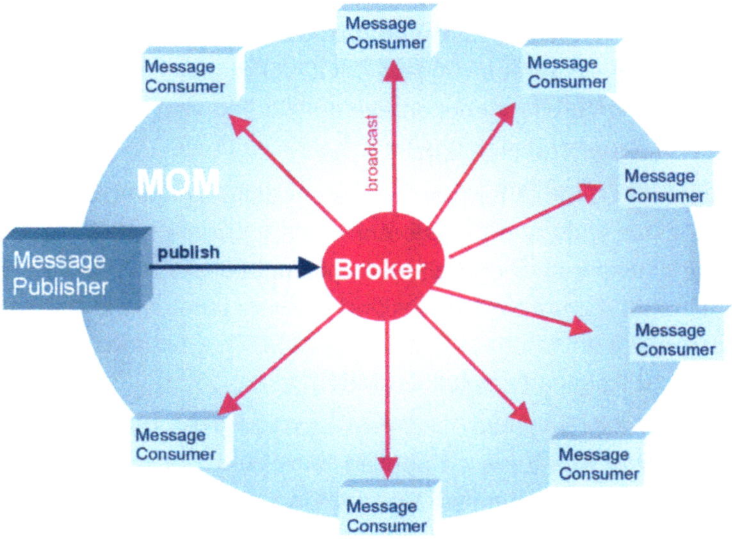

Fig. M-13. MOM architecture

MOMA – Message-Oriented Middleware Association. An international nonprofit association of vendors, users and consultants (http://www.moma-inc.org) dedicated to promoting the use of messaging to provide multiplatform, multitier message passing and message queuing services for distributed computing architectures. See also MOM.

MONET – Mobile Network and Applications. An international journal published quarterly by ACM and Baltzer focusing on portable computers and wireless networks. Some of the main topics include nomadic computing, appropriate algorithms, mobile data management, architectures of mobile and wireless networks, mobility management, mobile agents, standardization, planning, security, scalability and reliability of wireless networks, etc.

MONET – Multimedia Operating Systems and Networking. A research group located in the Department of Computer Science in the University of Illinois at Urbana–Champaign that is engaged in research into distributed multimedia systems.

MOO – MUD, Object-Oriented. A form of multiuser dungeon (see MUD) that contains an object-oriented language with which users can create areas and objects within the MOO. Generally, MOOs are more focused on communications and programming and less on games than MUDs are. See also OO and OOPL.

MOODS – Music Object-Oriented Distributed System. The project developed at the University of Florence focusing on providing music score editing and display via a suitable interface. In fact, MOODS is an integrated system of computer-based lectures for cooperative editing and visualization of music.

MorF – Male or female. The chat term.

MOSPF – Multicast OSPF. A form of link state routing algorithm that holds data about multicast islands and tunnels and adds that data to the usual routing information. Having knowledge about the complete topology it is possible to compute the best route from every island to every other island using the tunnels. See also Open Shortest Path First (OSPF). Compare with Distance Vector Multicast Routing Protocol (DVMRP).

MOSS – MIME Object Security Service. A protocol (RFC1848) for digital signatures and encryption services applied to MIME objects. MOSS is largely based on the Privacy-Enhanced Mail protocol (see PEM), but unlike PEM that requires users to have certificates, with MOSS users need only have a public/private key pair. See also MIME.

MOTD – Message Of The Day. A daily bulletin (see Fig. M-14) for users of a network, multiuser computer, or other shared system. In most cases, users are shown the message of the day when they log into the system.

MOTIS – Message-Oriented Text Interchange Standard. See Message Handling System (MHS).

MOV – Movie. Filename extensions for files that contain multimedia movies.

MOZ – Mozilla. A filename extension for a file that contains a Netscape cache.

MP – Multilink PPP. An extension of the Point-to-Point Protocol (see PPP) used for splitting a signal, sending it along multiple channels, and then reassembling it at the common destination. Also abbreviated as MPPP.

mp2 – MPEG layer 2 file. A filename extension for a file that contains MPEG 2 compressed audio. See also MPEG.

mp3 – MPEG layer 3 file. A filename extension for a file that contains MPEG 3 compressed audio. See also MPEG.

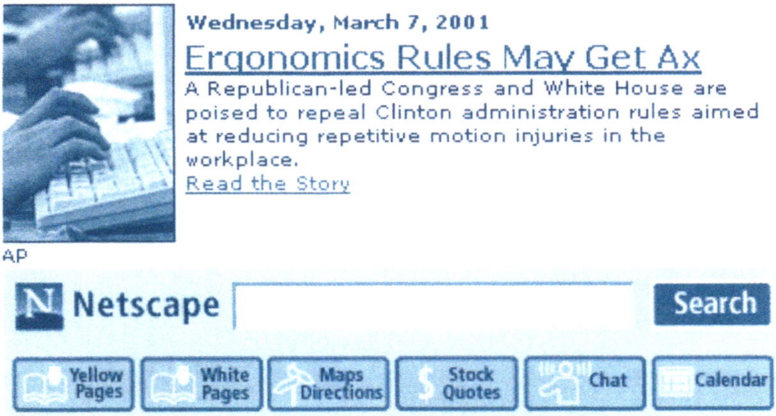

Fig. M-14. An example of a MOTD provided by messenger.netscape.com

MPC – Multimedia Personal Computer specification. A set of specifications for the minimum requirements for multimedia personal computers. Level 1 requires at a minimum a 386SX 16-MHz processor with 2-MB RAM, a 30-MB hard disk drive, and a CD-ROM drive with a sustained data transfer rate of 150 KBps. The maximum average seek time is 1 s and the MTBF is 10,000 h. Also, the computer must have 8-bit digital sound and an 8-note synthesizer with MIDI playback. MIDI, I/O, and joystick ports must be provided. The video display must have a minimum resolution of 640×480 in 16 colors. Level 2 is an improved version that requires a 25-MHz 486SX processor with 4-MB RAM, and 160-MB hard disk drive. A data transfer rate of 300 KBps supporting the CD-ROM is required. The computer must have 16-bit digital sound. A video display must support 65,536 colors.

MPE – MPEG. A filename extension for a file that contains MPEG animation.

MPE – Multiprogramming Environment. Hewlett-Packard operating system for HP 3000 Series computers.

MPEG – Motion Picture Experts Group. A bitstream standard since 1993 for compressed video and audio optimized to fit into a bandwidth of 1.5 Mbps. MPEG-1 algorithms allow better quality than VHS video. MPEG-2 (IS13818) is intended for higher-quality video-on-demand broadcast applications and runs at data rates between 4 and 9 Mbps. MPEG-4 is a low-bit-rate compression algorithm intended for 64-Kbps connections. Depicted in Fig. M-15 is MPEG's place among the communication and packing standards.

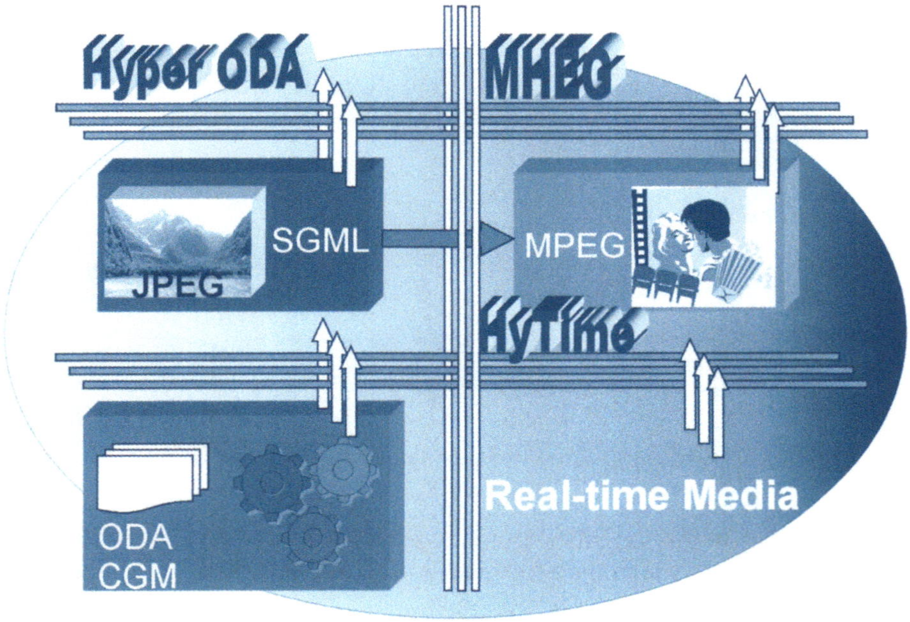

Fig. M-15. MPEG as a compression standard for real-time media

MPG – MPEG. A filename extension for a file that contains MPEG animation.

MPI – Message-Passing Interface. A proposal for the message-passing standard API that would allow developers to write portable message-passing applications.

MPI – Multiple Protocol Interface. The top part of the Link-Support Layer (see LSL) in the generic Open Data-link Interface (see ODI) for LAN drivers.

MPIF – Message-Passing Interface Forum. The organization considering the development of a message-passing interface (see MPI).

MPLS – Multi-Protocol Label Switching. A protocol architecture (RFC3031) that provides connection-oriented (see CO) and label-based switching based on IP routing and control protocols. This protocol attaches labels (4 or 8 byte) to IP and IPv6 protocols in the network layer, after the data-link layer headers, but before the network-layer headers. It allows a packet that enters the network at a particular router to be labeled differently than the same packet entering the network at a different router. Instead of network-layer header analysis, the label is used as an index into a table, which specifies the next hop, and a new label. The result is an easy way to make forwarding decisions, i.e. the next-hop router.

MPOA – Multiprotocol Over ATM. An ATM Forum standardization effort specifying how the existing and future network-layer protocols such as IP, IPv6, AppleTalk and IPX should run over an ATM network with directly attached hosts, routers and multilayer LAN switches. The new MPOA specification is a strong standard that provides multiprotocol support for ATM-based networks that are becoming more complex and difficult to manage. The proposed architecture consists of edge devices and route servers. An edge device would forward packets between the LAN and ATM networks, establishing ATM connections when needed, but would not be involved directly in routing. Route servers would be able to map a host address into the information needed by the edge device to establish a connection across the ATM network. For the query and response function, MPOA adopted and extended the Next-Hop Resolution Protocol (see NHRP).

MPP – Massively Parallel Processing. Data processing with a huge amount of data as inputs to parallel processors each executing a part of the required algorithm at the same time.

MPP – Microsoft Project Project. A filename extension for a file that contains a project made using Microsoft Project.

mpp – minutes per page. A measurement unit applied for printers used to measure the time required for a printer to finish printing one page.

MPPP – Multilink Point-to-Point Protocol. An Internet protocol that allows computers to establish multiple physical links to combine their bandwidths. This technology creates a virtual link with more capacity than a single physical link. See also MP.

MPR – Microsoft FoxPro. A filename extension for a file that contains compiled FoxPro code.

MPR – Multi-Port Repeater. A repeater (see R) used in an Ethernet network.

MPR – Multiprotocol Router. A set of software routing products that can route different protocols concurrently (for example TCP/IP stack, SNA stack or IPX/SPX stack).

MPT – Microsoft Project Template. A filename extension for a file that contains a Microsoft Project template.

MPT – Multipacket Transport. An adaptation layer developed by Microsoft that resides above the data-link layer of a network with large fixed-size packets.

MPTN – Multi-Protocol Transport Network. An IBM effort to develop software intended for gateways or end systems (see ES). MPTN's role is to translate transport-layer software from one protocol to another protocol (e.g. TCP/IP to SNA) so that only one transport protocol need be supported on the WANs.

MPX – Microsoft Project Export. A filename extension for a file that contains a Microsoft Project export.

MR – Magneto-Resistive. A hard drive technology.

MRP – Manufacturing Resource Planning. A system for planning and controlling the operational, engineering and financial resources of a manufacturing firm. Also known as MRP II, to distinguish it from the simpler version of MRP that covers only material requirements planning.

MRU – Maximum Receive Unit. The largest packet that can be received over a physical media between two nodes on the network. Compare with MTU.

MRU – Most Recently Used. A page, or block of memory, replacement strategy. Compare with LRU.

MS – Message Store. A general archive in the ITU-T X.400 MHS in which an e-mail can be held until the appropriate user retrieves it through a user agent (see UA), or until storage time for the mail is exceeded. See also MHS.

ms – millisecond. A measurement unit equal to one-thousandth of a second.

MS – Modeling and Simulation. The IASTED international conference focusing on Petri nets, artificial intelligence, expert systems, knowledge and fuzzy systems.

MSB – Most Significant Bit. The highest-order bit of a binary number, not including the sign bit. The bit with the greatest weight (2^{n-1}). Compare with LSB.

MSBDN – Microsoft Broadcast Data Network. A high-bandwidth broadcast network, capable of sending 2–25 Mbps.

MSC – Most Significant Character. The highest-order, or leftmost, character in a string. Compare with LSC.

MSC – Mobile Switching Center. In an Advanced Mobile Phone System (see AMPS), the name of a central computer in the AMPS cell to which all the telephones in the cell transmit. If the particular cell is too large, several MSCs may be needed. Also known as MTSO.

MSCDEX – Microsoft CD-ROM Extension. A driver that enables DOS and Windows 3.x systems to recognize and control CD-ROM players. In Windows 95, it is replaced by the driver called CDFS. See also CDFS.

MSCS – Mathematical Structures in Computer Science. The journal published by Cambridge University Press focusing on the applications of categorical, algebraic and geometric methods in computer science.

MSCS – Microsoft Cluster Server. A technology that supports clustering of two Windows NT servers in order to provide a single fault-tolerant server.

MSD – Most Significant Digit. The highest-order digit in a sequence of one or more digits. Compare with LSD.

MSDN – Microsoft Development Network. Microsoft digital library dedicated for developers that contains more than 1 GB of technical programming information, including sample code, documentation, practical examples, a glossary of terms, etc. Figure M-16 shows how it works. MSDN is available on CD and online (http://www.microsoft.com/msdn).

MS-DOS – Microsoft Disk Operating System. A single-task single-user operating system for personal computers with a command line interface. Pronounced “em-ess-doss”. See also DOS.

MSI – Medium-Scale Integration. A term describing a concentration of between 10 and 100 circuit elements on a single chip. See also LSI and SSI.

MSIE – Microsoft Internet Explorer. A very popular Web browser (see WWW) from Microsoft, introduced in October 1995. Later versions can incorporate advanced design and animation features into webpages and recognize ActiveX controls and Java applets (see applet).

MSN – Microsoft Network. An online service provided by Microsoft that supports electronic mail, chat forums, bulletin boards (see BBS), access to the Internet, various information services, information about new Microsoft products, etc.

MSNF – Multisystem Networking Facility. An IBM communications facility which allows more than one host to control a network.

MSP – Microsoft Paint. A filename extension for a file that contains a Microsoft Paint bitmap image.

MST – Minimum Spanning Tree. The shortest set of connections in a bridged network or in an internetwork.

MST – Mountain Standard Time. Time zone. UTC – 7.00 hours. See TZ.

MTA – Message Transfer Agent. The program responsible for delivering e-mail messages (see Fig. M-9). Upon receiving a message from another MTA or from a Mail User Agent (see MUA), it temporarily stores a message locally, and delivers it to an appropriate MUA or forwards it to another MTA. See also MHS and e-mail.

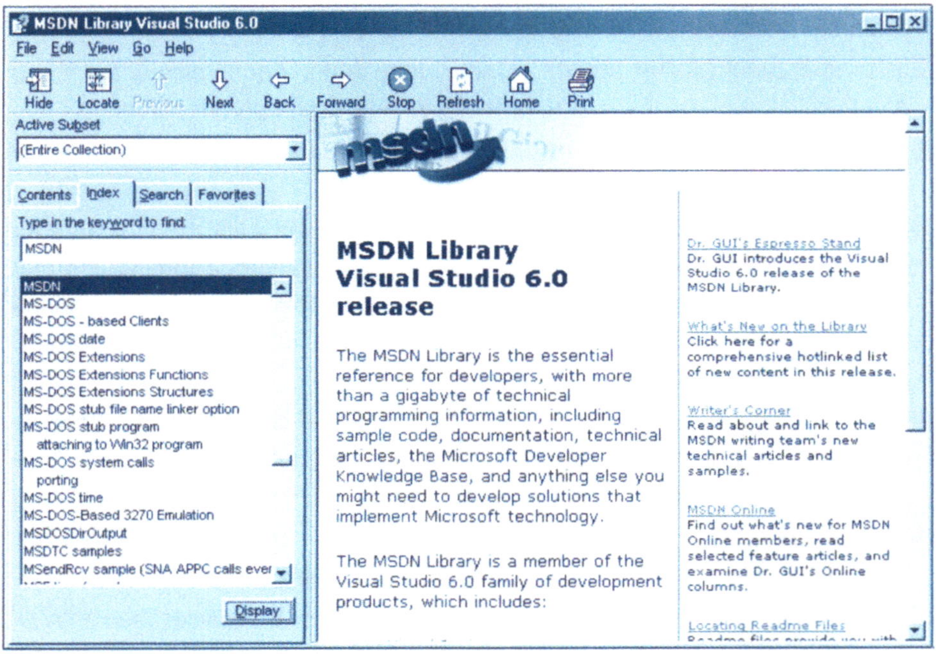

Fig. M-16. MSDN explanation page

MTBF – Mean Time Between Failures. The average time interval that will elapse before a hardware component fails and requires service. Usually, MTBF is expressed in thousands or tens of thousands of hours. The MTBF measure is part of almost every hardware price/performance analysis.

MTC – MIDI Time Code. A method of sending timing information between MIDI-capable devices. See also MIDI.

MTCS – Models for Time-Critical Systems. An international workshop focusing on models for time-critical systems. Some of the main topics include Z-specifications, Petri nets, software architecture, UML, formal reasoning, etc. The proceedings are published by Springer-Verlag (see LNCS).

MTE – Message Transfer Envelope. In the X.400 Message Handling System (see MHS), the term used for the delivery envelope which contains the information needed to deliver a message.

MTF – Microsoft Tape Format. A filename extension for a file that contains tape records readable using NT.

MTS – Message Transfer System. A worldwide application-independent store-and-forward service for message transfers. The primary purpose of the MTS is to "convey" messages from one user agent to another (see UA), as shown in Fig. M-9. Such messages are made up of "envelopes" and their contents. The envelope (see MTE) carries the information used during transfer of the message between the Message Transfer Agents (see MTA), i.e. within the MTS. The contents are the information for the User Agent. See also MHS and X.400. Compare with IPMS.

MTS – Microsoft Transaction Server. A Microsoft product that allows a developer to create components that contain data access and business logic and run them in a middle-tier component, such as an ORB. In addition, these components can create distributed transactions for modifying data in different data sources. Multitier and middle-tier terms are explained in the Enterprise Information Systems entry (see EIS).

MTSO – Mobile Telephone Switching Office. See Mobile Switching Center (MSC).

MTTR – Mean Time To Repair. The average time interval required to finish repairing a unit of hardware after it has failed. Usually expressed in several hours.

MTU – Magnetic Tape Unit. A type of magnetic storage unit that uses a magnetic tape as the data storage media. It has two reels between which the tape can pass and a read/write head located somewhere between the reels. The tape must be read or written to sequentially, not randomly as applies for a floppy disk or a hard disk.

MTU – Maximum Transfer Unit. The largest possible unit of data that can be sent to a given physical medium. If a packet is larger than an MTU, the packet must be fragmented and sent as two or more properly sized packets. See also PMTU.

MUA – Mail User Agent. A program which allows e-mail users to compose, send or read electronic mail messages (see Fig. M-17). Also, it is responsible for communication between the user and the Message Transfer Agent (see MTA). A user leaves its outgoing mail for the MUA to transfer it to its MTA for final delivery to the destination address (see Fig. M-9). Furthermore, the MUA receives incoming mails from its MTA to allow its user to read a mail message, store it, or delete it. See MHS.

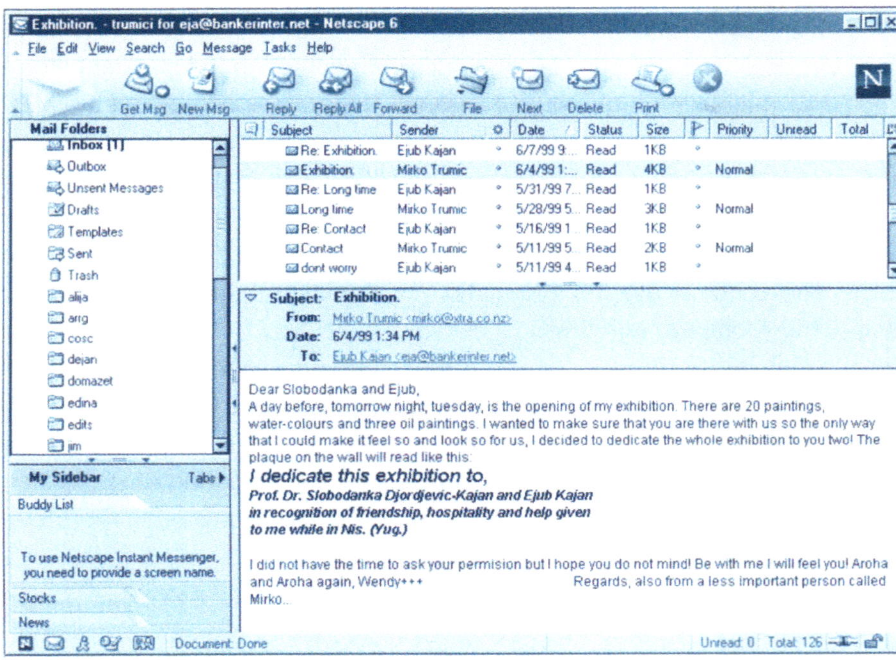

Fig. M-17. Netscape MUA user interface

MUD – Multi-User Dungeon (or Dimension). A virtual environment on the Internet in which multiple users simultaneously participate in a role-playing game and interact with each other in real time. Also called a multiuser simulation environment. See also MOO (MUD, Object-Oriented).

MULTICS – Multiplexed Information and Computing Service. A time-sharing operating system developed through the joint efforts of MIT, General Electric and Bell Telephone Laboratories in the mid-1960s. MULTICS introduced a lot of techniques in operating system design that were advanced for that period. One of the most notable was the exploitation of paging and segmentation to merge much of the memory and information-management functions. Also, special attention was given to security and privacy issues.

MUMPS – Massachusetts General Hospital Utility Multiprogramming System. A general-purpose programming language developed in the late 1960s with extensive DBMS support. It was originally used for medical records and was known as the Massachusetts General Hospital Utility Program. Now, the technique developed is widely used where multiple users access the same databases simultaneously (banks, stock exchanges, hospitals, etc.). It was standardized by ISO (ISO11756) and by ANSI (X11.1).

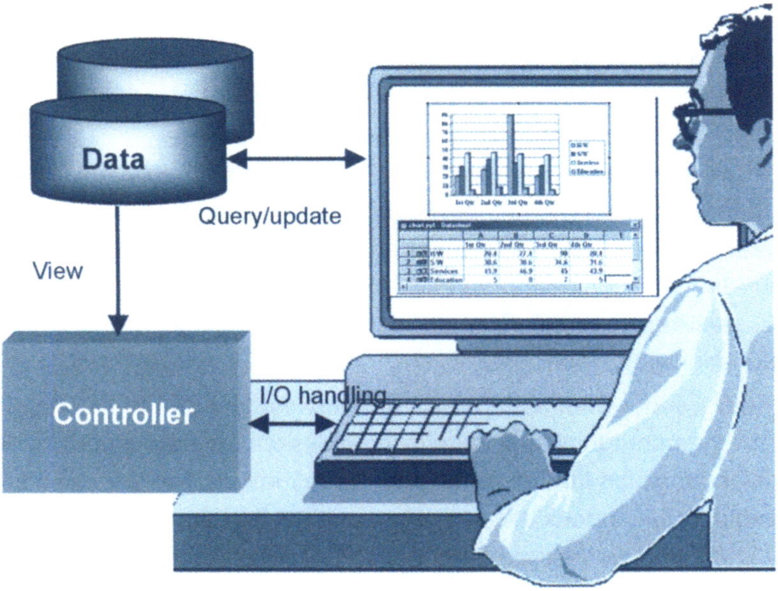

Fig. M-18. An example of a MVC

MUSE – Multi-User Simulated Environment. A kind of MUD with little or no violence. See also MOO and MUD.

MUSM – Miss you so much. The chat term.

MUX – Multiplexer. A device for selecting a single output from multiple inputs. Multiplexers are used to attach many communication lines to a smaller number of communication ports, or vice versa (DEMUX, demultiplexer).

mv – move. The UNIX command used to manage files. It allows UNIX files to be moved from one directory to another or be renamed.

MVC – Model View Controller. An approach to user interface design (see UI) in which the software used to show data is separated from the data itself. Thus, the data model can be independent of the desired view. In such a way, the same data may have a number of separate views each with an associated controller that handles user inputs and device interaction. An example of the MVC approach is shown in Fig. M-18, where the same numerical data appears in different views.

MVD – Multivalued Dependencies. A constraint in databases as a consequence of the first normal form (see 1NF) which disallows an attribute in a tuple having a set of values.

MVS – Multiple Virtual System. An IBM System 370 architecture operating system. Also known as OS/VS Release 2.

MWCN – Mobile and Wireless Communications Networks. An international workshop that serves as a forum for information exchange about recent and future developments in mobile and wireless networks. Some of the major topics include models of such networks, WLAN architectures, routing in mobile networks, mobility management and roaming, wireless security, mobile cellular Internet, mobile and wireless ATM networks, multiple-access techniques, satellite networks, IP routing for wireless and mobile hosts, information superhighways, etc.

MWM – Motif Window Manager. An X Window System client that provides window management functionality and some session management functionality. It provides functions that facilitate control (by the user and the programmer) of elements of window state such as placement, size, icon/normal display, and input-focus ownership. It also provides session management functions such as barring a client.

MX – Mail Exchange. A data structure applied in Internet DNS (see DNS) in order to assign which computer(s) can handle e-mail for a domain. See also DNS.

N

n – nano. An order of magnitude representing the value of 10^{-9}. See also nanosecond (ns).

N/A – Not Available (Applicable). A common term used in business letters or technical documentation used to indicate that something is not available yet, until the date given, or after the date given, or never. Sometimes also means "not applicable".

NA – Numerical Aperture. A term used in fiber optics (see FO) for the range of angles over which a fiber core can receive incoming light.

NAC – Network Access Controller. A device that provides access to a network.

NAI – Network Associates Inc. Probably the biggest company in the world focusing on data security (http://www.nai.com). Among other things, NAI offers antivirus programs (such as McAfee), PGP encryption, firewalls, etc. NAI Laboratories, formerly known as TIS, is deeply involved in research on advanced security (some projects are explained in this book).

NAK – Negative Acknowledgment. A control code (ASCII character 21) used as a signal that transmitted information has arrived incorrectly. Often represents a signal for retransmission.

NAMPS – Narrowband Advanced Mobile Phone System. A standard proposed by Motorola that advances the current AMPS cellular telephone standard and increases its capabilities and performance. See also AMPS.

a	b	a NAND b
0	0	1
0	1	1
1	0	1
1	1	0

Fig. N-1. The truth table for the Boolean function NAND

NAND – Not AND. The Boolean function representing the logical complement of AND that can be expressed as follows:

a NAND b = NOT (a AND b) = (NOT a) OR (NOT b)

NAND can form a complete set of Boolean functions on its own since it can be used to make any other Boolean function. The truth table is given in Fig. N-1.

NAPLPS – North American Presentation-Level-Protocol Syntax. A format for sending text and graphics over communication lines.

NAS – Network Application Support. A set of software products developed by DEC to integrate products on different systems at the application level. NAS is similar in concept to the System Application Architecture introduced by IBM (see SAA), but it differs in strategy, because NAS is designed for open systems, unlike SAA which is intended for IBM proprietary protocols.

NAS – Network Attached Storage. A standalone and separate storage device connected to a network.

NASI – NetWare Asynchronous Services Interface. A set of specifications for accessing communications servers across a network based on Novell NetWare.

NAT – Network Address Translator. A hardware device used to extend the Internet addresses already in use. It allows an organization with addresses that are not globally unique to connect to the Internet by translating those addresses into globally routable address space.

NAU – Network Addressable Unit. A term used in IBM SNA communications for an addressable network entity such as Logical Units (see LU) or Physical Units (see PU). Generally, NAUs provide upper-level network services. See also SNA.

NAUN – Nearest Active Upstream Neighbor. In Token Ring networks (see TR), the closest upstream network device from any given device that is still active. Each node in a TR network receives packets and tokens only from its NAUN.

NAWK – New AWK. An enhanced version of the pattern scanning and processing language AWK that has dynamic regular expressions and user-defined functions. See AWK.

NBF – NetBEUI Format. A transport-layer protocol used in OS/2-based network operating systems.

NBP – Name Binding Protocol. A transport-layer protocol used for mapping logical names to physical addresses around the AppleTalk network environment.

NBP – NetBIOS Protocol. An optimized implementation of NetBIOS that uses less memory.

NBS – Narrowband Sockets. A technology developed by Intel and Nokia to allow development of wireless messaging applications for mobile PCs and digital cellular telephones.

NBS – National Bureau of Standards. Part of the US Department of Commerce, now called the National Institute of Standards and Technology (see NIST).

NC – Network Computer. A computer that is equipped with the necessary hardware and software in order to be connected to a network.

NC – Numerical Control. A form of programmable automation in which the process is controlled by numbers, letters and symbols that form a program of instructions designed for a particular job. An operational NC system consists of a program, controller unit and machine tool. NC systems are part of CAM systems. They are widely used in industry today, especially in the metalworking industry. They can perform a wide variety of material-removal processes such as milling, drilling, boring, turning, sawing, etc. See also Computer-Aided Manufacturing (CAM) and Computer Numerical Control (CNC).

NCA – Network Computing Architecture. A collection of guidelines for distributed computing.

NCC – National Computer Centre. The body in the UK dedicated to automated software development for testing whether software products are compliant with X.400 and X.500, or not. The NCC has a counterpart in the US (see NVLAP).

NCC – Network-Centric Computing. An advanced computing and communication model that considers the whole network as a single computer with multiple processors and multiple memories. This model is based on delegation of functions to intelligent agents, software entities that carry out sets of operations on behalf of a user. At least seven management application areas based on intelligent agents for NCC model exist: systems and networks, mobile access, mail and messaging, information access and collaboration on shared documents, workflow and administration, electronic commerce (see EC), and adaptive UI. See also RP.

NCC – Network Control Center. A physical point within a network where various management and control functions are implemented.

NCCF – Network Communications Control Facility. A set of IBM software routines used for monitoring and controlling network functions and operations.

NCD – Norton Change Directory. The utility program in MS-DOS that allows the user to see the directory and to change its position in the directory tree.

NCF – Network Computing Framework. An architecture created to help design, deployment and management of e-business solutions.

NCITS – National Committee for Information Technology Standards. An organization in the US founded to produce voluntary consensus standards in several information systems areas, such as multimedia, information infrastructures, GIS, SQL3, security, programming languages, etc.

NCL – Network Control Language. A command-line interface language used by DEC in its DNA network architecture. See also Digital Network Architecture (DNA).

NCP – Network Control Protocol. Part of the PPP protocol that allows an independent way of negotiating network-layer options. NCP packets (in the PPP protocol field) are sent to configure the network layer once agreement on the PPP parameters has been achieved. Also, after the user has finished, NCP is used to tear down the network-layer connection and free up the IP address. See also Link Control Protocol (LCP) and Point-to-Point Protocol (PPP).

NCP – Network (NetWare) Core Protocol. A connection-oriented upper layer protocol inside the Novell NetWare network system. See Internet Packet Exchange (IPX) protocol.

NCR – National Cash Register. One of the major manufacturers of UNIX-based midrange servers (http://www.ncr.com), founded in 1884 as a mechanical cash register company by John H. Patterson. NCR is a worldwide company with 1100 offices in 130 countries. It specializes in data warehousing, with over 500 production data warehouses in use. Also, NCR is a world leader in open high-availability transaction processing systems. Years ago, the author had the opportunity of specializing at NCR, Wichita, Kansas. The memories of that occasion and people he met there are still alive and very pleasant.

NCS – Network Computing System. Architecture developed and promoted by Hewlett-Packard for implementing Remote Procedure Calls (see RPC) in a heterogeneous computer environment.

NCSA – National Center for Supercomputing Applications. One of the National Science Foundation (see NSF) supercomputing centers located in Urbana–Champaign, IL in the US (http://www.ncsa.uiuc.edu). It was founded in 1985 as part of the NSF, specializing in scientific visualization tasks. The NCSA is recognized all over the world as the birthplace of Mosaic, the first graphical Web browser. It is now involved in the High-Performance Computing and Communications project (see HPCC).

NCSA – National Computer Security Association. An education and information organization concerned with computer security issues. Founded in 1989 and based in Carlisle, Pennsylvania, NCSA supplies books on computer security and hosts an annual conference.

NCSC – National Computer Security Commission. The US government department focusing on the recent developments in the security of computer systems.

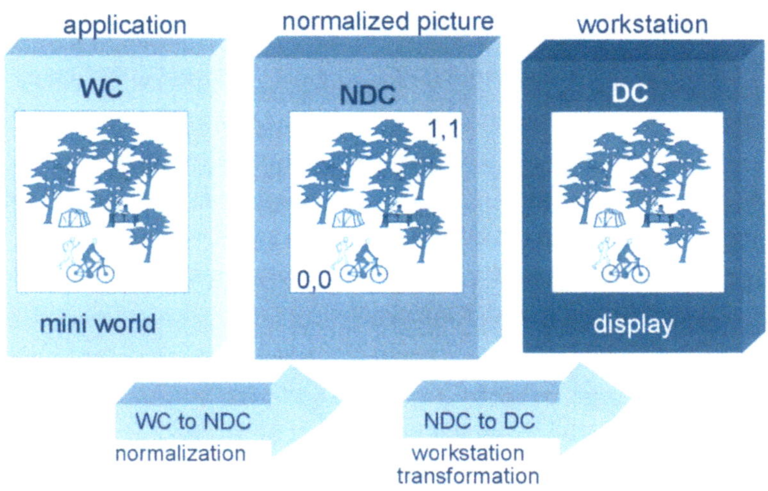

Fig. N-2. Device independence using NDC space

NDC – Normalized Device Coordinates. An intermediate coordinated system used in computer graphics that provides a uniform method of addressing different display spaces. In 2D graphics systems device independence is provided by two coordinate transformations, first from the world coordinate space (WC) to NDC, and then from NDC to device coordinate space (DC), as shown in Fig. N-2. Conventionally, this coordinate system is the unit square, where (0,0) is the bottom left-hand corner and (1,1) is at the top right. The NDC origin usually corresponds to the bottom left-hand corner of the display space. In a 3D graphics system, the number of transformations and coordinate spaces is bigger but the final transformation is always NDC–DC. See also Device Coordinate (DC) and World Coordinate (WC).

NDD – NetWare Directory Database. A database (commonly known as a directory) that contains the object information needed by the NetWare Directory Services (see NDS).

NDD – Norton Disk Doctor. A software utility developed and distributed by Symantec that allows automatic diagnostics and repair of disks. With NDD users are able to examine partition tables, boot records, files and directory structures, test the surfaces of disks, and compress disks.

NDIS – Network Driver Interface Specification. A standard interface developed by Microsoft and 3COM for network interface card (see NIC) drivers. NDIS enables any of the protocol stacks supported to communicate with any NDIS-compliant NICs and vice versa.

NDMP – Network Data Management Protocol. An open protocol for network-based backups of file servers that allows platform-independent data storage.

NDR – Network Data Representation. A standard network transmission format independent of the data-type format on any particular computer.

NDR – Nondestructive Readout. A reading technique that does not destroy the data read. In NDR, either a data update supports the reading or the storage technique is capable of retaining the data. Sometimes abbreviated NDRO.

NDRO – Nondestructive Readout. See NDR.

NDS – NetWare Directory Service. A global naming service used in NetWare that provides a global directory (see NDD, NetWare Directory Database) containing information about all the objects in a network.

NDT – Newfoundland Daylight Time. Time zone. UTC – 2.50 hours. See TZ.

NDT – Network Data Throughput. The actual rate at which data is transferred on a communications channel, normally specified in bits per second.

NE – Network Element. A system that supports a set of ATM network element functions (see NEF). An ATM NE may be realized as either a standalone device or a geographically distributed system.

NE – Not Equal to. An acronym often used in programming languages as a relational operator in logical expressions. See also EQ, LE, LT, GE and GT.

NEC – Nippon Electric Company. One of the largest computer equipment manufacturers in the world. Additional information is available from its homepage http://www.nec.com

NEF – Network Element Function. A function within an ATM entity that supports the ATM-based network transport services.

NEL – Network Element Layer. An abstraction of functions related specifically to the technology, vendor and the network resources or network elements that provide basic communications services.

NeMoW – Network Management on the Web. A project under development at GTE Laboratories in order to make next-generation Telephone Operations Network Integrated Control System (see TONICS). It provides network management capabilities that are accessible through a secure Web gateway.

NET – Near East (Yerevan) Time. Time zone. UTC + 4.00 hours. See TZ.

NetBEUI – NetBIOS Extended User Interface. An enhanced version of the NetBIOS protocol (pronounced "net-boo-ee") used by network operating systems such as LAN Manager, LAN Server and Windows for Workgroups and Windows NT. It formalizes the transport frame and includes additional functions. It operates at the lower-layer protocol stack (IEEE802.2). See also NetBIOS.

NetBIOS – Network Basic Input/Output System. An API and an upper-layer protocol used by applications on an IBM LAN, running MS-DOS, OS/2, or some UNIX versions, to request services from lower-level network processes. These services might include session establishment and termination, and information transfer. Other networking software packages have adopted NetBIOS and it is now widely emulated.

NetBSD – Network BSD. A free version of the BSD UNIX operating system developed as a result of a volunteer effort. NetBSD is highly interoperable, runs on many hardware platforms, and is nearly POSIX-compliant. See also BSD and POSIX.

NetCDF – Network Common Data Form. An interface for scientific data access, which implements a machine-independent, self-describing, extendible file format. For more information see http://www.unidata.ucar.edu/packages

netiquette – network etiquette. Principles of civility applied for netizens ("the Internet citizens"), perceived in sending electronic messages, such as e-mail and Usenet postings (RFC1853). The results of violating netiquette include being flamed and having one's name placed in the clumsy person filter or kill file. That means that users on the receiving side can block or filter out incoming messages or newsgroup articles from specified individuals. Unacceptable behavior includes: personal insults for no reason; posting of large amounts of irrelevant material; giving away the plot of a movie, television show or novel without warning; posting hateful material without encrypting it; and excessive cross-posting of a message to multiple groups without regard to whether the group members are likely to find it interesting. See Netizen.

Netizen – Network Citizen. A person who participates in online communication through the Internet and other networks, especially one who uses conference and chat services such as Internet news. Netizens must follow some written or unwritten policies on, for example, how to use a particular network (see AUP), or what kind of messages are not welcome (or not allowed), and they must avoid piracy, etc. See also netiquette.

NeWS – Network extensible Window System. A windowing environment based on PostScript developed by James Gosling and David Rosenthal. Also, it is the basis of the OpenLook user interface.

NEXT – Near-End Crosstalk. The leakage of a signal between adjacent wire pairs. Compare to FEXT.

NeXTSTEP – New Extended Technology Step. An object-oriented (see OO) variant of UNIX based on a microkernel architecture.

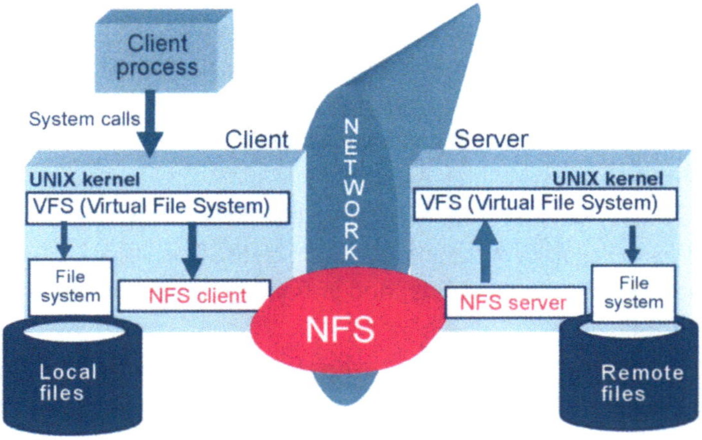

Fig. N-3. NFS architecture

NFS – Network File System. A distributed file system protocol suite operated at the application level, developed by Sun Microsystems, and defined in RFC 1094 (RFC1813 defines Version 3, RFC3010 defines Version 4), which allows a computer system to access files over a network as if they were on its local disks (see Fig. N-3). NFS relies on a remote procedure call mechanism (see RPC) to issue a request and external data representation (see XDR) to move information from one place to another. This protocol has been incorporated into products by more than 200 companies, and now it is a de facto Internet standard. See also Open Network Computing (ONC).

NFT – Newfoundland Standard Time. Time zone. UTC – 3.50 hours. See TZ.

NGC – Networked Group Communications. An international workshop focusing on networked group communications. Some of the major topics include multicast congestion control, routing, naming and address allocation, novel multicast architectures, multicast protocols, QoS, multipeer applications, group management techniques, etc. The proceedings are published by Springer-Verlag (see LNCS).

NGI – Next-Generation Internet. The joint project of the US university community, the US government and industry partners to accelerate the next stage of Internet development in academia. The Internet2 (or I2 project as it is also known), announced in October 1996, is bringing focus, energy and resources to the development of a new family of advanced applications to meet the emerging academic requirements in research, teaching and learning. A major goal is to develop at least two connected Internet testbeds connecting universities and federal research laboratories. One testbed of about 100 universities is projected to be about 100 times faster than today's Internet. A second testbed will include approximately 10 sites and will run about 1000 times faster than the Internet.

NGIO – Next-Generation Input/Output. An effort by Dell, Hitachi, Intel, NEC, Sun Microsystems and Siemens to develop technology for high-speed server communications (2.5 Gbps).

NGITS – Next-Generation Information Technologies and Systems. An international biennial workshop focusing on the next-generation information technologies. Some of the major topics include KBS, RDBMS, OODBMS, HDB-MS, ADBMS, DDBMS, information retrieval, data warehousing, workflow, ontologies, e-commerce, data mining, digital libraries, etc. The proceedings are published by Springer-Verlag (see LNCS).

NHRP – Next-Hop Resolution Protocol. A protocol used by routers to dynamically discover the MAC address of other routers and hosts connected to a network. The IETF draft specification defines a way for routers to learn network-layer addresses over networks that do not use broadcasts, such as ATM. NHRP uses a next-hop server (see NHS) to tell network clients, like routers, where the next hop toward a destination resides. These systems can then directly communicate without requiring traffic to use an intermediate hop, increasing performance in ATM, Frame Relay, SMDS and X.25 environments. Online information is available at ftp://ietf.org/internet-drafts/draft-ietf-rolc-nhrp-11.txt

NHS – Next-Hop Server. A server defined by the NHRP protocol that maintains the next-hop resolution cache tables containing the IP-to-ATM address mappings of associated nodes and nodes that are reachable through routers served by the NHS.

NI – Network Interactive. The online version of the IEEE Network magazine (http://www.comsoc.org/pubs).

NIAL – Nested Interactive Array Language. A high-level array-oriented procedural language based on the mathematical theory of arrays, developed at Queen's University at Kingston, Ontario, Canada. It combines APL data structures with LISP-style evaluation concepts and conventional control structure syntax.

NIC – Network Information Center. An organization that provides information, assistance and services to network users.

NIC – Network Interface Card. A common name for the boards that provide network communication capabilities to and from a computer system. Also called an adapter. NICs are distinguished from each other by the network architectures they support, implemented in chips on the boards.

NICE – Network Information and Control Exchange. An application-layer protocol used in the DECnet architecture for testing the network and for getting information about node configurations. See also DECnet.

NII – National Information Infrastructure. A project for an information superhighway across the US in the future. It will bring the satellite, terrestrial and wireless communication systems together in a virtual infrastructure capable of delivering content to homes businesses and other public and private institutions. The information content can be in the form of a database, a spreadsheet, the written word, a movie, music, a picture, software, etc., available using appropriate appliances and devices, as shown in Fig. N-4. More information can be found at http://sunsite.unc.edu/nii

NIKOS – New Internet Knowledge System. A text-based search engine developed by the California Polytechnic Institute and Rockwell.

NIM – Network Interface Module. See NIC (Network Interface Card).

NIP – Network Integrated Processing. A computing architecture intended for eliminating the distinctions between a processor and a network. NIP uses ATM or other high-speed LAN/WAN technology to build a distributed computing environment. NIP applications can use a geographically dispersed pool of CPU resources in order to aggregate the processing cycles needed for large-scale computing tasks.

NIR – Networked Information Retrieval. A common term for information retrieval (see IR) using networks. In this field there is a cooperative effort by the Internet Engineering Task Force (see IETF), the Association of European Research Networks (see RARE), and the Coalition for Networked Information (see CNI) to collect and disseminate information about the tools required, and to discuss and encourage cooperative development of current and future tools. In RFC1689, the following NIR tools are recognized: Alex, Archie, gopher, Hytelnet, Netfind, Prospero, VERONICA, and WAIS.

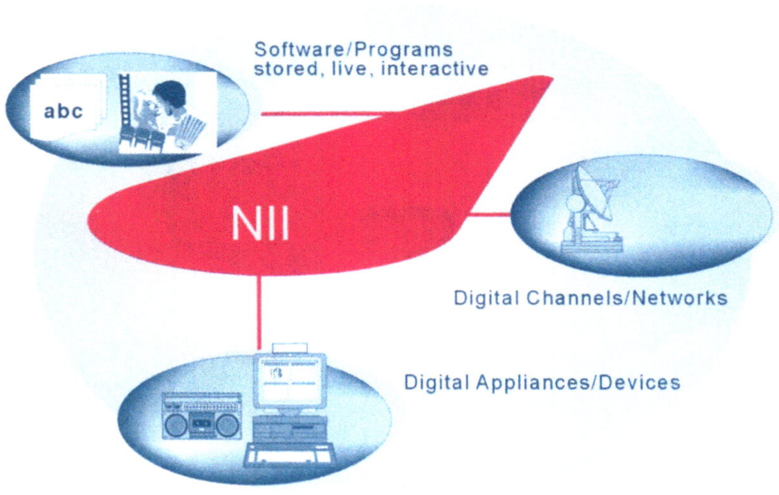

Fig. N-4. The building blocks and components of the NII

NIS – Networking and Information Systems. A journal published by Hermes France (http://www.editions-hermes.fr) which covers all areas of database and network technologies and their interconnections.

NIS – Network Information Services. A set of services generally provided by the Network Information Center (see NIC) to assist users in using the network.

NIS – Network Information System. A network naming and administration system developed by Sun Microsystems dedicated for UNIX-based LANs. It consists of a server, a library of client programs, and some administrative tools. Originally called YP (Yellow Pages). The later version is known as NIS+, and it has additional security.

N

NISB – Netscape Internet Service Broker. A CORBA-based Object Request Broker included in both Netscape Enterprise Server 3.0 and Netscape Communicator.

N-ISDN – Narrow-band ISDN. A kind of ISDN network based on 64-Kbps B channels and 16- or 64-KBps D channels (see 2B+D). It operates at, or below, 1.5 Mbps. Figure N-5 depicts a possible topology, where a small office company (see SOHO) is connected to an ISDN network using an appropriate network terminator (see NT-1). Up to eight ISDN devices can be connected to NT-1, similar to devices connected to a LAN. See also ISDN.

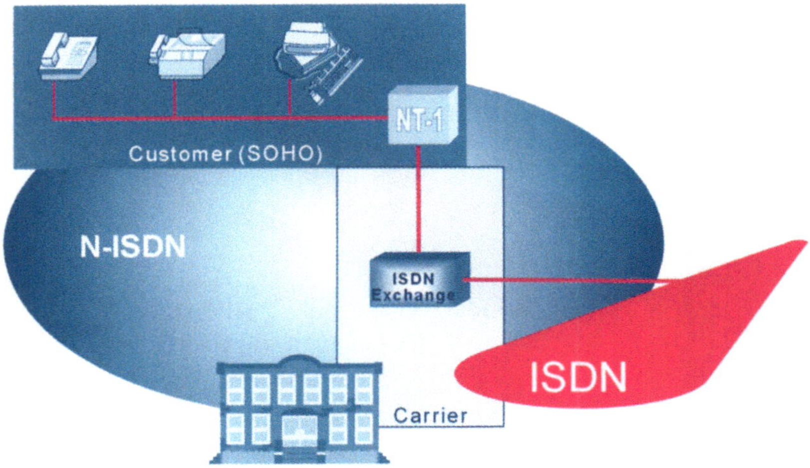

Fig. N-5. N-ISDN topology

NIST – National Institute of Standards and Technology. The US government agency (http://www.nist.gov) which specifies the US government procurement rules and has responsibility for the development of Federal Information Processing Standards (see FIPS).

NIU – Network Interface Unit. See NIC (Network Interface Card).

NLDB – Applications of Natural Language to Data Bases. An international conference focusing on the integration of databases and natural languages. The proceedings are published by Springer-Verlag (see LNCS).

NLP – Natural Language Processing. A common term for techniques that allow understanding and generation of a natural language by computers. Also, the name of an international conference focusing on NLP. The proceedings are published by Springer-Verlag (see LNAI).

NLQ – Near Letter Quality. A print mode available on dot-matrix printers that produces clearer darker characters than normal draft mode printing. Compare with Letter Quality (LQ).

NLS – National Language Support. A filename extension for files used for localization purposes.

NLS – Native Language System. A set of interfaces specified by X/Open for developing applications to run in different natural language environments.

NLSP – NetWare Link-State Protocol. A link-state protocol (see LSP) used in NetWare network environments.

NMA – Network Management Architecture. A common term used to refer to a vendor or products approach to managing a network. Also, the mainframe and centralized network management model developed by IBM.

NME – Network Management Entity. Part of the OSI network management model consisting of the software and/or hardware that allows a network node to collect, store and report data about the activities of the node.

NML – Network Management Layer. An abstraction of the functions provided by systems which manage network elements on a collective basis, i.e. end-to-end monitoring and controlling.

NMS – Network Management System. A name given to a system responsible for managing a network or its portion.

N

NN – Neural Networks. The IASTED international conference focusing on many disciplines of neural networks. Topics include genetic algorithms, fuzzy modeling, neural network architectures, complex systems, etc.

NNI – Network-to-Network Interface. An ATM Forum standard that defines the interface between two ATM switches that are both located in a private network or are both located in a public network. Compare with User Network Interface (UNI).

NNTP – Network News Transfer Protocol. A protocol defined in RFC977 by Brian Kantor and Phil Lapsley for distribution, inquiry, retrieval and posting of Usenet news articles over the Internet (see Fig. N-6). It allows news articles to propagate from one machine to another over a reliable connection (e.g. TCP) as well as remote news reading by poorly connected desktop computers. In the figure there are two fields in the NNTP command which are of common interest, the first addresses the NNTP command status, and the second is dedicated for the particular status of the command. As defined in RFC977, in general, 1xx codes may be ignored or displayed as desired;

code 200 or 201 is sent upon initial connection to the NNTP server depending upon posting permission; code 400 will be sent when the NNTP server discontinues service (by operator request, for example); and 5xx codes indicate that the command could not be performed for some unusual reason.

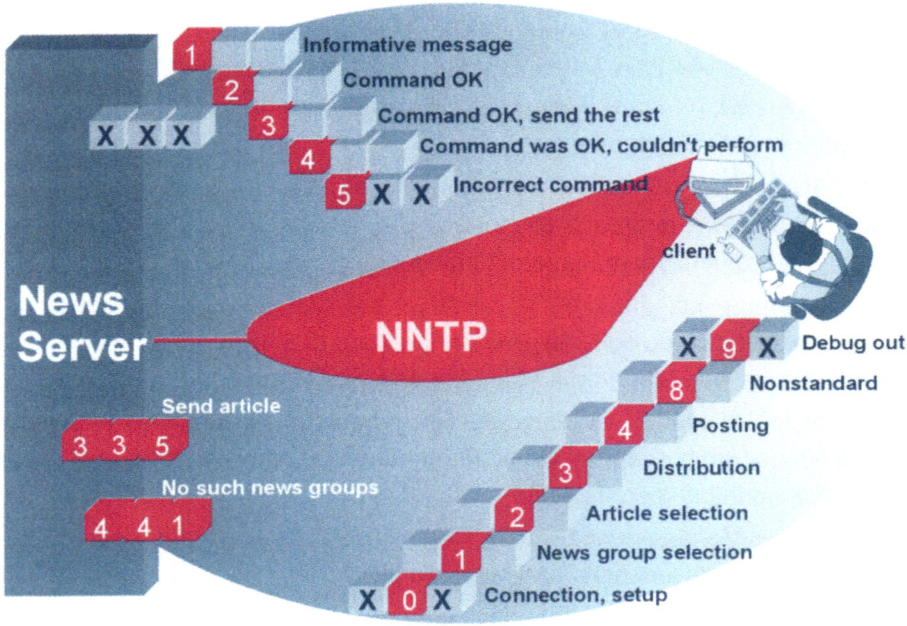

Fig. N-6. NNTP commands

NOC – Network Operations Center. A location from which the operation of a network or Internet is monitored. Additionally, this center usually serves as a clearinghouse for connectivity problems and efforts to resolve those problems. See also NIC.

NOR – Not OR. The Boolean function representing the logical complement of inclusive OR, that can be expressed as follows:

a NOR b = NOT (a OR b) = (NOT a) AND (NOT b)

NOR (the truth table is given in Fig. N-7) can form a complete set of Boolean functions on its own since it can be used to make any other Boolean function. For example: NOT a = a NOR a.

NORMA – No Remote Memory Access. Early distributed shared-memory systems in which there are no processors that can directly access any other processor's memory. Compare with Non-Uniform Memory Access (NUMA).

NOS – Network Operating System. A common term for operating systems with loosely coupled software on loosely coupled hardware distributed across a network. The users of such systems have the illusion that the entire network of computers is a single timesharing system, rather than a collection of distinct machines. The NOS coordinates the provision of services to the computers and other devices attached to the network. Examples of NOSs include LAN Manager, NetWare, NFS and VINES.

NP – No problem. The chat term.

a	b	a NOR b
0	0	1
0	1	0
1	0	0
1	1	0

Fig. N-7. Truth table for the Boolean function NOR

NPA – NetWare Peripheral Architecture. A Novell driver architecture consisting of a Host Adapter Module (see HAM) and a Custom Device Module (see CDM).

NPAP – Network Printing Alliance Protocol. A standard for a bidirectional protocol intended to be used for communication among printers distributed on a network.

NPC – Network Parameter Control. The set of actions taken by the network to monitor and control traffic for the Network-to-Network Interface (see NNI). The main purpose of the NPC is the protection of network resources from malicious action and unintentional misbehavior that can affect the Quality of Service (see QoS). See also UPC (Usage Parameter Control).

NPC – Normalized Projection Coordinates. An additional coordinate space that appears in 3D graphic systems such as GKS-3D and PHIGS before the final workstation transformation. See also Normalized Device Coordinate (NDC).

NPDA – Network Problem Determination Application. An IBM program that aids operators in finding network problems from a single point.

NPDU – Network Protocol Data Unit. The form into which the network layer of the OSI network architecture will format data for its use and recognition. See also OSI.

NPL – Non-Procedural Language. A language in which the set of rules defining the solution to the problem is applied rather than a series of operations to be executed. Also known as a declarative language. The language PROLOG falls into this category. Another widespread nonprocedural system is the spreadsheet program. See also PROLOG. Compare with Procedural Language (PL).

NREN – National Research and Education Network. The successor to NSFNET running at gigabits speeds, a part of the HPCC program designed to ensure US technical leadership in computer communications through research and development efforts in state-of-the-art telecommunications and networking technologies. See also HPCC.

NRN – No response necessary. The chat term.

NRZ – Non-Return-to-Zero. A scheme for encoding a binary datastream in which a signal transition occurs with every appearance of a binary 1 in the stream. Compare with NRZI.

NRZI – Non-Return-to-Zero Inverted. A scheme for encoding a binary datastream in which a signal transition occurs with every appearance of a binary 0 in the stream. Compare with NRZ.

NS – Name Server. A type of Resource Records (see RR) that marks the beginning of the DNS zone and supplies the domain name of a name server for that zone.

ns – nanosecond. One billionth (10^{-9}) of a second, a measure appropriate for computing speeds.

NSA – Next Station Addressing. An addressing mode used in FDDI in which an FDDI station can send a frame to the next station without knowing of the receiving station address. See also FDDI.

NSAI – National Standards Authority of Ireland. The standards body of Ireland.

NSAP – Network Service Access Point. The point at which the OSI network service is made available to a transport entity (see OSI and SAP). The NSAPs are identified by OSI network 20-byte addresses. NSAPs are also used in ATM networks.

NSAPI – Netscape Server API. A set of functions that can be used to interface with the Netscape Server. It allows an extension of the core functionality of the Netscape Server. It provides flexibility, control, efficiency and multi-platform solutions. NSAPI can provide database connectivity, customized logging, a personalized website for each client, custom user identification, alternative access control, etc.

NSB – National Standards Body. The organization in a country that is dedicated to developing and enforcing domestic standards in that country. Examples are BSI in the UK, AFNOR in France, CSA in Canada, etc.

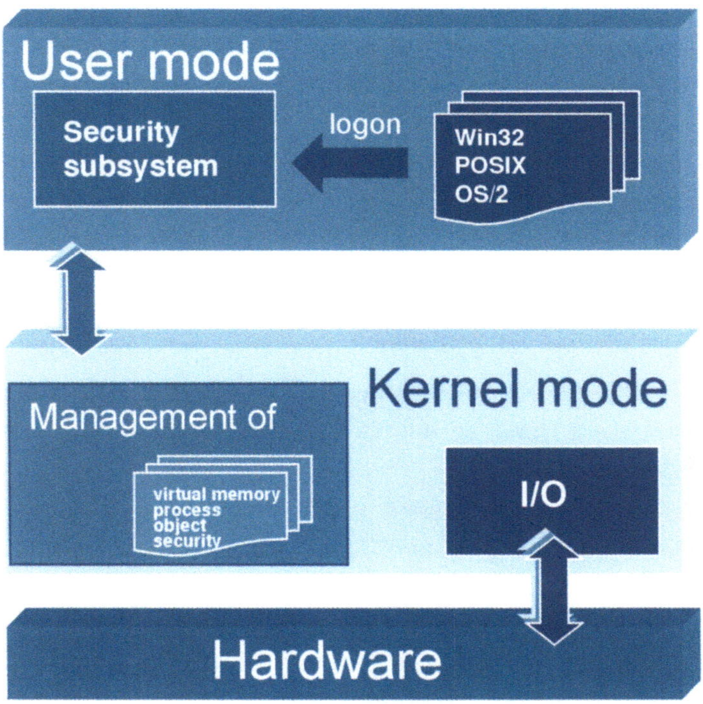

Fig. N-8. Windows NT architecture

NSF – National Science Foundation. A US government agency, the purpose of which is to fund science researchers, scientific projects, and infrastructure to improve the quality of scientific research. See also NSFNET.

NSFNET – National Science Foundation Network. A high-speed hierarchical "network of networks" in the US created in 1985 by the NSF to provide a network infrastructure for the research and education community within the

US, and also act as a testbed for network-related research. In April 1995, the NSF created a commercial infrastructure (see vBNS) that supports the very high performance needs of the research and education communities (initially at 155 Mbps).

NSI – NASA Science Internet. A NASA-wide network (http://nsipo.nasa.gov) that supports scientists and flight projects funded by NASA. Users include NASA sites, government facilities, and research and academic sites conducting NASA-funded research.

NSP – Network Service Protocol. A proprietary transport-layer protocol deployed in the DECnet architecture.

NT – New Technology. An operating system released by Microsoft in 1993. Unlike Windows (3.11 or 95), NT does not rely on MS-DOS, it is a completely self-contained operating system with a built-in GUI (see Fig. N-8). NT is a 32-bit multitasking operating system that features networking, symmetric multiprocessing, multithreading and security.

NT-1 – Network Terminator-1. An ISDN device that acts as an interface between an ISDN telephone line and one or more terminal adapters or terminal devices such as an ISDN telephone. See N-ISDN.

NT-2 – Network Terminator-2. See PBX (Private Branch Exchange).

NTAS – NT Advanced Server. A Windows NT advanced feature that can support additional client types, so remote PCs can get full access to the Windows NT network.

NTFS – New Technology File System. An advanced native file system within the Windows NT operating system. NTFS supports long filenames (up to 255 characters), file system recovery in the case of malfunction, automatic creation of a DOS-compatible filename, support for both FAT for DOS and HPFS for OS/2, and various features for the NT POSIX subsystem (see Fig. N-8). It also supports object-oriented applications. See also High-Performance File System (HPFS).

NTP – Network Time Protocol. A protocol defined in RFC1119 and RFC1305 that ensures accurate local timekeeping with reference to radio and atomic clocks located on the Internet. It is a very complex protocol capable of synchronizing distributed clocks within milliseconds over long time periods. A simpler version is known as the Simple Network Time Protocol (see SNTP).

NTT – Nippon Telegraph and Telephone Corporation. See 3G. Also see http://www.ntt.com

NUMA – Non-Uniform Memory Access. A kind of multiprocessor architecture with a single virtual address space that is visible to all CPUs with software-controlled caching. The key issue in NUMA software is deciding where to place each memory page to maximize performance. NUMA-based systems usually have a daemon process called the page scanner gathering periodical usage statistics about local and remote references. If the usage statistics indicate that a page is in the wrong place, the page scanner unmaps the page so that the next reference causes a page fault, allowing a new placement decision to be made. Compare with UMA. See also MPP and SMP.

NVE – Network-Visible Entity. A resource that is addressable through a network. Typically, an NVE is a socket client for a service available in a node. An NVE is identified by name, type and zone.

NVLAP – National Voluntary Laboratory Accreditation Program. One of the worldwide centers (http://www.ts.nist.gov/nvlap) located in the US involved in the development of automated suites for testing software compliance with ITU-T X.400 and X.500 specifications. NVLAP has a counterpart in the UK (see NCC).

NVM – Nonvolatile Memory. A type of memory, the contents of which are not lost after power-off. In the case of RAM, there is a specific name given (NVRAM).

NVoD – Near Video-on-Demand. A kind of Video on Demand (see VoD) where the user is capable of seeing the movie he/she wants, but the user has to wait for his/her video provider to start. Although the pause/resume is not available here, a viewer taking a little break can return and switch on another channel showing the same video but several minutes behind. In that case nothing will be missed, maybe some material will be repeated. Compare with VoD.

NVP – Normal Velocity of Propagation. A value indicating the signal speed in a network as a proportion of the theoretically maximum possible speed. Also known as VOP.

NVRAM – Nonvolatile RAM. See Nonvolatile Memory (NVM).

NWS – News. Filename extensions for files that contain news messages obtained using Microsoft Outlook Express.

NZDL – New Zealand Digital Library. A digital library (see DL) project developed by the University of Waikato and coordinated by Dr. Ian Witten. NZDL (http://www.nzdl.org) offers a huge collection of documents that are written in many different languages, including English, French, German, Arabic, Maori,

Portuguese and Swahili. Depicted in Fig. N-9 is one example of the available documents from the Historic New Zealand Newspapers Collection, The "Waka Maori" (The Canoe of Maori) newspaper.

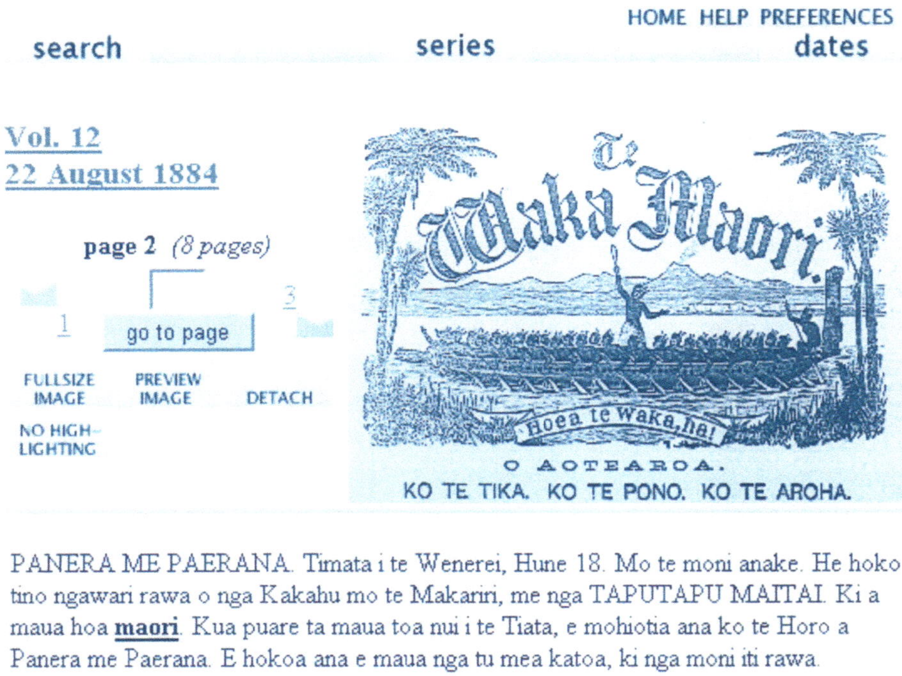

Fig. N-9. The Waka Maori from August 1884 stored in the NZDL

NZDT – New Zealand Daylight Time. Time zone. UTC + 13.00 hours. It applies during the New Zealand summer, i.e. the calendar winter.

NZST – New Zealand Standard Time. Time zone. UTC + 12.00 hours. See TZ.

O

OA – Object Adapter. Part of the Object Request Broker (see ORB) that provides services like generation and interpretation of object references, method invocation, object activation and deactivation, etc. See also BOA (Basic Object Adapter) and CORBA.

OA – Office Automation. A common term for performing office functions using computers and appropriate applications rather then manually.

OAB – Outlook Address Book. A filename extension for a file that contains a Microsoft Outlook address book.

OADF – Object Analysis and Design Facility. Part of OMG's Object Management Architecture (see OMA and OMG) which defines the interface and semantics for supporting the creation and manipulation of a core set of object models that define the structure, meaning and behavior of object applications.

OAI – Open Application Interface. An interface that can be used to program and change PBX operations. See also PBX.

OAL – OEM Adaptation Layer. The portion of Windows CE that must be provided by the hardware manufacturer to adapt Windows CE to that platform.

OAM – Operation, Administration and Maintenance. ATM Forum specification for cells used to monitor virtual circuits. OAM cells provide a virtual circuit-level loopback in which a router responds to the cells, demonstrating that the circuit is up, and the router is operational. OAM includes: fault and performance management (operations); addressing, data collection, and usage monitoring (administration); and analysis, diagnosis and repair of network faults (maintenance). The reference model, also known as the management-plane reference architecture, defines the aspects of an ATM point-to-point virtual circuit (see VC) that can be monitored and controlled using specialized OAM cells. The reference model divides a VC into five distinct layers, labeled F1 through F5. The F1 level defines the flow of cells at the lowest physical layer of the ATM stack. The F2 level defines the flow of cells at the SONET layer. The F3 level partially defines the flow between a virtual path (see VP) and a VC. The F4 level completes the definition of the traffic flow between a VP and a VC. Finally, the F5 level completes the definition of traffic flow from one ATM end-station to another. Also known as OA&M.

OARnet – Ohio Academic Resource Network. The Internet Service Provider (see ISP) in the US that connects a number of US sites, including the Ohio Supercomputer Center in Columbus, Ohio.

OBD – Office Binder. A filename extension for files that contain Microsoft Office binder templates. See also OBT.

OBEX – Object Exchange. A cross-application middleware product from Borland that provides communication services across applications, messaging services and platforms.

OBJ – Object file. A filename extension for files that contain object code.

OBT – Office Binder Template. A filename extension for files that contain Microsoft Office binder templates.

OC – Optical Carrier. A series of physical protocols defined for SONET optical signals. Generally, OC-n defines a SONET rate of n times 51.84 Mbps. In particular, OC-3, OC-12 and OC-48 define rates of 155.52 Mbps, 622.08 Mbps and 2488.32 Mbps, respectively.

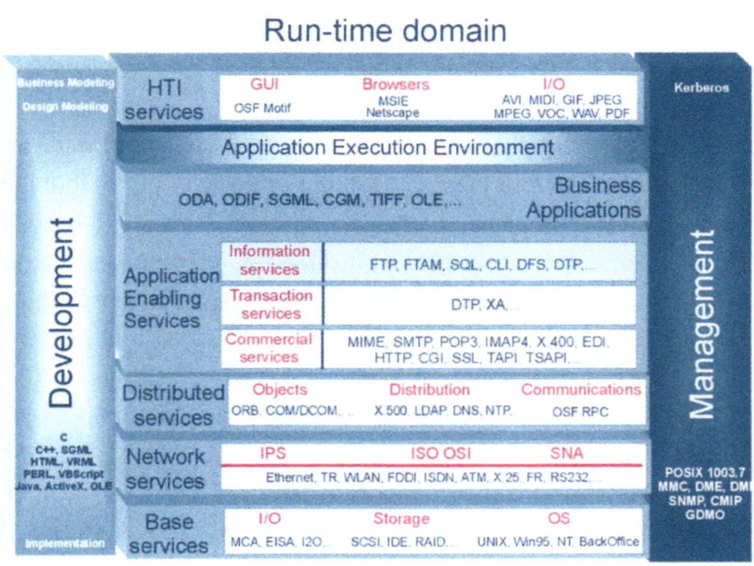

Fig. O-1. OCCA domains and some components inside domains

OCC – Open Cooperative Computing. NCR's customer-oriented technology strategy that allows users to make sound investments in their information systems that can increase later to meet their growing business requirements. OCC is supported by the appropriate foundation architecture (see OCCA).

OCCA – Open Cooperative Computing Architecture. A fundamental NCR architecture for building open cooperative computing systems. It serves as a repository of reusable standards and guidelines (see Fig. O-1) that can support the development, execution and management of enterprise information systems (see EIS) operating in complex distributed heterogeneous environments. The OCCA consists of three major domains, each representing closely related, but different, problems in information technology organizations. These are the development domain, the run-time domain and the management domain, as shown in Fig. O-1.

OCL – Object Constraint Language. An expression modeling formal language which is part of the Unified Modeling language (see UML).

OCLC – Online Computer Library Center Inc. A nonprofit membership organization that offers services for online cataloging and resource sharing. OCLC is connected to more than 10,000 libraries worldwide. OCLC also distributes online electronic journals (see EJO). Related information can be found at http://www.oclc.org

OCR – Optical Character Recognition. The process of recognition of printed or written characters by determining their shapes on the basis of detecting patterns of spots. Once the OCR reader has determined the shapes, a pattern-matching algorithm with a stored set of characters is used to translate the shapes into a form that the computer can manipulate.

OCSP – Online Certificate Status Protocol. An Internet standard (RFC2560) that specifies a protocol used to determine the status of a digital certificate. OCSP specifies the data that needs to be exchanged between an application checking the status of a certificate and the server providing that status.

OCX – OLE Custom Control (x). A filename extension for a file that contains ActiveX, previously known as OCX.

ODA – Office Document Architecture. The former name of the Open Document Architecture (see next entry ODA).

ODA – Open Document Architecture. An ISO standard (ISO8613) for describing documents. It allows text, graphics and facsimile documents to be transferred between different systems in an OSI environment. Three levels of document representation are defined: text-only data; text and graphical data from a word-processing environment; and text and graphical data from a desktop-publishing environment.

ODAPI – Open Database Application Programming Interface. A Borland product similar to Microsoft's ODBC, used to provide a standard way of sharing data between applications.

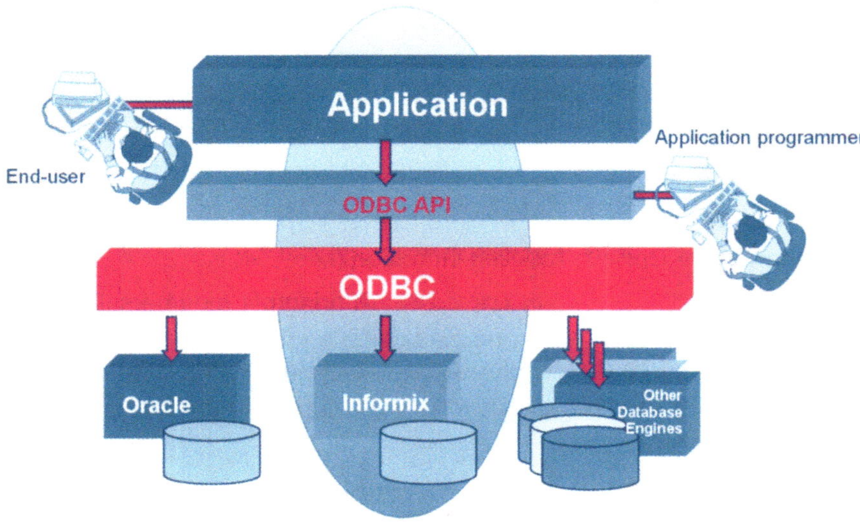

Fig. O-2. ODBC architecture

ODBC – Open Database Connectivity. A standard database middleware defined by the SQL Access Group to provide an application programming interface (see API) for accessing different database systems from Windows applications. There are interfaces for Visual Basic, Visual C++, AcuCOBOL, etc. ODBC basically defines an API, as shown in Fig. O-2, that client programs can use to connect to a database system and to issue SQL commands. An application program can use the same ODBC API to connect to any database engine registered. Each database system provides the appropriate driver that is controlled by the ODBC driver manager at the client side. A particular driver manager is responsible for connecting and communicating with the server, as well as for any data format translations that may be required. ODBC can work either in a single-tier or in a two-tier architecture, as shown in Fig. O-3. This example is based on AcuODBC, the product developed by AcuCORP (see COBOL) intended to support ODBC functionality for native COBOL files. Single-tier and multitier are explained elsewhere in the book (see EIS). ODBC is based on the SQL CLI. See also Call-Level Interface (CLI). Compare with IDAPI.

ODETTE – Organization for Data Exchange by Teletransmission in Europe. ODETTE provides standards for EDI messages, which can be exchanged by trading partners. These standards govern both the types of messages available and the structures which are applied to them. See also EDIFACT.

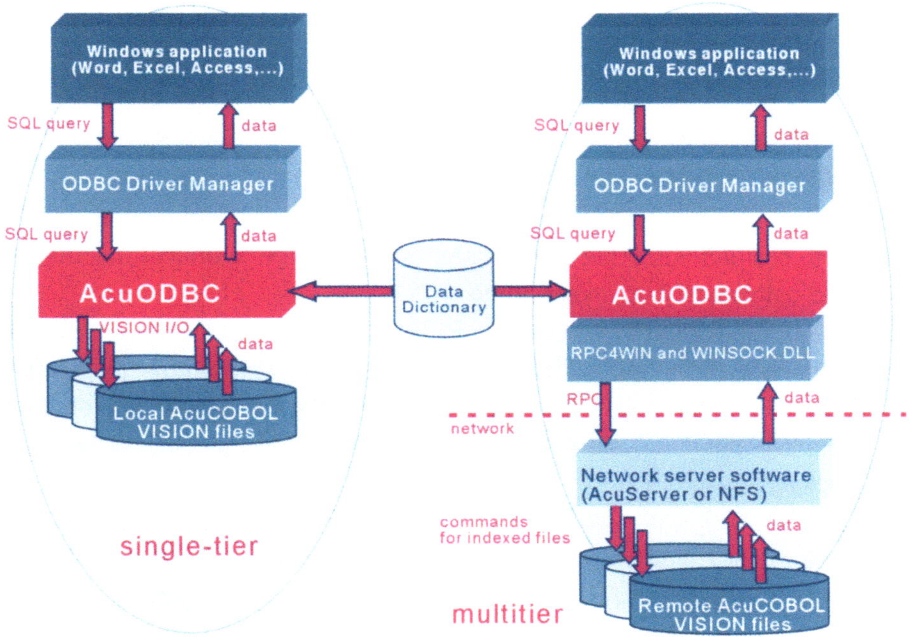

Fig. O-3. A single-tier (left) and a multitier (right) ODBC architecture

ODI – Open Data-link Interface. The architecture developed by Novell and Apple that provides a standard interface for device drivers. ODI connects LAN drivers, which are closely related to the NICs, and the upper-layer protocol stack. See also NIC. Compare with NDIS.

ODIF – Open (Office) Document Interchange Format. An ISO standard (ISO8613-5) for the ODA documents interchange format. The term "Office" in the parentheses refers to the older meaning of this acronym.

ODINSUP – ODI/NDIS Support. A Novell driver that can mediate between ODI and NDIS interfaces. See ODI and NDIS.

ODL – Object Definition Language. A language for describing a structure of objects developed by the Object Database Management Group (see ODMG). ODL has mappings defined for C++ and SmallTalk.

ODLAA – Open and Distance Learning Association of Australia. The professional association (http://www.odlaa.org) of members interested in the practice and administration of distance education and open learning. It is a non-profit organization managed by an Executive Committee of members operating in a voluntary capacity.

ODMA – Open Document Management API. An open specification for a platform-independent Application Programming Interface (see API) for client software used to access Document Management Systems (see DMS). The first ODMA specification appeared in 1994. Later on, ODMA was extended to integration with workflow systems.

ODMG – Object Database Management Group. A consortium formed by OODB vendors to standardize the data model and language interfaces for object-oriented databases (http://www.odmg.org).

ODP – Open Distributed Processing. A framework to standardize an OSI application layer in order to enable building of distributed systems in a multi-vendor environment. It defines multiple viewpoints which enable different participants to observe a system from suitable perspectives and suitable levels of abstraction.

ODT – Open Desktop. A collection of development tools and utilities from SCO integrated with the SCO UNIX operating system providing a full windowing system for an Intel x86-based PC. It includes a standard graphical interface based on OSF Motif. It also provides database, communications and network facilities. ODT is based on international standards.

OECC – Optoelectronics and Communications Conference. An international IEEE conference focusing on research, development and applications of optical communication systems and optoelectronics. Main topics include communication networks, optical systems and technology, optical fibers and cables, optical active and passive devices and modules, etc.

OEM – Original Equipment Manufacturer. A company which produces a piece of computer equipment or produces integrated systems using its own OEM products and/or purchased products from other OEMs. Compare with Value-Added Reseller (VAR).

OFB – Output Feedback. An operating mode for the Data Encryption Standard (see DES).

OFC – Open Financial Connectivity. The Microsoft specification for an interface between electronic banking services and Microsoft Money (personal financial software).

OFX – Open Financial Exchange. A specification used by financial institutions for electronic exchange of financial data. See also EDI.

OGC – Open GIS Consortium. The international standards organization dedicated to interoperable geoprocessing (http://www.opengis.org). As of March 1999, the OGC had 178 members. The OGC developed the OpenGIS specification (see OGIS). Now the OGC works closely with the ISO Technical Committee ISO TC211 (see ISO).

OGIS – OpenGIS specification. An open interface standard developed by the Open GIS Consortium (see OGC) that enables diverse geoprocessing systems to communicate across the Internet and other networks. OGIS consists of the Open Geodata Model (see OGM) and the OGIS services model, allowing OGIS-compliant software components to access data through standard interfaces stored according to the OGM.

OGM – Open Geodata Model. Part of the OpenGIS specification (see OGIS). It is a platform-independent high-level conceptual model for representing geographic features, supporting concepts of geodesy, temporality and geometry.

OH – Open Hook. A signal used to indicate that a telephone line is busy. External modems are usually provided with a LED indicator that shows the current OH signal state.

OHM – A measurement unit for electrical resistance (pronounced “oum”, represented by Greek omega, Ω). In fact, it is not an acronym, the name refers to German physicist Georg Simon Ohm (1787–1854) who discovered that voltage and electrical current are directly proportional in a metallic conductor if the temperature remains constant (known as Ohm’s law). So, 1 Ω = 1 V/1 A, the resistance of a conductor is 1 Ω if a constant voltage of 1 V across it causes a current of 1 A in it.

OHS – Open Hypermedia Systems. An international ACM workshop addressing the issues of integrated hypermedia functionality in existing tools in the computing environment. The proceedings are published by Springer-Verlag (see LNCS).

OID – Object Identity. A system-generated object identifier that is independent of the object state and any physical address in the memory.

OIR – Online Insertion and Removal. The possibility of adding, replacing or removing computer components without interrupting the system power, entering console commands, or causing other software or interfaces to shut down. Sometimes called hot swapping or power-on servicing.

OIS – Office Information Systems. See Office Automation (OA).

OKBC – Open Knowledge Base Connectivity. A protocol used for accessing knowledge bases (see KB) stored in Knowledge Representation Systems (see KRS).

OLAM – On-Line Analytical Mining. An architecture for constraint-based, multi-dimensional data mining of large databases and data warehouses (see DW).

OLAP – On-Line Analytical Processing. A category of database applications for decision support that allows query optimization and quick interactive examination of the results in various dimensions of data. Dr. Edgar F. Codd originally defined the term in 1993 in a white paper entitled "Providing OLAP to User-Analysts: An IT Mandate", but since then a lot of additional requirements were added.

OLB – OLE Object Library. A filename extension for files that contain OLE objects. See also OLE.

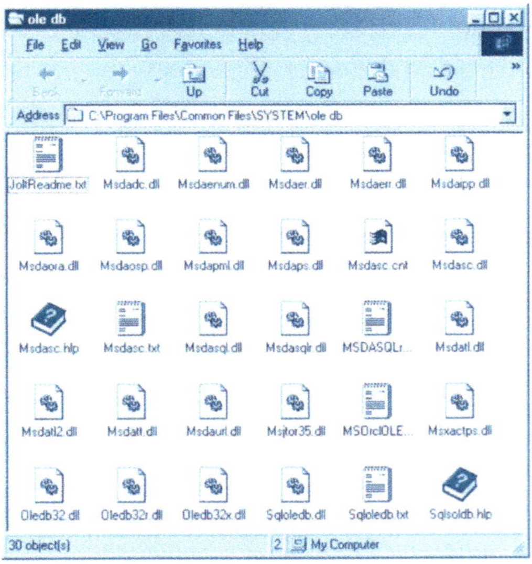

Fig. O-4. An example of an OLE folder

OLE – Object Linking and Embedding. A way to transfer and share information among applications (pronounced "olay"). The target information, an object, e.g. an image created using the CorelDraw program, is linked to a compound program, e.g. Microsoft Word. The Word document contains only a reference to the object. So, any further changes to the object will appear in the compound document. When an object is embedded in a compound document, the document contains a copy of the object; therefore, any further changes to the original object will not appear in the compound document unless the embedded object is updated. Actually, OLE is an object-oriented programming paradigm that replaces API functions with interface components called Window Objects. Each interface is a set of functions packaged together. These function groups do not limit or specify the implementation details; they are pure interface specifications and may be used by any programming language, including non-object-oriented programming environments. COM, DCOM and OLE are the central methods on which all Microsoft technologies, operating systems and applications are based. We should also mention OCX and ActiveX. In fact, there is no clear border between them. See also COM, DCOM and OCX. OLE is also the filename extension for a file or folder (see Fig. O-4) that contains OLE objects.

OLE DB – Object Linking and Embedding Database. A database architecture that provides universal integration over an enterprise network.

OLGA – Organic Land Grid Array. A type of heatsink used to cool Pentium III processors.

OLIT – OpenLook Intrinsic Toolkit. A software toolkit for the X Window System (see X).

OLTP – On-Line Transaction Processing. A category of database applications that requires high-concurrency support and clever techniques to speed up commit processing and to achieve a high rate of update transactions. See Transaction Processing (TP) and Distributed Transaction Processing (DTP).

OMA – Object Management Architecture. The conceptual object-oriented infrastructure upon which all Object Management Group specifications (see OMG) are based, as shown in Fig. O-5. OMA is entirely focused on providing an infrastructure and common facilities to support distributed objects. At a higher level, OMA could be considered a framework, since a collection of specified application, domain-specific, facility and service objects can be taken as an application framework, to be used in a variety of different applications. The operating system and other low-level facilities are outside the OMA scope. The heart of OMA is the Object Request Broker (see ORB) that acts as a switching center, locating objects, storing interface definitions and object implementations, and relaying messages between objects in a distributed heterogeneous environment. CORBA services are a low-level set of common object services (see CORBA). OMA is wider than CORBA.

OMF – Object Module Format. The standard developed by the Tool Interface Standards Committee (see TIS) that specifies the 32-bit relocatable object module format intended for 32-bit applications and tools for Intel architectures.

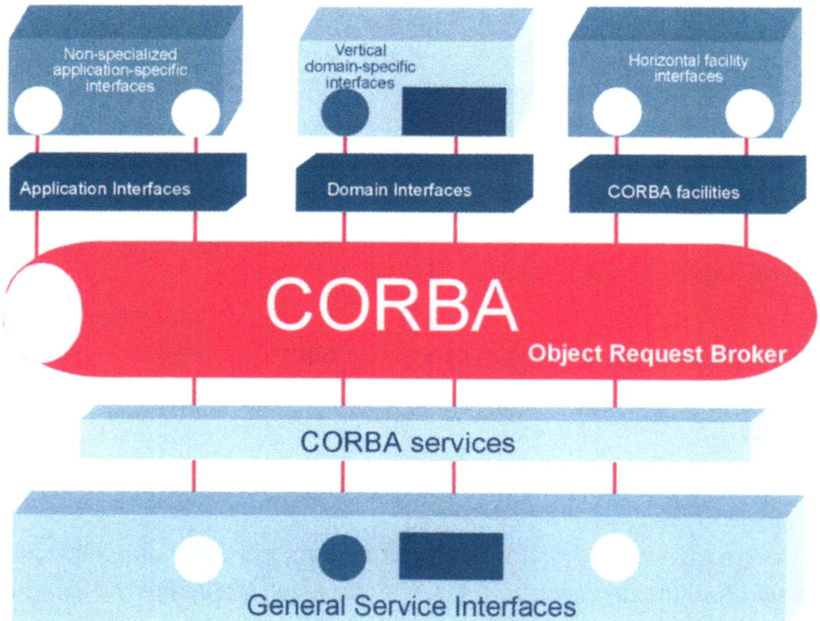

Fig. O-5. Object Management Architecture

OMG – Object Management Group. An international organization supported by over 750 members, including information system vendors, software developers, academic institutions and users (http://www.omg.org). Founded in 1989 by Data General, Hewlett-Packard, Sun, Canon, American Airlines, Unisys, Philips, Prime, Gold Hill, Soft-Switch and 3Com, OMG promotes the theory and practice of object-oriented technology in software development. OMG work is based on object orientation and distributed systems, the two technologies that will form the backbone of all software systems in the future. The organization's charter includes the establishment of industry guidelines and object management specifications to provide a common framework for application development. The primary goals are the reusability, portability and interoperability of the object-based software in distributed heterogeneous environments. Conformance to these specifications will make it possible to develop a heterogeneous applications environment across all major hardware platforms and operating systems. Today, OMG is by far the largest and most influential consortium in the software industry.

ONA – Open Network Architecture. A network service defined by the Federal Communications Commission (see FCC) to allow Regional Bell Operating Companies (see RBOC) to market add-on services in a network environment. Services include transaction processing, videotext, voice messaging, etc.

ONC – Open Network Computing. A distributed architecture from SunSoft, similar to the OSF Distributed Computing Environment (see DCE), with the major difference being the RPC functionality. The client and server translate all outgoing messages into the External Data Representation format (see XDR), and then translate all incoming messages from XDR to the native format. The NFS protocols are part of ONC. See also NFS.

ONP – Open Network Provision. An initiative in the European Union started in 1989 in order to harmonize national telecommunications regulations.

OO – Object-Oriented. A description applied to analysis, design, databases, computer technologies and programming. In the OO approach, also known as the OO paradigm, system decomposition is performed in such a way that the system is viewed as a collection of objects or object classes. An object is defined by a list of abstract attributes (often called instances) and a set of routines, often called "methods", which alter the state of that object. How abstract should these attributes be? They should be able to represent the essential features of an object without including background or unimportant features. Operations on the data must be performed via methods which are common to all instances of objects of a particular class. Thus, the interface to objects is well defined, and allows the code implementing the methods to be changed as long as the interface remains the same, i.e. as long as no other objects need ever be aware of the internal structure of a particular object.

OOA – Object-Oriented Analyses. A relatively new approach for method-based analyses that uses the object-oriented paradigm (see OO), developing an object-oriented model of the application domain. In general, the analysis is the decomposition of the problems into their component parts. The identified objects may or may not map directly into the system objects. Numerous OOA methodologies have emerged in the last 10 years. The best known is the Coad and Yourdon method considered to have been built upon the best concepts from information modeling, object-oriented programming languages and knowledge-based systems. OOA results in a five-layer model of the problem domain, where each layer builds on a previous layer. The five-step procedure, sometimes referred as SOSAS (Subjects, Objects, Structures, Attributes, Services), consists of the following steps:

1. Decompose the process (in Coad–Yourdon terminology, this stage is called Subjects): Look for structures, other systems, devices, events, rules, operational procedures, sites and organizational units.
2. Define structures (Objects): Look for relationships between classes and represent them as either general-to-specific structures or whole-to-part structures.
3. Define subject areas (Structures): Examine top-level objects within the whole-to-part hierarchies and mark these as candidate subject areas. Refine subject areas to minimize interdependencies between subjects.
4. Define attributes: Identify the atomic characteristics of the object as attributes of the object. Also look for associative relationships between objects and determine the cardinality of those relationships.
5. Define services (methods): For each class and object, identify all the services it performs, either on its own behalf or for the benefit of other classes and objects.

OOD – Object-Oriented Design. A process of mapping system requirements defined during the analysis of an object-oriented model. These requirements may or may not be structured around objects in the problem domain. Many OOD methods have been proposed. Generally, the object-oriented design process covers several activities, such as:

- identification of the objects in the system along with their attributes and operations;
- organization of objects into a cluster hierarchy which allows each object to be seen in relation to other objects;
- relationship identification between classes and objects which allows the establishment of exception handling for the interface of each object;
- implementation and testing of objects and object interfaces.

The primary tools used during OOD are class diagrams and class templates, object and timing diagrams, state-transition diagrams, operation templates, module diagrams and templates, and process diagrams and templates.

OODB – Object-Oriented Database. A database in which data is stored as objects and can be interpreted only using the methods specified by its class. The same programming language can be used for both data definition and data manipulation. Typically, an OODB can provide better support for keeping track of versions than relational databases can. See also OODBMS.

OODBMS – Object-Oriented Database Management System. A database management system capable of managing an OODB. See OODM.

OODM – Object-Oriented Data Model. A data model based on the object-oriented concepts that support new classes. It also supports inheritance (the ability of an object within the object hierarchy to inherit the data structure and behavior of the classes above it), polymorphism (allows different objects to respond to the same message in different ways), encapsulation (the ability to hide the object's internal details), etc.

OOGDM – Object-Oriented Geodata-Model. An extendible object-oriented data model for geoapplications. OOGDM supports both 2D and 3D Geographic Information System (see GIS) applications as well as raster and vector data. OOGDM objects have an identity, a state and a behavior. The possible states and the behavior of an object are defined by attributes and the set of methods corresponding to the class of the object.

OOGQL – Object-Oriented Geographic Query Language. SQL-like query language for querying databases based on OOGDM.

OOHDM – Object-Oriented Hierarchical Data Model. An object-oriented data model used for modeling DataWeb applications (see HDM).

OOK – On–Off Keying. Also known as Amplitude-Shift Keying (ASK).

OOL – Object-Oriented Language. See OOPL (Object-Oriented Programming Language).

OOP – Object-Oriented Programming. A programming technique based on the object-oriented concepts dedicated to improving productivity, quality and innovation in software development and to reducing programming time and maintenance.

OOPL – Object-Oriented Programming Language. A programming language based on the object-oriented concepts. The two dominant OOPLs are SmallTalk and C++, but object-oriented concepts have appeared also in other languages such as Ada, ALGOL, Java, etc.

OOPSLA – Object-Oriented Programming Systems, Languages and Applications. The annual ACM conference focusing on object-oriented technologies.

OOSD – Object-Oriented Structured Design. A design method based on the structured design that incorporates the essential features of the object-oriented approach. See OO.

OOUI – Object-Oriented User Interface. A kind of user interface that focuses users on objects, the "things" people use to accomplish their work. Users see and manipulate object-representations of their information allowing them to work more closely to the real-world way. Unlike OOP, where design is often dedicated to implementation details that must be hidden from the user, in OOUI design concentrates on objects that are perceived by users.

OPAC – Online Public-Access Catalog. A common term for a computerized system used to catalog and organize library material, replacing the old-fashioned card-based system in many libraries.

OpenGL – Open Graphics Library. A very portable software graphics library for rendering 3D graphics developed by Silicon Graphics Inc. (see SGI). It includes approximately 120 commands for drawing graphics primitives such as points, lines and polygons, and for lighting and animation. Commands for producing and manipulating higher-level 3D objects, such as cubes, pyramids, spheres, etc., are not included, but can be built from the existing primitives. OpenGL allows writing portable graphics applications that can be run on Windows PCs as well as on high-end graphics workstations. More information is available at http://www.sgi.com/Technology/openGL

OPeRA – Online Periodicals and Research Area. The IEEE online database (http://opera.ieee.org) that serves as a full guide to IEEE technical societies and IEEE periodicals. OPeRA consists of citation entries for all available papers in HTML format, and entire papers in PDF format.

OQL – Object Query Language. A new query language defined by the Object Database Management Group (see ODMG). It is an enhancement version of the SQL-92 standard. In addition to the expected integration into object-oriented languages and ORBs, OQL also allows object-oriented data mapping into non-object-oriented environments, such as RDBMs. A client application can be connected to an OQL either by ODBC or JDBC. It can use SQL commands that are directly translated into OQL commands. The other way is provided by CORBA. The data that is not object-oriented and legacy data are integrated using the wrapping method that hides the data from the CORBA object interfaces. The third method of OQL connection from the client application is a HTTP/HTML link. All of these ways are shown in Fig. O-6. See also CORBA, JDBC and ODBC.

ORB – Object Request Broker. The heart of the Object Management Architecture (see OMA) that provides the communication infrastructure for the OMA. It provides persistent storage for object implementation, distribution and installation of objects, database support for the interfaces supported by objects, and management of replicated objects in a distributed environment. The ORB is responsible for all of the mechanisms required to find the object implementation upon request, to prepare the object implementation to receive the request, and to communicate the data making up the request. The interface the client sees is completely independent of object location, programming language implementation, or any other aspect which is not reflected in the object's interface. There are many possible ORB implementations within CORBA, such as client- and implementation-resident ORB, server-based ORB, system-based ORB or library-based ORB, etc.

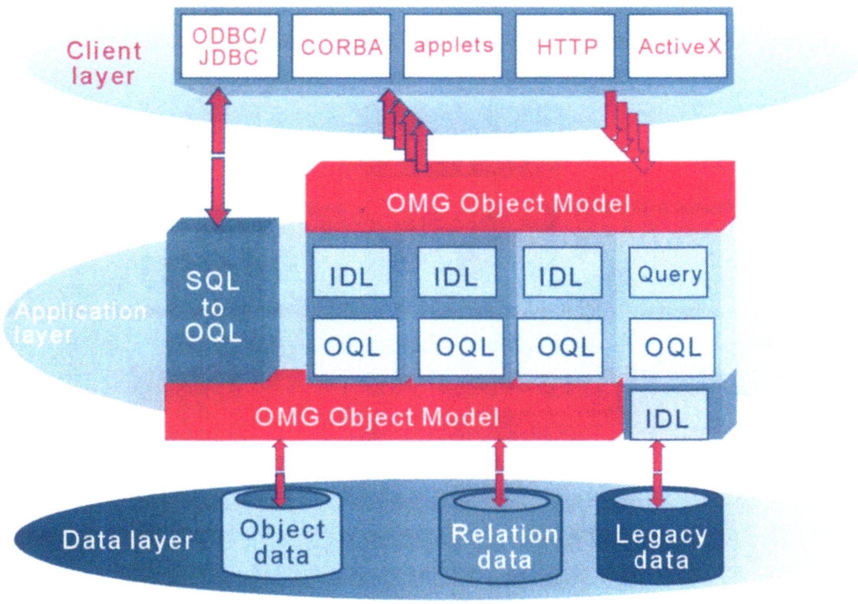

Fig. O-6. Architecture of an OQL-based application

OROM – Optical ROM. A storage method similar to CD-ROM.

ORPC – Object Remote Procedure Call. See DCOM (Distributed Component Object Model). See also RPC.

OS – Operating System. An organized collection of low-level software consisting of control routines for operating a computer and for providing an environment for the execution of programs. The operating system is also responsible for providing access to computer system resources such as files and input/output devices. Programs usually invoke the services of the operating system via system calls, while users may interact with the operating system using the system commands (see Fig. O-7). Operating systems can be classified as batch OSs, multiprogramming OSs, real-time OSs, time-sharing OSs, network OSs, distributed OSs, etc. Also, they are distinguished from each other by the degree of openness, i.e. how much they allow portability, scalability and interoperability (see PSI) of the application software and how much they are vendor-dependent, so they can range from proprietary (closed) to fully open operating systems. Examples of operating systems are BSD, AIX, Ameba, Coda, CP/M, Chorus, GCOS, KAOS, LINUX, MS-DOS, MINIX, MULTICS, Novell NetWare, OS/2, OS/400, QNX, UNIX, TACOMA, VMS, Windows NT, etc.

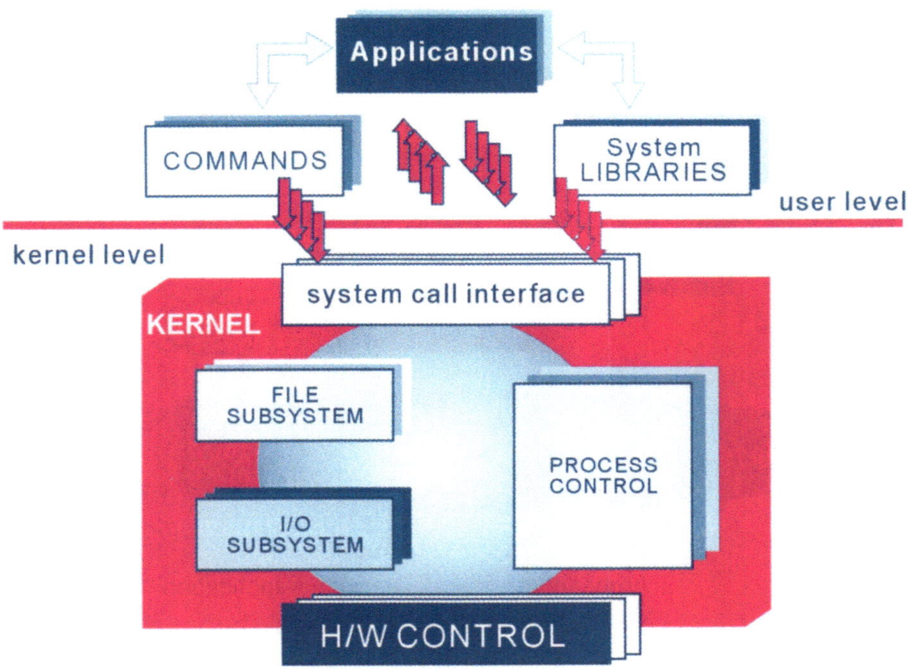

Fig. O-7. Block diagram of the OS kernel

OS/2 – Operating System/2. An IBM protected-mode virtual-memory multitasking operating system for personal computers based on the Intel processors. In addition to its own native applications, it can support Microsoft Windows applications. It also supports the Presentation Manager GUI. In October 1994, IBM released the OS/2 version known as Warp. The latest versions include support for electronic mail and web browsing via IBM Lotus Notes.

OS/400 – Operating System/400. The IBM operating system for RISC-based machines. It supports the AS/400 family (see AS) of computers.

OSAK – OSI Session Application Kernel. A DEC software product that modifies its DECnet session layer to the OSI session layer as defined by ISO standards. See also DECnet and OSI.

OSD – Open Software Description. A vocabulary used for describing software packages and their dependencies for heterogeneous clients, whether user-initiated ("pulled") or automatic ("pushed"). OSD specification allows software distribution across a network instead of using floppies or CDs. OSD has the ability to describe software dependencies in the form of a directed graph that can handle the situation where one component requires the presence of another to operate. It is based on the Extensible Markup Language (see XML). First and foremost, the OSD vocabulary can be used in a standalone XML document to declare dependencies between different software components for different operating systems and languages. Second, it can be used as a HTML reference, requiring additional software to be downloaded and installed for viewing the page. Third, potential use can provide automatic software distribution.

OSDI – Operating Systems Design and Implementation. The IEEE/ACM symposium focusing on the design, implementation and implications of systems software. Some of the major topics include operating systems, networking, distributed systems, parallel systems, mobile systems, embedded systems, and the influence of hardware development on systems and vice versa.

OSE – Open Systems Environment. A generic framework of standards which supports portable, scalable and interoperable applications. Referring to Fig. O-8, this model identifies five basic entities, as follows:

- the application software is software specific to an application, and is often referred to as an application program;
- the application platform is a set of resources, including hardware and software, that implements the services provided at the platform's interfaces;

- the communications provider is defined from the user's perspective, where universal connectivity is provided to the full set of information appliances and people, nationally and internationally;
- the external data storage media is a physical object, which can be used to store and play back data for an application platform or information appliance;
- people usually represent the users of services offered by the system.

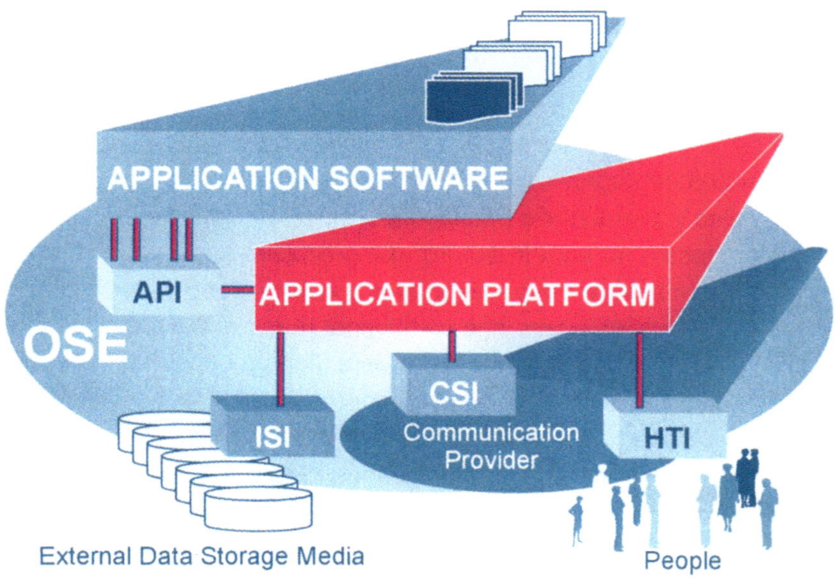

Fig. O-8. ISO OSE entities and interfaces

In addition, the OSE reference model includes four basic interfaces:

- the Application Programming Interface (API) is the interface between an application and an application platform, which is the immediate provider of all the services necessary for its execution;
- the Communication Service Interface (CSI) is the interface across which access to services and interaction between internal applications and external application platforms are provided;
- the Information Storage Interface (ISI) is the interface across which the external persistent data storage service is provided;
- the Human–Technology Interface (HTI) is the interface across which people interact with information technology.

OSF – Open Software Foundation. An international software development organization founded in 1988 by computer industry sponsors Apollo, Bull, DEC, Hewlett-Packard, Hitachi, Nixdorf and Philips. Membership is open to computer hardware and software vendors, educational institutions, government agencies, and other interested organizations worldwide. It is dedicated to defining specifications, developing leadership software, and making available an open, portable application environment. OSF defined the Distributed Computing Environment (see DCE), a graphical user interface Motif, an Architecture-Neutral Distribution Format (see ANDF) for mass distribution of applications, and also worked on an operating system OSF/1. Now, OSF is part of The Open Group (http://www.opengroup.org), combining forces with X/Open to deliver technology innovations and widespread adoption of open systems specifications. The Open Group has built an architectural framework (see TOGAF) for easier and more effective open systems information technology development.

OSG – Open Service Gateway. A commonly used software standard established by 15 of the world's biggest computer and telecommunication companies, for connecting consumer and small-business appliances. They can communicate with each other and with external networks over the Internet.

OSI – Open Systems Interconnection. The network architectural model developed by ISO and ITU-T (ISO7498) which consists of seven layers (see Fig. O-9), each specifying particular network functions such as addressing, flow control, error control, encapsulation, reliable message transfer, and network management. Each layer performs a service for the one above by requesting a service from the one below. Communication between systems is made by peer-to-peer communications (see P2P) within compatible OSI layers. The lower two layers are implemented in hardware and software, while the upper five layers are implemented only in software. However, the model does not prescribe how to implement any of the functions described. Generally, two communications models are incorporated: the horizontal one, dedicated to P2P communications, and the vertical one, intended for layer-to-layer communication on a single machine. The physical layer is directly connected to the physical medium between systems. It is responsible for sending and receiving streams of bits across the medium providing a physical connection between two systems. Also, it specifies the electrical characteristics of the interface (see Fig. O-10). The second layer, the data-link layer, controls data flow and performs error detection and correction. In short, this layer creates packets appropriate for the network architecture and topology being used.

Actually, two sublayers, the Logical Link Control (see LLC) and Media Access Control (see MAC) are defined. The network layer controls routing in the case of no direct connection between two end-systems and finds an intermediate system(s) that can relay the message forward to the destination. This layer involves address resolution protocols and routing protocols such as CLNP, IGP, IPX and X.25. The transport layer is responsible for monitoring the quality of service, which can be satisfied for both end-systems. It is crucial in different ways, because it sits between the upper layers (the application-dependent layers) and the lower layers (the network-, topology- and technology-based layers).

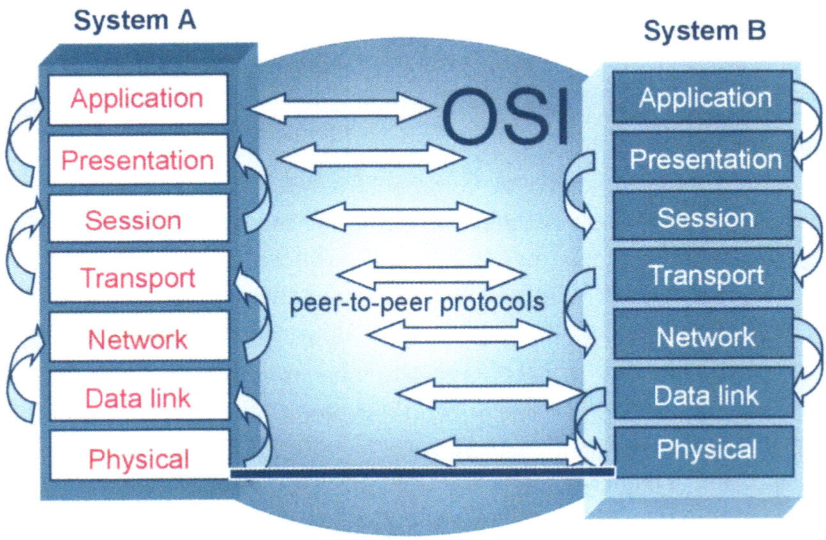

Fig. O-9. OSI Reference Model

This situation is depicted in Fig. O-10, where some representatives of network architectures use the common communication architectures below. In order to communicate on higher levels, it is required to use some of the routers, bridges or gateways, whatever is appropriate. At this level of P2P communications, five classes of protocols, known as TP0, TP1, TP2, TP3 and TP4, are defined (see TP). The fifth layer, called the session layer, is dedicated to a conversation agreement. In its peer-to-peer conversation, session layers negotiate the way the data should be sent, etc. These layers are also responsible for making sure that the connection is maintained until the transmission is complete, and ensuring that appropriate security has been used. The presentation layer is responsible for the character sets and symbols used and other common representation forms such as languages or alphabets. Finally, the application layer is specialized for different applications, but it is not the application itself. Examples include file transfer (see FTAM), e-mail (see X.400), directory services (see X.500), EDI, ODA, VT and network management (see CMIP). P2P communication is the ultimate goal in OSI. In order to accomplish that task OSI defines several important functions that are described elsewhere in the book (see PDU, PCI, SAP, SDU, etc.). Although the OSI reference model is used universally as a method for teaching and understanding network functionality, in practice it is a long way from achieving the Internet's efficiency and popularity.

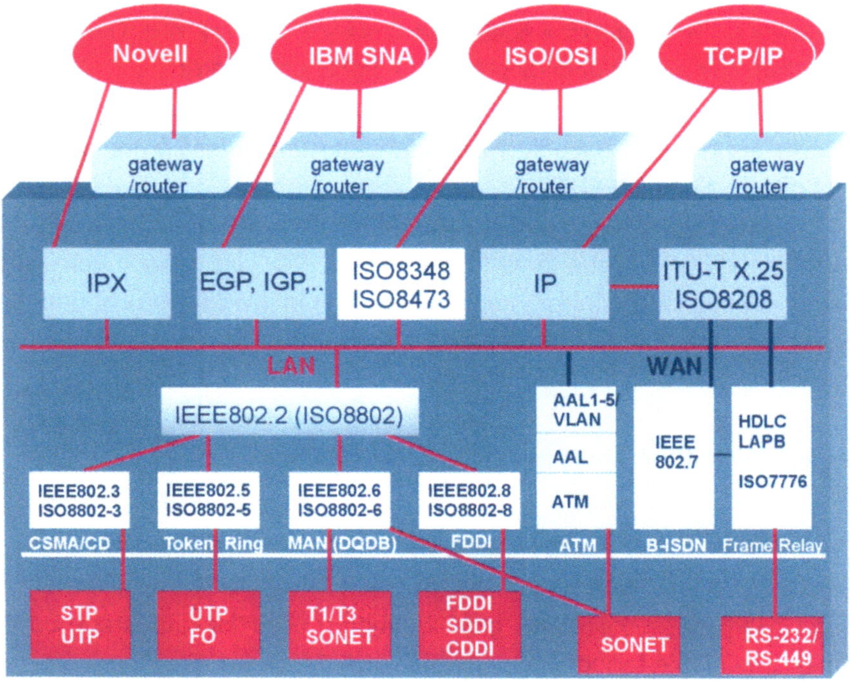

Fig. O-10. OSI layers in common with other network environments

OSInet – OSI network. A test network used by the National Bureau of Standards (see NBS) to test vendor conformance to OSI standards and specifications. See also OSI.

OSI/RM – Open Systems Interconnection/Reference Model. See Open Systems Interconnection (OSI).

OSLAN – Open System Local Area Network. The MS-DOS software that allows personal computers running MS-DOS to communicate with other systems on a LAN in an OSI environment and also via OSI transport-layer class 0 using TCP/IP (RFC1006). It may be used with network controller cards that support CSMA/CD Ethernet or Token Ring.

OSME – Open System Management Environment. An IBM implementation of X.400 messaging. See X.400.

OSPF – Open Shortest Path First. A hierarchical link state routing algorithm for the interior gateway protocol (see IGP) defined in RFC1583 and RFC1793. OSPF supports point-to-point lines between two routers and multiaccess networks (with multiple routers) with/without broadcasting. OSPF works by mapping the set of actual networks, routers and lines into a directed graph in which each arc is assigned a cost, i.e. a distance, a delay, etc. The shortest path is then computed depending on the weights on the arcs.

OSPM – Operating System Power Management. The term used to refer to an operating system that uses ACPI interfaces to implement power management policies. See also ACPI.

OSQL – Object-Structured Query Language. A language for the design and implementation of object-oriented databases. OSQL provides a rich set of constructs that allow definition, implementation and integration of information services in a distributed environment. It also provides a declarative query capability, similar to that provided by SQL for relational databases.

OSTC – Open System Testing Consortium. The European organization in charge of the X.400 test conformance development.

OTDR – Optical Time-Domain Reflectometer. A tool used in fiber optics (see FO) for testing the light signal.

OTOH – On the other hand. The chat term.

OTP – Open Trading Protocol. A global standard used for retail trade on the Internet. See also e-tailing.

OTP – One-Time Programmable. A special memory device that is manufactured as a blank recordable medium ready for programming once only.

OTPROM – One-Time Programmable ROM. See ROM and PROM.

OTS – Object Transaction Service. A definition of the interface that permits CORBA objects to participate in transactions. See also CORBA.

OTTOMH – Off the top of my head. The chat term.

P

p – package. A dynamic-link library (see DLL) used in Microsoft Visual C++.

P – Peta. An order of magnitude (10^{15}).

p – pico. An order of magnitude which denotes one-trillionth (10^{-12}). An example of its usage as a prefix is pF (picoFarad).

P2P – Peer-to-Peer. From an architectural point of view, P2P is a network consisting of two or more computers that use the same program or type of program to communicate and share data. Each computer, or peer, is considered equal in terms of responsibilities, and each acts as a server for the others in the network. In communications, P2P is used to assign interactions between devices that operate on the same communications level of a layered architecture. See also OSI (Open Systems Interconnection).

P3P – Platform for Privacy Preferences Project. A standard proposal for a protocol that should allow Internet users to control the type of information that is collected from sites visited. The mechanism is designed to inform users about the privacy policies of the services of websites. P3P enables websites to express their privacy practices in a standard format that can be retrieved automatically and interpreted easily by a user agent (web browser, browser plug-in, etc.). Thus, the users do not need to read the privacy policies at all the sites they visit. How does it work in practice? When a P3P-compliant client requests a resource, a P3P service sends a link to a machine-readable policy statement in which the organization responsible for the service declares its identity and privacy practices. The privacy policy enumerates the data elements that the service proposes to collect, and explains how each will be used, with whom data may be shared, and how long the data will be retained. Policies can be parsed automatically by the user agents (web browsers, browser plug-ins, or proxy servers) and compared with the privacy preferences set by the user. Depending on those preferences, a user agent may then simply display information for the user or take other actions.

P5 – Pentium/586. A codename for the Intel Pentium processor, before it was released.

P10 – Plot10. A filename extension for a file that contains a drawing made using the Tektronix Plot10 package.

PAB – Personal Address Book. Information stored in a local computer that contains all the address information for all possible recipients. It is used in e-mail systems to obtain an e-mail address usually using a recipient nickname (alias).

PABX – Private Automatic Branch Exchange. A kind of PBX that provides automatic switching. See PBX.

PAC – Privilege Attribute Certificate. A certificate used in a login procedure that specifies the privileges given to a user having a PAC.

PACE – Priority Access Control Enabled. A proprietary Ethernet architecture developed by 3COM in order to transmit time-sensitive data over Ethernet networks.

PACI – Partnership for Advanced Computational Infrastructure. A 10-year research program launched by the US National Science Foundation (see NSF) in 1999. The program is aimed at the creation of software that can handle real-world applications with minimal setups. Actually, two supercomputing centers are involved. The National Center for Supercomputing Applications (see NCSA) will focus on six application areas: chemical engineering, cosmology, hydrology, molecular biology, nanomaterials, and scientific instrumentation. The other supercomputing center located in San Diego will focus on molecular science, neuroscience, earth systems science, and engineering. The common aim is to integrate the applications into high-speed networks such as Internet2 and some of the US government networks.

PACIS – Pacific–Asia Conference on Information Systems. An international conference focusing on advanced applications of information systems. Topics of interest include e-business, e-marketplaces, EC, EDI and B2B systems, user behavior of online shopping, digital content creation, digital payment systems, digital copyright protection, BPR, groupware, workflow, etc.

PACS – Public Access Computer Systems Review. An online journal focusing on end-user computer systems in libraries.

PACT – Parallel Architectures and Compiler Theory. The IEEE/ACM international conference dedicated to recent research and development in parallel computing.

PAD – Packet Assembler/Disassembler. This is a typical black box element in packet-oriented networks. It serves to distinguish block-oriented data in a global environment from character-oriented data in a local environment. Its functionality is described by three CCITT recommendations, often referred to by the name triple X (see X.3, X.28 and X.29).

PADL – Practical Aspects of Declarative Languages. An international ACM workshop dedicated to the exchange of new ideas on recent and forthcoming issues in declarative language implementations. The proceedings of PADL workshops are published by Springer-Verlag (see LNCS).

PADS – Parallel and Distributed Simulation. An international workshop dedicated to presenting recent work on understanding parallel and distributed simulation techniques.

PAEB – Pan-American EDIFACT Board. The coordinating body on Electronic Data Interchange (see EDI) for the national standards organizations (see NSB) of North, Central and South America. See also AFEB, ANZEB and ASEB.

PAG – Property Page. A filename extension for a file that contains a Microsoft Visual Basic property page.

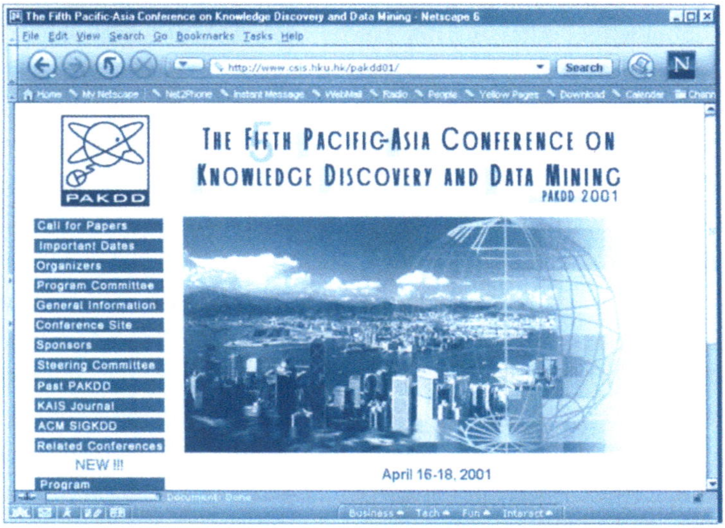

Fig. P-1. PAKDD 2001 homepage

PAKDD – Pacific–Asia Conference on Knowledge Discovery and Data Mining. An international conference focusing on knowledge discovery and data mining. Topics include the foundation and principles of data mining, data warehousing, mining in multidimensional databases, integration with data warehousing and OLAP, web-based mining, resource discovery on the Internet, rule induction and decision trees, performances and benchmarks of knowledge discovery systems, etc. (see Fig. P-1).

PAKM – Practical Aspects of Knowledge Management. An international conference focusing on the development and deployment of advanced business solutions for the management of knowledge and intellectual capital.

PAL – Palmtop Application Library. The freeware development library for HP100LX and HP200LX palmtops.

PAL – Phase Alternating Line. The European system used in TV and video techniques. It has 625 scan lines (576 of them only are displayed), an aspect ratio of 4:3, and 25 frames per second. Compare with NTSC.

PAL – Programmable Array Logic. A family of fuse-programmable logic integrated circuits. The output signals are the results of logical "OR" operations applied to a fixed number of logical "AND" operations performed on the input signals.

PAM – Pluggable Authentication Module. The new industry standard for integrated login. It allows a login procedure to integrate with different authentication mechanisms, such as the Kerberos, RSA or DCE authentication services.

PAM – Pulse Amplitude Modulation. A modulation technique which involves varying the amplitude of pulses of constant frequency and duration. With PAM, the pulse amplitude is changed according to the information being encoded. Compare with PCM, Pulse Duration Modulation (PDM), and Pulse Position Modulation (PPM).

PAP – Password Authentication Protocol. An authentication protocol defined in RFC1334 that allows point-to-point peers (see PPP) to authenticate each other. Basically, PAP is not a strong authentication method because passwords are sent over the network without any encryption and there is no protection against playback or repeated attacks. PAP works as follows:

1. After the link is established, the requestor sends a password and an id to the server.
2. The server either validates the request and sends back an acknowledgment, terminates the connection, or offers the requestor another chance.

PAP – Printer Access Protocol. A protocol used in AppleTalk networks for communication between nodes and printers.

PAR – Positive Acknowledgment with Retransmission. See ARQ.

PARAGON – Process-algebraic Analysis of Real-time Applications with Graphics-Oriented Notation. A tool for visual specification and verification of real-time systems, developed at the University of Pennsylvania.

PARC – Palo Alto Research Center. Xerox's research and development center (http://www.parc.xerox.com).

PART – Parallel and Real-Time Systems. The Australasian conference focusing on research into parallel and real-time systems and their applications. Some of the major topics include parallel programming, algorithms and architectures, mobile computing, network-based concurrent computing, object-oriented parallel and real-time computing, parallel I/O, multimedia systems, distributed operating systems, etc.

Fig. P-2. An example of PAT file deployments

PAS – Publicly Available Specifications. De facto standards with rules regarding their acceptability as parts of formal standards or as items referred to in formal standards. It is important that the process is open, the standard is agreed by consensus, there are adequate formal mechanisms for wide consultation, there are rigid change control procedures, and there are no problems with intellectual property rights.

pASP – pocket Active Server Pages. A scaled-down version of Active Server Pages (see ASP), optimized for server-side mobile channels scripting.

PAT – Pattern. A filename extension for a file that contains a CorelDraw pattern. Figure P-2 depicts a set of pat files applied to different shapes.

PAW – Physics Analysis Workbench. A general-purpose portable tool for physics data analysis and presentation. Also, there is an extension of PAW with an OSF Motif user interface named PAW++.

PB – Petabyte. The measurement unit for 10^{15} bytes.

PBX – Private Branch Exchange. A digital or analog telephone switchboard located at the subscriber premises and used to connect private and public telephone networks. See also PABX.

PC – Personal Computer. A computer designed for use by one person at a time. Also refers to a computer manufactured by IBM, or an IBM-compatible machine.

PCA – Policy Certification Authority. A part of the Privacy-Enhanced Mail standard (see PEM) for certifying the certification authorities; they are certified by the Internet Policy Registration Authority (see IPRA). Each PCA must clarify an official policy on registration and store it with IPRA. After that, these statements are signed by IPRA and made public.

P-CAV – Partial Constant Angular Velocity. A hard-disk technology that divides a disk into two zones. It varies the disk rotation (Constant Linear Velocity, see CLV) for the inner zone and then switches to a constant speed (see CAV) for the outer one. Also known as CAV/CLV.

PCB – Printed Circuit Board. A thin flat board made of an insulator material (plastic, fiberglass, etc.) onto which electronic components are mounted. There are two different techniques that can be applied: soldering pins passing through appropriate holes or surface mounting (see SMD). The connections between the components are made using metal strips, usually of copper, that are printed onto the surface of the board.

PCD – Photo CD. A filename extension for a file that contains a Kodak Photo CD image.

PC-DOS – Personal Computer Disk Operating System. The version of MS-DOS sold by IBM. It is very similar to MS-DOS, although the filenames of utility programs may differ. See also MS-DOS and DOS.

PCF – Pipeline Configuration File. A filename extension for a file that contains pipelines created using a pipeline editor.

PCH – Precompiled Header. A filename extension for a file that contains any C or C++ precompiled program ready to be included in the next development step. PCH files allow faster development, because stable lines of code compiled in PCH files do not require additional compilation and debugging.

PCI – Peripheral Component Interconnect. A specification for a self-configuring local bus introduced by Intel in 1993. It allows up to 10 PCI-compliant expansion cards to be installed in a computer. The PCI controller can exchange data with the system's CPU, either 32 bits or 64 bits at a time. A technique called bus mastering is applied to allow PCI-compliant adapters to perform tasks concurrently with the CPU. The core of a PCI card is a PCI chipset that uses either 5-V or 3.3-V logic. The PCI specification allows multiplexing, a technique that permits more than one electrical signal to be present on the bus at any time. PCI buses are not only applicable in desktop systems, they are also being reconfigured for industrial applications, embedded systems, laptops, mobile devices, etc. Compare with VLB.

PCI – Personal Communications Interactive. The online version of the IEEE Personal Communications magazine.

PCI – Protocol Control Information. The protocol information added by an OSI entity to the service data unit passed down from the layer above, altogether forming a protocol data unit (see PDU). Each layer adds its own PCI as the packet is passed down through the protocol stack. So, an application packet leaving the data-link layer has six PCIs attached, from the application, presentation, session, transport, network and data-link layers.

PCL – Printer Control Language. A generalized printer control language from Hewlett-Packard, used in its LaserJet, DeskJet and RuggedWriter printer lines. Also called the HP Printer Control Language. PCL uses scalable fonts and raster graphics, but is not implemented in a high-level language.

PCM – Pulse Code Modulation. A modulation signal technique that involves varying the amplitude of pulses. During modulation, the pulse amplitude is changed according to the information being encoded. PCM limits the pulse amplitudes to several predefined values. Compare with Pulse Amplitude Modulation (PAM), Pulse Duration Modulation (PDM), and Pulse Position Modulation (PPM).

P

PCMCIA – Personal Computer Memory Card International Association. An industrial organization (http://www.pcmcia.org) founded by a group of computer manufacturers and vendors to promote a common standard for PC-based peripherals and the appropriate slot designed to connect them. A PCMCIA slot can be one of three types, as follows:

- Type I: 3.3-mm-thick PC card, typically used for memory devices;
- Type II: 5-mm-thick PC card, also compatible with Type I cards, typically used for I/O devices;
- Type III: 10.5-mm-thick PC card, also compatible with Type I or Type II cards, typically used for devices whose components are thicker, such as rotating mass storage.

PCMCIA – People Can't Memorize Computer Industry Acronyms. Funny coincidence with an existing acronym (see above), which highlights the problem of the huge number of computer acronyms and abbreviations in use. Among other things, this book is intended to simplify people's orientation in this ever-growing world.

PCN – Personal Communications Network. A communication technology still under development, which will provide a small cordless phone to be used anywhere in the world in the same way as a static home phone is used, i.e. with only one phone number. As a user moves, the user's phone signal is picked up by the nearest antenna and then forwarded to a base station that connects to the wired network. This term is used everywhere in the world except in the US where it is called Personal Communication Services (PCS).

PCO – Point of Control and Observation. A place within a testing environment where the occurrence of test events is controlled, as defined by the particular abstract test method used.

PCR – Peak Cell Rate. In ATM networks, the maximum rate at which the sender plans to send cells. It is specified in cells per second and defined by the interval between the transmission of the last bit of one cell and the first bit of the next. See also QoS, MCR and SCR.

PCS – Personal Communications Services. See Personal Communications Network (PCN).

PCS – Plastic-Clad Silica. A type of optical fiber made using a glass core and plastic cladding.

PCS – Profile Connection Space. A device-independent color space used for color conversion and matching.

PCT – Picture file. A filename extension for a file that contains a picture.

PCT – Private Communication Technology. A security protocol developed to provide privacy over the Internet.

PCT – Program Comprehension Tool. A software engineering tool that allows an understanding of the structure and/or functionality of a program.

PCTE – Portable Common Tool Environment. An international ESPRIT project the results of which were first published in 1984. It is UNIX- and C-oriented, and is intended for general-purpose standardized software-engineering tool development. A later version of PCTE (PCTE+), released by ECMA, has been widely accepted as a de facto standard. See also ECMA and ESPRIT.

PCX – Picture any (X) image. A filename extension for a file that contains a picture that can be changed using the Paintbrush picture editor. As an example of a pcx file the author has decided to give the readers a wonderful view of Milford Sound, part of New Zealand's Fiordland National Park, one of the most beautiful fiords in the world. Rudyard Kipling called Milford Sound the Eighth Wonder of the World. See Fig. P-3.

Fig. P-3. Milford Sound in PCX format (March 1997)

PDA – Personal Digital Assistant. A common term describing a small lightweight handheld computer designed to provide specific personal help; its features generally include a basic editor, an appointments tracker, a calculator, and access to e-mails and the Internet. PDAs usually rely on flash memory instead of a power-hungry disk. Many PDA devices use a pen or another pointing device for interfacing, instead of a keyboard or a mouse. Some of them offer multimedia features. Communication abilities are provided by modem, cellular or wireless technology. All software is stored in ROM.

PDA – Public display of affection. The chat term.

PDAU – Physical Delivery Access Unit. A type of Access Unit (see AU) in the Message Handling System (see MHS) that provides a gateway between the Message Transfer System and the services involved in a physical delivery.

PDB – Program Database. A filename extension for a file that contains debugging information about a program developed using Microsoft Visual Studio tools.

PDC – Primary Domain Controller. In any local area network, the server that maintains the master copy of the domain's user accounts database and validates logon requests.

PDCS – Parallel and Distributed Computing and Systems. The IASTED international conference dealing with all aspects of distributed and parallel computing. Topics include parallel/distributed computing and operating systems, network design, real-time systems, data mining, tools and environments for software development, task scheduling, and routing algorithms.

PDD – Platform-Dependent Driver. A filename extension for a file in Microsoft Windows that contains the platform-specific layer for a built-in device driver.

PDDM – Parallel and Distributed Data Mining. An international workshop providing a forum for the presentation of original research results in the field of data mining in parallel and distributed environments.

PDE – Portable Development Environment. A project set up by Fujitsu Network Communication Systems in 1997. The project is aimed at building an enterprise infrastructure that would offer Internet-based support for the complete lifecycle of software products. The overall architecture of PDE can be viewed in IEEE Computer, May 1999 (pp. 38–47).

PDES – Product Data Exchange using STEP. A set of standards for communicating complete product models with sufficient information content to allow advanced CAD/CAM applications to interpret them. PDES is under development as a US standard, while STEP is under development as its international counterpart. See also CAD/CAM and STEP.

PDF – Portable Document Format. The native file format developed by Adobe to represent documents in a way independent of the original application software, operating system, and hardware used during document creation. PDFs are very suitable for electronic document publishing, because they are compact, and they are readable and printable in a WYSIWYG manner by any computer having Adobe Acrobat Reader (see Fig. P-4).

PDH – Plesiochronous Digital Hierarchy. A nearly synchronous (plesiochronous means almost synchronous) scheme for carrying digitized traffic over twisted-pair cabling. PDH evolved into other standards for digital hierarchies, such as SONET and SDH. See SONET and SDH.

PDI – Public Data Internet. A common name for Internet-based commercial networks without restrictions as to their use. PDI networks were designed to support wide-open Electronic Data Interchange (see Open-edi in EDI), but there are still limitations due to the current restrictions on networks connected to PDIs (e.g. corporate Intranets).

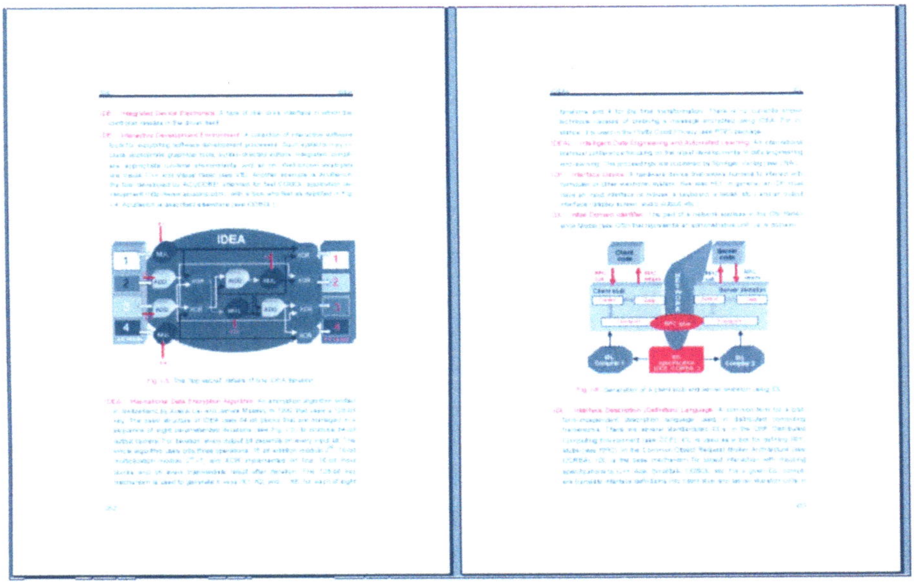

Fig. P-4. Part of a draft of this book in a PDF format

PDL – Page Description Language. A programming language, such as Adobe PostScript, which allows the appearance of a printed page to be described in a high-level device-independent way. A page description language describes the required formats for page size, layout, fonts, etc., but leaves the work of drawing characters and graphics to the output device itself. Printing then becomes a two-stage process: an application produces a description in the page description language, which is then interpreted by a specific output device. See also PostScript (PS).

PDM – Product Data Management. A strategy used in manufacturing to keep track of all the relevant data about a particular product. The components are entered into a database under a variety of classes according to the particular business requirements. Such components could include the Bill Of Materials (see BOM), classified drawings, assembly processes, etc. In addition, product data can be viewed according to the product structure, where the relationship between the components and parts in an assembly process can be recognized easily. With ISO9000 audit trail and conformance are fundamental requirements. Systems that support PDM are known as PDM systems or Engineering Data Management Systems (see EDMS).

PDM – Pulse Duration Modulation. A modulation technique which involves varying the duration of pulses. During the modulation, the pulse duration is changed according to the information being encoded. Sometimes called pulse width modulation or pulse length modulation. Compare with PAM, PCM and PPM.

PDN – Public Data Network. A network with a guaranteed bandwidth, operated either by a government (as in Europe) or by a private concern, for providing computer communications to the public, usually for a fee.

PDP – Parallel and Distributed Processing. A Euromicro workshop that focuses on advanced research in parallel and distributed computing. Some of the main topics include parallel and distributed systems, network-based computing, models and tools for parallel programming, advanced applications in the field, languages, compilers and run-time support systems, etc.

PDP – Programmable Data Processor. The DEC family of microcomputers. The best known model was the PDP-11.

PDPTA – Parallel and Distributed Processing Techniques and Applications. An international conference. Topics of interest include parallel and distributed applications and architectures, building block processors, reliability and fault-tolerance, real-time and embedded systems, parallel and distributed algorithms, object-oriented techniques and related issues, software tools for parallel and distributed platforms, Petri nets, high-performance computing in computational science, etc.

PDS – Partitioned Data Set. A data set that is divided into partitions of programs or data. Used in direct access storage devices (see DASD).

PDS – Processor-Direct Slot. A general-purpose expansion slot used in Macintosh computers.

PDS – Protected Distributed System. A distributed system that includes adequate acoustic, electrical, electromagnetic and physical safeguards to permit its use in the unencrypted transmission of classified information.

PDT – Pacific Daylight Time. Time zone. UTC – 7.00 hours. See TZ.

PDU – Protocol Data Unit. A common term for a discrete piece of information, a message unit (such as a packet or frame), exchanged between two protocol entities within a given communication layer. Every PDU has its own lifetime that indicates how many routers it can use before it must reach the destination. See also OSI.

PDV – Path Delay Value. The time required by a packet to travel the longest path across an Ethernet network.

PE – Portable Executable. The native executable format for the Microsoft Windows NT 32-bit operating system.

pel – picture element. An obsolete term for a picture element. See pixel.

PEM – Privacy-Enhanced Mail. The Internet e-mail standard defined in RFCs 1421 through 1424, which provides confidentiality, authentication and message integrity using various encryption methods. Unlike the optional solution in PGP, in PEM a message hash is computed using MD2 or MD5, and the key management is more structured. Keys are certified by certification authorities in the form of certificates, starting with the user's name, a public key, and the key's expiration date. Certificates include an MD5 hash signed by the certification authority's private key. PEM was applied to MIME in RFC1848 (see MOSS). See also Message Digest (MD), Policy Certification Authority (PCA) and MIME. Compare with PGP. See also RIPEM.

PEP – Protocol Extension Protocol. A proposed system to allow HTTP clients and servers to negotiate protocol extensions. The PEP demo code can be obtained online at http://www.w3.org/Protocols/PEP

PerfMon – Performance Monitor. A software tool available in Windows NT that allows analysis of the system's resource workloads. In particular, memory, disk I/O, CPU, objects, threads and processes can be monitored using PerfMon.

PERL – Practical Extraction and Report Language. An interpreted scripting language based on the C language and several UNIX utilities for parsing text files, extracting information and printing reports. Larry Wall at NASA invented PERL. See also CPAN. The website http://www.perl.com gives a detailed description of PERL.

PES – Packetized Elementary Stream. The output of an MPEG packetizer (either video or audio) having about 30 header fields and flags, including lengths, stream identifiers, encryption control, timestamps and CRC. See also MPEG.

PEX – Packet Exchange Protocol. A transport-layer protocol in a Xerox Network System (see XNS).

PEX – PHIGS Extension to the X Window System. A graphics standard which provides support to GKS-3D and PHIGS in a distributed X11 environment. PEX defines several new types of X11 resources which work together to support the implementation of GKS-3D and PHIGS. These resources can be configured differently to allow structure traversal at the server, structure traversal at the client, or a combination of both. In short, PEX allows developers to build network-transparent GKS-3D and PHIGS applications, which can be executed on a client and generate graphical outputs on a remote node in a heterogeneous network environment. See also X11, GKS-3D and PHIGS.

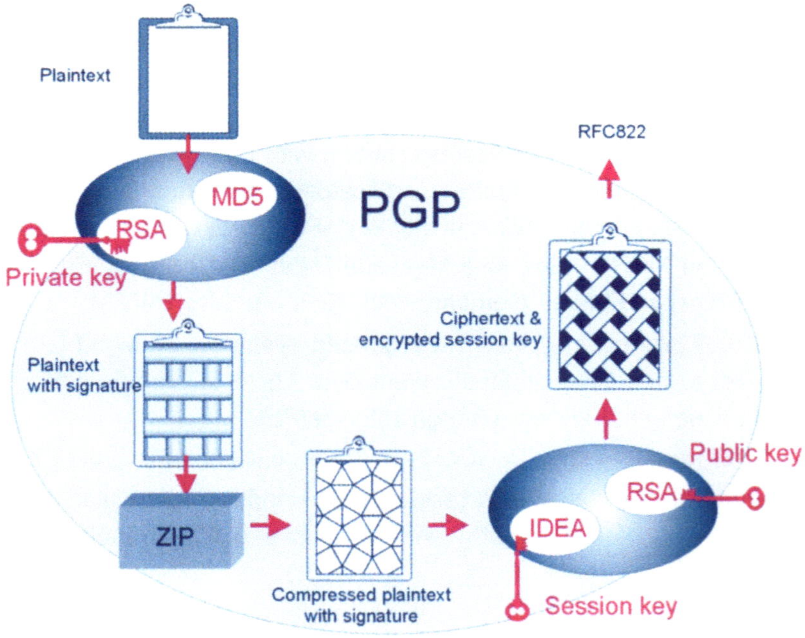

Fig. P-5. PGP in action to create a secure message

PG – Peer Group. A set of logical nodes that are grouped to create a routing hierarchy.

PGA – Pin Grid Array. A method for mounting chips on printed circuit boards (see PCB), especially for chips with very large numbers of pins. Compare with Dual In-line Package (DIP).

PGA – Professional Graphics Adapter. A video adapter introduced by IBM, especially for CAD applications. It allows 256 colors, displayed with a resolution of 640×480 pixels.

PgDn – Page Down. A key on the computer keyboard (usually in the numeric keypad), most often used in word-processing applications to scroll down the document by one screen, or page. Compare to PgUp.

PGP – Pretty Good Privacy. An e-mail security package that provides privacy, authentication, digital signatures, and compression. PGP with source code is easy to use and distribute free of charge via the Internet, BBSs and commercial networks. A commercial version is also available for those requiring support. It was written by Phil Zimmerman and published in 1995. PGP uses existing cryptographic algorithms such as RSA, IDEA and MD5. The format of a PGP message has three parts, containing the IDEA key, the signature and the message, respectively. PGP uses three keys: a public key associated with a person or a company which must be paired with a secret (private) key, a private key known only to the key's owner, and a session key generated at random every time a message is going to be encrypted (see Fig. P-5). IDEA and the session key are used to encrypt the message. RSA and the public key are used to encrypt the session key. PGP creates a digital signature using a private key and a message digest (see MD5). Additional information can be obtained at http://web.mit.edu/network/pgp-form.html or via ftp://src.doc.ic.ac.uk/package/pgp. See also IDEA and RSA. Compare with Privacy-Enhanced Mail (PEM).

P

PgUp – Page Up. A key on the computer keyboard (usually in the numeric keypad), most often used in word-processing applications to scroll up the document by one screen, or page. Compare to PgDn.

PHIGS – Programmer's Hierarchical Interactive Graphics System. The ISO standard for a 3D interactive graphics system (ISO9592). It defines a language-independent nucleus of a graphics system capable of being embedded in a language-dependent layer to provide an appropriate API for applications programming. The layer model of PHIGS is shown in Fig. P-6. PHIGS supports storage and manipulation of data in a centralized hierarchical data structure, known as the centralized structure store (see CSS). Structure elements can be either graphical data or application-specific data. By insertion and removal of structure elements structure editing can be achieved. The graphical output is built up from two groups of basic elements called output primitives and primitive attributes. The output primitives are abstractions of the basic actions a device can perform. The attributes control the properties of the primitives on a device (color, linetype, etc.). The graphical output on a workstation is produced by traversing a structure identified for display on that workstation and interpreting the structure elements. The workstation-independent stage of structure traversal involves mapping from modeling co-ordinates to a world coordinate system during which graphical structure elements can produce output primitives. The workstation-dependent stage then performs a transformation between four coordinate systems, WC, VRC, NPC and DC. Compare with GKS-3D.

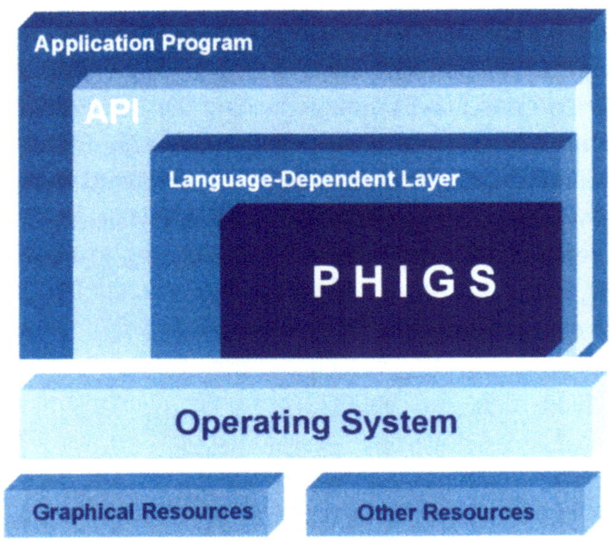

Fig. P-6. Layered model of PHIGS

PhSAP – Physical-layer Service Access Point. The point at which the OSI physical-layer service is made available to a data-link layer entity (see SAP).

PHY – Physical-layer protocol. One of the two sublayers of the FDDI physical layer. See also PMD. In ATM, the physical layer that provides cell transmission over a physical medium that connects two ATM devices.

PI – Primary In. One of the ports associated with a dual attached device in an FDDI network. See also FDDI.

PICMG – PCI Industrial Computer Manufacturers Group. An industrial consortium established to extend the PCI specification for use in industrial computing applications.

PICS – Platform for Internet Content Selection. A technology that enables users to filter the content they receive over the Internet. In particular, PICS is intended for the protection of children, preventing unguided Internet surfing (i.e. guarding against violent, indecent or inappropriate material). The rules that apply to the content filtering are password-protected in PICS rules files (see PCF). In addition to filtering out undesirable material, PICS can be used to screen sites according to whether they contain material of interest. Several rating systems, emphasizing different sets of criteria, are in use. Additional information can be obtained at http://www.w3.org/PICS

PICS – Protocol Implementation Conformance Statement. A statement made by the supplier of an implementation or system, stating which capabilities have been implemented for a given protocol.

PID – Personal Information Device. A common term for portable devices which provide information that is tailored and delivered directly to an individual. Such devices include, for example, Personal Digital Assistants (see PDA), notebooks, etc. In the near future, it is expected that any PID user will have access to the Internet from anywhere at any time.

PIF – Program Information File. A filename extension for files that contain information on how Microsoft Windows should run non-Windows applications.

PIM – Personal Information Manager. An application that usually includes an address book and organizes related information, such as notes, appointments and names, in a useful way.

PIM – Product Information Management. See PDM (Product Data Management).

P

PIM – Protocol-Independent Multicast. A multicast routing architecture that allows the addition of IP multicast routing to existing IP networks. PIM can be operated in two modes: dense mode (almost everyone wants to see the packets) and sparse mode (almost nobody wants to receive multicast datagrams). The PIM dense mode is data-driven and resembles typical multicast routing protocols. Packets are forwarded on all outgoing interfaces until pruning and truncation occur. In dense mode, the receivers are densely populated, and it is assumed that the downstream networks want to receive and will probably use the datagrams that are forwarded to them. The problem with using dense mode is its default-flooding behavior. The PIM sparse mode tries to constrain data distribution, so that a minimal number of routers in the network receive packets, i.e. they are sent only if they are explicitly requested. The problem with using the sparse mode is its reliance on the periodic refreshing of explicit joint messages and its need for a meeting point.

PIN – Personal Identification Number. A unique password code assigned to the authorized user, typically four digits long. It can be used through a telephone keypad, automatic teller machine or EFTPOS terminal, etc.

PINE – Program for Internet News and E-mail. A tool for reading, sending and managing electronic messages, developed at the University of Washington. It runs under UNIX and MS-DOS. It uses several Internet protocols such as SMTP, MIME, IMAP and NNTP. The message editor is very simple, easy to use, and offers justification, cut and paste, and a spellchecker as well. It can be downloaded via ftp://ftp.cac.washington.edu/mail/pine.tar.Z

ping – packet internet grouper. A program used to test the reachability of destinations by sending them an ICMP echo request and waiting for a reply. The term is used as a verb: "Ping host X to see if it is up!". The name actually comes from submarine active sonar technology, where a sound signal called a "ping" is broadcast, and surrounding objects are revealed by their reflections of the sound. Also the name of the UNIX utility that implements the ping protocol. See also Internet Control Message Protocol (ICMP).

PIR – Protocol-Independent Routing. A packet routing strategy that does not depend on the packet format and protocol being used.

PIU – Path Information Unit. An IBM SNA packet consisting of a transmission header and a basic information unit (see BIU). See also SNA.

pixel – picture element. The smallest addressable unit of information in raster graphics that can be displayed on the screen or printed by any raster printer. Pixel color can be coded with one or more bits, the bitmap ranging from a single black and white picture to a pixel map representing a full color image. A former short name for the term was "pel". Compare with voxel.

PIXIT – Protocol Implementation Extra Information for Testing. A statement made by the supplier of an Implementation Under Test (see IUT) which contains information about the IUT and its testing environment.

PJT – Project file. A filename extension for a file that contains a Visual FoxPro project (see Fig. P-7). Even if the user assigns another name to the project, the Visual FoxPro manager creates PJT and PJX files. See also PJX.

PJX – Project any (X) file. A filename extension for a file that contains a Visual FoxPro project (see Fig. P-7). Even if the user assigns another name to the project, the Visual FoxPro manager creates PJT and PJX files. See also PJT.

PKC – Public Key Cryptography. An international workshop focusing on all aspects (theoretical and practical) of public key cryptography. Some of the major topics include cryptoanalysis, encryption schemes and data formats, standards, the public key infrastructure, secure electronic commerce, etc.

PKI – Public Key Infrastructure. An Internet standard (RFC2150) that describes the management of the public key, and particular message formats for secure Internet messaging. See also PKIX.

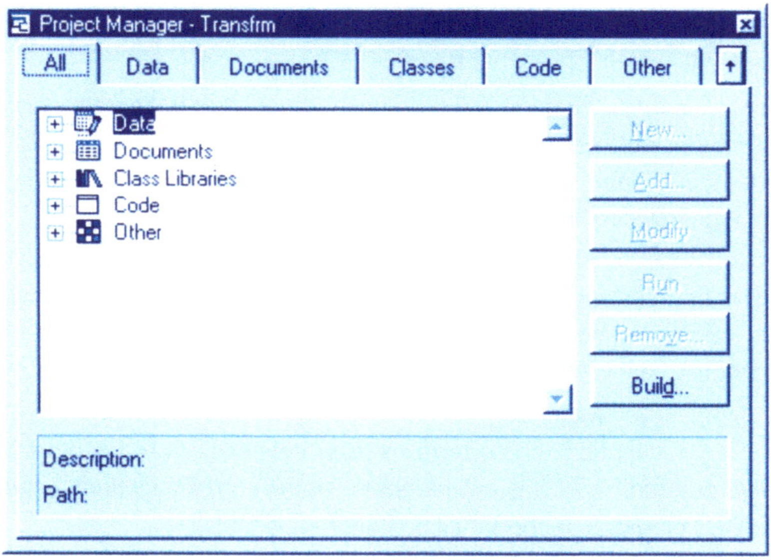

Fig. P-7. An example of a Visual FoxPro project file

PKIX – Public Key Infrastructure for X.509. The working group established in the fall of 1995 in order to develop Internet standards capable of supporting an X.509-based Public Key Infrastructure (see PKI).

PL – Procedural Language. A programming language in which the basic programming element is the procedure (a named sequence of statements, such as routines, subroutines or functions). The most popular representative languages are C, Pascal, BASIC, FORTRAN, COBOL and Ada. Compare with NPL.

PLCP – Physical-Layer Convergence Procedure. A function used in the DQDB architecture that maps higher-level packets into a uniform format for transmission in a particular configuration. See also DQDB.

PL/I – Programming Language I. A programming language developed by IBM in the mid-1960s. The primary motivation in developing PL/I was to produce a language that could satisfy as many application areas as possible, including scientific, commercial and systems programming areas. Thus, it brought together the key features of FORTRAN, ALGOL and COBOL. Because of this background, it is a very complex language that has never achieved widespread usage.

PLL – Phase-Lock Loop. A mechanism used to transfer timing information within a datastream. In order to derive this information, the receiving end locks its local clock.

PLP – Packet-Level Procedure. A full-duplex protocol that defines the means of packet transfer between an X.25 DTE and an X.25 DCE (see Data Terminal Equipment, DTE, and Data Circuit Equipment, DCE). It supports data-packet sequencing, flow control, error detection, and recovery.

PLS – Physical-Layer Signaling. The topmost component of the physical layer, serving as an interface between the MAC sublayer of the data-link layer and physical media. It also performs character encoding, transmission, reception and decoding, as well as optional isolation functions. See also OSI and MAC.

PLS – Primary Link Station. The term used in network environments that use the SDLC protocol. A PLS is a node that initiates communications either with another PLS or with a secondary link station (see SLS).

PLT – Pakistan Lahore Time. Time zone. UTC + 5.00 hours. See TZ.

PM – Physical Medium. A common term for several physical interfaces to an ATM element.

PM – Presentation Manager. The graphical user interface for OS/2.

PM – Preventive Maintenance. The care and servicing by personnel for the purpose of maintaining equipment and facilities in satisfactory operating condition, providing for systematic inspection, detection and correction of incipient failures, either before they occur or before they develop into major malfunctions.

PMA – Physical Medium Attachment. A device used to physically attach a node device to a network cable. The term is heavily used in LAN technology, and an Ethernet transceiver is a good example.

PMC – PCI Mezzanine Card. A family of low-profile mezzanine cards (IEEE 1386.1) for the VME bus, Futurebus, desktop computers and other computer systems with logical and electrical layers based on the PCI specification.

PMD – Physical-Medium-Dependent. The ATM sublayer that allows us to get the bits on and off the "wire" in order to support a uniform interface between ATM and the physical medium in both directions. Also, the FDDI sublayer that defines the characteristics of physical media, such as power levels, optical components, connectors, etc. See also PHY.

PMF – Parameter Management Frame. A type of Station Management frame (see SMT) used to read or write SMT Management Information Base objects (see MIB) used for remote management of the station.

PMMU – Paged Memory Management Unit. A hardware unit that performs memory access and management, used by different applications or by a virtual-memory operating system.

PMP – Point-to-Multipoint. The circuitry for distributing data such that a single end-point (usually a switch) acts as a root node to which numerous leaf nodes are connected. The root node may distribute information over a PMP and transmit copies to each of the leaf nodes. Likewise, leaf nodes can send information back to the root node, but they cannot relay information directly to other leaf nodes.

PMS – Pantone Matching System. A standard system of ink color specification. About 500 colors are specified.

PMS – Project Management and Scheduling. An international workshop focusing on the area of project management and scheduling. Some of the major topics include project management (network modeling, single and multi-project scheduling, resource management, uncertainty issues) and machine scheduling (single and parallel scheduling, scheduling of transportation robots, etc.).

PMTU – Path Maximum Transfer Unit. The largest possible unit of data that can be sent to given physical media located in the different networks in the path between the sending and the receiving ends. PMTU is determined by the smallest MTU anywhere in the path.

PNG – Portable Network Graphics. A file format (RFC2083) designed for online viewing applications, such as for viewing websites. It supports lossless, portable and compressed raster images. Also, the filename extension for related files. PNG can be obtained from http://www.w3.org/Graphics/PNG

PNI – Permit Next Increase. An Available Bit Rate (see ABR) service parameter. It is a one-bit flag controlling increases in the Actual Cell Rate (see ACR).

PNM – Physical Network Management. A common name for the maintenance and management of the physical infrastructure of a network.

PNNI – Private Network-to-Network Interface. A routing information protocol that allows different vendors' ATM switches to be integrated into the same network. PNNI automatically and dynamically distributes routing information, enabling any switch to determine a path to any other switch. See also ATM.

PNP – Plug and Play. See Plug and Play (P&P).

PO – Primary Out. One of the ports associated with a dual attached device in an FDDI network.

PODA – Piloting of Office Document Architecture. A European Strategic Programme for Research and Development in Information Technology (see ESPRIT) project.

PODC – Principles of Distributed Computing. The ACM SIGACT symposium focusing on all aspects of distributed computing.

POE – PowerOpen Environment. A standard that covers the Application Programming Interface (see API) and Application Binary Interface (see ABI) specifications based on the PowerPC architecture. It is compliant with other standards such as IEEE POSIX and X/Open XPG4. POE is hardware independent and can be applied to a range of systems, from laptop computers to supercomputers. Also, it provides network support, and an X Window System extension. See also POSIX and XPG.

POF – Plastic Optical Fiber. A fiber optics cable made from plastic rather than glass or silica. Plastic fiber has greater attenuation and dispersion than glass fiber, but the installation costs can be lower. The ATM Forum is working on specifications defining 50- and 155-Mbps operation over POF. See also ATM (Asynchronous Transfer Mode).

POFOD – Probability Of Failure On Demand. In a software reliability metric, the probability that the software will fail when a service request is issued.

POP – Point Of Presence. A site where a collection of telecommunications equipment exists, usually digital leased lines and multiprotocol routers.

POP3 – Post Office Protocol version 3. A simple protocol (RFC1225) used for fetching e-mail from a remote mailbox and storing it on the POP3 user's local machine, to be read or deleted later. It also includes login and logout procedures, using the user name and password to allow access to a private mailbox on a remote server. POP is useful for poorly connected mobile or home computers, which require the POP server, a "post office", to hold their mail until they can retrieve it. Compare with IMAP.

POPL – Principles of Programming Languages. The annual ACM symposium sponsored by the SIGPLAN and SIGACT groups which addresses fundamental principles in the design, definition, analysis and implementation of programming languages, systems and interfaces.

POS – Persistent Object Systems. An international workshop focusing on the design, implementation and use of persistent object systems. The proceedings are published by Springer-Verlag (see LNCS).

POS – Point Of Sale. Generally, the places in a store at which goods are paid for. From the computing point of view, this is usually some kind of electronic cash register equipped with a barcode reader, optionally with the EFTPOS terminal, etc.

POSIX – Portable Operating System Interface for UNIX. A set of IEEE (1003.0–1003.11) and ISO (9945-x) standards which defines the necessary functions and interfaces between application programs and the operating system, usually UNIX, in order to achieve full application portability. The required functions and standards are:

1. The POSIX Guide Project describes interoperability among POSIX standards, as well as the relationships with the standards of other bodies.
2. The System Services Interface defines standard interfaces for the most basic levels of the UNIX operating system.
3. The shell, tools and user utilities define the standard programming interface to the common UNIX tools.
4. The testing and verification standards define the conformance verification for IEEE1003.1.
5. Real-time extensions relating to real-time applications interfaces with IEEE1003.1.
6. The Ada language binding standard defines the POSIX standards relating to the Ada programming language.
7. The security extensions related to POSIX compliance with the US DoD Orange book (see TCSEC) are defined.
8. The system administration defines a standard set of administration tools.
9. The networking extensions include all the networking tools and functions, whether they are based on the OSI or TCP/IP protocol suites.
10. The FORTRAN language binding standard defines the POSIX standard in terms of the standard FORTRAN language.
11. The supercomputing functions related to the operating system requirements of large machines are defined.

P

12. The transaction processing standard addresses the issues of fast multiple transaction processing.

POSIX is not only suitable for the UNIX environment. It was created in a way that allows it to be implemented by other operating systems to accomplish the same goal, portability of application code among different operating systems and hardware platforms. See also PSI.

POST – Power-On Self-Test. A set of routines stored in a system's RAM that tests various system components immediately after power-on. If errors have occurred in the RAM, disk drives or keyboard, the POST routine warns the user with an appropriate message (usually a beep and a screen message indicating the relevant I/O address) to the standard output or standard error device. If there are no errors, the POST passes control to the bootstrap loader.

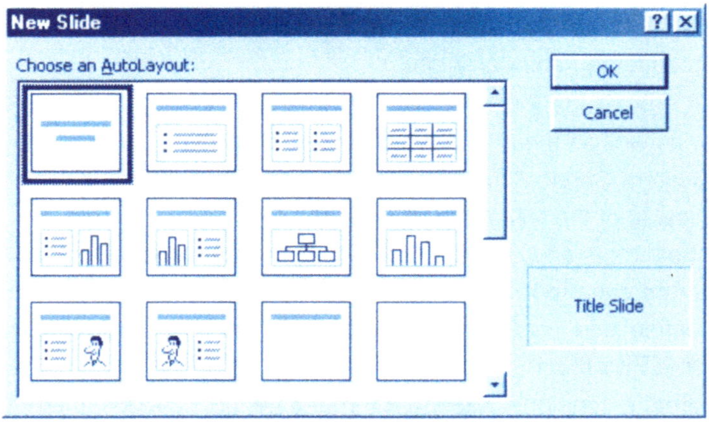

Fig. P-8. An example of a PowerPoint POT file

POT – PowerPoint Template. A filename extension for a file that contains a Microsoft PowerPoint template (see Fig. P-8).

POTS – Plain Old Telephone System. A common name for the conventional telephone services.

POWER – Performance Optimization With Enhanced RISC. The IBM name for the RISC architecture developed for the PowerPC platform (see PPC).

P&P – Plug and Play. A common attribute for hardware and software components that can be immediately used (played) just after installation (plug-in) without additional configuration. Also known as PNP.

PPA – PowerPoint Add-in. A filename extension for a file that contains Microsoft PowerPoint additions.

PPAM – Parallel Processing and Applied Mathematics. An international conference covering a broad variety of subject areas within parallel and distributed processing, including theory and applications. Topics include models of parallel and distributed computation, parallel and distributed architectures and algorithms, parallelization and mapping techniques, cluster computing and grids, numerical methods, optimization methods, etc. The proceedings are published by Springer-Verlag (see LNCS).

PPC – Pay Per Click. One of the bill methods used to charge Internet users.

PPC – PowerPC. A superscalar RISC-based microprocessor architecture developed in 1992 by IBM, Apple and Motorola. It has a 64-bit data bus and a 32-bit address bus. PowerPC is a registered trademark of IBM. There are several models on the market. PowerPC 601 is a 64-bit processor with 2.8 million transistors and a 32-KB on-chip cache. Its successors are the models 603, 604 and 620. See also POE, POWER and PPCO. You can find more information at http://fnctsrv0.chips.ibm.com/products/ppc/index.html

PPCO – PowerPC Organization. The IBM standard for ensuring compatibility among PowerPC-based systems built by different companies.

PPD – PostScript Printer Description. A filename extension for a file that contains information about a particular printer to be used for printing PostScript documents.

PPDP – Principles and Practice of Declarative Programming. An international ACM SIGPLAN conference focusing on declarative methods in programming and on the design, implementation and application of programming languages that support such methods. The proceedings are published by Springer-Verlag (see LNCS).

ppm – pages per minute. A rating of output capacity, associated particularly with laser printers. It measures the number of printed pages that a printer can produce in 1 min. For this rating, laser printer vendors' specifications assume that pages to be printed do not contain graphics or other special elements.

PPM – Portable Pixel Map. A color image file format that contains the width, height, maximum color component value, and (width×height) of pixels of a color map. All parts are separated by a blank space and the numbers are in a decimal ASCII representation.

PPM – Pulse Position Modulation. An encoding signal technique that involves varying the position of pulses. During modulation, the pulse positions are changed to reflect the information being encoded. Sometimes called pulse width modulation or pulse length modulation. Compare with PAM, PCM and PDM.

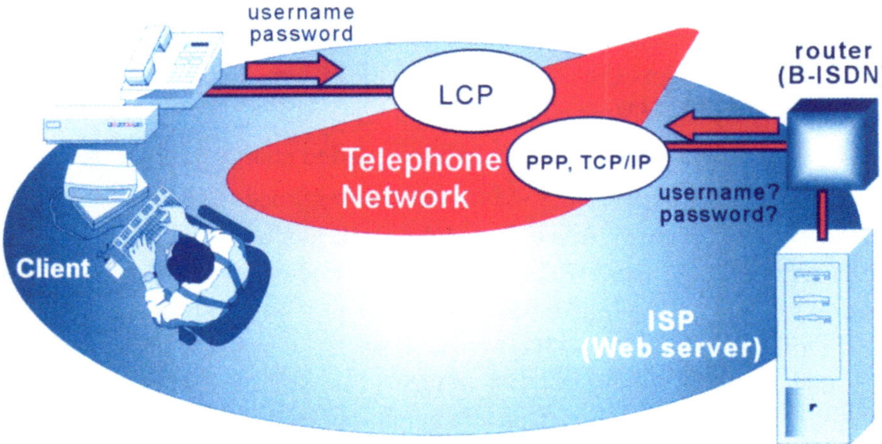

Fig. P-9. PPP functionality in brief

PPP – Point-to-Point Protocol. The Internet multiprotocol framing mechanism defined in RFC1661 (made obsolete by RFC2153) that provides a suitable solution for dial-up lines as well as for leased router-to-router lines (see Fig. P-9). PPP handles error detection, supports multiple protocols, allows IP addresses to be negotiated at connection time, permits authentication, etc. In addition to a framing method, PPP provides a link control protocol (see LCP) for bringing lines up, testing them, negotiating options, and bringing them down, and a set of network control protocols (see NCP) that provides network-layer independence. All PPP frames begin and end with the standard HDLC flag (01111110). After the start flag, the next byte represents the address field and is always set to the binary value 11111111 to indicate that all stations are to accept the frame. It is followed by the control field (defined in RFC1663), the protocol field which is used to tell what kind of packet it is (IP, IPX, LCP, NCP or XNS, among others), the payload field, and the checksum field (2-bytes or 4-bytes long).

PPQN – Pulses Per Quarter Note. A time format used in MIDI sequencers. See also MIDI.

PPS – Peripheral Power Supply. An auxiliary source of electricity used by a computer or a device as a backup in case of a power failure. See also UPS (Uninterruptible Power Supply).

PPS – PowerPoint Slide Show. A filename extension for a file that contains a Microsoft PowerPoint slide show.

Ppsh – Parallel port shell. A shell utility that allows downloads of binary images from the development workstation to the target machine.

PPT – PowerPoint. A filename extension for files created by Microsoft PowerPoint presentation software.

PRAM – Parameter Random-Access Memory. A small portion of Random-Access Memory (see RAM) used on Macintosh computers to store information about the way the system is configured. PRAM is pronounced "pee-ram".

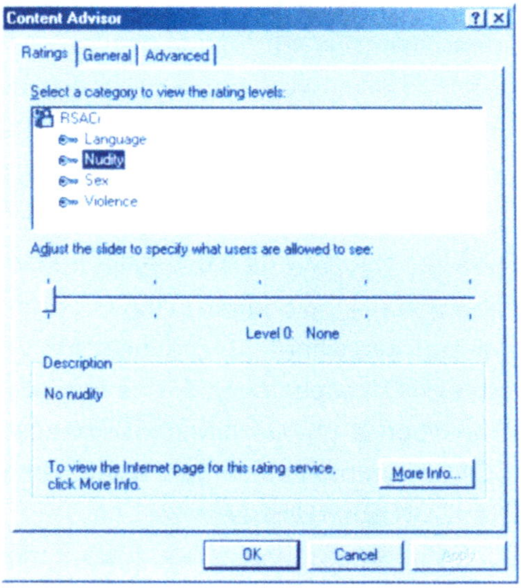

Fig. P-10. An example of a user interface used to fill rules into a PRF

PRD – Procedure Division. A filename extension related to files generated by AcuBench (see COBOL) that contain the COBOL "Procedure Division" paragraphs–sentences that are executed in the normal course of the COBOL program.

PRDC – Pacific Rim Dependable Computing. An international IEEE symposium focusing on research into dependable computing with particular emphasis on systems and software.

P

PREMO – Presentation Environment for Multimedia Objects. A new standard under development by ISO/IEC JTC1 SC24 that addresses the creation of, presentation of, and interaction with all forms of information using single or multiple media. The aim of PREMO is to provide a general framework, a reference model, for the presentation of multimedia data. PREMO complements the work of other emerging ISO standards on Multimedia, such as MHEG, HyperODA and HyTime. Typically, these standards deal primarily with aspects of the interchange of multimedia information. Also, an important aspect of PREMO is the use of object-oriented techniques using specifications developed elsewhere, such as CORBA, etc. Additional information can be found via the anonymous ftp://ftp.gmd.de/documents/iso/premo or at ftp://ftp.cwi.nl/pub/premo

PRF – PICS Rules File. A filename extension for a file that contains rules used to determine whether a site can be viewed (see Fig. P-10). See also Platform for Internet Content Selection (PICS).

PRF – Pseudo-Random Function. In cryptography, a function that follows a key, label and seed as input, and then produces an output of arbitrary length.

PRG – Program file. A filename extension for a file that contains Visual FoxPro program code.

PRI – Primary Rate Interface. A type of ISDN service that consists of a single 64-Kbps D channel plus 23 (T1), as applied in the US and Japan, or 30 (E1), as applied in Europe and elsewhere, B channels for voice or data. Also known as 23B+D and 30B+D, respectively. PRI is typically used for connections such as those between a private branch exchange (see PBX) and a central office (see CO), or an interexchange carrier (see IXC). Compare to BRI. See also B-ISDN, ISDN and N-ISDN.

PRIIA – Pacific Rim Intelligent Information Agents. An international workshop started in the year 2000 (Melbourne, Australia) focusing on intelligent software assistants on the Web and the Internet. Some of the major topics include declarative languages and models for intelligent information agents, methodologies, tools and techniques for intelligent information agents, multiagent architectures, mobile information agents, ontologies for information agents, adaptive information agents, intelligent personal information managers, etc.

PRIMA – Pacific Rim International Workshop on Multi-Agent Systems. An international workshop serving as a forum for the exchange of the latest technical advances in autonomous agents and multiagent systems. Some of the major topics include multiagent systems and their applications, agent architectures, agent programming languages, frameworks and toolkits, appropriate standards, conflict resolution and negotiation, metamodeling, metareasoning, evaluation of multiagent systems, multiagent programming and languages, etc. The proceedings are published by Springer-Verlag.

PRISM – Parallel Reduced-Instruction-Set Multiprocessing. HP/Apollo's term for its approach to the RISC architecture of the Domain computer. See also RISC.

PRMD – Private Management Domain. A Message Handling System (see MHS) operated by a private organization, such as a company or a university campus, etc.

PRN – Print file. A filename extension for a file that contains output data ready to be printed to the associated devices (local or remote printers, files, etc.).

PROLOG – Programming in Logic. A programming language developed in the early 1970s by Philippe Roussel at the University of Marseilles. Since then, many implementations have been produced and it has become an essential language in the field of artificial intelligence, although it has also been used in other application areas. It is one of the most famous nonprocedural languages available today. It can be considered as a language at a very much higher level than FORTRAN or ALGOL and their relatives. Programming in PROLOG involves the specification of a set of facts and rules to form a collection of knowledge on a subject. PROLOG offers simple and rapid solutions for a wide variety of problems, and it is easy to write accurate and readable programs.

PROM – Programmable Read-Only Memory. A kind of read-only memory (pronounced "prom") that allows data to be written using a device called a PROM programmer (also known as a PROM blaster or a PROM blower). There are a number of types, including OTPROMs (One-Time-Programmable, the process cannot be reversed), EPROMs (Erasable PROMs), UVEPROMs (Ultra-Violet-Erasable, they have an erasing window to allow UV light to erase the memory, and they can then be reprogrammed) etc. UVEPROMs are usually used during the prototype stage of design, and OTPROMs are usually used in the mass-production stage.

PRT – Puerto Rico and US Virgin Islands Time. Time zone. UTC – 4.00 hours. See TZ.

PS – PostScript. The best-known page description language. It was developed by Adobe Systems Inc. A program in PostScript gives a device-independent document description that can be displayed either on a display screen or a printer. PostScript uses scalable outline fonts that allow the creation of fonts of any size. Many modern printers support PostScript interpretation directly. Also, a filename extension for a file that contains a PostScript document. A popular utility for reading PS files is Ghostview. See also Page Description Language (PDL) and psz.

PS – Power Supply. An electrical device that transforms standard wall-outlet electricity (220 V AC in Europe, or 110 V AC in the US) into the lower voltages required by computer systems (e.g. 5–12 V DC). See also AC, DC and UPS.

ps – print status. UNIX command used to print the status information for processes.

PSAP – Presentation Service Access Point. The point at which the OSI presentation-layer service is made available to an application-layer entity (see OSI and SAP).

PSD – Photoshop Drawing. A filename extension for files that contain drawings made using the Adobe Photoshop package.

PSDN – Packet-Switching Data Network. A data network offering packet-switching (i.e. connectionless) data services. See also CL, PDN and PSN.

PSE – Packet-Switching Exchange. A term generally used to refer to a switch in an X.25 packet-switching network.

PSI – Perspectives on System Informatics. A forum for the presentation and in-depth discussion of advanced research directions in computer science. Topics include semantic-based program processing, automated software engineering, databases, knowledge-based systems, knowledge engineering, web publishing, electronic commerce, digital libraries, etc. The proceedings are published by Springer-Verlag.

PSI – Portability, Scalability, Interoperability. These common attributes deal with three crucial open-systems characteristics. Portability assumes application software portability among different computers without requiring source code changing. Scalability allows the application of the other two attributes to different levels of computers, from small systems to bigger ones, and vice versa, assuming the smallest one has the power to run a particular application. Finally, interoperability is the key attribute, and it involves different applications exchanging data, either among different hardware platforms or different operating systems, regardless of physical distance. Figure P-11 shows what we mean by PSI with open systems. Freedom of choice is an advantage that open systems offer computer users. Vendors can cooperate, protect their investments, and bring high-quality products to users at the same time, and application programmers can finally concentrate on the application problems instead of losing time adapting their applications for target machines.

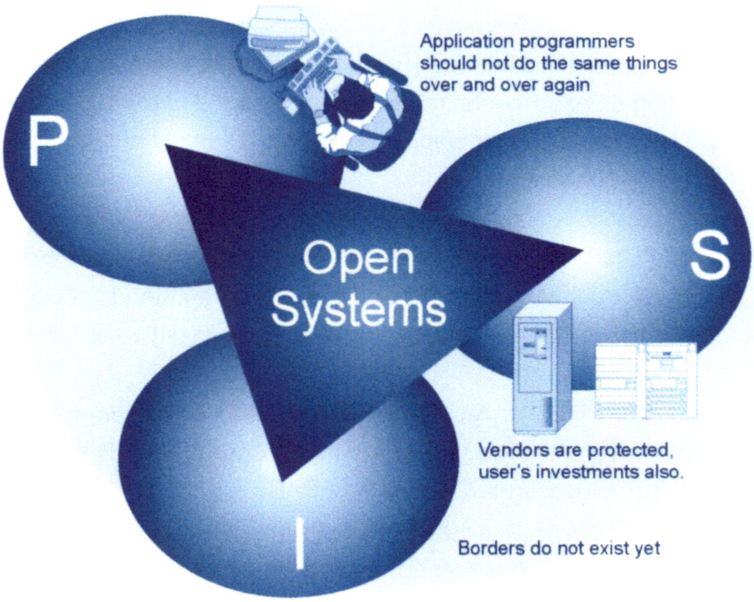

Fig. P-11. The PSI of Open Systems

PSK – Phase-Shift Keying. A modulation technique used for conversion of binary data into an analog signal comprising a single sinusoidal signal with a phase that varies according to the data being transmitted.

PSN – Packet-Switching Node. A dedicated computer, the purpose of which is to accept, route and forward packets in a packet-switching network.

PSN – Public Switched Network. A synonym for Public Switched Telephone Network (see PSTN).

PSP – Personal Software Process. Methods used to improve the quality of work of individual software engineers.

PSP – Photoshop file. A file name extension for an Adobe Photoshop file.

PSPDN – Packet-Switched Public Data Network. A public data network offering packet-switching data services.

PSRAM – Pseudo-Static Random-Access Memory. A type of Dynamic Random-Access Memory (see DRAM) with a built-in address multiplexer and refresh controller.

PST – Pacific Standard Time. Time zone. UTC – 8.00 hours. See TZ.

PST – Personal Message Store. A filename extension for a file that contains an object created by the user with a MAPI message store. See also MAPI.

PSTN – Public Switched Telephone Network. For years this technology has been aimed at transmitting human voice in a recognizable form. Nowadays, with the emerging developments in fiber technologies, PSTN has become an integral part of computer communications, while still maintaining its base as the public telephone system.

psz – PostScript zipped. A filename extension used for files containing zipped PostScript data. The data compression ratio achieved is approximately 4:1.

PT – Payload Type. A 3-bit field in the ATM cell header used to distinguish cells carrying management information from cells carrying user information. See also PTI.

PTF – Program Temporary Fix. An IBM term applied to a program sent to customers to temporarily solve the problem with a program already in use, while the program is further debugged. See also APAR.

PTI – Payload Type Indicator. An attribute of a Payload Type field (see PT) used to distinguish the various management cells and user cells.

PTI – Portable Tool Interface. See PCTE.

PTM – Pulse Time Modulation. A digital modulation technique that uses a time-dependent feature of a pulse (width, duration, etc.) to encode an analog signal into digital form.

PTMPT – Point-to-Multipoint. The main source for many destination connections.

PTS – Presentation Time Stamp. A timestamp that is inserted by the MPEG-2 encoder into the Packetized Elementary Stream (see PES) to allow the decoder to synchronize different elementary streams. See also MPEG.

PTSE – PNNI Topology State Element. A collection of PNNI information that is distributed among all logical nodes within a peer group (see PG). See also PNNI and PTSP.

PTSP – PNNI Topology State Packet. A type of Private Network-to-Network Interface (see PNNI) packet that is used for distributing PTSEs among logical nodes within a peer group. See also PG.

PTT – Postal, Telegraph and Telephone. A common name for many national providers of postal, telegraph and telephone services.

PU – Physical Unit. In IBM SNA terminology, a physical unit used to control the attached links and resources (logical units) of a node. See also SNA and Logical Unit (LU).

PUMA – Performance-oriented User-managed Messaging Architecture. A joint project between the Parallel Computing Sciences Department at Sandia National Laboratories and the Computer Science Department at the University of New Mexico. In short, PUMA is an operating system for massively parallel systems based on a message-passing kernel.

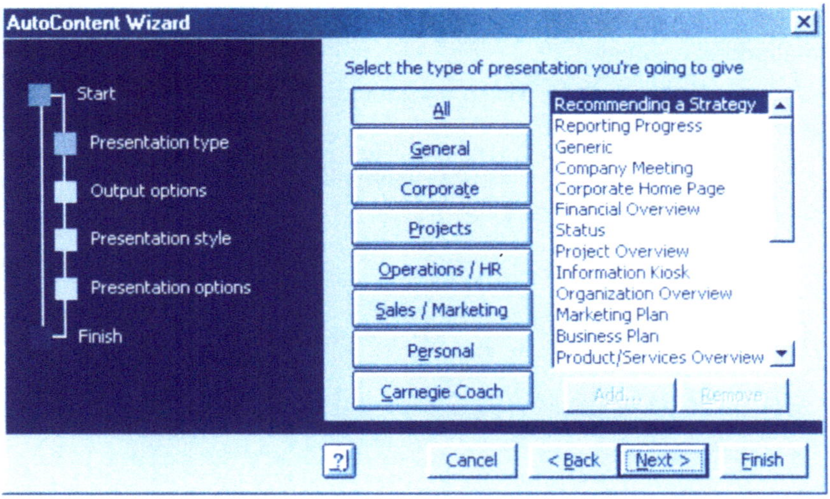

Fig. P-12. Microsoft PowerPoint wizard

PURL – Persistent Uniform Resource Locator. A service provided by OCLC that allows Internet users to avoid the 404 error: Document Not Found. This error usually appears after a familiar URL changes due to hardware reconfiguration, file system reconfiguration, organizational changes, and so on. Functionally, a PURL is a URL. However, instead of pointing directly to the location of an Internet resource, a PURL points to an intermediate resolution service. The PURL resolution service associates the PURL with the actual URL and returns that URL to the client. The client can then complete the URL transaction in the normal fashion. The assignment of PURLs is an intermediate step in the process whereby Uniform Resource Names (see

URN) are becoming an integral part of the Internet information architecture. The OCLC PURL service is available at http://purl.oclc.org. In addition, OCLC freely distributes its PURL source code, to aid in rapid wide distribution of this enabling technology. See 404.

PVC – Permanent Virtual Circuit. A virtual link with fixed end-points that are defined by the network manager in advance, so it is analogous to a leased line. A single virtual path may support multiple PVCs. See also Virtual Path (VP).

PVM – Parallel Virtual Machine. A portable software package that permits a heterogeneous collection of networked UNIX and/or NT computers to be used as a single large parallel computer. In such a way, individual PVM users can solve problems that overcome their own local hardware limitations at minimal additional cost.

pwd – print working directory. UNIX command used to print the name of the working directory.

PWZ – PowerPoint Wizard. A filename extension for a file that contains a Microsoft PowerPoint wizard (see Fig. P-12).

Q

QA – Quality Assurance. A widely used acronym related to those activities which should maximize the probability that a product (hardware and/or software) and its components will be manufactured according to the design specifications. Quality assurance is now closely related to the ISO9000 standards. ISO9000 is a set of standards that can be applied to a range of organizations from manufacturing through service industries. The most general standard is ISO9001, which applies to organizations which design, develop and maintain products. It describes various aspects of the QA process and defines which standards and procedures should exist within an organization. QA procedures in an organization should be documented in a quality manual that defines the quality process. The relationship between ISO9000, the quality manual and individual project quality plans is shown in Fig. Q-1.

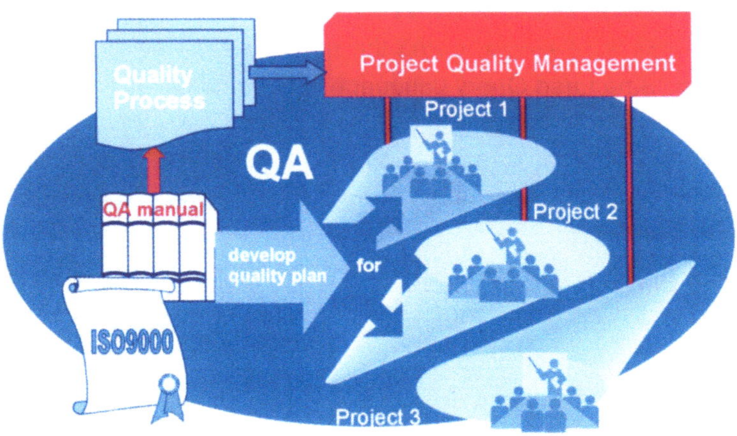

Fig. Q-1. ISO9000 and quality assurance

Quality assurance is usually managed by an independent team, to make sure that the people responsible for quality management have no responsibility for the project budget, schedule, etc. Many years ago, the author had the opportunity to transfer technical documentation from NCR, USA, to the UNIS factory in Mostar, Bosnia and Herzegovina. The QA documentation cover was marked with a devil chart to show that everyone else in the factory should be afraid of NCR QA team! See also SQA.

Q

QAM – Quadrature Amplitude Modulation. An encoding technique used by advanced modems that allows rates of 2400 bps or more. QAM works by amplitude modulation and phase modulation combining in order to create a so-called constellation pattern of amplitude and phase, i.e. a disposition of signal points, each representing one unique combination of bits.

QAM – Queued Access Method. A programming technique designed to provide an optimal information interchange between applications and input/output devices.

QAS – Quality Assurance Services. A certification body in the Asia–Pacific region (http://www.qas.com.au).

QBE – Query-By-Example. A simple-to-use query language implemented on several relational database management systems (see DBMS and RDBMS). Unlike most query and programming languages, QBE has a two-dimensional syntax. Queries look like tables. QBE queries are expressed "by example". Instead of requesting a procedure for obtaining the desired answer, the user gives an example of what is desired. The system generalizes this example to compute the answer to the query. From the user point of view, construction of the queries is very simple, giving the user a clear view of the database. Compare with Structured Query Language (SQL) and QUEL.

QBone – Q Backbone. Part of the Internet2 project (see NGI) with the goal of providing an interdomain testbed, where the engineering, behavior and policy consequences of new IP services can be explored. See also I2-DSI, QMA, QPS and SLS.

QD – Queuing Delay. In ATM networks, the delay imposed on a buffered ATM cell because the next network function or element is unavailable and cannot receive that cell.

QFC – Quantum Flow Control. A flow-control scheme for handling bursty applications. QFC uses ATM's available bit rate (see ABR) service, which allows instantaneous access to the unused bandwidth with very low cell loss. QFC uses a credit-based scheme, in which the quantity of cells allowed is determined by the space available in each receiver's buffers. Since credit-based schemes rely on the state of each receiver's buffers, they are best used on a hop-by-hop basis. For more information see http://www.qfc.org

QIC – Quarter-Inch Cartridge. A set of magnetic tapes and tape drives for data storage. Pronounced "kwik". More information can be obtained at http://www.qic.org

QLLC – Qualified Logical Link Control. An IBM data-link control protocol that allows SNA systems to operate over X.25 packet-switched networks.

QLT – Quality Logic Test. A common term for a test procedure performed by firmware on itself to check the quality of the integrated logic in the device.

QMA – QBone Measurement Architecture. A set of Quality of Service (see QoS) measurement requirements integrated into the QBone architecture (see QBone) in order to verify the service goals of the QBone Premium Services (see QPS).

QMF – Query Management Facility. A query-and-report-writing product developed by IBM that gives the user access to both the SQL and QBE query languages. It is designed to provide interactive relational database facilities for users with little or no data processing experience and to increase the productivity of data-processing professionals. An outstanding strength of QMF is that it offers its users a choice of two different means of entering queries: a command interface via SQL, or a table-driven interface via QBE. It is not suitable for general applications development. See also Structured Query Language (SQL) and Query-by-Example (QBE).

QofIS – Quality of Future Internet Services. An international workshop started in 2000 aimed at presenting and discussing the design and implementation techniques for Quality of Service (see QoS) engineering for Internet services. The proceedings are published by Springer-Verlag (see LNCS).

QoS – Quality of Service. A modern acronym related to ATM networks, and to the network and transport layer generally. It defines how to appropriately negotiate virtual circuits established by the transport layer and the network layer in order to arrange a successful communication acceptable to both sides. It takes a form similar to a contract, noting the traffic to be offered, the common service to be used, and the compliance requirements. To make this possible, the ATM standard defines a number of QoS parameters and their associated values as common terms to be negotiated. The mechanism for using and enforcing the QoS parameters is based on a specific algorithm (see GCRA, Generic Cell Rate Algorithm). There are five broad categories of quality-of-service classes. Class 1 specifies performance requirements and indicates that an ATM's quality of service should be comparable with the service offered by standard digital connections. Class 2 specifies the necessary service levels for packetized video and voice. Class 3 defines the requirements for interoperability with other connection-oriented protocols, particularly frame relay. Class 4 specifies the interoperability requirements for connectionless protocols, including IP, IPX and SMDS. Class 5 is effectively a "best-effort" attempt at delivery, and it is intended for applications that do not require a particular class of service. See also CDV (Cell Delay Variation), CDVT (Cell Delay Variation Tolerance), CER (Cell Error Rate), CLR (Cell Loss Ratio), CMR (Cell Misinsertion Rate), CTD (Cell Transfer Delay), MCR (Minimum Cell Rate), PCR (Peak Cell Rate), SCR (Sustained Cell Rate) and SECBR (Severely Errored Cell Block Ratio).

QPR – Query Program. A filename extension for a file that contains a Visual FoxPro-generated query program.

QPS – QBone Premium Service. Part of the QBone project that ensures transmission across QBone. That means that there should be almost no packet loss, low latency, low jitter, etc. See also QBone.

QPSK – Quadrature-Phase Shift Keying. A type of modulation method similar to Quadrature Amplitude Modulation (see QAM).

QPX – Query Program. A filename extension for a file that contains a Visual FoxPro-compiled query program.

QRY – Query file. A filename extension for a file that contains a Microsoft query.

qt – Quick Time. A filename extension for a file that contains a Quick Time Movie binary program. Quick Time Movie is the program developed by Apple that allows users to watch movies.

QTM – Quick Time Movie. A filename extension for a file that contains Apple Quick Time Movie motion pictures.

quadbit – Quadrate Bit. One of 16 possible 4-bit combinations used in some communications signals. Also known as a nibble.

QUEL – Query Language. A query language developed at the University of California, Berkeley. It allows the Ingres relational database management system to run under the UNIX operating environment. The language can be used either in a standalone manner, by typing commands to the QUEL processor, or embedded in the C programming language.

QUT – Queensland University of Technology. One of Australia's largest universities (http://www.qut.edu.au) located in Brisbane.

QWERTY – A keyboard layout (pronounced "kwer-tee"), named after the six leftmost characters in the top row of alphabetic characters on most keyboards. Compare with AZERTY.

R

R – Repeater. A device that operates at the physical layer of communications, used to regenerate and amplify signals in order to extend transmission distance. It is important to note that a repeater only overcomes the electrical restrictions of the media used, but cannot be used to increase the time limitations related to the topology used. It also links multiple segments of an Ethernet network in either a bus or star topology. Fully 802.3-compliant repeaters regenerate and retime the signal of each packet of information and automatically partition and isolate faulty segments when collisions occur on the network. A special kind of repeater is a hub, a wiring concentrator repeater that brings together the connections from multiple network nodes in a star topology. Unlike bridges (see B), routers (see next R) and gateways, which connect different networks at different layers, repeaters operate on the same network.

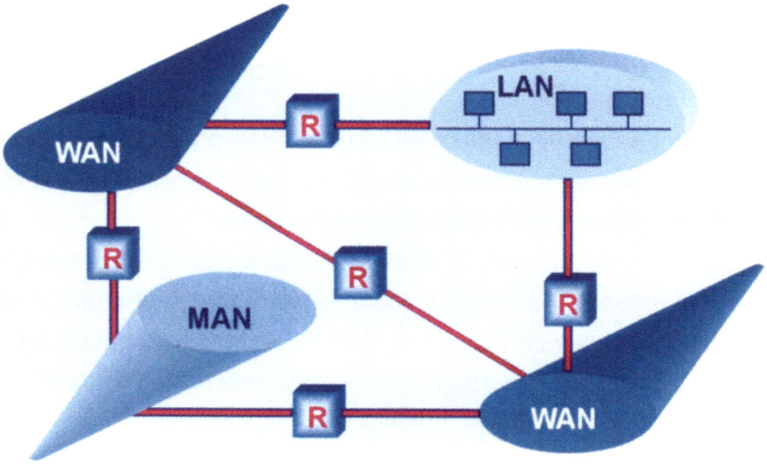

Fig. R-1. Routers in action, connecting different networks

R – Router. A device operating at the network layer that chooses the routing for packets across the network. This is a generic term and applies to such diverse devices as bridges (which pass packets from one physical LAN to another with almost no interpretation) and WAN gateways (which pass packets from one wide-area network to another, doing fragmentation and reassembly

R

as necessary). The role of routers is depicted in Fig. R-1, where routers are used to connect nodes on different networks. In general, routing algorithms are distinguished from each other by the general strategy used (distance vector or link state). Differences between them are explained elsewhere in the book (see DVP, LSA, OSPF, RIP, etc.). In addition, routing algorithms and routers can be compared using several important features, as follows:

- Convergence, i.e. how quickly the algorithm yields a route.
- Robustness, i.e. how the algorithm responds to an incorrect or missing packet. In other words, once a network has been put into operation it may be expected to run for years with no failures visible to end-users. So, one of the important features of any routing algorithm is its ability to reconfigure the network topology and traffic in the case where some router crashes for a while.
- Memory requirements, i.e. how much memory is required to store the necessary routing information.
- Load splitting, i.e. how easily the algorithm can support load splitting.
- Transmission speeds.
- Number of ports supported.
- The kind of networks supported, i.e. are they LAN-only routers or WAN-only routers, or both.
- Internal or external, i.e. are they standalone or built-in, etc.
- Network management, i.e. how many network monitoring and management capabilities are incorporated into a router.

RA – Robotics and Applications. The IASTED international conference focusing on the latest research on robotics, manufacturing and intelligent systems.

RACE – R&D for Advanced Communications in Europe. A major program, begun in 1987, on the development and diversification of the European Union's research and technology base in telecommunications.

RACE – Requirements Acquisition and Controlled Evolution. A "back-to-basics" approach to requirements engineering. The method is being pieced together through a series of intermediate research studies. In essence, the approach has been to establish the requirements for RACE, identify individual techniques that meet those requirements, experiment with the combined use of the techniques, and, finally, assemble the method.

RAD – Rapid Application Development. A common term for any software lifecycle designed to provide faster development and to take maximum advantage of recent software-development tools and techniques. Using the RAD method, the system is programmed and implemented in segments, rather than waiting until the entire project is completed for implementation. James Martin developed RAD.

RAD – Research and Advanced Development. The strategic development program from DEC. It includes several very powerful laboratories, such as:

- Cambridge Research Laboratory – Cambridge, MA, US (visualization, multimedia, information retrieval, speech recognition, distributed systems programming, etc.).
- Network Systems Laboratory – Palo Alto, CA, US (innovative internetworking systems).
- Systems Research Center – Palo Alto, CA, US (hardware, programming languages, user interfaces, networks, etc.).

RADAR – Radio Detecting and Ranging. An electronic instrument used for detection and ranging of distant objects that scatter or reflect radio energy.

RADIUS – Remote Authentication Dial-In User Service. The new protocol (RFC2865, RFC2866) giving the basis for future open standards-based exchange for all types of authentication data (e.g. PAP passwords, CHAP challenges and responses). Using RADIUS, a client can exchange authentication, access control, accounting, and device configuration information with a RADIUS server. The RADIUS server can authenticate the user/device using its database of user IDs and authentication parameters. The keyed-MD5 algorithm is used to provide authentication and integrity for the RADIUS messages and selective confidentiality for authentication parameters they might contain.

RAID – Recent Advances in Intrusion Detection. An annual international workshop focusing on the latest developments in the area of intrusion detection. The proceedings are published by Springer-Verlag (see LNCS).

RAID – Redundant Array of Independent (Inexpensive) Disks. A disk-storage architecture, also known as a drive array, with several disks working together. In the past, RAIDs were composed of small cheap disks, which were viewed as a cost-effective alternative to large expensive disks. Today, RAIDs are used for their higher reliability and higher data-transfer rate, rather than for economic reasons. Hence, the “I” in RAID now stands for independent, instead of inexpensive. The following RAID specifications, RAID levels, exist (see Fig. R-2):

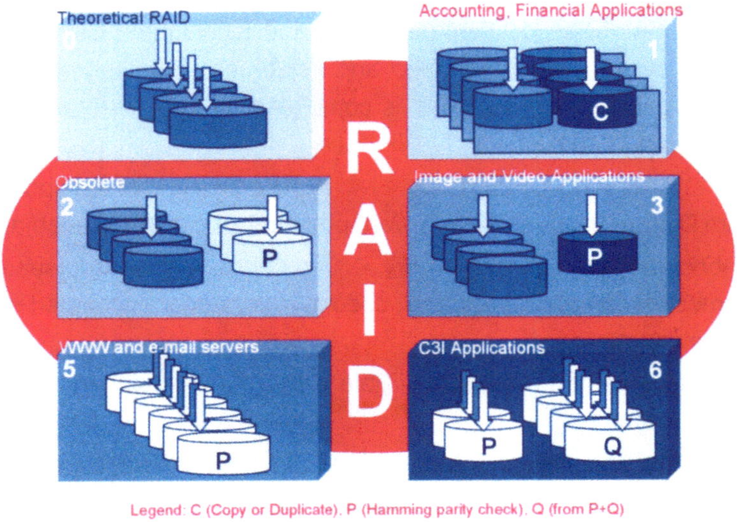

Fig. R-2. RAID levels

- 0: Also known as disk striping, refers to disk arrays in which every disk collects data in a fixed order, but with no redundancy mirroring or parity.
- 1: Also known as disk mirroring, meaning that every disk in the array has its own duplicate (C). In the case of a disk failure, data can be read from another. Thus, data can be lost only if the second disk fails before the first failed disk is repaired. RAID1 suits for applications that require high-availability, such as accounting software and the like.
- 2: A parallel array applies. Instead of having every disk duplicated as specified in RAID1, extra disks are used to store Hamming error-correction bits (P). If one of the disks fails, the remaining bits of the byte stored on the other disk and the associated error-correction bits can be used to reconstruct the damaged data. Made obsolete by RAID3 that offers a much cheaper solution.
- 3: A parallel array with bit-interleaved parity, it uses a single parity bit for error detection and correction. Instead of having every disk mirrored, it uses only one extra disk to save the parity calculated by disk controllers. In the case of failure, the damaged sector is known directly, so the re-construction of the damaged data requires the parity of the corresponding bits from the other disks to be computed and then that parity compared with the stored parity. RAID3 is suitable for high-throughput applications such as image and video editing.

- 4: An array with block-interleaved parity, it stores blocks just like in regular disks, without striping them across disks, but it keeps a parity block on just one separate disk. If one of the disks fails, the parity block can be used with the corresponding blocks from the other disks to restore the blocks of the failed disk. In practice, made obsolete by RAID5.
- 5: Also known as striping with parity. In other words data are distributed as in RAID4, but are also striped as in RAID0. Very useful for WWW and e-mail servers.
- 6: Also known as level 10 (read 1+0) or P+Q, where the level-5 strategy is applied by a level-1 mirroring scheme. It is useful for mission-critical applications such as C3I and the like.

The choice of RAID strategy depends on the application requirements, as discussed earlier. Thus, RAID0 is a great choice if high-performance I/O is required, otherwise levels 5 or 6 are recommended. Numerous improvements on the basic RAID schemes described here have also been proposed.

RAISE – Rigorous Approach to Industrial Software Engineering. A European Strategic Programme for Research and Development in Information Technology (see ESPRIT) project.

RAL – Rutherford Appleton Laboratory. A well-known research center in Europe (http://www.rl.ac.uk). Among others, RAL has a Department for Computation and Information, established in June 1996 when the Computing and Information Systems Department at RAL and the Theory and Computational Science Department at the Daresbury laboratory merged, together with some computing sections from other departments. The role of the department is to promote world-ranking scientific and engineering research by providing facilities and expertise in high-performance computation. It participates in UK and European Union research programs. Among other fields, it is involved in business processing, computer-supported cooperative work, multimedia, distributed information, formal methods and software technology, user interfaces, high-performance computing, knowledge engineering, virtual reality, etc. It is also part of W3C.

RAM – Random-Access Memory. A semiconductor-based memory (pronounced “ram”) that can store binary information capable of being read and written by microprocessors or other hardware devices. The speed of access does not depend on the location requested. RAMs can be either static (see SRAM) or dynamic (see DRAM). However, the term RAM is generally understood to refer to a volatile memory, which can be read or written equally quickly. In addition, most read-only memories (see ROM) are actually random-access but they are never referred to as RAM. Compare with EPROM, ROM and PROM.

RAMDAC – Random-Access Memory Digital-to-Analog Converter. A combination of three fast digital-to-analog converters with a small static RAM used as a single chip with some built-in graphics display adapters that translate the digital representation of a pixel into the analog information needed by the monitor to display it. Three DACs are needed to perform digital-to-analog conversion for each red, green and blue color value passed from the display memory. RAMDAC analog outputs go directly to the monitor, to three color guns. Pronounced “ram-dack”. See also CRT.

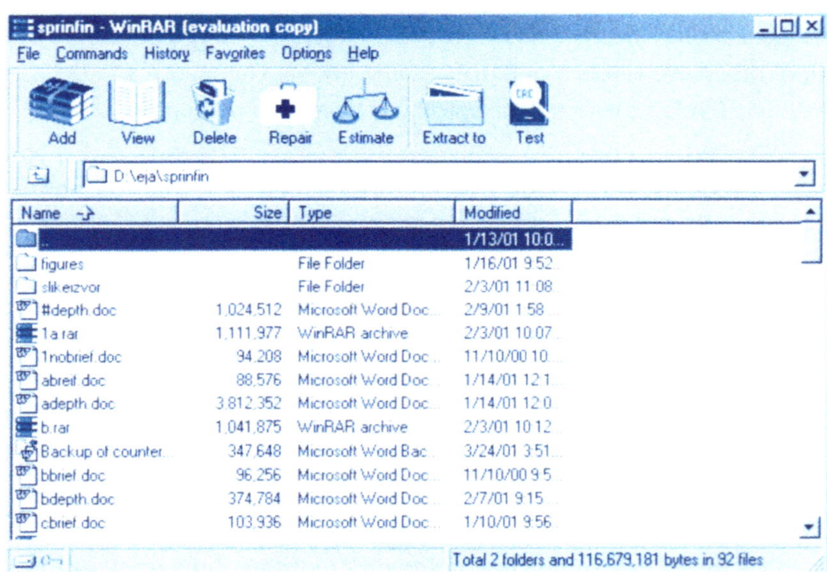

Fig. R-3. The menu for a RAR archive program

RAPI – Remote Application Programming Interface. An Application Programming Interface (see API) used to make function calls from a client application to a remote Windows CE-based device. RAPI runs over TCP/IP and Winsock. See also Winsock.

RAR – Roshal's Archive. A filename extension for a file that contains an archive. Also, the name of the executable file that invokes a RAR program (see Fig. R-3). RAR was developed by Eugene Roshal.

RARE – Réseaux Associés pour la Recherche Européenne. The European association of research networks, founded in 1986 as an association of European networking organizations and their users.

RARP – Reverse Address Resolution Protocol. A protocol (RFC903) that allows recognition of newly booted workstations via their unique Ethernet addresses. RARP maps a physical (hardware) address to an Internet address.

RAS – Remote-Access Server. A host on a local-area network that is equipped with modems to enable users to connect to the network over telephone lines.

RAS – Remote-Access Service. A service provided by Windows NT, which allows most of the services which would be available on a network to be accessed over a modem link. It involves dial-up and logon support. Windows NT includes a version of RAS that allows one user to access the network at a time. NT Advanced Server (see NTAS) allows up to 64 remote users.

RAS – Row-Address Strobe. A signal sent to a DRAM memory in order to tell it that an associated address is a row address. A data bit is stored in a cell, the location of which is determined by the column address and the row address. See DRAM. See also Column-Address Strobe (CAS).

RAW – Raw file. A filename extension for a file that contains a raw picture.

RBOC – Regional Bell Operating Company. A common name for any of the seven regional BOCs responsible for all local telephone services in the US. These are Ameritech, Bell Atlantic, Bell South, NYNEX, Pacific Telesis, Southwestern Bell Corporation and US West. Also known as "Baby Bell". See also BOC.

rcp – remote copy. A program and protocol provided in the Berkeley UNIX operating system (see BSD) that permits files to be copied from one computer to another. This protocol is often implemented on UNIX machines, but the protocol is general enough that non-UNIX machines may use it. However, rcp does not provide the word-length adaptability and flexibility that the FTP protocol does.

R&D – Research and Development. A common abbreviation for research and development activities, organizations, etc. Sometimes referred to as R/D.

RD – Receive Data. A signal line used in serial communications as the reception line for incoming information. In the full 25-pin RS-232C standard, RD is pin 3. In the abbreviated, 9-pin PC interface, RD is pin 2. See also Recommended Standard (RS) and Transmit Data (TD). Sometimes referred to as RXD.

RD – Routing Domain. A group of topologically contiguous systems all running one instance of a routing.

RDA – Radar Data Acquisition. Data acquisition using radar as sensors. A typical example of RDA acquisition is given in the HASIS entry. See also DAS (Data Acquisition System).

RDA – Remote Data Access. A standard developed to interconnect applications and databases. The standard originally attempted to cover any kind of data access and concerned itself only with effective dialog management, but the complexity involved with such a broad scope has required it to focus more on Structured Query Language (see SQL).

RDBA – Remote Database Access. See RDA (Remote Data Access).

RDBMS – Relational DBMS. A collection of programs that manages the complexity of a relational database, a database based on the relational model developed by Edgar F. Codd. Its conceptual structure is based on relations among tables. The tables are related to each other by maintaining common values in shared attributes. Well-known examples of RDBMS are Oracle, Ingres, Access, Informix, etc. See also DBMS (Database Management System).

RDF – Rate Decrease Factor. An Available Bit Rate (see ABR) service parameter that controls the decrease in the cell transmission rate.

RDF – Resource Description Framework. A W3C recommendation for using metadata to describe the data contained on the Web (text pages, graphics, audio files, video clips, and so on). RDF is associated with a new look at the future of the Web by its father, Tim Berners-Lee, known as the semantic Web. The key idea behind the semantic Web is that document descriptions should have some valuable information that will allow more accurate and efficient Web searching, by avoiding multiple meanings in search keywords. Berners-Lee said that in the future individual users and industry groups should work together to build their own consistent RDF vocabularies. Three object types make up the basic data model: resources, properties and statements. A resource may be an entire webpage, a part of a webpage, an entire website, or an object that is not directly accessible via the Web (e.g. a referenced journal article). Properties are specific aspects, attributes or relations used to describe a property. An RDF statement consists of a specific resource together with a named property and its value.

RDN – Relative Distinguished Name. The name of each component of the path in the X.500 naming scheme. All the RDNs originating in any given object must be distinct, but RDNs originating at different objects may be the same. Compare with DN (Distinguished Name). See also X.500.

RDO – Remote Data Objects. A collection of OLE objects inside Java Virtual Machine (see JVM) and Visual Basic (see VB) that allows control of ODBC sessions.

RDP – Reliable Datagram Protocol. An Internet standard protocol for reliably sending datagrams between user programs. This protocol is like UDP, but guarantees delivery and does retransmission as necessary. It is built on top of IP (see IP), and uses IP for datagram delivery.

RDRAM – Rambus DRAM. A byte-wide bus used for address, data and command transfers. The bus operates at very high speed, 500 million transfers per second. The chip operates synchronously with a 250-MHz clock.

RDS – Remote Data Services. RDS allows ADO-based applications to remotely access OLE DB components and data across multiple machines via the Internet or Intranets. RDS delivers a new Web data-access technology that allows developers to create datacentric applications within Active Data Object-enabled browsers such as Microsoft Internet Explorer. RDS provides the advantages of client-side caching of data results, an update capability for cached data, and integration of data-aware Active Data Object controls (see ADO).

RE – Requirements Engineering. The process of determining a complete, correct and clear specification of a future software-intensive system.

REG – Registration entity file. A filename extension for a file that contains a text description of the classes supported by a server application.

ReLaTe – Remote Language Teaching. A project that investigates the use of multimedia conferencing for distance learning of languages, being undertaken jointly by the University of Exeter and University College London. It involves a tutor teaching from a networked computer at one site, and students sitting at remote computers at the other sites. Each site is equipped with multimedia tools, such as a video camera and headsets with a combined microphone and earphones.

RELURL – Relative Universal (Uniform) Resource Locator. A form of URL in which the domain and some or all directory names are omitted, leaving only the document name and extension (and perhaps a partial list of directory names). The indicated file is found at a location related to the pathname of the current document. See also URL.

REN – Ringer Equivalent Number. A number that characterizes the on-hook impedance of equipment connected to the Public Switched Telephone Network (see PSTN).

REP – Requirements Engineering Process. An international workshop focusing on recent developments in requirements engineering (see RE).

REQUEST – Reliability and Quality of European Software. A European Strategic Programme for Research and Development in Information Technology (see ESPRIT) project.

RES – Resource file. A filename extension for a file that contains information about resources used by an application. Such information could be window positions, label definitions, etc. RES files are created by the resource compiler.

REX – Remote Execution. Part of the Open Network Computing (see ONC) architecture. It enables a user on one system to execute commands on another system in a distributed environment.

REXX – Restructured Extended Executor. A scripting language developed in 1979 by Mike Cowlishaw for IBM mainframes. In the meantime REXX has been improved several times, and now has Windows versions, as well as Object Rexx and NetRexx. See also REXXLA.

REXXLA – REXX Language Association. An independent organization (http://www.rexxla.org) dedicated to promoting the use and understanding of the REXX language (see REXX).

RF – Radio Frequency. A portion of the electromagnetic spectrum, the frequencies between 3 kHz and 300 GHz.

RFC – Request For Comment. Part of an open process prior to ANSI or ISO authorization of a standard. Actually, RFCs are described and floated by experts acting on their own initiative, so RFC documents are very often treated as standards rather than proposals. The RFC document series began in 1969. All Internet standards are written up as RFCs. Perhaps the single most influential one was RFC822, an e-mail Internet standard recommendation. RFCs can be found at a lot of websites, such as those of W3C (http://www.w3.org/DataSources/Archives/RFC.sites.html) and InterNIC (http://ds.internic.net/rfc).

RFD – Request For Discussion. A formal proposal for a discussion concerning the addition of a newsgroup to the Usenet hierarchy, the first step in a process that ends with a call for votes.

RFI – Radio-Frequency Interference. Unwanted "noise" in the radio frequency range (see RF), created by devices which emit electromagnetic waves, such as electric motors and fluorescent lights. RFI affects the quality of signals passing through some data transmission media.

RFP – Request For Proposal. An initial publication issued by a prospective software purchaser that describes details of a required system in order to attract offers by software developers to supply it.

RFS – Remote File System. A distributed file system, similar to the Network File System (see NFS), distributed with AT&T UNIX System V.

RFT – Request For Technology. Very similar to RFC. A common term describing the initial request for a new technology specification, usually issued by some organization (e.g. OSF). The main difference between RFTs and RFCs is that RFTs play more official roles in open processes, and more time is needed to change an RFT specification to a standard document than is required for an RFC. See also DP (Draft Proposal).

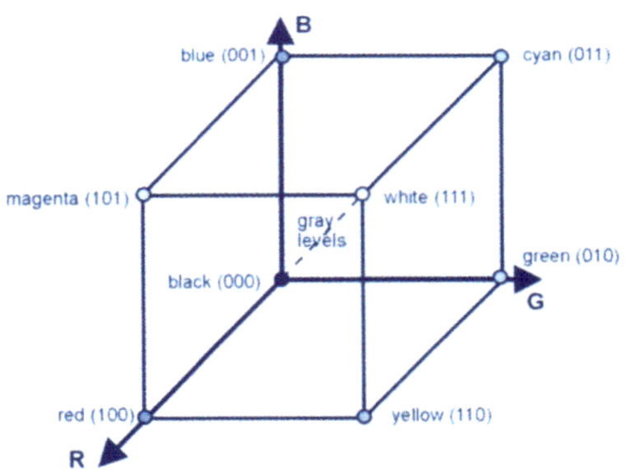

Fig. R-4. The RGB color model

RFTDCA – Revisable-Form Text DCA. A standard within the IBM Document Content Architecture (see DCA) for storing documents in such a way that the formatting can be changed by the receiver. Compare with FFTDCA.

RFU – Reserved for Future Use. A common term used to indicate that something has been reserved for future use. It is applied, for example, to blank pages in technical documents, to free pins on integrated circuits, etc.

RGB – Red, Green, Blue. An acronym for the red, green and blue colors representing one of the most common color models in use. The RGB color model is a unique cube subset of the 3D Cartesian coordinate system, as shown in

Fig. R-4. It uses the additive primaries method, mixing percentages of the three primary colors to get a desired color. The main diagonal of the RGB cube, with equal amounts of each primary color, represents the gray levels: black is (0,0,0), and white is at the opposite end of that cube diagonal (1,1,1). See also RGBA.

RGBA – Red, Green, Blue, Alpha. A color model that extends the RGB color model with a fourth component, alpha, which is used to control color blending. See also RGB.

RH – Request/Response Header. The part of the SNA data format that defines the type of data in the Response Unit (see RU).

RI – Ring Indicator. A signal used in serial communications (RS-232C) to tell the terminal or computer that the phone is ringing. Normally, RI is used with dial-up modems, in which case the receiving device can decide whether it wants to answer the call or not. In the full 25-pin RS-232C standard, RI is pin 22. In the abbreviated 9-pin PC interface, RI is pin 9. See also Recommended Standard (RS).

RIDE – Research Issues in Data Engineering. An annual international IEEE workshop focusing each year on some particular aspect of data engineering. The proceedings are published by IEEE CS Press.

RIF – Rate Increase Factor. Used in ATM networks to control the amount by which the transmission rate may increase upon receipt of an RM cell. See also Resource Management (RM).

RIFF – Resource Interchange File Format. A tagged file specification used to define standard formats for multimedia files.

RINEX – Receiver-Independent Exchange Format. A set of standard definitions and formats that allows GPS data to be exchanged and processed by different GPS receivers. See also Global Positioning System (GPS).

RIP – Raster Image Processor. A device (pronounced "rip"), consisting of chips, including a microprocessor, and software, that converts vector graphics and/or text into a raster (bit-mapped) image.

RIP – Routing Information Protocol. A distance vector routing protocol defined in RFC1058. See also Interior Gateway Protocol (IGP) and OSPF.

RIPEM – Riordan's Internet PEM. An implementation of the Privacy-Enhanced Mail (see PEM).

RIPSO – Revised Internet Protocol Security Option. The RFC1108 specification that defines an optional IP header field that contains a security classification

cation and a handling label. It allows the hosts and routers to label IP traffic according to a security level. According to the specified rules, the traffic may be accepted, rejected or forwarded by the routers along the way, or by the destination host.

RI/RO – Ring In/Ring Out. Ports in Token Ring multistation access units (see MAU). RI is a port through which another MAU can connect. On the other side, RO is a port through which the MAU can be connected to another MAU. See also TR (Token Ring).

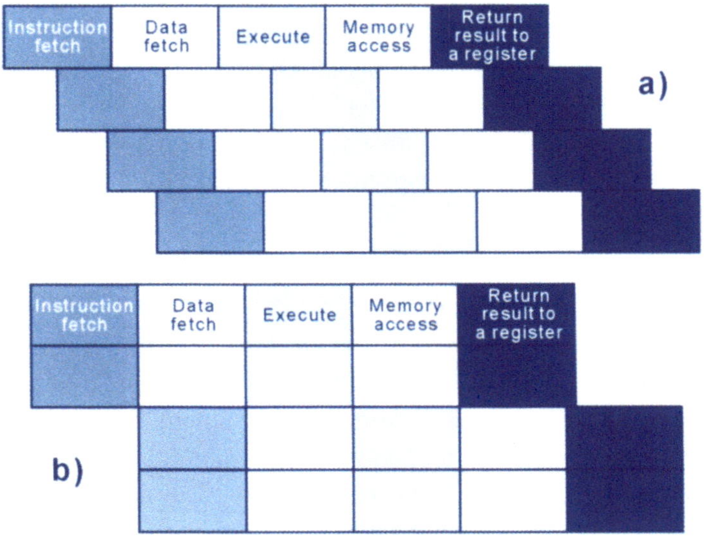

Fig. R-5. RISC architectures

RISC – Reduced-Instruction-Set Computer. A type of microprocessor design strategy (pronounced "risk") that focuses on rapid and efficient processing of a relatively small set of general-purpose instructions. Compare with CISC (Complex-Instruction-Set Computer). The features of RISC design include uniform instruction encoding, a homogenous register set, simple addressing modes, etc. The RISC architecture limits the number of instructions that are built into the microprocessor, but optimizes them so they can usually be carried out within a single clock cycle. Generally, RISC architectures can be superpipeline or superscalar, as shown in Fig. R-5a and b, respectively. The superpipelining approach assumes that the next instruction is going to be executed before the previous one is finished. The superscalar idea is borrowed from the world of supercomputers where parallel execution of two or more instructions is applied. From the microprocessor point of view that means an instruction can pass through the microprocessor via several different paths. In other words, it assumes that a superscalar CPU can have several ALUs, separated data caches and instruction caches, etc. Today, both architectures are used, sometimes in combination. Families of RISC chips include AMD 29000, MIPS R4000, IBM PowerPC 801 and RS10000, Intel i960, Motorola 88000, Sun SuperSPARC, Digital Alpha, etc.

RIT – Rate of Information Transfer. The amount of information transferred within a system in a unit of time.

RJ-xx – Registered Jack xx. A standard for modular connection that allows up to eight wires to be connected in a single connector. The jack is the female component of RJ, whilst xx stands for various available RJ configurations distinguished by the number of wire pairs used, wiring sequence, modifications applied, etc. The following are in common use: RJ-11, RJ-12 and RJ-45.

RJE – Remote Job Entry. An SNA application that is batch-oriented. In RJE environments, jobs are submitted to a computing facility, and the output is received later.

RL – Real life. The chat term. It refers to the time when a user is not chatting.

RLL – Run-Length-Limited encoding. A method for storing data on a disk. RLL translates patterns representing information in bits into codes rather than storing them bit by bit or character by character. The encoding scheme is built upon a "run-length" where changes in magnetic flux are based on a certain number of zeros occurring in sequence. See also ARLL and ERLL.

rlogin – remote login. A command, similar to Telnet, offered in most UNIX implementations, but the protocol is general enough so that non-UNIX machines may use it.

rm – remove. UNIX command that deletes files from a specified path.

RM – Resource Management. A mechanism used by the ATM Forum's explicit-rate flow control scheme that relies on special control cells. RM cells typically use no more than 3% of the network capacity, and they quickly convey information about congestion back to the source.

RM – Resource Manager. A part of the X/Open Distributed Transaction Processing specification (see DTP). A resource manager is responsible for ensuring integrity of the resources that it owns. This responsibility includes recovery from physical or logical damage, backing out of incomplete changes, and retrying operations. Typically, the RM is responsible for achieving ACID properties in distributed transaction processing. In addition, the RM provides synchronization services that allow multiple resource managers to act together to ensure that the resources they own retain their integrity. The RM is armed with services that provide a foundation for distributed transaction processing applications. There are functions that delineate a group of operations as a transaction, record a transaction's transactional state, finish the complete work or discard all operations, control the usage of resources involved on a transactional basis, facilitate the recovery of the system back to a known state following a failure, etc. See also ACID.

rmdir – remove directory. A UNIX command that deletes directories from a UNIX file-system tree.

RMI – Remote Method Invocation. The Java tool that allows the development of distributed objects. RMI involves invoking a method via a remote interface on a remote object with the same syntax used for invoking on a local object. RMI provides a simple and direct model for distributed computation with Java objects. These objects can be new Java objects, or can be simple Java wrappers around an existing API. It brings the power of Java safety and portability to distributed computing. RMI connects to the existing and legacy systems using the standard Java native method interface (see JNI). RMI can also connect to the existing relational database using the standard JDBC package. At the most basic level, RMI is Java's remote procedure call (see RPC) mechanism. RMI can use a natural, direct and fully powered approach to provide a distributed computing technology. The main features of RMI are: it's object-oriented; it has a mobile behavior; it's safe and secure; it's easy to write; it's easy to use; it supports legacy systems; it's 100% portable to any JVM; it has distributed garbage collection, and multithreading just as in parallel computing, etc. See also RP (Remote Programming).

RMM – Relationship Management Methodology. A DataWeb modeling method influenced by the Entity-Relationship (see ER) model and the Hypermedia Design Method (see HDM).

RMON – Remote Monitoring. Management Information Base (see MIB) agent specification described in RFC1271 that defines functions for the remote monitoring of networked devices. The RMON specification provides numerous monitoring, problem detection, and reporting capabilities. RMON is designed to supplement the management information obtained and used by the Simple Network Management Protocol (see SNMP).

RMS – Root Mean Square. The value of an AC voltage as it is actually measured.

RNG – Random Number Generator. The set of deterministic algorithms that produce numbers with certain distribution properties.

RO – Receive-Only device. Any device that can receive but cannot transmit data (e.g. a printer).

ROCOF – Rate of Occurrence Of Failures. The software reliability metric term which expresses the frequency of occurrence of unexpected behavior.

ROFL – Rolling on the floor laughing. The chat term.

ROI – Return on Investment. The business term that in general gives information on how successful some project was. ROI is expressed in terms of sales revenue and the money invested.

ROM – Read-Only Memory. A data storage device, a semiconductor-based memory with fixed contents loaded during manufacturing. In contrast to random-access memories, ROM chips retain their contents even when the power is switched off. ROMs are also used for storage of the lowest-level booting software. See also EEPROM, EPROM and PROM.

ROM BIOS – Read-Only Memory Basic Input/Output System. A set of routines stored in firmware that provides low-level simple input/output operations, shipped with IBM PCs and compatible computers. The BIOS takes 64 KB of address space beginning at location 0F0000H. In PS/2 computers, the available memory for BIOS is extended to double this size. See also BIOS (Basic Input/Output System).

ROP – Raster Operation. A Boolean operation used in computer graphics that combines values of the pixels in the source and destination bitmaps. See also BitBLT.

ROSE – Remote Operations Service Element. A remote procedure call protocol used in OSI message handling, and directory and network management (ISO9072) at the OSI application layer. In fact, ROSE is a general-purpose application-level service element (see ASE) that supports interactive cooperation between two P2P applications (see P2P). ROSE operations may be synchronous or asynchronous; also they may be confirmed, unconfirmed or partially confirmed.

ROT – Running Object Table. A globally accessible table on every computer that tracks the Microsoft OLE objects (see OLE).

RP – Remote Programming. An emerging technology in distributed computing based on intelligent mobile agents. Mobile agents can be considered as pieces of code with defined tasks which execute somewhere on the network and then return the requested results to the client (see Fig. R-6). The concept of agents has been investigated for almost 10 years, especially in the field of artificial intelligence. A general definition of what exactly an agent is supposed to be has not been reached yet. The following one is widely acceptable. An agent can be defined as a component of software and/or hardware capable of acting in order to accomplish tasks on behalf of its user.

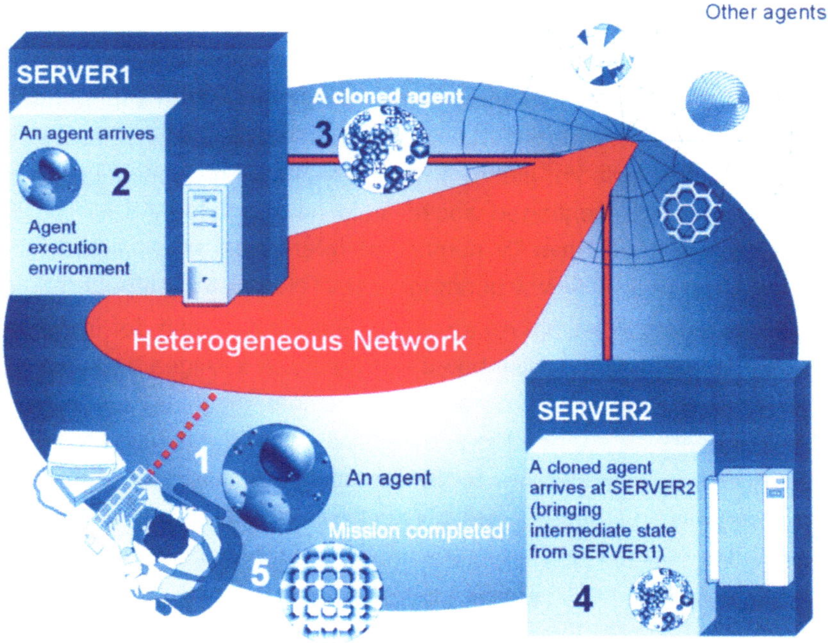

Fig. R-6. Conceptual model of remote programming

Mobile agents are those agents which have the ability to move across the network. In this way, remote programming allows a client to delegate a task to an agent, as shown in Fig. R-6. Computation by delegation allows the client and server to interact without using the network once the agent has arrived on the server. In addition, after processing the data on the remote server, an agent can decide, or it can be a part of its dedicated task, to compress the answers before shipping them back. The implications are obvious. The traffic across the network reduces significantly. For example, poorly connected clients using laptops can reach the data they want while at the same time holding their mobility at the required level; wireless users can have the ability to access data they need regardless of the bandwidth limitations; the possibility of errors is reduced, and so on. Furthermore, users can locally perform some other task(s) and not simply consume processing resources waiting for the RPC return. Instead, the client can call its agent on the remote server later on to ask if it has finished the delegated task, and if so it can just pick up the results or call again later. In order to support heterogeneity, it is often preferable to express an agent in an interpreted language such as Tcl, Telescript or Java. The total replacement of the RPC paradigm using a remote programming paradigm in the client/server design is not so straightforward. A more realistic approach is to use some kind of combination. See also RPC (Remote Procedure Call), RMI (Remote Method Invocation), C/S (Client/Server), DTP (Distributed Transaction Processing), JNI (Java Native Interface), etc. In any case, remote programming has a future. Mobile agents, mentioned above, also have a future. See Tcl (Tool Command Language), Java (a number of references are included in this book) or Telescript (http://www.genmagic.com/Telescript/Whitepapers/wp4).

RPC – Remote Procedure Call. An easy and popular paradigm for implementing a client/server model of distributed computing. A key idea behind RPC is the possibility of calling a program on a remote machine for execution, where even users do not need to know exactly what the execution machine is and where it is. In general, a request is sent to a remote system to execute a designated procedure, using arguments supplied, and the result is returned to the caller. There are many implementation variations, resulting in a variety of different, unfortunately incompatible, RPC protocols. The following example, based on the DCE RPC mechanism, explains it in brief (see Fig. R-7). The client calls a stub routine on its own machine that marshals a message containing the name of the procedure and all associated parameters, then passes such a message to the communication driver for transmission. A stub is a small program routine that substitutes for a longer program, possibly to be loaded later or located remotely. The server listens to the client's requirements coming via RPCs, and when they arrive the remote driver gives them to its own stub, which unpacks them and makes an ordinary procedure call to the server and returns them. ISO/IEC JTC1/ SC21/WG8 has agreed to accept the OSF specification of DCE RPC as the basis for its work in this area. See also DCE (Distributed Computing Environment).

RPCAPI – Remote Procedure Call Application Programming Interface. A part of the Open Network Computing (ONC) architecture. A high-level interface that a programmer can use to implement ONC RPC. See also Remote Procedure Call (RPC) and ONC.

RPCGEN – Remote Procedure Call Generator. A part of the Open Network Computing (ONC) architecture. A programming aid that automates parts of the RPC coding requirements. See also RPC and ONC.

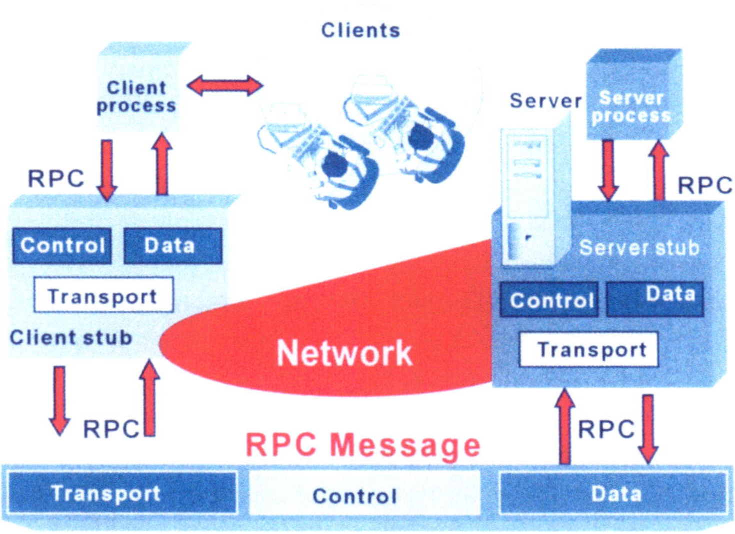

Fig. R-7. RPC mechanism

RPF – Reverse Path Forwarding. A routing method used for multidestination routing. Each packet contains either a list of destinations or a bitmap indicating the desired destinations. When a packet arrives at a router, the router checks all the destinations to determine the set of output lines that will be needed. The router then generates a new copy of the packet for each output line to be used and includes in each packet only those destinations that are to use the line. After a sufficient number of hops, each packet will carry only one destination and can be treated as a normal packet. The whole algorithm can be implemented as a subnet, or a tree built by RPF.

RPG – Remote Password Generator. A device that can be used to generate a unique password every time a user wants to log on to a network. The technique is closely related to PIN.

R

RPG – Report Program Generator. A programming language developed by IBM in the mid-1960s, intended for business applications development.

RPG – Role-playing games. A chat term applied in computer games where one or more players adopt a role and act it out in a virtual reality.

RPI – Rockwell Protocol Interface. A technology developed by Rockwell International in order to lower the cost of modems.

RPN – Reverse Polish Notation. A form of algebraic notation also called the postfix notation, in which the operators appear after the operands. For example, the algebraic expression (a+b)×(c–d) is written in postfix notation as ab+cd–×. The postfix notation is well-suited to stack-based architectures, but modern compilers have reduced this advantage considerably. The best-known language that has strictly postfix syntax is FORTH.

RPQ – Request for Price Quotation. A term in common use in business correspondence when someone is asked to offer merchandise or a service.

RPROM – Reprogrammable PROM. See EPROM.

RR – Resource Records. The Domain Name System (see DNS) data defined in RFC1035. RR consists of the domain name (Name), Class, Type and Data. RR types include addresses, the Canonical Name (see CNAME), the Start of Authority (see SOA), the Name Server (see NS), etc.

RS – Recommended Standard. A common name for a series of standards adopted by the Electronic Industries Alliance (see EIA). RS-232 is the most common asynchronous serial line standard (equivalent to ITU-T V.24 and V.28). It defines the specific lines and signal characteristics used by serial communications controllers to standardize the transmission of serial data between devices. The standard recognizes communication equipment either as Data Communication Equipment (see DCE) or Data Terminal Equipment (see DTE). DCE and DTE are distinguished from each other by the type of connector and by the transmitting and receiving pins. DCE should have a female connector and should use pins 2 and 3 for transmission (see TD) and receiving (see RD), respectively. DTE uses the opposite combination, has a male connector, and uses pins 2 and 3 as the RD and TD pins, respectively. The RS-232 interface is used in many types of applications for data communications, where relatively low performance is acceptable, and can be provided according to technical constraints. Typical examples include a connection between a computer and a terminal, a computer sending data to a nearby printer, a specialized device sending data to a computer, etc. RS-422, RS-423 and RS-449 are standards for serial communications with transmission distances over 15 m and faster data rates. The RS-485 standard has the highest performance and flexibility of this group of general-purpose EIA recommended standards. The key enhancement is that it supports true multidrop operation (up to 32 receivers and transmitters).

RS/6000 – RISC System/6000. Introduced in 1990, the RS/6000 is IBM's line of RISC-based engineering workstations and servers. It is delivered with OS/400 or the AIX operating system.

RSA – Rivest, Shamir, Adleman encryption. A public-key crypto system named after its inventors ("On Digital Signatures and Public Key Cryptography", April 1977 at MIT), Ronald Rivest, Adi Shamir, and Leonard Adleman. Their method is based on some principles from number theory. It works as follows:

1. Choose two large secret primes (a prime number is a number that has no division except for itself and 1), p and q (typically greater than 10^{100}).
2. Find the products $n = p \times q$ and $z = (p-1) \times (q-1)$.
3. Choose a number relatively prime to z and call it d.
4. Find e such that $e \times d = 1 \pmod z$.

These steps are used to compute the public key (e, n) and the private key (d, n) and must be followed with encryption. Plaintext (P) is divided into blocks of k bits, where k is the largest integer that satisfies $2^k < n$. To encrypt a k-bits-wide block P, the P is multiplied by itself e times, and the product is then divided by a modulus n leaving the remainder as a cipher text $C = P^e \pmod n$. In the reverse operation, it is necessary to determine $P = C^d \pmod n$. The security of the method is based on the difficulty of factoring large numbers. According to RSA's authors, factoring a 200-digit number requires 4 billion years of computer time. It is usually combined with DES or IDEA. The proper implementation of the RSA algorithm is well explained in RFCs 2314, 2315 and 2437. See also DES and IDEA.

R

RSFG – Route Server Functional Group. The group of functions performed to provide internetworking-level functions in an MPOA system. See also MPOA.

rsh – remote shell protocol. A protocol that allows a user to execute commands on a remote system without having to log in to the system. For example, rsh can be used to remotely examine the status of a number of access servers without connecting to each communication server, executing the command, and then disconnecting from the communication server.

RSI – Repetitive Strain Injury. An injury that may occur due to repeated physical movements of the hands and arms during keyboard or mouse use.

RSIP – Realm-Specific IP. An IETF protocol (RFC3102) intended to be deployed in router and client equipment working with IPv4.

RSN – Real soon now. The chat term.

RSVP – Resource Reservation Protocol. A protocol (RFC2205) that supports reservation of resources across an IP network using multicast routing with spanning trees (see SPA). Applications running on IP end systems can use RSVP to indicate to other nodes the nature (bandwidth, jitter, maximum burst, etc.) of the packet streams they wish to receive. It allows multiple senders to transmit to multiple groups of receivers, and permits individual receivers to switch channels freely, and optimize bandwidth use, while at the same time eliminating congestion. The acronym is not obvious. It comes from RSV (ReSerVation) and P (Protocol).

RTA – Rewriting Techniques and Applications. An international conference focusing on all aspects of rewriting. Some major topics include applications, foundations, frameworks, implementation techniques and semantics. The proceedings are published by Springer-Verlag (see LNCS).

RTAM – Remote Telecommunications Access Method. An IBM mainframe subsystem that handles application access and routing within the network.

RTDB – Real-Time Database. A database that deals with time-sensitive data. Such databases are typical for applications such as plant management, traffic control and scheduling, etc. In addition to data consistency, an imperative feature of any database, RTDB also requires the data to be temporally correct, since the contents of the database reflect the current status of the outside world. Furthermore, it also requires real-time query execution and update.

RTDBMS – Real-Time Database Management System. A DBMS that manages a real-time database (see RTDB).

RTE – Real-Time Executive. Operating system for the HP 1000 family of computers.

RTF – RichText Format. An interchange format for document exchange between Microsoft Word and other document preparation systems.

RTL – Register Transfer Language. A kind of Hardware Description Language (see HDL) used to describe the registers of a computer or digital system.

RTMP – Routing Table Maintenance Protocol. A transport-layer protocol in the AppleTalk protocol suite. RTMP is used for tracking and updating the information in the routing table for an internetwork.

RTOS – Real-Time Operating System. An operating system designed or optimized for the needs of a time-sensitive application.

RTP – Real-time Transfer Protocol. A protocol that allows support of real-time properties across the network.

RTS – Real-Time System. A computer system that operates in real time, characterized by stringent deadlines, high-throughput and high-reliability requirements. Real-time systems are used in very diverse application areas, such as, for example, air-traffic control, process control and mission-critical control. The crucial question for such systems is how fast each of them can respond to a change in input stimuli or the environment. The high-reliability requirement is complicated, because an RTS can fail not only because of software or hardware failure, but also because the system is unable to execute its critical workload in time. Typically, a guaranteed response within a short period of time is required; this is also known as a hard deadline. So, the response time must be less than the deadline, otherwise there is a risk that an RTS could fail with unrecoverable and probably catastrophic results.

RTS – Reliable Transfer Service. In an X.400 electronic mail network, RTS works together with Message Transfer Agents (see MTA) to ensure that the best possible route for a message is taken.

RTS – Request To Send. A signal used in serial communication to request permission to transmit. If the other side is ready to receive, it responds using a Clear to Send (see CTS) signal. In the full 25-pin RS-232C standard, RTS is pin 4. In the abbreviated 9-pin PC interface, RTS is pin 7. See also RS.

RTSA – Real-Time Structured Analysis. A structured analysis technique capable of modeling real-time aspects of software.

RTSE – Reliable Transfer Service Element. An OSI application service element (see ASE) used to handshake application protocol data units (see PDU) across the session service and TP0. See also Transport Protocol (TP).

RTSP – Real-Time Streaming Protocol. A proposed standard for controlling streaming data over the Web.

RTSS – Real-Time Systems Symposium. The IEEE symposium focusing on all aspects of real-time systems. Topics include operating systems, fault tolerance, databases, programming languages, tools, networks, architectures, case studies, performance modeling, applications, etc.

RTT – Round-Trip Time. Time required for a network communication to travel from the source to the destination and back. RTT includes the time required for the destination to process the message from the source and generate a reply. Some routing algorithms use RTT to calculate optimal routes.

RTTI – Run-Time Type Information. In C++, a mechanism that allows the determination of the type of an object during a program execution.

RU – Response Unit. The data portion of the IBM SNA format. See also SNA.

RUI – Request Unit Interface. In IBM SNA, a basic interface that allows programs to control logical units (see LU). RUIs also read and write data from/to RH, TH and RU SNA components. See also SNA, RH, RU and TH.

RVI – Reverse Vector Interrupt. A control sequence signal sent by a receiver back to a transmitter (during reception of transmitted data) requesting that transmission be stopped so that it (the receiver) can transmit a higher-priority message.

R/W – Read/Write. A common term addressing several things. It is applied to memory or to any device that can be both read from and written to. Also, R/W can refer to the types of operations that can be performed on a file. In this case reading and writing are both allowed.

RWX – Read, Write, Execute. An acronym for a three-bit combination that controls access writes in a UNIX file system. So, the eight possible combinations of RWX bits indicate whether a UNIX file is a read-only file, a write-only file, an execute-only file, or every combination of those three. RWX bits are also applied to user or group rights.

RXD – Receive Data. See RD (Receive Data).

RYO – Roll your own. The chat term ("Write your own program").

RZ – Return to Zero. A method of recording data on magnetic media. The neutral state is represented by the absence of magnetization. Also, an encoding communication technique. In RZ, the data pulses that represent binary 1 return to the binary 0 level in the middle of the time period allowed for the bit. That means that for every 1 there is a signal transition, which helps the receiver to synchronize with the incoming datastream. Compare with NRZ (Non-Return to Zero).

RZI – Return to Zero Inverted. The inverted counterpart of the RZ signal encoding (see RZ).

S

S4L – Spam for (4) Life. The chat term used to express the possibility that someone could be a victim of lifetime spamming. The word "spam" itself is a new word appearing in the vocabulary of netizens. Spam is a consequence of the growing use of Internet e-mail for everything, including bothering people and wasting their time by sending them different offers, advertisements, jokes, etc. which they actually do not want. According to techtarget (http://www.techtarget.com) the term "spam" comes from the Monty Python sketch "Spam spam spam spam spam ... spam, lovely spam, wonderful spam ...". Like the sketch, spam is an endless repetition of worthless text. See also Netizen.

SA – Source Address. A header field in many types of packets consisting of the address of the node sending the packet. For example, see HDLC. Compare with DA.

SA – Structured Analysis. See SSA (Structured System Analysis).

SAA – Systems Application Architecture. IBM's family of standard interfaces that enables software to be written independently of IBM hardware and operating systems, as depicted in Fig. S-1. SAA defines how an application interfaces with both the user and the supporting operating system. Under SAA, a program can be implemented on one type of IBM system and then easily moved to another type of IBM system. True SAA-compliant applications are compatible at the source level (before being compiled) with any SAA-compliant operating system. SAA has four main components, as shown in Fig. S-1. CPI, CUA and CCS are explained elsewhere in the book. The "Common Applications" part is the fourth main product-oriented component, and it is intended for developing common frameworks for the same kind of applications running on different platforms.

SAAL – Signaling ATM Adaptation Layer. The service that resides above the ATM layer. SAAL has two main sublayers: the common sublayer is where segmentation and reassembly of packets occurs; the service-specific sublayer is where reliable data-link protocols verify that signaling messages are received, or they are retransmitted otherwise.

SAB – Standards Activities Board. The IEEE Computer Society (see IEEE CS) board set up "to provide an organizational framework within which to develop broadly accepted, sound, timely and technically excellent standards that will advance the theory and practice of computing and information processing science and technology".

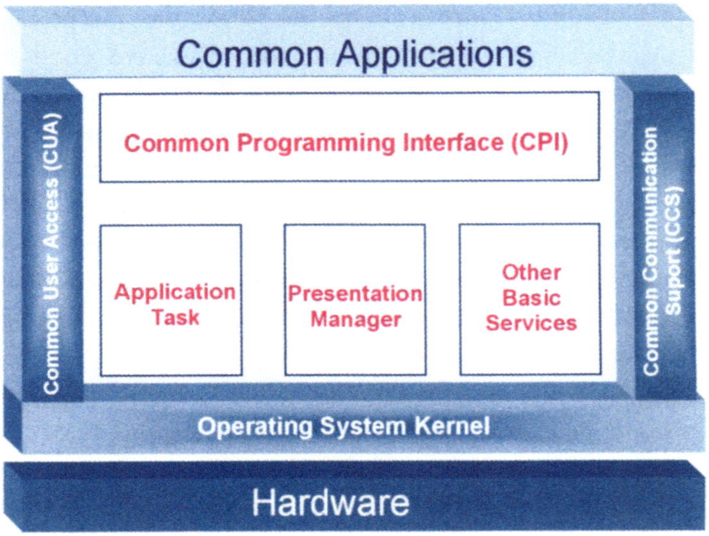

Fig. S-1. SAA components

SAC – Selected Areas in Cryptography. An annual workshop focusing on cryptography. The proceedings are published by Springer-Verlag (see LNCS).

SAC – Simplified Access Control. One of the two available access methods used in the ITU-T X.500 Directory Services. See also Basic Access Control (BAC) and X.500.

SAC – Single-Attached Concentrator. The FDDI or CDDI concentrator that connects to the network by being cascaded from the master port of another FDDI or CDDI concentrator. It also serves as a terminator for single-attachment stations (see SAS). See also Fiber Distributed Data Interface (FDDI) and Copper Distributed Data Interface (CDDI).

SAC – Symposium on Applied Computing. The ACM/SIGAPP symposium that deals with all areas of experimental computing and application development. The papers are published by the ACM/SIGAPP Applied Computing Review.

SACL – System Access Control List. An Access Control List (see ACL) that controls the generation of audit messages for attempts to access a secure object.

SAD – Systems Analysis Definition. The starting point for system design. It includes the analyses and identification of the requirements which the proposed system should meet. See also SSA (Structured System Analysis).

SADT – South Australia (Adelaide) Daylight Time. Time zone. UTC + 10.50 hours. It applies during the Australian summer, i.e. the calendar winter.

SAFER – Secure And Fast Encryption Routine. A byte-oriented block cipher algorithm developed in 1993 for Cylink Corporation. It has a variable number of rounds (maximum of 10, minimum of 6). Most recently, a version of SAFER, called SAFER SK-40, was announced, which uses a 40-bit key and has 5 rounds (thereby increasing the speed of encryption). This reduced-round version is secure against differential and linear cryptoanalysis in the sense that any such attack would require more effort than a brute-force search for a 40-bit key. SK denotes a strengthened key schedule.

SAG – SQL Access Group. A consortium of leading software and hardware companies working together (now under X/Open, known as X/Open SAG, see XSAG) to develop a standard SQL interface for database management systems and standard protocols for interoperability among clients and servers. The SQL Access Group is attempting also to accelerate the acceptance of the ISO Remote Database Access (see RDA) protocol.

SAGA – Stochastic Algorithms, Foundation and Applications. An international symposium started in 2001 in Budapest, Hungary. SAGA focuses on original research in the analysis, implementation, experimental evaluation, and real-world applications of stochastic algorithms. The proceedings are published by Springer-Verlag (see LNCS).

SAID – Security Association ID. A part of the IPv6 packet header 32-bit wide field reserved for encryption and authentication purposes.

SAIF – Spatial Archive and Interchange Format. A Canadian standard (pronounced "safe") for the exchange of geographic data. It allows sharing of spatial and spatiotemporal data. It also represents an efficient means of archiving such data in a vendor-neutral format. SAIF follows a multiple-inheritance, object-oriented paradigm. It makes a very strong distinction between the way information is described and the way it is encoded. At the most abstract level all information is defined as mathematical constructs, including tuples, lists, sets, enumerations and primitives. Using these as building blocks, SAIF introduces a number of spatial and temporal constructs.

SAINT – Symposium on Applications and the Internet. The IEEE international conference on Internet applications and the underlying technologies. Some of the major topics include agents on the Internet, collaboration technology, distributed applications, e-commerce, domain-specific languages, information retrieval and data mining, mobile computing, multimedia, etc. The proceedings are published by IEEE CS Press.

SAIS – Southern Association for Information Systems. An annual conference focusing on organizational or technical research in information systems planning, design, development, management, acquisition, implementation, usage or evaluation.

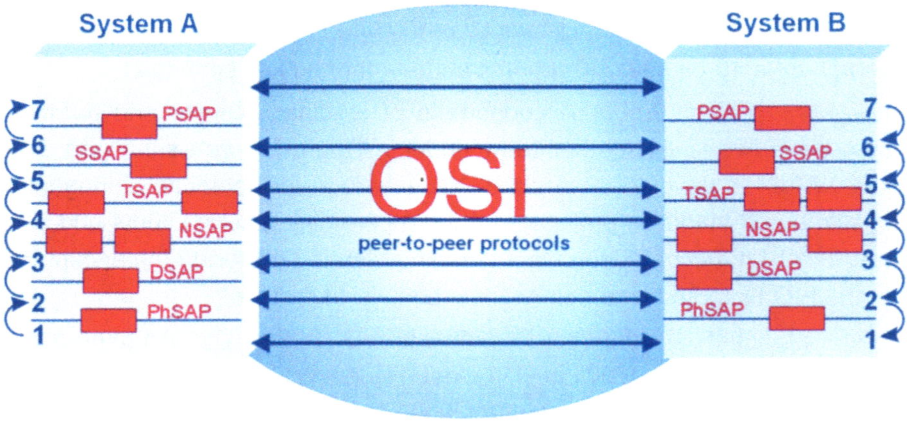

Fig. S-2. SAPs and their relation to OSI layers

SAN – Small Area Network. A network generally limited to tens of meters, which uses specialized communications methods and is applied in such areas as process control and other specific real-time computer applications. Compare with LAN, MAN and WAN.

SAN – Storage Area Network. An IBM high-speed special-purpose network used to interconnect different kinds of data storage devices and associated file servers. SAN supports disk mirroring, backup and restore, data migration between storage devices, and sharing of data among different servers in a network.

SAP – Service Access Point. The points at which the services of an OSI layer are made available to the next higher layer (see Fig. S-2). They are named according to the layer providing the services, e.g. NSAP for network layer,

TSAP for transport layer, etc. Normally, there is no ASAP, because there is no layer above the application layer. Each SAP has a unique address that is assigned by the IEEE standards office for common protocols. For example, AA, E0, F0 and F5, all in hexadecimal values, are the assigned numbers for the SNAP, IPX, NetBIOS and OSI network layers, respectively. See also Open Systems Interconnection (OSI), DSAP, NSAP, PhSAP, PSAP, SSAP and TSAP.

SAP – Service Advertising Protocol. A transport-layer protocol in NetWare environments, used by a service-providing node in a network (such as a file server or application server) to notify other nodes on the network that it is available for access. When a server boots, it uses the protocol to advertise its service; when the same server goes offline it uses the protocol to announce that it is no longer available.

SAP – Session Announcement Protocol. The IETF protocol (RFC2974) for announcements that define a binary header in front of the Session Description Protocol (see SDP) portion of an announcement.

SAP – Systems, Applications and Products in Data Processing. Founded in 1972 in Germany ("Systeme, Anwendungen, Produkte"), SAP provides e-business solutions for all types of industries. It's the world's largest interenterprise software company, and the world's third-largest independent software supplier overall (http://www.sap.de).

SAPI – Speech Application Programming Interface. A feature in Windows 95 and Windows NT that allows applications to include speech recognition or convert text to speech.

SAR – Segmentation And Reassembly sublayer. An ATM adaptation layer used to convert protocol data units (see PDU) into appropriate lengths, and formats them to fit the payload of an ATM cell. At the destination end-station, SAR extracts the payloads from the cells and converts them back into PDUs, which can be used by applications higher up the protocol stack. See also AAL.

SARA – Symposium on Abstraction Reformulation and Approximation. An international symposium focusing on all areas of artificial intelligence connected with abstraction, reformulation and approximation techniques. The proceedings are published by Springer-Verlag (see LNAI).

SAS – Single Attachment Station. A device attached only to the primary ring of an FDDI ring. Also known as a Class B station. Compare with DAS (Dual Attachment Station). See also FDDI (Fiber Distributed Data Interface).

SAS – Static Analysis Symposium. An international symposium focusing on high-performance implementations and verification systems of high-level programming languages. Some of the major topics include abstract interpretation, data flow analysis, complexity analysis, theoretical frameworks, compiler optimization, verification systems, program specialization, abstract domains, model checking, etc. The proceedings are published by Springer-Verlag (see LNCS).

SASE – Special Application Service Element. When used in connection with the ISO OSI layered network architecture it refers to a range of special services provided by the application layer. See also OSI.

SAST – South Africa Standard Time. Time zone. UTC + 2.00 hours. See TZ.

SAST – South Australia (Adelaide) Standard Time. Time zone. UTC + 9.50 hours.

SATAN – Security Administrator Tool for Analyzing (Auditing) Networks. An attack scanner invented by Wietse Venema (Eindhoven University of Technology) and Dan Farmer (Sun Microsystems) that helps UNIX system administrators. It was written using HTML files, UNIX shell scripts, C, PERL and other programs. SATAN recognizes several common networking-related security problems, and reports the problems without exploiting them. For each type of problem found, SATAN offers a tutorial that explains the problem and what its impact could be. On 5th April 1995, the first version of SATAN software was put out for general distribution all over the world. SATAN is an extensible open tool that allows users to add their own attack and analysis tools. However, the efficiency of SATAN is in doubt. SATAN is available from a number of FTP mirror sites. Some of them are listed below:

ftp://ftp.denet.dk/pub/security/tools/satan

ftp://ftp.ox.ac.uk/pub/comp/security/software/satan

ftp://coast.cs.purdue.edu/pub/tools/unix/satan

ftp://ftp.tisl.ukans.edu/pub/security

SAX – Simple API for XML. An event-based Application Programming Interface (see API) that allows parsing and interpretation of XML-based Web files. SAX is free for both commercial and noncommercial use. SAX parsers (in different languages, such as Python, C++, PERL, COM, etc.) are available at http://www.megginson.com/SAX/SAX1/applications.html

SBS – Small Business Server. An edition of the Microsoft SQL Server, the performance of which is typically limited to 50 concurrent users.

SC – Structural Computing. An international workshop focusing on the theoretical foundations of structural computing. Topics include new hypermedia domains, domain requirements for structural computing, structural computing as a school of thought, hypermedia infrastructure, etc. The proceedings are published by Springer-Verlag (see LNCS).

SCAM – SCSI Configuration Automatically. A subset of Plug and Play (see P&P) directions that provides P&P support for SCSI devices. See also SCSI.

SCCS – Source Code Control System. The version management tool under the UNIX operating system. In general, version management systems provide version and release identification, change history recording, storage management, etc. SCCS stores the first version of a system, with further versions specified in terms of how they differ from it, etc.

SCI – Scalable Coherent Interface. The standard (IEEE1596) for large multiprocessor systems and shared memory architectures. It is going to replace standard buses, overcoming their limitations in bandwidth and scalability. This is achieved by connecting processors and memories with a set of simplex point-to-point links in ring structures. Each single link allows packet-oriented transactions with an address, a command, and 0, 16, 64 or 256 bytes of data.

SCI – Science Citation Index. In general, a science citation index catalogs the citations in a scientific article, linking the article with the cited works. See also ACI (Autonomous Citation Index).

SCI – Systemics, Cybernetics and Informatics. An international conference focusing on information system development and management. The topics include virtual engineering, mobile/wireless computing, control systems, education and information systems, image, speech, acoustic and signal processing, etc.

SCO – Santa Cruz Operation. The company that supplies UNIX operating systems for Intel microprocessors. SCO was founded in 1979, with its headquarters in Santa Cruz, California (http://websco.sco.com). It also has offices all around Europe, as well as in Asia, Australia, Canada and Latin America.

SCP – Science of Computer Programming. An international journal published by Elsevier Science. The journal publishes research results in the areas of software system development, maintenance and use, including the software aspects of hardware design.

SCP – Session Control Protocol. A simple protocol, which lets a server and client have multiple conversations over a single TCP connection. The protocol is designed to be simple to implement, and is modeled on TCP. SCP's main service is dialog control. This service allows either end of the connection to establish a virtual session over a single transport connection. SCP also allows a sender to indicate message boundaries, and allows a receiver to reject an incoming session. SCP allows data to be sent when the session is established; the recipient does not confirm successful connection establishment, but may reject unsuccessful attempts. This simplifies the design of the protocol, and removes the need for latency for a confirmed operation. SCP has a fixed overhead of 8 bytes per segment.

SCR – Screen saver. A filename extension for a file that contains a Microsoft Windows screen saver (see Fig. S-3).

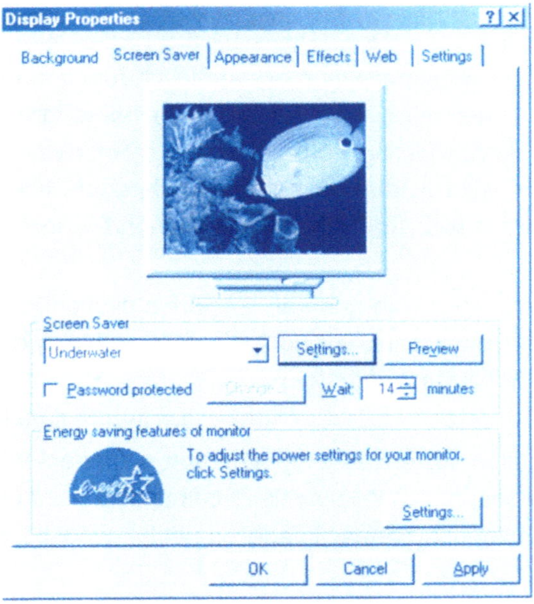

Fig. S-3. An example of an SCR file

SCR – Screen Section file. A filename extension generated by ACUCOBOL-GT as well as by AcuBench. SCR files contain Screen Section COBOL code. Because they exist separately, developers can easily merge their screen sections into existing applications. See also COBOL and IDE.

SCR – Signal-to-Crosstalk Ratio. A value that represents the decibel level (see dB) of the ratio between the signal propagated on the twisted-pair cable and the noise in the cable.

SCR – Sustained Cell Rate. One of the ATM QoS parameters that specifies how fast the user wants to send data. SCR is the expected cell rate averaged over a long time interval. See also QoS (Quality of Service).

SCS – SNA Character String. In SNA terminology, a type of data string where data characters and control characters are carried within the same transmission frame. SCS is used as a printing mode that allows various printing and formatting capabilities. See also System Network Architecture (SNA).

SCSA – Signal Computing System Architecture. An architectural framework for computer telephony systems (see CTI). The framework includes three layers: applications, the software model and the hardware model. The applications take charge of the media section of a call and the call flow. The software model provides programming interfaces for handling the media section of a call (see TAPI and TSAPI). The hardware model consists of appropriate bus protocols.

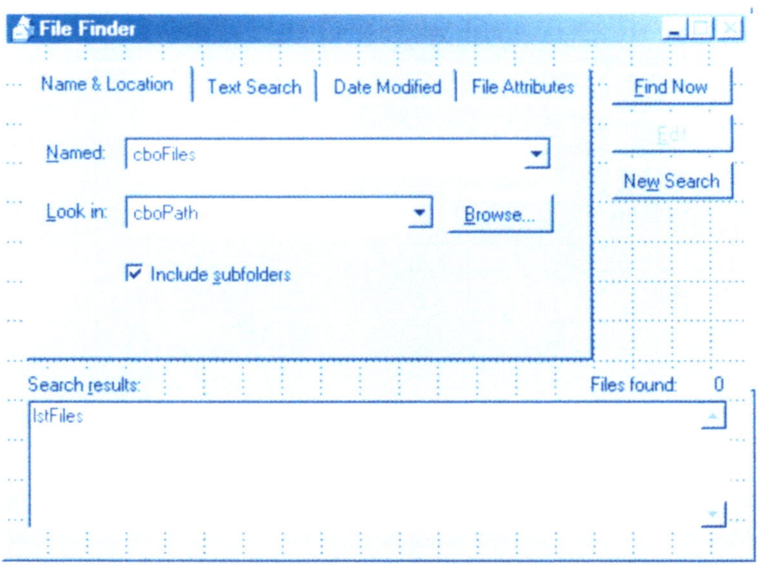

Fig. S-4. An example of an SCT (SCX) file

SCSI – Small Computer System Interface. A standard high-speed parallel generic interface (pronounced "scuzzy") defined by the ANSI X3T9.2 committee as ANSI standard X3.131-1986, and later on by ISO/IEC (ISO/IEC9316). A SCSI interface is used for connecting microcomputers to peripheral devices, such as disks, CD-ROMs and printers, as well as to other computers and

LANs. In SCSI, the physical characteristics of, for example, a hard disk, such as the number of cylinders, tracks and sectors, are hidden by the virtual device interface. SCSI can connect up to 7 devices to a single controller, with priority given to the device with the highest address. It can operate either in asynchronous or synchronous mode. The original standard is now called SCSI-1 to distinguish it from Wide SCSI (known as SCSI-2) and Fast SCSI (known as SCSI-3). In addition, SCSI devices can be daisy-chained, so that a single adapter can support a variety of devices. In that case every device in a daisy chain has its own address, and the last one has an adequate termination.

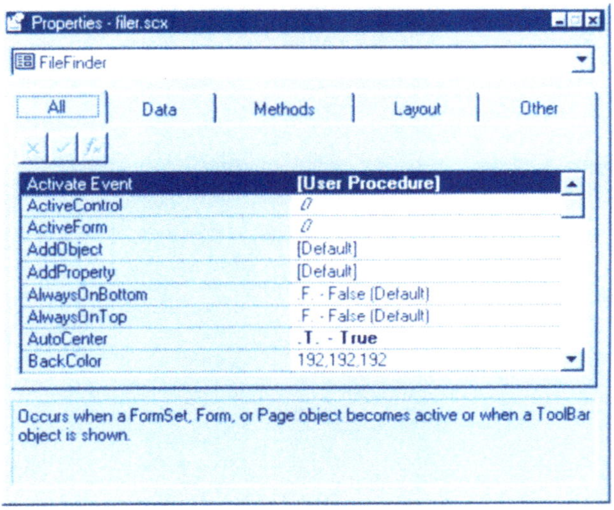

Fig. S-5. A part of an SCT (SCX) file that controls the objects in Fig. S-4

SCT – Screen Control Template. A filename extension for a file that contains a primary form memo generated using Visual FoxPro (see Figs. S-4 and S-5). Actually, Figs. S-4 and S-5 show parts of the same file. Figure S-4 shows an example of a screen developed for File Finder, whilst Fig. S-5 shows the properties of objects on the screen. See also SCX.

SCVP – Simple Certificate Validation Protocol. An Internet draft describing a protocol that allows a client to offload certificate handling to a server. The primary goal of SCVP is to make it easier for applications to deploy systems using the Public Key Infrastructure (see PKI).

SCX – Screen Control any (X). See SCT.

SD – Start Delimiter. A field in a Token Ring token (see TR).

SD – Structured Design. One of a number of systematic top-down design techniques used in software engineering, usually after structured analysis. See also SSA (Structured System Analysis).

SD2 – Sound Designer 2. See SDII.

SDII – Sound Designer II. An audio file format that can be monophonic or stereophonic.

SDDI – Shielded Distributed Data Interface. An implementation of the FDDI architecture and protocols over shielded twisted-pair cables (see STP). See FDDI. See also Copper Distributed Data Interface (CDDI).

SDH – Synchronous Digital Hierarchy. The European standard for high-speed data communications over fiber-optic media. The transmission rates range from 155.52 Mbps to 2.5 Gbps. SDH can improve network reliability and performance, and provides faster provision of new services such as ATM. The American version is called the Synchronous Optical Network (see SONET).

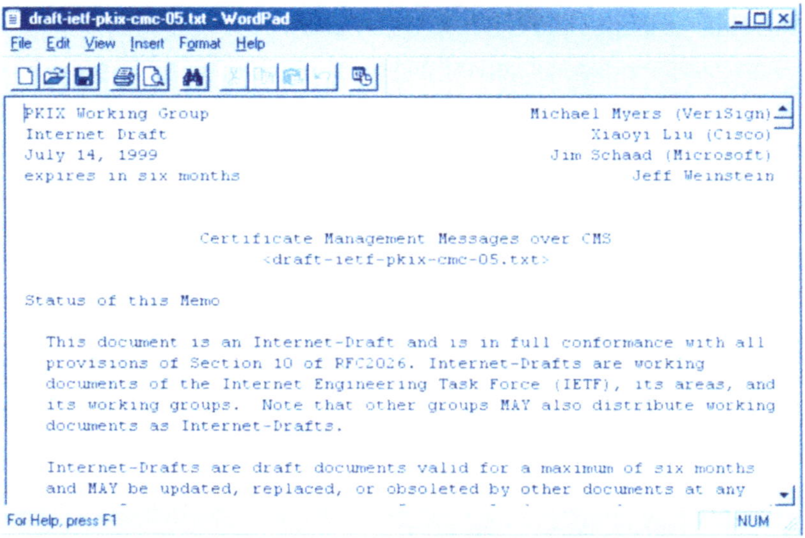

Fig. S-6. WordPad in action on a single document

SDI – Single Document Interface. A user interface architecture in Microsoft Windows that allows a user to work with just one document at a time. In order to work on another document, the user must first close the current document. A typical example of an SDI is WordPad (see Fig. S-6). Compare with MDI (Multiple Document Interface).

SDK – Software Development Kit. In general, any collection of software tools and associated documentation that helps developers to produce applications, e.g. the Microsoft software development kit for Windows NT 4.0, consisting of 12 CDs, which include the tools, services and infrastructure to enable a new generation of distributed Intranet and Internet applications. It includes:

- Distributed COM (see DCOM);
- Internet Information Server (see IIS);
- Microsoft NetShow, which provides an open software platform for live and online multimedia delivery over the Internet and intranets;
- Microsoft Index Server with a built-in search engine for all types of information retrieval and Java Virtual Machine;
- Microsoft Transaction Server;
- Active Directory that supports X.500, LDAP and DNS, all integrated with distributed security with Kerberos and SOCKS, etc.;
- Microsoft Management Console (see MMC).

The SDK platform also includes Windows NT Server 4.0, with Microsoft Internet Information Server, and BackOffice, a Microsoft integrated suite of server applications. Visual Basic, allowing easy development of ActiveX controls, Internet Studio, Visual J++ and Microsoft FrontPage are also included. Microsoft Content Replication System, Internet Chat Server, Internet Explorer, Internet Personalization System, Administration Kit, Internet Connection Wizard, NetMeeting, ActiveX Control Gallery and Control Pad are included as well. DirectX API, WebPost Wizard, ADO, Microsoft GIF Animator, and Microsoft Office Internet Assistant and Viewer are also available, etc.

SDL – Specification and Design Language. A language defined by the CCITT recommendation Z100, providing a tool for the unambiguous specification and description of telecommunication systems behavior. It also includes process control and real-time applications.

SDLC – Synchronous Data-Link Control. A technique developed in IBM for managing synchronous code-transparent bit-oriented serial data transfer organized in frames over a communication line. The connection line may be configured as point-to-point, multipoint or loop link, both switched or nonswitched. The precursor protocol of the ANSI ADCCP and ISO HDLC.

SDLC – Systems Development Life Cycle. The history of an information system divided into five phases: planning, analysis, architectural and detailed system design, implementation and maintenance. It is usually an iterative rather than a sequential process.

SDM – Space Division Multiplexing. An obsolete term related to the first automated form of multiplexing. It has been replaced with FDM and TDM. See FDM and TDM.

SDMI – Secure Digital Music Initiative. An organization (http://www.sdmi.org) formed in 1999 that brings together the recording industry and technology vendors to develop a specification for digital music security.

SDP – Session Description Protocol. The IETF protocol used to announce and initiate multimedia sessions.

SDRAM – Synchronous Dynamic Random-Access Memory. A form of DRAM, where a separate clock signal is added to the control signals.

SDT – Structured Data Transfer. An AAL1 data transfer mode where data is structured in blocks which are then segmented into cells for transfer. See also AAL.

SDTS – Spatial Data Transfer Standard. The US standard that provides a solution to the problem of spatial (i.e. geographic, cartographic, geological) data transfer from the conceptual level to the detailed state required for physical file encoding. SDTS addresses modeling spatial data concepts, data structures, and logical and physical file structures, as well as the meaningful data content and data quality.

SDU – Service Data Unit. A term used in the OSI Reference Model (see OSI) that applies to a unit of information from an upper-layer protocol that defines a service request to a lower-layer protocol.

SDX – Storage Data Acceleration (X). A technology developed by Western Digital that accelerates hard drive and CD-ROM data flow.

SE – Software Engineering. The computer science field concerned with the theories, methods and tools that are needed to develop software products. There are various models of the software lifecycle and many methods for different phases. Software engineering includes project management, software requirements engineering, analysis, definition and specification, software prototyping, software design, software reliability and reusability, software verification, validation and maintenance, re-engineering, cost estimation, etc. See also S/W (Software).

SE – Storage Engine. A part of Microsoft SQL Server. The SE is used for file management, concurrency control, building and reading the physical pages used to store data, managing the data buffers, logging and recovery.

SE – Switching Element. A device or a network node used to perform ATM switching functions based on the VPI or a VPI/VCI pair. See also VPI and VCI.

SEA – Security Extension Architecture. The W3C effort looking for an architecture for securing HTTP messages using three classes of protocol extensions: signature, encryption and key-exchange. These three modules can only be used in the exact order specified. Encryption and key-exchange may only be used once per message. See also PEP, SHTTP and S/MIME.

SEA – Software Engineering and Applications. The IASTED international conference that deals with the latest research and development in the field of software engineering and its applications (see SE, Software Engineering).

SEAL – Simple and Efficient Adaptation Layer. An ATM adaptation protocol, in the ATM Forum terminology named AAL5. SEAL supports ATM service classes C and D (see AAL). It determines whether AAL is offered a guaranteed delivery with flow control, or no guaranteed delivery. It also supports both message and stream modes. In the message mode, an application can pass a datagram of length 1 to 65,535 bytes to the AAL layer and have it delivered to the destination, either on a guaranteed or a best-effort basis.

SEAL – Software-optimized Encryption Algorithm. The binary additive stream cipher proposed in 1993.

SEC – Sponsor Executive Committee. The executive committee which coordinates all activities of the IEEE Portable Application Standards Committee (see PASC).

SECBR – Severely Errored Cell Block Ratio. A non-negotiable QoS parameter that specifies the fraction of an n-cell block for which m or more cells contain an error. See also QoS (Quality of Service).

SECC – Single-Edge Contact Cartridge. The packaging design for the Intel Pentium II processor. See also SECCII.

SECCII – Single-Edge Contact Cartridge II. The packaging design for the Intel Pentium III processor, which uses OLGA cooling. Also known as SECC2. See also OLGA.

SEDOS – Software Environment for the Design of Open Systems. An ESPRIT project. See ESPRIT.

SEE – Software Engineering Environment. A set of hardware and software tools which can act in combination in an integrated and coherent framework to provide support for the whole software development process from the initial specification through to testing and system delivery. See also IPSE (Integrated Project Support Environment) and SE (Software Engineering).

SEI – Software Engineering Institute. A research institute at Carnegie-Mellon University aimed at software technology transfer. SEI was established to improve the overall capabilities of the US software industry. See also CMM (Capability Maturity Model).

SEKE – Software Engineering and Knowledge Engineering. An international conference focusing on the application of either software engineering methods in knowledge engineering or knowledge-based techniques in software engineering.

SEPP – Secure Electronic Payment Protocol. See SET.

SEPP – Single-Edge Processor Package. A method of housing microprocessors.

SES – Severely Errored Seconds. A unit used to specify the error performance of T carrier systems. SES indicates a second that contains 10 or more errors, usually expressed as SES per hour, day or week. Compare with BER.

SES – Source-End Station. An ATM termination point, which is the source of ATM messages of a connection. It is used as a reference point for the Available Bit Rate Service (see ABR). See also DES (Destination End-Station).

SET – Secure Electronic Transactions. The protocol for electronic commerce (see EC) used to purchase products safely over the Internet. SET addresses five fundamental criteria to do that, as follows:

- Confidentiality of payment and ordering information. Consumers want to be sure that the information they are sending is going to be secure yet readily available to the people intended.
- Integrity of all transmitted data. It is impossible for anyone to change the encrypted “order”.
- Cardholder authentication. SET uses a system of digital signatures to make sure the cardholder is the legitimate user of the account.
- Merchant authentication. Verifying that the merchant is authorized to make transactions through the financial institution.
- Hardware and software independence. There is no monopoly relating to the right to use the protocol.

A credit card company (a financial institution) may offer SET. Once an account has been established, the user can go to a website, select a desired product, and send the order. The financial institution provides a certificate for its user. When the customer places an order, SET sends the merchant three things, all of which have the customer's own electronic "signature" attached to them: the order information (encrypted by the merchant's key); the payment information (encrypted with the bank's key); and the "message digest" that contains information about both the order and the payment information. Both Microsoft and Netscape are working with Visa and MasterCard to develop SET-compatible browsers.

SETI – Search for Extraterrestrial Intelligence. The computer-supported scientific effort to detect intelligent life elsewhere in the universe. More information is available at http://www.seti-inst.edu

S-F – Store-and-Forward. Applied to communication systems in which messages are received at intermediate routing points and recorded (stored). They are then transmitted (forwarded) to a further routing point or to the ultimate recipient (see MHS).

SF – SuperFrame. A DS1 framing format in which 24 DS0 timeslots plus a coded framing bit are organized into a frame which is repeated 12 times to form the SF.

SFL – Secure MIME Freeware Library. A reference implementation of the Secure MIME (see S/MIME) Cryptographic Message Syntax (see CMS).

SFT – System Fault Tolerance. A strategy used by Novell for protecting data. Three levels of SFT exist, as follows:

1. Read after write and verify.
2. Apply disk mirroring to the first level.
3. Apply 2nd strategy and duplicate servers.

SG – Signal Ground. Signal ground provides a common reference ground for both sides of a data communications link. In the full 25-pin RS-232C standard SG is pin 7. In the abbreviated 9-pin PC interface SG is pin 5. See also Recommended Standard (RS).

SGAM – Shared Global Allocation Map. In Microsoft SQL Server, a method used to record the allocation of currently used disk space (mixed and with at least one unused page). Each GAM covers 64,000 spaces with nearly 4 GB of data. Compare with GAM.

SGCP – Simple Gateway Control Protocol. An early effort (from 1998) made by Cisco and Bellcore in order to provide standardized mechanisms for gateways to permit voice, video and data traffic over large-scale IP networks. Later, SGCP was combined with the IP Device Control (see IPDC) effort to form the common mechanism known as the Media Gateway Control Protocol.

SGI – Silicon Graphics Inc. One of the leading manufacturers of workstations, servers and software for computer graphics and image processing (http://www.sgi.com).

SGML – Standard Generalized Markup Language. An international standard (ISO8879) for the definition of system-independent device-independent methods of representing text in electronic form.

SGMP – Simple Gateway Monitoring Protocol. A former network management protocol in the IP protocol suite. It was replaced by SNMP.

SGRAM – Synchronous Graphics Random-Access Memory. A type of synchronous DRAM (see SDRAM) optimized for use in graphics hardware. It is used in graphics-intensive operations such as 3-D rendering and full-motion video.

SGT – Singapore Time. Time zone. UTC + 8.00 hours. See TZ.

SHA – Secure Hash Algorithm. A message digest function that processes input data in 512-bit blocks and generates a 160-bit message digest. It is a government standard approved by the US National Institute of Standards and Technology (see NIST). Each output buffer is updated 80 times for each 512-bit-long input block. Each round of 20 rounds uses different mixing functions. Compare with MD (Message Digest).

shar – shell archive. A filename extension for a file that contains a UNIX shell archive.

SHF – Super-High Frequency. Transmission frequencies in the range 3–30 GHz.

SHTTP – Secure HTTP. A secure message-oriented protocol (RFC2660) designed for use in conjunction with HTTP. The SHTTP syntax mimics the HTTP syntax in an effort to ease integration with systems that already process HTTP. A SHTTP message consists of a request or status line (as in HTTP) followed by a series of RFC822-style headers followed by encapsulated content. Once the content has been recovered, it should be another SHTTP message, a HTTP message or simple data. The protocol emphasizes maximum flexibility in the choice of key management mechanisms, security policies and cryptographic algorithms by supporting option negotiation between parties for each transaction. SHTTP provides secure communication mechanisms in a HTTP client/server pair. The protocol provides symmetric capabilities to both the client and the server (i.e. equal treatment is given to both requests and replies, as well as to the preferences of both parties) while preserving the transaction model and the implementation characteristics of HTTP. The creation of an SHTTP message can be thought of as a function with three inputs: the cleartext message; the receiver's cryptographic preferences and keying material; and the sender's preferences and keying material. Any message may be signed, authenticated, encrypted, or any combination of these (including no protection). Multiple key management mechanisms are supported, including password-style manually shared secrets, public-key exchange and Kerberos ticket distribution. See also SSL. See the latest information at http://www.ietf.cnri.reston.va.us

SI – Système International d'Unités. International System of Units.

SIA – Semiconductor Industry Association. An association formed in 1977 primarily to represent the industry in tax and trade issues.

SICL – Standard Instrument Control Library. A platform-independent API for software, to control and test electronic instruments conforming to IEEE488.

SID – Security Identifier. A variable-length data structure used in Windows NT for unique identification of a user or a group in any NT implementation.

SIFT – Stanford Information Filtering Tool. The Internet searching machine (http://www.reference.com) that allows users to conduct searches and submit keywords; it skims thousands of Usenet news messages to find stories of interest. This free service also notifies users via e-mail once all the articles they have requested are available.

SIG – Special Interest Group. A number of ACM special interest groups in distinct areas of information technologies, as explained below. Each SIG organizes itself around those specific activities that best serve both its practitioners and research-based constituencies. It is usually up to SIGs to organize their own conferences and workshops as well as to produce newsletters and other publications. For more information see http://www.acm.org, or just check the following acronyms for the area of most interest to you.

SIG3C – SIG on Computing at Community Colleges. The ACM SIG focusing on the exchange of the experience of student education. SIG3C issues a quarterly publication called 3C Online.

SIGACT – SIG on Algorithms and Computation Theory. This ACM SIG specializes on the theoretical foundations of computer science. This includes algorithm design, parallel computation, VLSI design, cryptographic protocols computational geometry, machine learning, number theory, graph theory, etc. It publishes the quarterly newsletter ACM SIGACT.

SIGAda – SIG on Ada. The ACM SIG on the Ada programming language interested in understanding the scientific, technical and organizational aspects of Ada usage, standardization, environments, etc. Members of SIGAda receive the bimonthly newsletter ACM Ada Letters.

SIGAPL – SIG on the APL and J Languages. The ACM SIG interested in the development and application areas of the APL language and J (a relatively new form of APL). The quarterly published APL Quote Quad newsletter features independent reviews on vendor products. Also, it includes the complete proceedings from its annual conference. See also APL.

SIGAPP – SIG on Applied Computing. The ACM SIG oriented to innovative applications, technology transfer, strategic research, experimental computing, and the management of computing. The SIG Applied Computing Review newsletter is published twice a year.

SIGARCH – SIG on Computer Architecture. The ACM forum for interchange of ideas about future hardware architectures. Among other things, SIGARCH sponsors the annual International Symposium on Computer Architecture (see ISCA) and publishes the newsletter Computer Architecture News five times a year.

SIGART – SIG on Artificial Intelligence. The ACM SIG focusing on the study of human intelligence and its realization by computers. The main ideas are exchanged via the SIGART Bulletin which shows reviewed papers, announcements, correspondence, conference reports, reviews, and other things of interest.

SIGBIO – SIG on Biomedical Computing. The ACM SIG focusing on health and the biological sciences. The SIGBIO Newsletter is published quarterly.

SIGCAPH – SIG on Computers and the Physically Handicapped. The ACM SIG which promotes the professional interests of computing personnel with physical disabilities and the application of computing and information technology in solving relevant disability problems. The Computers and the Physically Handicapped newsletter is published three times a year.

SIGCAS – SIG on Computers and Society. The ACM SIG interested in the impacts of computers on society. It is active in developing an electronic forum through acm.org. Also, SIGCAS publishes a quarterly newsletter, Computers and Society.

SIGCHI – SIG on Computer–Human Interaction. The ACM SIG concentrating on research and development efforts in the design and evolution of user interfaces (see HCI, GUI and UI). It serves as a forum for the exchange of ideas among scientists in different fields (computers, psychology, social issues) and end-users. The SIGCHI Bulletin is published quarterly.

SIGCOMM – SIG on Data Communication. The ACM SIG focusing on network architecture, protocols, distributed systems and standard news. Five times a year SIGCOMM publishes the Computer Communication Review, which also includes the proceedings of its annual conference. Furthermore, SIGCOMM and IEEE together publish the ACM/IEEE Transactions on Networking journal (see TON).

SIGCPR – SIG on Computer Personnel Research. The ACM SIG focuses on the needs, interests and abilities of computer professionals, managers and end-users working with information technology. The SIGCPR Newsletter is published quarterly.

SIGCSE – SIG on Computer Science Education. The ACM SIG focusing on the development, implementation and evaluation of computer science programs and courses in universities. SIGCSE publishes a quarterly SIGCSE Bulletin, which includes the annual conference proceedings.

SIGCUE – SIG on Computer Uses in Education. The ACM SIG interested in using computers and related technology to aid the educational process.

SIGDA – SIG on Design Automation. The ACM SIG focusing on computer applications in electrical and electronic design, algorithms and techniques for computer-aided design, and the testing of such systems, etc. The SIGDA Network Server gives members online access. The SIGDA Newsletter is published twice a year.

SIGDOC – SIG for Documentation. The ACM SIG concentrating on documentation and user support for computer products and systems. The members of SIGDOC study processes, methods and technologies that can be applied for user support, either by paper or by electronic communication.

SIGecom – SIG on Electronic Commerce. The ACM SIG focusing on research and advanced applications relating to electronic commerce (see EC).

SIGGRAPH – SIG on Computer Graphics and Interactive Techniques. The ACM SIG interested in research, technology and applications in computer graphics and interactive techniques. SIGGRAPH provides two publications, the Video Review series, and the quarterly newsletter, Computer Graphics. Also, it organizes a SIGGRAPH annual conference.

SIGGROUP – SIG on Supporting Group Work. The ACM SIG interested in topics related to Computer-Supported Cooperative Work (see CSCW). Such topics include the integration of multiple computer-based tools and technologies and the impact on the human activities supported by these technologies.

SIGIR – SIG on Information Retrieval. The ACM SIG interested in all aspects of information storage, retrieval and dissemination. SIGIR Forum is published twice a year, and IR-L, a digest on information retrieval, is distributed regularly on the Internet.

SIGKDD – SIG on Knowledge Discovery in Data. The ACM SIG focusing on research and development on the processes and algorithms involved in knowledge discovery using all types of machine-readable data sources.

SIGMICRO – SIG on Microarchitecture. The ACM SIG interested in computer microarchitecture, especially features permitting instruction-level parallelism and their related implications for compiler design.

SIGMIS – SIG on Management Information Systems. The ACM SIG interested in the planning, design, development, implementation, maintenance, operation and management of business information technology. See also MIS (Management Information System).

SIGMM – SIG on Multimedia. The ACM SIG interested in all aspects of multimedia computing, communication, storage and applications.

SIGMOBILE – SIG on Mobility of Systems, Users, Data and Computing. The ACM SIG interested in the mobility of systems, users, data and computing. The research covers portable computers, wireless networks, nomadic computing, etc. The SIGMOBILE Newsletter is published four times a year.

SIGMOD – SIG on Management of Data. The ACM SIG interested in database technology. The SIGMOD Record is published quarterly.

SIGNUM – SIG on Numerical Mathematics. The ACM SIG interested in design, analysis and algorithms for numerical computation.

SIGOPS – SIG on Operating Systems. The ACM SIG interested in operating systems research and development. Operating System Review is published five times a year and includes conference proceedings.

SIGPLAN – SIG on Programming Languages. The ACM SIG focusing on the design, implementation and efficient use of programming languages. ACM SIGPLAN Notices is published monthly.

SIGSAC – SIG on Security, Audit and Control. The ACM SIG focusing on the theoretical foundations of system security

SIGSAM – SIG on Symbolic and Algebraic Manipulation. The ACM SIG focusing on practical and theoretical aspects of algebraic and symbolic mathematical computations. It includes related research in design, analysis, the application of algorithms, data structures, systems and languages.

SIGSIM – SIG on Simulation and Modeling. The ACM SIG focusing on the state-of-the-art in simulation and modeling. SIGSIM publishes the newsletter Simulation Digest.

SIGSOFT – SIG on Software Engineering. This ACM SIG focuses on all aspects of software development and maintenance. SIGSOFT publishes a bimonthly newsletter, Software Engineering Notes.

SIGSound – SIG on Electronic Forum on Sound Technology. The ACM SIG, which presents an electronic forum for the exchange of information on software, algorithms, hardware and applications for digitally generated and/or manipulated audio signals.

SIGUCCS – SIG on University and College Computing Services. The ACM SIG focusing on preparing its members to assist scholars in the effective use of technology.

SIGWEB – SIG on Hypertext, Hypermedia and Web. The ACM SIG focusing on multidisciplinary field of hypertext and hypermedia. Formerly SIGLINK.

SII – Systems Integration Interface. Used to define the proposed multivendor integration architecture sponsored by NTT of Japan, it relates to any set of standardized services that are used to interconnect computer-based systems.

SILK – Speech, Image, Language, Knowledge. The next-generation user interface metaphor, it's expected to replace the WIMP metaphor. The term highlights the four main future aspects of human–computer interaction.

SIMD – Single-Instruction Multiple Data. The processor architecture where many processing elements perform the same operations on different data.

SIMM – Single In-line Memory Module. A small circuit board used to hold surface-mounted memory chips (8, 16 or 32 MB). See also DIMM and SMT (Surface Mounting Technology).

SIP – Signal and Image Processing. The IASTED international conference focusing on all areas of signal and image processing.

SIP – Single In-line Package. A type of package for an electronic component in which all connectors come from one side of the package (e.g. transistors and resistors arrays).

SIPP – Simple Internet Protocol Plus. See IPv6 (Internet Protocol version 6).

SIPP – Single In-line Pin Package. See SIP.

SIR – Serial Infrared. A system developed by Hewlett-Packard for transmitting data between two devices up to 1 m apart using an infrared light beam. The infrared ports on the receiving and the sending devices must be aligned. Generally, SIR is used with laptops and many notebook computers, as well as with peripherals such as printers. See also infrared port (IR).

sixel – six pixels. A combination of the lower six bits of a byte to correspond to six vertical printer dots. The advantage of sixel is that the characters generated by using only the lower six bits stay within the displayable ASCII characters, so graphics data can be sent to the printer over virtually any type of data communications link.

SKCF – Strategic Knowledge and Concept Formation. An international workshop in the area of strategic knowledge and concept formation. Topics of interest include metaknowledge, representation of strategic knowledge, modeling and ambiguity of concept formation, concept design cognition, theoretical models of strategic knowledge in design, appropriate applications, empirical studies of design support, etc.

SLA – Service-Level Agreement. A contract between an Internet Service Provider (see ISP) and a customer that specifies what services the ISP will provide. Some measurable things that could be included in an SLA are: the number of simultaneous users, response time for help, dial-in access availability, usage statistics, etc.

SLD – Second-Level Domain. The portion of a Uniform Resource Locator (see URL) that identifies the specific administrative owner associated with an IP address. The SLD also includes the top-level domain name (see TLD). For instance, in "bankerinter.net", the TLD name is net, and the SLD name is bankerinter. See also DNS.

SLD – Slide file. A filename extension for a file that contains an AutoCAD slide.

SLED – Single Large Expensive Disk. A storage strategy, in contrast to RAID, which uses a single large disk to hold data.

SLI – Session-Level Interface. In SNA, a higher-level interface that facilitates the opening and closing of SNA sessions with host LU0, LU1, LU2 and LU3 applications. See also LU. Compare with RUI.

SLIP – Serial-Line Internet Protocol. A communication protocol (RFC1055) used to run IP over serial lines, such as telephone circuits or RS-232 cables connected to a modem, a predecessor of the Point-to-Point Protocol (see PPP).

SLS – Secondary Link Station. A node that serves as a slave node responding to communications initiated by a primary link station (see PLS), used in SDLC environments.

SLSI – Super-Large-Scale Integration. A term that refers to the density with which components are packed onto an integrated circuit. Generally, SLSI refers to the range 50,000–100,000 such components in a single integrated circuit.

SM – Shared Memory. A common memory unit that appears in multiprocessor architectures shared by several central processing units. Such architectures can be bus-based, where all processors use the same bus to access the shared memory, or ring-based, where the total address space is divided into a private part and a shared part, and is switched via multiple clusters. See also DSM, UMA and NUMA.

SM – Standby Monitor. A node in a Token Ring network (see TR) that is ready to take over the role of an active monitor (see AM) in case the AM fails.

SMAC – Source MAC. A MAC address specified in the source address field of a packet. Compare with DMAC (Destination MAC). See also MAC (Media Access Control).

SMAE – System Management Application Entity. The component used in OSI network management that implements the necessary services and functionality of network management at the OSI application level. See also CMIS, SMAP and SMASE.

SMAP – System Management Application Process. The software used in OSI network management that implements the network management in a single node. The single node in this particular case may be a regular station, a router, a bridge, an FEP, or another type of node. See also SMAE and SMASE.

SMART – Self-Monitoring, Analysis and Reporting Technology. A type of hard drive technology (see HDD) that monitors and reports impending drive failures.

SMASE – System Management Application Service Element. The component used in OSI network management that works as an agent or as a network manager for a system management application entity (see SMAE). SMASE relies on both a management service element (see CMISE) and a non-management service element (see ASE).

SMB – Server Message Block. A message protocol developed by Microsoft and used by some operating systems to share files. It allows client/server communication in heterogeneous environments (see C/S). SMB can be used on top of the TCP/IP, IPX and NetBEUI protocols. See also CIFS, an IETF counterpart of SMB.

SMC – Systems, Man and Cybernetics. An IEEE conference focusing on communications and controls through humans. Topics include systems science, systems engineering, computing and control, cybernetics, multimedia and communications, robotics and applications, etc.

SMD – Surface-Mount Device. A device that uses surface-mount technology (see SMT) for placement and electrical connection on an electronic circuit board.

SMDR – Station Message Detail Recording. Process whereby details of a telephone handset's use are centrally recorded. Used both for cost accounting and security. Often implemented as one of the functions of a Private Branch Exchange (see PBX).

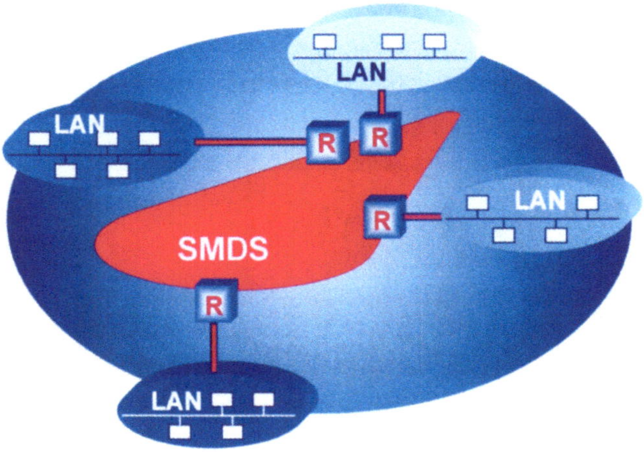

Fig. S-7. Interconnection between LANs using SMDS

SMDS – Switched Multimegabit Data Service. A connectionless high-speed datagram-based public data network service designed to connect together multiple LANs (see Fig. S-7), developed by Bellcore in the 1980s and deployed in the early 1990s by telephone companies as the basis of their data networks. It was the first broadband high-speed switched service offered to the public.

S

SME – Small-to-Medium Enterprise. A term used to identify organizations that are larger than SOHO-sized companies and smaller than enterprises. An SME has been defined by the European Union as a legally independent company with no more than 500 employees. See also SOHO.

SMF – Screen Metafile. A filename extension for files created by AcuBench that contain screens under development. See also COBOL.

SMF – Single-Mode Fiber. A fiber-optic cable in which the signal propagates in a single mode or path. Compare with MMF.

SMF – Standard MIDI File. The file format that allows users to exchange sequenced MIDI data between different software applications. There are two variants of the SMF format, called Type 0, which uses a single track of data, and Type 1, which uses multitrack data. See also MIDI.

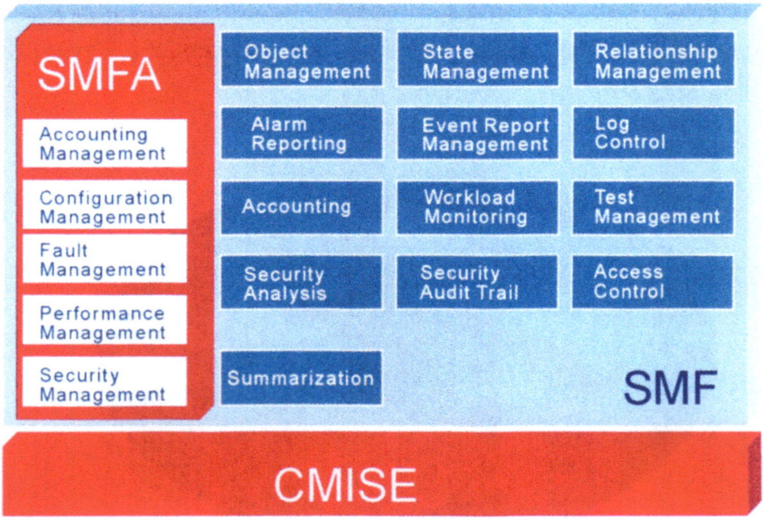

Fig. S-8. SMF functionality in its environment

SMF – System Management Function. The OSI management model that describes five major system management domains and the functions used by these domains. The domains, known as system management functional areas (see SMFA), are accounting management, configuration management, fault management, performance management, and security management, as depicted in Fig. S-8. SMF components rely on the CMISE to accomplish their work. SMF components, shown in Fig. S-8, are responsible for system management, as follows:

- Object management: Create, delete, examine and update objects.
- State management: Monitor object management states and report when these states are changed.
- Relationship management: Establish, monitor and view the relationships among objects.
- Alarm reporting: Provide information about errors or other inappropriate network operation.
- Event reporting: Select events to be reported and specify their destinations.
- Log control: Specify how to handle event logs.
- Security alarm reporting: Provide information related to network security.
- Security audit trail: Specify the events and their formats for recording in the security log.
- Access control: Control access to management operations.
- Accounting and workload monitoring: Keep track of resource usage, supervise accounting and billing.
- Summarization: A model for analyzing the network management.
- Test management: A model for testing network components.

SMFA – System Management Functional Area. Any of the five major domains that make up the OSI management model, as shown in Fig. S-8.

SMI – Self-Mounting Image. A filename extension for a file that contains a Macintosh disk image.

SMI – Structure of Management Information. One of the components in the IP management model. SMI covers the rules used to define the objects that can be accessed via the network management protocol inside the management information base (see MIB). These rules are defined in RFC1155. The representation of the objects uses a restricted version of ASN.1.

SMIL – Synchronized Multimedia Integration Language. A language (pronounced "smile") based on XML that provides TV-like content on the Web. Using SMIL, Web creators can define and synchronize multimedia elements (video, sound, still images). SMIL also allows team creation of a multimedia presentation where the presentation elements come from different sites and from different creators. See also XML. The first public draft of SML was released by W3C in November 1997.

SMILE – 3D Structure from Multiple Images of Large-scale Environments. An international workshop focusing on the visual acquisition of 3D models of real scenes and their application to virtual and augmented reality.

S/MIME – Secure (Signed) MIME. A standard for encrypted and digitally signed electronic mail that allows users to send encrypted messages and authenticate received messages. See also MIME.

SMIT – System Management Interface Tool. The software tool available in the IBM AIX operating system that allows the management of such systems. It consists of a set of ASCII commands and an appropriate GUI interface based on the X Window System. The main SMIT menu offers the following functions: software installation and maintenance, device connection and removal, spooler, security and user administration, system environment, performance and resource planning, etc. See also DSMIT (Distributed SMIT).

SMP – Symmetric Multiprocessing. A common term for two or more similar processors connected via a high-bandwidth link and managed by one operating system. Each processor has equal access to I/O devices. Also, each processor has an equal chance of getting a job from the associated operating system. Since the operating system divides the workload into tasks and assigns those tasks to the processors that are currently free, SMP reduces transaction time.

SMS – Short Messaging Service. A service similar to paging for sending up to 160-characters-long messages to mobile phones that use the Global System for Mobile communications (see GSM).

SMS – Storage Management Services. A collection of services for managing data storage and retrieval in the NetWare environment. These services are independent of operating systems and hardware.

SMS – System Management Server. A set of software tools developed by Microsoft used to manage personal computers in LAN. SMS runs under Windows NT, but also can manage DOS, Windows versions, OS/2 and MacOS clients.

SMSL – Standard Multimedia Scripting Language. The language under development that will provide an object-oriented interface between programming languages that can support the services required by SMSL and SGML/HyTime documents. The user will able to control the placement of graphics and video, the duration of their display, and playing of any accompanying audio. An important use for SMSL-based applications will be in developing interactive tutorials and maintenance manuals where different information is presented for different skill levels. To summarize, SMSL will provide key features for creating true multimedia. See also SGML and HyTime.

SMT – Simultaneous Multithreading. In RISC processors, a threading technique where instructions are simultaneously issued from multiple threads to the functional units (see FU) of a superscalar processor. See also RISC.

SMT – Software Methods and Tools. An international conference based around the experience reports of researchers and industrial practitioners actively involved in the development and use of software engineering methods and tools. The proceedings are published by IEEE CS Press.

SMT – Station Management. One of the four key FDDI layers (see Fig. S-9). It defines the configuration of the FDDI station, ring configuration and management, FDDI station insertion and removal, fault detection and reconfiguration, as well as the traffic statistics. See also FDDI, MAC, PHY and PMD.

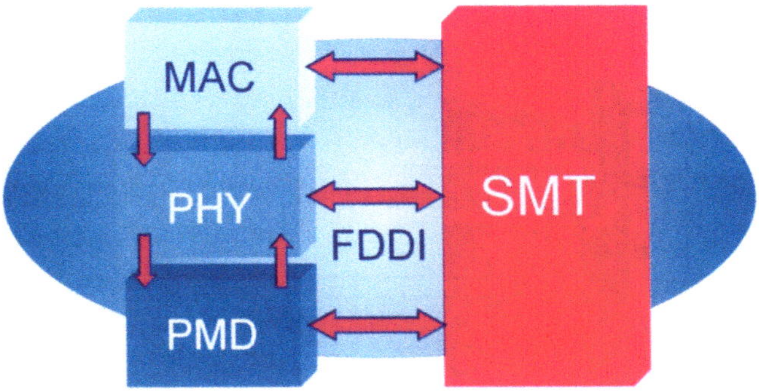

Fig. S-9. The four key FDDI component layers

SMT – Surface-Mount Technology. A method of manufacturing printed circuit boards where chips are fixed directly to the surface of the board instead of being soldered into predrilled holes.

SMTP – Simple Mail Transfer Protocol. A protocol used to transfer electronic mail between computers. It is specified in RFC821, with extensions specified in many other RFCs. It is a server-to-server protocol, so other protocols are used to access the messages. SMTP involves listening to port 25 in the destination machine. This e-mail daemon accepts incoming connections and copies messages from them into the appropriate mailboxes. See also e-mail and POP.

S/N – Signal-to-Noise ratio. An indication of the clearness and correctness of a communication link, measured in decibels. S/N represents the measure of power by which a signal exceeds the quantity of channel noise at the same point in transmission. Also abbreviated as SNR.

SNA – System Network Architecture. An IBM network architecture, born in 1974. It is a network framework that provides the infrastructure for network communications within an IBM environment. Because of its widespread use, SNA is a de facto standard. While it can use packet-switched networks for transport, SNA is mostly a circuit-switching rather than a packet-switching technology. However, SNA is not exactly a seven-layered architecture; the extended representation of SNA shown in Fig. S-10 gives an overall view of the SNA protocol stack which contrasts with the OSI protocol stack. The physical layer has the same purpose as in OSI networks, but it is not a part of the SNA specification. Thus, the SNA protocol stack (from bottom to top) begins with the data-link layer, where several protocols are used, such as BSC, SDLC, X.25 and LLC, as defined in IEEE802.2, etc.

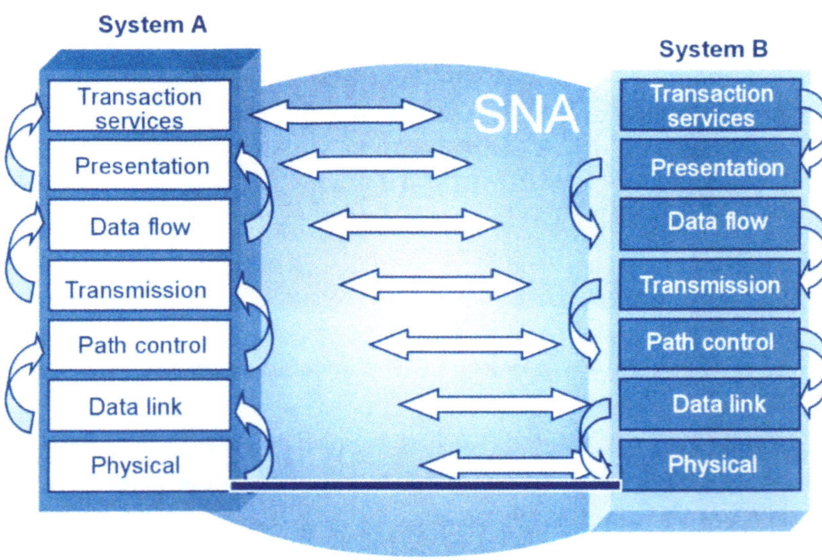

Fig. S-10. Extended SNA stack

The path control layer creates logical connections between the components associated with specific addresses (see NAU). This layer is also responsible for the physical routing. The transmission control layer is responsible for establishing, maintaining and terminating sessions between nodes. It also performs the automatic encryption and decryption of data. The data-flow control layer defines the general features of the connection. Such features include grouping data into bigger units, recovery after lost or error data transmissions definition of half-duplex or full-duplex connection, definition of the acknowledgement mechanism being used, etc. The presentation layer has a similar role as in an OSI network, making sure that data reaches its destination in the appropriate form. The transaction service layer is where applications communicate with each other.

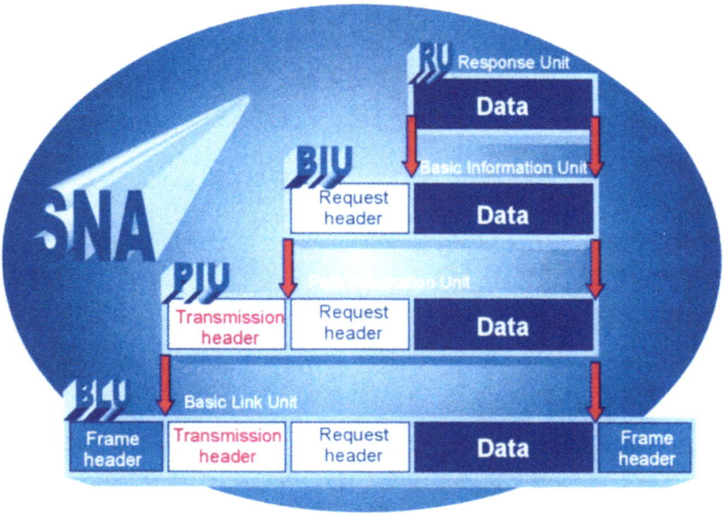

Fig. S-11. SNA packet encapsulation on a frame-oriented link

Figure S-11 shows the encapsulation that each layer applies to a message containing user data (see RU, Response Unit) being transmitted by an SNA node, assuming a frame-oriented data-link protocol (e.g. SDLC). There are many terms associated with SNA or within the SNA architecture that are explained elsewhere in the book. They include ACF, APPC, CICS, DDM, DCA, DIA, LU, NAU, NCP, PU, SAA, SDLC, SNADS and SSCP, etc. Compare with DNA, DSA, ONC and OSI.

SNAcP – Subnetwork Access Protocol. The type of protocol used at the lowest IONL sublayer that provides access and transfers data to a subnetwork. An example of an SNAcP protocol is X.25. See also IONL and SNDCP.

SNADS – System Network Architecture Distribution Services. A set of SNA services intended for delayed delivery (the delay is due to storage at intermediate switching points within a network) of data to its final destination. It uses the APPC protocol for data transport. See APPC (Advanced Program-to-Program Communication). See also SNA.

SNAP – Subnetwork Access Protocol. A version of the IEEE LAN logical link control frame (similar to the more traditional data-link level transmission frame) which allows the use of non-industry standard higher-level protocols.

SNC – Subnetwork Connection. In ATM networks, an entity that passes ATM cells transparently. It may be either standalone or a concatenation of SNCs and link connections.

SNDCP – Subnetwork-Dependent Convergence Protocol. The type of protocol used in the middle IONL sublayer that must be able to handle any problems relevant to the appropriate subnetwork. See also IONL. Compare with SNAcP and SNICP.

SNI – System Network Interconnection. An IBM-defined service that allows interconnection of SNA networks. See also SNA.

SNICP – Subnetwork-Independent Convergence Protocol. The type of protocol used in the highest IONL sublayer that must be able to provide routing and relaying capabilities in order to dispose data to its destination. An example of an SNICP protocol is the CLNP protocol. See also CLNP and IONL. Compare with SNAcP and SNDCP.

SNM – Simple Network Mail. A filename extension for a file that contains Netscape (Navigator or Communicator) mailbox. See also MBX.

SNMP – Simple Network Management Protocol. The Internet standard protocol developed to manage nodes on an IP network. The first version was defined in RFC1157. SNMPv2 (version 2) was defined in RFCs 1441 to 1452. The SNMP model of managed networks consists of four components, as follows:

- Managed nodes: They can be hosts, routers, bridges, printers, or other devices capable of communicating status information to the outside world. Such nodes must be capable of running an SNMP agent, the SNMP management process.
- Management stations: General-purpose computers running special management software that contains one or more processes that communicate with the agents over the network, issuing commands and getting responses.
- Management information: See MIB (Management Information Base).
- A management protocol.

SNOBOL – String-Oriented Symbolic Language. An interpretative string-processing language developed by Ralph Griswold in the mid-1960s. The acronym is not obvious. It comes from SN (StriNg), O (Oriented), BO (symBOlic), and L (Language).

SNPP – Simple Network Paging Protocol. A standard for sending one- and two-way wireless messages to pagers. SNPP is defined in RFC1861.

SNR – Signal-to-Noise Ratio. See S/N.

SNTP – Simple Network Time Protocol. A variant of the Network Time Protocol (see NTP) used to get the correct time from an official source and then pass this time information to subnet servers. SNTP is discussed in RFC2030.

SOA – Start Of Authority. A kind of Resource Record (see RR) that marks the beginning of a DNS zone, and typically appears as the first record in the name server for that domain.

SOAP – Simple Object Access Protocol. A protocol developed by Microsoft and a number of other companies that allows program-to-program communication independent of the operating system used. Information exchange in SOAP is based on the Extensible Markup Language (see XML) and HTTP. SOAP specifies exactly how to encode a HTTP header and an XML file so those programs can call each other and exchange data. Compare with IIOP and JRMI.

SOC – System On Chip. An emerging hardware technology representing the integration onto one chip of a complete system, consisting of the many integrated circuits that would normally be included in a printed circuit board system. SOC enables high-performance embedded processing solutions at a low single-chip cost.

SOCKS – Socket Secure. In short, SOCKS is a proxy system equipped with security, auditing, management, fault tolerance and alarm notification. However, SOCKS is not just another network firewall. It is a networking middleware system based on an agent technology that enables the safe use of enterprise networks on the Internet. From the technical point of view, SOCKS is used to establish a secure proxy data channel between two computers in a client/server environment. In a SOCKS network, all network application data flows through SOCKS, enabling SOCKS to collect, audit, screen, filter and control the network data, and create a rich network application data warehouse (see Fig. S-12). SOCKS5 supports a client-shared library for UNIX applications and a DLL for Windows applications.

SO DIMM – Small-Outline DIMM. A small version of the Dual In-line Memory Module (see DIMM) that has only 72 pins and can support only 32-bit transfer. SO DIMM chips are usually used in notebook computers.

SOFSEM – Software Seminar. An international conference devoted to the theory and industrial application of software systems. Different topics are selected every year. The proceedings are published by Springer-Verlag (see LNCS).

SOH – Start Of Header. A transmission control character used to signify the start of a transmission frame header.

SOHO – Small-Office/Home-Office. A term applied to the small-office or home-office environment with fewer than 50 employees. Also known as a virtual office. See also SME (Small-to-Medium Enterprise).

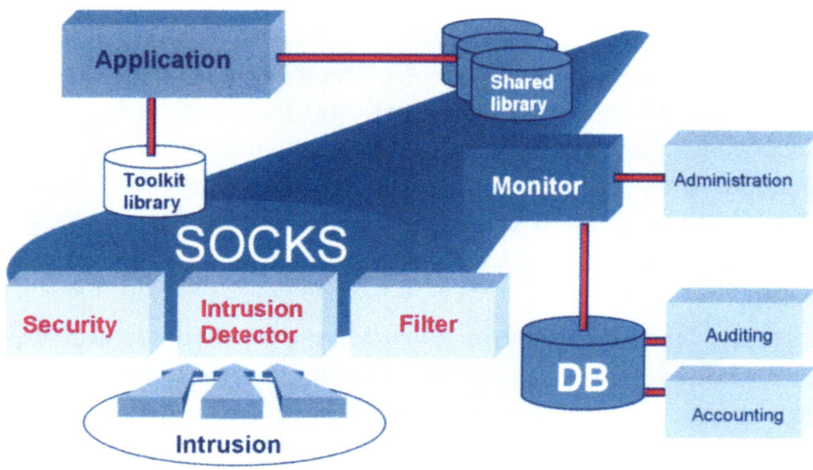

Fig. S-12. SOCKS in action

SOM – Start Of Message. A transmission framing character used in the BISYNC protocol to signify the start of a specific message. See also BISYNC.

SOM – System Object Model. The architecture developed by IBM that allows different applications to share binary code. Compare with COM (Component Object Model). See also DSOM.

SONET – Synchronous Optical Network. An international standard for high-speed data point-to-point communications over fiber-optic media. The transmission rates range from 51.84 Mbps to 2.488 Gbps. The European version of SONET is called the Synchronous Digital Hierarchy (see SDH). SONET is very suitable for supporting ATM-based services. SONET defines four layers:

- Photonic, that specifies cables, signals and components used.
- Section, where frames are created and correct transmission is monitored.

- Line, the layer responsible for frame delivery from one end of a line to another.
- Path, responsible for source–destination transmission.

SP – Stack Pointer. A register or a variable pointing to the top of a stack, a data structure which uses the LIFO algorithm. See LIFO (Last-In First-Out).

SPA – Spanning-Tree Algorithm. An algorithm, originally invented by DEC, that finds the most efficient path between segments of a multilooped bridged network; it allows redundant bridges to be used, for network flexibility. If a bridge fails, a new path to a redundant bridge is opened.

SPAA – Symposium on Parallel Algorithms and Architectures. The ACM annual symposium focusing on all areas of parallel algorithms and architectures, at all levels of parallelism from VLSI to supercomputers.

SPAG – Standards Promotion and Application Group. The group which was at the forefront of work on product conformance to formal standards and interoperability testing. The group introduced the SPAG "Product Support for Interoperability" (PSI) scheme. PSI has been taken over by the X/Open organization (see OSF and TOG). See also PSI.

SPAN – Space Physics Analysis Network. A computer network based on DECnet and maintained by NASA.

SPARC – Scalar Processor Architecture. The microprocessor architecture designed by Sun Microsystems with the intention of making it a de facto (industrial) standard. In keeping with their open philosophy, they passed responsibility for it to other companies, rather than manufacture it themselves. The evolution and standardization of SPARC is now directed by a nonprofit consortium. See also RISC (Reduced-Instruction-Set Computer).

SPARC – Standards Planning and Requirements Committee. An ANSI committee that helped write the 1977 database standard specifications. The committee suggested the three-level database architecture (see Fig. S-13) known as the three-schema architecture. The three levels are three different views of the data: external, conceptual and internal. The three-level database architecture allows a clear separation of the information meaning (conceptual view) from the external data representation and from the physical data structure layout. So, the architecture shown provides physical data independence and logical data independence.

SPC – Signal Processing and Communications. The IASTED international conference focusing on the recent developments in the field of signal processing and communications.

S/PDIF – Sony/Philips Digital Interface. A standard audio transfer file format.

SPDL – Standard Page Description Language. An international standard (ISO10180) page-independent device-independent page description language. It provides ASN.1 binary encoding and clear text representation. See also PDL.

SPE – Software – Practice and Experience. An international journal dealing with discussions on the practical experience with new and established software for both systems and applications.

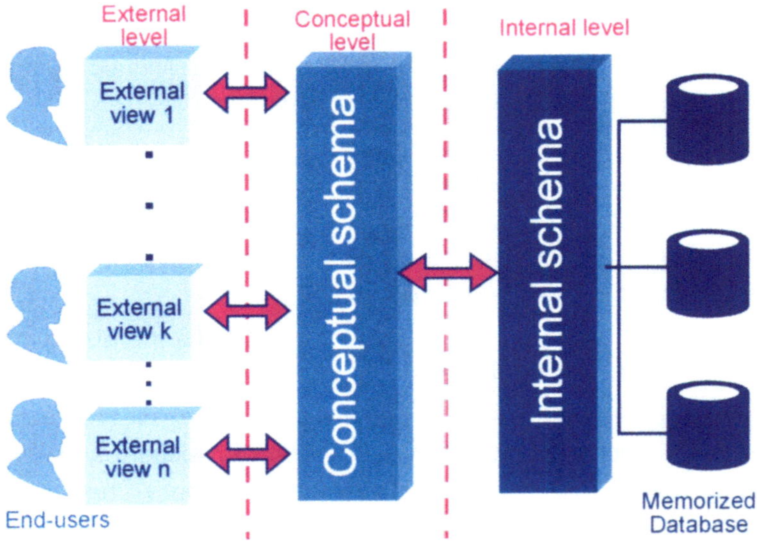

Fig. S-13. The three-schema architecture

SPE – Synchronous Payload Envelope. The user data inside the SONET frame. The SPE can begin anywhere within the frame, and can even span two frames. See also SONET.

SPEC – Standard Performance Evaluation Corporation. A nonprofit corporation registered in California and founded to establish, maintain and endorse a standardized benchmark set applicable to the latest generation of computers (http://www.spec.org).

SPECmark – Systems Performance Evaluation Cooperative benchmark. The measurement results, taking into account floating-point and/or integer operations, performed using some benchmark test. Some of the popular benchmarks are:

- SPEC CFP92: A benchmark suite containing 14 programs (12 are written in FORTRAN and 2 in the C language) performing floating-point computations. It can be used to estimate the CPU and memory performance as well as the compiler code that will be generated.
- SPEC CINT92: A benchmark suite that contains six benchmark programs in C, performing integer computations.
- SPEC fp92: It is used to estimate the single-tasking performance on a machine working with floating-point code.

SPF – Shortest-Path First. A routing algorithm that iterates based on the path length to determine the shortest-path spanning tree. Commonly used in link-state routing algorithms. Sometimes called Dijkstra's algorithm. See also SPA.

SPHIGS – Simple PHIGS. A subset of the 3D hierarchical standardized graphics system (see PHIGS) that operates on primitives defined in a floating-point abstract 3D world-coordinate system, independent of the type of display technology.

SPI – Service Provider Interface. The set of interfaces and functions implemented or used by Microsoft MAPI service providers. See also MAPI.

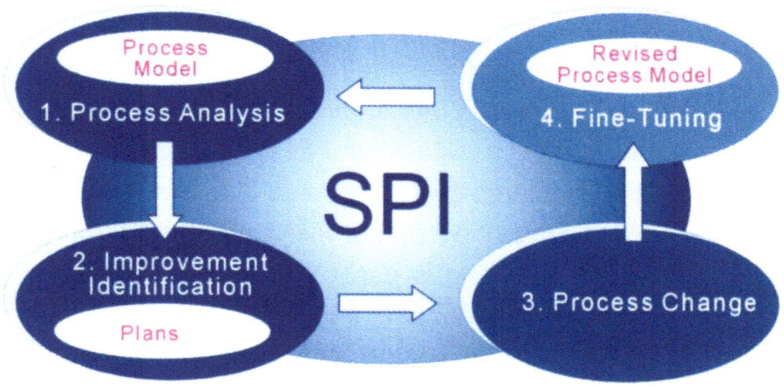

Fig. S-14. The simplified view of SPI

SPI – Software Process Improvement. An iterative strategy applied to understand existing processes and to change them in order to improve software quality and/or to reduce cost and development time. Although there is no common recipe for how SPI should be done, the key stages of SPI are known (see Fig. S-14). The first step is always a process analysis (1) that examines the existing processes and produces a process model. The process model is then used for understanding and documenting the process. As a result of this process understanding, in the next step it is possible to identify improvements (2) by eliminating existing bottlenecks and making appropriate plans which can then be used in the next phase, process change (3). Finally, there is a need for finetuning (4), i.e. eliminating minor problems that appear after the new process has been applied.

SPICE – Software Process Improvement and Capability Evaluation. An international initiative to support the development of an International Standard for software process assessment.

SPID – Service Profile Identifier. A number that uniquely identifies a B-channel on an ISDN network.

SPIFF – Still Picture Interchange File Format. A generic bitmap file format defined by ITU-T and ISO/IEC (IS10918-3) for the storage, compression, and interchange of color or grayscale continuous-tone and bitonal image data. SPIFF is capable of storing bitmap data containing pixels 1 to 32 bits in depth with a maximum image size of 4G×4G pixels. SPIFF data is always read and written using the MSB (big-endian) byte order. SPIFF supports both the JBIG and JPEG standards. See JBIG and JPEG. Compare with JFIF.

SPKI – Simple Public Key Infrastructure. A set of IETF protocols (RFC2692, RFC2693) intended to provide mechanisms for supporting security in a wide range of Internet applications that require the use of public key certificates.

SPOOL – Simultaneous Peripheral Operation On-Line. A term from the history of operating systems, before multitasking was introduced. Spooling essentially uses a disk as a very large buffer for reading as far ahead as possible on an input device and for storing output files until the output devices are able to accept them. So, spooling is capable of overlapping the I/O of one job with the computation of other jobs. In addition, spooling introduced a very important data structure, the job pool, with several jobs having been read and waiting on disk, ready to run.

SPP – Sequenced Packet Protocol. A protocol which exists in the XNS protocol suite (see XNS). It supports the reliable transmission of sequenced Internet packets between clients on the network. Compare with PEP (Packet Exchange Protocol).

SPR – Screen Program. A filename extension for a file that contains a Visual FoxPro program.

SPS – Standby Power Supply. A power source that can deliver a limited amount of power to a device in the case of a blackout. Also known as Standby UPS.

SPT – Spanning-Tree Algorithm. See SPA (Spanning-Tree Algorithm).

SPX – Screen Program any (X). A filename extension for a file that contains a compiled Visual FoxPro program.

SPX – Sequenced Packet Exchange. A connection-oriented transport protocol built on top of the Novell NetWare IPX protocol. The combination SPX/IPX performs an equivalent function to that of TCP/IP. See also IPX.

SPX/IPX – Sequenced Packet Exchange/Internet Packet Exchange. See SPX (Sequenced Packet Exchange) and IPX (Internet Packet Exchange).

SQA – Software Quality Assurance. The process for assuring the quality of a software product. It is concerned with defining how an organization aims to achieve software quality. It involves defining or selecting standards that should be applied to the software development process or software products. These standards must then be embedded into the development procedures, which may be supported by adequate tools. SQA not only ensures that the software is developed without faults and conforms to its specification. It has wider aims, dealing with a wide variety of software attributes, such as safety, security, reliability, resilience, robustness, understandability, testability, adaptability, modularity, complexity, portability, usability, reusability, efficiency, learnability, etc. See also QA.

SQE – Signal Quality Error. A test done at a point between the transceiver/MAU and the DTE to ensure that the collision detection circuit in the transceiver/MAU is working. The function must be disabled when a transceiver/MAU is attached to a repeater. If a transceiver/MAU, while transmitting, detects a collision, it sends the SQE signal to the repeater, or node, to which it is connected. This is also referred to as a heartbeat.

SQL – Structured Query Language. A database query language (pronounced "seequel" or "S-Q-L") based on work done by IBM in the 1970s. SQL was adopted by ANSI in 1986, and revised twice, in 1989 and 1992. SQL allows us to create a database and its table structures, to enter, correct, delete and update data within the database tables, and to explore the database contents. SQL is relatively easy to learn. It performs the required database functions by using a basic vocabulary of about 30 commands. The SQL development is not yet finished. The development of new SQL standards, which should support multimedia (see SQL/MM) and persistent complex objects (see SQL/PSM), is currently underway. SQL standards can be viewed at http://www.jcc.com/sql_stnd.html

SQL/CLI – SQL Call-Level Interface. An international standard that describes an implementation-independent client-level programming interface for accessing SQL databases. The SQL Access Group (see SAG) originally developed CLI. In 1993, SAG submitted CLI to the ANSI and ISO committees. It was completed as ISO/IEC 9075-3:1995. Also, it is a part of the Open Group Data Management Services defined by X/Open C451, 1995, which provides bindings for both the C and COBOL languages.

SQLJ – SQL Java. A set of programming extensions that allows Java programmers to put SQL statements in their programs. SQLJ has several parts, embedded SQL, specifications for calling Java static methods as SQL stored procedures (called SQL Routines), and SQL Types which allow Java classes to be used as SQL user-defined data types. See also SQL and JDBC.

SQL/MM – SQL Multimedia. An emerging SQL standard that allows SQL access to multimedia documents. See also SQL/PSM and MM.

SQL/PSM – SQL Persistent Storage Module. An extension of SQL under development (ISO9075-4) with a procedural language, multistatement and stored procedures, and external function and procedure call. It provides support for the object-oriented capabilities in SQL-3. Multistatement and stored procedures involve reduced network interactions with the client and enhanced security because users are not allowed to update database tables directly. A procedural language adds the power of traditional programming language through flow control statements (if–then–else, loops, begin–end, exception handling) and other programming constructs. External procedures and function calls allow a particular site or application to add their own database functions.

SQuID – Source Quench Introduced Delay. The use of an algorithm by a source computer in order to reduce its transmission speed to a rate acceptable to the destination computer.

SR – Source Routing. A bridged method whereby the source determines the route that subsequent frames will use.

SRAM – Static Random-Access Memory. A form of random-access memory (pronounced "ess-ram") where each bit is stored in a bistable flip-flop. SRAM holds the stored data as long as there is enough power available. SRAMs are usually reserved for use in cache memories. Compare with DRAM.

SRC – Semiconductor Research Corporation. The research organization (http://www.src.org) formed in 1982 aimed at coordinating academic research in the area of semiconductors.

SRC – Spiral Redundancy Check. A composite number transmitted with data and used for error checking purposes at the receiver.

SRE – Standard for Robot Exclusion. A standard that controls how "robots" catalog an Internet site. See also knowbots.

SRI – Stanford Research Institute. One of the largest independent research and technology development and consulting organizations in the world (http://www.sri.com). The SRI headquarters is located in Menlo Park, CA.

SRM – Software Release Management. The process through which software is made available to customers.

SRTS – Synchronous Residual Time Stamp. A clock recovery technique in which signals representing the difference between the source timing and a network reference timing signal are transmitted in order to reconstruct the source timing at the destination.

SS – Sampled Servo. A compact disk recording technique where the contents are stored on a single track. Compare with CCS.

SS7 – Signaling System 7. A family of standards developed for use in ISDN telephone systems that define message-transfer protocols, error and overload recovery, and call-related services. Also known as CCITT-7.

SSA – Serial Storage Architecture. An ANSI standard, proposed by IBM, for a high-speed interface to disk clusters and arrays. It allows 20 Mbps data rates in each direction.

SSA – Structured System Analysis. The method of designing a new information system or evaluating an existing one by analyzing a system, prior to taking some action. In computer systems development, analysis refers to the study of some business area or application, usually leading to the specification of a new system. The most important product of the system analysis is the structured specification document, called by different names, that is usually made up of data flow diagrams (see DFD), a Data Dictionary (see DD), data structure diagrams, and the description of a process.

SSADM – Structured System Analysis and Design Method. The British Standard BS7738 for an application development method that divides a project under development into modules, stages, steps and tasks, and provides the background for describing a project in a manner that is appropriate to the management of the project.

SSAP – Session Service Access Point. The point at which the OSI session-layer service is made available to a presentation-layer entity (see SAP).

SSCOP – Service-Specific Connection-Oriented Protocol. An additional AAL protocol, not covered by any of the AALs mentioned in the AAL description (see AAL), designed for simple end-to-end reliable transport connections; it's used only for control, not for data transmission.

SSCP – System Service Control Point. An SNA term. This is the software that manages the available connection services to be utilized by the NCP. There is only one SSCP in an SNA network and the software normally resides in the host processor. See also NCP and SNA.

SSCS – Service-Specific Convergence Sublayer. The part of the ATM convergence sublayer that is dependent upon the type of traffic that is being converted.

SSD – Symposium on Spatial Databases. An international symposium conference dealing with the handling of spatial data in databases. Topics include GIS, urban planning, geology, meteorology, astronomy, molecular biology, image retrieval by content, multimedia, etc.

SSI – Server-Side Include. A variable value that a Web server can include in a HTML file before it sends it to the requestor.

SSI – Small-Scale Integration. A concentration of fewer than 10 components on a single chip.

SSL – Secure Sockets Layer. A session-layer protocol developed by Netscape (a version of HTTP) that includes encryption, providing better security on the Internet. It provides mechanisms for server authentication and for user authentication as well. Also, it provides privacy and data integrity. SSL is a new protocol layer, just above TCP/IP and just below the application protocols. A HTTP transfer that is protected by SSL uses port 443 instead of the normal HTTP port 80. Also, it is identified by a special URL method called https. Via http://home.netscape.com it is possible to obtain the most recent version of SSL. It's also known by the IETF name Transport-Layer Security (TLS). See also HTTP, HTTPS and URL.

SSO – Single Sign-On. An approach to logons where a user is authorized to access all the resources on the network using a single user ID and password.

SSS – Server Session Socket. A field in an AppleTalk session-layer protocol that contains the number of the socket to which the packet is going to be sent.

SST – Solomon Islands Standard Time. Time zone. UTC + 11.00 hours. See TZ.

SST – Speech Science and Technology. An international conference focusing on all areas of speech science and technology.

SSTD – Symposium on Spatial and Temporal Databases. An international symposium that presents original research results in the areas of theoretical foundations, design, implementation and applications of spatial and temporal database technology. Some of the major topics include the management of moving objects, the spatial and temporal aspects of mobile computing, ontologies and taxonomies, database design, data semantics and models, query processing and indexing, appropriate data mining and data warehousing, active database technology, real-time databases, the use of spatiotemporal data for simulation, standards proposals, etc. The proceedings are published by Springer-Verlag (see LNCS).

STACS – Symposium on Theoretical Aspects of Computer Science. An international symposium that presents original and unpublished research on theoretical aspects of computer science. Some of the major topics include algorithms and data structures, computational geometry, cryptography, algorithmic learning theory, automata and formal languages, computational and structural complexity, deduction, etc. The proceedings are published by Springer-Verlag (see LNCS).

STARWEST – Software Testing Analysis and Review. An international conference that focuses on automated testing solutions, software testing, software quality assurance, and appropriate tools and techniques.

STC – System Time Clock. The master clock in an MPEG-2 encoder or decoder.

STD – Standard. A subseries of RFCs that specify Internet standards. The official list of Internet standards is contained in STD 1. See also RFC (Request For Comments).

STD – State Transition Diagram. A diagram consisting of circles to represent states and directed line segments to represent transitions between the states. One or more actions may be associated with each transition. The diagram represents a Finite State Machine. An example of an STD is given in Fig. S-15 which represents some states of processes inside an imaginary machine and the transitions between them.

STDA – StreetTalk Directory Assistance. The global network naming system used in Banyan's VINES. See also VINES.

STDIO – Standard Input/Output file. In C, a header file (see H) that contains declarations about input and output functions (stdio.h).

STDL – Structured Transaction Definition Language. X/Open specification C611 (1996) which describes the syntax and semantics of SDTL, a high-level language for developing portable and modular distributed transaction-processing applications for multivendor environments.

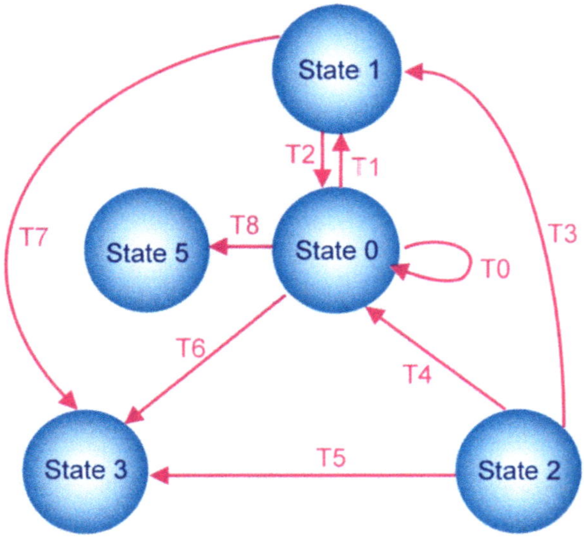

Fig. S-15. STD for an imaginary machine

STDM – Statistical Time-Division Multiplexing. A system developed to overcome some of the difficulties associated with regular time-division multiplexing (see TDM). STDM uses a variable time-slot length and allows channels to choose any free slot space.

STE – Section Terminating Equipment. A piece of SONET equipment that terminates a section of a link between a transmitter and a repeater, a repeater and a repeater, or a repeater and a receiver. STE is usually implemented in wide-area facilities. See also SONET.

STE – Spanning-Tree Explorer. A Source Route (see SR) bridging frame that uses the Spanning-Tree Algorithm (see SPA) in order to determine a route.

STE – Station Terminal Equipment. A term used to describe a gateway node between international packet-switched networks.

STEP – Standard for the Exchange of Product model data. An emerging standard which will be used to describe a product in a neutral format over its complete lifecycle in a hardware-independent way.

STM – Synchronous Transfer Mode. A B-ISDN communications method that transmits a group of different data streams synchronized with a single reference clock. All data are given the same amount of bandwidth. See also B-ISDN and ISDN.

STM-n – Synchronous Transfer Module n. A basic unit in the Synchronous Digital Hierarchy (see SDH) defined in increments of 155.52 Mbps, with n representing multiples of that rate. The most common values of n are 1, 2 and 4.

STP – Shielded Twisted Pair. Cabling with metal-backed Mylar, plastic or PVC covering to protect it from EMI and RFI. Compare with UTP (Unshielded Twisted Pair). See also EMI and RFI.

STP – Signaling Transfer Point. A high-speed reliable special-purpose packet switch for signaling messages in the SS7 network. See also SS7.

STRINGS – Statistical Report Integrated Generation Service. A CADDIA system for the production and dissemination of statistical information.

STS-n – Synchronous Transport Signal n. A set of SONET standards for transmission over OC-n optical fiber by multiplexing n STS-1 frames. STS-1 is the basic SONET channel with a data rate of 51.84 Mbps. See also OC-n and SONET.

STT – Secure Transaction Technology. The use of the Secure Sockets Layer (see SSL), Secure HTTP (see SHTTP), or both in online transactions, such as form transmission or credit card purchases.

STW – Search the Web. The chat term.

SUB – Substitute character. A transmission control character used in place of a character that is found to be in error.

sudo – superuser do. A UNIX utility that allows system administrators to give specific users permission, which they normally don't have, to use some system commands at the root level of the UNIX file hierarchy.

S

SunOS – Sun Operating System. Sun's operating system for its engineering workstations. SunOS is based on the AT&T and Berkeley versions of UNIX.

SUPER – Simply Unbeatable Palmtop Essentials Repository. The collection (http://www.super.net) of HP palmtop software.

SUT – System Under Test. The system being tested.

SVC – Switched Virtual Circuit. A virtual link, with variable end-points, established through an ATM network. Also, an X.25 term used to describe a packet-switched service similar to dial-up service. In other words, SVC is a circuit, or connection, that is established for a communication session, and that is terminated after the session is over. Compare with PVC (Permanent Virtual Circuit).

SVF – Simple Vector Format. This is a vector graphic format under development, which should support hyperlinks and layer information and which can be embedded into HTML. It includes points, polylines, rectangles, circles, arcs, cubic Bézier curves and text.

SVG – Scalable Vector Graphics. A W3C recommendation for a language intended for describing two-dimensional vector and mixed vector/raster graphics in XML. Three types of graphics objects, shapes, images and text, are allowed in SVG. Some of the main features of SVG are covered by the name itself. The term "scalability" in general is explained in the "PSI" entry; the term "scalable" here refers to an unlimited pixel size, a large number of users involved, or an unlimited number of applications etc. (see the original document at http://www.w3.org/TR/2000/03/WD-SVG-20000303). The term "vector" indicates another important attribute, the greater flexibility, i.e. the server side is vector-oriented, which allows rastering on the client side, and therefore less data needs to be sent over a network.

SVGA – Super VGA. A video display standard introduced by the Video Electronics Standards Association (see VESA) in 1989 for high-resolution color displays on IBM-compatible computers. Originally specified to have an 800×600 resolution, the VESA standard has been extended to include 1280×1024-pixel resolution. All SVGA cards are downward compatible, meaning that an SVGA adapter capable of supporting 1280×1024 resolution can also support the lower resolutions.

SVID – System V Interface Definition. The formal document from AT&T introduced in 1985 that specifies an operating system environment (UNIX) that allows users to create application software independent of any particular computer hardware. See also SVR4.

SVR4 – System V Release 4. The AT&T UNIX version released late in 1989 that merges XENIX and BSD UNIX with the standard POSIX-conforming UNIX system V. It is compliant with the X/Open XPG3 document, IEEE POSIX 1003.1 and ANSI C. See also BSD, XPG, POSIX and SVID.

S/W – Software. Frequently used abbreviation for the term "software", especially in a software producer's technical documentation as well as in fax or e-mail correspondence. Software is a set of computer programs that makes hardware work. The two main types of software are system software, such as operating systems, communication protocols and software tools, and applications, which perform the tasks for which people use computers. Also, several types of software are described based on their method of distribution. Software can be packed software, freeware public-domain software distributed free of charge, or shareware, which is also distributed free of charge for a period of time and then a registration fee (usually small) must be paid for continued use of the program. Figure S-16 depicts one of the widely used models for the software lifecycle, known as the waterfall model.

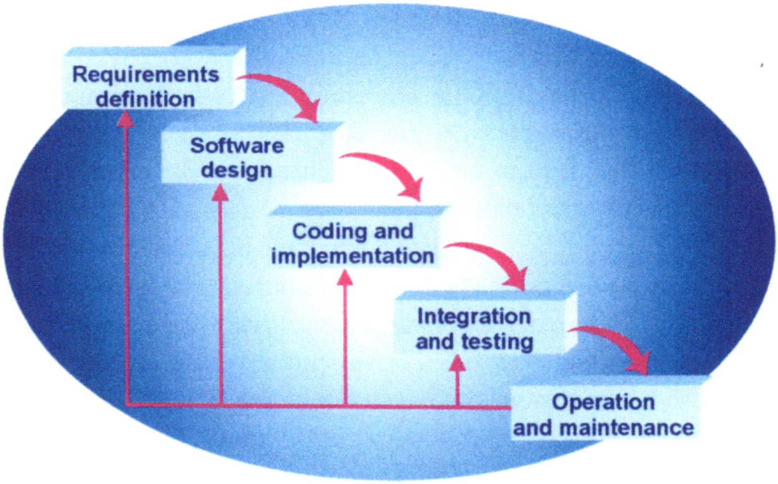

Fig. S-16. The waterfall model of the software lifecycle

It starts with the definition of a preferred concept for the software products (goals, constraints and user needs). Such requirement definitions are then used to design the overall software architecture, including data structures, interfaces, relationships between components, etc. The next stage includes coding of the necessary program units and verification that each program unit meets its specification. Then such program units are integrated and tested as a complete system in order to check whether the overall system requirements are met. If they are, the software is ready for delivery to the customer. After installation into the target hardware, it is put into operation. Typically some of the hidden errors are discovered during operation, and maintenance is required. Maintenance is also required if additional requirements appear later.

S

S/WAN – Secure Wide Area Network. A set of computers that communicate over a public network, but use security measures, such as encryption, authentication and authorization, to prevent their communications from being intercepted and understood by unauthorized users.

SWECC – Software Engineering Coordinating Committee. A joint ACM/IEEE-CS committee that coordinates working groups in the area of software engineering (see SE).

SWIFT – Society for Worldwide Interbank Financial Telecommunications. A network designed and operated to support the information transfer needs of banks and financial institutions.

SWISH – Simple Web Indexing System for Humans. A search machine that can use a number of keywords to search on the Web and return a list of documents containing all the keywords. The search is case-insensitive, but wildcards (*) can be used to simplify searching and Booleans (AND, OR, NOT) also can be used to refine the searches.

SWS – Silly Window Syndrome. A condition that can take place during window-based flow control (such as TCP). When SWS occurs, only small amounts of data are exchanged across the connection, instead of full-sized segments. It can be caused by either end: the receiver can advertise small windows, or the sender can transmit small amounts of data. For ways of avoiding SWS, see Stevens (1994).

SYN – Synchronizing character. A character used in synchronous communications that enables the sending and receiving devices to maintain the same timing.

SYSADM – System Administrator. A person responsible for coordinating the activities of the data processing function. Compare with SYSOP.

SYSOP – System Operator. A person responsible for the physical operations of a computer system or network resource. Compare with SYSADM.

T

T – Tera. An order of magnitude meaning 10^{12} in the decimal system or 2^{40} in the binary system. See TB and Tbps.

T – Tiny editor. A very small (tiny) freeware full screen editor.

T1/E1 – A digital transmission line with a capacity of 1544 Mbps. T1 is the name of that channel applied in the US, whilst E1 is the European name. There are also appropriate pairs for faster transmissions, such as T2/E2, T3/E3 and T4/E4, corresponding to 6312 Mbps, 44,736 Mbps and 274,176 Mbps rates, respectively.

TA – Terminal Adapter. A piece of equipment packed either as a standalone unit or as an interface card, used instead of a modem, that allows us to adapt Integrated Services Digital Network BRI (see ISDN and BRI) channels to existing pieces of terminal equipment, using, for example, RS-232.

TACAS – Tools and Algorithms for the Construction and Analysis of Systems. An international conference interested in rigorously based tools for the construction and analysis of systems. Some of the major topics include verification and construction techniques, test case generation, theorem proving and model checking, analytical techniques for real-time, hybrid and safety-critical systems, tool environments and architectures, applications and case studies. The proceedings are published by Springer-Verlag (see LNCS).

TACOMA – Tromso and Cornell Moving Agents. A distributed system developed jointly by Tromso and Cornell universities. The project is concerned with how to provide operating system support for agent-based computing. See also RP (Remote Programming) and NCC (Network-Centric Computing). Find more at http://dslab3.cs.uit.no:1080/Tacoma/index.html.

TAFIM – Technical Architecture Framework for Information Management. The US DoD architectural framework for information management based on IEEE POSIX 1003.0. TAFIM includes a breakdown of the Application Software, Application Platform and External Environment entities (see OSE) into service categories. The Application Software entity is divided into the mission area and support applications, which are further divided into the multimedia, communications, business processing, environment management, database utilities, and engineering support groups. The Application Platform entity recognizes the major service area, the mid-level service area, and the operating system services. Six groups of services are recognized, as follows:

- Software Engineering Services: languages, bindings, CASE tools and software lifecycle processes are included in the mid-level service area;
- User Interface Services: the mid-level service area includes user interface, graphical client/server, object management, and window management services;
- Data Management Services: data dictionary, data management system, and transaction processing;
- Data Interchange Services: document characters and symbols, raster images, mapping, compression, etc.;
- Graphics Services: raster, vector and device services;
- Communication Services: application, transport and network access.

All the Application Platform services mentioned above are supported by internationalization services, security services, and system management and distributed computing services. The External Environment entities are associated with networking, information interchange and users. TAFIM entities are connected using an appropriate API between the Application Software and the Application Platform, and using an external environment interface between the Application Platform and the External Environment. Compare with GOSE, OSE and TOGAF.

TAFN – That's all for now. The chat term.

TAG – Technical Advisory Group. An IEEE committee formed to provide general recommendations and technical guidance for other committees.

TAI – Temps Atomique International (International Atomic Time). The average number of ticks of the cesium 133 clocks since midnight on 1 January 1958, divided by 9,192,631,770. TAI is highly stable but there is a serious problem due to a discrepancy of the order of milliseconds between TAI and the mean solar day. The problem was solved by introducing leap seconds whenever the discrepancy grows to 800 ms. This correction provides another stable time referred to as Universal Time Coordinated (see UTC).

TALIP – Transactions on Asian Language Information Processing. The ACM journal that covers natural language processing of information in Asian languages and related disciplines.

TAM – Test Access Mechanism. On-chip hardware infrastructure used to transport test stimuli from the on- or off-chip hardware.

TAP – The Ada Project. A WWW site that serves as a clearinghouse for a wide variety of data related to women in computing. It is organized as a collection of links pointing to webpages containing information about women in computing, including conferences, references, academic issues, job announcements, etc. TAP also features a list of women in computer science to serve as encouragement for young women in the field. It has a section covering pioneering women in computing, with first place given to Ada Lovelace, who is widely recognized as being the first computer programmer (http://www.cs.yale.edu/homes/tap/tap.html).

TAPI – Telephony Application Programming Interface. A set of API functions provided by Microsoft in order to integrate PCs and telephone systems. TAPI supports conventional phone lines, PBX, ISDN and cellular technology. See also API, CTI, PBX and ISDN. Compare with TSAPI.

TAPOS – Theory and Practice of Object Systems. A journal published quarterly by Wiley that covers the important areas in the field of object technology.

tar – tape archive. The command under the UNIX operating system used to store and restore several files inside one tar file (for example a whole directory). Also, a filename extension for such an archive file.

tar.gz – tape archive gzipped. A combined filename extension for a file that has been archived using the tar command (see tar) and then gzipped (see gzip).

tar.z – tape archive zipped. A combined filename extension for a file that has been archived using the tar command (see tar) and then zipped.

TAXI – Transparent Asynchronous Transceiver/Receiver (X) Interface. See 4B/5B.

TB – Terabyte. A measurement unit used for high-capacity data storage (2^{40} bytes).

TB – Transparent Bridging. An IETF standard where bridge (see B) behavior is transparent to the data traffic. See also SPA.

TBE – Transient Buffer Exposure. A negotiated number of ATM cells that the network would like to limit the source-end to sending during startup.

TBO – Total Benefit of Ownership. A measurement model used to measure benefits of using computer technology in some area of business, expressed in dollars etc. Compare with TCO.

Tbps – Terabits per second. A measurement unit for high-speed data rates.

TC – Transactions on Computers. The IEEE monthly journal widely distributed to researchers, technical managers and educators all over the world.

TC – Transmission Control. A group of transmission control characters, which are used to facilitate or control data transmission. Examples are NAK and EOT.

TC – Transmission Convergence. An ATM physical sublayer above the PMD sublayer that handles all the issues related to determining where ATM cells begin and end in the bitstream. It is similar to the data-link layer in the ISO/OSI reference model. Also abbreviated as TCS. See also PMD (Physical-Medium-Dependent).

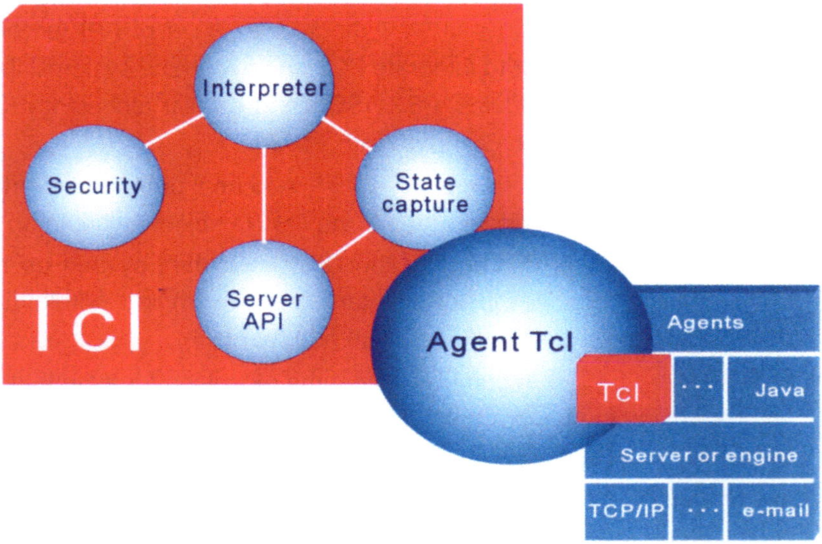

Fig. T-1. Agent Tcl architecture

TCAM – Telecommunications Access Method. An IBM mainframe subsystem that handles application access and routing within the network.

TCB – Trusted Computer Base. According to the Orange book, a TCB is the totality of protection mechanisms, including hardware, firmware and software, that together enforce a security policy. It consists of one or more components that together enforce a unified security policy for a product or a system. See TCSEC.

TCDE – Technical Committee on Data Engineering. A professional group sponsored by the IEEE CS that is focusing on the role of data in the design, development, management and utilization of information systems. The TCDE sponsors the International Conference on Data Engineering (see ICDE).

Tcl – Tool command language. A string processing highly portable secure language (pronounced "tickle"), developed by John Ousterhout in 1987. It is a powerful and easy-to-learn language. Tcl can be embedded in other applications and extended with user-defined commands. Furthermore, its extensions Safe Tcl, Agent Tcl and Tk are very popular tools for writing mobile agents for mobile computing (see NCC, Network-Centric Computing, and RP, Remote Programming). Agent Tcl is a simple itinerant-agent system that runs on UNIX workstations and allows rapid development of complex agents. It was developed by the Computer Science Department at Dartmouth College (http://www.cs.dartmouth.edu). Some of the leading researchers involved are Robert Gray, Daniela Rus and David Kotz. The Agent Tcl architecture has four levels (see Fig. T-1). These consist of an API for the available transport mechanisms, a server that accepts incoming agents and mediates in agent communications, an interpreter for each supported language, and the agents themselves. Agent Tcl authentication is based on the Pretty Good Privacy (see PGP) public-key cryptosystem.

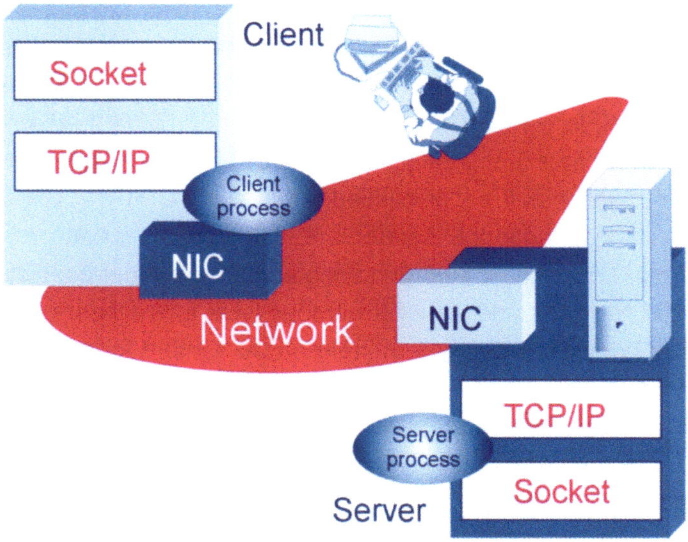

Fig. T-2. TCP sockets as end-to-end communication points

Tcl/Tk – Tool command language/Toolkit. An extension of the Tool command language (see Tcl) that provides commands for creating graphical user interfaces. Tk is event-driven and supports all the standard GUI features based on the WIMP metaphor (see WIMP).

TCM – Trellis-Coded Modulation. An improved form of quadrature amplitude modulation used by modems that work at or above 9600 bps. TCM encodes information as unique sets of Gbits associated with changes in both the phase and the amplitude of the carrier. TCM also introduces an extra set of points, the signal points that are grouped together, allowing the addition of a redundant error checking bit to each data set. The various shift-keying methods (see FSK and DFSK) may involve absolute or differential values. See also QAM.

TCNS – Thomas Conrad Network System. An implementation of the ARCnet architecture operated at 100 Mbps. See also ARCnet.

TCO – Total Cost of Ownership. A very popular term that describes the real cost of owning a personal computer. In addition to the original cost of the initial hardware and software configuration, TCO also includes upgrades, maintenance, and support and training costs. Compare with TBO.

TCP – Test Coordination Procedure. A set of rules used for coordination between the lower tester and the upper tester. TCPs may or may not be specified in an abstract test suite.

TCP – Transmission Control Protocol. An Internet standard transport-layer protocol defined in RFC793, RFC1122, and RFC1323. It is a connection-oriented protocol, in contrast to UDP, designed to provide a reliable end-to-end byte stream over an unreliable internetwork. It is part of the TCP/IP protocol suite, which will be discussed later (see TCP/IP). TCP service is obtained by having both the sender and the receiver create end points, called sockets (see Fig. T-2), each having a socket number consisting of the IP address of the host and a 16-bit number local to the host called a port. Two or more connections may terminate at the same socket. Port numbers below 256 are called well-known ports and they are reserved for standard services (such as FTP port 21, Telnet port 23, etc.). The full list is given in RFC1700. TCP provides reliability by sending and receiving data in the form of segments. The application data is broken into what TCP considers the best-sized chunks to send. The segment size is restricted by two limits. The first one is the IP payload (65,535-bytes long) and the second one is the maximum transfer unit of a particular network (see MTU). TCP entities use the sliding window protocol. So, when TCP sends a segment it maintains a timer waiting for the other end to acknowledge receipt of the segment. If an acknowledgement is not received in time, the segment is retransmitted. TCP also maintains an end-to-end checksum of its header and data to allow detection of any modification of the data during transmission. In the case of an invalid checksum, there is no acknowledgement at all, and the receiving end waits for the sender to retransmit on timeout. The TCP segments can arrive out of order. The receiving end of the TCP connection is responsible for passing received data in the correct order to the application. TCP (TCP/IP) encapsulation is shown in Fig. T-4. TCP does not recognize the contents of the data bytes at all. The interpretation of bytestream (binary data, ASCII, EBCDIC, etc.) is up to the applications at either end of the connection. See also CO (Connection-Oriented). Compare with UDP.

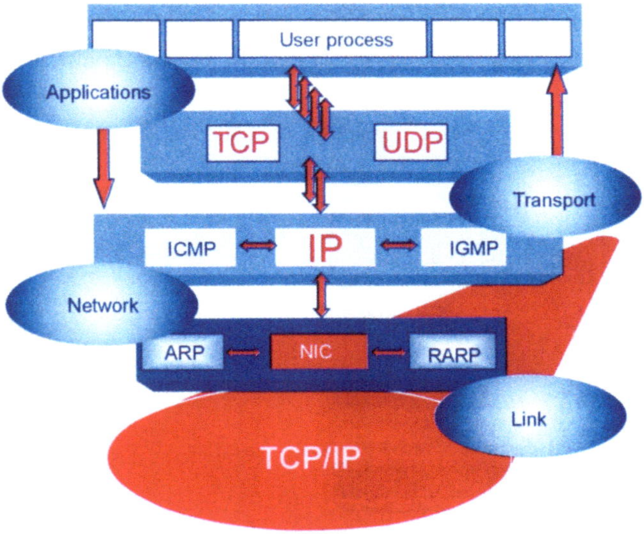

Fig. T-3. TCP/IP protocol suite (without the physical layer)

TCP/IP – Transmission Control Protocol/Internet Protocol. A common name for the most frequently used protocol suite, consisting of four layers (or five if a physical layer is included), as shown in Fig. T-3. The TCP/IP protocol suite allows full interoperability among computers of varying sizes, and basically forms a net and controls its functions. The corresponding layers are:

- The link layer which includes the device driver in the operating system and the corresponding network interface card (see NIC), as shown in Fig. T-3. It also includes the Address Resolution Protocol (see ARP) and Reverse ARP (see RARP) used only with certain types of network interfaces (Ethernet or Token Ring) to convert addresses between the IP layer and the network interface.

T

- The network layer handles the data path across the network. The main protocol here, the Internet protocol, and the others involved are described elsewhere in this book (see IP, ICMP and IGMP). This layer is sometimes called the Internet layer.
- The transport layer provides data flow between two end systems for the application layer above. In the TCP/IP, there are two different transport protocols, TCP and UDP. TCP provides reliable connection-oriented transmission, UDP offers no guarantee on the delivery of data. See TCP and UDP.
- The application layer handles the details of the applications, which can include File Transfer Protocol (see FTP), Telnet, Simple Mail Transfer Protocol (see SMTP), Simple Network Management Protocol (see SNMP), etc.

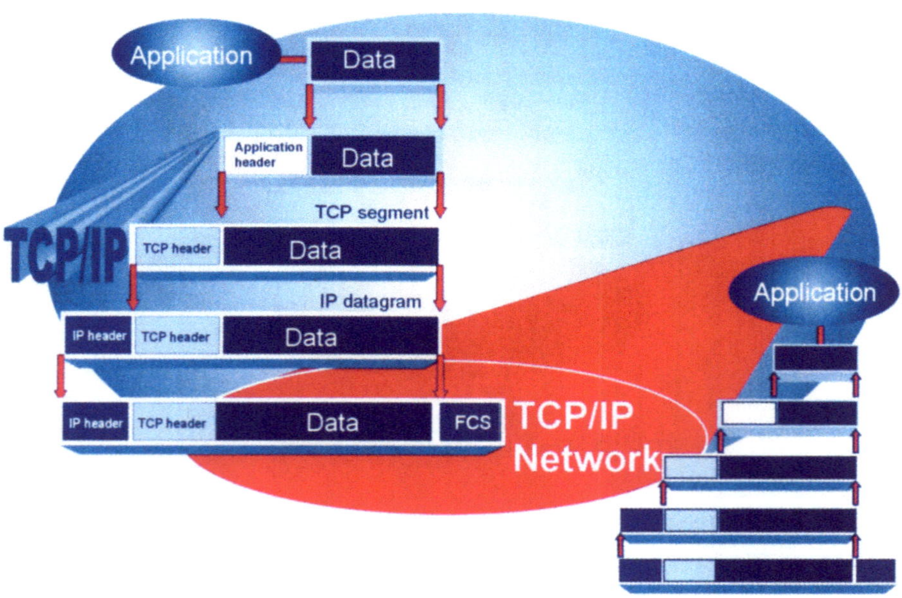

Fig. T-4. TCP/IP encapsulation

Comparing the TCP/IP protocol suite with the protocol suite introduced in the ISO Open System Interconnection Reference Model (see OSI), it is obvious that two layers, the presentation and session layers, are missing. However, this is not a serious disadvantage. First of all, the necessary presentation and session functions (for example, coding) are directly implemented in a particular TCP/IP application-level protocol. In addition, modern communication theory has already recognized that the 5-layer and the 7-layer communication models are not always suitable for new services implementation (see RP, Remote Programming). On the other hand, the communication scenario is very similar. When an application sends data using TCP/IP, the data is sent down the protocol stack (see Fig. T-4) through each layer, until it is sent in a stream of bits across the network. Each layer adds information to the data by preparing appropriate headers and sometimes trailers for the data that it receives. When a frame is received at the destination point, it moves in the opposite way up the protocol stack and all headers are removed one by one until the destination-application pure data is available in the same form in which it was sent by the source-application. This process is called TCP/IP encapsulation.

TCR – Tagged Cell Rate. An ABR service parameter that is used to limit the rate (10 cells/s) at which a source may send out-of-rate forward RM cells. See also ABR and Resource Management (RM).

TCS – Theoretical Computer Science. The journal published by Elsevier Science that publishes papers focusing on the nature of computation. Articles are organized in two sections. The first section covers algorithms, automata, complexity and games. The second section is devoted to semantics and the theory of programming. Also, the IFIP international conference focuses on similar computer science problems. The proceedings of IFIP TCS are published by Springer-Verlag (see LNCS).

TCS – Transmission Convergence Sublayer. See TC (Transmission Convergence).

TCS – Trusted Computer System. An automated information system, including all of the hardware, firmware and software that, by virtue of having undergone sufficient benchmark validation and testing, as well as acceptance and user testing, can be expected to meet the user's requirements for reliability, security and operational effectiveness with specified performance characteristics. See also TCB and TCSEC.

TCSEC – Trusted Computer Systems Evaluation Criteria. The US National Computer Security Council document, popularly known as the "Orange Book" issued in 1983, which defines a number of levels of security systems (see Fig. T-5). Later, in December 1985, it became US DoD standard 5200.28-STD, defining the criteria for trusted computer products. Figure T-5 shows four defined levels of security, A, B, C and D. Each level adds more features and requirements, as follows:

- D is a non-secure system in which no trust can be placed. D-class systems cover, for example, personal computers in an open office, or a multiuser system to which access can be gained without the need to know a password.
- C1 requires some kind of discretionary control such as user logon, but allows group IDs.
- C2 also requires discretionary control, such as individual logon with a password and an audit mechanism. Both C1 and C2 discretionary controls may result in a very insecure system if each user chooses to specify lax access permission for their objects. In any case, for most commercial systems, the C2 security level can satisfy all requirements.
- B1 requires DoD clearance levels.
- B2 guarantees the path between the user and the security system and provides assurances that the system can be tested and clearances cannot be downgraded.
- A1 involves a system characterized by a proven mathematical model.

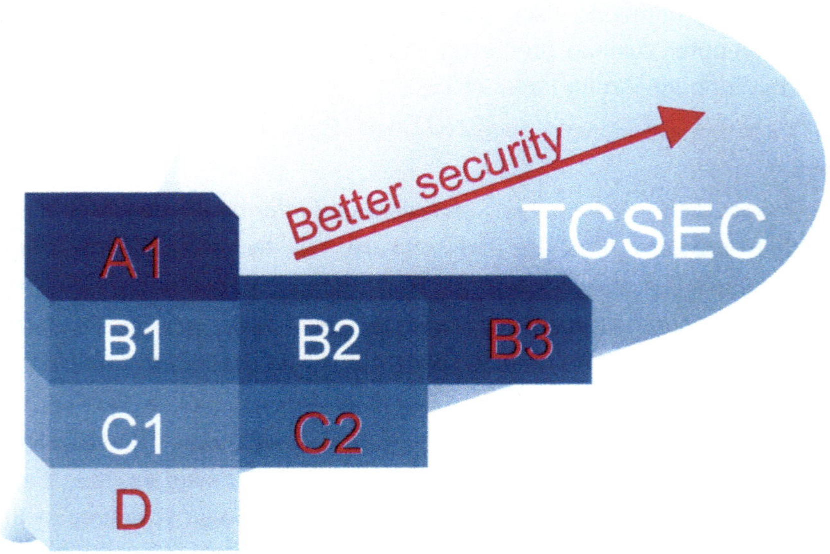

Fig. T-5. TCSEC levels of security

Furthermore, some policies must be added to a computer system so that it can be described as trusted or secure. The security policy protects the system and the data that it controls from unauthorized access. The accountability policy allows individual users to be identified, and their actions to be traced. Both policies, while implemented using a combination of hardware and software, require documentation, and must be testable in order that the whole system can pass evaluation criteria.

TCU – Terminal Control Unit. A device used to control a local group of terminals.

TD – Transmit Data. TD, a lead in the RS-232C interface, is used to transmit information across the interface. In the full 25-pin RS-232C standard, TD is pin 2. In the abbreviated 9-pin PC interface, TD is pin 3. See also RS and RD.

TDCC – Transportation Data Coordinating Committee. The former name of the Electronic Data Interchange Association (see EDIA).

TDD – Telecommunications Device for the Deaf. A machine that uses typed input and output, usually with a visual text display, to enable individuals with hearing or speech impairments to communicate over a telecommunications network. Such devices typically run at 300 bps.

TDDI – Twisted-pair Distributed Data Interface. A network architecture that implements FDDI on a twisted-pair copper-based cable (see CDDI). See also FDDI.

TDM – Time-Division Multiplexing. A type of multiplexing that combines separate channels into a single high-speed transmission. The transmission time is split into segments, each carrying elements of one signal. In other words, channels take turns to use the link. In the case of isochronal traffic, TDM becomes inefficient due to the allocation of time slots even when the channel has no data to transmit.

TDMA – Time-Division Multiple Access. A communication technique that uses a common channel multipoint broadcast for communication among multiple users by allocating unique time slots to different users. The duration of such an allocated time slot depends on the number of parties who want to transmit and on the relative significance of the party. It is used extensively in satellite systems, local-area networks, and physical security systems. See also TDM. Compare with CDMA (Cell Division Multiple Access) and FDMA (Frequency Division Multiple Access).

TDMS – Technical Document Management System. The system intended to support airline and aerospace industries in their maintenance and engineering activities by managing complex technical documents. It supports a variety of document representations, such as ASCII, CGM, PDF, SGML, XML, etc. All of these formats are described elsewhere in this book.

TDP – Tag Distribution Protocol. A protocol that runs over the connection-oriented (see CO) transport layer with guaranteed sequential delivery. It supports multiple network-layer protocols such as IP, IPX and AppleTalk.

TDR – Time-Domain Reflectometer. A test device capable of sending signals through a network medium to check cable continuity and other attributes. TDRs are used to find network problems in the physical layer. The term TDR is also used to refer to time-domain reflectometry as a diagnostic method used in the devices mentioned above.

TDS – Tabular Data Stream. An application-level datastream protocol used by Microsoft SQL Server for communication between client applications and SQL Server.

TE – Terminal Equipment. Any ISDN-compatible device that may be attached to the network, such as a telephone, fax or a computer.

TEn – Terminal Equipment type n (n=1,2). Used in ISDN terminology for a type of terminal equipment which is directly compatible with the ISDN network (TE1), or for a terminal which must be connected to the ISDN network via a specially designated point, normally an RS-232 or RS-449 interface (TE2). See also ISDN.

TEC – The Education Coalition. A nonprofit educational organization created in 1993 to serve the needs of the business and education communities. Its website (http://www.tecweb.org) provides information and resources on distance education and educational technology for teachers and students at all levels.

TEI – Text Encoding Initiative. An international research project funded by several organizations. Since 1988, the TEI has been working towards the definition of a suite of extensible guidelines and recommendations for use when encoding all kinds of text in machine-readable forms for all kinds of research purposes. The latest TEI specifications can by obtained at the ftp site ftp://ftp.info.ex.ac.uk

Telco – Telephone Company. A generic term for the local telephone operator in a given area. See also PTT.

Telnet – Teletype Network. A terminal emulation protocol that allows remote terminal-like connection to other computers on the Internet. Telnet runs on top of TCP/IP. It is defined by RFC854 and extended with options using many other RFCs.

TEMPEST – Transient Electromagnetic Pulse Emanation Standard. The standard that specifies the amount of electromagnetic radiation that a device may emit without compromising the information it is processing.

TEN – Trans-European Network. A European Commission project first outlined in 1994, for connecting and interoperating national networks. The project includes all kinds of communications, roads, rail networks, inland and maritime waterways, airports, as well as satellites and other IT-based communication networks.

Fig. T-6. Homepage of TERENA (with permission from TERENA)

TENNIS – Typical Example of a Needlessly Named Interface Standard. The name of the server used to prevent services from being captured by the network, thereby leading to a net fault. Of course, the acronym itself is a great one, easy to remember and easy to use, its extended title is a funny example of how abbreviations can be mysterious, after all. Another such acronym is TWAIN. There are many other acronyms that have differences between their explanations and usage. For example, DCE stands for Distributed Computing Environment, and for Data Communication Equipment, PCMCIA stands for Personal Computer Memory Card International Association, but it is also defined as People Can't Memorize Computer Industry Acronyms. This book is also designed to help professionals and inexperienced users overcome such misunderstandings.

TERENA – Trans-European Research and Education Networking Association. The organization that promotes information and telecommunications technologies development in Europe (http://www.terena.nl). TERENA was formed in October 1994, by the merger of RARE and EARN to promote and participate in the development of a high-quality international information and telecommunications infrastructure for the benefit of research and education. See Fig. T-6.

TEX – TeX file. A filename extension for a file that contains a TeX or LaTeX document.

Fig. T-7. A set of tex files used to fill several shapes

TEX – Texture file. A filename extension for a file that contains a texture (see Fig. T-7).

TFF – Tagged File Format. A file format in which data is tagged using standard headers that identify the data type and length.

TFIDF – Term Frequency – Inverse Document Frequency. A measurement method used in information retrieval (see IR), which is based on the statistics of words that are common to each string.

TFTP – Trivial File Transfer Protocol. A simplified version of FTP described in RFC783 and RFC1350 that allows files to be transferred from one computer to another over a network. It is used where user authentication and directory visibility are not required. TFTP uses UDP rather than TCP. See also FTP.

TGA – Targa Graphics Adapter. The Truevision file format that provides a common bitmap format for the storage of 16-, 24- and 32-bit images. Also, the brandname of a series of high-resolution video graphics boards.

TGIF – Thank God it's Friday. The chat term.

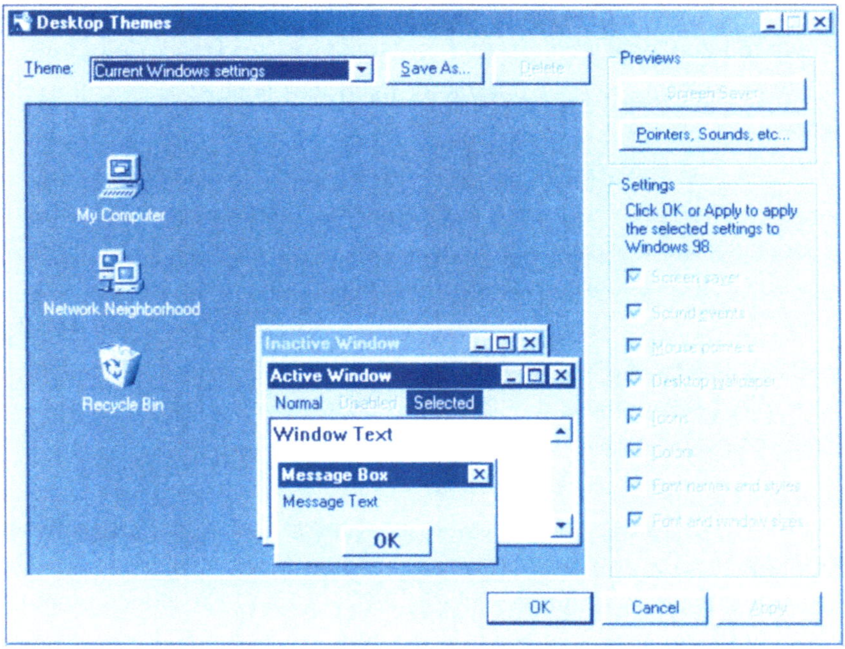

Fig. T-8. An example of a THEME file

TGS – Ticket Granting Service. A part of the Kerberos server (see KDC). TGS provides a token (ticket) for a client in order to verify that the sender has been recently authenticated using Kerberos. Tickets include the time of expiration and a newly generated session key for use by the client and the server.

TH – Transmission Header. The part of the SNA data format that defines the origin and destination of the message. See also System Network Architecture (SNA).

TH – Trojan Horse. In general, a well-known historical term applied to a person or group capable of going behind the enemy line (acting as something else) and then attacking. In computing, TH refers to a program that contains hidden instructions to destroy files, programs, etc., on a victim computer. THs are triggered by predefined circumstances such as dates, times, active tasks, etc.

THEME – Theme file. A filename for a file that contains a Microsoft Windows desktop theme (see Fig. T-8). Such files are usually used as screensavers or as desktop wallpapers.

THEnet – Texas Higher Education Network. A regional network in the US covering over 60 academic and research institutions in the Texas state area.

THT – Token Holding Time. A parameter used to adjust access to the FDDI network.

THX – Thanks. The chat term.

TI – Texas Instruments. A major company that produces microprocessors, semiconductors, measurement devices, etc. (http://www.ti.com). The first integrated circuit was demonstrated by TI researcher Jack Kilby in 1958.

TIA – Telecommunications Industry Association. An organization that develops standards relating to telecommunications technologies. Together, the TIA and the EIA have formalized standards, such as EIA/TIA-232 covering the electrical characteristics of data transmission. See also EIA.

TIA – Thanks in advance. The chat term.

TIA – The Internet Adapter. A shareware application that allows people with a UNIX shell account to use TCP/IP software such as Web browsers, POP mail clients, ftp clients and newsreaders on their own PC or Mac computers. TIA is a SLIP emulator that runs on the host computer and comes in versions that cover most of the UNIX operating systems used by providers. TIA comes in a number of versions, each compiled for a different operating system.

TIC – Token Ring Interface Coupler. In IBM terminology, the device that enables direct connection from a token ring network (see TR) to various mainframes.

TIC – Types in Compilation. An international workshop focusing on advanced type-based compilation techniques for modern programming languages.

TIFF – Tagged Image File Format. A popular file format used for raster bitmaps stored in tagged fields. It is commonly used for scanning, storage and interchange of grayscale graphic images. TIFF is in some cases the only format available for older programs (such as older versions of MacPaint), but most modern programs can save images in a variety of other formats, such as GIF or JPEG. Compare with GIF and JPEG.

TIGA – Texas Instruments Graphics Architecture. A PC video adapter architecture based on the Texas Instruments (see TI) 34010 graphics processor.

TINA – Telecommunications Information Networking Architecture. A common and open software architecture for the provision of telecommunication and information services. An important area of application of TINA is Intelligent Networks (see IN), where some functional entities can be distributed through a TINA service architecture. See also TMN. TINA is also the name of a related annual conference.

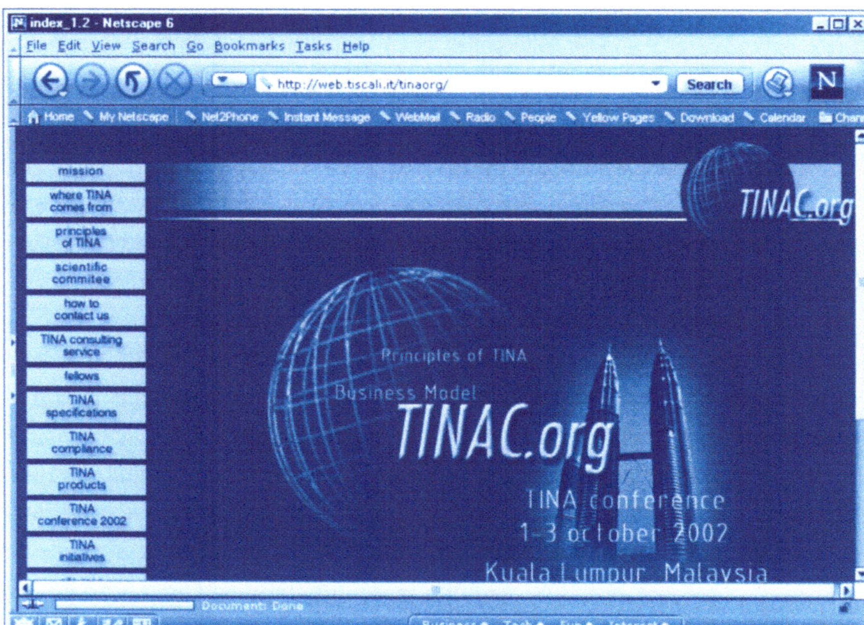

Fig. T-9. Homepage of TINAC (courtesy of TINAC)

TINAC – TINA Consortium. An industrial consortium (http://www.tinac.org) formed by over 40 leading network operators, and telecommunication and computer equipment manufacturers in order to define and validate the TINA architecture (see TINA). For the period 1998–2000, TINAC defined technical objectives for:

- Management of heterogeneous networks and services.
- Next-generation mobility and high-quality Internet/Intranet.
- Integration of legacy networks and services.
- Flexible advanced services portable over heterogeneous networks.

The Consortium Forum, consisting of representatives from all the member companies, is responsible for all the important decisions of TINAC, including reviewing and making decisions on both technical and administrative activities and the appointment of officers for the Consortium Administration Office and representatives on the Architecture Board. From 2001 TINAC has operated as the TINA International Scientific Committee (T-ISC). TINAC is also the name of the conference with the same topics. See Fig. T-9.

TIS – Tool Interface Standards Committee. An industry association founded to work on the software interfaces for the 32-bit Intel architecture.

TISSEC – Transactions on Information Systems Security. The ACM journal that covers original research papers and technical notes in all areas of systems security.

Tk – Toolkit. A standalone library for graphical user interface design developed by John Ousterhout, often used together with Tcl (see Tcl/Tk). It is very similar to OSF Motif. It is available for the X Window System, Microsoft Windows and the Mac.

TKDE – Transactions on Knowledge and Data Engineering. The IEEE bimonthly journal that covers state-of-the-art activities in the area of knowledge and data engineering. Some of the major topics include artificial intelligence techniques, knowledge and data engineering tools and techniques, parallel and distributed processing, database design and modeling, query design and implementation languages, system architectures, expert systems, integrity, security and fault-tolerance, etc.

TLA – Three-Letter Acronym. A common acronym that covers all acronyms consisting of three letters. The most common abbreviation technique is TLA, but there are also other acronyms in use (see FLA).

TLAP – TokenTalk Link Access Protocol. The data-link layer protocol used in the AppleTalk protocol suite.

TLB – Translation Lookaside Buffer. In some microprocessor architectures, a high-speed hardware lookup table used for the conversion of recently used virtual addresses into real addresses.

TLB – Type Library file. A filename extension for a file that contains the properties and methods of server objects. Such files are used by automation clients.

TLI – Transport-Layer Interface. A library of C functions implemented in UNIX System V that provides an API for the implementation of various networking protocols.

TLS – Thread Local Storage. A storage method used by multiple threads of the same process with just one index applied to store and retrieve a different value of each thread.

TLS – Transport-Layer Security. See SSL (Secure Sockets Layer).

TM – Transaction Manager. A part of X/Open Distributed Transaction Processing (see DTP), which allows an application to demarcate transactions and direct their completion. Transaction manager services include: starting a transaction, coordinating recoverable resources involved in a transaction, committing or rolling back transactions, controlling timeouts on transactions, monitoring their status, and chaining transactions together.

TM – Traffic Management. Mechanisms that control ATM traffic flow so that switches and end-stations are not overwhelmed and cells dropped. See also UPC (Usage Parameter Control) and CAC (Connection Admission Control).

TMI – Too much information. The chat term.

TMLA – Trademark License Agreement. The primary governing X/Open document for branding and providing the legal enforcement for the conditions of the X/Open branding program. Trademark law provides the legal basis for this agreement. Under the conditions of the TMLA, a vendor warrants that its product does in practice conform to the specifications for which conformance is claimed. It requires specific evidence of the conformance, such as test suites where these are available.

TMN – Telecommunications Management Network. Forthcoming standard for managed object classes and their properties, defined by ISO and ITU-T.

TMP – Temporary file. A filename extension in Microsoft Windows for a file or folder that contains temporary data.

TMP – Test Management Protocol. A protocol used in the test coordination procedures for a particular test suite.

TMR – Triple Modular Redundancy. The most commonly used technique to build fault-tolerant hardware. A hardware unit is replicated three (or sometimes more) times. The output of each unit is compared. If one of the units fails and does not produce the same output as the other units its output is ignored. The system works if two out of three units are operational.

TMSF – Tracks, Minutes, Seconds and Frames. A time format used in the Media Control Interface (see MCI) to express time in tracks, minutes, seconds and frames. TMSF is primarily used by CD audio devices.

TNC – Threaded Nut Connector. A connector similar to a BNC connector, except that the TNC is threaded and screws into the jack. See also BNC.

TNEF – Transport-Neutral Encapsulation Format. A proprietary file format used for RTF formatted message exchange between Microsoft Exchange and Outlook e-mail clients. Pronounced "tee-neff".

TNI – Trusted Network Interpretation. A document produced by the National Computer Security Commission (see NCSC), it states that the specification contained in the "Orange Book" will apply equally to network security. See also TCSEC.

TOCHI – Transactions on Computer–Human Interaction. The ACM journal that covers the field of human–computer interaction (see HCI).

TOCL – Transactions on Computational Logic. The ACM journal that covers the research field of computational logic used in computer science.

TOCS – Transactions on Computer Systems. The ACM journal that covers a broad range of research and development areas in the design, specification, realization, behavior and use of computer systems.

TODAES – Transactions on Design Automation of Electronic Systems. The ACM quarterly journal that publishes recent results on research and development in the area of electronic systems design automation. Some of the major topics include system design, high-level and logic synthesis, physical layout, design verification, system reliability, etc.

TODS – Transactions on Database Systems. The ACM journal published quarterly that covers all aspects of database research and development.

TOF – Time-Out Factor. An ABR service parameter used to control the maximum time permitted for sending forward RM cells before a rate decrease is required. See also ABR and Resource Management (RM).

TOF – Top-Of-File. A symbol used by a program to mark the beginning of a file, the first character in a sequential file, or the first indexed record in an indexed database.

TOG – The Open Group. The merger of the Open Software Foundation (see OSF) and X/Open.

TOG – Transactions on Graphics. An ACM SIGGRAPH journal that covers the area of computer graphics.

TOGAF – The Open Group Architectural Framework. A tool defined by The Open Group (see TOG) that describes a whole family of related architectures for building modern information systems. It consists of three parts:

- A technical reference model, which is similar to those given in TAFIM or OSE. Just like the ISO Open Systems Environment (see OSE), TOGAF recognizes three major entities, application software, an application platform, and an external environment, as well as two interfaces (API and EEI). Compared to OSE and TAFIM, the application software entity and external environment entities have the same roles as OSE entities. The application platform entity recognizes 9 services in the front plane (data interchange, data management, distributed computing, graphics and image processing, networking, operating systems, software engineering, transaction processing, user interfacing) and 3 services in the back plane (internationalization, security, and system and network management).
- A methodology for the development of an architecture based on the organization's business goals and leading to a selection of standards and products which integrate to meet the organization's needs within the constraints imposed by the existing systems.
- A list of standards, definitions and products, and the relations between them.

The architecture development process for designing a specific architecture consists of performing a requirements analysis (often connected to a business process, see BPR), making service allocations, selecting building blocks, and evaluating the resulting architecture.

TOIS – Transactions on Information Systems. The ACM journal focusing on the design, performance and evaluation of computer systems. Some major topics of TOIS include information retrieval and filtering, information interfaces, natural language processing, knowledge and information representation, multimedia information systems, networked information systems, social impacts of information systems, design and evaluation of information systems, etc.

TOMACS – Transactions on Modeling and Computer Simulation. The ACM scientific journal focusing on the area of computer simulation.

TOMS – Transactions on Mathematical Software. The ACM journal that publishes valuable research results focusing on the development, evaluation and use of mathematical computer programs.

TON – Transactions on Networking. The IEEE/ACM bimonthly journal that publishes articles about the state-of-the-art and practical applications of communication networks. Topics covered by the journal include network architecture and design, communication protocols, broadband networks, high-speed networks, network software and technologies, network services and applications, network operations and management, etc.

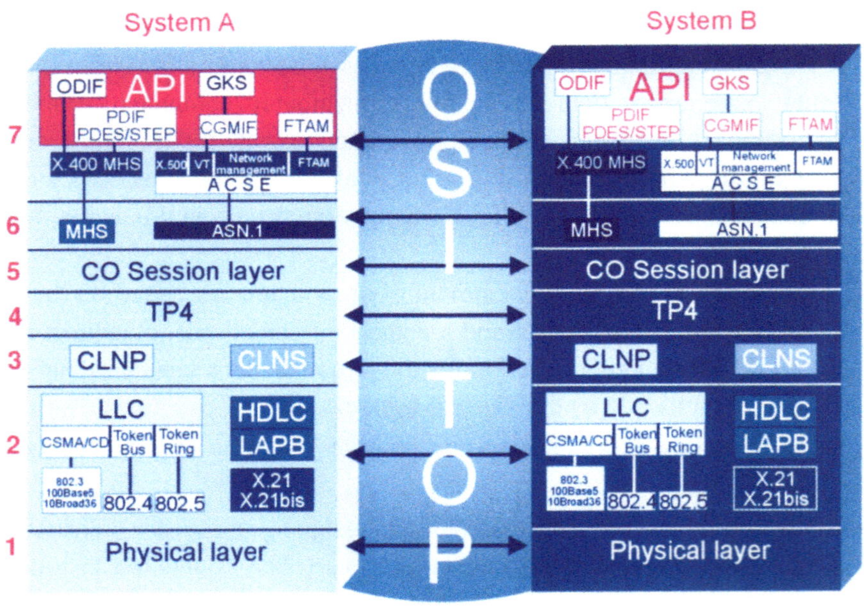

Fig. T-10. TOP protocol stack

TONICS – Telephone Operations Network Integrated Control System. An integrated network management system developed at GTE Laboratories. According to a journal article (IEEE Computer, March 1999) TONICS manages 5000 central-office switches, many thousands of SONET, ATM and frame relay devices, thousands of SS7 network elements, tens of thousands of X.25 and IP devices, etc.

TOOLS – Technology of Object-Oriented Languages and Systems. An international conference focusing on object-oriented technologies, held five times a year in either Europe, the US or the Asia–Pacific region.

TOP – Technical/Office Protocol. A protocol stack (see Fig. T-10) for office automation developed by Boeing following the OSI model. TOP provides several APIs that are built upon the application layer of the OSI Reference Model. These APIs are designed for a variety of files, such as PDIF, ODA/ODIF, CGMIF, GKS and FTAM. In the top three application-oriented OSI layers, TOP supports MHS, FTAM, Virtual Terminal (see VT), remote file access using FTAM, directory services using X.500, and the global OSI network management model. Following the picture shown in Fig. T-10, the layers below the application layer are all connection-oriented (see CO). See also MAP, PDIF, ODIF, CGMIF, GKS, SMF, TP4, CLNP, CLNS, LLC, HDLC, LAPB, CSMA/CD and FTAM.

TOPLAS – Transactions on Programming Languages and Systems. The ACM scientific journal that publishes research results on all aspects of the design, definition, implementation and use of programming languages and systems.

TOPS – Transparent Operating System. A type of local-area peer-to-peer network designed by Sun Microsystems that allows Apple Macintosh computers, PCs and Sun workstations to run on the same network.

ToS – Type of Service. A field in an IP packet header (see IP) that contains the kind of transmission desired. The desired transmissions can be distinguished from each other by delay, throughput and reliability.

TOSEM – Transactions on Software Engineering and Methodology. The ACM journal that publishes original and significant results in all areas of software engineering. The topics of TOSEM include models, languages, methods, mechanisms and tools for products and processes throughout software lifecycles.

TP – Transaction Processor. A software component in each computer in a distributed environment that requests data through a distributed database management system (see DDBMS). It is responsible for the execution and coordination of all database transactions issued by a local application that accesses data on any data processor.

TP – Transfer Price. A business term used by manufacturers and resellers in order to define the price of a product offered by a reseller. TPs vary depending on the specific agreement between the two sides. Typical discounts, often related to the suggested end-user prices (see EUP), approved by manufacturers range from 5% to 40% depending on the total marketing revenue of the reseller per fiscal year.

TP – Twisted Pair. A type of cable used on computer networks with wires which twist around each other. See also STP and UTP.

TP0–TP4 – Transport Protocol class 0–4. A series of ISO/OSI transport protocols. TP0 is a connection-oriented protocol (see CO), the simplest one, requiring neither error detection nor error correction. TP1 provides its own error detection. TP2 can support multiplexing transmissions. In addition to TP2, TP3 can also support multiplex transmissions, but includes the capabilities of TP1 and TP2. TP4 provides reliable connection-oriented data streams using datagrams. This protocol also handles error detection, synchronization and retransmission, just as TCP does.

TPAMI – Transactions on Pattern Analysis and Machine Intelligence. The IEEE journal published monthly that covers important results in the areas of pattern recognition, image analysis, computational models of vision, computer vision systems, artificial intelligence, learning, speech recognition, character and text recognition, understanding natural languages, expert systems, etc.

TPC – Transaction Processing Performance Council. An organization that has defined a series of benchmark standards for database systems. They are defined in great detail. They define the set of relations, and the sizes of the tuples. The number of tuples is not fixed, it is a multiple of the number of claimed transactions per second. The performance metric used is expressed in transactions per second (see TPS). There are four TPC benchmarks, known as TPC-A, TPC-B, TPC-C and TPC-D. TPC-A is used in applications that have multiple online terminal sessions, significant disk I/O, and require transaction integrity. The TPC-B benchmark was designed to test the core performance of database systems along with the operating system on which the DBMS runs. TPC-C is used to model more complex systems, and the TCP-D benchmark is used to test the DBMS performance on decision support queries. Additional information is available at http://www.tpc.org

TPD – Trailing Packet Discard. An intelligent packet-discard mechanism used with ATM Adaptation Layer 5 (see AAL) applications that permits an ATM switch to reduce retransmissions. When one or more of the cells in an AAL 5 frame is lost, the network marks subsequent cells so that a switch further down the line knows it can dump them, thus conserving bandwidth.

TPDDI – Twisted-Pair Distributed Data Interface. See CDDI.

TPDU – Transport Protocol Data Unit. A common term used sometimes for messages sent from the sending-end transport entity to a transport entity in the receiving-end transport layer.

TP-PMD – Twisted-Pair Physical-Medium-Dependent. An FDDI standard implemented on UTP cables and working at 100 Mbps.

TPS – Transactions Per Second. The metric used to express the power of the transaction processing system; it is usually used to refer to the speed of a DBMS and the speed of the supporting hardware and operating system. See TPC (Transaction Processing Performance Council). Furthermore, especially for business applications, cost is of great importance. Thus, the TPS benchmark is usually expressed in terms of the cost per TPS, rather than simply as pure TPS.

TPS – Transaction Processing System. A system capable of processing transactions. A transaction can be defined as a unit of program execution that accesses and possibly updates various data items. It can be done in a local or in a distributed environment (in that case, such systems are called distributed transaction processing systems, see DTP). A transaction usually results from the execution of a user program written in a high-level data manipulation language (see DML), programming language or SQL, etc. The ACID properties of transactions are required to ensure data integrity (see ACID).

TQM – Total Quality Management. An approach to quality management, developed by Joseph Juran, involving marketing, engineering, manufacturing, purchasing, etc. Defects should be defined through examining customer expectations. The focus is on prevention, detection and elimination of sources of defects. The Juran total quality management triangle involves quality control, planning and projects.

TR – Token Ring. A local area network formed in a ring (closed-loop) topology that uses token passing as a method of regulating traffic on the network. In a token ring network, a token exercising authority to transmit is passed from one station to the next in a physical circle. If a station has data to transmit, it takes the opportunity to catch the token, marks it as being in use, and inserts the data. The "busy" token, plus message, is then passed around the circle, delivers the data when it arrives at its destination, and is eventually returned to the sender. The sender removes the attached message and then passes the discharged token to the next station in the line. The term "token" is used for a short transmission frame that consists of a set of bits to define the start of the frame, a set of controlling bits, and a set of bits to define the end of the frame. This type of architecture works best with networks that handle heavy data traffic for many users. Token ring networks are defined in the IEEE-802.5 standards. Although TRs use a logical ring topology, actually they are organized in a star topology as shown in Fig. T-11, with central hubs (see MAU) equipped with Ring-In/Ring-Out ports (see RI/RO). As for any other LAN, Token Ring networks are limited in the distances that can be applied. Two limitations should be taken into consideration, lobe length and ring length, as shown in Fig. T-11. The lobe length represents the distance between a node and a MAU; the ring length is the distance between two adjacent MAUs. These limitations depend on the cabling, so the lobe length may vary from 45 m (UTP cabling) to 100 m (STP cabling). The ring length can reach up to 1 km using fiber-optic cables, whilst copper cables limit this distance to 30–40 m.

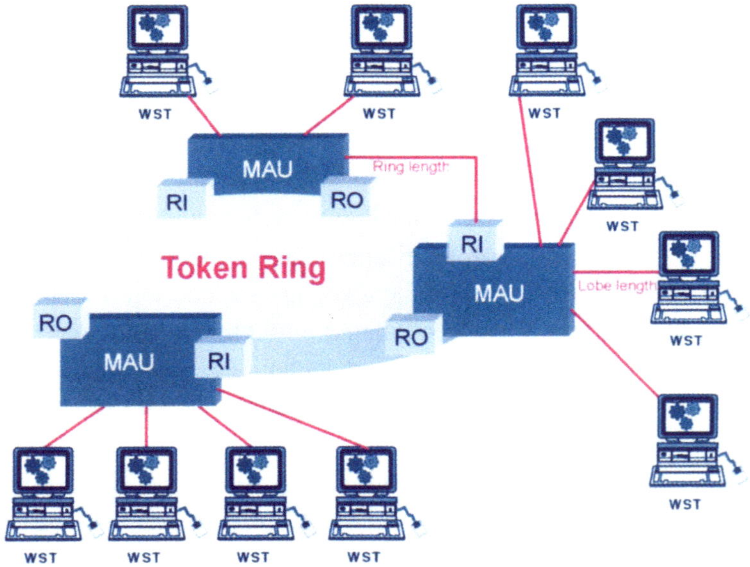

Fig. T-11. Token ring network

TRADIC – Transistorized Airborne Digital Computer. The first entirely transistorized computer.

Transceiver – Transmitter/Receiver. A device that can both receive and transmit a signal. It may be built into a network interface card (see NIC) or it may be a separate device. Also known as a MAU.

TRUSIX – Trusted UNIX. The Working Group formed by the US National Computer Security Center (see NCSC) in 1987. The primary goal of this group was to provide technical guidance to vendors and evaluators involved in the development of TCSEC Class B3 trusted UNIX systems. See TCSEC.

TS – Time Stamp. Stored data values used in distributed systems that represent the time at which some event occurred.

TS – Traffic Shaping. A mechanism that alters the traffic characteristics of a stream of ATM cells on a connection to achieve better network efficiency, while meeting the QoS aims.

TSA – Target Service Agent. A program used in NetWare networks that moves data between a host and a target server. In this case a host is any server with storage capabilities, and a target server is a server with data to be backed up or restored.

TSA – Time Stamp Authority. A trusted third party (see TTP) used to associate a datum (time stamp) with a particular point in time. In that case, a "proof-of-existence" for that particular datum at that instant in time is provided. See also TSP (Time Stamp Protocol).

TSAP – Transport Service Access Point. In the networking model, the end-point of the transport layer, where the application layer meets the transport layer. See SAP.

TSAPI – Telephony Services API. A set of functions developed by AT&T and Novell in order to provide Computer Telephony Integration (see CTI). Compare with TAPI.

TSDM – Temporal and Spatial Data Mining. An international workshop focusing on research and practice in knowledge discovery from datasets containing explicit or implicit temporal, spatial or spatiotemporal information. Some of the major topics include complexity, efficiency and scalability of temporal and spatial data mining algorithms, content-based searching, retrieval and discovery, data mining from GIS, spatial clustering methods, spatial data mining, etc. The proceedings are published by Springer-Verlag (see LNCS).

TSE – Transactions on Software Engineering. The IEEE scientific journal published monthly. TSE covers all aspects of valuable software engineering research and experience. See also SE (Software Engineering).

TSP – Time Stamp Protocol. Part of the Internet X.509 Public Key Infrastructure (see PKI) that uses the Time Stamp Authority (see TSA) in order to verify a message encrypted using a public key.

TSPI – Telephony Service Provider Interface. A tool for creating service providers under Microsoft Windows.

TSR – Terminate and Stay Resident. A program that remains loaded in memory even when it is not running, so that it can be quickly invoked for a specific task performed while another program is operating. Typically, these programs are used with non-multitasking operating systems, such as MS-DOS.

TSS – Television System Service. An interface designed to develop Windows 98-based applications that use broadcast TV.

TTCN – Tree and Tabular Combined Notation. The standardized test script notation for specifying abstract test suites.

TTD – Temporary Text Delay. A transmission control character defined by and used in the BISYNC protocol to signify a delay in the transmission of text components within an overall message. See also BISYNC.

TTF – TrueType Font. A font technology jointly developed by Apple and Microsoft which enables WYSIWYG printing by providing matching screen and printer representations supported in the operating system. TrueType is metrically compatible with PostScript Type 1 fonts (outline fonts) and provides greater hinting and character-set support. TrueType consists of two parts: the so-called "engine" built into the operating system that does the work of rasterizing and displaying the fonts, and the fonts themselves, which are stored in separate files on the hard disk and used as needed. Also the filename extension for the files containing the descriptions of such fonts.

TTL – Time To Live. A field in the IP header that indicates how long a particular packet should be allowed to survive before being discarded. A packet is initially sent with a nonzero TTL field, and each gateway that forwards the packet decrements the value in that field. Once the value reaches zero, a loop is assumed and the packet is discarded. It is primarily used as a hop count. See also IP (Internet Protocol).

TTP – Trusted Third Party. An entity in the network which is trusted by all other entities.

TTRT – Target Token Rotation Time. A parameter used in FDDI networks to specify how long it will take before every node on a network gets access to a token.

TTS – Transaction Tracking System. A software safety mechanism used in NetWare in order to protect file integrity in database applications.

TTTC – Test Technology Technical Council. A professional organization sponsored by IEEE CS focusing on testing in the area of electronics.

TTY – Teletypewriter. A low-speed communications device that consists of a keyboard and a printer. Early computers used teletypewriters as terminals. In UNIX, TTY (tty) represents the simplest terminal type.

TTYL – Talk to you later. The chat term.

TU – Thank you. The chat term.

TULIP – The University Licensing Program. A cooperative research project for networked delivery and use of journals, involving Elsevier Science and nine US universities.

TÜV – Technischer Überwachungsverein. Any of a number of German quality and safety compliance testers, organized regionally. See, for example, http://www.tuev-sued.de

TUXEDO – Transactions Under UNIX Extended for Distributed Operations. A distributed-transaction monitor that supports the design, configuration and operation of reliable distributed applications. On the server side, TUXEDO supports platforms ranging from Windows NT and Unix Ware to, for instance, HP-UX. The client side supports Windows, MS-DOS, OS/2, Macintosh and all versions of UNIX. Also, TUXEDO supports RDBMS, OODBMS, file managers and queue managers.

TVCG – Transactions on Visualization and Computer Graphics. The IEEE quarterly journal that publishes important research results and state-of-the-art papers on visualization and computer graphics topics. These include visualization techniques, methodologies, systems and software, information visualization, graphics systems, modeling, rendering, animation and simulation, user interfaces, virtual reality, visual programming, etc.

TWAIN – Technology Without An Interesting Name. The de facto standard interface between software applications and image-capturing devices such as scanners. Nearly all scanners contain a TWAIN driver, but only TWAIN-compatible software can use the technology.

twip – twentieth of a point. A screen-independent measurement unit used in Visual Basic statements for movement, drawings and other graphical operations. One centimeter is equivalent to 567 twips.

twm – tab window manager. A window manager for the X Window System (see X). It provides several forms of icon management, macros, user-specified keys, shaped windows, title bars, etc.

TWX – Teletypewriter Exchange. A text transmission service operating in the US and Canada that uses ASCII-coded characters.

TXD – Transmit Data. A line used to carry transmitted data from one device to another, such as from a computer to a modem. Pin number 2 in the RS-232C interface. Compare with RXD.

TZ – Time Zone. One of the longitudinal globe divisions in which clocks show the same time (see Fig. T-12). The time difference between the adjacent time zones is about 1 h (in some places 0.5 h). Examples of such time zones are GMT (Greenwich Mean Time), CET (Central European Time), NZST (New Zealand Standard Time), etc. The last two are shown in Fig. T-12. Computers are usually programmed to take into account the time zone in which the user is working.

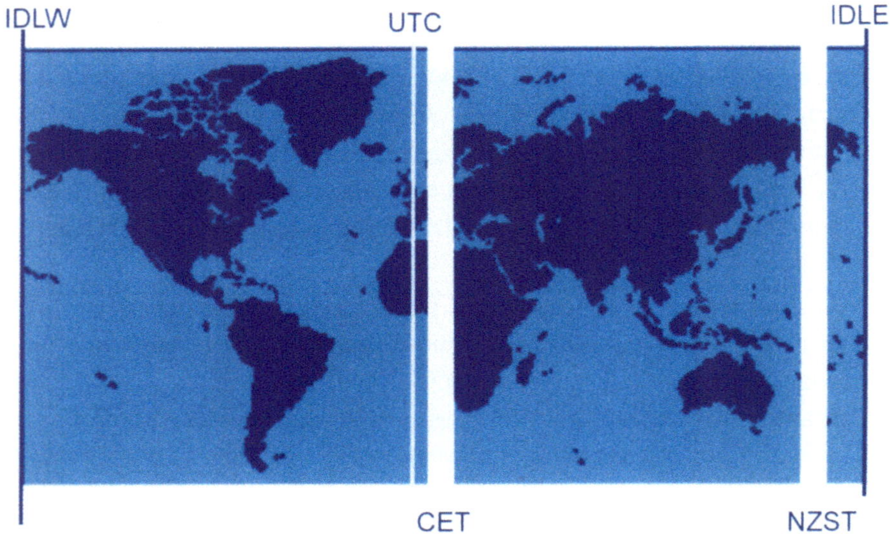

Fig. T-12. Two different time zones

TZD – Time Zone Data. A filename extension for a file that contains data about a time zone. See also TZ.

U

UA – User Agent. See Mail User Agent (MUA).

UAA – Unified Agent Architecture. A generic and open architecture for the creation, execution and interaction of software agents across networked computing platforms. The intention of this Internet Draft (see ID) is to create a reference model for the interoperation of heterogeneous agents and agent systems. Agents differ from each other by the degree of autonomy and authority they have (they can interact only with users, and/or with applications, and/or with other agents), by mobility, i.e. the degree to which the agents themselves travel through the network (fixed or mobile), and by intelligence, the degree of reasoning and learning behavior. The higher degrees of agent capability mentioned above require interaction with other agents. To do that, communication with other agents on possible different platforms may be required (see 3w). To learn more about mobile agents see RP (Remote Programming). See also KIF and KQML.

UADSL – Universal Asymmetrical Digital Subscriber Line. A specification proposed by UAWG relating to the development of ADSL specific chipsets, software and equipment. See also ADSL and UAWG.

UAIS – Universal Access in the Information Society. An international interdisciplinary journal (http://www.springer.de/journals/uais) focusing on the research aspects of the accessibility, usability and acceptability of information society technologies. The journal is published by Springer-Verlag.

UAL – User Access Line. In an X.25 network, the line that provides a connection between a DTE and a network. See also DTE.

UAM – User Authentication Method. In AppleTalk terminology, the UAM is assigned to a process that is capable of identifying the user for a file server before giving the user access to services.

UART – Universal Asynchronous Receiver/Transmitter. An integrated circuit (pronounced "u-art") used for serial communications. It contains a transmitter and a receiver, each clocked separately. Two computers, or a terminal and a computer each equipped with a UART, can communicate over a wire connection (see Fig. U-1). The parallel side of the UART is usually connected to the bus of the computer. When the computer writes a byte to the UART, the UART starts transmitting it over the serial line. The status register in the

UART can tell the computer if the UART is ready to receive another byte. The same register stores the signal that the computer has something to receive from the UART.

UAWG – Universal ADSL Working Group. An industrial organization established to accelerate the adoption and availability of high-speed digital Internet access for the mass market (http://www.uawg.org). See also UADSL.

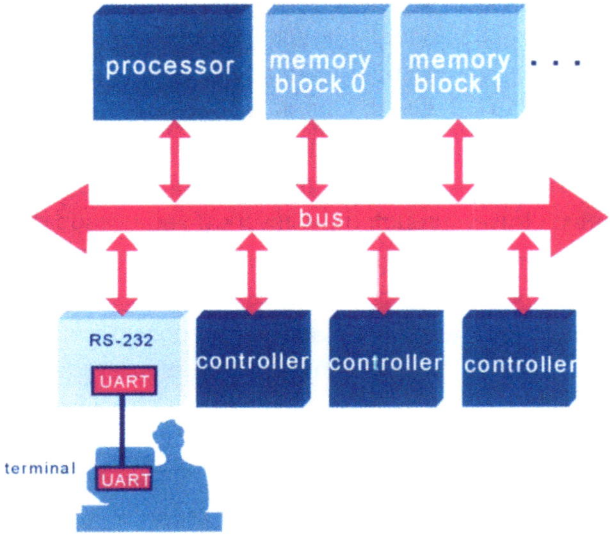

Fig. U-1. Communications via UART

UBO – User interface Business Objects. Part of the tiered architecture of the Lightweight Business Object Model (see LBOM). UBOs model business objects as class modules and provide properties and methods for the objects. UBOs are also responsible for data caching, allowing faster client-side data access. See also BPO and DABO.

UBR – Unspecified Bit Rate. An ATM service category which involves no guarantees of service. All UBR cells are accepted. If congestion occurs UBR cells are discarded without feedback to the sender. It is suitable for background file transfer.

UCISA – Universities and Colleges Information Systems Association. An organization involved in the development of academic, management and administrative information systems, providing a network of contacts and a powerful lobbying voice.

UCLA – University of California at Los Angeles. One of the most famous universities in the world (http://www.ucla.edu).

UCS – Universal Character Set. ISO/IEC standard 10646, also known as the "Universal Multiple-Octet Coded Character Set". It comes in two variants, a 16-bit called UCS-2 and a 32-bit variant called UCS-4.

UDA – Universal Data Access. The framework from Microsoft allowing the use of a single uniform API with databases from different software vendors. UDA provides database access to the Component Object Model (see COM). UDA consists of the high-level interface, ActiveX data objects (see ADO) and lower-level services (see OLE DB).

UDMS – Urban and Regional Data Management Symposium. An international symposium focusing on urban data management. The acronym comes from the Urban Data Management Society which organizes symposia at various locations in Europe in order to promote the development of information systems in local government.

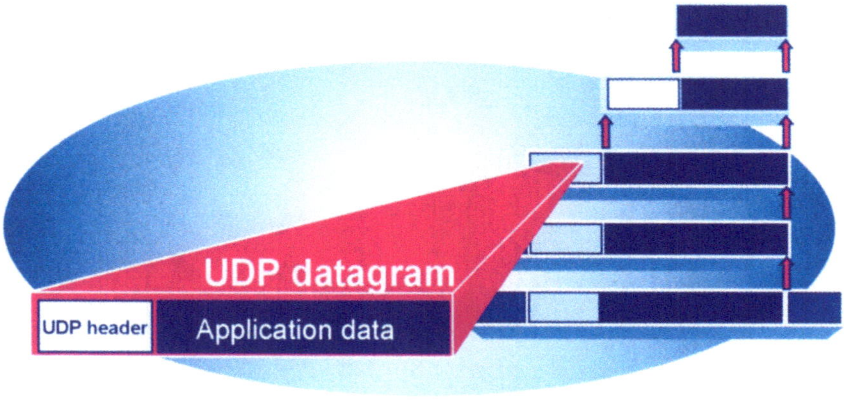

Fig. U-2. UDP encapsulation

UDP – User Datagram Protocol. A simple datagram-oriented transport-layer protocol defined by Jon B. Postel in RFC768 (1980). Each output operation produces exactly one UDP datagram, which causes one IP datagram to be sent. UDP is a connectionless protocol and it does not provide reliability. It sends the datagrams that the application writes to the IP layer, but there is no guarantee that they reach their destination. The application program must take care of all error processing and retransmission. The UDP header has four 20-byte-long fields consisting of the 16-bit source port number, the 16-bit destination port number, the UDP length, and the UDP checksum (optional). The maximum size of an IP datagram is 65,535 bytes. With an IP header of 20 bytes and a UDP header of 8 bytes, this leaves a maximum of 65,507 bytes of user data in a UDP datagram. However, most implementations require less than this, because the application program may be limited by its API, the operating system implementation of TCP/IP may be a limiting factor, etc. See Fig. U-2.

UDT – Uniform Data Transfer. The service used in the OLE extensions to Microsoft Windows that allows two applications to exchange data without either program knowing the internal structure of the other. See also Object Linking and Embedding (OLE).

UFID – Unique File Identifier. A file identifier used in distributed systems to refer to a file in all requests for file service operations.

UHF – Ultra-High Frequency. Transmission frequencies in the range from 300 to 3000 MHz.

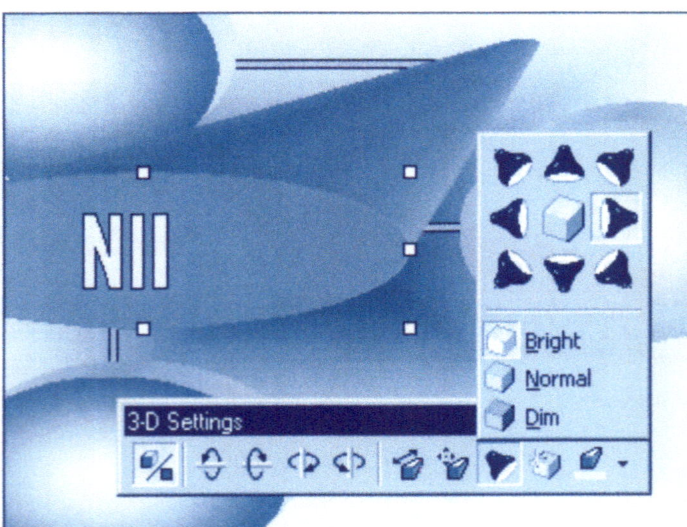

Fig. U-3. An example of a modern UI

UI – User Interface. The portion of a program with which a user interacts. The UI of a system is often a yardstick by which that system is judged. An interface that is difficult to use will, at best, result in a high level of user errors, and with user frustration this can produce more and more errors. The evolution of user interface design is described elsewhere (see GUI). The first-generation UIs were known as CUIs, because they were character-oriented (textual or form-based). Today, we have graphical-oriented (see GUI) interfaces with WYSIWYG attributes and built-in WIMP metaphors. An example of such an interface (PowerPoint 3D) is given in Fig. U-3. User interface design must take into account the needs, experience and capabilities of the system user. This is what we call user familiarity. The interface should use terms and concepts which are drawn from the experience of the anticipated class of users. In addition, the interface should be consistent, so comparable operations can be activated in the same way with minimal surprise. The interface should include mechanisms to allow users to recover from their errors (for example, an undo mechanism). A good user interface should also include some form of context-sensitive user guidance and assistance (online help). Today, GUI design based on the WIMP metaphor is very suitable for a number of applications; there are also a number of modern applications that require more advanced features. The main directions in modern interface design are recognized using a new UI metaphor (see SILK) with virtual reality (see VR), indirect manipulation, and demonstration interfaces, etc. See CAVE. See also WIMP and WYSIWYG.

UID – User Identifier. A term used in operating systems. This is a number or name that is unique to a particular user of a computer or group of computers that shares user information. The operating system uses UID to maintain a user's data structures (e.g. detail the owner of a file or process, control access rights, etc.).

UIDL – Unique ID Listing. A technique (RFC1725) used by a Post Office Protocol (see POP3) e-mail server to uniquely identify a mail message. It uses a fixed string of characters that is unique to the message even when the message has been deleted from the user's mailbox.

UIL – User Interface Language. A language for describing the initial state of a user interface. UIL specifies the widgets, gadgets and compound objects that make up the interface. It also identifies the subroutines to be called whenever the interface changes state as a result of user interaction.

UIMS – User Interface Management System. A system that supports the development and execution of user interfaces, usually on top of a windowing system. UIMS hides from application programmers the details of low-level services such as operating system or I/O devices. Naturally, it is a 4GL tool. Usually, it covers development, debugging and implementation tools for human-computer interaction design. UIMSs are distinguished from each other by several criteria, such as development stage, implementation mode, variable and expression types available during design, interaction with hardware and other system software, help organization, and testability, etc. See also UISRM.

UISRM – User Interface System Reference Model. A common name for the UIMS reference model, with actors and components as shown in Fig. U-4. It is important to note that the application programmer and the dialog designer don't have to be the same person. The end-user in this model can give the necessary suggestions, test the UI prototype, and, finally, be satisfied at the end of the development cycle. The reference model shown in Fig. U-4 divides the system into two parts: the dialog design and the run-time state. The structure of the dialog is designed to lie outside the application program. WYSIWYG tools help in the design of the look and feel of the screen, menus and dialogs. The dialog description can include previously described interactions from the common library, etc. The run-time version is created by linking the common library with the developed application code.

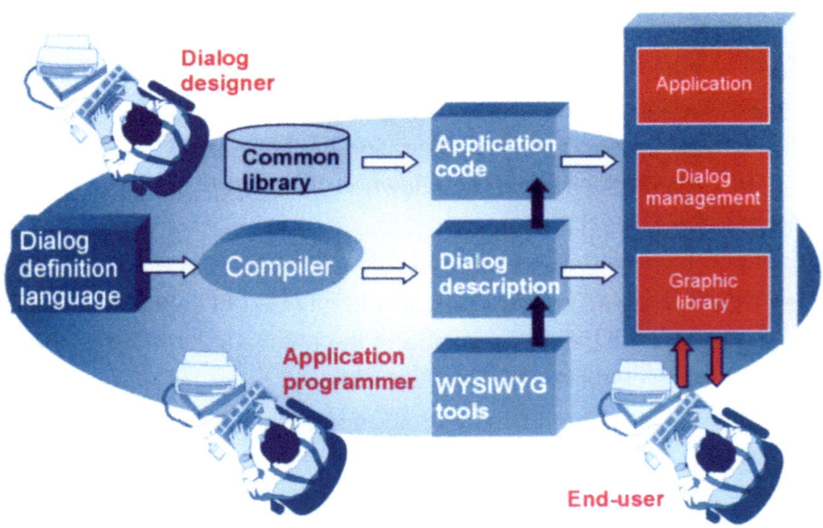

Fig. U-4. UIMS Reference Model

UIUC – University of Illinois at Urbana–Champaign. One of the major US universities (http://www.uiuc.edu) involved in several research projects which are outlined in the book (see, for example, DLI and HPPC).

UKERNA – UK Educational and Research Networks Association. An organization in the UK (http://www.ukerna.ac.uk) that manages the operation and development of the JANET networks under a Service Level Agreement with the Joint Information Systems Committee of the UK Higher Education Funding Council.

UL – Underwriters Laboratories. An independent agency in the US that tests product safety.

ULP – Upper-Layer Protocol. A protocol that operates at a higher layer in the OSI reference model relative to other layers in the protocol stack.

ULSI – Ultra-Large-Scale Integration. A reference to the density with which components are packed in an integrated circuit and to the fitness of the connections between them. It is not precisely defined, but it is generally used to refer to ICs having more than 100,000 components. Compare with VLSI.

UMA – Uniform Memory Access. In multiple-processor architectures, a model where multiple processors share a common memory bus with equal access times. Compare with NUMA.

UMA – Upper Memory Area. The portion of DOS memory between the first 640K and 1 MB. Compare with High Memory Area (HMA).

UMB – Upper Memory Block. A block of memory in the upper memory area (see UMA) that can be used for device drivers or TSRs. A UMB is allocated and managed by special memory manager programs, e.g. EMM386.EXE, etc. See also TSR.

UME – UNI Management Entity. The software residing in the ATM devices at each end of a UNI circuit that implements the management interface to the ATM network. See also UNI.

UML – Unified Modeling Language. A language developed jointly by Grady Booch, Ivar Jacobson and Jim Rumbaugh at Rational Software Corporation, California, with contributions from other leading software vendors and many users. The purpose of this language is specifying, visualizing, constructing and documenting the artifacts of software systems, and it can also be used for business modeling.

U

UNA – Upstream Neighbor's Address. In a token ring network (see TR), the unique address of the node from which a given node receives tokens.

UNC – Uniform Naming Convention. The system of naming files among computers on a network so that a file on a given computer will have the same pathname when accessed from any of the other computers on the network.

UNCLE – UNIX Net for Computer Security in Law Enforcement. The website designed as a resource and link to information on computer security reports and software for information professionals (http://www.fox.nstn.ca/~cookie).

UNI – Ente Nazionale Italiano di Unificazione. Italian national standards organization (http://www.uni.com).

UNI – User Network Interface. ATM Forum specification that defines an interoperability standard for the interface between ATM-based products (a router or an ATM switch) located in a private network and the ATM switches located within the public carrier networks. Also used to describe similar connections in Frame Relay networks. UNI 3.0 (1993), specifies the complete range of ATM traffic characteristics, including cell structure, addressing, signaling, adaptation layers, and traffic management.

UNL – Universal Networking Language. A research effort involving about 120 experts (computer science and linguistics) aimed at developing a language that would let people who speak different languages communicate electronically. They hope that their efforts should finalize in 2005, supporting languages spoken in 185 countries. UNL is intended to be an intermediary language serving as a translator between the sender's language and a vocabulary named Universal Word (see UW), and between UW and the receiver's language. This scenario has been chosen since direct translation between each of the 120 languages involved (spoken in 185 countries) would require software capable of handling more than 7000 sets of translations. Instead, the UNL requires only 120 sets of translations to be handled by the supporting software. When finished, UNL will introduce a new dimension in open communications (no language barriers).

UNMA – Unified Network Management Architecture. A network management architecture which adheres to the ISO/OSI network management recommendations. UNMA was defined by AT&T and works in any UNIX environment. It provides a framework that includes nine major network management functions: accounting management; configuration management; fault management; performance management; security management; integrated control; operations support; planning capability; and programmability. UNMA operates through five main components: a unified user interface that provides a graphics-based briefing of the network operation; an integrated network management; element management systems serving as local network managers; a network management protocol (see NMP); and network elements operating at the user level. See also OSI.

UNSM – United Nations Standard Message. A message exchanged to convey information related to specific transactions between partners engaged in EDI. See also UNTDID, EDED, EDCD, EDSD and EDMD.

UNSW – University of New South Wales. The largest and most famous university in Australia, founded in 1949 (http://www.unsw.edu.au) and located in Sydney.

UNTDID – United Nations Trade Data Interchange Directory. The directory designed to be used in and across different industries and applications for both national and international trade data interchange. In order to meet these requirements several segments and segment groups are defined as conditionals. Several interdependent documents are included in UNTDID. These include UN/EDIFACT Syntax Rules (ISO9735), EDED, EDCD, EDSD, EDMD, etc.

UOW – University of Wollongong. One of the most beautiful universities (http://www.uow.edu.au) in Australia. Founded in 1951, UOW today with 13,000 students is also one of the largest universities in that part of the world, featuring 9 faculties, 5 schools and 7 institutes.

UPC – Usage Parameter Control. A mechanism for protecting network resources from malicious or unintentionally damaging behavior by monitoring connection traffic for conformance to the service contract. Also called policing, usage parameter control involves checking such characteristics as the traffic burst size and rate.

UPC – Universal Product Code. A system of numbering commercial products using barcodes. A UPC consists of 12 digits: a number system character, a five-digit number identifying the manufacturer, a five-digit product code assigned by the manufacturer, and a modulo-10 check digit. Compare with EAN.

UPS – Uninterruptible Power Supply. A device connected between computerized equipment and a power source that ensures that electricity supply to the equipment remains available in the case of a blackout or, in general, any potentially damaging event. Modern UPSs are connected to, for example, a computer's serial port, and provide information such as the remaining battery time, allowing the computer to shut down before complete loss of power, etc. See also PS (Power Supply).

UQBT – University of Queensland Binary Translator. A project at the University of Queensland, Australia, to develop a static binary-translation framework that supports CISC, RISC and stack-based machines.

URC – Uniform Resource Characteristic. A URC is a set of attribute/value pairs describing an Internet object. URCs are not normally considered as short strings, but as sets of fields and values with some defined free formatting. A URC is a mechanism for resource description, which can be seen as an instance of the general issue of knowledge representation.

URI – Universal Resource Identifier. A common name for a WWW naming and addressing convention (defined in RFC1630 and RFC2396) that can be thought of as a generalized URL.

URI – University Research Initiative. A US DoD program that supports the Augmentation Awards for Science and Engineering Research Training (see AASERT) and other science and engineering education activities, including graduate fellowships and postdoctoral education. The program also provides for university research, and a university infrastructure for research and education in defense-critical fields. For instance, for the fiscal year 1997, the US DoD announced awards for 11 research topics in the area of US national defense.

URL – Uniform (Universal) Resource Locator. A worldwide unique Web Internet address for a particular webpage (RFC1808, RFC2368, RFC2396). There are three parts: the scheme (also called a protocol); the DNS name of the server on which the page is located; and the local name addressing the unique page (usually just a filename and the corresponding path on the machine where it resides). For example, the URL for the author's former homepage was: http://europa.elfak.ni.ac.yu/~ejub.The protocol is http, the DNS name of the host is specified by europa.elfak.ni.ac.yu, and the filename is ~ejub (actually ejub.html). In this case, ~ejub is used as a shortcut to the file ejub.html. Many sites use this shortcut addressing scheme. Another example is given in Fig. U-5. The Web user in this example is trying to find some information about DISA, the Document Interchange Standards Association (see DISA). He/she decides to use the Yahoo! search engine. By using the URL http://www.yahoo.com (step 1) and searching for the keyword "disa" (step 3), it is possible to find the target site in a few steps. For experienced Web users the normal choice would be to directly access the address, i.e. in the given example it is almost 100% certain that http://www.disa.org is the desired site, and an intermediate searching machine is not required. In any case, the process will deliver the addressed homepage to the Web user's computer. This URL scheme is open-ended in the sense that protocols other than http can be used (see WWW).

URN – Uniform Resource Name. A scheme for uniquely identifying resources that may be available on the Internet by name, without regard to where they are located. The specifications for the format of Uniform Resource Names are being developed by the Internet Engineering Task Force (see IETF).

USAN – University Satellite Network. A discipline-oriented network serving organizations which do research in the atmospheric and oceanographic sciences (http://ncar.usan.edu).

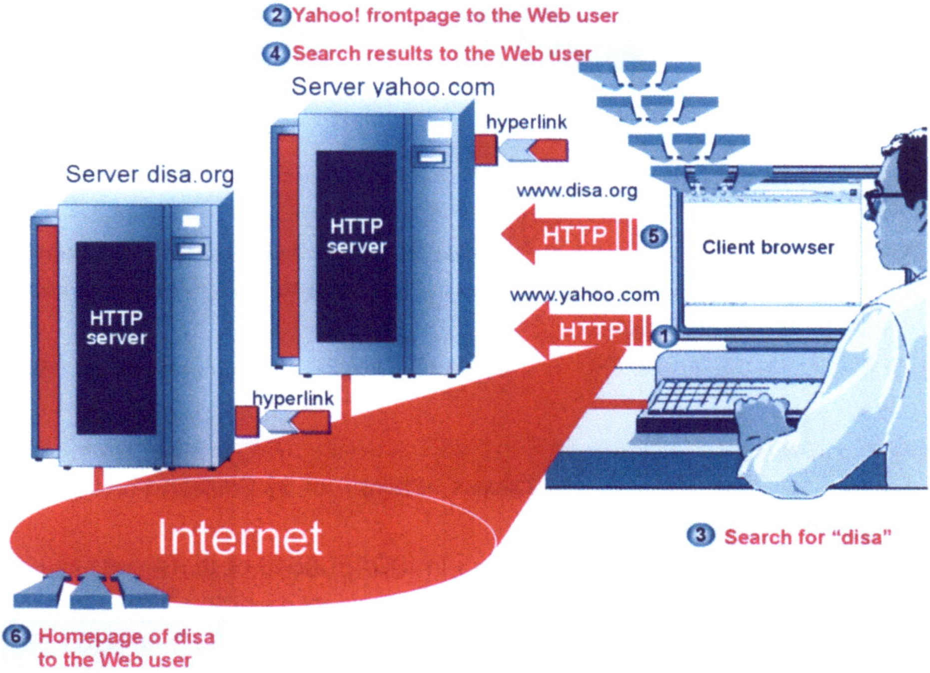

Fig. U-5. An example of how URLs work

USB – Universal Serial Bus. A standard introduced by Intel for communication between IBM PCs and external peripherals over inexpensive cable (at 15 Mbps). It supports up to 127 devices, such as external CD-ROM drives, printers, modems, mice and keyboards, as well as a daisy chain using the star multidrop topology. USB supports hot plugging and multiple datastreams. The website http://www.teleport.com/~usb provides additional information.

U

USDLA – US Distance Learning Association. A nonprofit association formed in 1987 by Patrick Portway, Dr. Smith Holt of Oklahoma State University, and Dr. Ralph Mills of California State University. The association's purpose is to promote the development and application of distance learning for education and training.

USDoD – US Department of Defense. See DoD.

USENET – Users Network. A distributed bulletin board (pronounced "yoos-net") supported mainly by UNIX System V and the people who post and read articles thereon. Initially implemented using UUCP and dial-up lines, now it has a much wider use. See also UUCP.

USG – UNIX Support Group. AT&T group founded in 1979 to support UNIX Version 7 and higher.

USL – UNIX System Laboratories. The software subsidiary of AT&T responsible for UNIX System V and related software.

USM – Unified Semantic Model. An extended version of the entity-relationship model (see ER) used to support geographic information systems developed at the University of Arizona.

USOC – Uniform Service Ordering Code. A commonly used sequence for wire pairs.

USRT – Universal Synchronous Receiver/Transmitter. An IC that contains both the receiving and transmitting circuits required for synchronous serial communication. Compare with UART.

UT – Upper Tester. The representation in ISO/IEC9646 of the means of providing, during test execution, control and observation of the IUT upper service boundary, as defined by the chosen abstract test method. See also IUT.

UTC – Universal Time Coordinated. The time at zero degrees of geographic longitude. Formerly known as Greenwich Mean Time (see GMT) or Zulu time. UTC is the basis for all modern civilian timekeeping. It is calculated using International Atomic Time and then coordinates with the apparent motion of the Sun. See also TAI and TZ.

UTOPIA – Universal Test and Operations Interface for ATM. An electrical interface that connects ATM devices in the bottom layer of the ATM reference model. See PHY.

UTP – Unshielded Twisted Pair. Cabling with insulation material like that commonly used with telephone cabling, but without a covering to protect it from EMI and RFI. The cable consists of at least two conductors twisted together, six twists per inch to minimize the effects of electromagnetic radiation. Compare with STP.

uucico – UNIX-to-UNIX copy-in copy-out. A program run under the UNIX operating system as a daemon process in order to perform the actions that have been requested by previous uucp or uux commands (see Fig. U-6). See also UUCP, uucp and uux.

UUCP – UNIX-to-UNIX Copy. Initially, a collection of programs run under the UNIX operating system (see Fig. U-6) that permitted one UNIX system to send files to another UNIX system via dial-up lines. Today, the term is more commonly used to describe the large network made up of these machines using the uucp protocol to pass USENET news and electronic mail. See also BNU, uucico, uucp, uux and uuxqt.

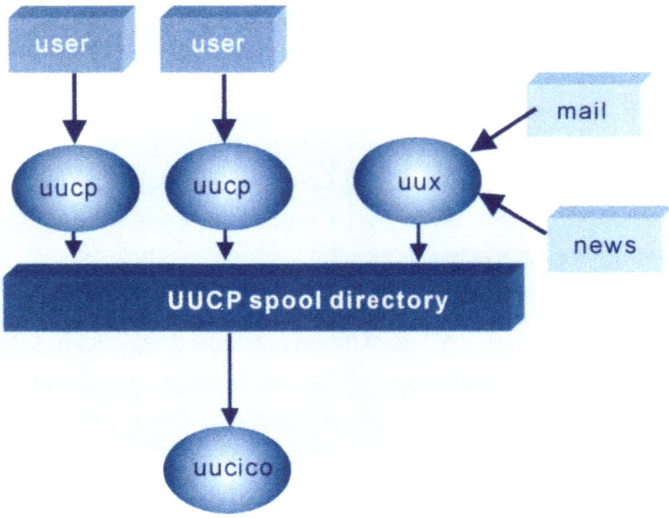

Fig. U-6. An overview of UUCP

uucp – UNIX-to-UNIX copy program. A UNIX utility, part of the UUCP collection, that can be invoked by users to copy a file from one system to another (see Fig. U-6). See also UUCP.

uudecode – UNIX-to-UNIX decode. A method for decoding ASCII files that have been encoded using uuencode.

uuencode – UNIX-to-UNIX encode. A method for converting binary files to ASCII so that they can be sent over the Internet via e-mail. See also uudecode.

UUID – Unique User Identifier. An element of the OSF DCE security services. It is a unique binary number associated with a principal. In DCE terminology, a principal is a user or process that needs to communicate securely. UUID is used in the DCE authentication process to check if the principal really is genuine. See DCE.

uuidgen – Unique User Identifier Generator. A utility program in Win32 SDK that generates unique UUIDs on the basis of the system time and the Network Interface Card (see NIC) identity number.

uux – UNIX-to-UNIX. A UNIX utility, part of the UUCP collection, that spools a command for execution on another UNIX system. In most cases, this process is started automatically by UNIX mail or UNIX news (see Fig. U-6). See also UUCP.

uuxqt – UNIX-to-UNIX execute. A UNIX utility, part of the UUCP collection, which executes files generated by uux (see Fig. U-6). See also UUCP and uux.

UVEPROM – Ultra-Violet-Erasable PROM. See PROM.

UW – Universal Word. A vocabulary designed to be an intermediate data source for the Universal Networking Language (see UNL). In the UNL project, UW would store the meanings of words in various languages (120 are currently being considered).

UW – You're welcome. The chat term.

UWIN – UNIX for Windows. A set of software tools that allows UNIX applications to run under NT and other Microsoft Windows environments (Win95, Win98). Commercial licenses can be obtained from Global Technologies (http://www.gtlinc.com or http://www.wipro.com). More information is also available at the AT&T site http://www.research.att.com/sw/tools/uwin:

V

V – Volt. A measurement unit for electric potential. The voltage between two points of a conducting wire carrying a constant current of 1 A (see A), when the power dissipated between these points is 1 W (see W).

V.nn – The common short name for ITU-T standards (see ITU), where "nn" represents a particular standard, as follows:

- V.17 – Fax transmission over dial lines at 14.4 Kbps rate.
- V.21 – Dial line modulation at 300 bps.
- V.22 – Dial line modulation at 1.2 Kbps.
- V.22bis – Dial line modulation at 2.4 Kbps.
- V.27bis – 4-wire leased line modulation at 4.8 Kbps.
- V.29 – 4-wire leased line modulation at 9.6 Kbps.
- V.32 – 2-wire leased line and dial line modulation at 9.6 Kbps.
- V.32bis – 2-wire leased line and dial line modulation at 14.4 Kbps.
- V.34 – 2-wire leased line and dial line modulation at 28.8 Kbps.
- V.34 – 2-wire leased line and dial line modulation at 33.6 Kbps.
- V.90 – 2-wire leased line and dial line modulation at 56 Kbps.
- V.110 – Specifies how data terminal equipment (see DTE) can be supported on an ISDN network.
- V.120 – Specifies how data terminal equipment can be supported on an ISDN network using a LAP-D-like protocol.

VA – VisualAge. An IDE developed by IBM for a variety of platforms, IBM and non-IBM as well. See also IDE (Interactive Development Environment).

VADD – VisualAge Developer Domain. A website that offers many services (the latest information, red books, white papers, software downloads, etc.) relating to VisualAge for Java (http://www7.software.ibm.com/vad.nsf).

VAFC – VESA Advanced Feature Connector. An open hardware interface defined by VESA for a high-bandwidth (150 Mbps) point-to-point connection that allows pixel data to be transferred between graphics and video systems.

VAIO – Video Audio Integrated Operation. The tradename for Sony's desktop and laptop personal computers.

VAN – Value-Added Network. A common term for a network that offers additional services to its users. Types of value-added services include message routing, resource management, conversion facilities, etc.

VAP – Value-Added Process. A process that runs on top of NetWare in order to provide additional services without interfering with the regular network operations.

VAR – Value-Added Reseller. A company that offers hardware and software on the market in a complete form, adding value through the integration of complete solutions, customer support, service, etc.

VAT – Visual Audio Tool. An X11-based audio teleconferencing tool. VAT allows users to conduct host-to-host or multihost audio teleconferences over an internetwork (multihost conferences require that the kernel supports IP multicasting). No special hardware, other than a microphone, is required for VAT. See also X.

VAX – Virtual Address Extended. The well-known DEC family of micro- and minicomputers. Pronounced "vaks".

VB – Visual Basic. A programming language provided by Microsoft (not exactly visual, see VPL). Visual Basic applications look like other Microsoft Windows applications. See also VBA.

VBA – Visual Basic for Applications. A shared development environment that enables developers to create user-oriented business solutions for Microsoft Office and other applications featuring VBA. VBA includes a language engine, a powerful editor, an Object Browser, and debugging tools (see IDE). Developers can use standard tools to employ the functionality of Microsoft Office and third-party software products to build vertical business solutions. The integrated development environment of VBA is a totally new environment for developers. The most significant aspect is that the new Visual Basic editor lies outside the host application. Therefore, developers can write code in VBA and view the results in the host application at the same time. Although the IDE lies outside the application, it runs in the same memory space as its host, and tight integration of event handling is included. VBA supports conditional compilation, so developers can set compilation flags within their code to control the actions of the applications at given points. Class modules are also important features provided by VBA. They allow user-defined objects to be treated as templates. Within a class module, developers can add common procedures that define custom methods and attributes for the object. When an instance of the class is created, developers can apply these custom methods and properties as they would for any object. Modules can be shared across projects using cut and paste or the export and import utility, etc. VBA also supports ActiveX controls. The first version of VBA appeared in 1994 in Microsoft Excel and Microsoft Project.

VBE – VESA BIOS Extensions. A VESA standard that defines a set of extensions to the VGA ROM BIOS.

vBNS – Very-high-speed Backbone Network Service. A network that links a number of supercomputer centers in the US. vBNS is the successor of the NSFNET. Also, vBNS is a part of the Internet2 (see I2) infrastructure.

VBP – Visual Basic Project. A filename extension for a file that contains Visual Basic project information.

VBR – Variable Bit Rate. One of the ATM service categories, divided into two subclasses, real-time and non-real-time. Real-time is intended for services that have variable bit rates combined with rigorous real-time requirements.

VBScript – Visual Basic Scripting Edition. A lightweight subset of the Visual Basic programming language which is Microsoft's answer to JavaScript. It is a scripting language targeting the Web. VBScript is available from Microsoft either in a binary distribution or in a source-level distribution. The binary distribution comes with a compiler and a set of runtime libraries and is available free of charge. VBScript is very similar to JavaScript. The underlying model is almost identical and the semantics are very close. The syntax is slightly different since VBScript code is derived from Visual Basic.

VBW – Visual Basic Workspace. A filename extension for a file that contains a Visual Basic workspace.

VBX – Visual Basic custom control (X). A software module that, when called by a Visual Basic application, produces a control that adds some desired feature to the application. A VBX is a separate executable file, usually written in C, that is dynamically linked to the application at runtime and can be used by other applications, including some not developed in Visual Basic. VBXs are still in use, but OCX and ActiveX controls have superseded it. See also Visual Basic (VB) and OCX.

VC – Virtual Circuit. A temporary connection established between two points in long-haul networks. Typical examples of such networks are X.25-based networks or frame-relay networks (see X.25 and FR).

VCB – Verb Control Block. A data structure used by SNA LUs when they communicate with each other. VCBs identify the verbs exchanged in LU–LU communications and supply information to be used by verbs (see LU).

VCC – Virtual Channel Connection. A logical circuit made up of virtual channels which carry data between two endpoints in an ATM network. Sometimes called a virtual circuit connection. A group of VCCs can be allocated for the same connection. In that case such a cluster is known as a virtual path connection (see VPC). See also VCI, VCL and VPI.

VCI – Video Cursor Interface. An interface defined by VESA for easy communication between SVGA and pointing devices.

VCI – Virtual Channel Identifier. A field in the ATM cell header (16-bits wide). The VCI and VPI are used to identify the next destination of a cell as it passes through a series of ATM switches on its way to its destination. ATM switches use the VPI/VCI fields to identify the next network VCL that a cell needs to move through on its way to its final destination.

VCL – Virtual Channel Link. A connection between two ATM devices. See VCC.

VCN – Virtual Circuit Number. A field in the X.25 header that identifies an X.25 virtual circuit. It allows the DTE to determine how to route a packet through the X.25 network. Sometimes called the LCI (Logical Channel Identifier) or the LCN (Logical Channel Number).

VCO – Voltage-Controlled Oscillator. An oscillator, the clock frequency of which is determined by the magnitude of the voltage delivered to its input.

VCPI – Virtual Control Program Interface. A specification for MS-DOS programs to allow access to extended memory under a multitasking environment (for example, Microsoft Windows) for 80386 and higher-level processors. Unlike DPMI, developed by Microsoft for the same purpose, VCPI was developed by several vendors and is not compatible with DPMI. See also DPMI.

VCT – Visual FoxPro Class Template. A filename extension for a file that contains a Visual FoxPro class library memo.

VCX – Visual FoxPro Class library file. A filename extension for a file that contains a Visual FoxPro class library.

VDD – Virtual Device Driver. A special type of device driver in Windows 95 that has direct access to the kernel of the operating system. Virtual device drivers are described using three-letter abbreviations beginning with “V” and ending with “D”; the middle letter indicates the type of device, such as “D” for a display, “P” for a printer, “T” for a timer, and “x” when the type of device is not relevant.

VDIF – VESA Display Information File. A uniform display specification defined by VESA which enables video controllers from different vendors to provide correct monitor timing and video signals to any connected VDIF-compliant display.

VDE – Verband der Elektrotechnik, Elektronik und Informationstechnik. German professional association for electrical, electronic and information technologies (http://www.vde.de).

VDL – Vienna Definition Language. A metalanguage developed for the formal algebraic definition of other languages. It contains both syntactic and semantic metalanguages. See also VDM (Vienna Definition Method).

VDM – Vienna Definition Method. A program development method based on formal specification using the Meta-IV language.

VDM – Virtual DOS Machine. Part of the Windows NT operating system (see NT) that provides support for DOS or for 16-bit Windows applications.

VDSL – Very-high-data-rate Digital Subscriber Line. One of four DSL technologies. VDSL delivers 13 Mbps to 52 Mbps downstream and 1.5 Mbps to 2.3 Mbps upstream over a single twisted copper pair. See DSL. Compare with ADSL, HDSL and SDSL.

VDT – Video Display Terminal. A common name for a type of terminal that consists of a keyboard, a screen (a monitor, VDU) and a communication port.

VDU – Video Display Unit. The device on which images generated by the computer's video adapter are displayed. Also called a monitor. See also CRT.

V.E.R.A. – Virtual Entity of Relevant Acronyms. A free online list of computer-oriented acronyms.

VERONICA – Very Easy Rodent-Oriented Net-wide Index to Computerized Archives. The comprehensive title/index of the world's Gopher servers. Because of VERONICA, the Gopher web is a search and retrieval system as well as a browsing system. It is popular because the ubiquitous Gopher client can both access the search server and provide immediate access to the discovered resources. VERONICA is easily accessed via any Gopher client. It offers various types of searches, ranging from single-keyword searches to Boolean queries of indefinite complexity.

VESA – Video Electronics Standards Association. An industry standards organization (http://www.vesa.org) concerned with graphic capabilities for IBM-compatible personal computers. Numerous standards have been defined by VESA. Some of these are described in this book. See SVGA, VAFC, VBE,

VCI (Video Cursor Interface), VDIF, VIAD, VIP (Video Interface Port), VLB, VMC and VP&D.

VFAT – Virtual File Allocation Table. The file system driver software used under Windows 95's File System Manager for accessing disks. VFAT is compatible with MS-DOS disks but runs more efficiently. For example, VFAT handles log file names (longer than 8 characters), runs in protected mode, and uses 32-bit code. Microsoft refer to VFAT as a driver because it should be installed by other operating systems which need access to VFAT. Compare with FAT.

VFP – Visual FoxPro. A database development system from Microsoft. In addition to the previous version known as FoxPro, Microsoft added object orientation (see OO) and client/server support (see C/S). Later, starting with version 5.0, ActiveX support was also provided.

VFS – VINES File System. A file system used in the VINES network operating system. VFS provides file access across the network, including support for several file systems commonly used. See also VINES.

VFW – Video For Windows. Full-motion video software developed by Microsoft that supports Audio Video Interleaved files (see AVI).

VGA – Video Graphics Array. A video adapter for PCs introduced by IBM in 1987. It supports 640 horizontal by 480 vertical pixels in 16 colors with a table of 262,144 colors. There is also a text mode with 720×400 pixels.

VHD – Very High Density. A term applied to storage devices to indicate a higher capacity than usual at a given time. See also VLDB.

VHDL – VHSIC Hardware Description Language. The IEEE1076 standard for a VHSIC hardware description language with an Ada-like syntax. See also VHSIC and VITAL.

VHE – Virtual Home Environment. An architectural concept in mobile computing that provides mobile users with the same environment as they have in their homes or offices.

VHF – Very High Frequency. The portion of the electromagnetic spectrum between 30 and 300 MHz.

VHSIC – Very-High-Speed Integrated Circuit. An integrated circuit that performs operations, usually logic operations, at a very high rate.

vi – visual interface. A popular text-based editor used under UNIX environments (pronounced "vee-aye").

VIAD – VESA Image-Area Definition. A standard method established by VESA for defining the usable image area for CRT displays.

VIF – Virtual Interface. A dynamic-link library (see DLL) used by Microsoft Multicast Router (see MMR).

VIFF – Visualization/Image File Format. A bitmap file format unlimited in both colors and image size, developed by Khoral Research and intended for use in the X Window System environment (see X). For further information look under http://www.khoros.unm.edu

VIM – Vendor-Independent Messaging. An API developed by Apple, Borland, Lotus, IBM, MCI, Oracle, Corel and Novell, intended for use between application programs and a variety of available messaging services. See also MAPI and XAPI.

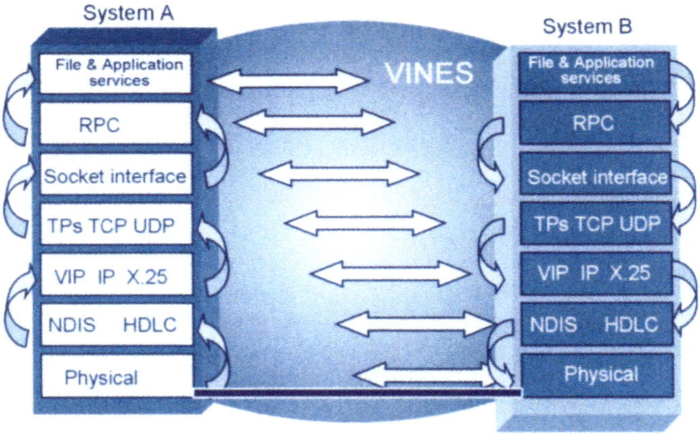

Fig. V-1. A simplified view of the VINES protocol stack

VINES – Virtual Integrated Network Service. A network operating system developed and marketed by Banyan Systems. It is built on a UNIX operating system, but also deals with other commonly used operating systems. Access to distributed files and directories is provided by the VINES file system (see VFS). In addition to its own protocol stack (see Fig. V-1), VINES provides optional support for OSI, TCP/IP and AppleTalk stacks. See also NOS (Network Operating System).

V

VINT – Virtual InterNetwork Testbed. The project that tests for simulation tools that could be implemented in the design and deployment of new wide area Internet protocols.

VIP – Video Interface Port. A standard defined by VESA for a dedicated physical connection between a graphics adapter and one or more third-party devices, such as video digitizers or MPEG decoders.

VIP – Virtual Internet Protocol. A protocol that provides host mobility on the Internet. VIP has the following features. It is scalable, to adapt to the scale of the network and the total number of mobile hosts; all packets avoid routing loops, except for the first packet which traverses the optimum route; and it is also tolerant in the case of lost control packets. VIP is a protocol that resolves a VIP address into a corresponding IP address. See also MH (Mobile Host).

VIR – Virus file. A filename extension for a file that is virus-infected, as identified by the Norton AntiVirus utility.

ViRGE – Video Rendering Graphics Engine. A family of 2D and 3D graphics accelerator chips from S3, introduced in 1995.

VIS – Viewable Image Size. A term that describes how much of a computer monitor is visible.

VIS – Visualization. The IEEE international conference focusing on interdisciplinary collaboration among developers and users of visualization techniques.

VITA – VMEbus International Trade Association. An industrial organization of VMEbus manufacturers that supports the PCI Mezzanine card standard. See also VME and PMC.

VITAL – VHDL Initiative Towards ASIC Libraries. An industry-based consortium, the objective of which is to accelerate the development of sign-off quality ASIC macrocell simulation libraries written in VHDL by exploiting existing methodologies of model development. VITAL is currently developing an IEEE standard for discrete-event digital simulation of fault-free electronic networks. See also ASIC and VHDL.

VKD – Virtual Keyboard Device. A built-in virtual device driver (see VDD) that controls the keyboard and allows keystrokes to be sent to the appropriate active application window.

VLAN – Virtual LAN. A group of devices on one or more LANs that are configured to work as a single LAN. In fact, they are located on a number of different LAN segments. Because VLANs are based on logical instead of physical connections, they are extremely flexible.

VLB – Ventura Library. A filename extension for a file that contains a Corel Ventura Library.

VLB – VESA Local Bus. A type of local bus architecture introduced by the Video Electronics Standards Association (see VESA). The VLB specification allows up to three VLB slots to be built into a motherboard. A VLB slot consists of a standard ISA, EISA or MCA connector plus an additional 16-bit MCA connector (see ISA, EISA and MCA). Video adapters, hard disk controllers and network adapters are types of VLB slots. Compare with PCI.

VLDB – Very Large Databases. A term sometimes used to describe databases that have data storage in the terabyte range (see TB). As always when technology improvements are involved, attributes like high, very high, very large, very fast, etc. are temporary attributes. Something that today looks very high or very large, tomorrow (in a reasonable sense) could be considered regular etc. There are also two more meanings associated with VLDB. First, VLDB is an annual international conference focusing on the most critical challenges and achievements in the research and practice of database applications and management. Second, VLDB is the name of the journal with the same topics, published by Springer-Verlag.

VLF – Very Low Frequency. The portion of the electromagnetic spectrum with frequencies between 3 and 30 kHz.

VLIW – Very Long Instruction Word. The term used to describe an assembly language instruction set implemented using a horizontal microcode. VLIW is sometimes classified as a type of static superscalar architecture (see RISC) in which units operate in parallel depending on the instruction contents.

VLM – Virtual Loadable Module. Software that runs in NetWare environments in order to provide communications between DOS workstations and the server.

VLSI – Very-Large-Scale Integration. This represents high technology in integrated circuit production with about 5000–50,000 transistors on a single chip.

VM – Virtual Machine. Software that mimics the performance of a hardware device, such as a program that allows applications written for an Intel processor to be run on a Motorola chip. The term is most frequently used with the Java programming language and Java environments. VM describes a software interface that acts between compiled Java binary code and the hardware platform where this code is executed (see JVM). The term VM is also used by IBM for any multiuser operating system with shared resources.

VM – Virtual Memory. An imaginary memory area, the abstraction of total memory required by a program. Operating systems that support virtual memory convert virtual addresses to real addresses during program execution (this process is called mapping). In the case of insufficient memory space, only those sections of code and data currently in use are mapped. The concept of virtual memory allows not only the execution of programs whose memory requirements exceed the physical capabilities of the main memory, but also an increase in the level of multiprogramming.

VMC – VESA Media Channel. An open software interface defined by VESA for transferring pixel data between two or more devices. See also VAFC.

VME – Versa Module Eurocard. An IEEE standard (1014) bus system first introduced in 1981 by Motorola, Philips, Thomson and Mostek.

VMM – Virtual Machine Manager. The 32-bit protected-mode operating system at the core of Windows 95.

VMS – Virtual Memory System. The operating system for VAX machines originated in 1979. It was renamed to OpenVMS.

VOC – Voice. A filename extension for a Creative Labs Sound Blaster audio file.

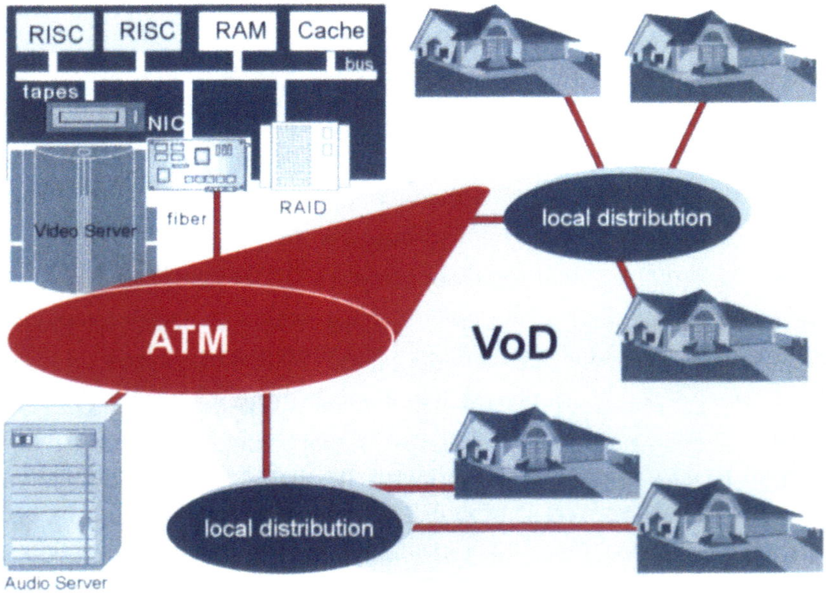

Fig. V-2. An overview of a video-on-demand system

VoD – Video-on-Demand. A system that allows remote selection of a movie at home, using the television set remote control. The general model is shown in Fig. V-2. At the center of the system is a high-bandwidth wide area backbone (ATM- or SONET-based). Thousands of local distribution providers are connected to that backbone. To have VoD (or even near video-on-demand, see NVoD), it is necessary to have video servers capable of storing and outputting a large number of movies simultaneously. The estimated number of movies made to date is close to 100,000, so the video server would need a huge amount of local storage to hold such a movie base. A normal (about 2-h duration) film compressed using MPEG-2 occupies about 4 GB of storage, so the total movie database would require 400 TB and that figure would increase daily. A video server capable of holding such a big database and supplying such VoD requirements would have to be a very powerful machine with one or more high-performance RISCS, and a shared main memory. It would also need a massive RAM cache to hold popular movies, a variety of storage devices (tape drives, optical jukeboxes, RAID disks), and some networking hardware, probably optical. All of that would have to be connected using an extremely high-speed bus (GBps). Possible solutions for a distribution network are given at other places in this book (see ADSL, FTTC, FTTH, FTTN and HFC). Finally, to see a chosen movie, a customer would have to be able to pick up the movie and put it on his/her TV set. To do that, customers' TVs would have to be connected either to so-called set-top boxes offered by the local network operator or to a personal computer with a card for decoding movies and picking them up from the local distribution network.

VoFR – Voice over Frame Relay. A specification developed by the Frame Relay Forum (see FR) in 1998 that defines frame formats and fragmentation for transmitting packetized voice over a frame relay network.

VoIP – Voice over Internet Protocol. The standard established by the VoIP Forum for sending audio data using IP on the Internet and within Intranets. The VoIP Forum is an industrial group run by several leading manufacturers in the area such as 3Com and Cisco.

VOP – Velocity Of Propagation. See Normal Velocity of Propagation (NVP).

VORD – Viewpoints for Requirements Definition. In software engineering, a method used in the viewpoint-oriented approach for software requirements analysis. The term VORD was introduced by Dr. Ian Sommerville and his associates (see Sommerville, 2000).

Vortal – Vertical Industry Portal. A portal website that provides information and resources for an industry.

VOTS – VAX OSI Transport Service. A transport-layer protocol used on VAX machines that follows the OSI Reference Model.

voxel – volume pixel. A basic unit of graphics information in three-dimensional space (see 3D). Compare with pixel.

VoxML – Voice over any (x) Markup Language. The markup language developed by Motorola that allows voice dialog with a website. A client program is called a voice browser.

VP – Ventura Publisher. A filename extension for a file that contains a document made using Ventura Publisher.

VP – Virtual Path. One of two types of ATM circuit identified by a VPI. A virtual path is a bundle of virtual channels, all of which are switched transparently across an ATM network based on a common VPI. See also VPI. Also, a sequence of names that is used to locate a file and that has the same form as a pathname in the file system, but is not necessarily the actual sequence of directory names under which the file is located. The part of a URL that follows the server name is a virtual path.

VPC – Virtual Path Connection. A cluster of logical connections (see VCC) between two entities in an ATM network. See also ATM.

VP&D – VESA Plug and Display. VESA standard for a digital interface and, optionally, an analog interface for video data.

VPD – Vital Product Data. The common name for data stored on a computer hard disk or the device itself for administration purposes.

VPI – Virtual Path Identifier. The 8-bit field in the header of an ATM cell. The VPI, together with the VCI, is used to identify the next destination of a cell as it passes through a series of ATM switches on its way to the destination. ATM switches use the VPI/VCI fields to identify the next VCL that a cell needs to transit on its way to the final destination. See also VCI and VCL.

VPL – Virtual Path Link. In ATM networks, a means of unidirectional transport of ATM cells between the point where a VPI value is assigned and the point where that value is translated or removed. See also VPI.

VPL – Visual Programming Language. A common term for any programming language that allows the user to specify a program in a two-dimensional or a multidimensional way. Programming is accomplished using visual techniques to express relationships or transformations to data. Such visual techniques include sketching, pointing and demonstrating via direct manipulation. In a typical dataflow VPL, the user would simply click on an input value, then click on an input port to the visual addition object to establish a relationship between the data and the function. According to the type and extent of visual expression used, VPLs may be icon-based, form-based or diagram languages. Naturally, visual languages have an inherent visual expression for which there is no obvious textual equivalent. They are usually designed for a specific application field, rather than as a general-purpose language. Despite their names, Visual Basic and Visual C are not visual programming languages.

VPN – Virtual Private Network. A computer network that appears to be a dedicated network to a particular set of users, whilst in fact using the infrastructure of public switched networks. Users of VPN communicate among themselves using some kind of encryption. Also, a wide area network made using permanent virtual circuits (see PVC) on another network, especially using ATM or frame relay technologies. See also Asynchronous Transfer Mode (ATM) and Frame relay (FR).

VR – Virtual Reality. Computer simulation that use 3D graphics, multimedia and other advanced techniques to allow the user to interact with the simulation. For instance, a service offering different types of corporate information can be presented by means of a virtual copy of an office building. A user can start in the lobby, where general information is provided, and then go to other "rooms" to find further information. The user sees the environment on display screens, possibly mounted in a special pair of goggles. Special input devices, such as gloves or suits fitted with motion sensors, detect the user's actions. See also CAVE and PARIS.

VRAM – Video Random-Access Memory. A fast memory (pronounced "vee-ram") used by video adapters. VRAM provides separate pins for the processor and video electronics. The processor accesses the VRAM in a way almost identical to DRAM access, but the video electronics accesses the memory bit by bit, which is more suitable for transferring pixel data to the screen. See also WRAM.

VRC – Vertical Redundancy Check. A parity check used in conjunction with a LRC in parallel data transfers. See also Longitudinal Redundancy Check (LRC).

VRC – View Reference Coordinates. A 3D device-independent coordinate system used to specify parameters for viewing transformations. It has three coordinate axes: the Z-axis denoted as N, Y-axis as V, and X-axis as U. Thus, it is usually called the UVN coordinate system. It is used in 3D graphics systems such as GKS-3D and PHIGS. The model of viewing transformation is based on a view reference point (VRP or VP), a point in the scene at which a pseudo (also called synthetic) camera is focused, defining the viewing direction of the camera, and the view plane onto which the scene is to be projected (see Fig. V-3). The window of the view plane is defined by two clippings, one of them lying in front of the view plane, the other one behind the view plane. Those two planes form the view volume, as shown in Fig. V-3.

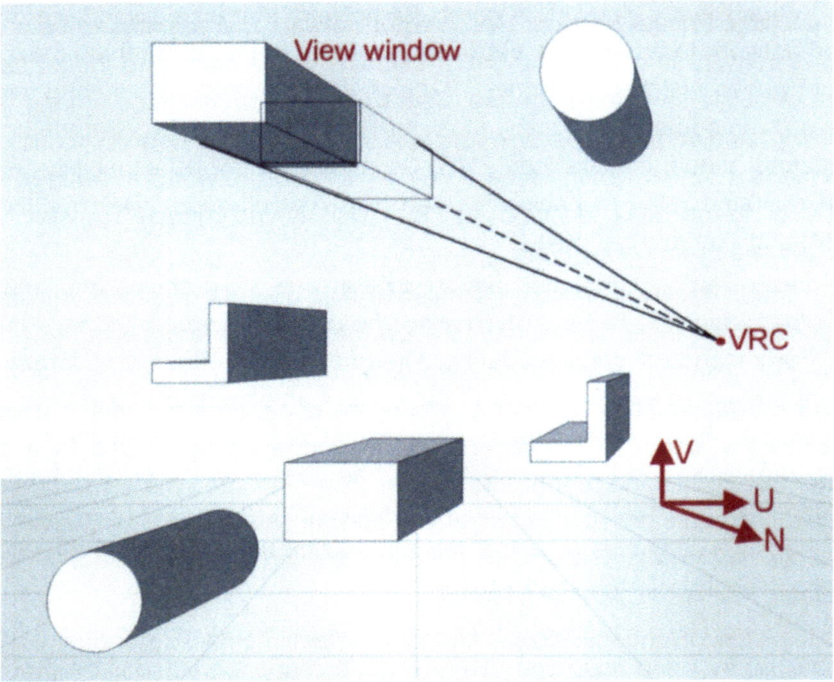

Fig. V-3. The model of viewing transformations

VRM – Voltage Regulator Module. A component that senses the voltage requirements of a microprocessor and ensures that the correct voltage is delivered.

VRML – Virtual Reality Modeling Language. The three-dimensional client standard on the Web that allows the description, manipulation and navigation of solid objects. VRML can create virtual 3D environments that users can move around in. VRML was created by Mark Pesce and Tony Parisi in 1994. VRML files can be created in a text editor, although CAD packages, modeling and animation packages, and VRML authoring software are the tools preferred by most VRML authors. VRML files reside on a HTTP server; links to these files can be embedded in HTML documents, or users can access the VRML files directly. To view VRML webpages, users need a VRML-enabled browser, such as WebSpace from Silicon Graphics, or a VRML plug-in for Internet Explorer or Netscape Navigator.

VRRP – Virtual Router Redundancy Protocol. Part of the Internet protocol (RFC2338) that allows the specification of a virtual IP address as a default router address on a LAN. Such an address is shared among the real routers, with one predetermined as the main router and the others used as backups.

VS – Virtual Scheduling. In ATM networks, an algorithm used to determine the conformance of an arriving cell.

VSAM – Virtual Storage Access Method. A file management system used in some IBM mainframe operating systems such as MVS and OS/390.

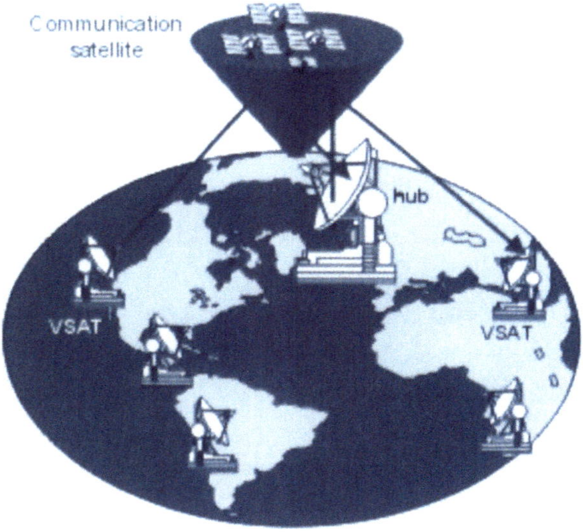

Fig. V-4. VSATs using a hub

VSAT – Very-Small-Aperture Terminal. A low-cost microstation on the ground used to contact a communication satellite. These tiny terminals have 1-m antennas and can deliver about 1 W of power. VSATs usually don't have enough power to communicate with each other. Instead, a special kind of groundstation, a hub, with a large antenna is used to relay traffic between VSATs (see Fig. V-4).

VSB – VME Subsystem Bus. An auxiliary bus used with the Versa Module Europe (see VME) bus.

VSD – Visio Drawing. A filename extension for a file that contains a drawing made using Microsoft Visio (see Fig. V-5).

VSDIR – Visual Studio Directory. A filename extension for a file that contains text information about items displayed using dialog boxes in a Microsoft Visual Studio.

VSIA – Virtual Socket Interface Alliance. An industrial organization formed by Fujitsu, Cadence, and Toshiba in September 1996 (http://www.vsi.org). With more than 200 members, the aim of VSIA is to establish and promote a unifying vision for the system chip industry and to develop the required technical standards in the field.

VST – Vietnam Standard Time. Time zone. UTC + 7.00 hours. See TZ.

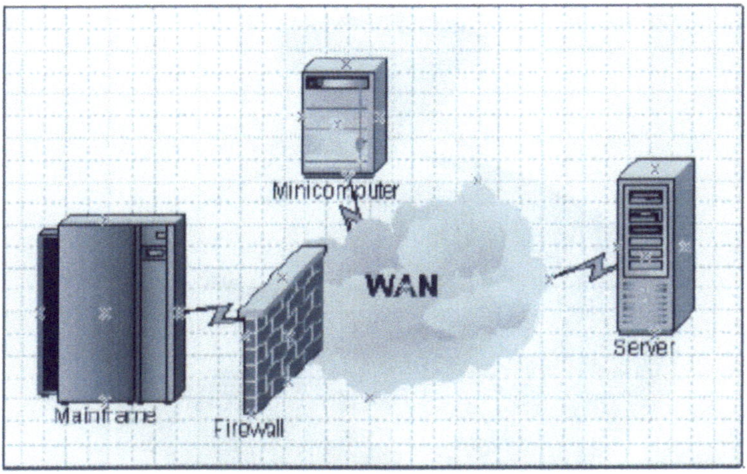

Fig. V-5. An example of a VSD file

VS/VD – Virtual Source/Virtual Destination. A method of flow control in available bit rate (see ABR) connections where ATM switch ports act as end points for regulating the flow of traffic. With VS/VD, one port acts as a virtual source and the next one acts as the virtual destination. When traffic has passed through one segment, that virtual destination then becomes the virtual source for the next hop. See also ATM.

VSX – Verification Suite for X/Open. Test suites that exist for many X/Open definitions. The successful completion of a formal test is usually a prerequisite for X/Open branding (see CAE). If X/Open does not specify a test suite for a component, there is no need to prove compliance at the time of branding, but the vendor is still required to warrant and demonstrate that the product conforms to the applicable X/Open definitions. For a number of X/Open definitions, X/Open itself has developed conformance test suites, which it has made available under license through a network of distributors. In other cases, for instance in the field of programming languages, where the X/Open specifications conform to international standards, X/Open indicates the test suites that have been developed to support the existing formal certification process.

VSZ – Visual Studio Wizard. A filename extension for a file that contains a Microsoft Visual Studio wizard.

VT – Video Terminal. See VDT (Video Display Terminal).

VT – Virtual Terminal. An application-layer service (ISO9040, ISO9041) in the OSI Reference Model (see OSI) that enables emulation of the behavior of a particular terminal. It allows an application to communicate with a remote system regardless of the type of hardware involved. Three classes of VT service are specified. The basic mode is a text-oriented service that provides line editing, scrolling and the other simplest terminal functions. In the forms mode, VT can emulate form-based terminals. The third mode is used to emulate graphics terminals.

VT – Virtual Tributary. A mechanism that allocates bandwidth in a SONET network by subdividing the basic SONET payload envelopes (51.84 Mbps) into lower-bit-rate envelopes. That allows a high-speed SONET connection to be broken down into multiple lower-speed channels. See also SONET.

VTAM – Virtual Telecommunications Access Method. IBM mainframe software that handles application access and routing within a network. It runs under the MVS and VM operating systems.

VTOA – Voice and Telephony Over ATM. The ATM Forum specification (see ATM) that addresses three methods of carrying voice over ATM networks. These are LAN services (desktop), WAN services (trunking) and mobile services.

VTOC – Volume Table Of Contents. An area on a disk or diskette that describes the location, size and other characteristics of each file, library and folder on the disk or diskette.

VTP – Virtual Terminal Protocol. A protocol used in the presentation and application layer in NetWare environments. See also VT (Virtual Terminal).

VTS – Virtual Terminal Services. An OSI upper-layer service used to define a common terminal format that might be shared between open systems. Defined in ISO9040. See also Virtual Terminal Protocol (VTP).

V&V – Verification & Validation. The generic name given to checking processes which ensure that software conforms to its specification and meets customer requirements. A system should be verified and validated at each stage of the software process using documents produced during the previous stage. See also IV&V.

VxD – Virtual any (x) Device driver. A filename extension for files containing virtual device drivers (see VDD).

W

W – Watt. The unit of power in the International System of Units. A Watt is the power required to do work at a rate of 1 Joule per second.

W3 – World-Wide Web. See WWW.

W3A – World-Wide Web Applets. A proposal for an API that describes an interface specification consisting of functions that WWW browser and external modules have to export in order to support dynamic linking of applets. See applet.

W3C – World-Wide Web Consortium. The main standardization body for the World-Wide Web (http://www.w3.org) created by MIT on 25 October 1994. MIT, INRIA and CERN run the consortium. W3C works with the global community to establish international standards that enable online commerce and communications all over the Internet. It also produces reference software.

WABI – Windows Application Binary Interface. A software package developed at Sun Microsystems that allows some Microsoft Windows applications to run under the X Window System. It works using translated versions of three core Windows DLLs (user, kernel and gdi) which redirect Windows calls to their Solaris equivalents. For other calls, WABI executes the instructions directly on the hardware (Intel chip), or emulates them. More information about WABI can be found at http://www.sun.com/solaris/products/wabi

WABI – Workshop on Algorithms in Bioinformatics. An international workshop focusing on discrete algorithms that address important problems in molecular biology, are based on sound models, are computationally efficient, and have been implemented and tested in simulations and on real datasets. The proceedings are published by Springer-Verlag (see LNCS).

WACK – Wait while Acknowledge. A transmission control signal which is issued by a receiver to indicate that it has received a transmitted set of information (byte, frame, block, etc.), but that it has not had time to establish its accuracy. Such a signal normally causes further transmission to be halted until a more useful decision can be made.

WADS – Workshop on Algorithms and Data Structures. An international forum that focuses on combinatorics, computational geometry, databases, computer graphics, and parallel and distributed computing. The proceedings are published by Springer-Verlag (see LNCS).

WADT – Workshop on Algebraic Development Techniques. An international forum for presenting and discussing research on the algebraic approach to system specification and development. The proceedings are published by Springer-Verlag (see LNCS).

WAE – Wireless Application Environment. An application framework on top of the Wireless Application Protocol stack (see WAP) for wireless terminals.

WAE – Workshop on Algorithm Engineering. An international workshop discussing all aspects of algorithm engineering, including implementation, experimental testing, and finetuning of discrete algorithms. The proceedings are published by Springer-Verlag (see LNCS).

WAI – Web Accessibility Initiative. An initiative hosted by W3C intended to ensure that the Web is accessible to people with disabilities.

WAI – Web Access Intermediaries. An IBM project that proposes a new approach to programming web applications in order to increase the Web's computational power, its flexibility and programmer productivity. The project is based on the so-called intermediaries, computational elements that lie along the path of web transactions. Intermediaries extend the web model to include content computation at client and workgroup proxies as well as at the server. This programming model provides a new degree of flexibility and allows web applications to do things that they could not do before. The architecture for intermediaries is known as Web Browser Intelligence (see WBI).

WAI – Web Application Interface. A CORBA-based programming interface that defines object interfaces to the HTTP request/response data and server information.

WAIBA – Wide Area Information Browsing Assistance. A shared TOG and DARPA project that finished in 1996, it allows users to create and share annotations to webpages, team-development webpages, and to display a user's browsing history.

WAIM – Web-Age Information Management. An international conference focusing on data, information and knowledge management in the age of the Internet and the Web. Some of the major topics are agent technology and information management, data mining and knowledge discovery, data and Web warehousing, databases and electronic commerce, emerging Web techniques, interoperability and heterogeneous systems, OLAP, multimedia information systems, parallel and distributed databases, transaction management, Web and database technology, workflow management, etc.

WAIS – Wide Area Information Service. An Internet service (pronounced "wayz") which helps to find a document using some part of its contents. Searching begins with a database selection, resulting in a list of hits with appropriate estimates of the correlation between the searching pattern used and the whole document. Matching documents are rank-ordered according to a simple statistical weighting scheme, which attempts to indicate the likely relevance. The information is accessible regardless of the format: text, formatted documents, pictures, spreadsheets, graphics, sound or video. The user may choose to view selected documents, or further refine the search. The results of a search may be used to successively refine future searches. WAIS databases may be accessed using WAIS, gopher and WWW clients (such as Mosaic), and via online services such as Delphi and AOL. WAIS software includes user interfaces for most platforms, and server software that provides automatic indexing of databases. With over 100 databases and a respective number of users worldwide, WAIS is rapidly becoming a standard for information distribution within the Internet environment.

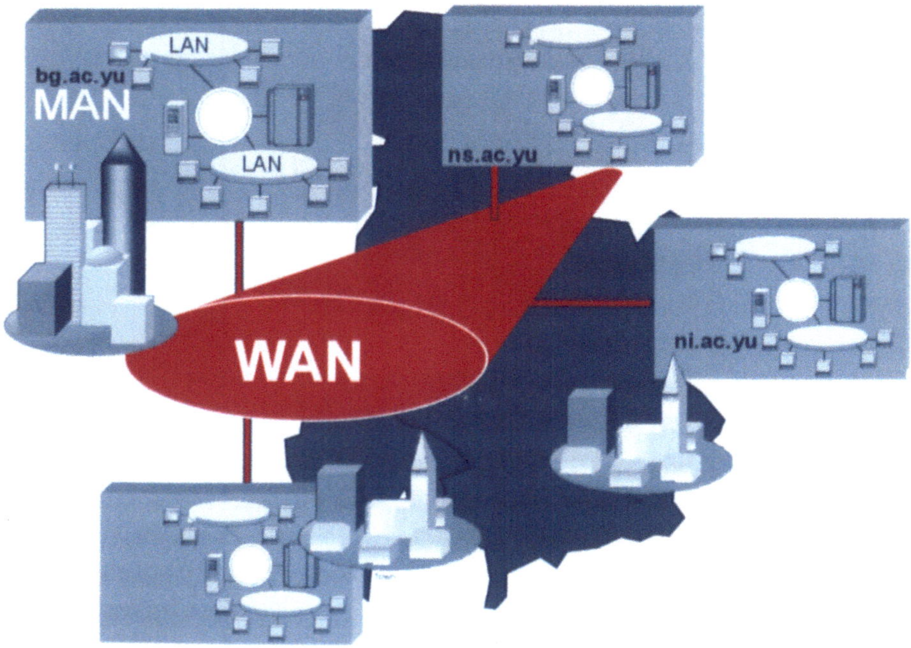

Fig. W-1. An example of a Wide Area Network

WAN – Wide Area Network. A kind of network distributed over a long distance or widely separated locations. There is no upper limit specified for the radius of a WAN. The main communication links in a WAN are provided by telephone company facilities or other network providers. Such links can be leased lines, satellite links or similar channels. Today WANs usually involve a number of local area networks (see LAN) and metropolitan area networks (see MAN) connected as shown in Fig. W-1. Examples of such WANs include the Yugoslavian Academic Network part of the Internet (domain ac.yu), the network of the National Bank, the YU TELECOM Network etc.

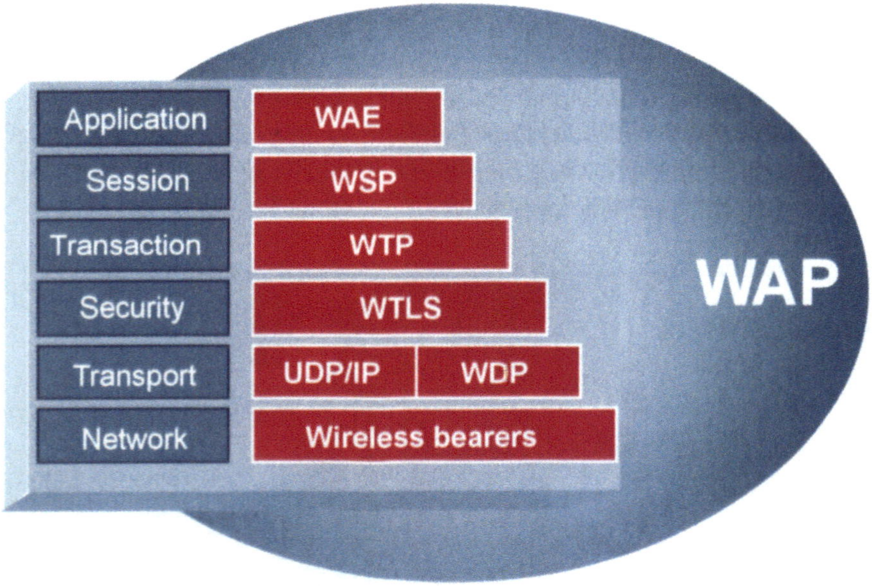

Fig. W-2. WAP stack

WAP – Wireless Application Protocol. A wireless communication protocol specified by the WAP Forum (Ericsson, Motorola, Nokia, Phone.com, AOL, AT&T, HP, IBM, Intel, Microsoft, and many others) that allows Internet access using mobile low-powered devices on different platforms. It includes the specifications for the transport (see WDP) and session (see WSP) layers, as well as for security (see Fig. W-2). WAP uses proxy technology to connect wireless technology with the Web. WAP was first released in June 1999. Website http://www.wapforum.org offers the latest information about WAP and the WAP Forum. See also WAE, WTLS, WML, WDP and WTP.

WARIA – Workflow and Reengineering International Association. A nonprofit organization (http://www.waria.com) concentrating on issues that are common to all users of workflows and those who are involved in the reengineering process in their organizations. See also WFM (Workflow Management) and BPR (Business Process Reengineering).

WAT – West Africa Time. Time zone. UTC + 1.00 hour. See TZ.

WATM – Wireless ATM. An initiative within the ATM Forum to develop a specification for transmitting ATM over wireless links. The goal is to develop a scheme for transporting voice, fax, data and video via wireless ATM links over satellite and microwave systems.

WATS – Wide Area Trunk Services. A telephone company service used to reduce the costs of long-distance calls. The best known example is the 1-800 system in the US.

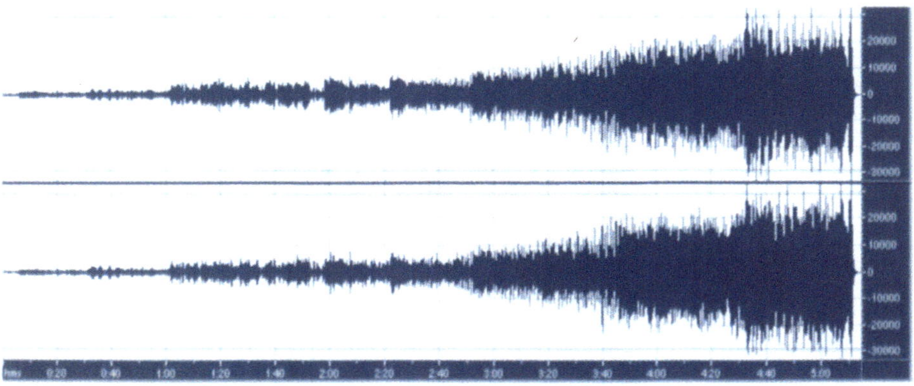

Fig. W-3. An example of a WAV format

WAV – Wave sound. A file format which Windows uses to store sounds as waveforms. Such files have the extension .wav. Depending on the sampling frequency, whether the sound is mono or stereo, and whether 8 or 16 bits are used for each sample, 1 min of sound can occupy as little as 644 KB or as much as 27 MB of storage. Figure W-3 shows Ravel's famous short ballet Bolero in .wav format.

WBC – Wideband Channel. A channel used in FDDI networks with a bandwidth of 6.144 Mbps.

WBEM – Web-Based Enterprise Management. An effort from the industry group of the same name (BMC Software., Cisco, Compaq, Intel and Micro-

W

soft) to allow administrators to use any Web browser to manage disparate systems, networks and applications. WBEM is designed to integrate existing standards, such as the desktop management interface (see DMI) for desktop and servers, SNMP for networks, and HTTP for communication over the Internet, into an architecture that can be managed using any Web browser. For additional information see http://wbem.freerange.com/wbem

WBI – Web Browser Intelligence. The WBI (pronounced "webby") architecture is a productive infrastructure for programming web applications using intermediaries (see WAI). It is a programming platform written in C++ and Java, that can be used to implement different types of intermediaries, from simple server functions to complex distributed applications. Compare with CGI, NSAPI and ASP. See http://www.cssrv.almaden.ibm.com/wbi

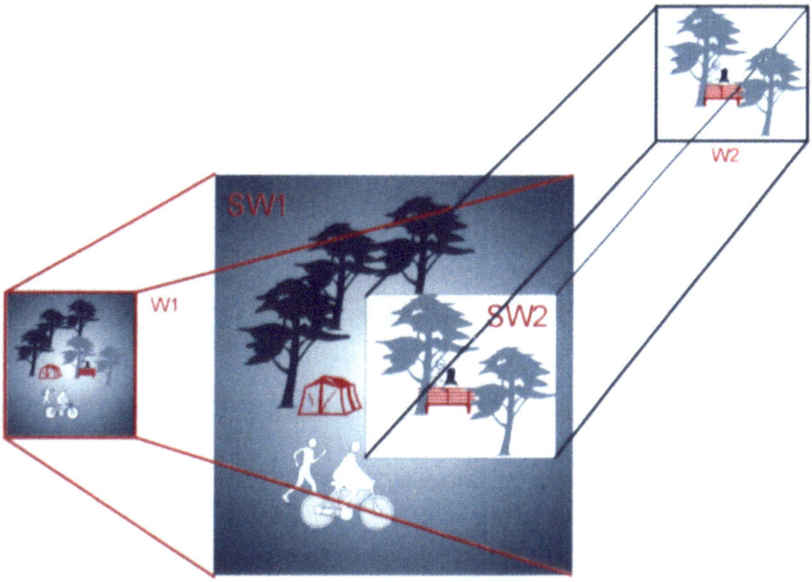

Fig. W-4. Clipping windows in WC space

WBK – Word Backup. A filename extension applied to backup versions of Microsoft Word documents (see WinWord and DOC). For example, if the original Word file has the name wdict.doc, its backup file has the name wdict.wbk.

WBMP – Wireless Bitmap. A filename extension for a file that contains a bitmap for transmission using the Wireless Application Protocol (see WAP).

WBS – Work Breakdown Structure. A method used to plan and manage the process of designing a product, producing it, and supporting it. A WBS is a mechanism for breaking work (generally related to some specific project) into smaller elements, which can be used for assigning resources, budgets, schedules, etc. The WBS provides a basis for project control.

WBT – Web-Based Training Information Center. The WBT is a nonprofit resource for individuals and organizations interested in developing and delivering training using Web technology. The aim of this site is to share nonproprietary information, stimulate creative ideas, and link to interesting training sites around the world.

WC – World Coordinates. The term originated in computer graphics. WC refers to an application coordinate space (infinite in all directions) in which the application chooses a finite rectangular window (scene window, SW) to describe a part of the real world (or a virtual world), usually called a scene (see Fig. W-4). Depending on the kind of graphic system in use, the chosen window is transformed (see NDC, for instance) to apply to an appropriate coordinate space and WST window (W).

WCC – World Computer Congress. The IFIP congress that covers all the important research areas in computer science. WCC2001 focused on IT foundations in the era of network and mobile computing, software architectures, telelearning, the state of the art in communication systems, issues of choice and quality of life in the information society, e-business, distributed and parallel embedded systems, and intelligent information processing. Figure W-5 shows the WCC2002 homepage.

WCNC – Wireless Communications and Networking Conference. The IEEE conference that covers the development and deployment of digital cellular personal communication systems and the full spectrum of supporting wireless technologies.

WD – Western Digital. See WDC.

WDC – Western Digital Corporation. A company founded in 1970 as a specialized semiconductor manufacturer, which today manufactures and sells microcomputer products including hard-disk drives (see HDD) for personal computers, integrated circuits, and circuit boards for graphics, storage, communications and logic functions (http://www.wdc.com).

WDL – Windows Driver Library. A collection of hardware device drivers for the Microsoft Windows operating system that were not included in the original Windows package.

WDM – Wavelength-Division Multiplexing. An alternative to frequency-division multiplexing (see FDM) for fiber-optic (see FO) channels. The idea used is not a new one. It's based on the refraction of light in a prism, as depicted in Fig. W-6. Two or more fibers meet at a prism, and each fiber uses a different energy band (the fibers use different internal angles, etc.). The beams pass through the prism, and are combined in a single shared fiber for transmission to a distant point, where they are split. It's a very useful technique because the bandwidth of a single fiber band is about 25,000 GHz, i.e. many channels can be multiplexed for long-haul routes. These WDM capabilities were demonstrated during a 1994 experiment when an AT&T research group achieved a datarate of 56.8 TBps/km using a 1420-km-long fiber and 16-channel WDM amplifiers approximately every 100 km.

Fig. W-5. WCC2002 homepage

WDMA – Wavelength-Division Multiple Access. This communication protocol is based on two channels, the narrow one is provided as a control channel to signal to the station, and the wide one is used for the output datastreams. The protocol supports three classes of traffic, constant-datarate connection-oriented traffic, variable-datarate connection-oriented traffic, and datagram traffic, used, for example, for uncompressed video, file transfer, or UDP packets, respectively.

WDP – Wireless Datagram Protocol. A part of the Wireless Application Protocol stack (see WAP) that works in a way similar to the classical UDP for the TCP/IP protocol stack, but supports most common wireless protocols in lower layers, such as CDMA, CDPD, GSM and TDMA.

WDSI – Western Decision Science Institute. An international symposium with main topics of global business, innovative education, accounting, information systems, e-commerce, etc. Unlike most conferences, WDSI has a permanent web address http://www.misnt.calpoly.edu/wds

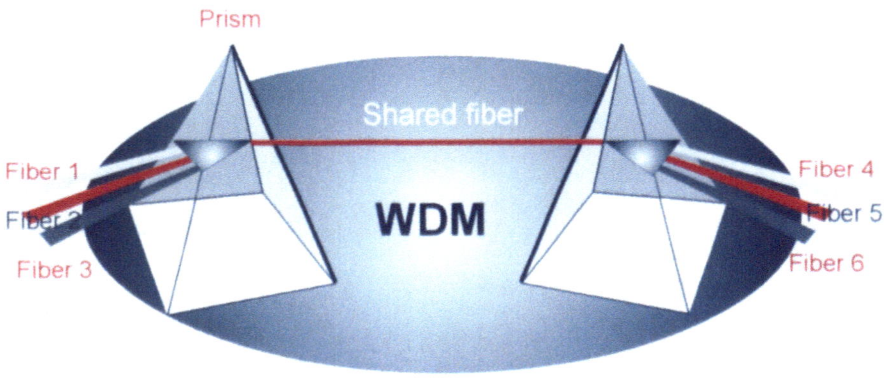

Fig. W-6. Wavelength-division multiplexing

wDSL – Wavelet Digital Subscriber Line. One of the available Digital Subscriber Line technologies (see xDSL) that offers significant improvements in digital bandwidth/carrier performance for existing copper telephone lines.

WDSS – Workstation-Dependent Segment Storage. The term "segment" is used here for a type of named data structure used by some graphics system (for example GKS) for grouping graphical output primitives. Such segments may be transformed, may be visible or invisible, highlighted, ordered front-to-back, deleted, renamed, etc. The term "workstation" is used here to describe an abstract graphical device, which can fall into one of the following six categories: output, input, output/input (outin), WISS, metafile input, or metafile output. Thus, WDSS refers to segment storage on an output or outin workstation. Segments cannot be moved from a WDSS to another workstation. Compare with WISS.

WDT – Watchdog Timer. A circuit used in Ethernet transceivers to ensure that transmission frames are never longer than the specified maximum length. Also, part of an operating system that sets various timers.

We-B – Working with e-Business. An international conference focusing on e-business, e-government and related fields. More information is available at the site in Fig. W-7.

WebDAV – Web Distributed Authoring and Versioning. A project undertaken by the group with the same name to define extensions to the HTTP protocol that allow webpages created using one web authoring tool to be revised using a different web authoring tool.

Fig. W-7. We-B 2001 homepage

WEBSIM – Web-Based Modeling and Simulation. An international conference intended to discuss the possibilities of the Internet and World-Wide Web as tools as well as objects for modeling and simulation. Some of the main topics include simulation systems and methodologies on the Web, coordination languages and systems, interface agents for system modeling and simulation, groupware, multimedia, standardization, etc.

Webzine – Web magazine. An electronic publication distributed primarily through the World-Wide Web, rather than as an ink-on-paper magazine. See also e-zine.

WECWIS – Workshop on E-Commerce and Web-Based Information Systems. An international workshop focusing on related technologies, management issues and solutions for e-commerce and the Internet. Topics include personalization and content management for electronic commerce (see EC) systems, real-time Internet delivering and scheduling protocols, content distribution, collaborative proxies, security for EC systems, data mining for EC systems, Web-based information systems, Java technologies for EC systems, QoS support, Web content hosting and replication, auction and negotiation technologies, collaborative commerce, etc.

WED – World E-mail Directory. A global online search engine database (http://www.worldemail.com) for e-mail addresses, URL and other information, with personal and business profiles from all over the world.

WEDT – Western European Daylight Time. Time zone. UTC + 1 hour. See TZ.

WEEB – Western Europe EDIFACT Board. The UN/EDIFACT board focuses on EDIFACT development in Western Europe.

WELL – Whole-Earth Electronic Link. A conferencing system based in San Francisco, California, that is accessible through the Internet and through dial-up access points in many major cities. WELL attracts many computer professionals, along with other people who enjoy participating in one of the Internet's most successful virtual communities. Because of the number of journalists and other prominent people who participate in the WELL, it has substantial influence beyond its own relatively small number of subscribers.

WET – Western European Time. The same time as that of UTC. See TZ.

WF – Web Farming. A new research area in Web applications focusing on systematic discovery and collection of Web data of interest to business for data warehouses (see DW). WF systems have three main goals:

- Discover and download webpages with relevant business data (i.e. potential markets, business partners, customers, competitors, etc.).
- Structure such data in a way that allows its integration into the existing data warehouse.
- Apply the above two goals in a systematic way to achieve strategic CIM.

WFC – Windows Foundation Classes. A set of class libraries used in application development using Visual J++.

WFM – Workflow Management. The computer-assisted management of business processes through the execution of software where the order of execution is controlled by a computerized representation of the business processes.

W

WFM – Works for me. The chat term.

WfMC – Workflow Management Coalition. An organization founded in August 1993 (http://www.wfmc.org) that defines industrial standards for workflow (see WFM) software.

WFW – Windows for Workgroups. An extension of Microsoft Windows 3.x that provides P2P networking capabilities (see P2P). WFW supports Ethernet and Token Ring networks. It also supports HyperTerminal, PhoneDialer, Sound Recorder, WordPad, etc.

WI – Web Intelligence. An Asia–Pacific conference focusing on artificial intelligence and advanced information technologies on the Web and Internet. Some of the major topics include Web human–media engineering, Web information management and retrieval, Web agents, Web mining and farming, Web-based applications, etc.

WIBNI – Wouldn't it be nice if. The chat term.

WIC – Women in Computing. An international conference that provides a forum for sharing the ideas and experiences of women studying and working in computing, education, and in the information technology and telecommunications industry.

WICSA – Working IEEE/IFIP Conference on Software Architecture. The joint IEEE/IFIP conference devoted to software architectures. Some of the main topics include theoretical foundations for software architectures (description languages, analysis methods, assessment, extraction, recovery, etc.), architecture in practice, computer-based software development, supported tools, economy-driven architectures, etc.

WID – Winsurf Intranet Development. A development kit used for easy integration of Microsoft Internet development tools, such as Visual Basic (see VB) or Visual Internet Developer with the Winsurf Mainframe Access system (see WMA) from Data Interface.

WIDL – Web Interface Definition Language. An API based on XML that allows Web applications to easily exchange data with one another across different platforms over the Web.

WIDM – Web Information and Data Management. An international workshop that covers research on how web information can be extracted, stored, analyzed and processed to provide useful knowledge to the end-users in various advanced database applications. Some of the major topics include data mining, web databases, web commerce, performance of web applications, advanced web applications, etc.

WIF – Wavelet Image File. A filename extension for files that contain WIF compressed data.

WIMP – Windows, Icons, Menus and Pointing devices. The most popular metaphor for user interface design (see UI and GUI). The display is partitioned into a series of (possibly overlapping) stacked windows, each running a separate task, each of them can be activated using a different icon (a small pictorial representation of the task), different operations can be chosen using menus, and the selection process is controlled by the pointing device (mouse etc.).

WIN – Wireless In-building Network. A wireless network dedicated to a single building. See also WLAN.

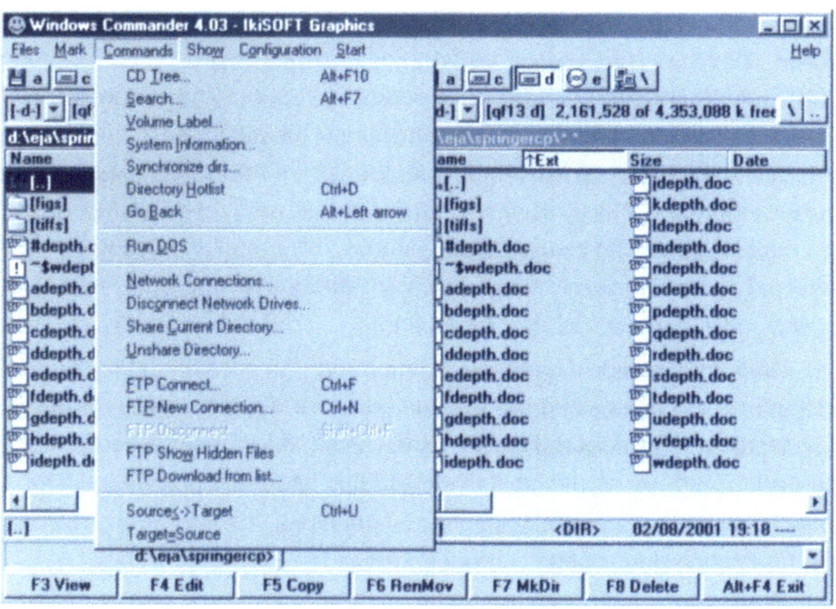

Fig. W-8. Windows Commander in action

Wincmd – Windows Commander. A utility program under Windows that allows a Windows file to be viewed, edited, copied, removed or deleted (see Fig. W-8). It is also possible, using Wincmd, to obtain an FTP connection to a remote machine and pick up a file from there and place it in a local folder.

WinG – Windows Games. An API intended for games in the Windows 95 environment. Under WinG, games can access the video frame buffer directly for increased speed.

WINS – Windows Internet Naming Service. A Windows NT Server method for associating a computer's host name with its address. Also called INS (Internet Naming Service). Compare with DNS.

WINSOCK – Windows Sockets. An API based on the BSD socket paradigm, specifically used with the Microsoft Windows family. This API specification defines an accepted industrial standard for Windows program development for TCP/IP networks. The curiosity of WINSOCK is that Microsoft has nothing to do with it. The specification is the result of work done by a large number of people from many different corporations to produce a single API capable of developing Windows-based network applications. Readers with a special interest in WINSOCK are welcome to use an anonymous ftp to log into SunSite.unc.edu and browse in the subdirectory /pub/micro/pc-stuff/ms-windows/winsock

WinWord – Word for Windows. The popular Microsoft word processor running on Microsoft Windows. It has many features required by modern text processors. In addition to WYSIWYG attributes, justification, a rich choice of fonts, cut and paste, and an undo mechanism, it allows the user to import different kinds of picture formats, create tables, and do spelling and grammar checks, and it has many other features. This book was produced using WinWord7. The look and feel of the WinWord user interface are shown in Fig. W-9. See also WP (Word Processing).

WISE – Web Information Systems Engineering. An international conference focusing on the engineering of Web-based information systems. Some of the major topics include databases and the Web, XML, Web security, transactions and workflow, modeling and metadata, information visualization, data mining and data warehousing, new services, development techniques, communications and mobile computing, etc.

WISE – Web-Integrated Software Metrics Environment. A WWW-based tool that provides a framework for managing software development projects across the Web. Programmers can log issue reports, track their status, and view project metrics using standard WWW browsers.

WISS – Workstation-Independent Segment Storage. A data structure used by some graphics systems (for instance, see GKS) that allows grouping of output primitives. Segments are stored in the WISS as long as it is open and active. That means that WISS is available only during run-time. Compare with WDSS.

WIT – W3 Interactive Talk. A form-based discussion system that allows discussion on W3 technical matters to be stored in a more structured fashion.

WITS – Workshop on Information Technologies and Systems. An international workshop that focuses on cutting-edge technologies in information systems.

Fig. W-9. WinWord in action used to develop this book

WIZ – Wizard file. A filename extension for a file that contains a wizard for a Microsoft Word document. An example is given in Fig. W-10, which depicts a WIZ file used to create an envelope.

WLAN – Wireless Local Area Network. A traditional local area network extended with a wireless interface to service small low-powered portable terminals capable of wireless access. The WLANs are further connected to a more extensive fixed network such as a LAN, WAN, the Internet, etc. The main component in the WLAN is the wireless interface card. This interface card can be connected to the mobile unit as well as to the fixed network. WLAN technology offers a medium for new applications introduced, with a growing market for portables. For instance, with WLANs it is possible to set-

W

up ad hoc networks, e.g. at a meeting or at other locations used only temporarily. A group of mobile users may establish an autonomous local area network anywhere, anytime, with negligible effort. The IEEE802.11 subcommittee was founded in 1990 in order to establish a global standard for WLANs. The functional requirements for a wireless LAN have been identified as follows: the protocol must handle fixed stations and portables as well as the mobile stations accessing the medium while in motion. The minimal functional bandwidth to be supported has been fixed at 1 Mbps.

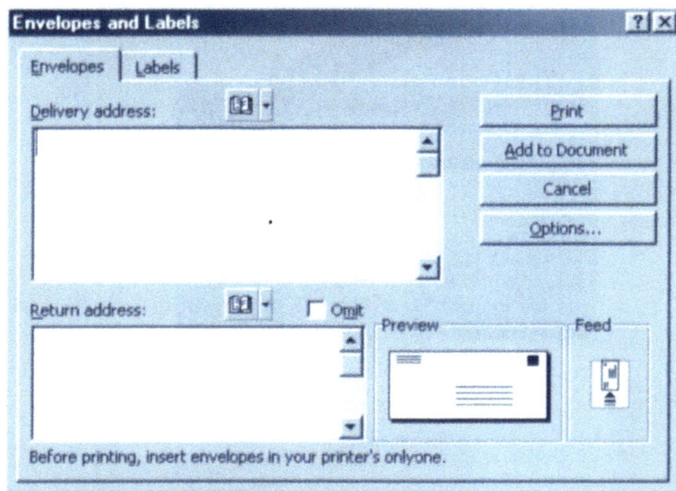

Fig. W-10. An example of a WIZ file

WMA – Winsurf Mainframe Access. A Web-to-host connectivity system developed by Data Interface. WMA resides on a Microsoft Windows NT server running Microsoft Internet Information Server (see IIS) and offers centralized management of Windows 95, 98 or NT clients accessing hosts. More information at http://www.di3270.com

WMCSA – Workshop on Mobile Computing Systems and Applications. The IEEE workshop focusing on advanced issues in mobile computing systems and applications.

WMF – Windows Metafile. The filename extension for a Windows metafile. This kind of file is used to exchange pictures among different applications running in the Microsoft Windows environment. Depicted in Fig. W-11 is an example of a WinWord import utility where a WMF made using the CorelDraw export utility (see CDR) is easily imported into a Word document.

WML – Wireless Markup Language. A markup language designed for the development of webpages that can be easily read using wireless devices with small screens and without keyboards. Also, a filename extension for a file that contains WML instructions.

WMLS – WML Script. A filename extension for a file that contains WML scripts.

WMS – Workflow Management System. See WFM (Workflow Management).

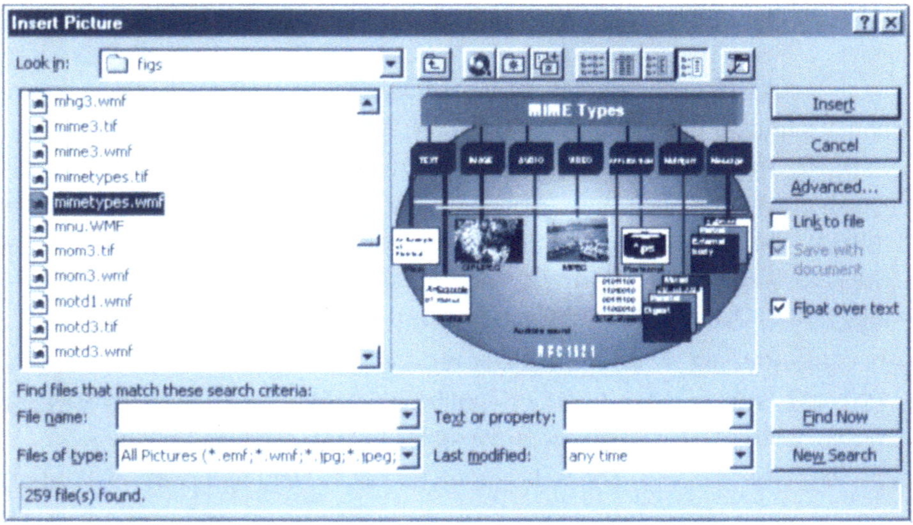

Fig. W-11. An example of a picture exchange using WMF

W/O – Without. A general abbreviation usually used in technical documentation to refer to the absence of a particular part or feature, etc. Also, w/o is used in business terminology. For example, equipment may be offered with or without some capabilities in certain circumstances, etc.

WOMBAT – Waste Of Money, Brains and Time. A common name for problems which are both profoundly uninteresting in themselves and are unlikely to benefit anyone even if solved. In contrast, the website wombat.doc.ic.ac.uk (named after the Australian marsupial, vombatus ursinus) offers a free-of-charge online dictionary of computing (see FOLDOC).

WOMPAT – Workshop on OpenMP Applications and Technologies. An international workshop focusing on open shared memory parallel programming OpenMP (see http://www.openmp.org) and its applications. The proceedings are published by Springer-Verlag (see LNCS).

W

WORM – Write-Once Read-Many. A type of optical disk that can be read and reread but cannot be modified after it has been recorded. WORM media have a significantly longer shelflife than magnetic media and thus are used when data must be preserved for a long time.

WOS – Workstation Operating System. A common name used for any of the native operating systems used on workstations (see WST). WOS may be represented using Microsoft Windows (any type), DOS, OS/2, SCO UNIX, LINUX, etc.

WOSA – Windows Open System Architecture. A set of application programming interfaces from Microsoft that is intended to enable Windows applications from different vendors to communicate with each other, such as over a network. The interfaces within the WOSA standard include Open Database Connectivity (ODBC), the Messaging Application Programming Interface (MAPI), the Telephony Application Programming Interface (TAPI), Windows Sockets (WINSOCK), and Microsoft Remote Procedure Calls (RPC). See also MAPI, ODBC, RPC, TAPI and WINSOCK.

WP – WordPerfect. A word processor for a variety of computers. The first version was sold in 1980 for Data General machines; later versions were sold for use with MS-DOS, Microsoft Windows and Macintosh computers.

WP – Word Processing. The act of entering and editing text using a word processor, an application program for manipulating text-based documents. Depending on the program and equipment used, word processors can display documents either in text or in graphics mode. Popular word processors on the market include WinWord, Ventura Publisher, QuarkExpress, LaTeX, WordPerfect, etc.

WPD – WordPerfect Document. A filename extension for a file that contains a document developed using WordPerfect (see WP).

WPG – WordPerfect Graphic. A filename extension for a file that contains graphics developed using WordPerfect.

WPI – Worcester Polytechnic Institute. The US university founded in 1865 and located in Worcester, Massachusetts (http://www.wpi.edu). In 2000, WPI produced more than 2700 graduates.

WPS – Workplace Shell. The graphical user interface for OS/2. Like the Mac OS and Windows 95, Workplace Shell is document-centric. Document files are displayed as icons; clicking on an icon starts the corresponding application, and the user can print a document by dragging the document's icon to a printer icon. The Workplace Shell uses the graphical functions of the Presentation Manager.

WPT – WordPerfect Template. A filename extension for a file that contains a WordPerfect template (see WP).

WQL – Web Query Language. A variant (subset) of Structured Query Language (see SQL) that allows Web-Based Enterprise Management (see WBEM) specific features. Unlike SQL, WQL is a retrieval-only language.

WRAM – Windows RAM. A special type of Video RAM (see VRAM) with better performance than conventional VRAM.

WRB – Web Request Broker. High-performance HTTP server from Oracle which allows client's requests to be directly translated into Oracle Database scripts (Oracle 7 and higher), and which automatically translates the results of the query back into HTML for delivery to the client browser. See http://www.oracle.com/products/websystem/webserver/html/ws2_info.html

WRI – Write document. A filename extension for a file that contains Microsoft Write (WordPad) document. WRI documents are very often used for so-called "Readme" documents.

WRK – Working storage. A filename extension for a file created using AcuBench (see COBOL) that contains the generated screen working storage variables. WRK files contain data items that allow the COBOL program to detect the actions that have been performed by the end-user. Compare with PRD and SCR files.

WSP – Wireless Session Protocol. A part of the Wireless Application Protocol (see WAP) stack that provides a consistent interface for client and server applications communicating in the WAP environment.

WST – Western Standard (Australia) Time. Time zone. UTC + 8.00 hours. No daylight saving applies in this zone.

WST – Workstation. A general-purpose computer designed to be used by one person at a time, which offers higher performance than that normally found in a PC, especially with respect to graphics, network capabilities, processing power and the ability to carry out several tasks at the same time. In a network environment, WST is a client machine usually running its own native operating system (see WOS) and the client side of application. There are also workstations without disks inside and consequently without operating systems. In such cases the term "diskless WST" is used and the necessary functions are booted from a server.

WTA – Wireless Telephony Application. An Application Programming Interface (see API) that allows application programmers to initiate phonecalls from the browser and respond to network events as they occur.

WTG –Way to go. The chat term.

WTLS – Wireless Transport-Layer Security. The security protocol implemented in the Wireless Application Protocol stack (see WAP) that secures, authenticates and encrypts data communication between the WAP gateway and mobile devices.

WTP – Wireless Transaction Protocol. A part of the Wireless Application Protocol (see WAP) stack that manages transactions between a user agent and an application server.

WTS – Web Transaction Security. The IETF working group dedicated to security services for HTTP. More information can be found at http://www.ietf.cnri.reston.va.us/html.charters/wts-charter.html

WU? – What's up? The chat term.

WUF? – Where are you from? The chat term.

WUSTL – Washington University in St. Louis. The US university in St. Louis (http://www.wustl.edu) with several research teams in computer science. Research areas include artificial intelligence, computational science, computer and system analysis, networking and communications, software systems, etc.

WVLSI – Workshop on VLSI. An international workshop focusing on the emerging trends and novel concepts in the area of very-large-scale integration technologies (see VLSI). See also SOC (System On Chip).

WWW – World-Wide Web. The World-Wide Web (also known as W3 or Web) was developed in 1992 by Tim Berners-Lee at CERN in order to pool human knowledge (as explained by Berners-Lee). To create the Web, he mixed together two existing ingredients to create something quite extraordinary. The base of the recipe was the Internet, to which Berners-Lee added hypertext (see HTML). The Web itself has changed almost everything on the Internet, the kind of users, the number of users, etc. (see Internet). The WWW merges the techniques of networked information and hypertext to make an easy but powerful global information system. W3 uses the concept of a seamless information space (the "web"), in which all objects exist, including those accessed using earlier protocols (WAIS, gopher, ftp, etc.). So that published information can be universally available, W3 relies on a common addressing syntax, a set of common protocols, and negotiation of data formats (see Fig. W-12). Thus, the Web has come to stand for a number of things, and these should be distinguished (Berners-Lee et al., 1994):

- The idea of a boundless information world in which all items have a reference by which they can be retrieved.
- The implemented address system required to make this world possible, despite involving many different protocols (see URL). A network protocol used by native Web servers giving performance and features not otherwise available (see HTTP).
- A markup language which every Web client is required to understand, and which is used for the transmission of basic things such as text, menus and simple online help information across the Internet (see HTML).
- The body of data available on the Internet, which can be accessed using bookmarks.

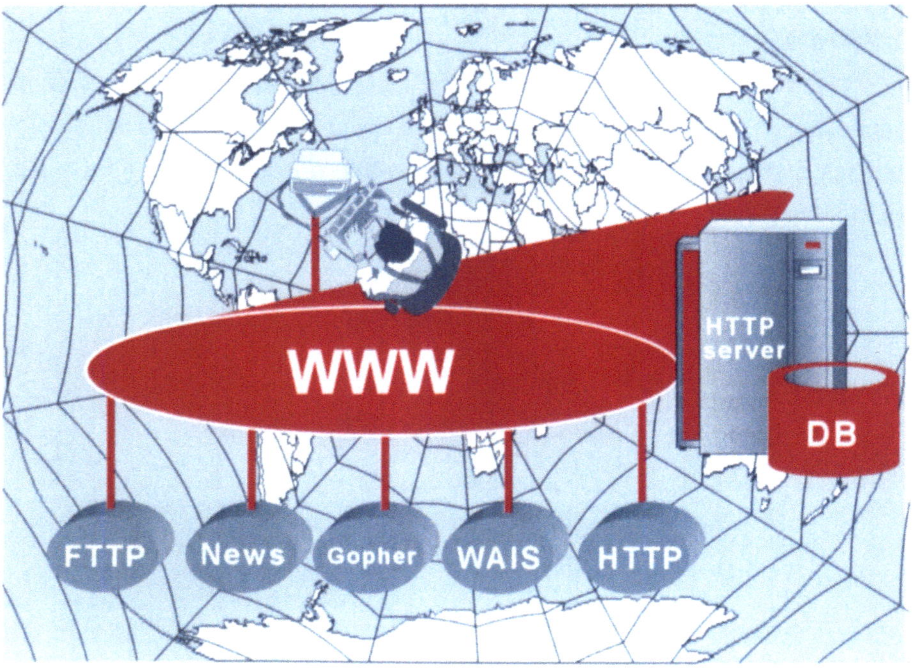

Fig. W-12. The parts of the WWW model

The user's view of the WWW world consists of documents, indexes and links to be used to find other documents. To follow a link, or to search an index, the reader uses a browser, a program capable of understanding HTML. To access the entire world of data, readers have only to know how to activate a browser, click with a mouse for the desired link, and enter a keyword if using a search engine etc. From the information provider's point of view, delivering information is as simple as running the Web server and pointing it at the existing directory structure. The server automatically generates the hypertext view of the required files to guide the user around.

WWWW – World-Wide Web Worm. One of the first automatic indexing tools for the WWW, developed in September 1994 by Oliver McBryan at Colorado University. The Worm created a database of 300,000 multimedia (see MM) objects, which can be searched using keywords via the WWW (http://www.cs.colorado.edu/home/mcbryan/WWWW.html).

WYSIAYG – What You See Is All You Get. Describes a user interface (pronounced "wiz-ee-ayg") with an unhappy variant of the UI WYSIWYG feature. WYSIAYG is used by advanced users who are familiar with the application goals but are not satisfied because of the UI's lack of depth. Compare with WYSIWYG.

WYSIWYG – What You See Is What You Get. A display method (pronounced "wiz-ee-wig") used in modern user interface design that shows documents and graphics on the screen as they will appear when printed. A typical example is given in Fig. W-9.

X

X – X Window System. A network-transparent windowing system developed by MIT (Athena project). At the same time, X represents a set of programming tools and a run-time environment. The main idea of the X system is based on the simple client/server (see C/S) relationship. The client and server run on different machines by default. X operates over TCP, typically using server ports starting with 6000.

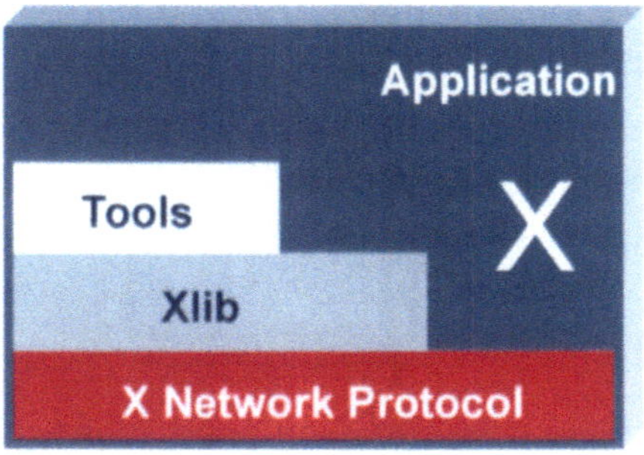

Fig. X-1. The architecture of the X system

The structure of the X system is shown in Fig. X-1. The X network protocol allows client/server communication. Messages exchanged between the client and the server in general fall into four categories: requests, replies, events and errors. More than one client can hold an open connection to the same server. Also, one client can simultaneously hold connections open with multiple servers. The Xlib library, written in the C language, allows the definition and drawings of windows, and event monitoring. X tools consist of widgets (window+gadget) and intrinsics. In short, a widget is responsible for showing something, while an intrinsic synchronizes communication between widgets and Xlib library routines. X supports all 16 raster operations (see BITBLT) supporting two picture forms: bitmaps and pixelmaps. The typical hardware requirements for X are shown in Fig. X-2. X runs under all modern UNIX implementations, including LINUX. The latest version, called X11, is described below. For more information about the X Window System, see two papers published in Software – Practice and Experience (Gettys et al., 1990; Scheifler and Gettys, 1990).

X.3 – The CCITT recommendation that specifies the service provided to an asynchronous (start/stop) device by a packet assembler/disassembler (see PAD).

X11 – X Version 11. The version of the X Window System released in June 1994. X11 introduced a new type of resource (graphics context) and visuals to support advanced high-power graphic displays. Also, X11 uses techniques termed bit gravity and window gravity for dynamic support of window size changing. In addition to the cut and paste mechanism, X11 uses a new technique, selection (primary, secondary and clipboard), to allow data exchange between different clients. X11, with its releases greater than or equal to 3, is a de facto standard for windowing and is associated with X/Open CAE, XPG, SVID and OSF documents. See also CAE, XPG, SVID and OSF.

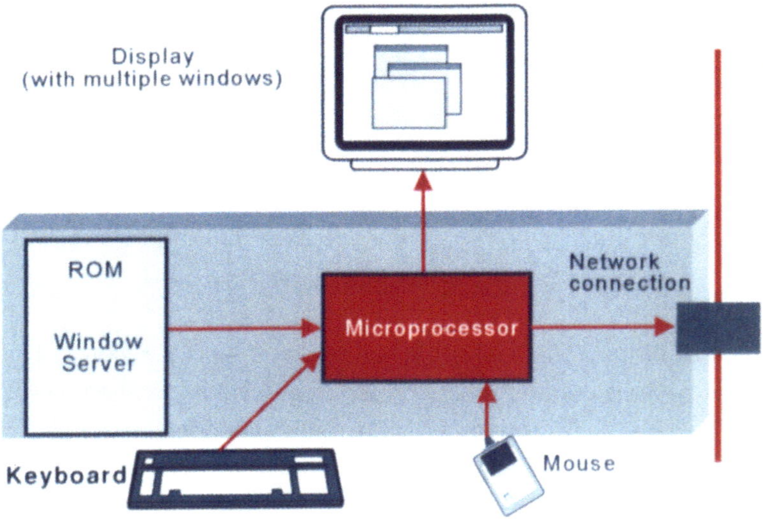

Fig. X-2. Typical hardware requirements for X terminal

X.21 – In data communications, the 21st CCITT recommendation in the X series, defining the connection of data terminal equipment to an X.21 public data network for digital leased and circuit-switched services.

X.25 – The CCITT standard that defines the interface between data terminal equipment (see DTE) and data communication equipment (see DCE) for workstations operating in packet-switching mode across public data networks. X.25 is used generically to describe packet-switching networks, which is misleading. The CCITT recommendation defines the interface only; it does not specify how the network should operate internally nor how it should be managed. Consequently, X.25 is not a uniform constant standard; rather it has many variations, none of which is guaranteed to operate with other X.25 set-ups.

X.28 – The CCITT recommendation that specifies the user interface between an asynchronous (start/stop) device and a packet assembler/disassembler device (see PAD).

X.29 – The CCITT recommendation that specifies the user interface between a DTE and a remote packet assembler/disassembler (see PAD).

X.121 – The 121st CCITT recommendation in the X series, defining a convention for the network user address (see NUA).

X.400 – A store and forward message handling system (see MHS) standard that allows for the electronic exchange of text as well as other electronic data such as graphics and fax data (ISO10021, 1990). Two main versions have appeared, known as CCITT (or ITU-T) MHS/84 and MHS/88. These are mainly provided by suppliers to allow internetworking between different electronic mail systems. X.400 has several protocols, defined to allow reliable transfer of information between User Agents and Message Transfer Agents (see MUA and MTA). In fact, ITU X.400 is a series of documents defining the MHS. X.400 itself is an overview document, X.402 describes the architecture, X.411 and X.413 describe the abstract services, X.419 describes the protocols, X.435 describes EDI functionality, etc.

X.435 – The ITU-T recommendation for a specialized application-level protocol that uses the X.400 MHS protocols in order to support EDI functionality.

X.500 – An international standard designed to provide a distributed global directory service (ISO9594, 1990). A directory service provides access to diverse kinds of information about users and resources in a network environment. It uses a naming system for identifying and organizing directory objects to represent this information. A directory object provides an association between attributes and values. The naming service is a fundamental facility in any computing system. In traditional systems, the naming service is seldom a separate service. It is usually integrated with another service, such as a file system, directory service, database, desktop, mail system, spreadsheet, etc. For example, a file system includes a naming service for files and directories. In the case of a distributed environment (enterprise system, for example, see EIS) there are several naming services that provide contexts for naming common entities in an enterprise, such as organizations, physical sites, human users and computers. Naming services are also incorporated in applications offering services such as file services, mail services, printer services, etc. Thus, a directory service enables information to be organized in a hierarchical manner to provide a mapping between human-understandable names and directory objects. X.500 contains a number of security features which are implemented in different paradigms in various servers. From the user point of view, the entire global X.500 directory is available on the local server. He/she can add, delete or modify information held in the directory, or issue search commands to locate individuals or information. Multiple objects can describe each entry in the directory, a group of attributes with values such as text strings, filenames or text-encoded photographs. X.500 is intentionally called a "directory service" instead of a "name service" to reflect the main distinction between it and name services like DNS or GNS that are described elsewhere (see DNS and GNS). Unlike those two services, which can only be used to resolve resource names that are known precisely, X.500 can satisfy imprecise queries in order to discover the names of other users or system resources. Although X.500 is specified as an application-level service in the OSI protocol suite (see ISO OSI), in fact its design is independent of any other OSI standard and therefore it can be viewed as a general-purpose directory service. See also DIB, DIT, DSA, DUA, X.509 and J2EE.

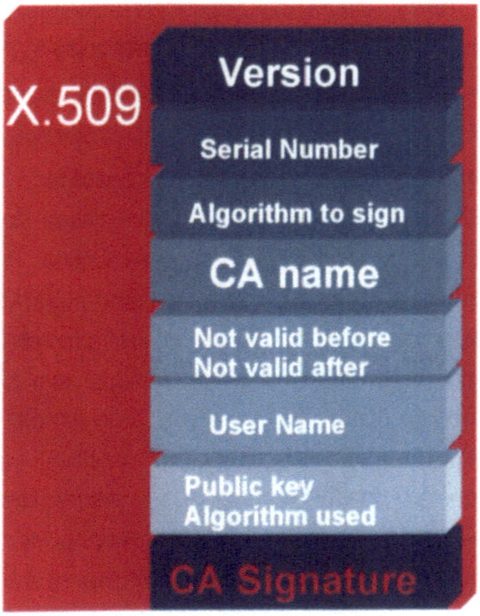

Fig. X-3. X.509 certificate

X.509 – The ITU-T recommendation (also ISO/IEC9594-8 standard) that defines the structure of the public-key certificate for message authentication and encryption (see Fig. X-3). See also CA (Certification Authority).

X.690 – The ITU-T recommendation (also ISO/IEC8825-1 standard) that defines the ASN.1 encoding rules. In particular, the Basic Encoding Rules (see BER), Canonical Encoding Rules (see CER), and Distinguished Encoding Rules (see DER) are specified.

X.800 – The ITU-T recommendation (also ISO7498-2 standard) that specifies the security architecture for the ISO/OSI Reference Model of communications (see OSI). The placement of security services and mechanisms within OSI layers are defined.

XA – Extended Architecture. A protocol which specifies the interface between a transaction manager and a multiple heterogeneous distributed DBMS in an On-Line Transaction Processing (see OLTP) environment. The XA interface is the bidirectional interface between a transaction manager and resource managers (see RM and TM).

XAP – X/Open Application Programming Interface. The X/Open specification that defines an application programming interface (see API) to the ISO OSI presentation layer (specifically to its connection-oriented services) including access to the ACSE application service element from the application layer. X/Open has defined this API as an interface for supporting portable implementations of application-specific OSI services and non-OSI applications.

XAPIA – X.400 API Association. An organization (http://www.xapia.org) established in December 1988 by the leading computer and communication vendors in order to develop API specifications for X.400 support. In 1990, X/Open and the XAPIA published three jointly developed documents: XDS, XOM and the X.400 API specification. In 1991, they published the "Guide to Selected X.400 and Directory Service APIs" and the "EDI Messaging Package" specification, and in 1992 they published the "Message Store API" specification.

xbm – X bitmap. A filename extension for files containing X bitmaps.

XBSFT – X/Open Bytestream File Transfer. The X/Open specification that defines a command line interface to a file transfer utility similar to ftp but using OSI FTAM. It also defines an FTAM protocol profile. Products providing this component functionality thus ensure the portability of any related software or human user that conforms to the interface defined in the specification. See also FTAM.

XBSS – X/Open Baseline Security Services. The X/Open specification covering a base set of security-related functionality to be provided by open systems, and the default settings of security-related parameters associated with such systems. XBSS addresses the concerns and priorities of private and public users of open systems who need assurance that such systems are capable of providing a reasonable level of protection against the sorts of disruptive events which commonly occur in the world of business and public administration. It is not intended for highly classified information security (military, governmental, etc.). XBSS is capable of running on standalone systems, interconnected homogeneous systems, and in distributed heterogeneous environments. See also TCSEC.

XCMF – X/Open Common Management Facilities. The X/Open specification that describes how standards-based open system administration applications can use common management services to facilitate the development of applications that significantly decrease the effort required in the administration of distributed systems. It is based on CORBA and defines a set of management facilities that are key to ensuring that system management applications and objects spanning multiple-vendors framework implementations may be defined and built.

XCPI-C – X/Open CPI-C. See CPI-C.

XCS – X/Open Calendaring and Scheduling. The X/Open specification that defines an API for calendaring and scheduling services.

XDCS – X/Open Distributed Computing Services. The X/Open framework for distributed computing, organized as a set of four layers, each layer providing a certain level of functionality in an enterprise-computing network, as follows:

- Operating System Services – They provide an environment for running distributed software on each node of the network.
- Communication Services – They provide the services that allow applications to communicate reliably across the network independently of the underlying network topology, networking protocols or data representations.
- Distribution Services – They provide a set of services that support consistency in distributed applications. These services address the fundamental issues in computing, including the processing model, the naming model, the security model and the management model.
- Application Services – They provide the enabling distributed system software to support the development of distributed applications.

In addition, there is a set of qualities (security, availability, manageability and internationalization) that apply to all services.

XDR – External Data Representation. A standard defined in RFC1014 by Sun Microsystems, used to encode the values in RPC call and replay messages. XDR defines numerous data types (unsigned integers, Booleans, floating-point numbers, fixed-length arrays, variable-length arrays, structures, etc.) and exactly how they are transmitted in an RPC message.

XDS – X/Open Directory Services. The X/Open document that defines an API for X/Open Directory Services (see CDS and GDS). This interface is designed to offer services that are consistent but are not limited to the X.500 and ISO9594 standards. When a call is made to one of the XDS procedures, XDS checks to see if the entry being manipulated is a CDS or GDS entry. In the case of a CDS entry, it works directly. In the case of a GDS entry, it makes the necessary XOM calls to get the job done. The XDS API consists of only 13 calls. XDS operates under OS/2, Windows NT, Windows 95, UNIX, and many other environments. The working configuration includes a utility (xm) that combines Modula-2 and Oberon-2 compilers, and the set of system files. See also XOM.

XDSA – X/Open Distributed Software Administration. The X/Open specification based on the IEEE1387.2 software administration standard. XDSA defines a software-packaging layout, a set of information maintained about the software, and a set of utility programs to manipulate that software and the information. XDSA specifies distributed operations without specifying the mechanism for how this is to be achieved. The Open Group has published a specification defining interoperability for XDSA that uses the DCE RPC mechanism. See also DCE (Distributed Computing Environment).

xDSL – Any (x) Digital Subscriber Line. A common term describing several Digital Subscriber Line technologies. It covers ADSL, DSL, HDSL, SDSL and VDSL. All of them are described elsewhere in this book.

XDSM – X/Open Data Storage Management. The X/Open specification that provides a set of APIs that use events to notify data management applications about operations on files. It enables such applications to store arbitrary attribute information with a file, to support managed regions within a file, and to control access to a file object. The interfaces and data structures described in XDSM are suitable for use in applications such as file backup and recovery, file migration and file replication.

XFA – XML Forms Architecture. A specification that describes secure capture, presentation, movement, processing, output and printing of information associated with electronic forms (see e-form).

XFDL – Extensible Forms Description Language. A document describing an XML syntax used for complex electronic forms (see e-form). The term complex here is associated with form attributes such as high-precision layout, integrated computations, input validation, multiple overlapping digital signatures, transaction records, etc.

XFN – X/Open Federated Naming. The X/Open specification that defines the model of a federated naming service and associated API. It also specifies the naming policies to be used in conjunction with this service. Furthermore, XFN provides integration with de jure and de facto naming standards such as X.500, DCE, DNS, ONC, etc.

XFTAM – X/Open FTAM. The X/Open specification that defines an API to the OSI FTAM protocol. XFTAM implements high-level file transfer and file management operations using the FTAM service and a service provider using the API. XFTAM thus allows the development of applications that are portable across OSI protocol stacks from a range of system vendors. See also FTAM and OSI.

XGKS – X Graphical Kernel System. An implementation of the Graphical Kernel System (see GKS) for use with the X Window System.

XHTML – Extensible Hypertext Markup Language. The W3C standard intended for semantic Web development that allows machines to understand page contents. XHTML was developed by reformulating HTML 4.0 in the Extensible Markup Language (see XML). See also RDF.

XID – Exchange Identification. In SNA an identification that is exchanged between SNA nodes so that they recognize each other. See also SNA.

XIE – X Image Extension. Extensions to the X protocol for handling images. See X (X Window System).

XIP – Execute In Place. The process of code execution directly from ROM, instead of from RAM.

XLA – Excel Add-in. A filename extension for a file that contains some additional Microsoft Excel features. Such features are made by another program while it's being installed.

XLB – Excel Toolbar. A filename extension for a file that contains a Microsoft Excel toolbar.

XLC – Excel Chart. A filename extension for a file that contains a Microsoft Excel chart.

XLD – Excel Dialog. A filename extension for a file that contains a Microsoft Excel dialog.

XLK – Excel Backup. A filename extension for a file that contains a backup copy of a Microsoft Excel document.

XLM – Excel Macro. A filename extension for a file that contains a Microsoft Excel macro.

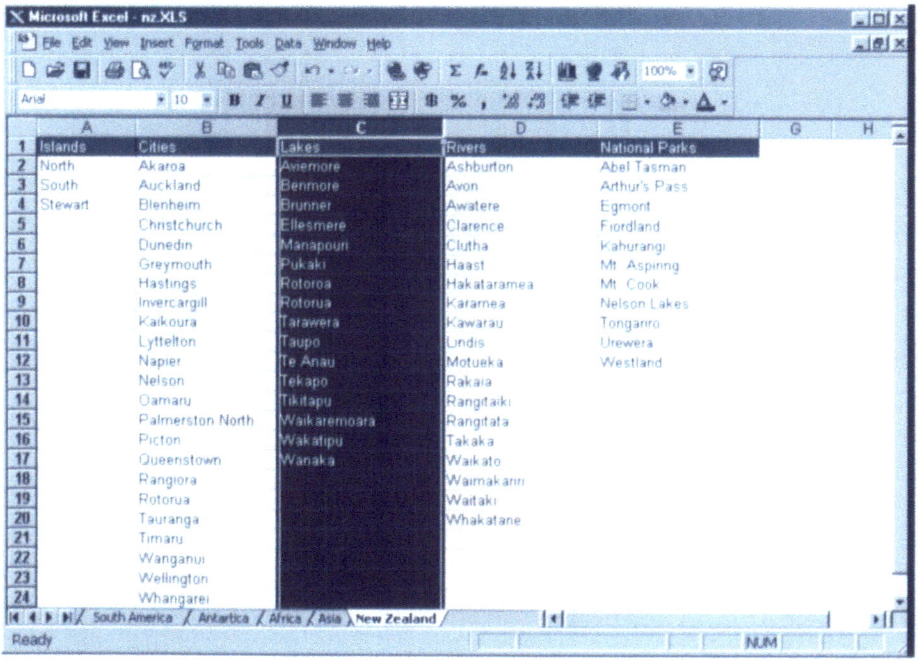

Fig. X-4. An example of an XLS file

XLS – Excel Worksheet. A filename extension for a file that contains an Excel worksheet (Fig. X-4).

XLT – Excel Template. A filename extension for a file that contains a Microsoft Excel template.

XML – Extensible Markup Language. A simple dialect of SGML defined to enable generic SGML to be served, received and processed on the Web in the same way as is now possible for HTML. XML was designed for ease of implementation and for interoperability with both SGML and HTML.

X

XMOG – X/Open Managed Object Guide. The X/Open guide intended to promote the development of management software that allows the administrator of a distributed system to manage a network of heterogeneous systems as a single logical system. The guide introduces the essential nature of managed objects, and the necessary framework for defining them. It discusses the managed object definition and development process, and explores the issues involved in registering them. It also discusses conformance testing.

XMPP – X/Open Management Protocol Profiles. The X/Open specification addressing communications using the CMIP and SNMP management protocols. See CMIP and SNMP.

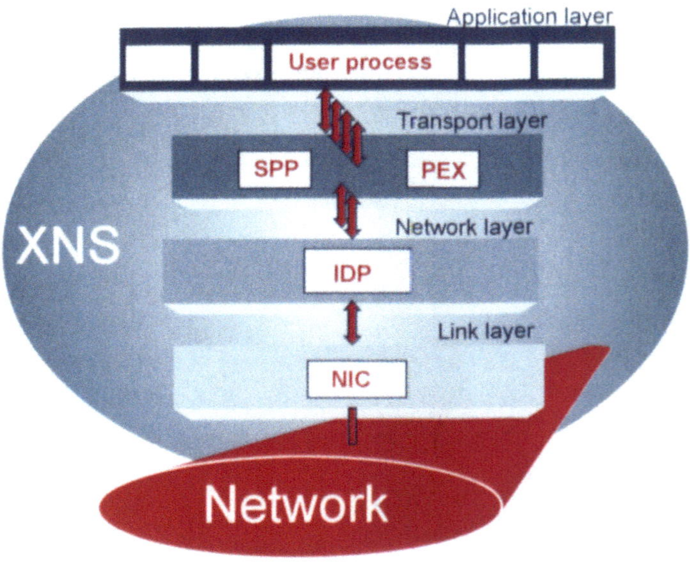

Fig. X-5. XNS protocol suite

XMPTN – X/Open Multi-Protocol Transport Networking. The set of X/Open specifications that offers a single long-term generic solution for the problem of multiple protocol and user types. The X/Open preliminary specifications for access node, address mapper and data formats, defining compensation protocols for distributed applications written for one transport provider but communicating over a different one.

XMS – Extended Memory Specification. The Microsoft specification for extended memory. See also EMS.

XMT – Transmit. A term applied to a signal used in serial communications.

XNFS – X/Open Network File System. The X/Open specification C218 that covers NFS (RFC1094), XDR (RFC1014) and RPC (RFC 1057). Although XDR and RPC are written as general-purpose specifications, their primary purpose within this document is in the context of NFS. The specification also defines a virtual file store, and a number of additional network monitoring and management features. It offers both protocols for interoperability and interfaces for application portability. See NFS (Network File System). See also XDR, XSI and RPC.

XNS – Xerox Network Services. The proprietary network architecture developed by Xerox Corp. in the late 1970s to integrate their office products and computer systems. XNS is similar to the TCP/IP protocol suite (see Fig. X-5). The most common protocols in use are IDP in the network layer (see IDP), and PEX and SPP in the transport layer (see PEX and SPP). The hardware interface to the link layer is usually an Ethernet adapter, although dial-up lines are also used.

XOM – X/Open Object Management. The X/Open specification that defines the API for the management of OSI objects. XOM is one of several specifications that X/Open originally developed in collaboration with the X.400 API Association (see XAPIA).

a	b	a XOR b
0	0	0
0	1	1
1	0	1
1	1	0

Fig. X-6. The truth table for the Boolean function XOR

XON/XOFF – Exchange On/Exchange Off. An asynchronous management technique which uses the XOFF control signal to tell the sender that the receiver is not ready to receive further data (usually because its buffer is full), or uses the XON control signal as a trigger for continuous sending until an XOFF appears on the communication line. The XON and XOFF characters are normally DC1 and DC3 control characters, respectively. Also known as the handshaking protocol.

XOR – Exclusive OR. The Boolean function with the truth table given in Fig. X-6.

XPG – X/Open Portability Guide. In general, XPG is the term given to the set of brandable items in the X/Open Common Applications Environment (see CAE) at a given moment in time, and it's supported by a branding program based on the CAE.

xpm – X11 pixelmap. An image file format for the X Window system (see X).

XSAG – X/Open SQL Access Group. An organization within X/Open, formed in late 1994 when the SQL Access Group (see SAG) transferred its activities and assets to X/Open.

XSM – X/Open Systems Management. The X/Open specification that provides an architectural overview of the Systems Management model, and identifies the various components of the model. It employs object-oriented techniques. It's a high-level model, which encompasses both the Object Management Group-compliant object-oriented technology (see OMG) and the OSI Network Management standards. It discusses the general properties of their interfaces and their means of interaction, and indicates an approach for the coexistence of both models.

XTI – X/Open Transport Interface. The X/Open specification that provides a standardized API for accessing a minimal set of OSI upper-layers functionality. This minimal set was designed by ISO to support basic communication applications, to open and close communications, and to send and receive messages, with a peer. Special attention is given to applications that are to be migrated from the Internet, or from the NetBIOS environment to an OSI environment, and for applications that are going to access the OSI transport layer. Thus, XTI is a single programming interface to a transport service that can be used in connection with a variety of transport protocol stacks – OSI transport protocols, including the minimum OSI upper-layers profile, the TCP or UDP protocols from the Internet Protocol Suite, SNA or NetBIOS. Products providing XTI functionality ensure the portability of any software that conforms to the transport interface defined in the XTI, and the connectivity of any software that conforms to the same protocol profiles as identified by the product supplier in the conformance statement questionnaire. See also XAP.

XTPI – X/Open Transport Provider Interface. An X/Open CAE specification upgrade that defines the message format underpinning XTI on stream-based systems. This definition should allow the production of portable transport provider implementations in stream-based environments. See also CAE.

xwd – X window dump. A program used to capture the visible part of an X window in an image file.

Y

Y2K – Year 2000. Shorthand for all the problems that could have occurred as a result of the date change from 31 December 1999 to 1 January 2000. The source of the problem was the fact that in the old computing days (from the beginning of computing up to the 1990s) both memory and disk resources were very expensive and the year 2000 looked very far away, so most programs stored only the last two digits of the year. The problem was widespread. It was not limited to a particular hardware, operating system, system software, application field, or even application. In the case of legacy systems, generally it applied to all these elements. Also, the problem had no national or political boundaries, and a real deadline was looming. Furthermore, the consequences of an unsolved Y2K are still mysterious, no one knows what might have happened, when and why. So, from the mid-1990s this was a nightmare for everyone seriously considering information technologies. Theoretically, it would have been possible to solve the Y2K problem by decreasing the system time by 28 years or using date binary encoding (for instance, DDMMYY=DDMMXX, etc.). Practically, the first solution was not appropriate because it would have led to the past, and to an era of isolated information islands and it would have caused new problems – for instance, who would take responsibility for time synchronization and how much would it cost, etc. The second solution has never been applied by computer manufacturers for old operating platforms. It is difficult to calculate how much money was really spent around the world to solve Y2K. The most important thing is that the problem was solved on time. The relevant international center under UN auspices (see IY2KCC) closed its offices on 1 March 2000, just after the leap date, confirming that the problem doesn't seriously exist any more. Of course, minor glitches may still occur, but most of them will never become public because they will be fixed by their owners, etc.

YaCC – Yet another Compiler-Compiler. A parser generator (yacc) that can be found on most UNIX systems. Also, the language used to describe the syntax of another language for yacc. In fact, yacc builds a parser while analyzing the grammar. The parser is a stack machine consisting of a large stack to hold current states, a transition matrix to derive a new state, a table of user-defined actions which are to be executed at certain points of recognition, and finally an interpreter to actually permit execution. The result is packaged as function yyparse(), which calls repeatedly on a lexical analyzer function yylex() to read standard input, and which returns "0" or "1" to indicate whether or not a sentence was presented as an input file. See also lex.

YACL – Yet Another Class Library. A C++ class library that offers high-level abstractions for common programming problems. Its class protocols are designed to be application-centered, minimize the amount of code a programmer must write, and provide adequate hooks for easy extensibility. Applications written using YACL are inherently portable across platforms, porting them is merely a matter of recompiling on the new platform.

YAD – Yet Another Decoder. A utility that helps to decode usenet binary attachments. See also USENET.

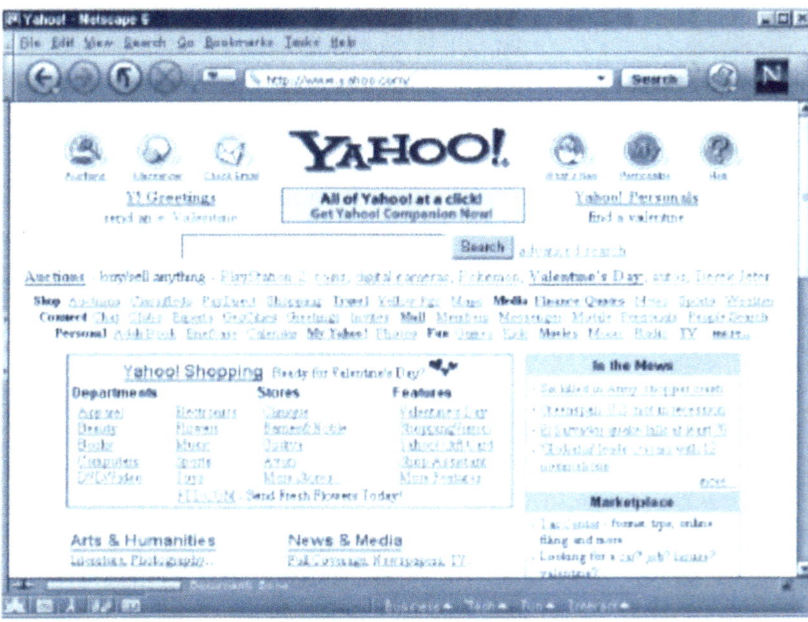

Fig. Y-1. YAHOO! frontpage (reproduced with permission of Yahoo! Inc.)

YAHOO! – Yet Another Hierarchical Officious Oracle. The site found at http://www.yahoo.com is probably the biggest hierarchical index on the Web (see Fig. Y-1). Originally developed at Stanford University, Yahoo! moved to its own site in April 1995.

YANTSWIBTC – You Also waNt To See What Is Behind The Curtain. This abbreviation is not in practical use, but anyway it has a historical value. First, the acronym is simply a confirmation that TLAs are not enough for all the computer subjects, and FLEAs can also be sometimes inadequate. Second, the given acronym, first introduced by Alan Morse and George Reynolds in a special issue of CACM, in April 1993, has a historical value in the theory of the modern user interface design.

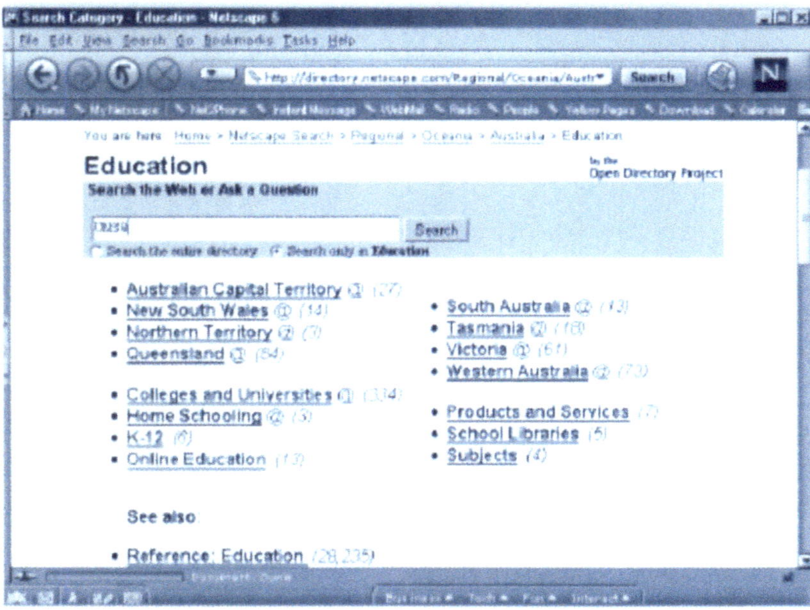

Fig. Y-2. An example from Netscape's Yellow Pages service

YAPP – Yet Another Authentication Protocol. A proposed standard from Microsoft intended to maintain user identification, authentication, authorization, and accounting policies.

YOO – Why Object Orientation. An international satellite workshop of CONCUR (International Conference on Concurrency Theory) focusing on object-oriented paradigm relevance to the theory of concurrency.

YP – Yellow Pages. In short, a common name for an addressing book, either printed or available online, that consists of names and addresses of phone subscribers, limited to a given area or available worldwide. Information is sorted according to products or services. Figure Y-2 shows how Netscape's

YP services work. Also, YP is the original name given to the Network Information System (see NIS).

Z

Z – Z notation. The formal specification notation (pronounced "zed") used for describing computer-based systems.

ZAI – Zero Administration Initiative. The popular term used for low-cost network administration. An example is ZAW.

ZAK – Zero Administration Kit. A set of tools, methodologies and guidelines for information technology managers that allows simplified implementation of centralized policy-based management. The ZAK limits end-user access to system files and unauthorized applications. Additional information about ZAK can be found at http://www.microsoft.com/windows.zak. See also ZAW.

ZAPP – Zero Assignment Parallel Processor. A virtual tree machine architecture, in which a process is dynamically mapped onto a fixed strongly connected network of processors communicating using message passing. ZAPP works as follows. Each node applies a divide and conquer function, which takes four arguments: primitive, solve, divide and combine, as described below:

- Primitive: takes a problem description and returns a "true" if it can be solved without division.
- Solve: takes a primitive problem description and returns its solution.
- Divide: takes a problem description and returns a list of smaller problem descriptions.
- Combine: returns the solution to a problem by combining a list of solutions of subproblems.

Each node has a copy of the code and one is given the initial problem description. Task distribution is done by process stealing where a process constructs a descriptor for each subtask and idle processors can steal a descriptor from a physically connected neighbor.

ZAW – Zero Administration for Windows. A key component of Microsoft's client strategy. The key capabilities of ZAW are:

- Automatic system update and application installation.
- Persistent caching of data and configuration information.
- Central administration and system lock.
- Application flexibility.

Actually, the term "zero administration" means zero administration for users. All administration is done on the server by the system administrator. The general-purpose framework for hosting administration tools is called the Microsoft Management Console (see MMC). The administrator also has a centrally controlled application environment where he/she can specify which applications users can access and at what level. Persistent caching enables high data availability, allowing mobile users to have access to information whether connected to the network or not. Furthermore, ZAW embraces the three-tier application model with a full implementation of active technologies (see SDK, Software Development Kit). With ZAW, administrators can tune the client environment to the exact needs of each user. See also ZAK. Microsoft's ZAW strategy is to offer a complete range of client solutions with maximum protection of previous investments, including support for a full range of devices.

ZBR – Zone Bit Recording. One of the hard-disk (see HD) recording techniques used to improve HD capacity and speed by eliminating wasted space. Tracks on the disk are grouped into zones based on their distance from the center of the disk, and each zone is assigned a number of sectors per track. The disk head moves from the innermost part of the disk to the outermost part of the disk, passing through different zones, each containing more sectors per track than the previous one. In that way, a more efficient usage of the larger tracks is possible. See also ZDR.

ZBTSI – Zero-Byte Time Slot Interchange. A control technique used in specific T1 systems where information on the locations of all-zero bytes is contained in a defined area of the transmission frame.

ZCAV – Zoned Constant Angular Velocity. A hard-disk technology (see HD) that divides a disk into several zones and controls the speed within each zone using a different clock frequency for each zone. See also CAV. Compare with ZCLV.

ZCLV – Zoned Constant Linear Velocity. A hard-disk technology (see HD) that divides a disk into several zones and controls the speed within each zone using a fixed clock frequency. See also CLV. Compare with CAV and ZCAV.

ZDL – Zero-Delay Lockout. A technology designed to prevent a beacon station from entering into a Token Ring (see TR) by locking out faulty stations.

ZDR – Zone Density Recording. A method of recording sectors on hard disks where there are more sectors in each outer track and progressively fewer sectors in the inside tracks. See ZBR, ZCAV and ZCLV.

ZIF – Zero Insertion Force. A kind of socket for integrated circuits that can be opened and closed by means of a lever or screw. When open, the chip may be placed in the socket without any pressure, and the socket is then closed, causing its contacts to grip the pins of the chip. Such sockets are used where chips must be inserted and removed frequently, such as in test equipment, or in PROM programmers, etc.

ZIP – Zig-zag Inline Package. A chip package, similar to a Dual-In-Line Package (see DIP), with the difference that there is only one row of pins, coming out of one side in an alternating pattern.

ZIP – Zone Information Protocol. In the AppleTalk protocol suite, a network-layer protocol for maintaining a mapping of the node names to the logical subnetworks (known as zones).

ZIS – Zone Information Socket. In an AppleTalk network, a socket (access point) associated with the zone information protocol (see ZIP) services.

ZIT – Zone Information Table. In an AppleTalk network, a ZIT is used to map home zone names associated with each subnetwork in a network or internetwork.

ZOPE – Z Object Publishing Environment. An open application server and website builder written in the Python language, for publishing objects rather than providing content that will be added to a webpage. ZOPE software has several major components, as follows:

- A "publisher" that publishes the objects using the ZOPE CGI protocol.
- A framework for the folders, files and images.
- An object database.
- A template for dynamic webpage generation.
- SQL methods and database adapters (Oracle, Sybase, ODBC, etc.).

Suggested Reading

In order to provide up-to-date information and a comprehensive point of view on modern computing acronyms, the author consulted a number of books, articles and webpages. The following list of the most frequently used references is just the tip of that iceberg, considering only those references used 10 or more times, or in some cases directly referenced in the text. Also, there are several reference books and articles which could help more familiar readers to gain a deeper view of the subject of interest. Other approaches would result in either no references at all (the practice in most dictionaries) or in thousands of references (maybe longer than the main body of the book). The given approach, together with the referenced webpages and RFCs in the book, will give readers enough options to find more information.

Agent-Oriented Techniques and Artificial Intelligence

[Djordjević-Kajan et al., 1997] Djordjević-Kajan S., Kajan E., Mitrović D., "Towards Active C3I Systems", Proc. 3rd Int. Conf. on Telecommunications in Modern Satellite, Cable and Broadcasting Services (TELSIKS'97), Niš, Yugoslavia, October 1997, pp. 411–420.

[Etzioni and Weld, 1995] Etzioni O., Weld D.S., "Intelligent Agents on the Internet: Fact, Fiction, and Forecast", IEEE Expert, Vol. 10, No. 4, August 1995, pp. 44–49.

[Finin and Labrou] Finin T., Labrou Y., "UMBC AgentWeb", University of Maryland, Baltimore County, http://www.cs.umbc.edu/agents

[Gray, 1997] Gray R.S., "Agent Tcl: A Flexible and Secure Mobile-Agent System", Dr. Dobb's Journal, March 1997, pp. 18–26.

[Harrison et al., 1995] Harrison C.G., Chess D., Kershenbaum A., "Mobile Agents: Are They a Good Idea?", IBM Research Report, RC 19887, 1995.

[Kajan, 1997] Kajan E., "Towards the Key Issues in Client/Server Computing for the Year 2000 and Beyond", Proc. 3rd Int. Conf. on Telecommunications in Modern Satellite, Cable and Broadcasting Services (TELSIKS'97), Niš, Yugoslavia, October 1997, pp. 811–814.

[Maes, 1994] Maes P., "Agents That Reduce Work and Information Overload", Communications of the ACM (CACM), Vol. 37, No. 7, July 1994, pp. 31–40.

[Mitrović and Djordjević-Kajan, 1995] Mitrović A., Djordjević-Kajan S., "Interactive Reconstructive Student Modeling: A Machine-Learning Approach", Int. J. of Human–Computer Interaction (IJHCI), Vol. 7, No. 4, 1995, pp. 385–401.

[Mitrović and Ohlsson, 1999] Mitrović A., Ohlsson S., "Evaluation of a Constraint-Based Tutor for a Database Language", Int. J. of Artificial Intelligence in Education (IJAIED), Vol. 10, Nos. 3–4, 1999, pp. 238–256.

[Mitrović et al., 2001] Mitrović A., et al., "Constraint-Based Tutors: A Success Story", Proc. 14th Int. Conf. on Industrial and Engineering Applications of Artificial Intelligence and Expert Systems, IEA/AIE-2001, Budapest, 4–7 June 2001, L. Monostori, J. Vancza, M. Ali (eds.), Lecture Notes in Artificial Intelligence (LNAI) 2070, Springer-Verlag, Berlin, Heidelberg, New York, 2001, pp. 931–940.

[Morreale, 1998] Morreale P., "Agents on the Move", IEEE Spectrum, Vol. 35, No. 4, 1998, pp. 34–41.

[Nwana, 1996] Nwana H.S., "Software Agents: An Overview", Knowledge Engineering Review, Vol. 11, No. 3, September 1996, pp. 1–40.

[Russell and Norvig, 1995] Russell S., Norvig P., "Artificial Intelligence: A Modern Approach", Prentice-Hall, 1995.

[White, 1996] White J., "Mobile Agents White Paper", General Magic, 1996, http://www.genmagic.com

[Wooldridge and Jennings, 1995] Wooldridge M., Jennings N., "Intelligent Agents: Theory and Practice", Knowledge Engineering Review, Vol. 10, No. 2, 1995, pp. 115–152.

[Wooldridge and Veloso, 1999] Wooldridge M.J., Veloso M. (eds.), "Artificial Intelligence Today: Recent Trends and Developments", Lecture Notes in Artificial Intelligence (LNAI) 1600, Springer-Verlag, Berlin, Heidelberg, New York, 1999.

Compression Techniques

[Witten et al., 1999] Witten I.H., Moffat A., Bell T.C., "Managing Gigabytes: Compressing and Indexing Documents and Images", 2nd ed., Morgan Kaufmann, 1999.

Computer Architectures

[Omondi, 1999] Omondi A.R., "The Microarchitecture of Pipelined and Superscalar Computers", Kluwer Academic, 1999.

[Stone, 1993] Stone H.S., "High-Performance Computer Architecture", Addison-Wesley, 1993.

Computer Graphics and Human–Computer Interaction

[Foley et al., 1996] Foley J.D., van Dam A., Feiner S.K., Hughes J.F., "Computer Graphics – Principles and Practice", 2nd ed., Addison-Wesley, 1996.

[Morse and Reynolds, 1993] Morse A., Reynolds G., "Overcoming Current Growth Limits in UI Development", Communications of the ACM (CACM), Vol. 36, No. 4, April 1993, pp. 72–81.

[Raskin, 2000] Raskin J., "The Humane Interface: New Directions for Designing Interactive Systems", Addison-Wesley, 2000.

[Salmon and Slater, 1987] Salmon R., Slater M., "Computer Graphics: Systems & Concepts", Addison-Wesley, Wokingham, UK, 1987.

Computer Networks and Protocols

[ATM Forum, 1993] ATM Forum Technical Committee, "ATM User–Network Interface (UNI) Specification", Prentice-Hall, 1993.

[Clark and Pasquale, 1996] Clark D., Pasquale J., "Strategic Directions in Networks and Telecommunications", ACM Computing Surveys, Vol. 28, No. 4, December 1996, pp. 679–690.

[Feibel, 1996] Feibel W., "Encyclopedia of Networking", 2nd ed., The Network Press, 1996.

[Jain, 1993] Jain R., "FDDI: Current Issues and Future Plans", IEEE Communications, Vol. 31, No. 9, September 1993, pp. 98–105.

[Kajan and Djordjević-Kajan, 1995] Kajan E., Djordjević-Kajan S., "Gigabit Networks for Open Computer Supported Cooperative Work", Proc. 2nd Int. Conf. on Telecommunications in Modern Satellite, Cable and Broadcasting Services (TELSIKS'95), Niš, Yugoslavia, October 1995, pp. 384–387.

[Singhal et al., 2001] Singhal S., et al., "The Wireless Application Protocol: Writing Applications for the Mobile Internet", Addison-Wesley, 2001.

[Stallings, 1999] Stallings W., "Data & Computer Communications", Prentice-Hall, 1999.

[Tanenbaum, 1996] Tanenbaum A.S., "Computer Networks", 3rd ed., Prentice-Hall, 1996.

Databases

[Chen, 1976] Chen P.P., "The Entity-Relationship Model: Toward a Unified View of Data", Transactions on Database Systems (TODS), Vol. 1, No. 1, January 1976, pp. 9–36.

[Codd, 1970] Codd E.F., "A Relational Model of Data for Large Shared Data Banks", Communications of the ACM (CACM), Vol. 13, No. 6, June 1970, pp. 377–387.

[Elmasri and Navathe, 2000] Elmasri R., Navathe S.B., "Fundamentals of Database Systems", 3rd ed., Addison-Wesley, 2000.

[Özsu and Valduriez, 1991] Özsu M.T., Valduriez P., "Distributed Database Systems: Where Are We Now?", IEEE Computer, Vol. 24, No. 8, August 1991, pp. 68–78.

[Özsu and Valduriez, 1999] Özsu M.T., Valduriez P., "Principles of Distributed Database Systems", Prentice-Hall, 1999.

[Rob and Coronel, 1995] Rob P., Coronel C., "Database Systems: Design, Implementation, and Management", 2nd ed., Thomson Learning, Course Technology, 1995.

[Silberschatz et al., 1996] Silberschatz A., Korth H., Sudarshan S., "Database System Concepts", 3rd ed., McGraw-Hill, 1996.

[Witten and Frank, 1999] Witten I.H., Frank E., "Data Mining: Practical Machine Learning Tools and Techniques with Java Implementations", Morgan-Kaufmann, 1999.

Distributed Systems

[Coulouris et al., 1994] Coulouris G., Dollimore J., Kindberg T., "Distributed Systems – Concepts and Design", 2nd ed., Addison-Wesley, 1994.

[Kajan, 1997] Kajan E., "Towards the Key Issues in Client/Server Computing for the Year 2000 and Beyond", Proc. 3rd Int. Conf. on Telecommunications in Modern Satellite, Cable and Broadcasting Services (TELSIKS'97), Niš, Yugoslavia, October 1997, pp. 811–814.

[OMG, 1995] Object Management Group (OMG), "The Common Object Request Broker Architecture and Specification", OMG, July 1995, http://www.corba.org/ or http://www.omg.org

[Özsu and Valduriez, 1991] Özsu M.T., Valduriez P., "Distributed Database Systems: Where Are We Now?", IEEE Computer, Vol. 24, No. 8, August 1991, pp. 68–78.

[Özsu and Valduriez, 1999] Özsu M.T., Valduriez P., "Principles of Distributed Database Systems", Prentice-Hall, 1999.

[Tanenbaum, 1995] Tanenbaum A.S., "Distributed Operating Systems", Prentice-Hall, 1995.

[Tanenbaum and van Steen, 2001] Tanenbaum A.S., van Steen M., "Distributed Systems: Principles and Paradigms", Prentice-Hall, 2001.

GIS

[Birkin et al., 1996] Birkin M., Clarke G., Clarke M., Wilson A., "Intelligent GIS: Location Decisions and Strategic Planning", GeoInformation International, 1996.

[Djordjević-Kajan et al., 1997] Djordjević-Kajan S., Kajan E., Mitrović D., "Towards Active C3I Systems", Proc. 3rd Int. Conf. on Telecommunications in Modern Satellite, Cable and Broadcasting Services (TELSIKS'97), Niš, Yugoslavia, October 1997, pp. 411–420.

[Mitrović and Djordjević, 1995] Mitrović D., Djordjević S., "An Open GIS Architecture for Inexpensive Hardware Platforms", Proc. AM/FM (Automated Mapping and Facilities Management) European Conf. X, Heidelberg, Germany, 18–20 October 1994, pp. 185–189.

[Mitrović and Djordjević-Kajan, 1996] Mitrović A., Djordjević-Kajan S., "Object-Oriented Paradigm Meets GIS: A New Era in Spatial Data Management", Proc. YUGIS (Yugoslavian GIS) Conf., Belgrade, March 1996, pp. 141–148.

[Worboys, 1997] Worboys M.F., "GIS: A Computing Perspective", Taylor & Francis, 1997.

Internet and WWW

[Berners-Lee, 1994] Berners-Lee T., "Universal Resource Identifiers in WWW", RFC1630, June 1994.

[Berners-Lee et al., 1994] Berners-Lee T., et al., "The World-Wide Web", Communications of the ACM (CACM), Vol. 37, No. 8, August 1994, pp. 76–82.

[CISCO] CISCO, "Dictionary of Internetworking Terms and Acronyms", http://www.cisco.com

[Comer and Stevens, 1995] Comer D.E., Stevens D.L., "Internetworking with TCP/IP. Vol. III: Client-Server Programming and Applications", Prentice-Hall, 1995.

[Deering and Hinden, 1998] Deering S., Hinden R., "Internet Protocol, Version 6 (IPv6) Specification", RFC2460, December 1998.

[Feibel, 1996] Feibel W., "Encyclopedia of Networking", 2nd ed., The Network Press, 1996.

[Fielding et al., 1999] Fielding R., et al., "HyperText Transfer Protocol – HTTP 1.1", RFC2616, June 1999.

[Krol and Hoffman, 1993] Krol E., Hoffman E., "What Is the Internet?", RFC1462, May 1993.

[Lange, 1999] Lange L., "The Internet", IEEE Spectrum, Vol. 36, No. 1, January 1999, pp. 35–40.

[Malkin, 1996] Malkin G., "Internet Users' Glossary", RFC1983, August 1996.

[Nesser, 1999] Nesser P., "The Internet and the Millennium Problem (Year 2000)", RFC2626, June 1999.

[Postel, 1994] Postel J., "Domain Name System Structure and Delegation", RFC1591, March 1994.

[Quarterman and Carl-Mitchell, 1996] Quarterman J., Carl-Mitchell S., "What Is the Internet, Anyway?", RFC1935, April 1996.

[Reynolds et al., 2001] Reynolds J., Braden R., Ginoza S., "Internet Official Protocol Standards", RFC2900, August 2001.

[Stevens, 1994] Stevens W.R., "TCP/IP Illustrated. Vol. 1: The Protocols", Addison-Wesley, 1994.

[Tanenbaum, 1996] Tanenbaum A.S., "Computer Networks", 3rd ed., Prentice-Hall, 1996.

Object-Oriented Techniques

[Booch, 1994] Booch G., "Object-Oriented Analysis and Design – With Applications", 2nd ed., Benjamin Cummings, 1994.

[Coad and Yourdon, 1991] Coad P., Yourdon E., "Object-Oriented Analysis", 2nd ed., Yourdon Press, 1991.

[Lee and Tepfenhart, 2001] Lee R.C., Tepfenhart W.M., "UML and C++ – A Practical Guide to Object-Oriented Development", 2nd ed., Prentice-Hall, 2001.

Open Systems

[Comerford, 1999] Comerford R., "The Path to Open-Source Systems", IEEE Spectrum, Vol. 36, No. 5, May 1999, pp. 25–31.

[Feibel, 1996] Feibel W., "Encyclopedia of Networking", 2nd ed., The Network Press, 1996.

[Gray, 1991] Gray P., "Open Systems – A Business Strategy for the 1990s", McGraw-Hill, 1991.

[Halsall, 1996] Halsall F., "Data Communications, Computer Networks, and Open Systems", Addison-Wesley, 1996.

[Kajan, 1994] Kajan E., "Open Systems: Concepts, Components, and Future Applications", Prosveta, Niš, Yugoslavia, 1994 (in Bosnian), http://www.knjizara.co.yu or http://www.plato.co.yu

[TOG] TOG (The Open Group), "Introducing TOGAF, The Open Group Architectural Framework", http://www.opengroup.org/architecture/togaf

Operating Systems

[Brinch Hansen, 2001] Brinch Hansen P. (ed.), "Classic Operating Systems – From Batch Processing to Distributed Systems", Springer-Verlag, Berlin, Heidelberg, New York, 2001.

[Davis and Rajkumar, 2001] Davis W.S., Rajkumar T.M., "Operating Systems: A Systematic View", 5th ed., Addison-Wesley, 2001.

[Silberschatz et al., 2001] Silberschatz A., Galvin P.B., Gagne G., "Operating System Concepts", 6th ed., Wiley, 2001.

[Tanenbaum, 1987] Tanenbaum A.S., "Operating Systems: Design and Implementation", Prentice-Hall, 1987.

[Tanenbaum, 1995] Tanenbaum A.S., "Distributed Operating Systems", Prentice-Hall, 1995.

[Tanenbaum, 2001] Tanenbaum A.S., "Modern Operating Systems", 2nd ed., Prentice-Hall, 2001.

Programming Languages and Programming Theory

[Aho et al., 1988] Aho A.V., Kernighan B.W., Weinberger P.J., "The AWK Programming Language", Addison-Wesley, 1988.

[Booch et al., 1998] Booch G., Rumbaugh J., Jacobson I., "The Unified Modeling Language User Guide", Addison-Wesley, 1998.

[Deitel et al., 2001] Deitel H.M., et al., "Advanced JAVA 2 Platform – How To Program", Prentice-Hall, 2001.

[Hall and Brown, 2001] Hall M., Brown L., "Core Web Programming", Prentice-Hall, 2001.

[Kernighan and Ritchie, 1988] Kernighan B.W., Ritchie D.M., "The C Programming Language", 2nd ed., Prentice-Hall, 1988.

[Knuth, 1998] Knuth D.E., "The Art of Computer Programming", Vols. 1–3, 3rd ed., Addison-Wesley, 1998.

[Martin, 1986] Martin J., "Fourth Generation Languages. Vol. II: Representative 4GLs", Prentice-Hall, 1986.

[Martin, 1986] Martin J., "Fourth Generation Languages. Vol. III: 4GLs from IBM", Prentice-Hall, 1986.

[McLaughlin, 2001] McLaughlin B., "Java & XML", 2nd ed., O'Reilly, 2001.

[Rumbaugh et al., 1998] Rumbaugh J., Jacobson I., Booch G., "The Unified Modeling Language Reference Manual", 2nd ed., Addison-Wesley, 1998.

[Stroustrup, 2000] Stroustrup B., "The C++ Programming Language: Special Edition", 3rd ed., Addison-Wesley, 2000.

[Wall et al., 2000] Wall L., Christiansen T., Orwant J., "Programming Perl", 3rd ed., O'Reilly, 2000.

[Watson, 1989] Watson D., "High-Level Languages and Their Compilers", Addison-Wesley, 1989.

Security

[Fraser, 1997] Fraser B., "Site Security Handbook", RFC2196, September 1997.

[Gray, 1991] Gray P., "Open Systems – A Business Strategy for the 1990s", McGraw-Hill, 1991.

[Lodin and Schuba, 1998] Lodin S.W., Schuba C.L., "Firewalls Fend off Invasions from the Net", IEEE Spectrum, Vol. 35, No. 2, February 1998, pp. 26–34.

[Menezes et al., 1996] Menezes A.J., van Oorschot P.C., Vanstone S.A., "Handbook of Applied Cryptography", CRC Press, 1996.

[Rivest et al., 1977] Rivest R.L., Shamir A., Adleman L., "On Digital Signatures and Public Key Cryptosystems", MIT Technical Memo 82, April 1977.

[Tanenbaum, 1996] Tanenbaum A.S., "Computer Networks", 3rd ed., Prentice-Hall, 1996.

Software Engineering and Software Tools

[Boehm, 1981] Boehm B., "Software Engineering Economics", Prentice-Hall, 1981.

[Boehm et al., 2000] Boehm B., et al., "Software Cost Estimation with COCOMO II", Prentice-Hall, 2000.

[Jacobson et al., 1999] Jacobson I., Booch G., Rumbaugh J., "The Unified Software Development Process", Addison-Wesley, 1999.

[Sommerville, 2000] Sommerville I., "Software Engineering", 6th ed., Addison-Wesley, 2000.

X Window System

[Gettys et al., 1990] Gettys J., Karlton P.L., McGregor S., "The X Window System, Version 11", Software – Practice and Experience, Vol. 20, No. S2, October 1990, pp. S2/35–S2/67.

[Scheifler and Gettys, 1990] Scheifler R.W., Gettys J., "The X Window System", Software – Practice and Experience, Vol. 20, No. S2, October 1990, pp. S2/5–S2/34.

Other Resources of Interest

[Kohn, 1997] Kohn G. (ed.), "The IEEE Standard Dictionary of Electrical and Electronics Terms", 6th ed., IEEE, 1997.

[Vlietstra, 2001] Vlietstra J., "Dictionary of Acronyms and Technical Abbreviations", 2nd ed., Springer-Verlag, Berlin, Heidelberg, New York, 2001.

[Woodcock et al., 1994] Woodcock J., et al., "Computer Dictionary", Microsoft Press, 1994.

Subject Index

List of Subjects

Agent-Oriented Techniques

Applications

Application Programming Interfaces

Architectures & Environments

Artificial Intelligence (AI)

Asynchronous Transfer Mode (ATM)

Business Terms

Chat & BBS Terms

Coding Schemas & Algorithms

Common Electronics Terms

Companies

Computer Graphics

Computer Science Fields

Computers & Systems

Conferences & Workshops

Control Characters

Databases

Devices

Distributed Processing & Systems

EDI & Electronic Commerce (EC)

Filenames & Formats

Formal Methods & Techniques

Hardware

Hardware Attributes

History of Computing

Human–Computer Interaction (HCI)

IEEE Standards

Information Systems

Institutes & Universities

Internet (Common Terms)

Internet Bodies & Organizations

Internet Protocols

Internetworking & Network Management

AM Active Monitor 33
AMP Active Monitor Present 34
AMT Address Mapping Table 35
ART Asynchronous Remote Takeover 42
ARTS Asynchronous Remote Takeover Server 42
AS Autonomous System 43
AToM ATM Management Objects 51
AToM MIB AToM Management Information Base 51
AURP AppleTalk Update Routing Protocol 52
B Bridge 55
BGP Border Gateway Protocol 61
BICI Broadband Inter-Carrier Interface 61
BIP Bit Interleaved Parity 62
BMTI Block Mode Terminal Interface 66
BN Bridge Number 66
BPDU Bridge Protocol Data Unit 67
Brouter Bridging router 68
CAU Controlled Access Unit 79
CBDS Connectionless Broadband Data Service 81
CBQ Class-Based Queuing 81
CIDR Classless InterDomain Routing 95
CMOT CMIP Over TCP 104
CNM Customer Network Management 105
CNR Complex Node Representation 105
COS Class Of Service 112
CRF Connection-Related Function 116
DE Discard Eligibility 141
DELNI Digital's Ethernet Local Network Interconnect 142
DESPR Digital Ethernet Single-Port Repeater 142
DESTA Digital Ethernet Station Adapter 142
DPA Demand Protocol Architecture 155
DTL Designated Transit List 163
DTS Digital Termination Service 165
DVMRP Distance Vector Multicast Routing Protocol 166
DVP Distance Vector Protocol 166
DXI Data Exchange Interface 168
ECN Explicit Congestion Notification 173
EGP Exterior Gateway Protocol 181
EIB Enterprise Information Base 181
EML Element Management Layer 185
EMS Element Management System 186
EPD Early Packet Discard 187
FC Feedback Control 196
FIX Federal Information Exchange 204
FUNI Frame User Network Interface 212
GIPR Gigabit IP Router 218
HMMA HyperMedia Management Architecture 233
HMMP HyperMedia Management Protocol 233
HMOM HyperMedia Objects Manager 234
HPR High-Performance Routing 236
IASG Internetwork Address Subgroup 243
IBMNM IBM Network Management 244
ICN Implicit Congestion Notification 248
internet internetwork 262
I-PNNI Integrated Private Network-to-Network Interface 269
I-POP I-WAY Point of Presence 269
IRDP ICMP Router Discovery Protocol 271
IWU Internetworking Unit 284
LAA Locally Administered Address 303
LBS LAN Bridge Server 308
LDCM LANDesk Client Manager 309
LIS Logical IP Subnet 312
LMI Local Management Interface 313
LMU LAN Manager for UNIX 314
LM/X LAN Manager for UNIX 314
LNNI LAN emulation Network-to-Network Interface 330
LSA Link-State Advertisement 317
LSP Link-State Packet 318
LSP Link-State Protocol 318
LSR Leaf Setup Request 318
LSRR Loose Source and Record Route 318
MAE Metropolitan Area Ethernet 324
MARS Multicast Address Resolution Server 326
MAU Multistation Access Unit 328
MIB Management Information Base 336
MICE Management Information Control and Exchange protocol 336
MLP Multilink Procedures 341
MMR Microsoft Multicast Router 342
Mn Management interface n 343
MOSPF Multicast OSPF 346
MP Multilink PPP 347

ISDN

ISO Standards

Job Professions & Titles

Journals & Other Publications

Local Area Networks (LANs)

Measurement Units, Methods & Terms

Memories

Microprocessors

Miscellany

Modulation Techniques

Multimedia

Network Architectures

Networks Are Everywhere

Network Types & Topologies

Object-Oriented Terms & Techniques

Open Systems

Operating Systems

Orders of Magnitude

Organizations & Consortia

OSI Reference Model

Physical Communications

Programming Languages

Programming Techniques

Protocols

Quality of Service (QoS)

Real-Time Systems (RTS)

Referenced People

Requests For Comment (RFCs)

Research Projects

Runtime Systems

Security

System Network Architecture (SNA)

Software Engineering

Software Tools

Standardization (de jure)

Storage Devices, Media & Technology

Telecommunications

Testing Environments & Procedures

Time Zones

UNIX Commands

Windows Technologies

World-Wide Web (WWW)

MIX
Papier aus verantwortungsvollen Quellen
Paper from responsible sources
FSC® C105338

If you have any concerns about our products,
you can contact us on
ProductSafety@springernature.com

In case Publisher is established outside the EU,
the EU authorized representative is:
Springer Nature Customer Service Center GmbH
Europaplatz 3, 69115 Heidelberg, Germany

Printed by Libri Plureos GmbH
in Hamburg, Germany